기도 맛들이기

-기도는 하느님의 뜻을 찾아내는 천체망원경이다

문석호 저

대양미디어

추 천 사

　이번에 발간되는 책, 『기도 맛들이기』는 기도에 매력을 느끼지 못하는 모든 신자들, 특히, 청소년들에게 도움을 주겠다는 취지로 발간되었습니다.

　기도의 정의, 기도방법, 기도목적 등을 설명하고, 하느님께 바치는 기도, 예수님께 바치는 기도, 성령님께 바치는 기도, 성모님께 바치는 기도 순서로 기도문을 배치하였습니다.

　요즘 글로벌 시대에 세계의 모든 젊은이들은 서로 만남과 교류가 언제 어디서나 쉽게 이뤄지고 있습니다. 세계의 젊은이들이 서로 같은 언어로 신앙을 고백하고, 기도한다면 더욱 친교가 활발해질 것입니다. 이 책을 통해 서울에서 개최되는 2027년 세계청년대회(WYD)에 참석하는 세계의 모든 청소년들이 함께 기도하면서, 하느님 안에서 하나가 되기를 기대해봅니다.

2025. 4. 25.
천주교 서울대교구
안경렬 몬시뇰

추 천 사

세례 받은 우리는 하느님의 자녀, 하느님 나라의 백성으로 부활하였습니다. 세상에 속하지 않고 하느님 나라에 속한 사람으로 사는 것이지요. 그러나 세상 안에서 살아야 하기에 어려움과 갈등의 연속입니다. 세상이 나를 끌어당길 때 우리는 눈을 감고 하느님을 부릅니다. 하느님께서는 예수님께 들려주셨던 소리를 우리에게도 들려주십니다.

"너는 내가 사랑하는 자녀, 내 마음에 드는 자녀이다."

기도는 우리에게 세상의 질서가 아니라 하느님의 질서에 따를 힘을 줍니다. 기도는 우리에게 세상이 원하는 대로가 아니라 하느님의 뜻에 따를 힘을 줍니다. "내가 세상을 이겼다."라고 하신 예수님의 외침이 우리의 환호가 될 것입니다.

이 책 『기도 맛들이기』를 통해 누구나 하느님 나라의 삶으로 발길을 옮기는 좋은 방법을 얻게 되기를 빕니다.

2025. 4. 20.
서울대교구 용평 청소년 수련장
김귀웅 토마스 신부

『기도 맛들이기』를 출판하면서

이번에 발간되는 『기도 맛들이기』는 영어로 대화하는데 어려워하거나, 신앙생활에서 기도가 버겁다고 생각하거나, 매력을 느끼지 못하는 신자들에게 도움을 주겠다는 취지로 만들었습니다.

저에게 기도는 하느님의 뜻을 찾아내는 천체망원경입니다. 하느님의 뜻은 성경, 특히 예수님을 통해 복음서에 완벽하게 계시되었습니다.

저는 "기도를 지탱해주는 10개의 기도기둥"에 따라 기도하고 있습니다. 10개의 기도기둥에 따라 기도하고 성경을 읽으며 하느님의 뜻을 아주 조금씩 경험하고 있습니다. 기도은총의 부산물도 있습니다. 주모경은 물론 니케아 신경, 묵주 기도, 미사 경본 일부 등 많은 기도문을 영어로 외우고 기도하는 은혜도 얻고 있습니다. 성무일도, 십자가의 길도 영어로 기도하고 있습니다. 기도 분심이 많이 줄었습니다.

주님의 뜻도 찾지 않으면서, 기도를 문제 해결의 방안이나 수단으로 받아들이는 사람들에게는 하느님을 아무 때나 호출하거나 부르거나 기도하면 달려오셔서 우리의 문제를 해결해 주시는 분으로 착각하게 됩니다. 기도는 하느님께 욕심을 드러내고 그 욕심을 채우는 것이 아닙니다. 10개의 기도기둥에 따라 기도하는 우리의 기도를 목이 타시도록, 애타게 기다리시는, 하느님께서 우리를 사랑해주시고, 우리에게 자비를 베풀어주시고, 우리를 보호해주시는 하느님이심을 제대로 경험하고 하느님의 뜻을 찾도록 허락하시는 것입니다.

또한, 기도는 저 스스로가 바뀌는 변화의 도화선이 되었습니다. 과거에는 1년 내내 365일 새벽 3시 반에 기상해서 하루도 빠지지 않고 새벽 평일 미사에 참석하였다고 우쭐해 하고, 저 자신을 드러내는 일에 빠졌습니다. 그런데, 이제는 주님 은혜 없이는 아무 것도 할 수 없는 미소한 존재라는 겸손을 배웠습니다. 저 스스로가 가라지 임을 예수님께 솔직히 고백하고, 주님, 저는 가라지에 불과합니다. 저도 밀이 되도록 도와주시라고 기도하고 있습니다.

"우리가 예수님 안에 머무르고 예수님 말씀이 우리 안에 머무르면, 우리가 청원하는 것은 무엇이든지, 우리에게 그대로 이루어질 것이라고" 하신 예수님 말씀(요한 15, 7)에 따라, 그런 삶을 살도록 저를 도와주는 것이 기도였습니다. 유혹에 빠지기 쉽고, 흐트러지기 쉬운 저의 마음을 예수님 성심(聖心)에 연결시켜 주님의 마음으로 아주 조금씩 채우도록 저에게 도움을 주었습니다.

기도는 저에게 희망이 피어 오르게 합니다. 꾸준히 인내하며 기도하면 예수님을 뵙고, 구원되리라는 희망으로 기쁩니다.

우리 자녀 수능 시험 잘 치르게 해 주십시오. 사업이 잘되게 해주십시오, 좋은 아파트로 이사가게 해 주십시오, 등 계속 저와 우리 가족만을 위한 "울타리 기도"에서 탈피했습니다. "이타적인 기도"를 하고 있습니다. 먼동이 틀 때, 새벽 아침 햇살이 온 누리에 퍼져나가듯이 어려운 이웃을 위한 보편지향기도를 많이 하고 있습니다.

하느님을 위해 무엇을 해드릴 것인가? 하느님을 기쁘시게 해드리기 위해 무슨 말씀을 드리고, 어떻게 봉사하고, 배려해야 하는지? 깊게 고민하는 기도도 하고 있습니다. 이타 기도를 통해 빛으로 나아가는 기도, 덕을 쌓는 기도, 진명덕화(進明德化)의 기도를 하고 있습니다.

이 책을 통해 서울에서 개최되는, 2027년 서울 가톨릭 세계 청년 대회(WYD) 참가자들은 물론이고, 가속화되는 글로벌화에 따라 더욱 치열해지는 무한 경쟁에 대비하는 어린 중학생부터, 청년, 성인 등 모든 독자들이, 기도생활을 맛들이는데 도움이 되기를 바랍니다.

2025. 4. 20. 부활 대축일에
삼성동 서재에서 문석호 안드레아

Contents

Introduction

A. Prayer and Devotion

How do I pray? Various forms of prayer are presented in the Catechism of the Catholic Church (CCC 2623-2649). These various forms include prayer of blessing or adoration, prayer of petition, prayer of intercession, prayer of thanksgiving, and prayer of praise.

What is meditation? Meditation is a Christian practice of prayer dating back to the early Church. As the Catechism states: "Meditation is above all a quest. The mind seeks to understand the why and how of the Christian life, in order to adhere and respond to what the Lord is asking." By meditating on the Gospels, holy icons, liturgical texts, spiritual writings, or "the great book of creation," we come to make our own that which is God's. "To the extent that we are humble and faithful, we discover in meditation the movements that stir the heart and we are able to discern them. It is a question of acting truthfully in order to come into the light: "Lord, what do you want me to do?" (CCC 2705-2706). Meditation is an essential form of Christian prayer, especially for those who are seeking to answer the vocational question, "Lord, what do you want me to do?" Spiritual reading of Sacred Scripture, especially the Gospels, is an important form of meditation. This spiritual reading is traditionally called lectio divina or divine reading. Lectio divina is prayer over the Scriptures.

The first element of this type of prayer is reading (lectio): you take a short passage from the Bible, preferably a Gospel passage and read it carefully, perhaps three or more times. Let it really soak-in. The second element is meditation (meditatio). By using your imagination enter into the Biblical scene in order to "see" the setting, the people, and the unfolding action. It is through this meditation that you encounter the text and discover its meaning for your life. The next element is prayer (oratio) or your personal response to the text: asking for graces, offering praise or thanksgiving, seeking healing or forgiveness. In this prayerful engagement with the text, you open yourself up to the possibility of contemplation. Contemplation (contemplatio) is a gaze turned toward Christ and the things of God. By God's action of grace, you may be raised above meditation to a state of seeing or experiencing the text as mystery and reality. In contemplation, you come into an experiential contact with the One behind and beyond the text.

What are devotions?

Popular devotions are expressions of love and fidelity that arise from the intersection of one's own faith, culture and the Gospel of Jesus Christ. As Saint John Paul II said in 2001: Genuine forms of popular piety, expressed in a multitude of different ways, derives from the faith and, therefore, must be valued and promoted. Such authentic expressions of popular piety are not at odds with the centrality of the Sacred Liturgy. Rather, in promoting the faith of the people, who regard popular piety as a natural religious expression, they predispose the people for the celebration of the Sacred Mysteries. The correct relationship between these two expressions of faith must be based on certain firm principles, the first of which recognizes that the Liturgy is the center of the Church's life and cannot be substituted by, or placed on a par with, any other form of religious expression. Moreover, it is important to reaffirm that popular religiosity, even if not always evident, naturally culminates in the celebration of the Liturgy towards which it should ideally be oriented. This should be made clear through suitable catechesis" (Address to the Congregation for Divine Worship and the Discipline of the Sacraments, September 21, 2001).

B. Prayer and Worship

"For me, prayer is a surge of the heart; it is a simple look turned toward heaven, it is a cry of recognition and of love, embracing both trial and joy." CCC, no. 2558, citing St. Therese of Lisieux, Manuscripts Autobiographies, C 25. Descriptions of prayer are abundant throughout Christian history. "True prayer," wrote St. Augustine, "is nothing but love." Prayer should arise from the heart. "Prayer," said St. John Vianney, "is the inner bath of love into which the soul plunges itself." "Everyone of us needs half an hour of prayer each day," remarked St. Francis de Sales, "except when we are busy—then we need an hour." Definitions of prayer are important, but insufficient. There is a huge difference between knowing about prayer and praying. On this issue, the Rule of St. Benedict is clear, "If a man wants to pray, let him go and pray." St. John Damascene gave a classic definition of prayer: "Prayer is the raising of one's mind and heart to God or the requesting of good things from God" (CCC, no. 2559, citing St. John Damascene, De Fide Orth. 3, 24). The Catechism clearly defines prayer as a "vital and personal relationship with the living and true God" (CCC, no. 2558). Prayer is Christian "insofar as it is communion with Christ" (CCC, no. 2565), and a "covenant relationship between God and man in Christ" (CCC, no. 2564). It is important to remember that we understand prayer through our celebration of the Sacraments and in the Liturgy of the Hours. The word liturgy comes from a Greek term meaning "public work or work done on behalf of the people." A work, then, done by an individual or a group was a liturgy on behalf of the larger community. All the worshipers are expected to participate actively in each liturgy, for this is holy "work," not entertainment or a spectator event. Every liturgical celebration is an action of Christ the High Priest and of his Mystical Body, which is the Church. It therefore requires the participation of the People of God in the work of God. Liturgy is centered on the Holy Trinity. At every liturgy the action of worship is directed to the Father, from whom all blessings come, through the Son in the unity of the Holy Spirit. We praise the Father who first called us to be his people by sending us his Son as our Redeemer and giving us the Holy Spirit so that we can continue to gather, to remember what God has done for us, and to share in the blessings of salvation. # Copyright of (A) and (B) © 2010 United States Conference of Catholic Bishops, Washington, D.C. Used with permission. All rights reserved.

Chapter 1 기도의 정의, 목적, 방법, 기도시간

A. 기도의 정의

기도라는 말이 성경에서 처음 쓰여진 곳은 민수기 11장 2절 말씀입니다; 백성이 주님의 귀에 거슬리는 불평을 하였다. "주님께서 그것을 들으시고 진노하셨다. 그러자 주님의 불이 그들을 거슬러 타올라 진영 언저리를 삼켜 버렸다. 백성이 모세에게 부르짖었다. 그리하여, 모세가 주님께 기도하자 불이 꺼졌다. 그래서 그곳의 이름을 타브에라라고" 하였다. 주님의 불이 그들을 거슬러 타올랐기 때문이다.(Now the people complained bitterly in the hearing of the LORD; and when he heard it his wrath flared up, so that the LORD's fire burned among them and consumed the outskirts of the camp. But when the people cried out to Moses, he prayed to the LORD and the fire died out. Hence that place was called Taberah, because there the fire of the LORD burned among them). 모세 오경 시대의 "기도"는 주로 재앙, 역경 등을 없애 주시고, 적을 물리쳐 주시고, 복을 주시라고, 청하는 "청원기도"가 대부분이었습니다.

구약의 모세부터 신약에 이르기까지 하느님을 믿는 사람들의 기도는 예수님 안에서 완성되었습니다. 예수님께서는 기도의 달인이셨습니다. 기도의 모범이셨습니다. 기도는 예수님의 존재 전체에 깊이 뿌리내리고 있었습니다. 예수님께서는 공생활 동안, 결정적인 일과 중요한 사명 등을 이행하시기 전에 기도하셨습니다. 홀로, 밤에, 산에 오르셔서 기도하셨습니다. 예수님 삶의 전체가 기도였다고 할 수 있습니다. 예수님의 기도는 우리 모두의 구원을 위한 기도, 우리의 고통에 동참하시는 기도였습니다. 또한, 하느님 아버지께 대한 감사와 확신의 기도, 믿음의 기도였습니다. 하느님으로부터 청한 것을 받기 전에, 청한 것을 주시는 하느님께 드리는 감사와 신뢰의 기도였습니다. 마지막으로, 예수님의 기도는 겟세마니 동산에서 성부이신 하느님 아버지께 자신을 바치는 기도였습니다. 성부 하느님께 예수님 자신을 온전히 바치는 기도였습니다. 가장 완벽한 기도, 주님의 기도도 우리에게 가르쳐 주셨습니다.

따라서 그리스도인의 모든 기도도 감사와 신뢰의 기도가 되고 주님께 우리 자신을 봉헌하는 기도가 되어야 합니다. 그렇게 하기 위해서는 먼저 하느님과 예수님의 뜻이 무엇인지 알아내고, 말씀을 귀담아 듣고, 하느님과 예수님께 청하고 싶은 내용도 말씀 드리며, 은총도 청하면서, 예수님의 기도 관행을 따르고 참여하고, 적극 동참하는 것입니다. 우리 주 예수님께서 하시는 기도의 연장이라고 할 수 있습니다.

바오로 사도가 정의한 기도의 속성 가운데 하나도 "기도는 우리 주 예수 그리스도의 하느님, 영광의 아버지께서 우리에게 지혜와 계시의 영을 주시어 우리가 그분을 알게 되고, 우리 마음의 눈을 밝혀 주시어, 그분의 부르심으로 우리가 지니게 된 희망이 어떠한 것인지, 성도들 사이에서 받게 될 그분 상속의 영광이 얼마나 풍성한지 우리가 알게 되기를 기도하는 것입니다."라고 하면서 우리가 마음의 눈을 떠서 하느님을 알고 예수님을 아는 것이 기도라고 하였습니다. (에페 1, 17-18)

성인들은 기도를 어떻게 정의하고 있는지 살펴보겠습니다. 성 요한 다마세노는 기도는 "하느님께 마음과 정신을 올려 드리는 것이요, 하느님께 좋은 것을 청원하는 것이라고 정의하였습니다. (Prayer is the raising of one's mind and heart to God or the requesting of good things from God. 미국 가톨릭교리서 2559항) 성 에로니모와 성 아우구스티노는 기도를 하느님과의 대화라고 하였습니다. 성 금구 요한은 하느님과의 친교, 니사의 성 그레고리오는 하느님과의 친밀함으로 설명하기도 하였습니다. 한편, 성 요한 비비안네 사제는 죄로 더럽혀진 우리의 몸과 영혼과 마음을 씻어주는 사랑의 목욕물이라고 정의하였습니다.

그런데, 우리는 기도의 정의를 무엇이라고 생각하고 어떻게 기도하고 있습니까? 우리가 기도할 때 하느님의 뜻은 무엇인지 구하지도 않고 알아보려고 하지도 않고, 한껏 부풀어오른 교만의 꼭대기에서 또는 자신의 뜻만을 고집하고 자기 욕심과 의지대로 멋대로 기도하지 않습니까? 또는 하느님의 뜻이 무엇인지 하느님의 뜻을 알아내려고 먼저 노력하면서 겸손하면서도 참회하는 마음 깊은 곳에서 우러나오는 정성된 마음으로 공손하게 기도하고 있습니까? 겸손한 마음으로 기도하는 것을 하느님께서는 기뻐하십니다. 겸손은 기도의 기초공사입니다. 건물을 건축하는데 기초공사가 부실하면 건물은 무너질 위험에 처할 수 있습니다. 올바른 기도가 되기 위해서는 무엇보다도 겸손한 마음으로 기도해야 합니다. 겸손하게 참회하는 마음으로 바치는 기도를 하느님께서는 즐거이 받아주실 것입니다. 그런데, 하느님의 뜻도 제대로 모르고 올바른 방법으로 기도하는 것조차 몰라도, 겸손하게 하느님께 아뢰면, 기도의 은총을 받을 것입니다. (미국 가톨릭 교리서 2559항, 로마 8, 26)

성녀 소화데레사는 기도에 대해 이렇게 말하고 있습니다. "저에게 기도는 저의 마음을 감싸주고 따뜻하게 휘감아주는 것입니다. 가장 단순하게 저의 시선과 마음을 하늘에 계신 하느님께 돌리는 것이 저의 기도입니다." 저의 마음 안에 있는 모든 시련과 기쁨을 보듬으면서 하느님의 정체성과 하느님의 뜻을 알아차리고 하느님 사랑을 알아낸 다음에 저의 내적 마음을 하느님께 소박하게 말씀 드리고 표출해 드리곤 하였습니다. (소화데레사 C 25항)

하느님께서는 어린이와 같이 천진난만 기도, 계산되지 않은 기도, 이해타산이 없는 기도는 응답을 해 주십니다. 소화데레사 성녀가 수녀원에 입회한지 얼마 되지 않았을 때, 사형수 프란치니가 병자성사(종부성사)를 받지 못하고 사형 집행을 받게 되었다는 뉴스를 듣고, 하느님께 다음과 같은 단순한 기도를 하였습니다. 하느님, 프란치니가 병자성사를 받고, 깨끗한 영혼과 몸으로 사형 집행을 받게 하여주시기를 기도 드립니다. 프란치니가 병자성사를 받지 않으면, 지옥에 떨어질 수 있습니다. 하느님, 프란치니가 지옥에 떨어지지 않도록 도와주세요. 제가 수녀원에 입회한지도 얼마 안되었습니다. 하느님, 부족한 저의 기도를 들어주시고, 제가 걱정하지 않게 해주세요. 그런데, 얼마 후, 신문 기사에 사형수 프란치니는 십자가에 세 번 친구하고 사형장으로 갔다는 기사가 실렸습니다. 하느님께서 소화데레사 성녀의 기도를 허락하여 주신 것입니다. 사형수 프란치니는 하느님께 모든 것을 맡기고 형장으로 갔다는 이야기입니다.

우리가 기도하기 전에 하느님의 뜻이 무엇인지 먼저 알아내려고 노력하면 성령님께서도 올바른 방식으로 기도할 줄 모르는 우리를 대신하여 하느님께 기도하여 주십니다. 왜냐하면, 하느님께서는 우리가 청하지도 않은 우리의 바램을 들어주시겠다고 목이 타시도록 갈증을 느끼시면서 우리가 하느님께 기도하기를 간절히 원하고 계시기 때문입니다. 기도는 우리의 바램과 청원을 전부 들어주시고 애정으로 허락하시겠다는 하느님의 애타는 갈증과 우리 모두의 목마름이 서로 만나는 것입니다.(성 아우구스티노). 하느님께서는 우리가 기도하기를 목이 타시도록 간절히 원하고 계시지만, 우리가 기도하지 않는 것이 문제입니다.

아우구스티노 성인은 "기도가 우리의 마음속에서 여러 가지 방법으로 이뤄지는 하느님과의 인격적인 만남이요, 친교며, 하느님과의 일치요, 하느님께서 우리에게 베푸시는 애정이라고" 하면서 "기도는 애정을 다하여 하느님께 나아가고자 하는 사랑으로 가득 찬 행위"라고 하였습니다.

그런데, 아우구스티노 성인은 기도에 대해 이렇게 경고하였습니다. 많은 말을 줄이고, 기도 횟수는 많이 가지라고 하였습니다. 교회 활동을 오래하다 보면 판에 박히고 틀에 박힌 기도가 청산유수처럼 나오는 수가 있습니다. 형식적인 습관으로 바뀐 기도, 마음은 다른 곳에 있는데 입으로만 하는 기도, 정성 없이 하는 기도, 이와 같은 청산유수 기도는 기도의 생명력을 잃게 됩니다. 청산유수 기도는 주님께서 우리 안에 계시기가 어렵게 만듭니다. 주님과 동행하는데 방해가 될 수 있습니다. 멋진 말로 포장하여 기도하는 것은, 그들에게는 의미가 없는 기도가 될 수 있습니다. 아우구스티노 성인이 예수님 말씀처럼 중언부언하지 말아야 한다고 권고한 것은 (마태 6, 7; 코헬렛 5, 1-2) 말이 많으면 어리석은 소리도 나오게 되어 있기 때문입니다. 많은 말 대신에 기도횟수를 많이 가지라는 권고입니다. 예를 들어, 처음 시작할 때는 아침, 낮, 저녁 하루 세 번 5분씩 기도하다가, 기도가 익숙해지면 기도횟수를 다섯 번, 아홉 번 등으로 늘리는 것입니다.

기도가 하느님과의 인격적인 만남, 친교, 애정, 일치라는 관점에서 오리게네스 성인도 "기도는 하느님의 현존을 의식하여 그분과 대화하고 그분을 바라보는 것이라고" 설명하였습니다.

기도생활은 삼위일체 하느님의 현존 안에서 이뤄지는 삶의 일상적인 관행입니다. 우리가 매일 숨을 쉬지 않고서는 살아갈 수 없듯이 우리의 영혼도 기도생활이 전혀 없다면 메마르고 죽어갈 것입니다.(미국가톨릭 교리서 2565항) 바오로 사도도 우리 안에서 활동하시는 하느님의 권능으로 우리가 청하거나 상상하는 모든 것보다 훨씬 더 풍성하게 주실 수 있는 분은 하느님이시라고 하였습니다. 우리의 기도생활을 통해 살아계신 하느님과의 생생한 인격적인 관계, 친밀한 사랑과 애정의 관계를 맺을 수 있을 때 우리의 영혼도 건전하게 성장 할 수 있기 때문입니다.(에페 3, 14-20, 마태 6, 8) 기도생활을 통해 우리가 하느님 아버지를 "아빠, 아버지"라고 부르고, 교제하고, 친교를 맺으며 하느님과 동행하며 사는 것도 하느님의 애정과 은총으로 주어진 것입니다. 우리는 우리를 하느님의 자녀로 삼도록 해 주시는 영을 받았습니다. 이 성령의 힘으로 우리가 "아빠, 아버지" 하고 외치는 것입니다.(마르 14, 36; 로마 8, 15; 갈라 4, 6) 기도를 통해 하느님 아버지를 "아빠"라고 부르는 것은 사랑의 극치요, 애정과 친밀감의 절정이 되고, 하느님의 현존을 의식할 수 있고, 하느님과 동행하는 것입니다.

B. 평신도가 바라본 기도의 정의

첫째, 저에게 기도는 하느님의 뜻을 바라보고 찾아내는 망원경입니다. 보이지 않는 하느님의 뜻을 기도라는 영적 대형 망원경으로 바라보고 알아내는 것입니다. 주님을 우리 안에 모시고, 동행하며, 하느님의 뜻을 알기 위해서는 기도해야 합니다. 거창한 기도, 남에게 드러내는 기도가 아니라, 조용히 침묵 속에 드리는 작은 기도를 자주 드릴 때에 하느님의 뜻을 알 수 있습니다. 성경 말씀을 묵상하면서 기도하는 것도 좋습니다.

둘째, 저에게 기도의 의미는 "기도를 지탱해주는 10개의 기도기둥"에 따라 하느님께 말씀 드리는 것입니다. 기도는 우리가 청원기도로 하느님께 말씀 드린 것을 얻어내는 수단이나 도구로 한정되어 있지 않음을 배우는 것입니다. 기도를 문제 해결의 방안이나 수단으로 받아들이는 사람들에게는 하느님을 아무 때나 호출하거나 부르면 달려오셔서 우리의 문제를 해결해 주시는 분으로 착각하고 있습니다. 더구나, 제멋대로 고집하고 살다가, 방황하고 방종하며 죄 중에 살다가, 10계명도 제대로 지키지 않고, 세상의 욕망대로 살면서, 하느님의 힘을 빌려서 우리가 원하는 것을 얻어 내려고 한다면, 그것은 하느님 보시기에 옳은 기도, 좋은 기도가 아닙니다. 하느님은 알라딘 요술램프가 아닙니다. 10개의 기도기둥에 따라, 겸손하게 기도하면, 우리가 원하는 것, 미처 청하지 못했던 것도 하느님께서 덤으로 허락하여 주십니다.

셋째, 기도는 하느님께 욕심을 드러내고 그 욕심을 채우려는 것이 아니라, 하느님께서 우리를 사랑해주시고, 우리에게 자비를 베풀어주시고, 우리를 보호해주시는 하느님이심을 제대로 경험하도록 허락하시는 것입니다. 기도는 우리가 필요한 것을 얻지 못해도, 우리가 대화하는 하느님이 우리의 훌륭한 아버지 아빠 이시라는 것을 신뢰하고, 만나고, 경험하도록 해주시는 은총입니다. 기도 응답을 받지 못해도, 기도는 하느님을 굳게 신뢰하는 저의 믿음이 성장하도록 도와주고 연단(鍊鍛)이 되었습니다. 하느님 아버지와 기도에서 만나는 시간은 아깝지도 않고, 손해 보는 시간도 아니고, 실패를 맛보는 시간도 아니고, 의미 없는 시간도 아닙니다.

넷째, 기도는 "우리가 예수님 안에 머무르고 예수님 말씀이 우리 안에 머무르면, 우리가 청원하는 것은 무엇이든지, 우리에게 그대로 이루어질 것이라고" 하신 예수님 말씀(요한 15, 7)이 저의 삶의 핵심이 되도록 그런 삶을 살도록 도와주곤 하였습니다. 하느님과 일치를 이루는 삶을 살면서 기도해야 기도 응답을 잘해 주신다는 것을 저는 굳게 믿고 있습니다. 우리의 삶과 생명에 영원한 가치를 유일하게 주실 수 있는 예수님과 일치를 이루지 못하고 제멋대로 삶을 살아가는 경우, 우리들의 삶은 결국 공허한 것으로 끝난다는 것을 예수님께서 가르쳐 주신 것입니다. 예수님 말씀이 우리 안에 머무르게 하려면 끈기 있게 꾸준하게 성경 공부를 먼저 하여야 합니다. 우리의 영혼을 살찌게 도와주는 성경 공부를 해야 하느님의 뜻도 알아차릴 수 있습니다.

조선시대 시인 김득신의 일화가 있습니다. 그는 그의 묘비에 이런 글을 써달라고 하였답니다. "재주가 남만 못하다고 스스로 한계를 짓지 마라. 모든 것은 노력하는데 달렸을 따름이다." 김득신은 독수기를 썼는데, 독수기란 만 번 이상 읽은 책의 목록과 서평으로 총 36권의 목록을 작성하였다고 합니다. 정말, 놀라운 일입니다. 학자인 "주자"도 경서를 수천 번을 읽어야 정통할 수 있다고 하였습니다. 세종대왕도 구양수와 소동파의 글을 천백 번 읽었다고 합니다. 그러나, 하느님의 뜻은 성경을 읽고 외우는 것만으로 온전히 얻어지는 것이 아닙니다. 백경천도(百經千禱)라는 말이 있습니다. 마음에 와 닿는 성경구절을 백 번 읽고 천 번 기도해야 온전한 믿음을 얻을 수 있고 하느님 뜻도 알 수 있다는 뜻입니다. 그만큼 성경을 많이 읽고 많이 기도하라는 뜻입니다.(예금통장을 불타는 아궁이에 던져버려라, MJ미디어, 146쪽)

예수님 말씀(요한 15, 7)이 예수님을 항구하게 따르고, 순종하여, 우리 안에 머무르도록 하게 한다면, 미래에 대한 두려움을 느끼지 않게 되고, 하느님의 뜻도 깨닫게 된다는 것입니다. 기도는 저에게 있어서, 저의 삶을 하느님의 뜻에 조율할 수 있는 은총의 시간이 되었습니다. 그래서, 저는 하느님의 뜻을 깨닫고, 하느님의 뜻에 맞게 올린 기도는 하느님께서 틀림없이 들으시고 우리의 도움이 되고 은총이 됨을 굳게 믿고 있습니다.

다섯째, 기도는 저 스스로가 바뀌는 변화의 도화선이 되었습니다. 유혹에 빠지기 쉽고, 흐트러지기 쉬운 저의 마음을 하느님의 성심(聖心)에 연결시켜 하느님의 마음으로 충전하도록 도움을 저에게 주었습니다. 우리는 수시로 하느님의 뜻이 무엇인지? 하느님의 마음이 무엇인지? 알아 차리도록 노력해야 합니다. 하느님의 말씀과 뜻에 우리의 마음과 기도 지향을 일치시켜야 합니다. 하느님의 마음으로 우리 마음을 연결하였을 때, 우리가 얻는 행복감이 있습니다. 세상을 이기적이고도 편협한 저의 마음으로만 한정하고 살았을 때는 좁은 눈으로만 바라보게 되었습니다. 그런데, 하느님의 마음으로 저의 마음이 연결되면, 저는 하느님 마음으로 세상을 넓게 바라볼 수 있었습니다. 아내, 자녀, 가난한 이웃 등도 하느님의 눈으로 바라볼 수 있게 되었습니다. 우리가 기도하는 목적의 하나도 현실을 바라보는 우리의 입장과 내면을 변화시키는 것입니다. 우리의 마음이 하느님 말씀으로 연결되면, 우리에게 필요한 것은 하느님께서 거저 주시는 선물입니다.

여섯째, 기도는 저에게 희망이 피어 오르게 합니다. 제가 저의 삶을 사는 동안 희망적인 일도 많았지만, 과거를 회상해 보면, 때로는 풍랑을 만나 침몰할 것처럼 절망적인 일과 난관들이 중첩되어 힘들었습니다.

의학적으로, 사람은 밥을 먹지 않아도 4주간 정도를 버틸 수 있지만, 희망이 없는 사람은 이미 영적으로 죽은 사람입니다. 그런데, 저는 중학교 시절 읽은 쇠렌 오뷔에 키르케고르(1813~1855, 덴마크의 실존주의 철학자)의 "죽음에 이르는 병"에서 "절망"이 인생에서 가장 위험하고, 죽음에 이르는 병이라는 것을 알고부터 무슨 난관이 있더라도 절망에 빠져서는 안 된다고 살아왔습니다. 그러다가, 성경을 읽으면서 하느님께서 우리에게 활기찬 미래와 평화와 희망과 행복과 영원한 생명을 주신다는 말씀을 알고 기도에 맛들이기 시작하였습니다.(예레 29, 11) 저에게 "미래와 희망"이 없다면 얼마나 불행하고 쉽게 낙담하는 삶을 살아갈까? 하고 생각해 봅니다. 그런데, 저는 기도로 희망을 주시는 하느님을 아주 조금씩 경험하는 은총을 얻게 되었습니다.

아브라함은 희망이 없어도 희망하며, "너의 후손들이 저렇게 많아질 것이다." 하신 말씀에 따라 "많은 민족의 아버지"가 될 것을 믿었습니다.(로마 4, 18) 희망을 굳게 믿었기 때문에 아브라함에게 하느님 말씀이 이뤄진 것입니다.

저도 기도를 드릴 때마다 "저의 소망을 있는 그대로 하느님께 내어 놓기를 배우게 해주십시오." 하고 말씀 드립니다. 그러면, 저의 모든 희망, 감정, 느낌과 청원까지도 전부 하느님 앞에 쏟아내는 방법을 배우게 해주십니다. 기도할 때마다, 더 큰 기쁨으로 하느님을 환영하도록 해주십니다. 장래에 성취될 저의 희망과 청원도 아브라함의 희망과 같이 성취시켜 주실 것이라고 굳게 믿고 있습니다. 제가 기도를 하면 하느님의 섭리와 은총을 아주 조금씩 체험하게 됩니다. 하느님을 만나는 경험도 조금씩 하게 됩니다. 저의 희망이 하나 둘 성취되는 경험도 조금씩 하게 됩니다. 제가 하느님을 굳게 신뢰하고 하느님께 희망을 두는 것, 그 자체가 하느님께서 저에게 주신 은혜로운 선물이요 은총입니다.

C. 기도의 원칙

기도는 결코 의심하는 일없이 믿음을 가지고 하여야 합니다. 의심하는 사람은 바람에 밀려 출렁이는 바다 물결과 같습니다. 그러한 사람은 하느님에게서 아무것도 받을 생각을 하지 말아야 합니다. 그는 두 마음을 품은 사람입니다.(야고 1, 6~8) 기도하는 마음의 자세는 하느님을 굳게 신뢰하고, 인내하고, 기도에 대한 응답을 반드시 받는다는 확신을 가져야 합니다.

기도에는 기도를 지탱해주는 다음과 같은 10개의 기도기둥이 있습니다. 우리가 가장 신뢰할 수 있고, 우리 생명의 창조주시며, 우리 생명을 주관하고 계시는 하느님께 흠숭지례(欽崇之禮)를 바치고(Adore), 찬양하고(Praise), 찬미 드리고(Bless), 공경하고(Honor), 영광을 드리고(Glorify), 환호하고(Acclaim), 경배 드리고(Worship), 하느님께서 베풀어 주신 은혜에 감사를 드리고(Give thanks), 전구를 드리고(중보기도라고도 함, Intercession), 청원을 드리는(Petition) 10개의 기도 기둥입니다. 저는 9개의 기도기둥에 따라 기도한 다음에, 마지막으로 하느님께 청원기도를 드리곤 합니다.

흠숭지례(欽崇之禮)를 바치는(Adore) 것은, 하느님을 하느님이요, 창조주시며 구세주로 인정하는 것입니다.(The adoration means that we acknowledge God as God, Creator and Savior. 보성사, 영어기도서 190페이지).

우리를 창조하신 하느님의 위대하심과, 우리를 악에서 구해주신 예수 그리스도의 권능을 드높이는 것입니다. 흠숭을 바치면 우리를 겸손하게 해주시고, 우리의 청원기도에 대한 확신도 주십니다. "흠숭기도의 내용을 좀 더 잘 이해할 수 있는 기도 모범이 있어 소개합니다." 카르투지오 "귀고" 수도원장의 흠숭 기도입니다. 귀고 원장은 가장 깊이 있는 관상기도를 경험한 분입니다.

하느님께서는 얼마나 많은 즙을 포도 한 알에서 짜내시는지요. 하느님께서는 얼마나 많은 물을 옹달샘에서 길어 올리시는지요. 얼마나 작은 불씨 하나로 큰 불로 불타오르게 하시는지요. 제 영혼은 메마르고 연약하여 저 혼자 기도할 수 없지만, 하느님께서는 메마른 저의 영혼에서 수천 마디 기도를 짜내십니다. 제 영혼은 너무 강팍해서 혼자서는 사랑을 할 수 없지만, 하느님께서는 그것에서 당신과 저의 이웃을 위해 무한한 사랑을 길어 올리십니다. 제 영혼은 너무 차갑고 냉혹해서 저 혼자서는 아무 기쁨도 누릴 수 없지만, 하느님께서는 제 안에 하늘나라를 미리 맛보는 기쁨의 샘이 샘솟게 하십니다. 제 영혼은 너무 연약해서 혼자서는 아무 믿음도 없지만, 하느님께서 주시는 힘과 은총으로 저의 믿음은 높이 자라납니다. 기도와 사랑과 기쁨과 믿음으로 하느님께 감사 드립니다. 저로 하여금 늘 기도하고 사랑하고, 기뻐하고 신실하고도 충실하게 하느님만을 믿고 의지하게 하여주소서.

찬양하는(Praise) 것은 "무엇보다 신속하게 하느님께서 참 하느님이심을 인정하는 기도입니다. (Praise is the form of prayer which recognizes most immediately that God is God.) 찬양은 하느님께서 하시는 일 때문만이 아니라, 참 하느님이시기에 사랑하고, 참 하느님이시기에 찬양을 드리는 것입니다. 찬양 시편인 시편 148편에는 "찬양"이라는 단어가 10번 나옵니다.

찬미 드리는(Bless) 것은 하느님께서 주신 선물에 대한 응답입니다. (The prayer of blessing is man's response to God's gifts.) 하느님께서 우리 모두를 축복하여 주시고, 복을 내려주신 것에 대한 보답입니다. 모든 복의 근원이신 하느님께 드리는 우리들의 응답입니다. 기적을 일으키는 기도입니다. 은총에 대한 응답기도입니다. 어떤 어려움이나 불행에 직면해도, 기도하는 사람이 되면 불행을 행복으로 바꿔주시고, 치유의 기적도 베푸십니다.

공경하는(Honor) 것은 하느님을 의지하고, 우리의 삶 전부를 하느님께서 주관하시고, 도와주시고, 인도해 주시는 분이심을 믿고, 하느님 은혜를 입으로 시인하고 고백하는 것입니다. 하느님께 공손하게 순종하면서 받들어 모시는 것입니다.

영광을 드리는(Glorify) 것은 하느님께서, 하느님으로서 본래 가지고 계신 영광에 추가적으로 더해지는 것이 아니라, 하느님의 존재와 속성이 인간과 피조물 가운데 드러나고 인정되었다는 뜻입니다. 하느님의 영광은 본질적이고도, 고유한, 내재적 영광(Intrinsic Glory)입니다. 하느님께서는 본질적으로 영광스러운 분이시며, 그분의 영광은 피조물에 의해 추가되거나 감소되지 않습니다. 예를 들어, 시편(19, 1)에서 "하늘은 하느님의 영광을 이야기하고 창공은 그분 손의 솜씨를 알리네"라고 했을 때, 이 말은 하느님께서 창조하신 세상이 하느님의 영광을 증가시키는 것이 아니라, 이미 존재하는 하느님의 영광을 피조물인 인간이 드러내고 나타낸다는 의미입니다.

환호하는(Acclaim) 것은 미사 또는 기도에서 하느님의 구원을 바라거나 하느님의 신성을 드러내는 간절한 간구입니다. 하늘에 계신 성모 마리아와 천사와 성인들과 혼연일체가 되어 기뻐서 큰 소리로 하느님께 드리는 간절함과 기도입니다. 예를 들어, 복음 환호송(기쁜 소식, 복음을 맞이하며 환호하는 노래;   미사전례에서 주례자나 봉사자의 인사 또는 초대에 대한 회중의 응답을 나타내는 인사와 기도, 그리고 신앙을 고백하는 짤막한 성경 문구 등)을 노래하거나 말함으로써 신자들은 복음에서 자신들에게 말씀하실 주님을 환영하고 환호하며 주님께 대한 믿음을 고백하는 것입니다.

경배는(Worship) 하느님께서 하늘과 땅에서 모든 피조물로부터 받으시는 것입니다. 몸과 마음을 다하여 숭배하는 것입니다. 인류는 모두 하느님께 경배 드리기 위해 창조되었습니다.(미국 성무일도) 공적 예배는 교회 전례에서 예수님의 파스카 신비를 기념하면서 하느님께 봉헌하는 것입니다.(Public worship is given to God in the church by celebration of the Paschal Mystery of Christ in the liturgy.) 예수님께서도 "주 너의 하느님께 경배하고." 그분만을 섬겨라. (You shall worship the Lord, your God, and him alone shall you serve. 루카 4, 8). 하고 말씀하셨습니다.

성경에서는 창세기 22장에서 최초로 Worship이라는 단어가 표기되었습니다. (Abraham said to his servants: "Stay here with the donkey, while the boy and I go on over there. We will worship and then come back to you. 창세 22, 5)" 오늘날에는 성령으로 거듭난 사람들이 바치는 것이 경배입니다. 경배 예식의 하나는 피를 바치는 전례에서 예물을 바치는 전례로 변경되었음을 의미합니다.

감사를 드리는(Give thanks) 것은 감사할 일은 말할 것도 없고, 모든 슬픔과 기쁨도 너그럽게 수용하며 하느님께 드리는 것이 감사입니다.

저는 3시 반에 기상해서 성무일도를 바치고 교회로 걸어가, 교회 마당에서 묵주기도를 봉헌합니다. 교회 야간 관리 근무자가 4시 50분경 교회 문을 열어주면 성체조배로 미사 준비를 합니다. 그리고, 성경을 읽고 묵상합니다. 쳇바퀴 돌듯이 일상을 보내고 있는 것 같지만 매일매일 새로운 은혜가 새록새록 합니다. 그래서, 하느님께 감사 드립니다. 지난 2024년 한 해 365일 하루도 빠지지 않고 3시 반에 기상을 하고 교회에 갔습니다. 그것도 하느님께 감사 드렸습니다.

그리고, 매월 말일이 되면 제가 한번도 빠지지 않고 드리는 평범한 기도가 있습니다. 하느님, 부족함과 허물이 많은 제가 미사에 참석할 수 있도록 은총을 주셔서 충심으로 감사 드리고 있습니다.

더구나, 하느님께서 제가 봉헌한 청원기도의 일부를 받아드리시지 않으시고 기도응답을 하여 주지 않으신 것도 감사 드리고 있습니다. 하느님께서 저에게 허락하지 않으신 청원기도를 묵상하고 저 자신을 조심스럽게 성찰하곤 합니다. 하느님, 부족함과 허물이 많은 저의 부실한 기도, 때로는 제멋대로 생각하고 드린 저의 기도를 들어주시지 않고, 응답하여 주시지 않은 것에 대해서도 하느님께 감사를 드렸습니다. 다음달에는, "기도를 충실히 더 잘 준비하고 하느님 뜻에 맞는 기도를 드리도록 노력하겠습니다."라고 기도하고 있습니다.

하느님께서 저의 기도에 응답을 하시지 않은 것, 저의 기도를 들어주시지 않은 것을, 곰곰이 생각해보고 성찰해보면, 제가 부끄럽게 낭비한 시간, 이기지 못한 유혹들, 연약함과 낙담 속에 하느님께 불평한 것, 친구들, 교우들과의 인간관계와 봉사 활동, 친교 과정에서 제가 저지른 잘못, 때로는 제가 우쭐함을 드러내었고, 저 자신의 영광을 드러냈던 것, 저에게 맡겨진 교회 일의 소홀함에서 비롯된 것이었습니다. 또한, 저의 기도 방법이 잘못되어 잘못 구한 결과라는 것도 알게 됩니다.

우리 모두 개개인이 정성 없이 자기의 욕망을 채우기 위해 제멋대로 바치는 모든 청원 기도를 하느님께서 전부 받아 주신다면, 세상이 의롭지 못하고, 얼마나 혼탁해지고 추해지고 무질서한 세상이 될지 상상이 됩니다. 그나마, 하느님께서 저의 일부 기도를 허락하지 않으셨기에 제가 더 많이 겸손함을 배우게 되었고 저를 돌아보고, 저의 기도가 옳은 기도인지, 성찰할 수 있는 은총의 시간이 되었습니다. 하느님께서 저의 기도를 들어주시지 않았기에, 저의 욕심과 하느님의 뜻을 식별하도록 저의 지혜의 안목도 넓어졌습니다. 그래서 하느님께 더 많이 진심으로 감사 드리고 있습니다.

전구를 드리는 기도는(중보기도라고도 함, Intercession) 성모 마리아, 천사, 성인, 가족, 지인 등의 도움으로 우리의 바램이 하느님께 전달되기를 바라는 기도입니다. 우리 자신과 다른 사람을 위한 기도입니다. 예수님께서도 죄인들과 우리 모두를 위해 하느님께 전구의 기도를 드리셨습니다. 전구를 드리는 기도는 나(자아)를 넘어 이웃사랑을 실천하는 사랑의 통로입니다.

여기서 우리는 전구를 드리는 기도(중보기도)에 관한 바오로 사도의 생각을 상기할 필요가 있습니다. 바오로 사도는 믿음이 강한 우리는 믿음이 나약한 이들의 약점을 그대로 받아 주어야 하고, 자기 좋을 대로 해서는 안 됩니다. 우리는 좋은 일이 생기도록, 교회의 성장이 이루어지도록, 저마다 이웃이 좋을 대로 해야 합니다. 그리스도께서도 당신 좋으실 대로 하지 않으시고, "당신을 모욕하는 자들의 모욕이 제 위로 떨어졌습니다.(로마 15, 1-3)"라고 말하면서, 바오로 사도는 "전구를 드리는 기도"가 우리의 이웃이 성장하고, 우리의 이웃이 좋아지도록 하는 기도라고 설명한 바가 있습니다. 예수님의 양부이신 성 요셉께 전구를 드리는 기도를 (Memorare) 할 때마다, 기도 응답을 많이 받았다는 아빌라의 대 데레사 수녀님의 기도 경험은 지금까지 널리 알려져 왔습니다.

청원기도를 드리는(Petition) 것은 개인이나 공동체의 지향이 이뤄지도록 하느님께 비는 기복기도입니다. 하느님 앞에 인간은 단지 피조물일 뿐이라는 한계를 말씀 드리는 것이 청원기도 입니다. 기복기도는 좋은 것입니다. 그러나, 의롭지 않은 방법으로 바치는 기도, 이기적으로 바치는 기도, 하느님 보시기에 합당하지 않은 방법으로 바치는 기도를 청원기도로 바쳐서는 안됩니다.

저의 기도에는 세 가지 3C 원칙이 있습니다. 첫 번째, 하루도 거르지 않고, 365일 기도를 계속하는(Continually) 것입니다. 부족함이 많은 제가 빠짐없이 기도를 1년 내내 계속하면 하 느님의 성품을 조금씩 닮게 해주십니다. 두 번째, 새벽, 낮, 저녁 등 교회가 정한 시간에 꾸준하게 (Consistently) 기도에 전념하는 것입니다. 제가 꾸준하게 기도하면 하느님의 시선으로 삶을 살아가도록 조금씩 은총을 주십니다. 세 번째 기도 시간을, 예를 들어, 새벽에 한 시간, 정오 무렵 15분, 저녁 한 시간 등 기도 시간의 분량을 변함없이(Constantly) 일관되게 할 수 있도록 정하고 기도하는 것입니다. 저는 언제나 변함없이, 일관되게 기도하면 예수님과 함께 동행하는 영원한 생명의 길이 열릴 것이라고 굳게 믿고 있습니다.

3C 원칙으로 기도하는데 도움이 되는 성경 구절을 소개하겠습니다.

우리는 항상 성령님 안에서 온갖 기도와 간구로 기도해야 합니다. 그렇게 할 수 있도록 인내를 다하고 모든 신자들을 위하여 간구하며 깨어 기도해야 합니다.(에페 6, 18 Constant prayer) 어떠한 경우에든 감사하는 마음으로 기도하고 간구하며 여러분의 소원을 하느님께 아뢰어야 합니다.(Under any circumstances, by prayer and petition, with thanksgiving, make your requests known to God. 필리 4, 6) 끊임없이 기도하십시오. 모든 일에 감사하십시오. (Pray continually; give thanks in all circumstances; Pray without ceasing. 1 테살 5, 17-18)

고통을 겪는 사람도 기도해야 합니다.(야고 5, 13) "희망 속에 기뻐하고 환난 중에 인내하며 기도에 전념하십시오(Rejoice in hope, endure in affliction, persevere in prayer; Rejoice in affliction, persevere or consistent in prayer.로마 12, 12)"라고 한 것은 바오로 사도가 "꾸준하게 기도해야 한다고" 신자들에게 가르쳤던 기도의 핵심가치입니다.

또 다른 기도 원칙이 있습니다.
첫 번째 기도원칙은, 중세 수도원에서 적용한 기도원칙입니다. 중세 수도원에서는 기도를 전투와 중노동에 비유하였습니다. 지금까지의 우리의 기도가 소극적인 기도였다면, 수도원에서 적용한 기도원칙을 적용하여 적극적이고도 공격적인 기도를 하여야 합니다. 예를 들면, 가난에 처한 형제 자매들에게 물질적인 도움을 주지 않고 단순히 기도만 하는 것은 죽은 믿음의 결과입니다. 능동적이고도 공격적인 기도를 드려야 합니다. 예를 들어, "지난해 교무금을 월 10만원 책정했습니다. 금년에는 제가 15만원을 낼 수 있도록 검소하게 살아가게 허락하여 주시옵소서. 빈첸시오회에도 가입하여 봉사하도록 은총을 더하여 주시옵소서."

가난한 사람들에게 음식과 옷을 주고 금전적인 도움을 주고 나누는 것도 이웃사랑이지만, 적정한 교무금을 내는 것도 공동체 차원의 좋은 이웃사랑 실천의 하나입니다. 이런 적극적인 기도를 봉헌함으로써 우리가 세상을 조금씩 바꿔나가야 합니다. 총알이 날아오는 전투에 참가한 것처럼 긴장하고 기도하여야 합니다. 예를 들어 "주님, 제가 가정 형편이 어렵지만, 주님을 위해 성전 건축 헌금도 많이 책정하겠습니다." 이런 기도가 적극적인 기도요, 중노동에 비유된 기도입니다. 하느님 마음에 드시는 기도요, 하느님 사랑의 실천입니다.

우리 자녀 수능 시험 잘 치르게 해 주십시오. 사업이 잘되게 해주십시오, 좋은 아파트로 이사가게 해 주십시오, 등 계속 나와 우리 가족만을 위한 "울타리 기도"에서 탈피해야 합니다. "이타적인 기도"를 해야 합니다. 먼동이 틀 때, 새벽 아침 햇살이 확 퍼져나가듯이 어려운 이웃을 위한 "햇살기도"나 보편지향기도를 해야 합니다. 그래야, 기도의 은총이 아침 햇살처럼 모든 사람들에게 골고루 퍼져나갈 것입니다.

하느님을 위해 무엇을 해드릴 것인가? 하느님을 기쁘시게 해드리기 위해 무슨 말씀을 드리고, 봉사하고, 배려해야 하는지? 깊게 고민하고, 충실하게 정성을 다해 드리는 기도가 매우 중요합니다. 이타기도를 통해 빛으로 나아가는 기도, 덕을 쌓는 기도, 진명덕화(進明德化)의 기도를 하여야 합니다.

두 번째, 기도는 하느님께서 우리에게 직접 은총을 내려주시는 요술 방망이가 아님을 알아야 합니다. 우리가 기도하고 구하는 것이 우리의 우상이 되어 버리게 한다면, 그것은 욕정을 채우는 기도가 될 것입니다.(야고보4, 2~3) 예를 들어, 물질, 명예, 성공, 권력 등 우리가 추구하는 그 모든 것이 사실은 우리의 우상이 되어 버리는 경우가 많습니다. 삼구(三仇)가 되는 것입니다. 사실 우리에게 유익한 그 모든 것들이 전부 우리의 우상이 될 수 있는 가능성이 많습니다. 우리의 물질이 우상이 되어 버리고, 성공이 우상이 되어 버리게 되면, 결국 하느님은 수단이 되어 버리는 것입니다. 하느님을 왜 찾습니까? 우리는 우리가 정말 갈망하는 것, 하느님께서 기뻐하시는 최고의 영적 가치를 지닌 것을 얻기 위해 기도해야 합니다. 우리의 세속적 욕망을 얻기 위한 수단과 방법으로 하느님을 수단화시키는 것은 하느님께서 원하시는 것이 아닙니다. 우리가 헌신하고 희생하는 것 없이, 우리가 노력 없이 하는 기도가 욕정으로 하는 기도가 될 수 있을 것입니다. 시험공부는 하나도 하지 아니하면서, 하느님 앞에 기도하기를 "하느님, 저의 자녀가 수능에 합격하게 해 주세요." 하는 기도를 한다거나, 자녀들을 위해서, 그 아이들의 말에 귀를 기울이기 위해서, 아이들에게 인내하고 참고 견디면서, 그 아이들과 대화하는 시간을 가지려고 하지도 않고, 그들의 마음을 알아주려고 하는 그런 시간을 가지려고 하지도 않고, 그들의 아픔과 절규에 대해서 귀 기울이려고 하는 그런 마음을 가지지도 않은 채, 그냥 하느님 앞에 나와서 "하느님, 저의 자녀가 공부 잘하게 해주세요. 저의 자녀가 성공하고, 출세하게 해 주세요"라고 기도만 하는 것은 그야말로 욕심으로 구하는 기도가 될 것입니다.

우리 자녀가 믿음으로 바로 서게 만드는 기도를 하기 원한다면, 그냥 기도만 하고 있을 것이 아니라, 그 아이와 진정한 이야기를 나누고, 대화를 해야 되고, 마음을 어루만져 줘야 되고, 그들의 마음을 얻어야 하고, 귀를 기울이는 노력을 해야 합니다. 공부를 게을리하는 자녀가 수능시험에서 좋은 성적을 내도록 기도할 것이 아니라, 아침에 일찍 일어나 공부하도록 근면함과 성실함과 지혜를 주시도록 기도하고, 부모 스스로가 모범을 보이는 것이 중요합니다.

스스로는 변하려는 노력이 전혀 없이, 자신의 희생과, 헌신과 노력은 아무것도 하지 않은 채, "하느님, 우리 남편이 예수님 마음으로 변하게 해주세요, 우리 레지오 단원이 봉사 잘하게 도와주세요, 우리 연령회 회원들이 열심한 신자가 되게 해 주세요."라고 기도하는 것은 옳은 기도가 아닙니다. 교회의 활성화와 발전을 위해서 기도는 하지만, 실제로 교우가 새로 이사와도 아는 척도 하지 않고, 정말 선교하려고 하는 마음도 없고, 아무런 노력도 하지 않은 채, 그냥 우리 교회 공동체는 사랑이 넘치는 교회가 되게 해 주십시오. 자신과 다른 모습을 가지고 있는 사람들을 향해서 이해하려고 하는 노력도 없이, 우리 교우들이 변하게 해주십시오, 또는, 우리 교회만 잘 되게 해달라고 하는 기도들은 다 욕망으로 구하는 기도일 뿐입니다. 하느님 앞에서 드리는 참된 기도는 아닙니다.

그렇다고, 기도를 중단해야 한다고 하는 이야기는 아닙니다. 기도를 시작하기 전에, 기도의 제목을 보면, 늘 아쉽고 늘 부족한 기도의 제목일 수밖에 없고, 죄 중에서 드리는 기도일 수밖에 없고, 욕망 가운데 드리는 기도일 수밖에 없지만, 그럼에도 불구하고 우리는 마음을 고쳐 먹고, "제가 옳은 일을 하도록 저부터 변하겠습니다." 하고 하느님 앞에 기도하는 것이 옳습니다.

우리에게 하느님은 어떤 분이십니까? 하느님은 시험 감독관처럼, 우리의 기도가 믿음에 합당한 기도인지, 또 죄악 가운데 혹은 욕망과 욕정으로 드리는 기도인지를 엄격하게 따지시는 분이 아니십니다. 하느님께서는 우리의 기도를 "불합격 기도" 또는 "합격한 기도"라고 판정하시는 그런 냉혹한 하느님, 무심한 판정관 역할을 하시는, 하느님이 아니시고, 우리의 연약함을 아시고, 외 아들을 십자가에 내어주시기까지 우리를 사랑하신, 그리고 우리 죄인들과 대화하기를 원하시고 듣기를 원하시는 하느님이십니다. 하느님께서는 우리의 모든 부족함을 전부 아시기 때문에, 중단 없이 참된 기도를 계속 봉헌하도록 회개하고, 변화하고, 성찰해야 합니다. 당신의 친 아드님마저 아끼지 않으시고 우리 모두를 위하여 내어 주신 분께서, 어찌 그 아드님과 함께 모든 것을 우리에게 베풀어 주지 않으시겠습니까? 하고, 말씀해 주셨습니다. (로마 8, 32) 그러므로 부족하여도 정성껏 주님 앞에 나아가 기도하는 노력을 성실하게 하여야 하고, 기도하는 가운데 우리의 기도 제목들이 혹시 우상이 되고 있는지? 아닌지? 살펴보면서 기도하면 좋습니다.

세 번째, 우리가 처한 환경, 신분, 생활 조건 등을 바꿔주시도록 기도하는 것이 아닙니다. 하느님, 제가 사업을 실패해서 부도가 났습니다. 이럴 때, 교회 감실 앞에서, 눈물을 흘리면서 신세한탄을 하는 것도 한 두 번은 좋지만, 신세한탄을 계속하는 기도는 하느님께서 좋아하시는 진정한 기도가 아닙니다. 기도는 삶의 개선과 건전한 미래와 희망의 쟁취를 위한 기도가 되어야 합니다. 우리는 기도를 전쟁에 임한 군인같이 해야 합니다. 험한 세상을 스스로 먼저 정면 돌파해야 합니다. 주님, 이번에 제가 사업실패를 경험했습니다만, 더 이상 눈물 흘리지 않겠습니다. 연약하게 눈물 흘리지 않겠습니다. 다만, 하느님께서 제가 재기할 수 있도록 지혜를 허락하여 주시옵소서. 제 힘으로 노력하고 극복하도록 하겠습니다. 물질적인 도움이 아니라, 지혜로서 하느님께서 도와주시기를 기도 드리는 것이 합당한 기도요, 적극적인 기도입니다.

하느님께서는 사람들이 하느님을 부르며 다가가서 하느님께 기도하면 그들의 기도를 들어주시 겠다고 말씀하셨습니다.(예레 29, 12) 우리가 무엇이든지 하느님의 뜻에 따라 하느님께 청하면 하느님께서 우리의 청원기도를 들어주신다는 것입니다.(마태, 7, 7~8) 그러나, 우리는 항상 기도하면서 지금, 우리가 하느님께 봉헌하는 기도가 하느님의 뜻이나 예수님의 뜻에 합당한 것인지 성찰해보고, 우리 자신의 힘과 지혜로 극복할 수 있도록, 지혜를 청하는 기도가 더 중요합니다.

소화데레사 성녀는 겸손한 마음, 어린이와 같은 마음으로 기도하곤 하였습니다. 소화데레사 성녀는 글을 모르는 어린아이처럼 주님께 원하는 모든 것을 간절히 말씀 드리면 하느님께서는 항상 기도를 허락해 주셨다고 합니다. 소화데레사 성녀는 아름다운 기도문을 찾기 위해 기도관련 책자, 기도서, 성경 등을 찾지 않았다고 합니다. 소화데레사 성녀의 이 말씀은 기도가 복잡하다 거나, 어렵다거나, 기도가 익숙하지 않다거나, 교구나 교회에서 만든 복잡한 기도문(기도 내용) 을 따르기가 어렵다고 핑계를 대거나, 기도하기를 겁내거나 주저하는 우리들에게 위로가 되는 좋은 말씀입니다.

기도는 우리가 처한 환경, 신분, 생활 조건 등을 하느님께서 확 바꿔주시도록 기도하는 것이 아니라, 소화데레사 성녀의 기도처럼 단순함과 간절함이 필요합니다. "제가 직면한 문제들을 제 스스로 극복하겠습니다."라는 간절함과 결단력이 있는 기도가 필요합니다.

네 번째, 기도를 숙제 하듯이 의무적으로 해서는 안됩니다. 예를 들어, 평일 새벽미사에 반드시 참례할 의무는 없는 것입니다. 다만, 우리 마음 깊은 곳에서, 예수님을 반드시 만나고야 말겠다는 간절함이 있을 때, 새벽미사에 가면 좋습니다. 기복적인 신앙에서 숙제 하듯이 의무적으로 기도한다면 기도의 열매나 응답을 얻기는 어렵습니다. 내가 교회에서 직책을 맡았으니까 새벽미사에 가야하고, 사제에게 잘 보이기 위해 미사참례를 하는 것이라면 예수님을 만날 수가 없습니다. 정성된 마음으로 꾸준하게 기도하는 것이 하느님 보시기에 더 좋은 기도입니다.

D. 기도의 목적

하느님께서는 시편 27장, 시편 44장, 시편 86장, 시편 102장, 시편 139장, 마태오 복음(6, 8; 마태, 7, 7~8)처럼 우리의 몸, 마음, 생각, 정신 안에 있는 모든 바램, 청원을 알고 계십니다. 하느님을 흠숭하고 찬미하고 찬양하는 마음, 참회하는 마음, 감사하는 마음, 간구하고 청원하는 마음 등 우리의 내면에 있는 마음, 희망, 청원 등을 속속들이 전부 알고 계십니다. 우리가 기도하는 것과 기도하고자 마음에 둔 것을 전부 알고 계십니다. 그럼에도 불구하고, 하느님께서는 모든 사람들이 정해진 특정 시간에 또는 화살기도와 같이 즉흥적으로 하느님께 흠숭의 기도, 찬미의 기도, 감사의 기도, 청원 기도 등을 바치기를 원하고 계십니다.

우리는 일상생활에서 만나는 모든 위험, 역경, 곤경에 직면하여, 다음과 같이 하느님께 기도할 수 있습니다. "하느님, 제게 무슨 일이 일어나고 있는지 하느님께서는 너무 잘 알고 계십니다. 그렇지만, 지금 저에게는 오로지 기댈 곳이 하느님 밖에 아무도 없습니다. 저를 도와주십시오. 하느님께서 저에게 하시는 말씀에 귀를 활짝 열고 듣겠습니다. 귀를 활짝 열고 하느님 말씀을 들어야 하느님과 맺은 사랑의 관계, 하느님과의 사랑의 친교를 더욱 굳건히 하고 발전시킬 수 있기 때문입니다. 기도는 하느님께 말씀 드리는 것으로 시작하되, 하느님 말씀을 듣고 성실하게 경청하는 것으로 끝내야 합니다. 하느님, 저는 부족함이 많은 주님의 종입니다. 하느님께서 저를 통해 이루시고자 하는 것과 하느님의 뜻을 겸손하게 듣겠습니다. 기도가 하느님과의 대화이므로, 청하기 전에, 그리고 모든 것을 청한 다음에 하느님의 말씀을 잘 듣고, 경청하고 하느님의 뜻이 무엇인지 아는 것이 좋은 기도입니다. 경청 그 자체로도 좋은 기도입니다.

첫 번째, 기도의 목적은 주일과 의무 축일 미사에 빠지지 않고 반드시 참례하기 위해, 그리고, 개인 기도를 위해 우리의 귀한 시간을 하느님께 내어드리는 것입니다. 가장 먼저 시간을 내어서, 우리가 가장 신뢰할 수 있고 우리 생명의 창조주시며, 우리 생명을 주관하시고 계시는 하느님께 흠숭지례(欽崇之禮)를 바치고(Adore), 찬양하고(Praise), 찬미 드리고(Bless), 공경하고 (Honor), 영광을 드리고(Glorify), 환호하고(Acclaim) 하느님께서 베풀어 주신 은혜에 감사를 드려야 합니다(Give thanks). 아버지의 이름이 거룩하게 빛나시도록 찬양, 찬미 등을 하지 않고, 달랑 청원 기도만 바친다면, 기도의 정성은 반감된다고 할 수 있습니다. 하느님 아버지의 이름이 거룩하게 빛나시도록 하는데 있어서, 중요한 것은 주일과 의무 축일 미사에 빠지지 말고 반드시 참례하여 하느님께 공적으로 예배를 드리는 것입니다. 미사에서 하느님을 만나는 것입니다. 하느님을 만나 하느님께 우리의 마음, 감정, 생각, 바램, 사랑 등을 전부 맡겨드리고, 우리의 고통, 기쁨, 슬픔, 감사, 상처, 걱정, 병고 등도 전부 말씀 드리고 정성껏 간절히 기도하는 것입니다. 기도 속에서 하느님과의 친밀한 관계(친교)를 더욱 굳건하게 다질 수 있습니다. 하느님과 친교를 나누는데 있어서 돈, 규정, 특별한 예식 등은 중요하지 않습니다. 오로지 우리의 귀한 시간을 하느님께 내어드리는 정성과 충절과 거룩함이 요구됩니다. 하느님께서는 우리를 거룩하게 살도록 부르셨습니다.(1 테살 4, 7) 우리가 먼저 거룩하게 살아야 하느님 아버지의 이름이 거룩하게 빛나시도록 해드릴 수 있습니다.

그러나, 우리가 지극정성으로 하느님을 찬양하고, 찬미가를 부른다 해서, 여러 행태의 신심활동과 봉사를 하였다고 해서, 성지 순례를 하고, 전례에 빠짐없이 참례했다고 해서, 하느님 아버지의 이름을 완벽하게 거룩하게 빛나시도록 해드릴 수는 없습니다. 이런 일들은 모두가 하나의 수단일 뿐입니다. 하느님의 이름이 거룩하게 빛나시도록 하기 위한 목적은 우리의 인간적인 생각과 애정을 그리스도교적인 생각과 애정으로 거룩하게 변화시키는 것입니다. 신앙을 가진다는 것은 하느님께 온전히 우리 자신을 맡겨드리고 살아가는 것입니다. 우리 삶의 근본적인 방향을 하느님께 향하고 하느님의 신성을 닮겠다는 삶에 전력투구해서 헌신하겠다는 뜨거운 결단입니다. 우리는 교회 안에서만, 전례를 거행할 때만, 교회에서 봉사할 때만, 거룩한 신자 행세를 해서는 안됩니다. 가정 안에서 직장에서, 사회에서 언제 어디서나 하느님 보시기에 좋은 신자, 충실한 신자가 되어야 하느님 아버지의 이름을 거룩하게 빛나시도록 해드릴 수 있습니다. 하느님 보시기에 좋은 신자가 되어 하느님께 우리의 시간을 정성껏 내어드릴 때, 하느님께서는 더없이 기뻐하실 것입니다.

"하느님 아버지께서는 우리가 청하기도 전에 무엇이 필요한지 알고 계십니다.(마태 6, 8)" 바오로 사도도 "우리 안에서 활동하시는 예수님의 힘으로, 우리가 청하거나 생각하는 모든 것보다 훨씬 더 풍성히 이루어 주실 수 있다고 하셨습니다.(에페 3, 20) 이러한 가르침은 우리가 하느님께 무엇을 청원할 수 있는지 고민하게 합니다. 이미 하느님께서는 우리에게 필요한 것을 우리보다 더 잘 아시고, 우리가 굳이 청하지 않아도 그것을 주십니다. 그러한 하느님께 청원기도가 무슨 소용이 있겠습니까? 하거나, 또는, 하느님께서 졸고 계시거나 주무시고 계셔서, 기도로 우리 목소리를 높이고, 주무시고 계신 하느님을 깨어드려야 비로서 응답하시는 것이 아니라면, 하느님께 청원기도가 무슨 필요가 있겠습니까? 하고 질문할 수 있습니다.

이와 같은 질문에 대하여, 장 칼뱅(프랑스어 Jean Calvin 개혁주의 신학자, 영어 표기 존 칼빈

John Calvin)은 다음과 같이 답변하고 있습니다. 첫 번째, 기도는 하느님을 찾고, 사랑하며, 하느님을 흠숭하고 경배하고, 하느님께 영광을 드리도록 우리 마음을 불타오르게 도와주는 것입니다. 그러므로, 기도해야 합니다. 두 번째, 기도는 하느님 앞에 내어 놓기 부끄러운 우리의 잘못된 욕망, 탐욕, 바램, 죄, 마귀 등이 우리 마음에 들어오지 못하도록 막아 주는 방패입니다.

기도를 하지 않으면 우리 마음과 생각, 우리 몸이 마귀들의 놀이터가 될 수 있습니다. 기도를 해야 마귀들의 유혹을 물리칠 수 있습니다. 기도는 우리 소망과 희망을 하느님께서 보시도록 사실대로 내놓기를 배우게 해줍니다. 기도는 우리 마음을 하느님 앞에 쏟아내고 적나라하게 드러내는 방법을 배우게 해줍니다. 세 번째, 기도는 하느님께서 베풀어주시는 모든 은총을 감사, 찬미, 찬양으로 받게 해주십니다. 우리의 삶이 하느님을 흠숭하고, 감사 드리고, 찬미, 찬양하는 마음으로 살게 해줍니다. 네 번째, 기도를 해야, 하느님께서 우리의 기도에 응답하셨음을 알게 되고, 무한하신 하느님의 은총을 깨닫게 해주시고, 하느님의 사랑과 자비를 더 간절히 바라게 해주십니다. 하느님, 제가 은총을 받을 자격이 없는데 기도를 허락하여 주시니, 감개무량합니다. 이 죄인을 불쌍히 여겨 주시옵소서. 다섯 번째, 우리의 기도로 얻은 은총과 축복을 장래의 더 큰 은총과 축복으로 보답하여 주실 것이라는 밝은 희망을 안겨줍니다. 여섯 번째, 기도는 하느님의 섭리를 체험하게 해줍니다. 하느님을 만나는 경험을 하게 됩니다. 기도는 하느님께서 우리에게 거저 주시는 선물을 알게 하시고, 하느님의 섭리를 경험하게 해주십니다.

이와 같은 이유 때문에, 우리는 하루 일과 중, 귀한 시간을 내어서 청원기도를 드릴 수 있고, 또, 마땅히 드려야 합니다. 청원기도는 우리와 하느님과의 관계를 훨씬 더 돈독하게 하여 주기 때문입니다. 모든 기도의 목적은 하느님과 사랑의 관계를 맺는 친교이며, 청원기도의 궁극적인 목적도 이와 다르지 않습니다. 우리의 청원기도에 대하여 응답을 받지 못하더라도, 하느님과 우리는 이 기도로써 어떤 좋은 관계를 형성하게 됩니다. 그러한 의미에서 응답 받지 못하는 청원기도는 없다고 말하는 것입니다.

청원기도에서 어떤 일이 일어나는지 살펴보기로 합니다. 우리는 청원기도로 하느님께 희망을 아룁니다. 그러면, 하느님께서는 우리의 청원을 들으시고, 당신의 마음, 사랑의 마음을 우리에게 전해 주십니다.

두 번째 기도의 목적은 하느님께 감사를 드리는 것입니다. 식사 전, 후 기도를 바칠 때마다, 하느님의 각종 은총이 허락될 때마다, 감사기도를 드려야 합니다. 한편, 미사 가운데 감사기도에서 주례사제는 "우리 주 하느님께 감사합시다."라고 우리를 초대합니다. 기도는 무엇보다 하느님께서 베풀어 주신 사랑과 은총에 감사 드리는 것입니다. 감사하는 마음으로, 진정으로 뉘우치면서, 통회하면서, 용서를 청하면서, 부족함을 인정하면서, 하느님의 자비와 사랑을 청하면서, 그리고 우리의 일상생활에 필요한 것을 겸손하게 청하는 마음으로 하느님께 감사를 드리는 것입니다. 감사기도의 예를 들어보겠습니다. 주님, 부족함과 허물이 많은 제가, 오늘, 하느님께 기도를 드릴 수 있는 시간을 허락해 주셔서 감사 드립니다. 평화롭고 건강한 가운데, 매일의 일상을 허락하여 주시고 마무리 할 수 있음을 감사 드립니다. 저에게 하루 하루 일용할 양식을 주시는 것도 감사 드립니다. 저에게 사랑하는 가족을 주셔서 감사합니다. 가족들이 완벽해서가 아니라 가족들을 통해 하느님의 사랑을 알 수 있게 해주셔서 감사합니다. 자주, 제 마음에 시기, 무관심, 미움, 저주, 질투, 증오 등의 어두움이 생깁니다. 불평, 불만, 증오, 죄로 가득 찬 차가운 마음이 제 영혼을 어지럽힐 때도 있습니다. 그럴 때마다 하느님께서 저를 사랑하시도록 허락하여 주시고, 저도 하느님께 감사드릴 수 있도록 허락하여 주시기를 기도 드립니다. 하느님께서 저에게 베풀어 주시는 사랑이 크다는 것을 압니다. 그 사랑을 저의 가슴으로 느낄 수 있도록 도와주시기를 기도 드립니다. 하느님의 사랑으로 제가 모든 증오, 시기, 미움 등 악습을 과감히 버리고, 제 마음에 진정한 감사가 끊이지 않도록 간절히 기도 드립니다. 감사를 잊고 불평, 불만, 시기, 증오, 저주, 미움, 질투가 생기고, 유혹과 죄의 종이 될 때에도 하느님의 사랑을 느낄 수 있도록 허락하여 주시기를 기도 드립니다. 범사에 항상 감사 드리며, 감사가 넘쳐나는 삶을 허락하여 주시기를 기도 드립니다.

세 번째 기도의 목적은 깨어있는 것입니다.

기도를 영혼의 호흡이라고도 하는데, 기도를 하지 않아, 영혼의 호흡이 없기 때문에, 우리가 영적으로 잠들고 있다면, 우리는 예수님의 재림을 더 이상 기대하지도 못하는 영적 죽음이라는 사망 선고를 이미 받은 것입니다. 영적 사망 선고를 받은 사람은 예수님의 재림을 필요로 하지도 않고 기다리지도 않는 사람들입니다. 그렇지만, 우리가 죽음에 도달하기 전에, 사망선고를 받기 전에, 인생을 마감하기 전에 영적 죽음에 떨어질 필요는 없습니다. 깨어있지 않고, 세속의 세상살이에 만족하여 현재의 삶을 더 오래 누리고 싶은 욕망이 커질수록, 영원한 생명과 하느님 나라의 행복에 대한 열정은 사그라들고 기도할 수 없기 때문입니다. 흥미진진한 세속의 육적 유혹으로 소돔과 고모라의 사람들처럼 탐욕을 채우기 위해, 육의 눈은 항상 말똥말똥 뜨고 있고, 육의 욕망을 채우기 위해 혈안이 되어 있지만, 영적인 눈을 가진 사람들은 눈을 지긋이 감고 묵상하면서 하느님을 찾아 나선 사람들이며, 깨어있고 기도하는 사람들입니다. 코린토 신자들이 예수님께서 다시 나타나시기를 간절히 기다린 것처럼, 우리도 코린토 신자들의 마음과 같이 항상 깨어 있어야 합니다. 미리 영적 죽음에 떨어질 필요는 없습니다.

하느님께서는 깨어 기도하는 사람들에게 하늘 문을 열어주십니다. 여기서, 예수님의 세례 받으실 때의 장면을 보겠습니다. "온 백성이 세례를 받은 뒤에 예수님께서도 세례를 받으시고 기도를 하시는데, 하늘이 열렸습니다.(루카 3, 21)." 하늘 문이 열리는 또 다른 모습을 보겠습니다. "너희는 십일조를 모두 창고에 들여놓아 내 집에 양식이 넉넉하게 하여라. 그리고 나서 나를 시험해 보아라. 만군의 주님께서 말씀하신다. 내가 하늘의 창문을 열어 너희에게 복을 넘치도록 쏟아 붓지 않나 보아라.(말라키 3, 10)" 이 성경 구절이 영광스럽게 오실 예수님을 간절히 기다리는 우리 모두가 항상 영적으로 깨어있는데 도움이 되기를 희망합니다.

영적 죽음으로 잠든 상태에서 깨어나기 위해서는 기도해야 합니다. 영적으로 깨어 있는 상태에서, 우리가 드리는 기도는 죽은 우리의 영혼이 하느님을 다시 바라볼 수 있게 해줍니다. 스마트 폰, 인공지능, 인공지능을 가미한 로봇 등에 마음을 빼앗겨 눈이 먼 우리 영혼의 눈은 하느님 나라와 영원한 생명을 바라보지 못하고 있습니다. 그래서, 신앙생활이 점점 더 버겁게 느껴지고 짐처럼 느껴지기도 합니다. 그러니까, 자연스럽게 일상생활에서 기도도 점점 사라지고 있습니다. 이럴 때일수록 우리 영혼의 시선을 하느님께 고정시키고 깨어 기도 드려야 합니다.

예수님께서 이미 하늘나라에 있는 모든 성인들과 함께 재림하실 때 우리 모두 하느님 우리 아버지 앞에서 흠 없이 거룩한 사람으로 나설 수 있게 되기를 빕니다.(1 테살 3, 13) 바오로 사도의 말씀처럼, 우리는 다시 오실 예수님을 맞이할 사람들입니다. 그런데, 만약 우리 삶에서 기도가 사라져 버렸고, 고해성사도, 하느님과 함께하는 미사시간도, 신앙생활의 모든 것이 부담스럽다고 생각한다면 예수님을 다시 만날 때, 희망과 기쁨 속에서 예수님을 맞이할 수 있을까요? 예수님 앞에서 고개도 들지 못할 것입니다. 그러므로, 우리는 항상 깨어 있으면서 기도해야 합니다. 예수님께서도 "너희는 앞으로 일어날 이 모든 일에서 벗어나 사람의 아들 앞에 설 수 있는 힘을 지니도록 늘 깨어 기도하여라"(Be vigilant at all times and pray that you have the strength to escape the tribulations that are imminent and to stand before the Son of Man. 루카 21, 36)고 말씀하셨습니다.

우리는 하느님과 맺은 좋은 관계가 무너졌다면 깨어 기도하는 삶을 시작해야 합니다. 기도는 하느님의 존재와 권능을 겸손하게 인정하는 것입니다. 또한, 우리 생명의 주관자가 하느님 이시라는 것을 고백하는 것입니다. 항상, 하느님을 우리 삶의 첫 자리에 모시는 마음이 기도입니다. 기도는 우리를 내버리시지도 않고, 포기하시지도 않고, 떠나시지도 않는 하느님의 사랑을 깨닫게 해 줍니다. 기도하는 사람은 영원한 생명의 가치를 깨닫고 우리 삶이 구원으로 나아갈 수 있게 해 주는 길을 찾은 사람들입니다. 기도하는 사람은 하느님으로부터 힘을 얻습니다. 깨어 기도하는 삶을 통해 예수님을 우리 구원자로 맞이할 수 있는 영적 힘을 크게 키워 나갔으면 좋겠습니다.

E. 기도 방법

기도하는 방법은 여러 가지가 있습니다. 환경, 일정, 상황, 시간, 성향 등에 따라 우리는 다양한 방법으로 자기 자신만의 개인기도를 바칠 수 있습니다. 개인기도는 우리 자신의 어려움, 불편함, 고통, 곤란함, 불행 등을 우리 자신과 다른 사람의 유익함과 행복을 위한 희생과 봉헌의 기도로 바치는 것입니다. 바오로 사도도 유익함과 기쁨을 위한 기도를 하였습니다. "이제 나는 여러분을 위하여 고난을 겪으며 기뻐합니다. 그리스도의 환난에서 모자란 부분을 내가 이렇게 그분의 몸인 교회를 위하여 내 육신으로 채우고 있습니다.(콜로새 1, 24) 그러므로, 우리는 크고 작은 어떤 고통도 연옥 영혼들을 위해 개인기도를 할 수 있습니다. 또한, 가족, 친지, 친구들을 위해 개인기도를 바칠 수 있습니다. 우리가 희생봉헌을 위해 개인기도를 바칠 때, 우리의 참 자신을 발견할 수 있으며 마음의 평화도 얻을 수 있습니다. 예수님도 따로 개인기도를 하시려고 혼자 산에 오르셨습니다.(마태 14, 23) 우리가 혼자 하는 기도는 하느님과 친밀한 교감과 친교를 나눌 수 있습니다.

여러 명이 함께 공동으로 기도하는 것은 아름다운 기도입니다. 숫자에는 힘이 있습니다. 한 사람이 기도하는 것보다, 예를 들어, 천 명이 힘을 모아 기도하면 기도의 효과는 천오백 명이 기도한 것과 같은 풍선효과가 있을 것입니다. 예수님께서도 두 사람이나 세 사람이 내 이름으로 모인 곳에는 나도 함께 있겠다고 하셨습니다.(마태 18, 19-20) 미사 전에 교회 공동체가 미사 준비 기도(성월 기도 등)을 함께 봉헌하는 것, 레지오 단원이 함께 기도하는 것, 연령회 회원들이 함께 기도하는 것 등은 하느님을 찬미하고 주님께 영광을 드리며 은사를 받을 수 있는 은혜로운 공동기도입니다. 더구나, 교회 공동체가 함께 봉헌하는 미사성제는 가장 거룩하고 제일 중요한 으뜸기도로서, 여러 명이 함께 봉헌하는 공동기도입니다. 가족이 함께 기도하는 것도 하느님 보시기에 아주 은혜로운 일입니다. 자녀와 하느님과의 관계를 성장시켜 줍니다. 함께 기도하는 가족은 하느님 안에 함께 머물게 됩니다. 처음부터 거창하게 가족이 함께 기도하기 보다는 식사 전, 후 기도를 함께 시작하고 차츰 기도에 맛들이면 묵주기도를 함께 하여, 함께 기도하는 기도의 맛을 점진적으로 느끼도록 하여야 합니다.

모든 기도 방법 중에서 교회가 의무적으로 요구하는 유일한 한가지는 미사참례입니다. 미사 참례에서 함께 기도할 때, 주님께서 당신 잔치에 초대하신 모든 신자들의 공동체가 부활하신 예수님을 미사에서 만나게 됩니다.(가톨릭 교회 교리서 1166항) 이 거룩한 희생제사와 하나되어 드리는 기도는 엄청난 힘을 가진다고 프란치스코 살레시오 성인도 말씀하셨습니다. 살레시오 성인께서는 미사를 그리스도교 신앙의 중심이라고 강조하셨습니다. 우리는 미사전례 참례로서 하느님께 훨씬 더 가까이 갈 수 있습니다.

예수님께서도 "낙심하지 말고 끊임없이 기도해야 한다고 말씀해 주셨습니다.(Then he told them a parable about the necessity for them to pray always without becoming weary. 루카 18, 1). 끊임없이 기도한다는 뜻의 의미를, 쉽게 예를 들면, 가장 중요한 기도,

정기적인 기도로서 으뜸기도인 미사 참례에 모든 정성을 다해 한번도 빠지지 않고 정성껏 참례하는 것입니다. 미사는 개인적 신심이 아니라, 교회 공동체의 기도입니다. 그래서, "그리스도인의 모든 기도는 전례에서 시작되고 전례로 완성된다."고 하는 것입니다.(가톨릭 교회 교리서 1073항) 미사는 구원의 신비를 재현하는 가장 거룩한 전례이며 신앙의 중심입니다. 따라서, 미사 전례는 개인의 신심이 아니며 교회 신앙 공동체의 가장 거룩한 기도이므로, 미사 전례에 참여하는 것은 아무리 강조해도 지나치지 않습니다.

F. 기도 종류

가장 으뜸 기도인 미사 전례(The Mass is our greatest prayer.)와 예수님께서 가르쳐 주신 주님의 기도, 성모송, 영광송, 성체조배, 성시간, 시간 전례(성무일도), 묵주기도, 삼종기도, 식사 전과 후 기도, 사도신경, 니케아 신경, 십자가의 길 기도, 감사 기도 등 소리기도(염경기도)가 있습니다. 혼자 또는 공동으로 바칠 수 있습니다. 소리는 그저 스쳐가는 소리가 아니라, 하느님께 건네는 정성된 말입니다. 따라서, 소리기도를 바칠 때, 정성을 다해 온 마음으로 바쳐야 합니다.

묵상기도가 있습니다. 침묵 중에 하느님 말씀을 듣고 하느님 뜻을 알아차리고, 하느님 뜻을 마음에 새기며 마음으로 바치는 마음기도입니다. 묵상자료는 성경, 전례기도문, 신심서적, 성화상, 거룩한 기도 등입니다. 특히, 그리스도의 생애에 있었던 4대 복음을 통해 묵상할 수 있고, 묵주기도, 렉시오 디비나, 영적독서, 창작활동, 희생봉헌, 성가대 봉사 등 다른 방법을 통해서도 묵상할 수 있습니다.

묵상을 통해 마음을 고요히 하고 겸손하게 하고 하느님 뜻이 무엇인지? 찾으려고 노력하면 성령님께서 우리를 도와주십니다. 겸손이 기도의 토대입니다.(Humility is the foundation of prayer. 미국 가톨릭교리서 2559항) 겸손하게, 최 우선적으로 하느님의 뜻을 찾으면 하느님의 음성도 들을 수 있습니다. 하느님의 음성을 듣게 되면 우리의 마음을 움직이는 감동을 발견하게 되고 발견한 것을 실천할 수 있습니다.

관상기도가 있습니다. 침묵 중에 주님께 몸과 마음과 정성을 다해 바라보는 것이며 하느님과 단 둘만의 시간을 갖는 것입니다. 우리 내면에서 말씀하시는 하느님의 말씀에 귀 기울여 듣는 들음의 기도입니다. 목숨까지도 하느님을 위해 바치겠다는 일치의 기도, 비움의 기도입니다. 관상기도는 하느님의 성품으로 우리 자신을 전부 채우는 기도입니다. 관상기도는 하느님의 선물이요 은총입니다. 하느님의 성품으로 우리 자신을 채우는 방법에 대해서는 예수님께서 이렇게 비유를 들어 말씀하셨습니다. 예수님께서는 "내가 주는 평화는 세상이 주는 평화와 같지 않다."라고 하셨습니다.(요한 14, 27) 예수님께서 우리 안에 계시고, 우리가 예수님 안에 있을 때, 우리는 예수님과 완전히 결합하여 예수님의 인품과 성품으로 완전히 채워지게 됩니다. 그때에 우리는 완전히 충만하여 결핍 없는 상태가 되고, 예수님께서 거저 주시는 평화로운 상태가 되는 것입니다. 왜냐하면, 예수님과 함께 있을 때, 모든 것이 완전하고 완벽하여 손실이나 손상된 부분이나 결핍된 부분이 전혀 없게 됩니다. 또한, 서로 다투거나, 싸우거나 전쟁을 할 필요도 없는 것입니다. 주님께서 주시는 평화 가운데 살면, 일상 생활에서 겪는 그 어떤 억압, 불안, 위험, 죄악, 우리 마음 속을 집요하게 헤집어 놓는 악마의 모략, 흉계, 유혹, 어둠, 전쟁도 하느님에게서 우리를 떼어 놓을 수가 없습니다. 더군다나, 주님의 평화 가운데 살면 주님과 함께 사는 우리들을 악마나 그 어느 누구도 어찌하지 못한다는 굳센 믿음을 가져야 합니다. 주님께서 주시는 평화에 대한 믿음으로 주님과 일치를 이루고 주님 안에 머무는 것이 관상이요, 주님께서 주시는 평화로움 속에 사는 것이 관상이며 우리 자신을 주님의 성품으로 완전히 채우는 것입니다.

어떤 자매가 교회의 성체조배 회원들이 함께하는 월 정례 조배가 끝난 후에, 옆에서 함께 조배를 한 형제에게 말하기를 "저는 성체조배를 하면서 성경을 읽고, 조배 기도문을 읽고 청원기도 등을 바쳤는데, 제가 보기에 형제님은 아무것도 안 하신 것 같은데, 무엇을 하셨어요?. 형제님이 대답하기를, 저는 하느님만 바라보았습니다. 하느님께서도 저를 바라보셨어요. 하느님을 바라보면 어떤데요? 하느님을 바라보고, 하느님의 뜻에 저의 마음을 일치하도록 노력합니다. 제 마음이 주님의 마음과 일치를 이루면, 비로소 제가 희망하는 것을 주님께 말씀 드립니다. 지금, 제 마음이 이렇습니다. 저의 마음이 이런 저런 이유로 속상합니다. 잔소리 많이 하는, 저의 부인도 정말 밉습니다. 저에게 돈을 빌려간 후, 돌려주지 않는 친구도 밉습니다. 저 자신도 부족함과 허물이 많습니다. 그래서 저의 마음 속이 더 좁아졌습니다. 너그럽지 못합니다. 그러나, 이런 모든 문제들이 하느님 뜻대로 해결되기를 바랍니다. 이렇게, 하느님과 합쳐지는 기도가 관상기도입니다.

시간 전례(성무일도 Liturgy of Hours) 기도가 있습니다. 아침기도 낮기도, 저녁기도, 끝 기도로 구성되어 있습니다. 여기서 "시간"이라는 뜻은 기도에 걸리는 시간을 뜻하는 것이 아니라 특정한 시간(하루의 일정한 시간, 예를 들면 아침기도는 아침 6시에 바치는 것)을 의미합니다.

그리스도의 생애를 묵상하는 묵주기도가 있습니다. 1단(영어로는 10개를 의미하는 Decade)에서 5단까지 예수님의 강생(탄생), 수난, 빛, 부활 등을 묵상합니다. 환희의 신비(Joyful Mysteries 월요일, 토요일에 기도함), 고통의 신비(Sorrowful Mysteries 화요일, 금요일), 영광의 신비(Glorious Mysteries 수요일, 일요일) 빛의 신비(Luminous Mysteries 목요일)가 있습니다. 성인이 되신 요한 바오로 2세 교황께서는 묵주기도를 복음의 요약이라고 하였습니다. 묵주기도 5단을 한꺼번에 바칠 수 없는 경우에는 나머지 기도를 별도의 시간을 내서 바칠 수 있습니다. 묵주를 집에 두고 온 경우에는 손가락을 꼽으며 바칠 수도 있습니다.

렉시오 디비나(Lectio Divina, 성 독서) 기도가 있습니다. 성경 구절을 여러 번 읽으면서 묵상하고 기도하며 관상하는 기도입니다. 첫 번째 단계(읽기, Reading, Lectio)에서는 성경을 두 세 번 반복하여 천천히 읽습니다. 소리 내어 읽을 수 있습니다. 읽으면서 마음에 와 닿는 단어나 간단한 문장을 발견하는 것입니다. 두 번째 단계(묵상, Meditation, Meditatio)에서는 전체 내용을 소가 위에서 되새김질 하듯이 마음 속으로 여러 번 음미해 봅니다. 묵상은 성경 공부가 아니므로 성경 말씀 내용에 집중하여 그 심오한 의미를 여러 번 되새겨봅니다. 세 번째 단계(기도, Prayer, Oratio)는 성경 말씀에 대한 우리의 응답입니다. 우리가 성경을 읽고, 묵상하고 느낀 내용을 말씀 드리고, 하느님께 모든 것을 맡겨드리는 것입니다. 네 번째 마지막 단계(관상, Contemplation, Contemplatio)에서는 성경 말씀을 읽고, 묵상하고 기도 드렸던 내용을 실천할 수 있도록 하느님과 일치하는 시간을 갖는 것입니다. 관상은 직역하면 하느님을 바라보는 것입니다만, 관상은 하느님과 합쳐지는 기도입니다. 하느님과 우리가 합쳐지는 기도입니다. 하느님을 우리 안에 모시고, 우리 자신을 온전히 하느님께 내어드리는 것입니다. 하느님과 일치하기 위해 우리 자신을 전부 비우고, 버리고, 하느님의 성품(신성)으로 채우는 것입니다.

즉흥적인 기도(화살 기도)가 있습니다. 때와 장소를 가리지 않고 언제든지 할 수 있는 기도입니다. 기도에 익숙하지 않은 신자, 세례를 받은 지 얼마 되지 않은 신자가 바치면 좋은 기도입니다. 우연히 성당 앞을 지나가다가 잠시 성당에 들어가 성체 앞에서 짧은 시간을 내서 기도할 수 있습니다. 길을 걸어가다가, 비행기, 여객선, 기차, 버스 등에서 주모경, 묵주기도 등을 바치는 것입니다. 화살기도는 "간결하게, 자주, 집중하여(Briefly, Frequently, Intensively)" 드리는 기도입니다. 화살 기도를 드리려면 집중과 마음의 단순함과 간단함이 요구된다는 사실은 더 말할 나위도 없습니다. 화살 기도를 할 때, 주님의 기도를 모든 기도의 시작점으로 사용하는 것도 좋은 방법입니다. 마치 갓난 어린아이가 젖을 찾듯, 단순하게 바치는 기도입니다. 화살기도에 맛들이고 자주하게 되면, 모든 기도에 통달할 수 있습니다.

9일기도(Novena)는 끈기가 필요한 기도 입니다. 9일기도는 9일간 연속으로 바치거나 특정 요일에 9주간 연속으로 바치는 기도입니다. 보통 대축일 9일 전에 9일기도를 시작합니다. 병자들의 치유를 기도지향으로 루르드의 성모님께 바치는 9일기도, 세계 전쟁 종식과 평화와 죄인들의 회개를 위해 파티마의 성모님께 9일 기도를 바칠 수 있습니다. 자신이나 가족이 직면한 상황이 너무 절망적이라고 생각되면, 다시 말해 희망이 전혀 없다고, 의사나 전문가가 이야기했을 때, 12제자의 한 분이신 성인 "유다 타대오 사도"에게 전구의 9일기도를 바칠 수 있습니다. 다만, 성령 강림 대축일 전 9일기도를 시작하였는데, 극심한 독감, 질병, 사고 등으로 하루 기도를 못하였다면, 다음 날 두 번 기도하면 됩니다. 하루 기도를 못하였다고 걱정할 필요가 없습니다. 빠지지 않고 정성껏 기도하는 것도 중요하지만, 얼마나 몸과 마음을 다해 정성껏 기도하느냐? 하는 것이 더 중요합니다.

삼종기도(The Angelus)와 부활 삼종기도(Queen of Heaven)는 혼자 또는 여럿이 공동으로 함께 기도할 수 있습니다. 보통 하루 중 아침 6시, 정오 12시, 오후 6시 세 번 기도합니다. 장소에 관계없이 어디서나 할 수 있는 기도입니다.

G. 겸손 호칭기도(Litany of Humility)

마음이 온유하고 겸손하신, 오 예수님! 저의 기도를 들어주소서.

존경 받고 싶은 욕망에서 예수님 저를 구하소서
사랑 받고 싶은 욕망에서 예수님 저를 구하소서
격찬 받고 싶은 욕망에서 예수님 저를 구하소서
영예를 받고 싶은 욕망에서 예수님 저를 구하소서
칭찬 받고 싶은 욕망에서 예수님 저를 구하소서
다른 사람보다 더 선호 받고 택함 받기를 바라는 욕망에서 예수님 저를 구하소서
남을 상담해주려는 욕망에서 예수님 저를 구하소서
인정받고자 하는 욕망에서 예수님 저를 구하소서
모욕 당하는 두려움에서 예수님 저를 구하소서
경시 당하는 두려움에서 예수님 저를 구하소서
질책 받는 고통의 두려움에서 예수님 저를 구하소서
중상모략 비방 당하는 두려움에서 예수님 저를 구하소서
타인으로부터 잊혀지는 두려움에서 예수님 저를 구하소서
비웃음 당함의 두려움에서 예수님 저를 구하소서
부당한 대우와 학대 받음의 두려움에서 예수님 저를 구하소서
의심받는 두려움에서 예수님 저를 구하소서
예수님 다른 이들이 저보다 더 많은 사랑을 받기를 갈망하는
은총을 허락하소서. 예수님 다른 이들이 저보다 더 높이 존경
받기를 갈망하는 은총을 허락하소서
예수님, 세상 사람들이 보기에 다른 이들이 높아지고 제가 낮아지기를
갈망하는 은총을 허락하소서
예수님 다른 이들은 선택 받고 저는 제외되도록 갈망하는
은총을 허락하소서
예수님 다른 이들은 칭찬받고 저는 눈에 띄지 않도록 갈망하는 은총을 허락하소서

예수님 모든 일에서 다른 이들이 저보다 우선적으로 선호되고 택함
받도록 갈망하는 은총을 허락하소서
제가 마땅히 거룩해져야 할 정도로 거룩하다면 다른 사람들이 저보다
더 거룩해지도록 갈망하는 은총을 허락하소서. 아멘.

2019년 6월 13일 프란치스코 교황은 전 세계에 파견되어 있는 교황대사들과 교황청에서 만난 자리에서 겸손의 기도를 봉헌하라고 권고하였습니다.

겸손의 기도(Litany of Humility)는 성 비오 10세 교황 당시 교황청 국무원장을 역임한 라파엘 메리 델 발(Rafael Merry del Val, 1865-1930) 추기경이 만든 기도문입니다.

라파엘 메리 델 발 추기경의 "겸손의 기도"는 단순한 기도문 이상의 가치를 지닙니다. 우리 인간의 마음속 깊은 곳에 자리한 욕망들과, 우리 마음 안에 자리한 세 종류의 악마를 어떻게 물리치고 어떻게 우리가 자유로워질 수 있는가에 대한 응답과 같습니다. 겸손의 기도는 영혼의 울림을 통해 우리가 인간으로서, 어떻게 해야 겸손하게 되는지를 가르쳐줍니다.

겸손의 기도는 욕망으로부터의 해방을 가져다 줍니다. 겸손의 기도는 모든 기도의 토대가 됩니다. 존경, 사랑, 칭찬, 명예, 영예, 재물 욕, 성욕 등은 인간이라면 누구나 원하는 것입니다. 이는 자연스럽고 본능적인 욕구로 보입니다. 하지만, 이 욕구가 커질수록 우리를 타인에게 종속시키고, 결국 욕망이 커질수록 내면의 평화도 빼앗깁니다. 우리는 "얼마나 존경 받는가?" "얼마나 사랑 받는가?"와 같은 질문들은 우리 자신을 평가 받는 기준이 됩니다. 그러나, 이러한 평가기준은 우리를 끊임없는 불안, 경쟁, 결핍 속으로 몰아넣는 악순환을 겪고 있습니다.

라파엘 메리 델 발의 기도는 이러한 악순환에서 벗어나도록 초대합니다. 예를 들면, 존경 받고자 하는 욕망에서 해방되는 것은 단순히 욕망을 버리는 것을 의미하지 않습니다. 그것은 진정한 자유를 찾는 일입니다. 더 이상 타인의 인정이나 칭찬에 의존하지 않는 것. 이것이 바로 겸손이 지닌 진정한 자유요, 해방의 힘입니다.

겸손의 의미를 알아보겠습니다.
謙자는 "겸손하다, 겸허하다"라는 뜻을 가진 글자입니다. 謙자는 言(말씀 언)자와 兼(겸할 겸)자가 결합한 모습입니다. 兼자는 벼 다발을 손에 쥐고 있는 모습을 그린 것으로 "아우르다, 겸하다"라는 뜻을 갖고 있습니다. 인격과 소양이 두루 갖춰진 사람은 자신을 낮추고 말을 공손하게 합니다. 그래서 謙자는 "겸하다"라는 뜻을 가진 兼자와 言자를 결합해 "말에 인격과 소양이 두루 갖추어져 있다"라는 의미입니다.

遜자는 겸손할 손. 뜻을 나타내는 "책받침(辶=辵) 쉬엄쉬엄 가다, 부(部)와 음(音)을 나타내는 동시(同時)에 달아나다(孫遜)의 뜻을 가진 孫(손)으로 이루어짐. "달아나다, 전(轉)하여, 사양하다."의 뜻. (네이버 사전)

겸손한 사람은 자기가 겸손하면서도 정작 자기가 겸손한 사람인 것을 모르는 사람입니다. 겸손한 사람은 상대방을 존경하고 높여 주는 사람이며, 말을 예의 바르고 공손하게 합니다. 상대방이 자기 자랑만을 일방적으로 늘어 놓아도 함께 즐거워해주는 사람입니다. 부자이면서도 가난한 척하는 사람은 겸손한 사람이 아니고 자기를 비하하는 사람입니다. 겸손은 보통 사람들에게는 미덕이지만, 지식인이면서도 모르는 척하는 사람, 재능이 있으면서도 재능이 없는 척하는 사람은 겸손한 사람이 아닙니다. 역시, 자기를 비하하는 사람입니다. 자기 재물을 어려운 이웃에게 남 모르게 나눠주는 부자가 겸손한 사람입니다. 지식인이 남 모르게 자기의 지식을 재능 기부로 이웃에게 거저 나눠주는 사람이 겸손한 사람입니다. 모든 소유, 재물, 재능, 지혜, 학식, 건강 등이 하느님께로부터 왔으며, 하느님 소유이고, 우리가 잠시 보관하고 관리하는 충실한 청지기임을 인정하는 것이 겸손의 출발점입니다.

예수님께서 비유로 들려주신 성경 속의 겸손에 대하여 알아보겠습니다. 바리사이와 세리 두 사람이 기도하러 성전으로 갔습니다. 유명한 바리사이와 세리의 기도입니다.

바리사이의 기도는 감사기도였습니다. 그러나 바리사이는 스스로 의롭다고 확신하며, 자신보다 부족한 다른 사람들을 업신여기면서 잘난체하며 기도를 바쳤습니다. 그는 스스로 의롭다고 생각하기에 하느님 앞에서 "꼿꼿이 서서" 기도하였습니다. 감사기도이지만, 세리와 비교하며 자신의 의로움을 마음껏 자랑하고 과시하였습니다.(루카 18, 9-14)

그의 눈은 하느님을 바라보거나 자신의 내면을 성찰하지도 않았습니다. 하느님이나 자신에게 향하지 않고, 오로지 세리의 약점을 파고드는데 향하였고, 세리를 죄인으로 단죄하고 세리의 죄를 정 조준하였습니다. 반면에 세리는 "하늘에 계신 하느님을 향하여 눈을 들어 기도할 엄두도 내지 못하고 가슴을 치며" 하느님의 자비를 청합니다. 그의 눈은 하느님 앞에서 한없이 부족하다고 느끼고 자기 자신을 향합니다. 의롭게 되어 돌아간 사람은 마음이 겸손하고, 자기의 잘못과 죄를 뉘우치며 집으로 돌아간 세리입니다.

의로움은 스스로 얻는 것이 아니라 하느님에게서 주어지는 것입니다. 의로움은 겸손하고 회개하며, 자기를 낮추고, 참회하는 사람들에게 하느님께서 거저 주시는 것입니다. 다른 이들과 비교해서 의로운 것이 아니라 하느님께서 의롭다고 인정해 주시는 것입니다. 의로움을 구원이라는 말로 바꾸어서 이해해도 마찬가지입니다. 구원은 스스로 쟁취하거나 다른 이들과 비교해서 얻어지는 것이 아니라, 하느님으로부터 선물로 주어지는 것입니다.

겸손하지 못한 "교만"은 다른 사람이 아닌 오로지 하느님을 적으로 대합니다. 교만을 제외한 다른 악한 행동과 죄는 잘못을 저지른 사람에게 그 벌이 돌아가거나 다른 사람들에게 영향을 끼칩니다. 하지만 교만으로 가득 찬 마음만은 하느님을 직접 대적하기에, 하느님께서는 이것을 적으로 간주하십니다. 겸손이 아닌 "교만"으로 부풀어 오르면 언제나 하느님의 것을 자신의 것인 양 주장하려고 하기 때문입니다." (브라가의 마르티누스 "교만" 7.)

교만하고 오만불손한 사람은 간이 부어있으며 간이 몸 밖으로 나와있는 것입니다. 이 세상의 모든 만물이 하느님께서 창조하신 하느님의 소유물인데, 하느님을 무시하고, 하느님의 소유물마저도 자기 것이라고 주장하는 독선과 교만으로 살아가기 때문입니다.

어느 교회든지 10년 동안 교회에 다니고, 봉사를 하고 섬기면, 신부, 목사, 장로, 집사, 또는 사목회의 간부 등 봉사자가 되었든, 신자가 되었든, 그들은 예외 없이 바리사이가 된다는 우스개 소리가 있습니다. 대개 10년이 경과되면 그들은 무엇을 좀 안다고, 다른 신자들을 가르치려 들고, 그들은 편견(prejudice, bias)과 선입견(stereotype, preconception, preconceived notion, preconceived opinion)의 노예가 되어 뒷담화를 즐기고, 예수님의 자리를 차지하려 들고, 시선을 하느님에게 돌리지도 않습니다.

자기의 단점을 성찰하거나 찾아내지도 않고 오히려 감추려 들고 있습니다. 그들의 시선은 다른 선량한 신자들의 단점을 찾는데 혈안이 되어있으며 정조준하고 있습니다. 우리 마음 안에는 세 종류의 마귀가 있습니다. 그 마귀들이 우리를 유혹하고 있습니다. 마귀들은, 하느님께 영광을 드리는 것이 아니라, 자기의 특출함과 영광을 드러내려고 하는 것입니다. 예를 들면, 미사전례에서 절은 통일되고 일치되어야 합니다. 그런데, 복사나 수녀님은 미사 중에 절을 하지 않는데 혼자 계속 자주 절을 하여, 자기 잘난 체를 하고, 자기를 과시하며, 공동체의 화합을 해치는 신자들이 있습니다. 교회에 잘 나오지 않던 신자가 갑자기 나와서 제대 앞이나 감실 앞에서 큰 절을 하거나 미사 전례 중에 과도한 절을 하는 사람은 십중팔구 교회 신자들을 유혹하여 이단교회로 낚아채가는, 이단의 일꾼이요, 낚시꾼들입니다. 순진한 신자들, 세례를 받은 새로운 신자들은, 이단의 낚시꾼들을 조심해야 합니다.

성경에서 알려주는 겸손의 속성에 대해 알아보겠습니다. 오만과 교만이 가득하면 수치와 욕됨이 오고 불행을 자초하지만, 겸손한 이에게는 지혜가 따르기 때문에 인생을 올바로 인도합니다. (잠언 11, 2) 영광에 앞서 겸손이 있습니다. 겸손이 영광과 존귀의 길잡이입니다.(잠언 15, 33) 파멸에 앞서 교만이 있고 멸망에 앞서 오만한 정신이 있다.(잠언 16, 18) 가난한 사람들과 겸손하게 지내는 것이 거만하고 오만하며 교만한 사람들과 지내는 것보다 낫다는 하느님 말씀입니다.

나는 드높고, 거룩한 곳에 좌정하여 있지만, 겸손한 이들의 넋을 되살리고, 뉘우치는 이들의 마음을 되살리려고, 뉘우치는 이들과, 겸손한 이들과 함께 있습니다.(이사야 57, 15) 하느님께서는 겸손한 마음을 기뻐하시며, 뉘우치고 통회하는 사람들과 함께 계시겠다고 약속하십니다.

나는 마음이 온유하고 겸손하니 내 멍에를 메고, 나에게 배워라. 그러면 너희가 안식을 얻을 것이다.(마태 11, 29) 예수님을 본받아 겸손하게 살아가도록 가르쳐주십니다. 겸손과 온유를 다하고 인내심을 가지고 사랑으로 서로 참아주며, 성령께서 평화의 끈으로 이루어 주신 일치를 보존하도록 애쓰십시오.(에페 4, 2) 겸손과 온유는 교회 소공동체 안에서 사랑과 용서를 이루는 기초가 됩니다. 겸손한 마음으로 서로 남을 자기보다 낫게 여기십시오.(필리 2, 3) 이기심, 자만, 오만, 교만을 버릴 때, 다른 사람이 자기보다 낫다고 높이 존경할 때, 겸손한 마음이 우리 마음을 차지합니다. 그러나 하느님께서는 더 큰 은총을 베푸십니다. 그래서 성경은 이렇게 말합니다. "하느님께서는 교만한 자들을 대적하시고 겸손한 이들에게는 은총을 베푸십니다."(야고4, 6) 여러분은 모두 겸손의 옷을 입고 서로 대하십시오. 하느님께서는 교만한 자들을 대적하시고 겸손한 이들에게는 은총을 베푸십니다. 그러므로 하느님의 강한 손 아래에서 우리 자신을 낮추면 하느님께서 우리를 높여주실 것입니다.(1베드 5, 5-6) 하느님께 선택된 사람, 거룩한 사람, 사랑 받는 사람답게 마음에서 우러나오는 동정과 호의와 겸손과 온유와 인내를 입으십시오.(콜로 3, 12) 겸손은 하느님께서 선택하신 신자들이 하느님 자녀로서 갖추고 있는 영성이자 품성입니다.

정중례(鄭重禮)로 90도로 절을 하거나 무릎을 꿇고 하느님을 찬양하고, 찬미 드리고, 흠숭하는 것 등도 중요하지만, 하느님께 모든 정성을 다해 우리의 선한 마음을 충심으로 숙이고 겸손하게 마음을 낮추는 것이 더 중요합니다.

H. 기도의 시작 점

청원기도를 시작하기 전에 무슨 기도를 하여야 하나요? 성호경을 긋고 곧바로 청원기도를 하기보다는 먼저 시작기도를 한 다음에 청원기도를 하는 것이 좋습니다.

(1) 주님의 기도가 가장 좋은 시작기도입니다. 먼저 주님의 기도를 시작 기도로 바친 후, 다음에 청원기도를 할 수 있습니다.
(2) 시편과 성가를 기도의 시작점으로 삼는 것도 기도의 좋은 방법입니다. 예를 들면, 주님 제

입시울을 열어주소서, 제 입이 주님의 찬양을 널리 전하오리다.(시편 51, 17) 하느님 어서 오시어 저를 구하소서. 주님 어서 오시어 저를 도우소서.(시편 70, 2)

(3) 일을 시작하며 드리는 기도(Come Holy Spirit, 오소서 성령님)를 기도의 시작점으로 삼을 수 있습니다.

I. 하느님의 뜻에 합당한 기도란?

기도는 하느님의 뜻에 합당하게 드려야 합니다. 지금까지 우리의 뜻과 기도지향과 의지만을 고집하는 기도목적으로 기도하였다면, 이제부터는 하느님의 뜻이 우리 안에서 이루어지는 기도로 서서히 변화되는 기도를 드려야 합니다.

하느님의 뜻이 무엇인지를 먼저 알아내고, 알아낸 하느님의 뜻이 우리 안에서 이루어지는 기도를 하느님께서 들으시기를 좋아하실 것입니다. 우리는 기도 안에서 우리를 사랑하시는 하느님을 만납니다. 이 만남에서 하느님을 우리 삶의 가장 윗자리로 모시고 있습니다. 하느님을 위해 우리 자신을 하느님께 봉헌하고 몸과 마음과 영혼을 모두 하느님께 내어드리고 있습니다. 하느님으로부터 받은 은총에 감사 드리며, 우리의 소망과 청원도 말씀 드리지만 하느님의 뜻에 우리 자신을 온전히 맡겨드리는 것입니다.

우리는 삶에서도 하느님의 뜻을 실천하도록 초대받은 사람들입니다. 초대받은 사람답게 성모님처럼 하느님의 뜻이 무엇인지 먼저 알아차려야 합니다. "보십시오. 저는 주님의 종입니다. 말씀하신 대로 저에게 이루어지기를 바랍니다. (Mary said, "Behold, I am the handmaid of the Lord. May it be done to me according to your word." 루카 1, 38). 그러므로, 우리의 기도가 하느님 뜻과 예수님의 가르침에 맞는지 돌아보는 것이 중요합니다. 우리의 이기심을 충족시키는 기도가 되어서는 안됩니다. 입과 머리로만 기도하고, 하느님 아버지의 뜻을 염두에 두지 않고, 우리의 바램과 요구 사항만 기도하는 것은 우리를 부끄럽게 하는 것입니다. 그러므로, 기도하기 전에 "하느님의 뜻이 무엇인지 알게 하여 주십시오." 하면서 우리 내면을 성찰하고 기도를 하는 것이 좋습니다. 우리를 사랑하시는 하느님의 뜻을 앎으로서 하느님과 함께하고 하느님을 만나는 것이 기도의 목적입니다.

세상의 모순, 질병, 고통, 예상하지 못한 일, 만남과 이별 등 일상생활의 모든 일들을 어떻게 분명하게 설명할 수 있겠습니까? 그럴듯한 이유나 구실을 붙일 수야 있겠지만, 사실 그것이 하느님의 뜻인지 자신의 생각인지 확신할 수 없는 것입니다. 다만, 우리는 유한한 인간으로서 믿음을 가지고 전지전능하신 하느님의 뜻을 찾는 인생의 순례 여정을 묵묵히 겸손하게 걸어갈 뿐입니다.

하느님의 뜻을 찾은 욥의 이야기를 들어보겠습니다. 욥은 하느님의 뜻을 찾아 모험에 나섰습니다. 욥의 눈으로는 무고한 의인의 고통과 그 어떤 이유도 찾을 수 없는 불행의 원인을 설명할 수 없었습니다. 욥은 그저 하느님을 만나 자신의 고통을 토로하고, 이 고통과 불행의 이유와 의미와 하느님의 뜻을 묻고자 하였습니다. 이에 대하여 결국 하느님께서 응답하십니다. 하느님의 답변은 인간의 기준으로는 이해할 수 없는 하느님의 위대하심입니다. 세상을 창조하시고 다스리시는 하느님의 위대하심은 우리가 온전히 이해할 수 없는 심오한 신비입니다. 고통과 불행, 행복 등에 관한 하느님의 뜻을 유한한 인간 사고의 틀 안에 가두기보다, 인간의 이해를 넘어서는 하느님의 위대하심을 인정하고, 불확실성 안에서 확실한 믿음을 가지고 담대하게 그리고 겸손하게 하느님께 나아가는 것이 우리 신앙인의 올바른 태도일 것입니다. 그런 태도를 보일 때 우리가 알 수 없는 고통과 불행, 행복 등의 신비와 하느님의 뜻을 아주 조금이나마 이해하게 될 것입니다.

우리의 뜻을 포기하고 하느님의 뜻을 알아내고 알아차리며 하느님의 뜻을 겸손하게 받아드릴 때, 우리의 내면에서 은은하게 솟아오르는 희열과 기쁨도 만끽할 수 있습니다. 우리의 뜻과 교만을 포기할 때, 진정한 예수님의 협력자가 되고 예수님의 친구요, 형제로, 성장하게 됩니다. 궁극적으로 우리의 인생은 하느님의 뜻을 찾아가는 희망의 순례 여정입니다. 순례 여정에서 우리가 할 말은 가급적 줄이고 하느님의 말씀을 듣고 하느님의 뜻이 무엇인지 알아내기 위해 경청을 잘해야 합니다. 경청을 잘해야 하느님께 대한 신앙을 잘 표현할 수 있고, 참 자신(자아)를 발견할 수 있으며, 하느님께서 주시는 평화도 얻을 수 있습니다. 그래야 하느님의 뜻을 잘 알아내고, 실천하고 하느님의 진정한 협력자가 될 수 있습니다. 올바른 기도 준비는 그 자체가 이미 훌륭한 기도이며, 잘 듣는 경청 또한 훌륭한 기도입니다.

J. 하느님의 뜻이 무엇인지 식별하는 방법

하느님께 우리의 청원기도를 다 말씀 드렸다면, 하느님께서 하시는 말씀을 정성껏 경청해야 합니다. 하느님께서 우리 마음 속에 무엇을 말씀하실까? 잘 들어야 합니다. 우리의 청원기도가 하느님의 뜻에 부합되는지 살펴보아야 합니다. 그러나, 하느님의 뜻은 음성으로 들려오지 않습니다. 하느님께서는 쉬지 않으시고 계속 말씀하시지만, 우리의 청각 주파수와 지각 주파수가 하느님의 주파수와 맞지 않아서 들을 수가 없습니다. 우리의 청각 주파수와 지각주파수를 하느님의 주파수와 맞추기 위해서 다음과 같이 하실 것을 권유해 드립니다.

매일매일 일정분량의 성경을 읽고 묵상하는 것입니다. 저는 우리나라에 100주간 성경공부 과정이 처음 도입되었을 때, 100주간 성경공부 과정에서(학습과정은 121주간 공부하는 프로그램임) 결석을 한 번하여 정근상을 받았습니다. 안경렬 몬시뇰께서 직접 100주간 봉사자로 봉사하시고 가르쳐 주셨습니다. 지금까지 만난 사목자 중에서 가장 훌륭하신 분이셨습니다. 주임 신부께서 성경공부의 봉사자로 자원하신 분은 아마 우리나라 천주교회에서 유일하신 분이라고 사료됩니다. 우리들의 멘토 역할도 집안의 아버지 처럼 해 주셨습니다. 그때, 공부하면서 깨달은 것은 "하느님의 뜻"은 전부 성경 안에 있다는 것과, 너무 성경에 대한 지식이 부족함을 실감하였습니다. 그래서, 하느님의 뜻에 맞게 기도하기 위해서는 성경공부를 꾸준히 해야 하겠다고 결심하였습니다. 그 뒤에 100주간 봉사자로 두 번 봉사하였습니다. 성경 공부는 벼락치기 공부로 해서는 자기 것으로 소화할 수가 없습니다. 매일 겸손한 마음으로 정성껏 일정 분량의 성경을 꾸준히 읽고, 소가 위에서 되새김질을 하듯 묵상하는 것이 좋습니다.

예를 들어, 하루에 두 시간 성경을 읽고, 묵상하고 두 시간 기도하는 것이 좋습니다. 성경공부를 계속하다 보면 수시로 성경말씀이 떠오르게 하시기도 하고, 하느님과 예수님께서는 성경을 통해 우리의 일상 삶 속에서 끊임없이 우리에게 말을 건네오시기도 합니다. 그런데, 하느님께서 말씀하시지 않는 것이 아니라, 우리가 듣지 못하는데 문제가 있습니다. 그 문제를 해결하기 위해 "하느님, 하느님께서 저에게 끊임없이 말씀하실 것인데, 하느님 말씀을, 그 음성을 놓치지 않고 살아가게 해주십시오. 저는 지금까지 사람들의 말, 소음, 그리고 우리 마음 안의 내면의 소리만을 들으면서 살아왔습니다.

그런데, 그 소리들이 너무 커서 하느님의 음성이 묻혀버리고 들리지 않습니다. 제가 세속의 소음 소리에 너무 익숙하다 보니까, 하느님의 목소리가 점점 들리지 않고, 마침내는 전혀 들리지 않고 있습니다. 오늘, 제가 하느님의 목소리를 듣지 못하는 이유는 하느님께서 침묵하시는 것이 아니라, 제 마음이 세속의 욕망과 정욕과 세상의 소리로 가득 차 있기 때문입니다. 하느님 제 마음이 소음으로 시끄럽지 않게 해주십시오. 세상의 소음에 끌려 다니지 않게 해주시고, 하느님의 음성을 들을 수 있는 영적인 눈과 귀를 열어 주십시오. 부족함과 허물이 많은 제가 무엇이 하느님의 음성인지 식별할 수 있는 지혜를 허락하여 주시기 바랍니다.

AI 인공지능 시대에는 가짜 뉴스 등 더 많은 말이 들리는 시대입니다. 그래서, 무엇이 하느님의 음성이고 무엇이 세상의 소리인지? 가짜 뉴스인지? 식별할 수 있는 지혜가 저에게는 너무 필요합니다. 그 지혜로 하느님의 소리를 듣고 싶습니다.

하느님께서는 이렇게 말씀하실 것입니다. "정말, 네가 성경공부 한다고, 힘들었겠구나. 나는 네가 때로는 친구, 지인, 직장 사람들, 가족들하고 심한 갈등을 겪고 있는 것도 알고 있다. 더구나, 네가 스마트폰 등에 몰두하고, 세상의 온갖 욕정과 정욕의 노예가 되고 정신이 팔려 내 목소리를 들으려고 하지 않는 것도 잘 알고 있다. 나는 네가 처한 환경, 심정, 네 마음 전부 속속들이 이해하고 있단다. 나는 네가 그 어려움을 극복할 수 있고, 나의 목소리를 침묵 가운데 들으려고 할 것으로 너를 믿고 있단다." 덧붙여서 하느님께서 다음과 같은 말씀을 하실 것입니다. "너희들은 내 목소리를 잘 경청하여야 한다." 그러므로, 기도에서 중요한 것은 "하느님을 바라보는 시간과 침묵도 필요하고, 청원기도를 드리는 시간도 필요하고, 무엇보다 하느님의 말씀을 듣기 위해 우리 마음을 여는 시간도, 하느님의 뜻을 알아내는 시간도, 그리고 하느님의 뜻에 맞게 기도하는 시간이 필요합니다."

아무리 복잡하고 바쁜 일정 속에서도 성경을 읽고 묵상하여 하느님 말씀을 듣는 것을 삶의 최우선 순위로 삼아야 합니다. 성경 말씀을 통해서만 하느님 음성을 들을 수 있는 기초가 되기 때문입니다. "하느님, 저에게 필요한 것은 하느님 음성을 놓치지 않고, 단연코 반드시 하느님 말씀을 잘 듣고, 하느님 아버지의 뜻을 찾겠다는 것이 저의 확고한 각오입니다."라고 하느님께 기도 전에 말씀 드리는 것이 좋습니다.

미국의 복음 전도사 드와이트 무디(Dwight Lyman Moody)도 하느님의 뜻을 아는 것이 매우 중요함을 이렇게 이야기 하고 있습니다. "기도는 자기 필요와 욕심에 의하여 하느님을 자기 편으로 만드는 것이 아니라, 하느님의 뜻에 우리 자신을 맞추는 일이다"라고, 하면서 하느님의 뜻을 아는 것이 기도에서 중요함을 강조하였습니다.

토마스 아 켐피스(Thomas à Kempis, 독일 가톨릭 사제)는 주님의 뜻에 대하여 이렇게 말하고 있습니다. "오 주님, 주님께서는 무엇이 최선인지 아십니다. 모든 일을 주님의 뜻대로 이루소서. 주님께서 선택하신 것을, 주님이 선택하신 양만큼, 주님께서 선택하신 순간에 저의 기도를 들어주시기를 청합니다." 주님께서 원하시는 곳에 저를 두시고, 적당하다고 생각하시는 대로 저를 다루소서. 저는 주님의 손 안에 있는 미소한 존재입니다. 주님의 뜻대로 인도하소서. 저는 무슨 일이든 할 수 있는 준비된 주님의 종입니다. 저 자신이 아니라 주님의 뜻을 실천하고 주님만을 위해 살기 원합니다.

예수님께서도 완벽하게 하느님의 뜻을 구하는 기도를 하셨습니다.(마태 6, 10; 26, 39; 마르 14, 36; 루카 22, 42, 요한 5, 30; 6, 38). 우리도 항상 하느님의 뜻이 온전히 이루어지도록 바라고 기도해야 합니다.

K. 하느님의 뜻에 관한 프란치스코 교황의 강론

프란치스코 교황께서는 하느님의 뜻을 찾는 데는 언제나 불확실성이 있기 때문에 하느님의 뜻을 찾기가 쉽지 않다고 하였습니다. 그런데, 교황께서는 만일 하느님의 뜻을 찾았다고, 너무나 확실하게 말하는 사람들은 하느님이 아니라 자기 자신을 위해서 하느님을 이용하는 것이라고 말씀하십니다.

하느님의 뜻을 찾고 알게 된 사람들은 천성이 너무 겸손하고, 스스로의 존재가 하느님 앞에서는 아무 존재도 아니라고 여기기 때문에, 하느님의 뜻을 찾은 것을 자랑하지도 않고, 과시하지도 않으면서, 조용히 하느님 뜻을 실천하는 사람입니다.

매사에 하느님을 찾고 발견하려는 일에는 항상 불확실성의 영역이 남아 있습니다. 누군가가 하느님을 확실히 만났다고 주장하면서도 불확실성의 그림자가 드리우지 않는다면, 무엇인가 잘못된 것이라고 프란치스코 교황께서는 말씀하신 것입니다. 인간은 "초월적이면서도 범접할 수 없는 하느님의 신비"를 완전히 알 수 없는 존재입니다. 그러므로, 너무 쉽게 하느님의 뜻을 찾았다고 단정해서는 안됩니다. 하느님의 뜻을 발견하거나, 알고자 노력할 뿐이고, 그런 노력 덕분으로 숨겨진 하느님의 뜻을 아주 조금씩 찾고 깨달을 수 있을 뿐입니다. 그렇기 때문에 기도를 하기 전에, 하느님의 뜻을 찾기 위해 철저히 준비해야 합니다.

하느님의 뜻을 찾기 위해 좋은 방법은 "우리가 예수님 안에 머무르고 예수님 말씀이 우리 안에 머무르면, 우리가 청원하는 것은 무엇이든지, 우리에게 그대로 이루어질 것이라고" 하신 예수님 말씀(요한 15, 7)이 우리 삶의 핵심이 되도록 그런 삶을 살도록 노력하는 것입니다.

하느님과 일치를 이루는 삶을 살면서 기도 준비를 해야 기도 응답을 주시고, 하느님의 뜻도 알게 해주신다는 것입니다. 기도는 하느님과 일치하고, 하느님과 하나가 되기 위한 사랑의 대화입니다. 대화를 잘 하기 위해서는 대화 전에 철저히 준비하여야 합니다. 성경을 읽고, 예수님의 말씀이 우리 마음속에 머물도록 하고, 묵상하는 모든 내용도 기도를 잘하기 위한 준비가 되도록 노력해야 합니다. 대화 시에 하느님을 배려하고 하느님 말씀을 잘 경청해야 합니다.

L. 기도 장소로 좋은 곳 (어디에서 기도해야 하나요?)

기도는 사사로이 하는 개인 기도도 중요하지만, 미사참례, 성시간 참여, 교회 차원의 피정 참여 등 공동으로 하는 기도가 훨씬 더 중요합니다. 공동으로 하는 기도장소는 교회가 되어야 합니다. 교회는 기도하는 집이므로 교회가 가장 바람직한 기도장소라고 할 수 있습니다.

교회(성전)은 하느님께서 "하느님의 거룩한 이름을 머무르게 하시려고" 선택하신 곳입니다.(신명 26, 2) 이름은 인격, 존재감, 계시를 의미하고 있습니다. 하느님께서 "하느님의 거룩한 이름을 머무르게 하시려고" "교회라는 거룩한 이름을" 교회에 붙여 주신 것입니다. 그래서 교회를 기도하는 집이라고 하는 것입니다.

그렇지만, 차선책으로 피정센터에서 기도할 수 있고, 가정의 조용한 방이나 공간을 기도장소로 활용하는 것도 바람직합니다. 물론, 비행기, 기차, 버스 등에서 기도할 수 있고, 걸어가면서도 기도할 수 있습니다.

M. 기도 시간(언제 기도해야 하나요?)

기도는 우리 자신의 가장 중요한 시간, 소중한 시간, 값진 시간을 하느님께 내어드리는 것입니다. 모든 정성된 마음으로 시간이라는 자신의 귀한 재물을 하느님께 드리는 것이요, 가장 선한 마음을 가지고 우리의 시간을 하느님께 드리는 것입니다.

그러므로, 하느님을 우리 삶의 가장 윗자리에 모시고, 하루의 일과에서 하느님께 드리는 기도 시간이 하느님께 드리는 맏물(First Fruit)이 되도록 해야 합니다. 하루 중 가장 값지고 소중한 시간에 기도하는 것이 좋습니다. 그래야 하느님께서는 지혜롭다는 사람들, 슬기롭다는 사람들, 많은 예언자, 그리고 임금들이 보려고 하였지만 보지 못하였고, 들으려고 하였지만 듣지 못한 하느님의 신비와 은총을 우리에게 드러내실 것이고, 우리가 보고 듣고, 얻을 수 있게 허락하여 주실 것입니다.

예를 들어, 아침 잠에서 깨어나면 하느님께, "잠을 잘자고 일어날 수 있도록 해주셔서 하느님께 감사 드립니다."하고 화살기도를 드립니다. 그런 다음, 성무일도나 아침기도로 하루를 시작하고, 성무일도 끝 기도나 통회기도로 하루를 마무리하는 기도로 봉헌할 수 있습니다.

우리의 인생(삶)은 하느님께서 우리 개개인에게 주신 시간의 길이만큼 사는 것입니다. 인생의 삶은 시간으로 구성된 것이므로 매 시간마다 우리에게 주어진 시간을 우리의 활동으로 바꾸는 것입니다. 그런데, 신자로서 우리의 시간을 무엇과 바꾸며 살고 있습니까? 스마트폰, TV 등에 시간을 투자하고 빼앗기고 있습니까?

스마트폰 등에 시간을 빼앗겨 기도하지 않았고, 교만해서 기도하지 않았고, 몰라서 기도하지 않았고, 때로는 너무 바쁘다는 핑계로 기도하지 않았고, 교회에서 봉사했다는 이유와 구실로 기도하지 않았습니다. 그럼에도 불구하고 하느님께서는 매일 매일 우리에게 은총을 주시고, 너무 좋은 것들로 채워주셨습니다. 그러므로, 하느님 은총에 보답하기 위해, 우리의 소중한 시간을 할애하여 기도 드려야 합니다.

하느님께서는 우리를 환난, 고난, 병고, 불행에 빠지도록 하시는 분이 아니십니다. 모든 행복을 주십니다. 그러므로, 우리의 가장 값진 시간을, 기도 시간으로 바꿔서, 하느님께 기도기둥에 따라 기도 드려야 합니다. 우리의 시간을 학문과 바꾸고 매진하여 공부하면 학자나 교수가 될 것입니다. 그런데, 우리가 우리의 귀한 시간을 무엇으로 바꾸고 있는지 생각하지 않고, 파도에 휩쓸리듯이, 바람에 날리듯이 목적 없이 살아간다면, 우리 인생의 시계가 멈추고, 심장이 멈추고, 호흡이 정지되는 죽음을 맞이할 때, 크게 후회를 하게 될 것입니다. 우리 모두 후회하는 삶을 살지 않기 위해서는 우리의 시간의 일부를 기도시간으로 바꿔야 합니다.

하느님께서는 오늘도 우리 각자에게 공평하게 하루 24시간이라는 값진 시간을 주셨습니다. 그 소중한 시간을 우리 인생에서 가장 소중한 것, 즉, 우리 생명을 구하는 일의 하나인 기도에 정성껏 시간을 할애하는 것이 우리에게 매일의 시간을 허락하여 주신 하느님께 대한 충실한 감사의 표현이 될 것입니다. 또한, 정성껏 우리가 매일 바치는 기도는 예수님께서 운영하시는 기도 은행에 저금을 하는 것입니다.

그러므로, 우리 자신을 위해 타임 푸어(Time poor) 상태에서 탈출하여 하느님께 끈기 있게 기도해야 영원한 생명을 얻을 수 있습니다.

종교 개혁자 마르틴 루터 (Martin Luther, 1483-1546)는 하루를 시작하고 마칠 때에 2시간씩 기도하고 성경 공부를 하였고, 기도를 최우선의 일로 삼았다고 합니다. 그는 기도에 관해 "나는 나중에 한 시간 동안 기도할 거야. 오늘 내가 처리할 일을 먼저하고 기도해야지"라고 한다면, 그런 생각들은 기도가 아닌 다른 일에 우선적으로 시선을 돌리게 되어, 그날 마땅히 바쳐야 할 기도를 할 수 없게 된다고 경고하였습니다.
마르틴 루터는 세례를 받고 새롭게 신자가 된 경우에는, 처음부터 오랜 시간 기도하려고 하면, 곧 지쳐버리거나 기도를 포기하므로 기도는 간단하게, 청원기도 내용을 요점만 강렬하게 하되, 자주 기도하라고 권유하였습니다.

N. 언제나 허전함과 부족함만 남는 기도

저의 몸은 하느님의 성전이고 성령님께서 제 안에 계십니다.(1코린3, 16; 6, 19) 하늘과 땅, 우주를 꽉 채우고 계시는 성령님께서 제 안에도, 제가 가는 곳 어디든지, 계심을 믿습니다. 그럴 때마다 성령님께 말씀 드립니다. 성령님, 기도 생활을 해도, 저의 지혜와 정성이 부족하여 허전함과 부족함이 가득 찰 때가 많습니다.

무엇보다, 노력한다고 했지만, 저 자신을 성찰해보니까, 저 자신의 절제와 정성과 변화가 부족했습니다. 저 자신을 드러내려고 하는 욕심도 줄지 않고 있습니다. 그러다 보니까, 때로는 제가 주님께 기도 드린 내용이 미흡하고 궁색한 내용도 많았습니다.(요한6, 7-9) 또한, 저의 기도가 가끔은 물에 빠진 베드로처럼 절망 속에서의 절규였지만, 되돌아보면, 그 절규가 저의 욕심을 채우려는 것이었습니다.(마태 14, 30) 이제부터, 저는 토빗과 같이 탄식할 일이 있어도 좌절하지 않고 꿋꿋하게 기도하겠습니다.(토빗 3, 1-6) 욥과 같이 하느님께는 어떠한 계획도 불가능하지 않음을 다시금 마음에 굳게 새기고, 하느님을 사랑하고 경외하는 마음으로 심기일전하여 정성껏 기도생활을 하겠습니다.(욥기 42, 1-6)

마르타의 동생, 마리아처럼 주님의 발치에 앉아 예수님의 말씀을 듣고 성실하게 경청하고 실천하겠습니다. 기도하기 전에 성경을 묵상하고, 주님의 뜻을 알아내는데 귀 기울이겠습니다. (루카 10, 39-42) 하느님의 뜻은 전부 성경에 있음을, 특히, 예수님을 통해 계시해주신 복음서에 있음을 굳게 믿고 있습니다. 마르타의 동생, 마리아처럼 성경에 하느님의 뜻이 전부 있음을 신뢰하고, 그 보물을 캐내도록 더욱 노력하겠습니다. 평생 직업이 어부였던 베드로와 같이 우쭐대거나 교만하지 않고 순명하는 마음으로 기도의 그물을 던지겠습니다.(요한 21, 6) 지금까지 명예, 욕심, 이기심 등을 채우기 위한 저의 이기적인 기도는 성령을 받기에 합당한 지혜로운 기도가 아니었습니다.(루카 11, 13) 예수님께서는 광야에서 유혹을 받으셨을 때, 성경말씀으로 유혹을 식별하시고 모두 물리치셨습니다. 저도 예수님을 닮아 삶에서 만나는 유혹을 물리치고 주님의 뜻에 맞는 기도(로마 12, 2; 1요한 5, 14), 성령을 받기에 지혜로운 기도를 하겠습니다. 하느님을 사랑하는 기도, 이웃을 사랑하는 기도, 이웃을 용서하는 기도를 하겠습니다. 하느님의 소리를 경청하겠습니다.(요한12, 28) 하느님의 음성을 듣도록 영적인 귀를 활짝 열어놓고 기도하겠습니다. 하느님의 소리를 듣는 사람들은 천성이 너무 겸손하고, 스스로의 존재가 하느님 앞에서는 아무 존재도 아니라고 여깁니다. 저도 하느님의 소리를 듣는다 해도 자랑하지 않고, 과시하지도 않겠습니다. 성모님처럼 조용히 마음에 간직하고, 하느님 뜻에 맞게 기도하겠습니다.

무엇보다도 성모님처럼 청할 것은 청하되 기도의 응답은 오로지 하느님께 온전히 맡겨드리는 신뢰와 겸손의 자세로 기도에 매진하겠습니다. 성모님의 순명의 자세를 본받겠습니다.(루카 1, 38: 요한 2, 1-5)

Chapter 2 Important Catholic Prayers

A. The Sign of the Cross(성호경)

In the name of the Father, and of the Son, and of the Holy Spirit. Amen.

성호경(聖號經)

(1) 천주교 신자는 어떠한 기도를 바치든지 성호경으로 시작하고, 기도가 끝난 때에도 언제나 성호경으로 끝냅니다. 성호경의 의미는 우리가 모든 기도를 바칠 때, 가정이나 직장에서 일을 시작할 때, 우리가 식사를 시작하기 전, 식사를 끝냈을 때, 잠자기 전에, 아침에 일어났을 때, 수능시험 등 모든 시험을 보기 전 등, 모든 기도나 동작이나 행동이 우리의 힘으로 하는 것이 아니고, 성부와 성자와 성령의 이름으로 한다는 뜻입니다. 성호경은 예수님께서 직접 우리에게 가르쳐 주신 삼위일체 교리이며 삼위일체 신앙고백입니다.

(2) 군인은 군복을 입음으로써, 군인이라는 신분을 나타내고, 올림픽에서 금메달을 수상한 선수들은 자기 나라의 국기로 자기나라를 홍보하고 있습니다. 마찬가지로 천주교 신자는 성호경으로 하느님을 경배하고, 흠숭하고, 찬미하고, 찬양하고, 공경하는 천주교 신자임을 알리고 선교하는 것입니다.

(3) 성호경은 하느님은 한 분이시나, 성부와 성자와 성령은 하느님께서 세 분이란 뜻이 아니고 세 위격(位格)을 가지고 계시다는 뜻입니다. 예수님께서 가르쳐 주신 삼위일체 교리입니다. 그러므로 천주교 신자는 성호경을 바침으로써 신앙을 고백하는 것입니다. 위(位 Person, 사람, 보이지 않는 분을 세는 방법; 라틴어 페르소나 persona; 그리스어 휘포스타시스 ὑπόστασις)

(4) 천주교 교회는 성호경을 정성껏 바칠 때마다, 바치는 사람들에게 특별한 은사를 베풀어주십니다. 성호경을 한번 바칠 때마다 한대사(限大赦: 小罪 소죄, 작은 죄 하나를 용서받는 것)을 받도록 허락하여 주셨습니다. 성호경은 스스로를 축복하는 준성사라고 할 수 있습니다.

(5) 성호경은 신앙의 갑옷(Armor of Faith)이요, 선의의 방패(Shield of Good Will)이며, 그리고 전쟁에 나가는 군인의 철모(Helmet of the Soldier)와 같습니다. 총알과 포탄이 빗발치는 전쟁터에서 군인이 철모를 쓰고 있지 않다면 100% 전사할 위험에 노출되는 것입니다. 그러므로, 우리는 성호경을 바칠 때마다 일상생활에서 만나는 각종 위험에서 보호받을 수 있는 위험방지 통장에 저금을 하는 것과 같은 은총을 얻을 수 있습니다.

(6) 성호경 기도는 십자가 표시로 예수님 사랑을 기억하는 것입니다.

(7) "아멘 Amen"은 "굳은, 확실한"이라는 의미의 히브리어 형용사였으나 후세대에 "진실로, 그렇게 되기를"이라는 뜻으로 사용되었습니다. 즉, 기원(祈願)을 뜻하는 부사로 사용하고 있습니다. 4대 복음

서에서도 예수님께서 아주 중요한 진리를 말씀하실 때, "아멘, 아멘" 하시면서 "진실로, 진실로"라고 말씀하셨습니다. 오늘날 우리가 아멘으로 응답하는 것은 "하느님께 진실을 맹세한다든지, 혼자 바치든지 공동으로 바치든지 기도에 동의하고 기도대로 이뤄지기를 바란다는 뜻을 표시하고 있습니다". 기도가 "그대로 허락되게 하여 주십시오"하고 간구하는 기도이자, 저도 그 기도에 능동적으로 참여하여 "기도의 한 몫을 분담하였다"는 신앙고백입니다.

B. The Lord's Prayer(주님의 기도)

Our Father who art in heaven, hallowed be Thy name.
Thy kingdom come. Thy will be done on earth, as it is in heaven.
Give us this day our daily bread, and forgive us our trespasses,
as we forgive those who trespass against us, and lead us not into temptation,
but deliver us from evil. Amen.

주님의 기도(祈禱)

(1) 주님의 기도는 복음 전체의 요약입니다. 주님께서는 기도의 관행(마태 6, 5-8; 7, 7-11; 18, 19-20, 루카 11, 5-13; 18, 1-8)도 말씀하시면서 "청하여라, 찾아라, 문을 두드려라,"하고 꾸준히 기도하도록 허락하셨습니다. 모든 신자들이 그들이 처한 상황에 맞는 독특한 청원기도, 보편지향 기도와 중재기도(중보기도) 등 모든 기도를 할 때에는 가장 합당하면서도 완벽한 주님의 기도를 먼저 바치고 청원기도 등을 바치도록 권고하고 있습니다. 왜냐하면, 주님의 기도는 청원기도 등 모든 기도의 단단한 토대가 되고 기초가 되기 때문입니다. 주님의 기도에는 놀라운 신비가 있습니다. 주님의 기도를 세세하게 음미하면, 주님의 기도는 우리가 바친 모든 청원 기도 등 모든 기도와 우리가 바치려는 모든 청원기도 등이 이미 전부 함축되어 있는 완벽한 기도이기 때문 입니다. (미국 주교회의 홈페이지)

(2) 주님의 기도에서 우리는 우리가 올바로 바라는 것뿐만 아니라 순서대로 우리의 바램이 이뤄지도록 주님께 청합니다. 주님의 기도는 우리가 주님께 청할 일들을 우리에게 가르쳐 줄뿐만 아니라 우리가 어떤 순서로 우리의 바램을 청해야 하는지도 가르쳐줍니다.

(3) 한편, 산상설교는 삶의 가르침인데 반해, 주님의 기도는 단순히 기도입니다. 그렇지만, 성령님께서는 주님의 기도와 산상설교에서, 그리고 두 가지 모두에서 우리 삶에 생기를 불어넣어주는 내면의 변화를 통해서 새로운 유형의 청원기도를 할 수 있도록 허용해 주신 것입니다. 예수님께서는 이와 같은 새로운 삶을 복음 말씀을 통해 우리에게 가르쳐 주신 바가 있습니다. 예수님께서는 우리가 기도로서 이 새로운 바램을 청원기도로 청하도록 가르쳐 주신 것입니다. 다만, 예수님 안에서 우리가 올바로 살아갈 수 있느냐 없느냐는 우리의 기도가 예수님 보시기에 올바른 기도인지, 하느님 뜻에 맞는지에 달려있습니다.

(4) 예수님께서 가르쳐 주신 주님의 기도는 하늘에 계신 하느님 아버지께 드리는 일곱 가지 청원으로 이루어집니다. 처음 세 가지는 종말론적 청원들입니다. 하느님 아버지의 이름과 나라와 뜻이 구현되는 결정적인 때가 오기를 청원하는 것입니다. 하느님 아버지의 나라가 이 세상에 온전하게 오시는 때가 되면, 그분의 이름은 모든 피조물의 영광과 찬미 속에 거룩하게 드러날 것이고 하늘과 땅은 더 이상 하느님과 인간의 영역으로 나뉘지 않는 하나의 세상, 즉, 하느님 아버지의 뜻이 그대로 이루어지는 하느님 나라가 될 것입니다. 이는 이미 예수님의 구원활동으로 이미 시작된 하느님의 다스림이 온전히 실현되기를 간절히 바라는 자녀들의 기도라고 할 수 있습니다. 나머지 네 가지 청원은 일인칭 우리와 관련된 청원들입니다. 이처럼 주님의 기도는 하느님 나라와 그분의 다스림이 온전히 실현되기를 바라는 기도입니다. 사실, 우리들은 세속적인 문제들을 더 염려하고, 걱정하고 그것들을 훨씬 더 삶의 우선 순위에 놓고 청원기도를 할 때가 많습니다. 그러나, 하느님께서는 이미 그것들을 알고 계십니다. 마태 복음서에서 예수님께서는 이렇게 말씀하고 계십니다. "너희 아버지께서는 너희가 청하기도 전에 무엇이 필요한지 알고 계신다."(마태 6, 8) 우리가 진실로 하느님께 청하고 기도 드려야 하는 것은 "하느님 아버지의 나라가 오시는 가운데 우리가 하느님의 백성으로서 그분 나라에 속하고 그분의 자녀가 될 수 있도록 허락하여 주시기를 하느님에게 간절히 청해야 하는 것입니다." 그런 다음에, 육체적인 강건함을 위한 양식과 구원에 필요한 영적 양식(주님의 말씀, 성찬례를 통한 주님의 몸과 피를 받아 모시는 것), 용서, 그리고 구원을 방해하는 악의 세력에서 신앙을 굳건히 지켜낼 수 있는 지혜, 지식, 용기, 굳센 힘 등을 하느님께 청하는 것이 바람직합니다. "하늘에 계신 우리 아버지"의 뜻은 첫 번째, 하느님께서 보내주신 성령의 가르침, 성령의 은총, 성령의 인도를 받는 우리들은 모두 하느님의 자녀라는 의미입니다. 이와 관련하여 바오로 사도도 다음과 같이 이야기하고 있습니다. "여러분은 사람을 다시 두려움에 빠뜨리는 종살이의 영을 받은 것이 아니라, 여러분을 자녀로 삼도록 해주시는 영을 받았습니다. 이 성령의 빛으로 우리가 "아빠, 아버지"하고 외치는 것입니다.(로마 8, 15) 그러므로, 우리는 항상 하느님으로부터 구원받았음을 확고하게 믿어야 합니다. 그러기 위해서는 우리의 나약함에서 우리를 굳건히 일으켜 주시는 하느님 은총을 우리 안에서 가장 먼저 인식하고 믿어야 합니다. 그래야만, 하느님의 자녀로서 확신을 가지고 하늘에 게신 우리 아버지를 "아빠, 아버지"하고 외칠 수 있습니다.(갈라4, 6) 기도는 하느님 품 안에 안기는 것이라고 말할 수도 있습니다. 그러므로, 기도를 통해 하느님께서 우리를 하느님 품 안에 포근하게 안아주심을 느낄 때에, 하늘에 계신 하느님 아버지의 사랑을 경험할 수 있습니다. 우리는 하느님 아버지의 사랑을 경험하기 전에 사제의 얼굴에서 하느님과 예수님의 얼굴을 보아야 합니다. 두 번째, "우리 아버지"라고 부를 때마다 하느님의 자녀답게 살겠다는 굳은 결심을 하여야 합니다. 그리고, 주님의 기도를 비롯하여 모든 기도를 바칠 때마다, 우리 아버지의 자녀로서 하느님 아버지께서 우리의 기도를 반드시 허락하여 주신다는 확고부동한 믿음을 가지고 기도하여야 합니다. 혹시, 하느님께서 우리의 기도를 들어주시지 않으시거나, 거절하시거나, 침묵하시고 계시다고 생각하고 우리가 제멋대로 생각하는 한계 상황에 빠져서 허우적댈 수가 있습니다. 이러한, 절망과 함께 하느님께서 기도를 들어주시지 않는다는 고통의 한

가운데 있을수록 하느님 아버지의 존재를 부정하고, 의심하고, 분해서 울부짖고 교회를 떠날 수도 있습니다. 비록, 하느님께서 우리의 기도를 거부하시고, 침묵하시며 어떤 응답도 없으시고, 우리의 부르짖는 절규에, 우리의 간절한 청원기도에 전혀 미동도 보이지 않으시고, 귀조차 기울이지 않으시는 것처럼 보이는 절망의 순간에도 하느님, 아버지께서는 우리에게 훨씬 더 좋은 것을 예비하시고 계시다는 확고한 믿음을 가져야 합니다. 이럴 때일수록, 우리의 기도내용과 방법이 하느님 보시기에 미흡하다는 성찰을 하고, 조용히 기도내용을 점검하면서 일관되게 하느님 보시기에 좋은 기도, 하느님 뜻에 맞는 기도를 봉헌하면 하느님께서 반드시 기도를 허락하여 주신다는 신앙을 간직하고 끈기 있게 포기하지 말고, 정성껏 기도를 하여야 합니다. 우리 곁에서 우리를 포기하지 않으시고, 지켜보시고, 보호해주시며, 우리 기도를 끝까지 듣고 계시는 하느님 아버지의 현존을 염두에 두고, 모든 정성을 다해 하느님을 사랑하고 기도해야 합니다

The Lord's Prayer "is truly the summary of the whole gospel." "Since the Lord… after handling over the practice of prayer, said elsewhere, 'Ask and you will receive,' and since everyone has petitions which are peculiar to his circumstances, the regular and appropriate prayer (the Lord's Prayer) is said first, as the foundation of further desires. The Lord's Prayer is the most perfect of prayers. In it we ask, not only for all the things we can rightly desire, but also in the sequence that they should be desired. This prayer not only teaches us to ask for things, but also in what order we should desire them (St. Thomas Aquinas, STH II- II, 88, 9). The Sermon on the Mount is teaching for life, the Our Father is a prayer; but in both the one and the other the Spirit of the Lord gives new form to our desires, those inner movements that animate our lives. Jesus teaches us this new life by his words; he teaches us to ask for it by our prayer. The rightness of our life in him will depend on the rightness of our prayer. From the Catechism of the Catholic Church; 2761. page 662.

C. The Hail Mary(성모송)

Hail Mary, full of grace, the Lord is with you. Blessed are you among women, and blessed is the fruit of your womb, Jesus.
Holy Mary, Mother of God, pray for us sinners, now and at the hour of our death. Amen.

(1) "Beginning with Mary's unique cooperation with the working of the Holy Spirit, the churches developed their prayer to the holy Mother of God, centering it on the Person of Christ manifested in His mysteries. In countless hymns and antiphons

expressing this prayer, two movements usually alternate with one another: the first "magnifies" the Lord for the "great things" He did for His lowly servant and through her for all human beings. The second entrusts the supplications and praises of the children of God to the Mother of Jesus, because she now knows the humanity which, in her, the Son of God espoused. From the Catechism of the Catholic Church; 2675. page 642.

(2) Hail Mary(or Rejoice Mary): The greeting of the angel Gabriel opens this prayer. It is God himself who, through his angel as intermediary, greets Mary. Our prayer dares to take up this greeting to Mary with the regard God had for the lowliness of his humble servant and to exult in the joy he finds in her(Lk 1:48; Zeph 3:17b).

(3) Ave Maria.마리아님 賀禮하나이다. 하례: 아랫사람이 윗사람(성모님)에게 축하하여 예의를 보이는 것이다.

(4) Hail : to greet gladly, cheerfully, with delight, with joy or enthusiastically: rejoice over; The crowd hailed the Most Blessed Virgin Mary with joy: to acclaim or acknowledge; The faithful hailed the Most Blessed Virgin Mary as their Mother: to attract the attention of someone by shouting or gesturing; to hail a taxi or to hail a passing ship.

D. Glory Be(영광송)

Glory to the Father, and to the Son, and to the Holy Spirit. As it was in the beginning, is now, and will be forever. Amen.

영광송(榮光頌)

영광이 성부와 성자와 성령께
처음과 같이 이제와 항상 영원히. 아멘.

(1) 밑줄 부분에서 고개를 숙입니다. 현재 우리 나라에서 행해지는 절은 크게 서서 하는 절과 앉은 절로 나누어집니다. 선절은 서 있는 자세에서 하는 절입니다. 그 형태는 똑바로 선 자세에서 조용히 고개나 허리를 굽히는 것으로 그 굽히는 정도로 존경의 깊이를 표시합니다. 서서 절을 하는 방법은 세 가지가 있습니다. 화장실이나 목욕탕 또는 대중이 많은 장소, 회의 중 등에서 지인이나 윗사람 등을 만났을 때 인사하는 목례, 존경하는 직장의 상사 등에게 45도로 허리를 굽혀서 하는 경중례(輕重禮), 하느님 등 자기가 믿는 신, 부모님, 스승에게 90도로 허리를 굽혀서 하는 정중례(鄭重禮)가 있습니다. "영광이 성부와 성자와 성령께"는 삼위일체 하느님께 흠숭을 드리는 것이요, 모든 영광을 바치는 것이므로, 90도로 허리를 굽혀 절하는 것이 바람직합니다.

(2) 영광송은 언제 바치나요? 영광송은 모든 기도가 끝나서 더 이상 바칠 기도가 없을 때 바치는 기도
입니다. 예를 들면, "젊은이를 위한 본기도"를 바친 다음 성모님께 전구를 하고, 성인들께 전구의 기
도를 한 다음, 마지막으로 "성당의 주보 성인이신, 성 안드레아 저희를 위하여 빌어주소서"하고 기
도한 다음에 바치는 기도가 영광송입니다. 물론, 강의를 시작할 때, 시작기도로 영광송 만을 바칠
수도 있습니다.

E. The Nicene Creed(니케아 신경)

I believe in one God, the Father almighty, maker of heaven and earth, of all things
visible and invisible.

I believe in one Lord Jesus Christ, the Only Begotten Son of God, born of the Father
before all ages. God from God, Light from Light, true God from true God, begotten,
not made, consubstantial with the Father; through him all things were made. For us
men and for our salvation he came down from heaven, and by the Holy Spirit was
incarnate of the Virgin Mary, and became man. For our sake he was crucified under
Pontius Pilate, he suffered death and was buried, and rose again on the third day in
accordance with the Scriptures.

He ascended into heaven and is seated at the right hand of the Father. He will come
again in glory to judge the living and the dead and his kingdom will have no end.

I believe in the Holy Spirit, the Lord, the giver of life, who proceeds from the Father
and the Son, who with the Father and the Son is adored and glorified, who has
spoken through the prophets.

I believe in one, holy, catholic and apostolic Church.

I confess one Baptism for the forgiveness of sins and I look forward to the resurrection
of the dead and the life of the world to come. Amen.

† 한 분이신 하느님을 ◎ 저는 믿나이다.

전능하신 아버지, 하늘과 땅과 유형무형한 만물의 창조주를 믿나이다.

또한 한 분이신 주 예수 그리스도, 하느님의 외아들, 영원으로부터 성부에게서 나신 분을 믿나이다.

하느님에게서 나신 하느님, 빛에서 나신 빛, 참 하느님에게서 나신 참 하느님으로서,

창조되지 않고 나시어 성부와 한 본체로서 만물을 창조하셨음을 믿나이다.

성자께서 저희 인간을 위하여, 저희 구원을 위하여 하늘에서 내려오셨음을 믿나이다.

(밑줄 부분에서 모두 고개를 깊이 숙인다)

<u>또한 성령으로 인하여 동정 마리아에게서 육신을 취하시어 사람이 되셨음을 믿나이다.</u>

본시오 빌라도 통치 아래서 저희를 위하여, 십자가에 못 박혀 수난하고 묻히셨으며, 성서 말씀대로 사흘날에 부활하시어 하늘에 올라, 성부 오른편에 앉아계심을 믿나이다. 그분께서는 산 이와 죽은 이를 심판하러 영광 속에 다시 오시리니 그분의 나라는 끝이 없으리이다. 또한 주님이시며 생명을 주시는 성령을 믿나이다. 성령께서는 성부와 성자에게서 발하시고, 성부와 성자와 더불어 영광과 흠숭을 받으시며, 예언자들을 통하여 말씀하셨나이다. 하나이고 거룩하고 보편되며, 사도로부터 이어오는 교회를 믿나이다. 죄를 씻는 유일한 세례를 믿으며, 죽은 이들의 부활과 내세의 삶을 기다리나이다. 아멘.

AD 325년 니케아 공의회와 381년 콘스탄티노플 공의회에서 결정된 것을 결합하여 만든 니케아 신경은 신앙고백이다. 보통 주일과 대축일에 사용된다. 구원 역사 전체의 요약인 신경은 기쁜 소식에 대한 응답이다. 신경은 회중이 그리스도의 메시지에 충실히 머물러 있음을 가리킨다. 한자리에 모인 신자들은 신앙고백을 함으로써 신앙의 신비인 성체성사를 시작하기 전에 독서들에서 들었고 강론을 통해 해설된 하느님의 말씀에 동의함을 아울러 고백한다. (출처 : 서울대교구 가톨릭정보)

E-1. The Apostles' Creed(사도신경)

I believe in God, the Father almighty, Creator of heaven and earth, and in Jesus Christ, his only Son, our Lord, (At the words that follow, up to and including the Virgin Mary, all bow.) who was conceived by the Holy Spirit, born of the Virgin Mary, suffered under Pontius Pilate, was crucified, died and was buried; he descended into hell; on the third day he rose again from the dead; he ascended into heaven, and is seated at the right hand of God, the Father almighty; from there he will come to judge the living and the dead. I believe in the Holy Spirit, the holy Catholic Church, the communion of saints, the forgiveness of sins, the resurrection of the body and life everlasting. Amen.

전능하신 천주 성부 천지의 창조주를 저는 믿나이다.
그 외아들 우리 주 예수 그리스도님 성령으로 인하여 동정 마리아께 잉태되어 나시고 본시오 빌라도 통치 아래서 고난을 받으시고 십자가에 못박혀 돌아가시고 묻히셨으며 저승에 가시어 사흘날에 죽은 이들 가운데서 부활하시고 하늘에 올라 전능하신 천주 성부 오른편에 앉으시며 그리로부터 산 이와 죽은 이를 심판하러 오시리라 믿나이다. 성령을 믿으며 거룩하고 보편된 교회와 모든 성인의 통공을 믿으며 죄의 용서와 육신의 부활을 믿으며 영원한 삶을 믿나이다. 아멘

F. Act of Faith(신덕송)

O my God, I firmly believe that You are one God in three divine Persons, Father, Son, and Holy Spirit. I believe that your divine Son became man and died for our sins and that he will come to judge the living and the dead. I believe these and all the truths which the Holy Catholic Church teaches because you have revealed them who are eternal truth and wisdom, who can neither deceive nor be deceived. In this faith I intend to live and die. Amen. # The key point of the Act of Faith is to express to the Lord: our faith in his merciful love and his real presence in the Eucharist. You can come up with your own prayer or use a more traditional version like this "Act of Faith."(USCCB).

G. Act of Hope(망덕송)

O Lord God, I hope by your grace for the pardon of all my sins and after life here to gain eternal happiness because you have promised it who are infinitely powerful, faithful, kind, and merciful. In this hope I intend to live and die. Amen.

H. Act of Love(애덕송)

O Lord God, I love you above all things and I love my neighbor for your sake because you are the highest, infinite and perfect good, worthy of all my love. In this love I intend to live and die. Amen. Prayers(F, G, H) excerpted from the Compendium of the Catechism of the Catholic Church. Copyright ©2005 - Libreria Editrice Vaticana.

I. Act of Contrition

Oh My God, I am heartily sorry for having offended You, and I detest all my sins because of Your just punishments, but most of all because they offend You, my God, Who are all good and deserving of all my love. I firmly resolve with the help of Your grace to sin no more and to avoid the near occasion of sin. Amen.

J. The Angelus(삼종기도)

V/. The Angel of the Lord declared unto Mary,
R/. And she conceived of the Holy Spirit.

Hail Mary⋯

V/. Behold the handmaid of the Lord,

R/. Be it done unto me according to your Word.

Hail Mary⋯

V/. And the Word was made flesh,

R/. And dwelt among us.

Hail Mary⋯

V/. Pray for us, O holy Mother of God,

R/. That we may be made worthy of the promises of Christ.

Let us pray : Pour forth, we beseech you, O Lord, your grace into our hearts: that we, to whom the Incarnation of Christ, your Son, was made known by the message of an angel, may by his Passion and Cross be brought to the glory of his Resurrection. Through the same Christ, our Lord. Amen.

○ 주님의 천사가 마리아께 아뢰니 ● 성령으로 잉태하셨나이다. (성모송)

○ "주님의 종이오니 ● 그대로 제게 이루어지소서!" (성모송)

○ 이에 말씀이 사람이 되시어 ● 저희 가운데 계시나이다. (성모송)

○ 천주의 성모님, 저희를 위하여 빌어주시어

● 그리스도께서 약속하신 영원한 생명을 얻게 하소서.

† 기도합시다. 하느님, 천사의 아룀으로 성자께서 사람이 되심을 알았으니

성자의 수난과 십자가로 부활의 영광에 이르는 은총을 저희에게 내려주소서.

우리 주 그리스도를 통하여 비나이다. ◎ 아멘.

안젤루스(Angelus)라 함은 라틴기도 첫 단어가 안젤루스로 시작하기 때문이다.

Angelus.천사. Angelorum.복수2격. 라틴기도 첫 단어가 안젤루스로 시작하기 때문이다. 미국식 발음은 앤절러스이다. Excerpted from Catholic Household Blessings and Prayers, revised edition ©2007 United States Conference of Catholic Bishops. All rights reserved by the USCCB. Short history of the Angelus; The modern form as we know it appears for the first time—according to J. Fournée in his "The History of the Angelus." The Angel's Message to Mary —in The Little Office of the Blessed Virgin Mary (Officium parvum BMV), printed in Rome during the time of Pope Pius V (1566-1572), and also in the Manuale Catholicorum (Handbook for Catholics) by the Jesuit St Peter Canisius, published in Antwerp in 1588. In older manuals of devotion, according to the date of their publication, the Angelus may mention Pope Benedict

XIV (14 September 1742) and Pope Leo XIII (15 March 1884) as its great promoters.
Taken from: L'Osservatore Romano, Weekly Edition in English, 4 September 2002, page 6. L'Osservatore Romano is the newspaper of the Holy See.

K. Regina Caeli (Queen of Heaven) 부활 삼종기도

V/. Queen of heaven, rejoice, alleluia.

R/. The Son whom you merited to bear, alleluia,

V/. has risen as He said, alleluia.

R/. Pray for us to God, alleluia.

V/. Rejoice and be glad, O Virgin Mary, alleluia!

R/. For the Lord has truly risen, alleluia.

† Let us pray:

O God, who through the resurrection of your Son, our Lord Jesus Christ, did vouchsafe to give joy to the world; grant, we beseech you, that through his Mother, the Virgin Mary, we may attain the joys of everlasting life.

Through the same Christ our Lord. Amen.

○ 하늘의 모후님, 기뻐하소서. 알렐루야. ● 태중에 모시던 아드님께서, 알렐루야.

○ 말씀하신 대로 부활하셨나이다. 알렐루야.

● 저희를 위하여 하느님께 빌어주소서. 알렐루야.

○ 동정 마리아님, 기뻐하시며 즐거워하소서. 알렐루야.

● 주님께서 참으로 부활하셨나이다. 알렐루야.

† 기도합시다. 하느님, 성자 우리 주 예수 그리스도의 부활로 온 세상을 기쁘게 하셨으니

성자의 어머니 동정 마리아의 도움으로 영생의 즐거움을 얻게 하소서.

우리 주 그리스도를 통하여 비나이다. ◎ 아멘.

Regina.女王, 모후님. caeli. (소유격) 하늘의. caelum.(주격) sky, heaven, 하늘.

Chapter 3 Major Prayers to God and Jesus

A. Act of Reflection

O Lord, help me to examine fully the sins I have committed today in thought, word, and deed, and through any unfulfilled duty, and make me aware of those faults that have become habits. Amen.

B. Act of Charity

O my God, I love you with my whole heart and above all things, because you are infinitely good and perfect; and I love my neighbor as myself for love of you. Grant that I may love you more and more in this life and in the next for all eternity. Amen.

C. Offering

O Lord, from love You created me, giving me a soul and body, commanded me to serve You and to help my neighbor. Now, sinful though I am, I offer You my mind and heart, and beg you to receive them as my offering of praise and devotion. Amen.

D. Morning Offering(아침 기도)

O Jesus, through the Immaculate Heart of Mary, I offer you my prayers, works, joys, and sufferings of this day for all the intentions of your Sacred Heart, in union with the Holy Sacrifice of the Mass throughout the world, for the salvation of souls, the reparation of sins, the reunion of all Christians, and in particular for the intentions of the Holy Father this month. Amen. # (1) This prayer was written in 1844 by Fr. François-Xavier Gautrelet. Prayer source: From Catholic Household Blessings and Prayers. # (2) This prayer has numerous variations, but the main idea is to start your day giving to God everything you may encounter during the upcoming day.

E. An Evening Prayer(저녁기도)

I adore You, my God, and I love You with all my heart. I thank You for having created me, for having made me a Christian, and for having preserved me this day. Forgive me for whatever evil I have done today. If I have done anything good, be pleased to accept it. Protect me this night and deliver me from all dangers. May your grace be always with me and with those I love. Amen. # The above evening prayer has numerous variations and is similar to that of "A prayer for protection."

A Prayer for Protection: O My God, I adore Thee and I love Thee with all my heart. I thank Thee for having created me, for having made me a Catholic and for having watched over me this day. Pardon me for the evil I have done this day; and if I have done any good, deign to accept it. Watch over me while I take my rest and deliver me from danger. May Thy grace be always with me. Amen.

F. Blessing before Meals

† Bless us, O Lord, and these Your gifts, which we are about to receive from Your bounty, through Christ our Lord. Amen.

G. Grace after Meals (Thanksgiving after Meals)

† We give You thanks for all Your benefits, Almighty God, who lives and reigns forever and ever. And may the souls of the faithful departed, through the mercy of God, rest in peace. Amen.

H. Prayer after Meals

† Almighty God, we give You thanks for all Your benefits bestowed on us. Amen. Blessed be the name of the Lord, now and forever. May the souls of the faithful departed, through the mercy of God, rest in peace. Amen. # Prayer source: The prayer book of the Catholic Bishops Conference of Korea. (page 18).

I. Grace after Meals (Thanksgiving after Meals)

† We give You thanks for all Your benefits, O Almighty God, who lives and reigns forever and ever. Amen. Vouchsafe, O Lord, to reward with eternal life, all those who

do us good for Your name's sake. Amen.

V. Let us bless the Lord.

R. Thanks be to God.

May the souls of the faithful departed, through the mercy of God, rest in peace. Amen. # Prayer source: http://www.rercglasgow.org. In the United States of America, Catholics rarely pray Grace After Meals these days, but this traditional prayer is well worth reviving. While Grace Before Meals asks God for His blessing, Grace After Meals is a prayer of thanksgiving for all of the good things that God has given us, as well as a prayer of intercession for those who have helped us. And Grace After Meals is an opportunity to call to mind all those who have died and to pray for their meals. # Bless: to invoke God's favor on something. Gifts: in this case, the food and drink before us. Bounty: something found in generous amounts. Benefits: in this case, kind actions or gifts. Vouchsafe: to grant something, especially to someone who doesn't deserve it on his own. Faithful departed: those who have died in a state of grace; usually used specifically to refer to those currently in Purgatory. Rest in peace: in Latin, Requiescat in pace; to enter into the presence of God in Heaven, having finished one's penance in Purgatory.

J. Prayer after Meals

We thank You, Christ our God, for You have satisfied us with the good things of Your earth. Do not deprive us of Your heavenly kingdom but as You appeared to Your disciples, O Savior, granting them peace-come also to us and save us. Lord have mercy. (Three times) Give the blessing. Blessed is our God who, through His grace and loving kindness, is merciful to us and nourishes us from the abundance of His gifts, always, now and ever, and forever. Amen. # Prayer source: https://www.ewtn. com/library/prayer/byzpray.txt. Byzantine Catholic Prayer. Copyright ©2017 Eternal Word Television Network, Inc. Irondale, Alabama. All rights reserved.

K. The Blessed Sacrament

Lord Jesus, at the Last Supper as You sat at table with Your Apostles, You offered Yourself to the Father as the spotless lamb, the acceptable gift that renders perfect praise to Him. You have given us the memorial of Your Passion to bring us its saving power until the end of time. In this great Sacrament You feed Your people and strengthen them in holiness, so that the human family may come to walk in the light of one faith, and in one communion of love. We are fed at Your table and grow into Your risen likeness. Lord Jesus, You are the Eternal and True Priest Who established this unending sacrifice. You offered Yourself as a Victim for our deliverance and You taught us to offer it throughout time in memory of You. As we eat Your Body that You gave for us, we grow in strength. As we drink Your Blood that You poured out for us, we are washed clean. Lord Jesus, let the power of Your Eucharist pervade every aspect of our daily lives. Let Your consecration transform all our actions and all the events of each day into supernatural agents that form Your Mystical Body. Amen. Copyright ©2003, 1997 by Catholic Book Publishing Corp., N.J. All rights reserved."

L. St. Thérèse's "Act of Oblation to Merciful Love"

Offering of myself as a Victim of Holocaust to God's Merciful Love, O My God! Most Blessed Trinity, I desire to Love You and make you Loved, to work for the glory of Holy Church by saving souls on earth and liberating those suffering in purgatory. I desire to accomplish Your will perfectly and to reach the degree of glory You have prepared for me in Your Kingdom. I desire, in a word, to be saint, but I feel my helplessness and I beg You, O my God! to be Yourself my Sanctity! Since You loved me so much as to give me Your only Son as my Savior and my Spouse, the infinite treasures of His merits are mine. I offer them to You with gladness, begging You to look upon me only in the Face of Jesus and in His heart burning with Love. I offer You, too, all the merits of the saints (in heaven and on earth), their acts of Love, and those of the holy angels. Finally, I offer You, O Blessed Trinity! the Love and merits of the Blessed Virgin, my Dear Mother. It is to her I abandon my offering, begging her to present it to You. Her Divine Son, my Beloved Spouse, told us in the says of His mortal life: "Whatsoever you ask the Father in my name he will give it to you!" I am certain, then, that You will grant my desires; I know, O my God! that the more You want to give, the more You make us desire. I feel in my heart immense desires and it is with confidence I ask You to come and take possession of my soul. Ah! I cannot receive Holy Communion as often as I desire, but, Lord, are You not all-powerful? Remain in me as in a tabernacle and never separate Yourself from Your little victim. I want to console You for the ingratitude of the wicked, and I beg of you to take away my freedom to displease You. If through weakness I sometimes fall, may Your Divine

Glance cleanse my soul immediately, consuming all my imperfections like the fire that transforms everything into itself. I thank You, O my God! for all the graces You have granted me, especially the grace of making me pass through the crucible of suffering. It is with joy I shall contemplate You on the Last Day carrying the scepter of Your Cross. Since You deigned to give me a share in this very precious Cross, I hope in heaven to resemble You and to see shining in my glorified body the sacred stigmata of Your Passion. After earth's Exile, I hope to go and enjoy You in the Fatherland, but I do not want to lay up merits for heaven. I want to work for Your Love Alone with the one purpose of pleasing You, consoling Your Sacred Heart, and saving souls who will love You eternally. In the evening of this life, I shall appear before You with empty hands, for I do not ask You, Lord, to count my works. All our justice is stained in Your eyes. I wish, then, to be clothed in Your own Justice and to receive from Your Love the eternal possession of Yourself. I want no other Throne, no other Crown but You, my Beloved! Time is nothing in Your eyes, and a single day is like a thousand years. You can, then, in one instant prepare me to appear before You. In order to live in one single act of perfect Love,

I OFFER MYSELF AS A VICTIM OF HOLOCAUST TO YOUR MERCIFUL LOVE, Asking You to consume me incessantly, allowing the waves of infinite tenderness shut up within You to overflow into my soul, and that thus I may become a martyr of Your Love, O my God! May this martyrdom, after having prepared me to appear before You, finally cause me to die and may my soul take its flight without any delay into the eternal embrace of Your Merciful Love. I want, O my Beloved, at each beat of my heart to renew this offering to You an infinite number of times, until the shadows having disappeared I may be able to tell You of my Love in an Eternal Face to Face! Amen. Marie, Françoise, Thérèse of the Child Jesus and the Holy Face, unworthy Carmelite religious. This 9th day of June, Feast of the Most Holy Trinity, In the year of grace, 1895. # Prayer Source: *Story of A Soul*, translated by Fr. John Clarke, O.C.D. Copyright © 1976 by Washington Province of Discalced Carmelites, ICS Publications, 2131 Lincoln Road, N.E., Washington, DC 20002 U.S.A., pp. 276-278.

M. Act of Consecration of the Human Race to the Sacred Heart of Jesus (예수 성심께 천하만민을 바치는 기도)

Most sweet Jesus, Redeemer of the human race, look down upon us, humbly prostrate before Thine altar. We are Thine and Thine we wish to be; but to be more surely united with Thee, behold each one of us freely consecrates himself today to Thy Most Sacred Heart. Many, indeed, have never known Thee; many, too, despising Thy precepts, have rejected Thee. Have mercy on them all, most merciful Jesus, and draw them to Thy Sacred Heart. Be Thou King, O Lord, not only of the faithful who have never forsaken Thee, but also of the prodigal children who have abandoned Thee, grant that they may quickly return to their Father's house, lest they die of wretchedness and hunger. Be Thou King of those who are deceived by erroneous opinions, or whom discord keeps aloof and call them back to the harbor of truth and unity of faith, so that soon there may be but one flock and one shepherd. Be Thou King of all those who even now sit in the shadow of idolatry or Islam, and refuse not Thou to bring them into the light of Thy kingdom. Look, finally, with eyes of pity upon the children of that race, which was for so long a time Thy chosen people; and let Thy Blood, which was once invoked upon them in vengeance, now descend upon them also in a cleansing flood of redemption and eternal life. Grant, O Lord, to Thy Church, assurance of freedom and immunity from harm; give peace and order to all nations, and make the earth resound from pole to pole with one cry: Praise to the Divine Heart that wrought our salvation: to it be glory and honor forever. Amen.

This Act of Consecration of the Human Race to the Sacred Heart of Jesus is also recited on the Feast of Christ the King, the last Sunday of the liturgical year (that is, the Sunday before the First Sunday of Advent), in the traditional calendar (still used in the Traditional Latin Mass), and the last Sunday in October (the Sunday immediately before All Saints Day). Traditionally, the Act of Consecration was preceded by exposition of the Blessed Sacrament (which remained exposed during the Act of Consecration) and followed by the recitation of the Litany of the Sacred Heart and benediction. This form of the Act of Consecration of the Human Race to the Sacred Heart of Jesus is occasionally incorrectly ascribed to Pope Pius XI, who, in his encyclical Quas Primas(1925), established the Feast of Christ the King. While Pius XI commanded in that same encyclical that the Act of Consecration be made on the Feast of Christ the King, the text presented here was sent by Pope Leo XIII to all the

bishops of the world in 1899, when he promulgated his encyclical Annum Sacrum. In that encyclical, Leo asked that such a consecration be made on June 11, 1900. Whether Leo himself wrote the text of the prayer, however, is not clear. While the text is meant to be recited publicly in a church, if your parish does not make the Act of Consecration on the Feast of Christ the King you can recite it privately or with your family, preferably in front of an image of the Sacred Heart of Jesus (You can learn more about the history of devotion to the Sacred Heart of Jesus in The Feast of the Sacred Heart of Jesus). A shortened form of the Act of Consecration of the Human Race to the Sacred Heart of Jesus, omitting the penultimate paragraph with its prayers for the conversion of non-Christians, is often used today.

N. Act of Spiritual Communion(신령성체 기도)

My Jesus, I believe that You are present in the Most Blessed Sacrament. I love You above all things, and I desire to receive You into my soul. Since I cannot at this moment receive You sacramentally, come at least spiritually into my heart. I embrace You as if You were already there and unite myself wholly to You. Never permit me to be separated from You. Amen. # This prayer was composed by St. Alphonsus Maria de' Liguori(AD 1696-1787).

영적 영성체(신령성체) 기도

저의 예수 그리스도님,
저는 주님께서 지극히 거룩하신 성체 안에 계심을 믿나이다. 저는 세상의 모든 것 위에 주님을 사랑하오며, 주님의 성체를 제 영혼 안에 영하기를 간절히 구하나이다. 지금 이 순간, 성사적으로 주님 성체를 영할 수 없더라도, 적어도 영적으로 만이라도 저의 마음 안에 오소서. 저는 주님께서 이미 제 안에 계시고, 저와 주님께서 완전히 일치된 것처럼 주님을 포옹해드리고 있습니다. 결코 주님에게서 떨어나가지 않게 허락하여 주시옵소서. 아멘

성체는 미사 때만 영할 수 있나요? 성체성사는 교회가 봉헌하는 미사성제 안에서 이뤄집니다. 따라서 영성체는 미사 때 영하는 것이 일반적입니다. 그러나 미사 밖에서도 영성체를 할 수 있습니다. 거동이 불편한 병자나 어르신 등 미사에 참여하기 힘든 신자들은 자기가 거주하는 집이나, 병원, 양로원 등에서 영성체를 할 수 있습니다. 사제는 이러한 신자들을 위해 성체를 모셔 가 영성체를 해주는데 이를 "병자 영성체(봉성체)"라고 합니다. 바로 이러한 목적에서 미사 때 축성한 성체를 감실에 보존하는 관습이 생겼습니다. 현재 우리나라의 거의 모든 본당은 정기적으로 병자 영성체를 실시하고 또한 미리 소속 본당에 연락하면 병자 영성체를 할 수 있습니다. 그리고 어떤 원인이든지 죽을 위험 중에 있는 신자들은

병자성사와 노자 성체로 기력을 얻을 수 있습니다.(교회법 제911 · 918 · 921조)

영적 영성체(신령성체)와 모령성체는 무엇인가요? 교회는 신자가 영성체를 할 수 없는 경우에 성체에 대한 믿음과 사랑을 지니고 성체를 모시고자 원한다면 성체성사의 효과를 얻을 수 있다고 가르칩니다. 이를 "영적 영성체(신령성체 神領聖體)라고 부릅니다. 반대로 신자가 대죄(큰 죄)를 저질러서 영성체를 해서는 안 될 경우임에도 성체를 받아 모시는 경우가 있습니다. 이를 "모령성체"(冒領聖體)라고 합니다. 모령성체는 은총의 지위에 있지 않은 신자가 스스로 중죄 중에 있음을 의식하면서 영성체를 하는 경우입니다. 모령성체는 성체에 대한 불경한 태도이며, 중죄에 해당합니다. 그러므로 은총의 지위에 있지 않은 신자는 영성체 하기 전에 하느님께 죄의 용서를 받고 교회와 화해해야 합니다. 비록 죄를 짓고 고해 성사를 미처 받지 못했더라도 영적 영성체를 받을 수 있습니다. 다만, 지은 죄에 대한 진정한 회개를 이루고, 가능해지면 즉시 고해 성사를 받겠다는 마음이 있어야 영적 영성체의 모든 풍요로운 효과를 받아 누릴 수 있을 것입니다. 그렇다면 영적 영성체만으로 충분하므로 성사적 영성체는 불필요할까요? 그것은 아닙니다. 성체는 원래 받아 모시라고 존재하는 것이고, 성사적 영성체 안에 이미 영적 영성체도 존재하는 것입니다. 그래서 원래 이 둘은 하나입니다. 그러므로 고해 성사를 받고 미사에 대한 제한이 완화되면, 성당에 가서 미사에 참례하여 직접 성체를 모셔야 할 것입니다.

사제가 없어서 미사를 거행하지 못하고 말씀 전례만 거행할 경우, 병고나 다른 여러 가지 이유에서 미사에 참여하지 못하는 경우, 대죄 중에 있으면서 고해성사를 받지 못해 영성체를 할 수 없는 경우, 혼인 무효 장애 때문에 지속해서 성체를 모시지 못하는 경우, 또는 아직 세례를 받지 않은 예비 신자일 경우에 영적 영성체(신령성체)를 할 수 있습니다. 특별한 경우이기는 하지만 미사 중에 축성된 빵(제병)이 모자라서 영성체를 하지 못하는 경우도 여기에 해당합니다. 이처럼 영성체를 하지 못하는 신자들이 영적 영성체(신령성체)를 하는 것입니다. 영적 영성체(신령성체)는 지극한 성체 신심의 또 다른 표현으로서 성체를 모시지 않고 마음으로 성체를 모셔도 같은 효과가 있다는 믿음입니다. 2020년 3월 19일, 프란치스코 교황께서 성 요셉 대축일 미사를 봉헌하시던 중, 전 세계 신자들에게 성체조배의 중요성을 강조하시면서, "영적 영성체(신령성체)를 하십시오!"라고 강력하게 권고하셨습니다. 코로나19의 전 세계 대유행으로 인하여 많은 지역에서 미사가 제한되어, 성체를 직접 받아 모시지 못하는 때에도, "영적 영성체(신령성체)"의 중요성이 더욱 강조되고 있었습니다. 성체를 직접 받아 모시는 것을 "성사적 영성체(communio sacramentalis)"라고 합니다. 반면에, 성체를 직접 받아 모실 수 없는 상황에서 뜨거운 사랑과 원의로 주님과 하나 되어 그리스도의 몸을 영적으로 받아 모시고자 간절히 기도하면 실제 영성체 한 것과 같아지는데, 이것을 "영적 영성체(communio spiritualis)" 혹은 "신령성체"라고 부릅니다. 토마스 아퀴나스 성인은 "물로 세례를 받기 전에 원의로써 세례(화세)를 받을 수 있는 것처럼, 성사적 영성체를 받기 전에 영적으로 성체를 받아 모실 수 있다."라고 하였습니다. 또한, 성체를 '천사의 양식'이라고 부르듯이, 영적 영성체를 천사들이 성체를 받아 모시는 방법이라고 하였습니다. 트리엔트 공의회에서도 영적 영성체의 효과를 정식으로 인정하였습니다. 영적 영성체는 마음을 모으고 주님과 하나 되어 성체를 모시려는 올바른 원의만 가진다면 언제 어디서든 가능하다고 합니다. 다만, 가장 좋은 것은 직접 성체를 바라볼 수 있는 성체조배나 성체강복 때 이루는 것입니다. 이러한 전례 중에 말씀을 봉독하고 묵상하며 성체를 바라보고 또 축복을 받으면서 영적 영성체를 가장 효과적으로 이룰 수 있습니다. 또한, 코로나19 사태가 벌어진 시기와 같이 미사가 불가능한 시기에는 텔레비전 생방송이나 인터넷 스트리밍 영상을 보면서 영적 영성체를 이루는 것이 특별히 권장됩니다. 한편, 우리가 기도함으로써 은총을 얻고 주님과 일치한다는 것은 잘 알면서도 가톨릭 신자들이 온 세계 방방곡곡 천주교 성당에서 시간마다 인류의 구원을 위해 봉헌되는 미사 성제에 영적으로 참례하여 영적 영성체(신령 성체)를 함으로써 얻는 영적 은총에 대해 잘 모르는 것은 유감스럽고 아쉬운 일입니다. 합당한 준비를 하고 미사 참례하면서 성체를 실제로 받아 모시면 제일 좋지만 그렇지 못할 때는 꼭 영적 영성체(신령 성체)라도 하는 좋은 습관을 갖도록 하는 것이 좋습니다. 영성체를 하지 못한다고 미사참례마저 하지 않는 신자들을 가끔 볼 수 있습니다. 그러나 이러한 태도는 바람직하지 않습니다. 영성체를 하지 못하더라도 미사에 참례하고 영적 영성체(신령성체)를 함으로써 그리스도와 일치를 이루도록 노력해야 합니다.

어떤 방법으로 성체께 공경을 드리나요? 성체에 대한 공경의 첫 자리를 차지하는 것은 은총 가운데 미사에 온전히 참례하고 성체를 모시는 영성체입니다. 영성체 외에도 성체 현시, 성체조배, 성체강복, 성체거동, 성체대회 그리고 성시간 등의 유형으로 미사 밖에서도 성체께 공경을 드릴 수 있습니다. 초세기 신자들은 영성체를 위해 엄격한 규정들을 지켜야만 했으며, 이러한 분위기 속에서 성체에 대한 공경이 자연스레 생겨났습니다. 그러나 지나치게 엄격한 규정으로 영성체하는 사람의 수가 줄어들고, 영성체 대신 성체를 바라보는 공경 형태의 신심이 발달하였습니다. 13세기부터 성체조배를 통한 성체 공경 신심이 교회 안에 빠르게 퍼져 나갔습니다. 그리고 성체거동, 성체 현시, 성체 강복이 교회에서 성체 공경의 한 형태로 나타나기 시작하였습니다.

성체 현시는 성광을 이용하여 성체를 볼 수 있는 형태로 제대 위에 모셔 놓고 신자들이 기도하고 묵상하며 그리스도와 일치하도록 이끌어줍니다. 성체 현시를 마칠 때는 성체 강복이 이뤄지고 그 다음 성체는 감실에 모셔집니다. 성체조배는 감실 안에 모셔져 있거나 현시된 성체 앞에서 개인적 또는 공동체적으로 경배를 드리는 신심 행위입니다. 성체거동은 성체를 모시고 하는 행렬로서 "성체 행렬"이라고도 부르며, 초대 교회 때부터 대표적 성체 공경 신심 행사입니다.

성체대회는 성체에 대한 공경의 특수한 표현 중 하나로서, 교회 전체 구성원의 일치를 드러내는 신심 행이며, 성체성사의 신비를 기념하고자 성체 신비의 특정한 주제를 심화하고 사랑과 일치 속에서 공적으로 성체에 대한 경배를 표현하는 모임입니다. 성체대회는 지역별, 국가별로 개최되기도 하며, 전 세계적 행사로는 세계성체대회가 있습니다. 일반적으로 개인이나 공동체가 성당에서 성체께 공경을 드리려면 성체조배를 하거나 성시간에 참여하는 것이 바람직합니다.

Four steps of Spiritual Communion:
1) Make an act of faith: come up with your own prayer or use a traditional one to

express the Lord our faith in his real presence in Eucharist.

2) Make an act of love: say a prayer that expresses your love and gratitude to the Lord. Thank Him for his infinite love as well.

3) Express your desire to receive Him: as you are not able to physically receive the Lord, express your desire to receive Him in your heart.

4) Invite Jesus to come into your heart: with a humble and contrite heart we ask the Lord to come to us just as He would if we were able to receive the sacrament.

St. Pope John Paul II, in his encyclical, Ecclesia de Eucharistia (A Eucharistic Church), of April 2003, encouraged the practice of spiritual communion, "which has been a wonderful part of Catholic life for centuries and recommended by saints who were masters of the spiritual life." St. Thomas Aquinas also defined a Spiritual Communion as "an ardent desire to receive Jesus in the Most Holy Sacrament [in Communion at Mass] and in lovingly embracing Him as if we had actually received Him." We can make a Spiritual Communion such as this one below during Mass, or before our Lord in the Blessed Sacrament, or anywhere else where the Spirit moves you. Oh Jesus, I turn toward the holy tabernacle where You live hidden for love of me. I love you, O my God. I cannot receive you in Holy Communion. Come, nevertheless, and visit me with Your grace. Come spiritually into my heart. Purify it. Sanctify it. Render it like unto Your own. Amen. Lord, I am not worthy that Thou should enter under my roof, but only say the word and my soul shall be healed. This last sentence is drawn from Matthew's Gospel (Matt 8:6), in which a Roman Centurion expressed his deep faith in our Lord's healing powers (in this case to cure his servant rather than his soul). Jesus was quite moved by the soldier's faith, and healed his servant at once. Christ might not answer us quite so instantaneously, but rest assured, He can and will respond to anyone who comes to Him in love and humility for His Divine assistance. After all, didn't He say in the Sermon on the Mount, concerning the power of prayer, "Ask, and it shall be given you: seek, and you shall find"(Matt 7:7) # The source of this information: From www.ourcatholicprayers.com.

O. Anima Christi(예수님의 영혼께 대한 기도)

Soul of Christ, sanctify me. Body of Christ, save me. Blood of Christ, inebriate me. Water from the side of Christ, wash me. Passion of Christ, strengthen me. O good Jesus, hear me. Within Your wounds hide me. Separated from You, let me never be. From the evil one protect me. At the hour of my death, call me. And close to you bid me; That with Your saints, I may be praising You forever and ever. Amen. The Anima Christi is a prayer from around the 14th century. It is still widely used after receiving the body and blood of Our Lord, Jesus Christ in Holy Communion. "I love You, O my God, and my only desire is to love You until the last breath of my life. I love You, O my infinitely lovable God, and I would rather die loving You, than live without loving You. I love You, Lord and the only grace I ask is to love You eternally. My God, if my tongue cannot say in every moment that I love You, I want my heart to repeat it to You as often as I draw breath." (St. John Vianney). This well-known prayers dates origin from the first half of the fourteenth century and was enriched with indulgences by Pope John XXII in the year 1330. All the manuscripts practically agree as to these two facts so there can be no doubt of their exactness. In regard to its authorship all we can say is that it was, perhaps, written by John XXII. Of this we are not certain, as this Pope has been falsely accredited with similar pious compositions, and a mistake could easily be made of confounding the one who gave the indulgence with the real author. The Anima Christi was and is still generally believed to have been composed by St. Ignatius Loyola, as he puts it at the beginning of his "Spiritual Exercises" and often refers to it. This is a mistake, as has been pointed out by many writers, since the prayer has been found in a number of prayer books printed during the youth of the saint and is in manuscripts which were written a hundred years before his birth (1491). James Mearns, the English hymnologist, found it in a manuscript of the British Museum which dates back to about 1370. In the library of Avignon there is preserved a prayer book of Cardinal Peter De Luxembourg, who died in 1387, which contains the Anima Christi in practically the same form as we have it today. It has also been found inscribed on one of the gates of the Alcazar of Seville, which brings us back to the times of Don Pedro the Cruel (1350-69). This prayer was so well known and so popular at the time of St. Ignatius, that he only mentions it in the first edition of his "Spiritual Exercises", evidently supposing that the exercitant or reader already knew it. In the later editions, it was printed in full. It was by assuming that everything in the book was written by St. Ignatius that it came to be looked upon as his composition. All this has been told at length by Guido Dreves (Stimmen aus Maria-Laach LIV, 493) and B. Baesten (Précis Historiques, XXXII, 630).

The source of this information: From the Catholic Encyclopedia.

P. The Holy Face(거룩한 얼굴)

O Blessed Face of my kind Savior, by the tender love and piercing sorrow of Our Lady as she beheld You in Your cruel Passion, grant us to share in this intense sorrow and love so as to fulfill the holy will of God to the utmost of our ability. Amen. # This is the prayer of Blessed Maria Pierina de Micheli.

Q. Christ Candle of Hope Prayer(예수님께 초를 밝히며 드리는 희망의 기도)

God, our loving Father, you sent your Son, Jesus Christ, into this world to counter all the forces of evil: sin, suffering and death, and to overcome evil with the force of good; hatred with the power of love, your great love for us in Jesus. Help us never to curse the darkness, but to join with you in bringing Your light into this world, the light that is Your Son, born of the Virgin Mary, in Bethlehem. Help us to be instruments of your light and love by doing one special act of kindness or by being your special instrument of reconciliation this New Year. May the Christ Candle we light symbolize our desire to bring light into a world of darkness and hope into a world of despair. We ask this through Christ our Lord. Amen. # Once again, Bishop Robert J. Baker is encouraging Catholics to celebrate their faith with the Christ Candle of Hope during the Christmas season. Christmas is the celebration of the breaking through history of the greatest event of all time — the birth of the Son of God into our world, who was victorious over all the forces of evil, past, present, and future. Can we not enable the force of good that Christ brought into this world by his birth to impact our lives in our own day and time — this Christmas? Hope is the virtue that enables us to experience now the reign of Christ. Hope unites past, present and future by bringing Christ's activity to bear on the present moment. I, as your bishop, invite our clergy, religious, and laity to join together again this Christmas season in a symbolic gesture of hope in the face of all the temptations to negativity and hopelessness. As we have done in the past, can we use again in our churches this Christmas season the Christ Candle that is often lit during Christmas Mass? It may or may not be situated in the center of the Advent wreath with its four Advent candles that had previously been lit each Sunday of Advent. The Christ Candle can be brought up during the Offertory procession after the homily, Creed, and Prayers of the Faithful. The celebrant of the Christmas Mass may have in his homily comments about concrete ways of doing something positive this Christmas in one's life to counter the negativity in the world.

As the Christ Candle is being brought to a position in the sanctuary and placed, possibly in the center of the Advent wreath, a prayer can be offered; an invitation is made to all in the congregation to commit toward doing something constructive, some random act of kindness, as soon as possible; and finally the Christ Candle is lit as a symbol of our prayer and constructive action, a Christmas symbol of hope, that is envisioned as bringing a little light into the darkness of the world in which we live. People are then invited to have their own Christ Candle of Hope in their homes to be lit at their main Christmas dinner, after the opening prayer and after everyone in the household has a chance to think about doing one positive, constructive action to better the world in which we live during the Christmas season. Families might consider continuing to light the Christ Candle at their main dinner and offering the prayer above during the twelve days of Christmas, or even longer, until the Feast of the Baptism of the Lord, the liturgical end of the Christmas season. This Christmas season, in your church, in your home, offer up a prayer; make a commitment; light a candle of hope for the church and for the world. The above "Christ Candle of Hope Prayer" is a possible prayer to be used before lighting the Christ Candle. # The source of this information: From http://themiscellany.org/2006.

R. Litany of Humility(겸손 호칭기도)

O Jesus! meek and humble of heart, Hear me.
From the desire of being esteemed, Deliver me, Jesus.
From the desire of being loved ⋯
From the desire of being extolled ⋯
From the desire of being honored ⋯
From the desire of being praised ⋯
From the desire of being preferred to others ⋯
From the desire of being consulted ⋯
From the desire of being approved ⋯
From the fear of being humiliated ⋯
From the fear of being despised ⋯
From the fear of suffering rebukes ⋯
From the fear of being calumniated ⋯
From the fear of being forgotten ⋯

From the fear of being ridiculed …

From the fear of being wronged …

From the fear of being suspected …

That others may be loved more than I, Jesus, grant me the grace to desire it.

That others may be esteemed more than I …

That, in the opinion of the world,

others may increase and I may decrease …

That others may be chosen and I set aside …

That others may be praised and I unnoticed …

That others may be preferred to me in everything …

That others may become holier than I, provided that I may become as holy as I should……Amen. # This prayer was composed by Rafael Cardinal Merry del Val (1865-1930).

S. Novena to the Divine Child Jesus

Divine Child Jesus, we believe in You; We adore You; and we love You; have mercy on us, sinners. We've come to this Temple in response to your love. We've come in response to your mercy and grace. We are here because You invited us to come before You and to pour out the cares of our hearts to You since You deeply care for each of us. We remember Your words to the disciples: Ask and you shall receive. Seek and you shall find. Knock and the door shall be opened. Trusting in your infinite goodness and trusting that You always keep your promise, we now ask this intention which we pray in the silence of our hearts…(silently mention the request). Thank you, Divine Child Jesus, for listening attentively to our prayers all the time. We hope that You will ask this before Our Heavenly Father. And, if what we ask for may not be good for our salvation and sanctification, we trust that you will grant us instead what we truly need, so that one day we may be with You for all eternity enjoying that ultimate happiness of Heaven.

Divine Child Jesus, bless and protect us.

Divine Child Jesus, bless and lead us.

Divine Child Jesus, bless and provide for us.

All this we ask through the intercession of your Holy Mother, Mary, and in Your powerful and Most Holy Name, Jesus. Amen. # A nine days' private or public devotion in the Catholic Church to obtain special graces. The octave has more of the festal character; to the novena belongs that of hopeful mourning, of yearning, of prayer. The number nine in Holy Writ is indicative of suffering and grief(St. Jerome, in Ezech., vii, 24; P.L., XXV, 238, cf. XXV, 1473). The novena is permitted and even recommended by ecclesiastical authority, but still has no proper and fully set place in the liturgy of the Church. It has, however, more and more been prized and utilized by the faithful. Four kinds of novenas can be distinguished: Novenas of mourning, of preparation, of prayer and the indulgence novenas, though this distinction are not exclusive. # The Information source: From the Catholic Encyclopedia. .

A "Novena" consists of acts of devotion, performed on nine consecutive days, to obtain a particular grace of either spiritual or temporal nature. These acts of devotion may consist of vocal prayers (for instance, nine "Hail Mary," followed by a "Hail, Holy Queen," or any other short prayer, or nine "Glory be to the Father," or a fixed number of ejaculatory prayers whilst at work, etc.); reception of the holy sacraments; acts of mortification (for example to refrain from unnecessary talk, to abstain from a particular kind of food we have a craving for, to break off sleep, and to spend this time in a pious manner, not to take a very comfortable posture while at prayer, etc.). A person may choose the acts of devotion for himself, or better still, have them determined by his spiritual director. Particular care should be taken to avoid even the least voluntary venial sin and fault. By a Novena pious Catholics prepare themselves for the feasts of our Lord, the Blessed Virgin or a particular saint; or pay honor to a special mystery of our holy religion. The first Novena was made by the Blessed Virgin and the Apostles, at the command of our Lord Himself. It lasted from the Ascension of Christ into Heaven until the descent of the Holy Spirit on the feast of Pentecost. # The information source: From www.ecatholic2000.com.

T. Prayer while visiting the Most Blessed Sacrament(성체를 방문하면서 드리는 기도)

This prayer was written by St. Alphonsus Liguori. # St. Padre Pio(AD 1887-1968) recited this prayer daily.
이 기도문은 Chapter 10 Eucharistic Adoration에 있음.

U. Stations of the Cross or The Way of the Cross (십자가의 길); This was written by Saint Alphonsus Maria de' Liguori.

(a) Preparatory Prayer:

1) Kneeling before the altar, make an Act of Contrition, and form the intention of gaining the indulgences, whether for yourself or for the souls in Purgatory.

2) Then say:

My Lord Jesus Christ, You have made this journey to die for me with love unutterable, and I have so many times unworthily abandoned You; but now I love You with my whole heart, and because I love You, I repent sincerely for having ever offended You. Pardon me, my God, and permit me to accompany You on this journey. You go to die for love of me; I wish also, my beloved Redeemer, to die for love of You. My Jesus, I will live and die always united to You. Dear Jesus You go to die for very love of me; Let me bear You company; I wish to die with You.

(b) Prayer at each Station

First Station: Jesus Is Condemned To Death

V. We adore You, O Christ, and we bless You.
R. Because by Your holy Cross, You have redeemed the world.

Consider how Jesus, after having been scourged and crowned with thorns, was unjustly condemned by Pilate to die on the Cross.
My adorable Jesus, it was not Pilate, no, it was my sins that condemned You to die. I beg You, by the merits of this sorrowful journey, to assist my soul in its journey towards eternity. I love You, my beloved Jesus; I love You more than myself; I repent with my whole heart of having offended Thee. Never permit me to separate myself from Thee again. Grant that I may love You always; and then do with me what You will.

Our Father, Hail Mary, Glory be.
Dear Jesus, You(Thou dost) go to die
For very love of me: Ah! let me bear You(Thee) company; I wish to die with Thee.
V. Have mercy on us, O Lord.

R. Have mercy on us.

At the Cross her station keeping,
Stood the mournful Mother weeping,
Close to Jesus to the last.

Second Station: Jesus carries His Cross

V. We adore You, O Christ, and we bless You.
R. Because by Your holy Cross, You have redeemed the world.

Consider how Jesus, in making this journey with the Cross on His shoulders, thought of us and for us offered to His Father the death He was about to undergo.

My most beloved Jesus, I embrace all the tribulations that You have(Thou hast) destined for me until death. I beg You(beseech Thee), by the merits of the pain You suffered(Thou didst suffer) in carrying Your(Thy) cross, to give me the necessary help to carry mine with perfect patience and resignation. I love You(Thee), Jesus, my love; I repent of having offended Thee. Never permit me to separate myself from Thee again. Grant that I may love Thee always; and then do with me what You will(Thou wilt).

Our Father, Hail Mary, Glory be.
Dear Jesus, You(Thou dost) go to die
For very love of me:
Ah! let me bear You(Thee) company; I wish to die with Thee.
V. Have mercy on us, O Lord.
R. Have mercy on us.
Through her heart, His sorrow sharing, All His bitter anguish bearing, Lo! the piercing sword had passed!

Third Station: Jesus Falls the First Time

V. We adore You, O Christ, and we bless You.
R. Because by Your holy Cross, You have redeemed the world.

Consider this first fall of Jesus under His cross. His flesh was torn by the scourges,

His head crowned with thorns, and He had lost a great quantity of blood. He was so weakened that He could scarcely walk, and yet He had to carry this great load upon His shoulders. The soldiers struck Him rudely, and thus He fell several times in His journey. My beloved Jesus, it is not the weight of the cross but of my sins, which have made Thee suffer so much pain. Ah, by the merits of this first fall, deliver me from the misfortune of falling into mortal sin. I love Thee, O my Jesus, with all my heart; I repent of having offended Thee. Never permit me to offend Thee again. Grant that I may love Thee always; and then do with me what Thou wilt.

Our Father, Hail Mary, Glory be.
Dear Jesus, You(Thou dost) go to die
For very love of me:
Ah! let me bear You(Thee) company; I wish to die with Thee.
V. Have mercy on us, O Lord.
R. Have mercy on us.

O, how sad, and sore distressed,
Now was she, that Mother Blessed of the sole-begotten One.

Fourth Station: Jesus Meets His sorrowful Mother

V. We adore You, O Christ, and we bless You.
R. Because by Your holy Cross, You have redeemed the world.

Consider the meeting of the Son and the Mother, which took place on this journey. Jesus and Mary looked at each other, and their looks became as so many arrows to wound those hearts which loved each other so tenderly.

My most loving Jesus, by the sorrow Thou didst experience in this meeting, grant me the grace of a truly devoted love for Thy most holy Mother. And thou, my Queen, who were overwhelmed with sorrow, obtain for me by thy intercession a continual and tender remembrance of the Passion of thy Son. I love Thee, Jesus, my Love. I repent of ever having offended Thee. Never permit me to offend Thee again. Grant that I may love Thee always; and then do with me what You will(Thou wilt).

Our Father, Hail Mary, Glory be.

Dear Jesus, You(Thou dost) go to die

For very love of me:

Ah! let me bear You(Thee) company; I wish to die with Thee.

V. Have mercy on us, O Lord.

R. Have mercy on us.

Woe begone, with heart's prostration, Mother meek, the bitter passion saw she of her glorious Son.

Fifth Station: Simon Cyrene helps Jesus to carry the Cross

V. We adore You, O Christ, and we bless You.

R. Because by Your holy Cross, You have redeemed the world.

Consider that the Jews, seeing that at each step Jesus, from weakness, was on the point of expiring and fearing that He would die on the way, when they wished Him to die the ignominious death of the cross, constrained Simon the Cyrenian to carry the cross behind Our Lord.

My most sweet (My beloved) Jesus, I will not refuse the cross as the Cyrenian did: I accept it, I embrace it. I accept in particular the death that Thou hast destined for me with all the pains which may accompany it. I unite it to Thy death and I offer it to Thee. Thou hast died for love of me; I will die for love of Thee and to please Thee. Help me by Thy grace. I love Thee, Jesus, my love; I repent of having offended Thee. Never permit me to offend Thee again. Grant that I may love Thee always; and then do with me what You will(Thou wilt).

Our Father, Hail Mary, Glory be.

Dear Jesus, You(Thou dost) go to die

For very love of me:

Ah! let me bear You(Thee) company; I wish to die with Thee.

V. Have mercy on us, O Lord.

R. Have mercy on us.

Who could mark, from tears refraining, Christ's dear Mother uncomplaining, in so great a sorrow bowed.

Sixth Station: Veronica wipes the face of Jesus

V. We adore You, O Christ, and we bless You.
R. Because by Your holy Cross, You have redeemed the world.

Consider that the holy woman named Veronica, seeing Jesus so afflicted and His face bathed in sweat and blood, presented Him with a towel, with which He wiped His adorable face, leaving on it the impression of His holy countenance.
My most beloved Jesus, Thy face was beautiful before, but in this journey it has lost all its beauty, and wounds and blood have disfigured it. Alas, my soul also was once beautiful, when it received Thy grace in Baptism; but I have disfigured it since with my sins. Thou alone, my Redeemer, canst restore it to its former beauty. Do this by Thy Passion, O Jesus. I repent of having offended Thee. Never permit me to offend thee again. Grant that I may love Thee always, and then do with me what Thou wilt.

Our Father, Hail Mary, Glory be.
Dear Jesus, You(Thou dost) go to die
For very love of me:
Ah! let me bear You(Thee) company; I wish to die with Thee.
V. Have mercy on us, O Lord.
R. Have mercy on us.

Who, unmoved, behold her languish, underneath His Cross of anguish, mid the fierce, unpitying crowd?

Seventh Station: Jesus falls the second time

V. We adore You, O Christ, and we bless You.
R. Because by Your holy Cross, You have redeemed the world.

Consider the second fall of Jesus under the cross - a fall which renews the pains of all the wounds of the head and members of our afflicted Lord.

My most gentle Jesus, how many times Thou hast pardoned me, and how many times I have fallen again, and begun again to offend Thee! Oh, by the merits of this new fall, give me the necessary helps to persevere in Thy grace until death. Grant that in all temptations which assail me, I may always commend myself to Thee. I love Thee, Jesus, my Love with my whole heart; I repent of having offended Thee. Never permit me to offend Thee again. Grant that I may love Thee always, and then do with me what Thou wilt.

Our Father, Hail Mary, Glory be.
Dear Jesus, You(Thou dost) go to die
For very love of me:
Ah! let me bear You(Thee) company; I wish to die with Thee.
V. Have mercy on us, O Lord.
R. Have mercy on us.

For this people's sins rejected, She her Jesus, unprotected, saw with thorns, with scourges rent.

Eighth Station: The women of Jerusalem weep over Jesus

V. We adore You, O Christ, and we bless You.
R. Because by Your holy Cross, You have redeemed the world.

Consider that those women wept with compassion at seeing Jesus in so pitiable a state, streaming with blood, as He walked along. But Jesus said to them, "Weep not for Me, but for your children."

My Jesus, laden with sorrows, I weep for the offenses that I have committed against Thee, because of the pains which they have deserved, and still more, because of the displeasure which they have caused Thee, Who hast loved me so much. It is Thy love, more than the fear of hell, which causes me to weep for my sins. My Jesus, I love Thee more than myself; I repent of having offended Thee. Never permit me to offend Thee again. Grant that I may love Thee always, and then do with me what Thou wilt.

Our Father, Hail Mary, Glory be.
Dear Jesus, You(Thou dost) go to die

For very love of me:

Ah! let me bear You(Thee) company; I wish to die with Thee.

V. Have mercy on us, O Lord.

R. Have mercy on us.

Saw her Son from judgment taken, her beloved in death forsaken till His Spirit forth He sent.

Ninth Station: Jesus falls the third time

V. We adore You, O Christ, and we bless You.

R. Because by Your holy Cross, You have redeemed the world.

Consider the third fall of Jesus Christ. His weakness was extreme, and the cruelty of His executioners excessive, who tried to hasten His steps when He had scarcely strength to move.

Ah, my outraged Jesus, by the merits of the weakness that Thou didst suffer in going to Calvary, give me strength sufficient to conquer all human respect and all my wicked passions, which have led me to despise Thy friendship. I love Thee, Jesus, my Love, with my whole heart; I repent of having offended Thee. Never permit me to offend Thee again. Grant that I may love Thee always, and then do with me what Thou wilt.

Our Father, Hail Mary, Glory be.

Dear Jesus, You(Thou dost) go to die

For very love of me:

Ah! let me bear You(Thee) company; I wish to die with Thee.

V. Have mercy on us, O Lord.

R. Have mercy on us.

Fount of love and holy sorrow, Mother, may my spirit borrow somewhat of your woe profound.

Tenth Station: Jesus is stripped of His Garments

V. We adore You, O Christ, and we bless You.
R. Because by Your holy Cross, You have redeemed the world.

Consider the violence with which the executioners stripped Jesus. His inner garments adhered to His torn flesh, and they dragged them off so roughly that the skin came with them. Compassionate your Saviour thus cruelly treated, and say to Him:
My innocent Jesus, by the merits of the torment which Thou hast felt, help me to strip myself of all affection to things of earth, in order that I may place all my love in Thee, Who art so worthy of my love. I love Thee, O Jesus, with my whole heart; I repent of having offended Thee. Never permit me to offend Thee again. Grant that I may love Thee always, and then do with me what Thou wilt.

Our Father, Hail Mary, Glory be.
Dear Jesus, You(Thou dost) go to die
For very love of me:
Ah! let me bear You(Thee) company; I wish to die with Thee.
V. Have mercy on us, O Lord.
R. Have mercy on us.

Unto Christ, with pure emotion, raise my contrite heart's devotion, love to read in every wound.

Elevens Station: Jesus is nailed to the Cross

V. We adore You, O Christ, and we bless You.
R. Because by Your holy Cross, You have redeemed the world.

Consider how Jesus, after being thrown down on the cross, extended His hands and offered to His eternal Father the sacrifice of His life for our salvation. These barbarians fastened Him with nails, and then, raising the cross, left Him to die in anguish on this infamous gibbet.

My Jesus, loaded with contempt, nail my heart to Thy feet, that it may ever remain there to love Thee and never quit Thee again. I love Thee more than myself; I repent of having offended Thee. Never permit me to offend Thee again. Grant that I may love Thee always, and then do with me what Thou wilt.

Our Father, Hail Mary, Glory be.
Dear Jesus, You(Thou dost) go to die
For very love of me:
Ah! let me bear You(Thee) company; I wish to die with Thee.
V. Have mercy on us, O Lord.
R. Have mercy on us.

Those five wounds were smitten on Jesus. Mother! in my heart be written, deep as in your own they be.

Twelfth Station: Jesus is raised upon the Cross and dies

V. We adore You, O Christ, and we bless You.
R. Because by Your holy Cross, You have redeemed the world.

Consider how Thy Jesus, after three hours of agony on the cross, consumed at length with anguish, abandons Himself to the weight of His body, bows His head and dies.
(kneel)
O my dying Jesus, I kiss devoutly the cross on which Thou didst die for love of me. I have merited by my sins to die a miserable death, but Thy death is my hope. Ah, by the merits of Thy death, give me grace to die, embracing Thy feet and burning with love for Thee. I commit my soul into Thy hands. I love Thee with my whole heart; I repent of having offended Thee. Never permit me to offend Thee again. Grant that I may love Thee always, and then do with me what Thou wilt.

Our Father, Hail Mary, Glory be.
Dear Jesus, You(Thou dost) go to die
For very love of me:
Ah! let me bear You(Thee) company; I wish to die with Thee.
V. Have mercy on us, O Lord.
R. Have mercy on us.

You my Saviour's Cross who bear, and Your Son's rebuke who share. Let me share them both with You.

Thirteenth Station: Jesus is taken down from the Cross

V. We adore You, O Christ, and we bless You.
R. Because by Your holy Cross, You have redeemed the world.

Consider how, after the death of Our Lord having expired, two of His disciples, Joseph and Nicodemus, took Him down from the Cross and placed Him in the arms of His afflicted Mother, who received Him with unutterable tenderness and pressed Him close to her bosom.
O Mother of Sorrow, for the love of this Son, accept me for thy servant, and pray to Him for me. And Thou, my Redeemer, since Thou hast died for me, permit me to love Thee; for I wish but Thee, my Jesus; and I repent of having offended Thee. Never permit me to offend Thee again. Grant that I may love Thee always, and then do with me what Thou wilt.

Our Father, Hail Mary, Glory be.
Dear Jesus, You (Thou dost) go to die
For very love of me:
Ah! let me bear You(Thee) company; I wish to die with Thee.
V. Have mercy on us, O Lord.
R. Have mercy on us.
In the Passion of my Maker, be my sinful soul partaker, weep till death, and keep with Thee.

Fourteenth Station: Jesus is laid in the sepulcher

V. We adore You, O Christ, and we bless You.
R. Because by Your holy Cross, You have redeemed the world.

Consider that the disciples carried the body of Jesus to bury it, accompanied by His holy Mother, who arranged it in the sepulcher with her own hands. They then closed the tomb, and all withdrew.

Ah, my buried Jesus, I kiss the stone that encloses Thee. But Thou didst rise again the third day. I beseech Thee, by Thy resurrection, make me rise glorious with Thee at the Last Day, to be always united with Thee in Heaven, to praise Thee and love Thee forever. I love Thee , and I repent of ever having offended Thee. Never permit me to offend Thee again. Grant that I may love Thee always, and then do with me what Thou wilt.

Our Father, Hail Mary, Glory be.
Dear Jesus, You (Thou dost) go to die
For very love of me:
Ah! Let me bear You(Thee) company; I wish to die with Thee.
V. Have mercy on us, O Lord.
R. Have mercy on us.
Mine with you be that sad station. There to watch the great salvation wrought upon the atoning tree.
To complete the devotion of the Stations, say the "Our Father, Hail Mary and Glory Be" five times, in honour of the Passion of Jesus Christ, and once for the intention of the Holy Father.
Prayer to Jesus Christ crucified: Behold, O kind and most sweet Jesus, I cast myself upon my knees in Your sight, and with the most fervent desire of my soul, I pray and beg You to impress upon my heart lively sentiments of faith, hope and charity, with true contrition for my sins, and a firm purpose of amendment: while with deep affection and grief of soul, I ponder within myself and mentally contemplate Your five most precious Wounds; having before my eyes the words which David spoke in prophesy: "They have pierced My hands and My feet; I can count all My bones."
#1: The faithful who, after receiving Communion, recite this prayer before a picture of Christ Crucified may gain a plenary indulgence on any Friday in Lent and a partial indulgence on other days of the year, with the addition of prayers for the Holy Father's intention.
#2: Those who devoutly make the Stations of the Cross, may gain a plenary indulgence. Those who are lawfully hindered from making the Stations of the Cross, may gain the same indulgence if they read and meditate on the Passion and Death of our Lord for at least one half-hour(no.63).

V. The Sacrament of Confession; Guide for Confession

(a) How to go to confession

1) A Pastoral Exhortation on the Sacrament of Penance and Reconciliation; God's Gift of Forgiveness

Dear Brothers and Sisters in Christ: "Peace be with you!" With these words, the Risen Lord greeted his frightened Apostles in the Upper Room on the day of his Resurrection. They were troubled, anxious, and fearful—much like each one of us at some point in our lives. Christ repeated the words, "Peace be with you." But then he added, "Receive the holy Spirit. Whose sins you forgive are forgiven them" (Jn 20:19-23). What an extraordinary gift! The Risen Lord was proclaiming that all the suffering he had just endured was in order to make available the gifts of salvation and forgiveness. He wanted the Apostles to receive these gifts. He wanted them to become apostles of this forgiveness to others. In the Sacrament of Penance and Reconciliation, also called confession, we meet the Lord, who wants to grant forgiveness and the grace to live a renewed life in him. In this sacrament, he prepares us to receive him free from serious sin, with a lively faith, earnest hope, and sacrificial love in the Eucharist. The Church sees confession as so important that she requires that every Catholic go at least once a year.(Catechism of the Catholic Church, nos. 1457-1458) The Church also encourages frequent confession in order to grow closer to Christ Jesus and his Body, the Church. By the grace of the Holy Spirit, we seek forgiveness and repentance, let go of patterns of sin, grow in the life of virtue, and witness to a joyful conversion. Since the graces of the sacrament are so similar to the purpose of the New Evangelization, Pope Benedict XVI has said, "The New Evangelization…begins in the confessional!" (Pope Benedict XVI, Address to the Annual Course on the Internal Forum Organized by the Apostolic Penitentiary). We bishops and priests are eager to help you if you experience difficulty, hesitation, or uncertainty about approaching the Lord in this sacrament. If you have not received this healing sacrament in a long time, we are ready to welcome you. We, whom Christ has ordained to minister this forgiveness in his name, are also approaching this sacrament, as both penitents and ministers, throughout our lives and at this special moment of grace during Lent. We want to offer ourselves to you as forgiven sinners seeking to serve in the Lord's name.

During Lent—in addition to the various penitential services during which individual confession takes place—we bishops and priests will be making ourselves available often for the individual celebration of this sacrament. We pray that through the work of the Holy Spirit, all Catholics—clergy and laity—will respond to the call of the New Evangelization to encounter Christ in the Sacrament of Penance and Reconciliation. Come to the Lord and experience the extraordinary grace of his forgiveness! "He said to him, 'My son, you are here with me always; everything I have is yours. But now we must celebrate and rejoice, because your brother was dead and has come to life again; he was lost and has been found.'" (Lk 15: 31-32)

2) The procedure to go to confession.

May the Passion of Our Lord Jesus Christ, the intercession of the Blessed Virgin Mary and of all the saints, whatever good you do and suffering you endure, heal your sins, help you grow in holiness, and reward you with eternal life. Go in peace. –Rite of Penance, no. 93

1 PREPARATION: Before going to confession, take some time to prepare. Begin with prayer, and reflect on your life since your last confession. How have you—in your thoughts, words, and actions— neglected to live Christ's commands to "love the Lord, your God, with all your heart, with all your soul, and with all your mind," and to "love your neighbor as yourself" (Mt 22:37, 39)? As a help with this "examination of conscience," you might review the Ten Commandments or the Beatitudes (Ex 20:2-17; Dt 5:6-21; Mt 5:3-10; or Lk 6:20-26).

2 GREETING: The priest will welcome you; he may say a short blessing or read a Scripture passage.

3 THE SIGN OF THE CROSS: Together, you and the priest will make the Sign of the Cross. You may then begin your confession with these or similar words: "Bless me, Father, for I have sinned. It has been [give days, months, or years] since my last confession."

4 CONFESSION: Confess all your sins to the priest. If you are unsure what to say, ask the priest for help. When you are finished, conclude with these or similar words: "I am sorry for these and all my sins."

5 PENANCE: The priest will propose an act of penance. The penance might be prayer, a work of mercy, or an act of charity. He might also counsel you on how to

better live a Christian life.

6 ACT OF CONTRITION: After the priest has conferred your penance, pray an Act of Contrition, expressing sorrow for your sins and resolving to sin no more. A suggested Act of Contrition is:

My God, I am sorry for my sins with all my heart. In choosing to do wrong and failing to do good, I have sinned against you whom I should love above all things. I firmly intend, with your help, to do penance, to sin no more, and to avoid whatever leads me to sin. Our Savior Jesus Christ suffered and died for us. In his name, my God, have mercy. (Rite of Penance, no. 45)

7 ABSOLUTION: The priest will extend his hands over your head and pronounce the words of absolution. You respond, "Amen."

8 PRAISE: The priest will usually praise the mercy of God and will invite you to do the same. For example, the priest may say, "Give thanks to the Lord for he is good." And your response would be, "His mercy endures for ever" (Rite of Penance, no. 47).

9 DISMISSAL: The priest will conclude the sacrament, often saying, "Go in peace."

(b) How to go to Confession

1) A Brief Examination of Conscience based on the Ten Commandments. I am the Lord your God: you shall not have strange Gods before me. Have I treated people, events, or things as more important than God? You shall not take the name of the Lord your God in vain. Have my words, actively or passively, put down God, the Church, or people? Remember to keep holy the Lord's Day. Do I go to Mass every Sunday (or Saturday Vigil) and on Holy Days of Obligation (Jan. 1; the Ascension; Aug. 15; Nov. 1; Dec. 8; Dec. 25)? Do I avoid, when possible, work that impedes worship to God, joy for the Lord's Day, and proper relaxation of mind and body?

Do I look for ways to spend time with family or in service on Sunday? Honor your father and your mother. Do I show my parents due respect? Do I seek to maintain good communication with my parents where possible? Do I criticize them for lacking skills I think they should have? You shall not kill. Have I harmed another through physical, verbal, or emotional means, including gossip or manipulation of any kind? You shall not commit adultery. Have I respected the physical and sexual dignity of others and of myself? You shall not steal. Have I taken or wasted time or resources that belonged to another? You shall not bear false witness against your neighbor. Have I gossiped, told lies, or embellished stories at the expense of another? You shall not covet your neighbor's spouse. Have I honored my spouse with my full affection and exclusive love? You shall not covet your neighbor's goods. Am I content with my own means and needs, or do I compare myself to others unnecessarily?

2) A Brief Examination of Conscience based on the Catholic social teaching Life and Dignity of the Human Person
- Do I respect the life and dignity of every human person from conception through natural death?
- Do I recognize the face of Christ reflected in all others around me whatever their race, class, age, or abilities?
- Do I work to protect the dignity of others when it is being threatened?
- Am I committed to both protecting human life and to ensuring that every human being is able to live in dignity?

Call to Family, Community, and Participation
- Do I try to make positive contributions in my family and in my community?
- Are my beliefs, attitudes, and choices such that they strengthen or undermine the institution of the family?
- Am I aware of problems facing my local community and involved in efforts to find solutions? Do I stay informed and make my voice heard when needed?
- Do I support the efforts of poor persons to work for change in their neighborhoods and communities? Do my attitudes and interactions empower or disempower others?

Rights and Responsibilities

- Do I recognize and respect the economic, social, political, and cultural rights of others?
- Do I live in material comfort and excess while remaining insensitive to the needs of others whose rights are unfulfilled?
- Do I take seriously my responsibility to ensure that the rights of persons in need are realized?
- Do I urge those in power to implement programs and policies that give priority to the human dignity and rights of all, especially the vulnerable?

Option for the Poor and Vulnerable

- Do I give special attention to the needs of the poor and vulnerable in my community and in the world?
- Am I disproportionately concerned for my own good at the expense of others?
- Do I engage in service and advocacy work that protects the dignity of poor and vulnerable persons?

The Dignity of Work and the Rights of Workers

- As a worker, do I give my employer a fair day's work for my wages? As an owner, do I treat workers fairly?
- Do I treat all workers with whom I interact with respect, no matter their position or class?
- Do I support the rights of all workers to adequate wages, health insurance, vacation and sick leave? Do I affirm their right to form or join unions or worker associations?
- Do my purchasing choices take into account the hands involved in the production of what I buy? When possible, do I buy products produced by workers whose rights and dignity were respected?

Solidarity

- Does the way I spend my time reflect a genuine concern for others?
- Is solidarity incorporated into my prayer and spirituality? Do I lift up vulnerable people throughout the world in my prayer, or is it reserved for only my personal concerns?
- Am I attentive only to my local neighbors or also those across the globe?

- Do I see all members of the human family as my brothers and sisters?

Care for God's Creation
- Do I live out my responsibility to care for God's creation?
- Do I see my care for creation as connected to my concern for poor persons, who are most at risk from environmental problems?
- Do I litter? Live wastefully? Use energy too freely? Are there ways I could reduce consumption in my life?
- Are there ways I could change my daily practices and those of my family, school, workplace, or community to better conserve the earth's resources for future generations? # Copyright © 2013, United States Conference of Catholic Bishops, Washington, DC. All rights reserved. Permission is hereby granted to duplicate this work without adaptation for non-commercial use. Scripture excerpts used in this work are taken from the New American Bible, rev. ed. ©2010, 1991, 1986, 1970 Confraternity of Christian Doctrine, Inc., Washington, DC. All rights reserved. No part of this work may be reproduced or transmitted in any form or by any means, electronic or mechanical, including photocopying, recording, or by any information storage and retrieval system, without permission in writing from the copyright owner.

(c) Prayer before Confession

1) My Lord and God, I have sinned. I am guilty before You. Grant me the strength to say to Your minister what I say to You in the secret of my heart. Increase my repentance. Make it more genuine. May it be really a sorrow for having offended You and my neighbor rather than a wounded love of self. Help me to atone for my sin. May the sufferings of my life and my little mortifications be joined with the sufferings of Jesus, Your Son, and cooperate in rooting sin from the world. Amen. Copyright ©2003, 1997 by Catholic Book Publishing Corp., N.J. All rights reserved.
2) O my God, help me to make a good confession. Mary, my dearest Mother, pray to Jesus for me. Help me to examine my conscience, enable me to obtain true sorrow for my sins, and beg for me the grace rather to die than to offend God again. Lord Jesus, light of our souls, who enlightens every man coming into this world, enlighten my conscience and my heart by Thy Holy Spirit, so that I may perceive all that is displeasing to Thy divine majesty and may expiate it by humble

confession, true contrition, and sincere repentance. Amen. #This was written by St. Alphonsus Liguori.

3) Invocation of the Holy Spirit

O Holy Spirit, source of all light, Spirit of wisdom, of understanding, and of knowledge, come to my assistance and enable me to make a good confession. Enlighten me, and help me now to know my sins as one day I shall be force to recognize them before Thy judgment seat. Bring to my mind the evil which I have done and the good which I have neglected. Permit me not to be blinded by self-love. Grant me, moreover, heartfelt sorrow for my transgressions, and the grace of a sincere confession, so that I may be forgiven and admitted into Thy friendship. Amen. # No Copyright ©. The source of this invocation: From St. Charles Borromeo Catholic Church, Picayune, MS and org.

(d) Prayer of the Penitent

1) My God, I am sorry for my sins with all my heart. In choosing to do wrong and failing to do good, I have sinned against You whom I should love above all things. I firmly intend, with Your help to do penance, to sin no more, and to avoid whatever leads me to sin. Our Savior Jesus Christ suffered and died for us. In His name, my God, have mercy. Amen.

2) Lord Jesus, You opened the eyes of the blind, healed the sick, forgave the sinful woman, and after Peter's denial confirmed him in your love. Listen to my prayer: forgive all my sins, renew your love in my heart, and help me to live in perfect unity with my fellow Christians that I may proclaim your saving power to all the world. Lord Jesus, Son of God, have mercy on me, a sinner. Amen. # Copyright ©2003, 1997 by Catholic Book Publishing Corp., N.J. All rights reserved.

3) Other approved acts of contrition and prayer of the penitent

Psalm 25:6-7:

Remember your compassion and your mercy, O Lord, for they are ages old. (You showed long ago.) Remember no more the sins of my youth (Do not recall the sins and failings of my youth); remember me according to your mercy, because of your goodness, Lord. (In your mercy remember me, Lord, because of your goodness.)

Psalm 51:4-5:

Thoroughly wash away my guilt, and from my sin cleanse me.
For I know my transgressions; my sin is always before me.

Luke 15:18; 18:13:

Father, I have sinned against heaven and against you. I no longer deserve to be called your son; treat me as you would. O God, be merciful to me, a sinner.

Or: Father of mercy, like the prodigal son I return to you and say: "I have sinned against you and am no longer worthy to be called your son." Christ Jesus, Savior of the world, I pray with the repentant thief to who you promised Paradise: "Lord, remember me in your kingdom." Holy Spirit, fountain of love, I call on you with trust: "Purify my heart, and help me to walk as a child of light."

Prayer: Lord God, forgive all my sins, renew your love in my heart, help me to live in perfect unity with my fellow Christians that I may proclaim your saving power to all the world.

Or: Lord God, in your goodness have mercy on me: do not look on my sins, but take away all my guilt. Create in me a clean heart and renew within me an upright spirit.

Or: Lord Jesus, Son of God, have mercy on me a sinner.

Or: Lord Jesus, you chose to be called the friend of sinners. By your saving death and resurrection free me from my sins. May your peace take root in my heart and bring forth a harvest of love, holiness, and truth. # Source of these acts of contrition and prayer of the penitent: From Rite of Penance/Rite for Reconciliation of Individual Penitents. Copyright ©1974. International Committee on English in the Liturgy, Inc. All rights reserved.

(e) Prayer after Confession

My dearest Jesus, I have told all my sins as well as I could. I tried hard to make a good confession. I feel sure that You have forgiven me. I thank You. It is only because of all Your sufferings that I can go to confession and free myself from my sins. Your Heart is full of love and mercy for poor sinners. I love You because You are so good to me. My loving Savior, I shall try to keep from sin and to love You more each day. My dear Mother Mary, pray for me and help me to keep my promises. Protect me and do not let me fall back into sin. Almighty God, kneeling before Your Divine Majesty, I adore You and because You command me, I dare approach Your divine Heart. But what shall I say if You do not enlighten me with a ray of Your divine light? Speak to my soul, O Lord, and command me to listen to Your voice. Enlighten my will to put Your words into practice. Pour Your grace into my heart; lift up my soul weighed down by my sins; raise my mind to heavenly things, so that earthly desires may no longer appeal to me. Speak to my soul with Your divine omnipotence, for You are my salvation, my life, and my peace, in time and in eternity. Strengthen me with the grace of Your Holy Spirit and give Your peace to my soul that I may be free from all needless worry and care. Help me to desire always that which is pleasing and acceptable to You so that Your Will may be my will, Grant that I may rid myself of all unholy desires, and that for Your love I may remain unknown in this world, and be known only to You. Do not permit me to attribute to myself the good that You perform in me and through me, but rather, referring all honor to Your majesty, may I glory only in my weakness, so that renouncing sincerely all vain glory which comes from the world, I may aspire to the true and lasting glory which comes from you. Amen.

Mother Cabrini, much like St. Paul, wishes to glory in her weakness towards the end of this prayer. (St. Paul once wrote concerning his hardships in spreading the Gospel "I will glory in my infirmities, that the strength of Christ may dwell in me⋯ For when I am weak I am strong" 2 Cor 12:9-10.) She lived her life filled with missionary zeal for Christ and in Christ, (her motto was "I can do all things in Him"), overcoming obstacles for His sake. For example, she made numerous trips by boat between Italy and America to bring new sisters for her houses even though she had a great fear of the ocean. (This was way before airplane travel, remember.) She clearly wished to give Jesus free reign to show His love through her, so that her will could be united with His. In this regard, she once wrote that she would go anywhere or do anything to communicate His love to those who didn't know Him or had forgotten Him. Fittingly enough, she abhorred vainglory, that temptation to excessive pride which is a most subtle and deadly snare for the religious. For example, think of those snobbish Scribes and Pharisees Jesus denounced in the Gospels who craved attention and prestige more than serving God and others (as poignantly described in Chapter 23 of Matthew's Gospel, among other places.). Yet vainglory can afflict any of us. Our egos can often get in the way of doing God's work, when we wish to advance our own needs and pleasures at His expense. Mother Cabrini clearly views herself in this prayer more like the publican in the famous parable, a sinner asking God for Mercy, rather than the Pharisee boasting about his sanctimoniousness (Luke 18:9-14). Keep in mind that such humility, like sanctity itself, is not just for those who have been canonized as saints! We must adopt this attitude of being God's loving humble servants as well. We cannot get to heaven solely on our own strength. As Jesus said in His Last Supper discourse "I am the vine and you are the branches. He who abides in me and I in him, he bears much fruit; for without me you can do nothing"(John 15:5). We need to turn to God constantly for his help, grace, guidance and, yes, forgiveness in confession! In this regard, there are a couple of sentences in Mother Cabrini's prayer you might wish to memorize to when you feel most at odds with yourself or with the world around you: "Speak to my soul, O Lord, and command me to listen to Your voice. Enlighten my will to put Your words into practice. Pour Your grace into my heart; lift up my soul weighed down by my sins; raise my mind to heavenly things. Amen." # This prayer after confession was written by St. Frances Xavier Cabrini , a nun who helped found the Missionary Sisters of the Sacred Heart. This was a religious institute dedicated to serving many community needs, most notably those of Italian immigrants to America in the late 19th and early 20th centuries. Under her care, 67 religious houses, schools, and charitable institutions such as orphanages and hospitals were established throughout the United States, Italy, England and even in Central and South America from 1880 until her death in 1917. Mother Cabrini made such an impact that she became the first American citizen to become a saint! (Although she was born in Italy, she was naturalized in 1909.) She expresses some wonderful saintly attitudes in her prayer below that we should all try to have as well: a genuine sense of contrition for sins, great humility, a hunger for holiness and being in one with God, and a healthy disdain for the spiritual affliction known as vainglory.

Chapter 4 Prayers to the Holy Spirit

A. Pentecost Veni Sancte Spiritus: Prayer to the Holy Spirit 성령 송가

Come, Holy Spirit, and send down from heaven the ray of Your light. Come, Father of the poor, come, giver of gifts, and come, light of the heart. Best Consoler and sweet guest of the soul, refresh us. Rest in work, shade in heat and solace when we are in tears. O blessed eternal light, fill the innermost hearts of Your faithful. Without Your help, there is nothing in us, nothing that is not harmful. Cleanse our faults, water the dry land and heal what is taken ill. Soften our hardened heart (=Bend what is inflexible), warm what is cold and straighten what is crooked(=correct what goes astray). Give to Your faithful, those who trust in You, the sevenfold gifts. Grant to render a service for the reward of virtue, open the door of salvation wide and grant us eternal blessing and joy. Amen.

성령 송가

오소서, 성령님. 주님의 빛, 그 빛살을 하늘에서 내리소서. 가난한 이 아버지, 오소서 은총 주님, 오소서 마음의 빛. 가장 좋은 위로자, 영혼의 기쁜 손님, 저희 생기 돋우소서. 일할 때에 휴식을, 무더위에 시원함을, 슬플 때에 위로를. 영원하신 행복의 빛, 저희 마음 깊은 곳을 가득하게 채우소서. 주님 도움 없으시면, 저희 삶의 그 모든 것, 해로운 것, 뿐이리라. 허물들은 씻어 주고, 메마른 땅 물 주시고, 병든 것을 고치소서. 굳은 마음 풀어 주고, 차디찬 맘 데우시고, 빗나간 길 바루소서. 성령님을 굳게 믿고, 의지하는 이들에게, 성령 칠은 베푸소서. 덕행 공로 쌓게 하고, 구원의 문 활짝 열어, 영원복락 주옵소서.

Solemnity of Pentecost we conclude the fifty days of Eastertide and commemorate the pouring forth of the Holy Spirit who sent the Apostles on mission to proclaim the Gospel. On this Solemnity let us unite our hearts in prayer. Before the Pentecost there is to be a novena of the Pentecost Veni Sancte Spiritus.

B. Come, Holy Spirit (오소서 성령님)

V. Come, Holy Spirit, fill the hearts of Your faithful.

R. And enkindle in them the fire of Your love.

V. Send forth Your Spirit and they shall be created.

R. And You shall renew the face of the earth.

Let us pray:

O God, Who by the light of the Holy Spirit, instructed (or taught) the hearts of the faithful. In the same Spirit, help us to know what is truly right and always to rejoice in Your consolation. Through Christ our Lord. Amen.

오소서 성령님(일을 시작하며 바치는 기도)

○ 오소서, 성령님. 저희 마음을 성령으로 가득 채우시어 저희 안에 사랑의 불이 타오르게 하소서. ● 주님의 성령을 보내소서. 저희가 새로워지리이다. 또한 온 누리가 새롭게 되리이다.

† 기도합시다.

하느님, 성령의 빛으로 저희 마음을 이끄시어, 바르게 생각하고 언제나 성령의 위로를 받아 누리게 하소서. 우리 주 그리스도를 통하여 비나이다. ◎ 아멘.

C. Veni, Sante Spiritus(Come, Holy Spirit, Creator Blest)

Come, Holy Spirit, Creator come, from Your bright heavenly throne; come, take possession of our souls, and make us all Your own. You who are called the Paraclete, best gift of God above; the living spring, the living fire, sweet unction and true love. Thou who art sevenfold in Thy grace, finger of God's right hand; His promise, teaching little ones to speak and understand. O guide our minds with Thy blest light, with love our hearts inflame; and with Thy strength, which ne'er decays, confirm our mortal frame. Far from us drive our deadly foe; true peace unto us bring; and through all perils lead us safe beneath Thy sacred wing. Through Thee may we the Father know, through You, the eternal Son, and You, the Spirit of them both, thrice-blessed Three in One. All glory to the Father be, with his co-equal Son; the same to Thee, great Paraclete, while endless ages run. Amen.

오소서 성령님, 복되신 창조주님.

오소서 성령님. 오소서, 창조주시여. 성령님의 빛나는 하늘 어좌에서 오소서; 오셔서, 저희의 영혼을 차지하시고 저희 모두를 당신 소유로 만들어 주소서. 당신의 이름은 파라클리토, 티없이 높으신 하느님의 가장 좋은 선물; 생명의 샘, 생명의 불, 달콤한 기름이시며 참사랑이십니다.

당신은 일곱 가지 은총 지니신, 하느님 아버지의 오른 손가락; 성부의 언약으로 작은 어린이들이 말하고 이해하도록 가르치십니다. 오, 당신의 복된 빛으로 저희 마음을 인도하여 주시고, 당신의 사랑으로 저희 마음 불타오르게 하소서. 결코 썩지 않는 당신의 힘으로 저희의 육신(몸)은 반드시 죽어야 할 운명임을 확실히 깨닫게 하여주소서. 생명을 앗아가는 원수들 저희에게서 멀리멀리 쫓아주시고, 참 평화 저희에게 내려주소서. 그리고 모든 위험을 뚫고서 당신의 거룩한 날개아래로 안전하게 인도하소서. 당신의 힘을 입어 성부를 알고, 영원하신 성자도 그 힘으로 알게 하소서. 성부와 성자께로 좇아나시는 성령님도 그 힘으로 알게 하소서. 지극히 복되시고 찬미 받으시는 분, 세 위격이시지만 한 분이신 분.
하느님 아버지, 모든 영광 받으시옵소서.
성부와 동격이신 성자께서도 모든 영광 받으시옵소서.
위대하신 파라클리토 성령께서도 세세 대대로 영원토록 모든 영광 받으시옵소서. 아멘,

D. Prayer to the Holy Spirit

O Holy Spirit, Divine Paraclete, Father of the poor, Consoler of the afflicted, and Sanctifier of souls, behold us prostrate in Your presence. We adore You with the deepest submission and we repeat with the Seraphim who stand before Your throne; "Holy, holy, holy!" You filled the soul of Mary with immense graces and inflamed the hearts of the Apostles with holy zeal; enkindle our hearts with Your love. You are a supernatural light; enlighten us that we may understand eternal things. You appeared as a dove; grant us purity of life. You came as a wind full of sweetness; disperse the storms of passions that rise in us. You appeared as a tongue; teach us to sing Your praises without ceasing. You came forth in a cloud; cover us with the shadow of Your protection. O Bestower of heavenly gifts, vivify us by Your grace, sanctify us by Your love, and govern us by Your infinite mercy, so that we may never cease blessing, praising, and loving You now during our earthly lives and later in heaven for all eternity. Amen.

E. Prayer to the Holy Spirit

Holy Spirit of light and love, you are the substantial love of the Father and the Son; hear my prayer. Bounteous Bestower of most precious gifts, grant me a strong and living faith which makes me accept all revealed truths and shape my conduct in accord with them. Give me a most confident hope in all divine promises which prompts me to abandon myself unreservedly to you and your guidance. Infuse into me a love of perfect goodwill, and act according to God's least desires. Make me love not only my friends but my enemies as well, in imitation of Jesus Christ who through you offered himself on the Cross for all people. Holy Spirit, animate, inspire, and guide me, and help me to be always a true follower of You. Amen. # Prepared by St. Augustine of Hippo(AD 354-430). Especially we may pray this prayer during the Easter season.

F. St. Augustine's Prayer to the Holy Spirit

Breathe into me Holy Spirit, that all my thoughts may be holy. Act in me, O Holy Spirit, that my work, too, may be holy. Draw my heart, O Holy Spirit, that I may love but what is holy. Strengthen me, O Holy Spirit, to defend all that is holy. Guard me, then, O Holy Spirit, that I always may be holy. Amen.

G. St. Pius X's Prayer to the Holy Spirit

Holy Spirit, divine Spirit of light and love. I consecrate to You my understanding, my heart and my will, my whole being for time and for eternity. May my understanding be always submissive to Your heavenly inspirations and to the teachings of the Holy Catholic Church, of which You are the infallible Guide. May my heart be ever inflamed with love of God and of my neighbor; may my will be ever conformed to the divine Will, and may my whole life be a faithful imitation of the life and virtues of Our Lord and Savior Jesus Christ, to whom with the Father and You, Holy Spirit, be honor and glory forever. Amen.

H. Cardinal Mercier's Prayer to the Holy Spirit

O Holy Spirit, Soul of my soul, I adore You. Enlighten, guide, strengthen and console me. Tell me what I ought to do and command me to do it. I promise to be submissive in everything that You permit to happen to me, only show me what is Your will. Amen. This prayer is part of A Secret of Sanctity by Cardinal Mercier in which he said plainly: "I am going to reveal to you a secret of sanctity and happiness. If every day during five minutes, you will keep your imagination quiet, shut your eyes to all things of sense, and close your ears to all the sounds of earth, so as to be able to withdraw into the sanctuary of your baptized soul, which is the temple of the Holy Spirit, speaking there to that Holy Spirit saying: "O Holy Spirit, Soul of my soul …" If you do this, your life will pass happily and serenely. Consolation will abound even in the midst of troubles. Grace will be given in proportion to the trial as well as strength to bear it, bringing you to the gates of Paradise full of merit. The submission to the Holy Spirit is the Secret of Sanctity."

I. To the Holy Spirit through Mary

Holy and Divine Spirit! Through the intercession of the Blessed Virgin Mary, Your Spouse, bring the fullness of Your gifts into our hearts. Comforted and strengthened by You, may we live according to Your Will and die praising Your infinite mercy. Through Christ our Lord. Amen. Come, Holy Spirit! Come, by the means of the powerful intercession of the Immaculate Heart of Mary, Your well-beloved Spouse!

J. Prayer for the Consecration to the Holy Spirit

Most Holy Spirit, receive the consecration that I make of my entire being. From this moment on, come into every area of my life and into each of my actions. Thou art my Light, my Guide, my Strength, and the sole desire of my heart. I abandon myself without reserve to Thy divine action, and I desire to be ever docile to Thine inspirations. O Holy Spirit, transform me, with and through Mary, into another Christ Jesus, for the glory of the Father and the salvation of the world. Amen. # This prayer was written by Fr Felix de Jesus Rougier.

K. Act of Consecration (Oblation) to the Holy Spirit

On my knees before the great multitude of heavenly witnesses, I offer myself body and soul to Thee, eternal Spirit of God. I adore the brightness of Thy purity, the unerring keenness of Thy justice and the might of Thy love. Thou art the strength and light of my soul. In Thee I live and move and have my being. I desire never to grieve Thee by unfaithfulness to grace, and I pray with all my heart to be kept from the smallest sin against Thee. Make me faithful in every thought, and grant that I may always listen to Thy voice, watch for Thy light, and follow Thy gracious inspirations. I cling to Thee and give myself to Thee, and I ask Thee by Thy compassion to watch over me in my weakness. Holding the pierced feet of Jesus, looking at His five Wounds, trusting in His Precious Blood and adoring His opened side and stricken Heart, I implore Thee, adorable Spirit, Helper of my infirmity, so to keep me in Thy grace that I may never sin against Thee with the sin which Thou wilt not forgive. Grant to me the grace, O Holy Spirit, Spirit of the Father and of the Son, to say to Thee always and everywhere, "Speak, Lord, for Thy servant hears." Amen. # This oblation was recited by Cardinal Newman after a prayer.

L. Prayer for the Seven Gifts of the Holy Spirit

We beg the all-merciful Father through Thee, his only-begotten Son made man for our sake, crucified and glorified for us, to send upon us from his treasure-house the Spirit of sevenfold grace, who rested upon Thee in all his fullness: the spirit of wisdom, enabling us to relish the fruit of the tree of life, which is indeed Thyself; the gift of understanding: to enlighten our perceptions; the gift of prudence, enabling us to follow in Thy footsteps; the gift of strength: to withstand our adversary's onslaught; the gift of knowledge: to distinguish good from evil by the light of Thy holy teaching; the gift of piety: to clothe ourselves with charity and mercy; the gift of fear: to withdraw from all ill-doing and live quietly in awe of thy eternal majesty. These are the things for which petition. Grant them for the honor of Thy holy name, to which, with the Father and the Holy Spirit, be all honor and glory, thanksgiving, renown, and lordship forever and ever. Amen. # This prayer was written by St. Bonaventure.

M. Prayer for the Seven Gifts of the Holy Spirit

O Lord Jesus Christ, Who, before ascending into heaven, didst promise to send the Holy Spirit to finish Your work in the souls of Your Apostles and Disciples, deign to grant the same Holy Spirit to me, that He may perfect in my soul the work of Your grace and Your love. Grant me the Spirit of Wisdom that I may despise the perishable things of this world and aspire only after the things that are eternal, the Spirit of

Understanding to enlighten my mind with the light of Your divine truth, the Spirit of Counsel that I may ever choose the surest way of pleasing God and gaining Heaven, the Spirit of Fortitude that I may bear my cross with You, and that I may overcome with courage all the obstacles that oppose my salvation, the Spirit of Knowledge that I may know God and know myself and grow perfect in the science of the Saints, the Spirit of Piety that I may find the service of God sweet and amiable, the Spirit of Fear that I may be filled with a loving reverence towards God, and may dread in any way to displease Him. Mark me, dear Lord, with the sign of Your true disciples and animate me in all things with Your Spirit. Amen. Copyright © 2017 Eternal Word Television Network, Inc. Irondale, Alabama. All rights reserved. The above prayer touches on all of them. You have heard of a gift that keeps on giving? The Prayer for the Seven Gifts of the Holy Spirit spells out with wonderful clarity some of the ways these gifts can bring us closer to our Lord through His Spirit. In the Sacrament of Confirmation, as described here, the priest seals each of us with the Gift of the Holy Spirit. Yet we receive not just one gift in this rite but seven according to traditional church teaching! First referenced in the book of Isaiah (11:2), these are commonly known as wisdom, knowledge, understanding, counsel, piety, fortitude, and the fear of the Lord (this last one is meant to foster in us a healthy respect for His justice.). The ⋯⋯ touches on all of them: We may partake of all these Gifts as we follow the Holy Spirit in prayer, the sacraments, studying scripture, and of course, in imitating Christ in our actions by showing others His goodness and His love. In so doing, may we all, as St. Paul put it, "be filled with the Holy Spirit" (Eph 5:16) just as we have been sealed with His Gift!.

N. Prayer to the Holy Spirit by Leo XIII

O Holy Spirit, Creator, generously help the Catholic Church. By your supernatural power strengthen and confirm her against the assaults of the enemy. By your love and grace renew the spirit of Your servants whom You have animated – that in You they may glorify also the Father and His only Son, our Lord. Amen.

O. Novena of the Seven Gifts of the Holy Spirit

Forward: The novena in honor of the Holy Spirit is the oldest of all novenas since it was first made at the direction of Our Lord Himself when He sent His apostles back to Jerusalem to await the coming of the Holy Spirit on the first Pentecost. It is still the only novena officially prescribed by the Church. Addressed to the Third Person of the Blessed Trinity, it is a powerful plea for the light and strength and love so sorely needed by every Christian.

a) Act of Consecration (Oblation) to the Holy Spirit; To be recited daily during the Novena; Please refer to Chapter 3, (K).
b) Prayer for the Seven gifts of the Holy Spirit: This prayer shall be found at the Chapter 3, (M).

The Novena begins on the day after the Solemnity of the Ascension, Friday of the 6th Week of Easter, even if the Solemnity of the Ascension is transferred to the 7th Sunday.

First day (Friday after Ascension or Friday of 6th Week of Easter)

Holy Spirit! Lord of Light! From Your clear celestial height, Your pure beaming radiance give!
The Holy Spirit.
Only one thing is important; eternal salvation. Only one thing, therefore, is to be feared; sin? Sin is the result of ignorance, weakness, and indifference. The Holy Spirit is the Spirit of Light, of Strength, and of Love. With His sevenfold gifts He enlightens the mind, strengthens the will, and inflames the heart with love of God. To ensure our salvation we ought to invoke the Divine Spirit daily, for "The Spirit helps our infirmity. We know not what we should pray for as we ought. But the Spirit Himself asks for us." Prayer: Almighty and eternal God, Who hast vouchsafed to regenerate us by water and the Holy Spirit, and hast given us forgiveness all sins, vouchsafe to send forth from heaven upon us your sevenfold Spirit, the Spirit of Wisdom and Understanding, the Spirit of Counsel and Fortitude, the Spirit of Knowledge and Piety, and fill us with the Spirit of Holy Fear. Amen.
Our Father and Hail Mary once. Glory be to the Father Seven times. Act of Consecration and prayer for the Seven Gifts of the Holy Spirit.

Second day (Saturday of 6th Week of Easter)

Come. Father of the poor. Come, treasures which endure; Come, Light of all that live!

The Gift of Fear

The gift of Fear fills us with a sovereign respect for God, and makes us dread nothing so much as to offend Him by sin. It is a fear that arises, not from the thought of hell, but from sentiments of reverence and filial submission to our heavenly Father. It is the fear that is the beginning of wisdom, detaching us from worldly pleasures that could in any way separate us from God. "They that fear the Lord will prepare their hearts, and in His sight will sanctify their souls."

Prayer: Come, O blessed Spirit of Holy Fear, penetrate my inmost heart, that I may set you, my Lord and God, before my face forever, help me to shun all things that can offend You, and make me worthy to appear before the pure eyes of Your Divine Majesty in heaven, where You live and reign in the unity of the ever Blessed Trinity, God world without end. Amen. Our Father and Hail Mary once. Glory be to the Father Seven times. Act of Consecration and prayer for the Seven Gifts of the Holy Spirit.

Third day (7th Sunday of Easter or transferred Ascension)

Thou, of all consolers best, visiting the troubled breast, dost refreshing peace bestow.

The Gift of Piety

The gift of Piety begets in our hearts a filial affection for God as our most loving Father. It inspires us to love and respect for His sake persons and things consecrated to Him, as well as those who are vested with His authority, His Blessed Mother and the Saints, the Church and its visible Head, our parents and superiors, our country and its rulers. He who is filled with the gift of Piety finds the practice of his religion, not a burdensome duty, but a delightful service. Where there is love, there is no labor.

Prayer: Come, O Blessed Spirit of Piety, possess my heart. Enkindle therein such a love for God, that I may find satisfaction only in His service, and for His sake lovingly submit to all legitimate authority. Amen. Our Father and Hail Mary once. Glory be to the Father Seven times. Act of Consecration and prayer for the Seven Gifts of the Holy Spirit.

Fourth day (Monday, 7th Week of Easter)

Thou in toil art comfort sweet, pleasant coolness in the heat, solace in the midst of woe.

The Gift of Fortitude.

By the gift of Fortitude the soul is strengthened against natural fear, and supported to the end in the performance of duty. Fortitude imparts to the will an impulse and energy which move it to undertake without hesitancy the most arduous tasks, to face dangers, and to endure without complaint the slow martyrdom of even lifelong tribulation. "He that shall persevere unto the end, he shall be saved."

Prayer: Come, O Blessed Spirit of Fortitude, uphold my soul in time of trouble and adversity, sustain my efforts after holiness, strengthen my weakness, give me courage against all the assaults of my enemies, that I may never be overcome and separated from Thee, my God and greatest Good. Amen. Our Father and Hail Mary once. Glory be to the Father Seven times. Act of Consecration and prayer for the Seven Gifts of the Holy Spirit.

Fifth day(Tuesday, 7th Week of Easter)

Light immortal! Light Divine! Visit Thou these hearts of Thine, and our inmost being fill!

The Gift of Knowledge

The gift of Knowledge enables the soul to evaluate created things at their true worth--in their relation to God. Knowledge unmasks the pretense of creatures, reveals their emptiness, and points out their only true purpose as instruments in the service of God. It shows us the loving care of God even in adversity, and directs us to glorify Him in every circumstance of life. Guided by its light, we put first things first, and prize the friendship of God beyond all else. "Knowledge is a fountain of life to him that possess it."

Prayer: Come, O Blessed Spirit of Knowledge, and grant that I may perceive the will of the Father; show me the nothingness of earthly things, that I may realize their vanity and use them only for Thy glory and my own salvation, looking ever beyond them to Thee, and Thy eternal rewards. Amen. Our Father and Hail Mary once. Glory be to the Father Seven times. Act of Consecration and prayer for the Seven Gifts of the Holy Spirit.

Sixth day (Wednesday, 7th Week of Easter)

If Thou take Thy grace away, nothing pure in man will stay, all his good is turned to ill.

The Gift of Understanding:

Understanding, as a gift of the Holy Spirit, helps us to grasp the meaning of the truths of our holy religion. By faith we know them, but by Understanding we learn to appreciate and relish them. It enables us to penetrate the inner meaning of revealed truths and through them to be quickened to newness of life. Our faith ceases to be sterile and inactive, but inspires a mode of life that bears eloquent testimony to the faith that is in us; we begin to "walk worthy of God in all things pleasing, and increasing in the knowledge of God."

Prayer: Come, O Spirit of Understanding, and enlighten our minds, that we may know and believe all the mysteries of salvation; and may merit at last to see the eternal light in Thy Light; and in the light of glory to have a clear vision of Thee and the Father and the Son. Amen. Our Father and Hail Mary once. Glory be to the Father Seven times. Act of Consecration and prayer for the Seven Gifts of the Holy Spirit.

Seventh day (Thursday, 7th Week of Easter)

Heal our wounds--our strength renews; On our dryness pour Thy dew, and wash the stains of guilt away.

The Gift of Counsel

The gift of Counsel endows the soul with supernatural prudence, enabling it to judge promptly and rightly what must be done, especially in difficult circumstances. Counsel applies the principles furnished by Knowledge and Understanding to the innumerable concrete cases that confront us in the course of our daily duty as parents, teachers, public servants, and Christian citizens. Counsel is supernatural common sense, a priceless treasure in the quest of salvation. "Above all these things, pray to the Most High, that He may direct thy way in truth."

Prayer: Come, O Spirit of Counsel, help and guide me in all my ways, that I may always do Thy holy will. Incline my heart to that which is good; turn it away from all that is evil, and direct me by the straight path of Thy commandments to that goal of eternal life for which I long. Amen .Our Father and Hail Mary once. Glory be to the Father Seven times. Act of Consecration and prayer for the Seven Gifts of the Holy Spirit.

Eighth day (Friday, 7th Week of Easter)

Bend the stubborn heart and will; melt the frozen and warm the chill. Guide the steps that go astray!

The Gift of Wisdom

Embodying all the other gifts, as charity embraces all the other virtues, Wisdom is the most perfect of the gifts. Of wisdom it is written "all good things came to me with her, and innumerable riches through her hands." It is the gift of Wisdom that strengthens our faith, fortifies hope, perfects charity, and promotes the practice of virtue in the highest degree. Wisdom enlightens the mind to discern and relish things divine, in the appreciation of which earthly joys lose their savor, whilst the Cross of Christ yields a divine sweetness according to the words of the Savior: Take up thy cross and follow me, for my yoke is sweet and my burden light.

Prayer: Come, O Spirit of Wisdom, and reveal to my soul the mysteries of heavenly things, their exceeding greatness, power and beauty. Teach me to love them above and beyond all the passing joys and satisfactions of earth. Help me to attain them and possess them forever. Amen. Our Father and Hail Mary once. Glory be to the Father Seven times. Act of Consecration and prayer for the Seven Gifts of the Holy Spirit.

Ninth day (Saturday, Vigil of Pentecost)

Thou, on those who evermore Thee confess and Thee adore, in Thy sevenfold gift, Descend; Give Them comfort when they die; Give them life with Thee on high; Give them joys which never end. Amen

The Fruits of the Holy Spirit

The gifts of the Holy Spirit perfect the supernatural virtues by enabling us to practice them with greater docility to divine inspiration. As we grow in the knowledge and love of God under the direction of the Holy Spirit, our service becomes more sincere and generous, the practice of virtue more perfect. Such acts of virtue leave the heart filled with joy and consolation and are known as Fruits of the Holy Spirit. These Fruits in turn render the practice of virtue more attractive and become a powerful incentive for still greater efforts in the service of God, to serve Whom is to reign.

Prayer: Come, O Divine Spirit, fill my heart with Thy heavenly fruits, Thy charity, joy, peace, patience, benignity, goodness, faith, mildness, and temperance, that I may never weary in the service of God, but by continued faithful submission to Thy inspiration may merit to be united eternally with Thee in the love of the Father and the Son. Amen. Our Father and Hail Mary once. Glory be to the Father Seven times. Act of Consecration and prayer for the Seven Gifts of the Holy Spirit. Copyright © 2017 Eternal Word Television Network, Inc. Irondale, Alabama. All rights reserved.

P. Novena of the Holy Spirit; # This Novena was written by St Alphonsus Liguori(1696–1787).

Meditations for Each Day of the Novena, beginning with the Feast of the Ascension (This Novena can be prayed throughout the year). The novena of the Holy Spirit is the chief of all novenas because it was the first that was ever celebrated, and that by the Apostles and Mary in the upper room, and was distinguished by so many remarkable wonders and gifts, principally by the gift of the same Holy Spirit, a gift merited for us by the Passion of Jesus Christ himself. Jesus himself made this known to us when he said to his disciples that if he did not die, he could not send us the Holy Spirit: 'If I go not, the Paraclete will not come to you; but if I go, I will send him to you (John 16:7). We know well by faith that the Holy Spirit is the love that the Father and the eternal Word bear one to the other; and therefore the gift of love, which the Lord infuses into our souls, and which is the greatest of all gifts, is particularly attributed to the Holy Spirit, as St. Paul says, 'the charity of God is poured forth in our hearts by the Holy Spirit, who is given to us (Rom.5: 5). In this novena, therefore, we must consider, above all, the great value of divine love, in order that we may desire to obtain it, and endeavor by devout exercises, and especially by prayer, to be made partakers of it, since God has promised it to him who asks for it with humility: Your Father from heaven (will) give the good Spirit to them that ask him! (Luke 11: 13).

Meditation 1. Love Is a Fire that Inflames the Heart

God had ordered, in the ancient law, that there should be a fire kept continually burning on his altar: "The fire on the altar shall always burn (Lev. 6:12)." St. Gregory says that the altars of God are our hearts, where he desires that the fire of his divine love should always be burning; and therefore the eternal Father, not satisfied with having given us his Son Jesus Christ to save us by his death, would also give us the Holy Spirit, that he might dwell in our souls and keep them constantly on fire with love. And Jesus himself declared that he had come into the world on purpose to inflame our hearts with this holy fire, and that he desired nothing more than to see it kindled: "I have come to set the earth on fire: and how I wish it were already blazing! (Luke 12:49)." Forgetting, therefore, the injuries and ingratitude he received from men on this earth, when he had ascended into heaven he sent down upon us the Holy Spirit. Oh, most loving Redeemer, thou dost, then, love us as well in Thy sufferings and ignominies as in Thy kingdom of glory! This is why the Holy Spirit chose to appear in the upper room under the form of tongues of fire: "And there appeared to them parted tongues as it were of fire (Acts 2:3)." And therefore the Church teaches us to pray: 'May the Holy Spirit, we beseech Thee, O Lord, inflame us with that fire which our Jesus Christ came to cast upon the earth, and which he ardently desired should be enkindled. This was the holy fire which has inflamed the saints to do such great things for God, to love their enemies, to desire contempt, to deprive themselves of all earthly goods, and to embrace with delight even torments and death. Love cannot remain idle and never says, 'This is enough. The soul that loves God, the more she does for her beloved the more she desires to do, in order to please him and to attract to herself his affections. This holy fire is enkindled by mental prayer. If, therefore, we desire to burn with love for God, let us love prayer; that is the blessed furnace in which this divine ardor is enkindled.

Affections and prayers: O my God, up to now I have done nothing for Thee Who hast done so much for me. My coldness could well make Thee cast me away from Thee. But, O Holy Spirit, make warm what is cold. Deliver me from my lack of fervor and make me burn with the desire to please Thee. I now wish to deny all that pleases me. I would rather die than displease Thee in the least thing. To Thee Who hast appeared in the form of fiery tongues, I consecrate my tongue that it may not offend Thee again. Thou didst give it to me to praise Thee, but I, I have used it to injure Thee and cause others to offend Thee. I am sorry for my sins. For the love of Jesus Christ Who honoured Thee so much by His tongue when He walked this earth, grant that henceforward I may honor Thee by praising Thee, by asking often for Thy help and by speaking of Thy goodness and the infinite love Thou deserve. I love Thee, my supreme Good. I love Thee, O loving God. O Mary, most beloved Spouse of the Holy Spirit, obtain for me this holy fire.

Meditation 2. Love Is a Light That Enlightens the Soul

One of the greatest evils which the sin of Adam has produced in us is that darkening of our reason by means of the passions which cloud our mind. Oh, how miserable is that soul which allows itself to be ruled by any passion! Passion is, as it were, a vapor, a veil which prevents our seeing the truth. How can he fly from evil who does not know what is evil? Besides, this darkness increases in proportion as our sins increase. But the Holy Spirit, who is called 'most blessed light, is he who not only inflames our hearts to love him through his divine splendor but also dispels our darkness and shows us the vanity of earthly things, the value of eternal goods, the importance of salvation, the worth of grace, the goodness of God, the infinite love which he deserves and the immense love which he bears us. 'The sensual man perceive not these things that are of the Spirit of God (I Cor. 2:14). A man who is absorbed in the pleasures of the world knows little of these truths and therefore, unfortunate that he is, loves what he ought to hate and hates what he ought to love. St. Mary Magdalene of Pazzi exclaimed: 'Oh, love not known! Oh, love not loved! And St. Teresa said that God is not loved because he is not known. Therefore the saints were always seeking light from God: 'Send forth Thy light; illuminate my darkness; open Thou my eyes. Yes, because without light we cannot avoid precipices nor find God.

Affections and prayers: Holy and Divine Spirit, I believe that Thou art true God, yet one God with the Father and the Son. I adore Thee and acknowledge Thee as the Giver of those lights which make me know the evil I have done in offending Thee and the obligation I have to love Thee. I thank Thee for these lights. I am sorry for having offended Thee. I have deserved to be left in darkness, but I see that I am not yet abandoned by Thee. Continue, O eternal Spirit, to enlighten my mind. Make me know still more Thy infinite goodness. Give me strength now to love Thee with all my heart. Add grace upon grace so that I may be gently drawn to Thee and compelled to love none but Thee. I ask for this grace through the merits of Jesus Christ. I love Thee, infinite Goodness, I love Thee more than myself. I will be all Thine. Accept me and do not permit me to be separated from Thee again. O my Mother, Mary, help me always by thy intercession.

Meditation 3. Love Is a Fountain That Satisfies

Love is also called a living fountain, fire, and charity. Our blessed Redeemer said to the Samaritan woman: He that shall drink of the water that I will give him, shall not thirst for ever (John 4:13). Love is the water which satisfies our thirst; he who loves God really with his whole heart neither seeks nor desires anything else, because in God he finds every good. Therefore, satisfied with God, he often joyfully exclaims, 'My God and my all! My God, Thou art my whole good. But the Almighty complains that many souls go about seeking for fleeting and miserable pleasures from creatures and leave him, who is the infinite good and fountain of all joy: 'They have forsaken me, the fountain of living water, and have dug to themselves cisterns, broken cisterns, that can hold no water (Jer. 2:13). Therefore God, who loves us and desires to see us happy, cries out and makes known to all: 'If any man thirst, let him come to me, and drink (John 7:37). He who desires to be happy, let him come to me; and I will give him the Holy Spirit, who will make him blessed both in this life and the next. 'He that believeth in me (He goes on to say), 'as the scripture said, out of his belly shall flow rivers of living water (John 7:38). He, therefore, who believes in Jesus Christ and loves him shall be enriched with so much grace that from his heart (the heart, that is the will, is the belly of the soul) shall flow many fountains of holy virtues, which shall not only serve to preserve his own life, but also to give life to others. And this water is the Holy Spirit, the substantial love which Jesus Christ promised to send us from heaven after his ascension: 'Now this he said of the Spirit which they should receive, who believed in him: for as yet the Spirit was not given, because Jesus was not yet glorified (John 7:39). The key which opens the channels of this blessed water is holy prayer, which obtains every good for us in virtue of the promise, 'Ask, and you shall receive. We are blind, poor, and weak; but prayer obtains for us light, strength, and abundance of grace. Theodoret said: 'Prayer, though but one, can do all things. He who prays receives all he wants. God desires to give us his graces; but he will have us pray for them.

Affections and prayers: Lord, give me this water. Yes, Lord Jesus, I will say to Thee like the Samaritan woman: give me this water of divine love that I may turn away from this world and live only for Thee Who art so lovely. 'Water that which is dry. My soul is like a dry land where nothing but the briars and thorns of sin grow. Ah! give me, before I pass out of this world, an outpouring of divine grace to make my soul fruitful in works worthy of Thy heavenly glory. O Fountain of living water, O supreme Good, too often have I left Thee for the corrupt waters of this earth which have deprived me of Thy love. Why did not death overtake me before I offended Thee? In the future I will seek nothing but Thee, O my God. Assist me and grant that I may be faithful to Thee. Mary, my hope, keep me ever under thy protection.

Meditation 4. Love Is a Dew Which Fertilizes

Thus does Holy Church teach us to pray: 'May the infusion of the Holy Spirit cleanse our hearts, and fertilize them by the interior sprinkling of his dew. Love fertilizes the good desires, the holy purposes, and the good works of our souls: these are the flowers and fruits which the grace of the Holy Spirit produces. Love is called dew, because it cools the heart of bad passions and of temptations. Therefore the Holy Spirit is called refreshment and pleasing coolness in the heat. This dew descends into our hearts in time of prayer. A quarter of an hour's prayer is sufficient to appease every passion of hatred or of inordinate love, however ardent it may be: He brought me into the cellar of wine, he set in order charity in me (Cant. 2: 4). Holy meditation is the cellar where love is set in order, so that we love our neighbor as ourselves and God above everything. He who loves God loves prayer. He who does not love prayer will find it morally impossible to overcome his passions.

Affections and prayers: O holy and Divine Spirit, I will no longer live to myself. I will spend the remaining days of my life in loving and pleasing Thee. For that purpose I beseech Thee to grant me the gift of prayer. Come into my heart and teach me how to pray as I ought. Give me strength not to neglect prayer when my soul is weary and dry before Thee. Give me the spirit of prayer, that is, the grace to pray always and to say those prayers that are most agreeable to Thy divine Heart. My sins have endangered my salvation, but I understand from so many kindnesses in my regard that Thou wish me to be saved and to become a saint. I will become a saint to please Thee. I love Thee, O supreme Good, O my Love and my All. I give myself wholly to Thee. O Mary, my hope, protect me.

Meditation 5. Love Is a Repose That Refreshes

LOVE is also called in labor rest, in mourning comfort. Love is repose that refreshes, because the principal office of love is to unite the will of the lover to that of the beloved one. To a soul that loves God, in every affront it receives, in every sorrow it endures, in every loss which happens to it, the knowledge that it is the will of its beloved for it to suffer these trials is enough to comfort it. It finds peace and contentment in all tribulations merely by saying, This is the will of my God. This is that peace which surpasses all the pleasures of sense, the peace of God, which surpass all understanding (Phil. 4:7). St. Mary Magdalene of Pazzi merely by saying The will of God was always filled with joy. In this life everyone must carry his cross. But as St. Teresa says, the cross is heavy for him who drags it, not for him who embraces it. Thus our Lord knows well how to strike and how to heal: He wound, and cure as Job said (5:18). The Holy Spirit, by his sweet unction, renders even ignominies and torments sweet and pleasant: Yea, Father; for so hath it seemed good in Thy sight (Matt. 11:26). Thus ought we to say in all adversities that happen to us: So be it done, Lord, because so hath it pleased Thee. And when the fear of any temporal evil that may befall us alarms us, let us always say: Do what Thou wilt, my God; whatever Thou dost, I accept it all. And it is a very good thing to offer oneself thus constantly during the day to God, as St. Teresa did.

Affections and prayers: O my God, how often have I opposed and despised Thy will to do my own. I am sorry for this evil more than for any other. Henceforward, O Lord, I will love Thee with all my heart. Speak, Lord, for Thy servant hear. Make me know what Thou wouldst have me do and I will do it all. I will always desire and love nothing but Thy will. O Holy Spirit, help my weakness. Thou art goodness itself: how can I love anything but Thee? Ah! may Thy holy love draw my whole heart to Thee! I leave all things to give myself entirely to Thee. Accept me and help me. O my Mother Mary, I trust in thee.

Meditation 6. Love Is the Virtue Which Gives Us Strength

Love is strong as death (Cant. 8:6). As there is no created strength which can resist death, so there is no difficulty for a loving soul which love cannot overcome. When there is a question of pleasing its beloved, love conquers all, losses, contempt, and sorrow. Nothing is so hard, but that the fire of love can conquer it. This is the most certain mark with which to know if a soul really loves God, if it is as faithful in love when things are adverse as when they are prosperous. St. Francis de Sales said that God is quite as amiable when he chastises as when he consoles us, because he does all for love. Indeed, when he strikes us most in this life, then it is that he loves us most. St. John Chrysostom esteemed St. Paul in chains more fortunate than St. Paul caught up into the third heaven. Hence the holy martyrs in the midst of their torments rejoiced and thanked the Lord, as for the greatest favor that could fall to their lot, that of having to suffer for his love. And other saints, where there were no tyrants to afflict them, became their own executioners by the penances which they inflicted upon themselves in order to please God. St. Augustine says that for that which men love, either no labor is felt, or the labor itself is loved.

Affections and prayers: O God of my soul, I pretend to love Thee, and yet I do nothing for Thy love. Would it not be a sign that I love Thee not, or very little? But send me the Holy Spirit, O Jesus, the Holy Spirit Who will give me strength to suffer for Thy love and do something for Thee before I die. I pray Thee, O my beloved Redeemer, let me not die now, cold and ungrateful to Thee as I have been. Though I have committed so many sins for which I should be in hell, grant me the courage to love suffering, to do something for Thee. O my God, Whose nature is all goodness and love, Thou desire to be the guest of my soul from which I have so often driven thee. Oh! come and dwell in it: be Thou its Master and make it all Thine. I love Thee, O my Lord, but if I love Thee Thou art already with me, since St. John assures us that he who abides in love abides in God and God in him, Thou art within me then, O my God. Make my love more ardent still. Bind me with stronger chains that I may desire, seek and love nothing but Thee. Let me never be separated from Thy love. I desire to be all Thine, O my Jesus. O Mary, my Queen and Advocate, obtain for me love and perseverance.

Meditation 7. Love Causes God to Dwell in Our Souls

The Holy Spirit is called Sweet Guest of the soul. This was the great promise made by Jesus Christ to those who love him, when he said: If you love me, keep my commandments. And I will ask the Father, and he shall give you another Paraclete, that he may abide with you forever. The Spirit of truth ⋯ shall abide with you, and shall be in you (John 14: 5-17). For the Holy Spirit never forsakes a soul if He is not driven away from it; he does not forsake, unless he be first forsaken. God, then, dwells in a soul that loves him. But he declares that he is not satisfied if we do not love him with our whole heart. St. Augustine tells us that the Roman Senate would not admit Jesus Christ into the number of their gods because they said that he was a proud god, who would have none other beloved but himself. And so it is. He will have no rivals in the heart that loves him; and when he sees that he is not the only object loved, he is jealous (so to speak). St. James writes of those creatures who divide up with him the heart which he desires to have all to himself: Do you think that the scripture said in vain: To envy doth the spirit covet which dwell in you (James 4: 5). In short, as St. Jerome says, Jesus is jealous, Zelotypus est Jesus. Therefore the heavenly spouse praises that soul which, like the turtledove, lives in solitude and hidden from the world (Cant. 1: 9). Because he does not choose that the world should take a part of that love which he desires to have all to himself, therefore he also praises his spouse by calling her a garden enclosed (Cant. 4: 12), a garden closed against all earthly love. Do we doubt that Jesus deserves our whole love? He gave himself wholly to you, says St. John Chrysostom, he left nothing for himself. He has given you all his blood and his life; there is nothing left to give.

Affections and prayers: I understand, O my God, that Thou want me to be all Thine. Many times have I driven Thee from my soul, but Thou didst not shrink from returning to be united to me again. Ah! take possession of my entire self, for today I give myself wholly to Thee. Do Thou accept me, O Jesus, and do not permit that I should again live in the future, no, not even for a moment, without Thy love. Thou seek me and I seek none but Thee. Thou love me and I love Thee. Since Thou love me, bind me to Thyself that I may never abandon Thee. O Mary, Queen of heaven, I trust in thee.

Meditation 8. Love Is a Bond Which Binds

As the Holy Spirit, who is uncreated love, is the indissoluble bond which binds the Father to the eternal Word, so he also unites the soul with God. Charity is a virtue, says St. Augustine, uniting us with God. Hence, full of joy, St. Laurence Justinian exclaims: Love, your bond has such strength that it is able to bind even God and unite him to our souls. The bonds of the world are bonds of death; but the bonds of God are bonds of life and salvation (Ecclus.6:31), because the bonds of God by means of love unite us to God, who is our true and only life. Before the coming of Jesus Christ, men fled from God and being attached to the earth refused to unite themselves to their Creator. But a loving God has drawn them to himself by the bonds of love as he promised through the prophet. O see: I will draw them with the cords of Adam, with the bands of love (11: 4). These bands are the benefits, the lights, the calls to his love, the promises of paradise which he makes to us, the gift which he has bestowed upon us of Jesus Christ in the sacrifice of the cross and in the sacrament of the altar, and finally, the gift of his Holy Spirit. Therefore the prophet exclaims, loose the bonds from off thy neck, O captive daughter of Zion (Isa 52: 2). Oh my soul, you who are created for heaven, loose yourself from the bonds of earth, and unite yourself to God by the bonds of holy love: Have charity, which is the bond of perfection (Col 3: 14). Love is a bond which unites with herself all other virtues and makes the soul perfect. Love, and do what Thou wilt, said St. Augustine. Love God, and do what you wish, because he who loves God tries to avoid causing any displeasure to his beloved and seeks in all things to please him. Affections and prayers: O my dear Jesus, Thou hast put me under a sweet obligation to love Thee, and how much it has cost Thee to win my love! I would be an ungrateful wretch if I loved Thee little after that, or if I let creatures share my heart with Thee Who hast given Thy life and Thy blood for me. I wish to detach myself from everything and place all my affections in Thee alone. But I am weak and unable to realize this desire. Thou Who hast inspired it, help me to bring it into effect. O my beloved Jesus, pierce my heart with the arrows of Thy love so that it may sigh ever after Thee and be melted in Thee! Thou alone I seek, Thou alone may I always seek. None but Thee may I desire and find! My Jesus, I desire only Thee and nothing more. Grant that I may repeat it always during my life, and especially at the moment of my death: I desire only Thee and nothing more. O my Mother Mary, from henceforward make me desire nothing but God.

Meditation 9. Love Is a Treasure Containing Every Good

Love is that treasure of which the Gospel says that we must leave all to obtain it, because love makes us partakers of the friendship of God, an infinite treasure to men which they use, become the friends of God (Wis. 7:14). Oh man, says St. Augustine, why, then, do you go about seeking for good things? Seek that one good alone in which all other good things are contained. But we cannot find God, who is this sovereign good, if we do not forsake the things of the earth. St. Teresa writes, Detach your heart from creatures, and you will find God. He who finds God finds all that he can desire: Delight in the Lord, and he will give thee the requests of thy heart (Ps. 36: 4). The human heart is constantly seeking after good things that may make it happy; but if it seeks them from creatures, however much it may acquire, it will never be satisfied; if it seeks God alone, God will satisfy all its desires. Who are the happiest people in this world, if not the saints? And why? Because they desire and seek only God. A tyrant offered gold and gems to St. Clement, in order to persuade him to renounce Jesus Christ. The saint exclaimed with a sigh, Is God to be put into competition with a little dirt? Blessed is he who knows this treasure of divine love, and strives to obtain it. He who obtains it will of his own accord divest himself of everything else, that he may have nothing else but God. When the house is on fire, says St. Francis de Sales, all the goods are thrown out of the windows. And Father Paul Segneri the Younger, a great servant of God, used to say that love is a thief which robs us of all earthly affections, so that we can say, And what else do I desire but thee alone, my Lord?

Affections and prayers: I have not lived for Thee in the past, O my God, but rather for myself and my own gratifications. I have accordingly turned my back upon Thee, my supreme good. But I take heart at these words of Jeremias: 'The Lord is good to the soul that seek him. He says then that Thou art all goodness for him who seeks Thee. O my beloved Lord, I know well the evil I have done in going away from Thee and I am sorry for it with all my heart. I know the infinite treasure we find in Thee. I will profit by this light that Thou give me. I leave all things and choose Thee for my only love. My God, my love, my all, I love Thee, I sigh after Thee, I desire Thee. Come, O Holy Spirit, come and consume in me by Thy sacred fire every affection that is not for Thee. Make me all Thine and grant me the grace to overcome everything in order to please Thee. O Mary, my Advocate and Mother, help me by thy prayers.

Novena Resolution: The more we love God, the more holy we become. St. Francis Borgia says it is prayer that introduces divine love into the human heart and mortification that withdraws the heart from the world and renders it capable of receiving this holy fire. The more there is of the world in the heart, the less room there is for holy love: 'Wisdom is [not to be] found in the land of them that live in delights (Job 28: 12-13). Hence the saints have always sought to mortify as much as possible their self-love and their senses. The saints are few, but we must live with the few if we will be saved with the few. St. Bernard says, 'That cannot be perfect which is not singular. He who would lead a perfect life must lead a singular one. But above all, in order to become saints, it is necessary to have the desire to be saints; we must have the desire and the resolution. Some are always desiring, but they never begin to put their hands to the work. 'Of these irresolute souls, says St. Teresa, 'the devil has no fear. On the other hand, the saint said, 'God is a friend of generous souls. The devil tries to make it appear to us as pride to think of doing great things for God, it would indeed be pride in us if we thought of doing them all by ourselves, trusting in our own strength; but it is not pride to resolve to become saints trusting in God and saying, 'I can do all things in him who strengthen me. (Phil 4: 13). We must therefore be of good courage, make strong resolutions, and begin. Prayer can do everything. What we cannot do by our own strength, we can do easily with the help of God, who has promised to give us whatever we ask of him: 'You shall ask whatever you will, and it shall be done unto you. (Jn 15: 7).

Affections and Prayers: Sweet Redeemer of my soul, Thou desire to be loved by me and Thou command me to love Thee with all my heart, and with all my heart I desire to love Thee, O my Jesus. I will even go so far as to say to Thee: O my God, such is the trust I have in Thy mercy that my sins do not inspire me with fear, since I hate and detest them above every other evil. I know besides that Thou remember not the offences of one who repents and who loves Thee. Nay more, since I have offended Thee more than others, I wish to love Thee more than others. O my Lord, Thou want me to be a saint and I wish to become one in order to please Thee. I love Thee, infinite Goodness. I give myself entirely to Thee. Thou art my one good, my only love. Do not turn me away, O my love. Make me all Thine. Do not permit me to displease Thee again. Grant that I may sacrifice myself entirely for Thee, as Thou hast sacrificed Thyself entirely for me. Mary, most loving and beloved Spouse of the Holy Spirit, obtain for me love and faithfulness. Amen.

Chapter 5　Prayers to the Trinity and Other Payers

A. Offering to the Trinity

Most holy and adorable Trinity, one God in three Persons, I praise You and give You thanks for all the favors You have bestowed upon me. Your goodness has preserved me until now. I offer You my whole being and in particular all my thoughts, words and deeds, together with all the trials I may undergo this day. Give them Your blessing. May Your Devine Love animate them and may they serve Your greater glory. I make this morning offering in union with the Devine intentions of Jesus Christ Who offers Himself daily in the holy Sacrifice of the Mass, and in union with Mary, His Virgin Mother and our Mother, who was always the faithful handmaid of the Lord. Glory be to the Father, and to the Son, and to the Holy Spirit. Amen.

B. The Most Holy Trinity

Most blessed Trinity, Father, Son and Holy Spirit, behold us kneeling in Your Divine presence. We humble ourselves deeply and beg of You the forgiveness of our sins. We adore You, almighty Father, and with all our hearts we thank You for having given us Your Divine Son Jesus to be our Redeemer. We adore You, Word of God, Jesus our Redeemer, and with all our hearts we thank You for having taken human flesh upon Yourself and having become priest and victim for our redemption in the sacrifice of the Cross, a sacrifice that, through Your great love, You renew upon our altars. We adore You, Divine Spirit, and with all our hearts we thank You for having worked the unfathomable mystery of the Incarnation of the Word of God with such great love for us, a blessing that is being continually extended and increased in the Sacrament of the Eucharist. By this adorable mystery grant us and all poor sinners Your holy grace. Pour forth Your sacred gifts upon us and upon all redeemed souls. Amen. (A)& (B) Copyright ©2005 , 2003, 1997 by Catholic Book Publishing Corp., N.J.

C. Angelic Trisagion(삼성송 三聖誦; holy를 세 번 반복해서 하느님을 찬미하는 기도)

In the name of the Father, and of the Son, and of the Holy Spirit. Amen.

V. Lord, open my lips.

R. And my mouth shall declare Thy praise.

V. O God, come to my assistance.

R. O Lord, make haste to help me.

V. Glory be to the Father, and to the Son, and to the Holy Spirit,

R. As it was in the beginning, is now and will be forever. Amen.

The decade below is recited three times, once for each member of the Trinity.
All: Holy God! Holy Strong One! Holy Immortal One, have mercy upon us.
V. Our Father, Who art in heaven, hallowed be Thy name. Thy kingdom come, Thy will be done, on earth as it is in heaven. Give us this day our daily bread and forgive us our trespasses as we forgive those who trespass against us. And lead us not into temptation, but deliver us from evil. Amen.

The following part of the decade is repeated nine times.
V. To Thee, O Blessed Trinity, be praise, and honor, and thanksgiving, forever and ever!
R. Holy, holy, holy Lord, God of hosts. Heaven and earth are filled with Thy glory.
V. Glory be to the Father, and to the Son, and to the Holy Spirit,
R. As it was in the beginning, is now and will be forever. Amen.

End of Decade
Antiphon

God the Father un-begotten, only-begotten Son, and Holy
Spirit, the Comforter; holy and undivided Trinity, with all
our hearts we acknowledge Thee: Glory to Thee forever. Amen.
V. Let us bless the Father, and the Son with the Holy Spirit.
R. Be praised and exalted above all things forever. Amen.

Let us pray,

Almighty, ever-living God, who has permitted us Thy servants, in our profession of the true faith, to acknowledge the glory of the eternal Trinity, and in the power of that majesty to adore the Unity, grant, that by steadfastness in this same faith, we may be ever guarded against all adversity: through Christ our Lord.

All: Amen

All: Set us free, save us, and vivify us, O Blessed Trinity! # This devotion to the Blessed Trinity is the official prayer of the Order of the Blessed Trinity, otherwise known as the Trinitarians. The devotion has been recited by them and their affiliates for centuries in praise of the Trinity. # No Copyright ©

D. Prayer for Divine Guidance through the day

Lord, God Almighty, You have brought us safely to the beginning of this day. Defend us today by Your mighty power, that we may not fall into any sin, but that all our words may so proceed and all our thoughts and actions be so directed, as to be always just in Your sight. Direct, we beg You, O Lord, our actions by Your holy inspirations, and carry them on by Your gracious assistance, that every prayer and work of ours may begin always with You, and through You be happily ended. Amen. # No Copyright ©

E. The Santus

Holy, holy, holy, Lord God of hosts.

Heaven and earth are full of Thy glory.

Hosanna in the highest. Blessed is He who comes in the name of the Lord.

Hosanna in the highest. #The Santus has been a part of the Mass from the first century and its Jewish roots go back even farther.

The first part of chant is based on Isaiah 6:3 and Daniel 7:10.

The second part is based on Mt 21:9.

The chant unites our voices with those of the saints and angels in heaven into one song of praise of God.

F. Novena to the Holy Trinity

I adore Thee, O my God, one God in three Persons; I annihilate myself before Thy Majesty. Thou alone art being, life, truth, beauty, and goodness. I glorify Thee, I praise Thee, I thank Thee, and I love Thee, all incapable and unworthy as I am, in union with Thy dear Son Jesus Christ, our Savior and our Father, in the mercifulness of His heart and through His infinite merits. I wish to serve Thee, to please Thee, to obey Thee, and to love Thee always, in union with Mary Immaculate, Mother of God and our Mother, loving also and serving my neighbor for Thy sake. Therefore, give me Thy Holy Spirit to enlighten, correct, and guide me in the way of Thy commandments, and in all perfection, until we come to the happiness of heaven, where we shall glorify Thee forever. Amen. Glory be (7 times) (Indulgence 300 Days: # This was prepared by Pius X, April 18, 1906)

G. Prayer to the Most Holy Trinity

Omnipotence of the Father, help my weakness, and deliver me from the depth of misery. Wisdom of the Son, direct all my thoughts, words and actions. Love of the Holy Spirit, be Thou the source and beginning of all the operations of my soul, whereby they may be always conformable to the divine will. Amen. (Indulgence 200 days. # This was composed by Leo XIII).

H. In Praise of the Trinity

With our whole heart and voice we glorify Thee, we praise Thee, we bless Thee, God the Father unbegotten, the only-begotten Son, the Holy Spirit, the Paraclete, the holy and undivided Trinity. For Thou art great, and dost wonderful things: Thou alone art God. To Thee be praise, to Thee glory, to Thee thanksgiving forever and ever, O blessed Trinity! Amen. # Prayer source: From Roman Missal.

I. Aspiration

Do you feel too pressed for time to pray? These short prayers (also known as aspirations) can help! They're easy to learn. A good many of them are easy to memorize as well! They can provide you with a great way to stay in touch with our Lord and our Blessed Mother, especially for those times you feel most at your wit's end! At times like these when it seems like nothing is going right don't lose hope! You can stay close to Jesus and Mary with these aspirations, many of which come from old prayer books. (These prayers are great in good times or bad!) Be inspired by with these short prayers by our Lord's words: "pray always" (Luke 21:36) and by St. Paul's as well: "pray without ceasing" (1 Thes 5:17)! Here's a good one to both our Lord and his Blessed Mother, for starters: Jesus, Mary, I love you. Save souls!(Aspiration). Here's a good one to the Holy Spirit. This one is especially good when said with any prayer to the Holy Spirit, but is good all on its own, especially in those times you feel most in need of His counsel, comfort, and strength! O Holy Spirit, sweet Guest of my soul, abide in me and grant that I may ever abide in Thee(Aspiration). These prayers are meant to help us continually turn our thoughts toward God.

This one is also very powerful: Holy Spirit, command me to do Your will(Aspiration). This next one comes especially recommended by Jesus Himself! He once told Sister Mary of St. Peter, a French Carmelite nun in 1844. "Oh, if you only knew what great merit you acquire by saying even once 'Admirable is the name of God' in the spirit of reparation for blasphemy!" We've grouped these other aspirations into the following categories:

I-1. Aspirations to our Lord

(It has been noted, incidentally, that a very good effective prayer is just to say the name of God and Jesus!)
Jesus, I love You; Jesus, have mercy on me; Jesus, make Your will mine!
Blessed be God!
Blessed be the name of the Lord!
Divine Heart of Jesus, convert sinners, save the dying, and deliver the holy souls in purgatory.
Eucharistic Heart of Jesus, increase in us our Faith, Hope and Charity.

I-2. Aspirations to Our Lord in the Blessed Sacrament

Jesus, my God, here present in the Sacrament of Thy love, I adore Thee.
O Jesus in the Blessed Sacrament, have mercy on us.

O Jesus, in the most holy Sacrament, have mercy on us.

Praised and adored forever be the most holy Sacrament.

We adore Thee. Thou true Bread of angels. # I, I-1 and I-2 © Our Catholic Prayers All Rights Reseved.

Chapter 6 Marian Prayers (성모님께 봉헌하는 기도)

A. The Prayer Of Mary (The Magnificat: 성모님의 노래)

My soul proclaims the greatness of the Lord,
my spirit rejoices in God my Savior
for he has looked with favor on his lowly servant.
From this day all generations will call me blessed:
the Almighty has done great things for me,
and holy is his Name.

He has mercy on those who fear him
in every generation.
He has shown the strength of his arm,
he has scattered the proud in their conceit.

He has cast down the mighty from their thrones,
and has lifted up the lowly.
He has filled the hungry with good things,
and the rich he has sent away empty.

He has come to the help of his servant Israel
for he remembered his promise of mercy,
the promise he made to our fathers,
to Abraham and his children forever. (Lk. 1:46-55)
(Glory be)

B. The Prayer Of Mary; Prayer to the Virgin Mary in the Holy Month (성모성월 기도).

The Prayer Of Mary (The Magnificat 성모님의 노래 (Lk 1:46-55)

My soul proclaims·········to Abraham and his children forever (Glory be).

Let us pray,
Lord Jesus Christ, Who leads us to God the Father, granted us the Virgin Mary, Mother of God, to become our mother and set her as our mediator. We beg You, through the intercession of the Holy Mary, that we may receive and enjoy all the graces that we ask of You. Amen.

C. The Litany of the Blessed Virgin Mary(성모 호칭 기도)

Lord, have mercy on us.

Christ, have mercy on us.

Lord, have mercy on us.

Christ, hear us.

Christ, graciously hear us.

God, the Father of Heaven, have mercy on us.

God the Son, Redeemer of the world, have mercy on us.

God the Holy Spirit, have mercy on us.

Holy Trinity, One God, have mercy on us.

Holy Mary,	pray for us.
Holy Mother of God,	pray for us.
Holy Virgin of virgins,	pray for us.
Mother of Christ,	pray for us.
Mother of divine grace,	pray for us.
Mother most pure,	pray for us.
Mother most chaste,	pray for us.
Mother inviolate,	pray for us.
Mother undefiled,	pray for us.
Mother most amiable,	pray for us.
Mother most admirable,	pray for us.
Mother of good counsel,	pray for us.
Mother of our Creator,	pray for us.
Mother of our Savior,	pray for us.
Virgin most prudent,	pray for us.

Virgin most venerable,	pray for us.
Virgin most renowned,	pray for us.
Virgin most powerful,	pray for us.
Virgin most merciful,	pray for us.
Virgin most faithful,	pray for us.
Mirror of justice,	pray for us.
Seat of wisdom,	pray for us.
Cause of our joy,	pray for us.
Spiritual vessel,	pray for us.
Vessel of honor,	pray for us.
Singular vessel of devotion,	pray for us.
Mystical rose,	pray for us.
Tower of David,	pray for us.
Tower of ivory,	pray for us.
House of gold,	pray for us.
Ark of the covenant,	pray for us.
Gate of heaven,	pray for us.
Morning star,	pray for us.
Health of the sick,	pray for us.
Refuge of sinners,	pray for us.
Comforter of the afflicted,	pray for us.
Help of Christians,	pray for us.
Queen of Angels,	pray for us.
Queen of Patriarchs,	pray for us.
Queen of Prophets,	pray for us.
Queen of Apostles,	pray for us.
Queen of Martyrs,	pray for us.
Queen of Confessors,	pray for us.
Queen of Virgins,	pray for us.
Queen of all Saints,	pray for us.
Queen conceived without original sin,	pray for us.
Queen assumed into heaven,	pray for us.
Queen of the most holy Rosary,	pray for us.
Queen of Peace,	pray for us.

Lamb of God, who takes away the sins of the world,
spare us, O Lord.
Lamb of God, who takes away the sins of the world,
graciously hear us, O Lord.
Lamb of God, who takes away the sins of the world,
have mercy on us.
V. Pray for us, O holy Mother of God.
R. That we may be made worthy of the promises of Christ.
Let us pray:
O God, whose only-begotten Son, by his life, death and resurrection has purchased for us the rewards of eternal salvation; grant, we pray you, that meditating upon these mysteries in the most holy Rosary of the Blessed Virgin Mary, we may imitate what they contain, and obtain what they promise. Through Christ our Lord. Amen.

D. Memorare

Remember, O most gracious Virgin Mary, that never was it known that anyone who fled to your protection, implored your help or sought your intercession, was left unaided. Inspired by this confidence, I fly to you, O Virgin of virgins, my Mother; to you do I come, before you I stand, sinful and sorrowful. O Mother of the Word Incarnate, despise not my petitions, but in your mercy hear and answer me. Amen. (# The Memorare is a famous prayer of St. Bernard of Clairvaux).

E. Prayer to Our Lady, Help of Christians(Feast Day 24th May)

Most Holy Virgin Mary, Help of Christian, how sweet it is to come to your feet imploring your perpetual help. If earthly others cease not to remember their children, how can you, the most loving of all mothers forget me? Grant then to me, I implore you, your perpetual help in all my necessities, in every sorrow, and especially in all my temptations. I ask for your unceasing help for all who are now suffering. Help the weak, cure the sick, and convert sinners. Grant through your intercessions many vocations to the religious life. Obtain for us, O Mary, Help of Christians, that having invoked you on earth we may love and eternally thank you in heaven. Amen. # This prayer was written by St. John Bosco; John Bosco, also known as Giovanni Melchiorre Bosco and Don Bosco(AD1815-1888).

F. Litany to Our Lady of Fatima(Feast Day May 13)

Our Lady of Fatima, pray for our dear country.

Our Lady of Fatima, sanctify our clergy.

Our Lady of Fatima, make our Catholics more fervent.

Our Lady of Fatima, guide and inspire those who govern us.

Our Lady of Fatima, cure the sick who confide in thee.

Our Lady of Fatima, console the sorrowful who trust in thee.

Our Lady of Fatima, help those who invoke your aid.

Our Lady of Fatima, deliver us from all dangers.

Our Lady of Fatima, help us to resist temptation.

Our Lady of Fatima, obtain for us all that we lovingly ask of thee.

Our Lady of Fatima, help those who are dear to us.

Our Lady of Fatima, bring back to the right road our erring brothers.

Our Lady of Fatima, give us back our ancient fervor.

Our Lady of Fatima, obtain for us pardon of our manifold sins and offenses.

Our Lady of Fatima, bring all men to the feet of thy Divine Child.

Our Lady of Fatima, obtain peace for the world.

O Mary conceived without sin, pray for us who have recourse to thee. Immaculate Heart of Mary, pray for us now and at the hour of our death. Amen.

Let Us Pray:

O God of infinite goodness and mercy, fill our hearts with a great confidence in Thy dear Mother, whom we invoke under the title of Our Lady of the Rosary and our Lady of Fatima, and grant us by her powerful intercession all the graces, spiritual and temporal, which we need. Through Christ our Lord. Amen. No Copyright ©

F-1. Novena Prayers to Our Lady of Fatima

Day 1 – Our Lady of Fatima Novena

O Most Holy Virgin Mary, you came to Fatima to reveal the graces that come from praying the Holy Rosary to three little shepherd children. Inspire us with a sincere love of this devotion so that, like the shepherd children, it is not a burdensome task but a life-giving prayer. May our prayers and meditations on the mysteries of our redemption bring us closer to your Son, Our Lord Jesus Christ. Like the children of Fatima, we want to bring God's word to others. Give us the strength, O Lord, to overcome our doubts so that we may be messengers of the Gospel. We know that Jesus lives in our hearts and we receive Him in the Eucharist. Lord Jesus, the miracles, prophecies and prayers that Your Mother brought to us at Fatima amazed the whole world. We are certain of her closeness to You. We ask through the intercession of Our Lady of Fatima that you graciously hear and answer our prayers. Especially··· (Mention your intentions here···)

Our Lady of Fatima, Pray for us! Our Lady of the Rosary, Pray for us!

Immaculate Heart of Mary, Pray for us!

"From famine and war, deliver us." Amen.

Day 2 – Our Lady of Fatima Novena

O Most Holy Virgin Mary, you came to Fatima to reveal the graces that come from praying the Holy Rosary to three little shepherd children. Inspire us with a sincere love of this devotion so that, like the shepherd children, it is not a burdensome task but a life-giving prayer. May our prayers and meditations on the mysteries of our redemption bring us closer to your Son, Our Lord Jesus Christ. Our Lady of Fatima, we pray that we may be like you and follow your example. We pray for all those who face oppression, that they will find peace. We pray and give thanks for all the blessings we enjoy. Lord Jesus, the miracles, prophecies and prayers that Your Mother brought to us at Fatima amazed the whole world. We are certain of her closeness to You. We ask through the intercession of Our Lady of Fatima that you graciously hear and answer our prayers.

Especially··· (Mention your intentions here···)

Our Lady of Fatima, Pray for us! Our Lady of the Rosary, Pray for us!

Immaculate Heart of Mary, Pray for us!

"From nuclear war, from incalculable self-destruction and from every kind of war, deliver us." Amen.

Day 3 – Our Lady of Fatima Novena

O Most Holy Virgin Mary, you came to Fatima to reveal the graces that come from praying the Holy Rosary to three little shepherd children. Inspire us with a sincere love of this devotion so that, like the shepherd children, it is not a burdensome task but a life-giving prayer. May our prayers and meditations on the mysteries of our redemption bring us closer to your Son, Our Lord Jesus Christ. Our Lady of Fatima, today, we pray for an end to the suffering and injustice that plague so many parts of the world. Through the power of the Lord, you performed a miracle at Fatima and made the sun dance for thousands of people to see. Please intercede for those who are suffering. Lord Jesus, the miracles, prophecies and prayers that Your Mother brought to us at Fatima amazed the whole world. We are certain of her closeness to You. We ask through the intercession of Our Lady of Fatima that you graciously hear and answer our prayers. Especially··· (Mention your intentions here···)

Our Lady of Fatima, Pray for us! Our Lady of the Rosary, Pray for us!

Immaculate Heart of Mary, Pray for us!

"From sins against the life of man and from its very beginning, deliver us." Amen.

Day 4 – Our Lady of Fatima Novena

O Most Holy Virgin Mary, you came to Fatima to reveal the graces that come from praying the Holy Rosary to three little shepherd children. Inspire us with a sincere love of this devotion so that, like the shepherd children, it is not a burdensome task but a life-giving prayer. May our prayers and meditations on the mysteries of our redemption bring us closer to your Son, Our Lord Jesus Christ. Our Lady of Fatima, let us pray today for humility to seek forgiveness for our sins and make amends for our misdeeds. Lord Jesus, the miracles, prophecies and prayers that Your Mother brought to us at Fatima amazed the whole world. We are certain of her closeness to You. We ask through the intercession of Our Lady of Fatima that you graciously hear and answer our prayers. Especially··· (Mention your intentions here···)

Our Lady of Fatima, Pray for us! Our Lady of the Rosary, Pray for us!

Immaculate Heart of Mary, Pray for us!

"From hatred and from the demeaning of the dignity of the children of God, deliver us." Amen.

Day 5 – Our Lady of Fatima Novena

O Most Holy Virgin Mary, you came to Fatima to reveal the graces that come from praying the Holy Rosary to three little shepherd children. Inspire us with a sincere love of this devotion so that, like the shepherd children, it is not a burdensome task but a life-giving prayer. May our prayers and meditations on the mysteries of our redemption bring us closer to your Son, Our Lord Jesus Christ. Our Lady of Fatima, may we offer everything we do today to our Lord. As we make this offering, we think of people who are affected by our actions each day. We ask God to help us be motivated by love and compassion. Lord Jesus, the miracles, prophecies and prayers that Your Mother brought to us at Fatima amazed the whole world. We are certain of her closeness to You. We ask through the intercession of Our Lady of Fatima that you graciously hear and answer our prayers. Especially··· (Mention your intentions here···)

Our Lady of Fatima, Pray for us! Our Lady of the Rosary, Pray for us!

Immaculate Heart of Mary, Pray for us!

"From every kind of injustice in the life of society, both national and international, deliver us." Amen.

Day 6 – Our Lady of Fatima Novena

O Most Holy Virgin Mary, you came to Fatima to reveal the graces that come from praying the Holy Rosary to three little shepherd children. Inspire us with a sincere love of this devotion so that, like the shepherd children, it is not a burdensome task but a life-giving prayer. May our prayers and meditations on the mysteries of our redemption bring us closer to your Son, Our Lord Jesus Christ. Our Lady of Fatima, sometimes we live in fear and we are too afraid to let go of our anxieties. We want to be God's instruments to achieve His will and to bring Him glory. Today we ask through your intercession, that Jesus help us to trust in Him like the children at Fatima. Lord Jesus, the miracles, prophecies and prayers that Your Mother brought to us at Fatima amazed the whole world. We are certain of her closeness to You. We ask through the intercession of Our Lady of Fatima that you graciously hear and answer our prayers. Especially··· (Mention your intentions here···)

Our Lady of Fatima, Pray for us! Our Lady of the Rosary, Pray for us!

Immaculate Heart of Mary, Pray for us!

"From readiness to trample on the commandments of God, deliver us." Amen.

Day 7 – Our Lady of Fatima Novena

O Most Holy Virgin Mary, you came to Fatima to reveal the graces that come from praying the Holy Rosary to three little shepherd children. Inspire us with a sincere love of this devotion so that, like the shepherd children, it is not a burdensome task but a life-giving prayer. May our prayers and meditations on the mysteries of our redemption bring us closer to your Son, Our Lord Jesus Christ. Our Lady of Fatima, show us how to pray always. Teach us how to speak to God as a friend. Help us to make time for silence in our hectic days so that we may listen to what God has to tell us. Throughout the business of our days, help us remember God and have our hearts centered on Him. Lord Jesus, the miracles, prophecies and prayers that Your Mother brought to us at Fatima amazed the whole world. We are certain of her closeness to You. We ask through the intercession of Our Lady of Fatima that you graciously hear and answer our prayers. Especially⋯ (Mention your intentions here⋯)

Our Lady of Fatima, Pray for us! Our Lady of the Rosary, Pray for us!

Immaculate Heart of Mary, Pray for us!

"From attempts to stifle in human hearts the very truth of God, deliver us." Amen.

Day 8 – Our Lady of Fatima Novena

O Most Holy Virgin Mary, you came to Fatima to reveal the graces that come from praying the Holy Rosary to three little shepherd children. Inspire us with a sincere love of this devotion so that, like the shepherd children, it is not a burdensome task but a life-giving prayer. May our prayers and meditations on the mysteries of our redemption bring us closer to your Son, Our Lord Jesus Christ. Our Lady of Fatima, today we pray for your Son to come to our aid and end the suffering and wars throughout the world. Help us to be like the children at Fatima; loving, trusting and faithful. May we pray to bring peace to our own world in our own small way by choosing to love and trust in the Lord.

Lord Jesus, the miracles, prophecies and prayers that Your Mother brought to us at Fatima amazed the whole world. We are certain of her closeness to You. We ask through the intercession of Our Lady of Fatima that you graciously hear and answer our prayers. Especially⋯ (Mention your intentions here⋯)

Our Lady of Fatima, Pray for us! Our Lady of the Rosary, Pray for us!

Immaculate Heart of Mary, Pray for us!

"From the loss of awareness of good and evil, deliver us." Amen.

Day 9 – Our Lady of Fatima Novena

O Most Holy Virgin Mary, you came to Fatima to reveal the graces that come from praying the Holy Rosary to three little shepherd children. Inspire us with a sincere love of this devotion so that, like the shepherd children, it is not a burdensome task but a life-giving prayer. May our prayers and meditations on the mysteries of our redemption bring us closer to your Son, Our Lord Jesus Christ. Our Lady of Fatima, thank you for appearing to the children at Fatima and delivering messages that are still relevant to us today. We pray again and again for peace in the world and for an end to war. May we continue to pray and sacrifice as you requested. Lord Jesus, the miracles, prophecies and prayers that Your Mother brought to us at Fatima amazed the whole world. We are certain of her closeness to You. We ask through the intercession of Our Lady of Fatima that you graciously hear and answer our prayers. Especially··· (Mention your intentions here···)

Our Lady of Fatima, Pray for us! Our Lady of the Rosary, Pray for us!

Immaculate Heart of Mary, Pray for us!

"From sins against the Holy Spirit, deliver us, deliver us." Amen. # A very small portion of these daily prayers (in quotes) is taken from St. John Paul II, and the content is from: L'Osservatore Romano. Weekly Edition in English on May 24, 1982. L'Osservatore Romano is the newspaper of the Holy See.

G. Novena In honor of Mary, Help of Christians 15th to 23rd May.

First Day: O Mary, you readily agreed to the Angel's request when you were asked to be the mother of God's Son, and throughout your life your one desire was to do the will of your Father in heaven. Help me always to be obedient and humble. May I, like you, always have the generosity to follow Jesus, wherever he calls.

Hail Mary, full of grace···

V. Pray for us, O Immaculate, Help of Christians.

R. That we may be made worthy of the promises of Christ.

Let us pray, Heavenly Father, place deep in our hearts the love of Mary, our help and the help of all Christians. May we fight vigorously for the faith here on earth, and may we one day praise your victories in heaven. Lord God, grant this through our Lord Jesus Christ, your Son who lives and reigns with You and the Holy Spirit, One God forever and ever. Amen.

Second Day: O Mary, by your visit to your cousin, Saint Elizabeth, you joyfully spread the good news of the coming of Jesus into the world. May many young people generously follow your example, and give their lives totally to the service of your Son as priests, brothers and sisters. Amen.

Third Day: O Mary, ever since the wedding feast of Cana you have always been the powerful help of all those who have asked your aid and protection. By your prayers, keep me free from all dangers and help me always to rise above my faults and failings. Amen.

Fourth Day: O Mary, by your presence at the foot of the cross, you comforted and strengthened your son as he offered his life to the Father. Be with me at the hour of my death, and lead me quickly to the joys of your Son's kingdom in heaven. Amen.

Fifth Day: O Mary, by your presence in the upper room you strengthened and encouraged the apostles and disciples as they waited for the coming of the Holy Spirit at Pentecost. May I always be open to the gifts of the Spirit, and may my faith always be deep and living. Amen.

Sixth Day: O Mary, throughout her long history you have always defended your Son's Church from the attacks of her enemies. Be with her again in our days. Help each one of us to be her loyal subjects and to work without ceasing for that unity of peace and love for which your Son so fervently prayed. Amen.

Seventh Day: O Mary, you have always been the special guide and protector of Saint Peter's successor, the Bishop of Rome. Keep our present Holy Father in your loving care. Defend him from all harm and give him all those gifts he needs to be the faithful shepherd of your Son's flock. Amen.

Eight Day: O Mary, the wonderful way you helped Saint John Bosco's work to grow and spread shows that you have a great love for the young. As you watched over the child Jesus at Nazareth, so now watch over all young people, especially those most in need, and help them to grow daily in love of your Son. Amen.

Ninth Day: O Mary, you so often showed great courage during your life here on earth. Help all those who are suffering pain and persecution as they try to worship your Son. Obtain for me a deep love of Jesus, so that my life may always be pure, my service of others generous and loving, and my death a truly happy one. Amen. Mary, help of Christians, pray for us! Amen. # This Novena was prepared by SALESIANS of Don Bosco Ireland.

H. We fly to your patronage

We fly to your patronage, O holy Mother of God; despise not our petitions in our necessities, but deliver us always from all dangers, O glorious and blessed Virgin. Amen. # Copyright © 2003, 1997 by Catholic Book Publishing Corp., N.J. All rights reserved.

I. Prayer in Honor of the Immaculate Conception

ANT. This is the rod in which was neither knot of original sin, nor rind of actual guilt.
V. In thy conception, O Virgin! You were Immaculate.
R. Pray for us to the Father, Whose Son thou didst bring forth.

Let us Pray
O God, Who, by the Immaculate Conception of the Virgin, didst prepare a worthy habitation for Thy Son, we beseech Thee, that as by the foreseen death of that same Son, Thou didst preserve her from all stain, so too thou wouldst permit us, purified through her intercession, to come unto Thee. Through the same Christ our Lord. Amen. # On March 31, 1876 Pius IX authorized the above antiphon, versicle and prayer in honor of the Immaculate Conception of the Blessed Virgin Mary. The above prayer is the collect for the feast of the Immaculate Conception (Dec. 8). From the Raccolta #410. (S. C. Ind. Dec. 14, 1889; S. P., March 15, 1934).

J. How to Pray the Rosary

The Rosary, though clearly Marian in character, is at heart a Christocentric prayer. In the sobriety of its elements, it has all the depth of the Gospel message in its entirety, of which it can be said to be a compendium. It is an echo of the prayer of Mary, her perennial Magnificat for the work of the redemptive Incarnation which began in her virginal womb. With the Rosary, the Christian people sits at the school of Mary and is led to contemplate the beauty on the face of Christ and to experience the depths of his love. Through the Rosary the faithful receive abundant grace, as though from the very hands of the Mother of the Redeemer. From on the Most Holy Rosary······(Rosarium Virginis Mariae). The Rosary is a Scripture-based prayer. It begins with the Apostles' Creed, which summarizes the great mysteries of the Catholic faith. The Our Father, which introduces each mystery, is from the Gospels. The first part of the Hail Mary is the angel's words announcing Christ's birth and Elizabeth's greeting to Mary. St. Pius V officially added the second part of the Hail Mary. The Mysteries of the Rosary center on the events of Christ's life. There are four sets of Mysteries: Joyful, Sorrowful, Glorious and—added by St. Pope John Paul II in 2002—the Luminous. The repetition in the Rosary is meant to lead one into restful and contemplative prayer related to each Mystery. The gentle repetition of the words helps us to enter into the silence of our hearts, where Christ's spirit dwells. The Rosary can be said privately or with a group.

The Five Joyful Mysteries are traditionally prayed on Mondays, Saturdays, and, during the season of Advent, on Sundays:
1. The Annunciation
2. The Visitation
3. The Nativity
4. The Presentation in the Temple
5. The Finding in the Temple

The Five Sorrowful Mysteries are traditionally prayed on Tuesdays, Fridays, and, during the season of Lent, on Sundays:
1. The Agony in the Garden
2. The Scourging at the Pillar

3. The Crowning with Thorns

4. The Carrying of the Cross

5. The Crucifixion and Death

The Five Glorious Mysteries are traditionally prayed on Wednesdays and, outside the seasons of Advent and Lent, on Sundays:

1. The Resurrection

2. The Ascension

3. The Descent of the Holy Spirit

4. The Assumption

5. The Coronation of Mary

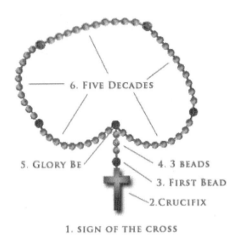

The Five Luminous Mysteries are traditionally prayed on Thursdays:

1. The Baptism of Christ in the Jordan

2. The Wedding Feast at Cana

3. Jesus' Proclamation of the Coming of the Kingdom of God

4. The Transfiguration

5. The Institution of the Eucharist

Praying the Rosary

Familiarize yourself and/or your group with the prayers of the rosary.

1. Make the Sign of the Cross.

2. Holding the Crucifix, say the Apostles' Creed.

3. On the first bead, say an Our Father.

4. Say one Hail Mary on each of the next three beads.

5. Say the Glory Be

6. For each of the five decades, announce the Mystery (perhaps followed by a brief reading from Scripture) then say the Our Father.

7. While fingering each of the ten beads of the decade, next say ten Hail Mary's while meditating on the Mystery. Then say a Glory Be.

   (After finishing each decade, some say the following prayer requested by the Blessed Virgin Mary at Fatima: O my Jesus, forgive us our sins, save us from the fires of hell; lead all souls to Heaven, especially those who have most need of your mercy.)

8. After saying the five decades, say the Hail, Holy Queen, followed by this dialogue and prayer:

V. Pray for us, O holy Mother of God.

R. That we may be made worthy of the promises of Christ.

Let us pray: O God, whose Only Begotten Son, by his life, Death, and Resurrection, has purchased for us the rewards of eternal life, grant, we beseech thee, that while meditating on these mysteries of the most holy Rosary of the Blessed Virgin Mary, we may imitate what they contain and obtain what they promise, through the same Christ our Lord. Amen.

(A prayer to St. Joseph may also follow.) Conclude the Rosary with the Sign of the Cross.

The Joyful Mysteries

The Annunciation:

For parents facing an unexpected pregnancy, that they lovingly accept the precious life God has entrusted to their care.

The Visitation:

That the family and friends of expectant parents might reach out and support them as they prepare to meet their child face to face.

The Nativity:

That the love of the Blessed Mother and the Christ Child may be a source of strength for every expectant mother, especially mothers living in poverty, and that they both will be surrounded by joy and love.

The Presentation:

That fathers of young children will model St. Joseph in devoutly practicing their faith, so that they lead their children to God by their words and example.

The Finding of Jesus in the Temple:

For all children who have been lost and forgotten, that they may be led to a place where they are treasured, protected and loved.

The Luminous Mysteries
The Baptism of Jesus in the River Jordan:
That all baptized Christians will be open to the
Holy Spirit and bear witness to the sanctity of life.

The Wedding Feast at Cana:
For all husbands and wives, that they treasure the priceless gift of married love by generously accepting children through procreation and adoption.

The Proclamation of the Kingdom of God:
That those who pray and work for greater respect for human life will be guided by the Beatitudes and reveal the face of Christ to others.

The Transfiguration:
That our world will be transfigured by the witness of faithful Christians so that all may understand the priceless value of every human being.

The Institution of the Eucharist:
That through our worthy reception of the Eucharist and frequent Eucharistic Adoration, Jesus will teach us to love sacrificially the least and neediest among us.

The Sorrowful Mysteries
The Agony in the Garden:
For all who are suffering from abandonment or neglect, that compassionate individuals will come forward to offer them comfort and aid.

The Scourging at the Pillar:
That the victims of violence, torture and slavery will be delivered from their suffering, find healing and know that God is close to them.

The Crowning with Thorns:
That the persecution of Christians will end in a new era of tolerance and respect for

the religious freedom and conscience rights of all.

The Carrying of the Cross:
For all who labor under burdens that seem too great to bear—due to illness, age, poverty, cruelty or injustice—that our prayers and aid will lighten their crosses.

The Crucifixion:
For an end to the death penalty and for the release of all prisoners of conscience and all who have been wrongfully convicted.

The Glorious Mysteries
The Resurrection:
For all who have lost loved ones, and especially for parents of a child who was miscarried, aborted or stillborn, that they will find peace in the promise of the Resurrection.

The Ascension:
For all who struggle with addictions, that through Christ's triumph and ascent into glory, they may triumph over their temptations, and gain strength and peace.

The Coming of the Holy Spirit:
That the Holy Spirit will open the minds and hearts of those who now reject the Gospel of Life and allow them to be convinced of the truth and goodness of all that the Church professes concerning human life.

The Assumption of Mary:
For mothers who have died at the hands of abortion providers, that they may experience reconciliation and together with their children know God's peace.

The Coronation of Mary:
For all mothers, that they might come to know the wonder of their vocation.

K. Prayer to St. Joseph after the Rosary

Introduction: This prayer to St. Joseph—spouse of the Virgin Mary, foster father of Jesus, and patron saint of the universal Church—was composed by Pope Leo XIII in his 1889 encyclical, Quamquam Pluries⋯ He asked that it be added to the end of the Rosary, especially during the month of March and October, which is dedicated to the Rosary. The prayer is enriched with a partial indulgence (Handbook of Indulgences, conc. 19), and may be said after the customary Salve Regina and concluding prayer. It may also be used to conclude other Marian devotions.

Prayer: To you, O blessed Joseph, do we come in our tribulation, and having implored the help of your most holy Spouse, we confidently invoke your patronage also. Through that charity which bound you to the Immaculate Virgin Mother of God and through the paternal love with which you embraced the Child Jesus, we humbly beg you graciously to regard the inheritance which Jesus Christ has purchased by his Blood, and with your power and strength to aid us in our necessities. O most watchful guardian of the Holy Family, defend the chosen children of Jesus Christ; O most loving father, ward off from us every contagion of error and corrupting influence; O our most mighty protector, be kind to us and from heaven assist us in our struggle with the power of darkness. As once you rescued the Child Jesus from deadly peril, so now protect God's Holy Church from the snares of the enemy and from all adversity; shield, too, each one of us by your constant protection, so that, supported by your example and your aid, we may be able to live piously, to die in holiness, and to obtain eternal happiness in heaven. Amen.

L. Prayer to the Blessed Virgin Mary for the Peaceful Unification of the Korean Peninsular

O Most Blessed Virgin Mary, Mother of Mercy, at this most critical time, we entrust the Republic of Korea to your loving care. Most Holy Mother, we beg you to reclaim this land for the glory of your Son, Jesus Christ. Overwhelmed with the burden of the sins of our nation, we cry out to you from the depths of our hearts and seek refuge in your motherly protection. Look down with mercy upon us and touch the hearts of the political leaders in both South and North Korea. Open our minds to the great worth of human life and to the responsibilities that accompany human freedom. Free all politicians of both South and North Korea from the falsehoods that lead to a lack of reflection, ignorance, forgetfulness, obstinacy, prejudice, error, perversion, indifference, sinful inclinations, over sentimentality, attachment, fickleness, inconsistency, stubbornness, evil of abortion and threaten the sanctity of family life. Grant our country the wisdom to proclaim that God's law is the foundation on which this nation was founded, and that He alone is the true source of our cherished rights to life, liberty, peace and the pursuit of happiness on the whole Korean Peninsula. O Merciful God, give us, all Koreans the courage to reject the culture of death. Grant us the strength to build a new culture of life through conceiving in us good taste, feelings and inclinations. O dispenser of His graces, present to Your Divine Son the petition for which we are making, Most Blessed Virgin Mother, intercede for us that our country through peaceful unification in the Korean peninsula will support life for each individual at every stage, uphold family life, and influence other countries throughout the world to love God above all else and neighbor as self, to serve Him, and to live for Him alone. Time and time again you have given us your gracious assistance, and thus we humbly and gratefully acknowledge you as our patron. Most Generous Blessed Virgin Mary, conceived without sin, pray for all Korean who have recourse to you and all those who do not have recourse to you. May our God of power and mercy shine His light upon our country and the whole world. Amen.

M. Litany: Mary, Mother of Life

Mary, Mother of all Life, help us to respect human life from the moment of conception to the moment of natural death. R: Mary, pray for us.

Mary, Mother of Compassion, You showed us how valuable a single life can be; Help us to guard and protect the lives of all people entrusted to our care. R: Mary, pray for us.

Mary, Mother of the Child Jesus, with St. Joseph you formed the Holy Family. Guard and protect all families in this earthly life. R: Mary, pray for us.

Mary, Mother Most Holy, You sanctified the vocation of motherhood; Pour out your heavenly aid on all mothers and help them to be holy. R: Mary, pray for us.

Mary, Mother of Sorrows, Simeon's prophecy foretold that a sword of suffering would pierce your heart; Bring comfort and hope to all mothers who suffer over their children. R: Mary, pray for us.

Mary, Full of Grace, You had a choice in responding to God's call; help us always to say "Yes" to the will of God in our lives, and strive always to do whatever he tells us. R: Mary, pray for us.

Mary, Comforter of the Afflicted, Pour forth your heavenly grace on all who are in need of God's healing, especially those involved in abortion; Help them to experience the love and mercy of Christ, your Son. R: Mary, pray for us.

Mary, Intercessor and Advocate, we lift up the poor, the displaced, the marginalized and vulnerable members of society; Help them to never abandon hope, but to place their trust in the God who gave them life. R: Mary, pray for us.

Mary, Mother of the Word Incarnate, you bore in your womb him whom the heavens cannot contain; Help us to bear witness to Christ by the example of our lives and show the world the extravagant love of God. R: Mary, pray for us.

All: Remember, o most gracious Virgin Mary, that never was it known that anyone who fled to your protection, implored your help, or sought your intercession was left unaided. Inspired with this confidence, we fly unto you, O Virgin of virgins, our Mother. To you we come, before you we stand, sinful and sorrowful. O Mother of the Word Incarnate, despise not our petitions, but in your mercy hear and answer them. Amen. Copyright ©2010 United States Conference of Catholic Bishops, Washington, D.C. Used with permission. All rights reserved.

Chapter 7 The Order of Mass

The Mass is our greatest prayer:

At the Last Supper, our Savior instituted the Eucharistic sacrifice of His Body and Blood. He did this in order to perpetuate the sacrifice of the Cross throughout the ages until He should come again. Thus, the Mass is: (a) the true sacrifice of the New Covenant, in which a holy and living Victim is offered, Jesus Christ, and we in union with Him, as a gift of love and obedience to the Father; (b) a sacred meal and spiritual banquet of the children of God; (c) a Paschal meal, which evokes the passage (pass over) of Jesus from this world to the Father; it renders Him present and makes Him live again in souls, and anticipates our passage to the Kingdom of God; (d) a communitarian meal, that is, a gathering together of the Head and His members, of Jesus and His Church, His Mystical Body, in order to carry out a perfect Divine worship. Thus, the Mass is the greatest prayer we have. Through it we give thanks and praise to the Father for the wonderful future He has given us in His son. We also ask forgiveness for our sins and beg the Father's blessing upon us and all human beings.

The Order of Mass

1) The Introductory Rites:

a) The Mass is made up essentially of two movements or rites: the Liturgy of the Word and the Liturgy of the Eucharist. It also includes preliminary, known as the introductory rites and concluding rites. Acts of prayer and penitence prepare us to meet Christ as He comes in Word and Sacrament. We gather as a worshiping company to celebrate our unity with Him and with one another.

b) When the people are gathered, the Priest approaches the altar with the ministers while the Entrance Chant is sung. When he has arrived at the altar, after making a profound bow with the ministers, the Priest venerates the altar, which represents Christ, with a kiss (or bow) and, if appropriate, incenses the cross and the altar. Then, with the ministers, he goes to the chair. When the Entrance Chant is concluded (or Antiphon provides us with the theme of the day), the Priest and the faithful, standing, sign themselves with the Sign of the Cross, while the Priest, facing the people, says: In the name of the Father, and of the Son, and of the Holy Spirit. The people reply: Amen.

c) Then the Priest, extending his hands, greets the people, saying: The grace of our Lord Jesus Christ, and the love of God, and the communion of the Holy Spirit be with you all. Or: Grace to you and peace from God our Father and the Lord Jesus Christ. Or: The Lord be with you. The people reply: And with your spirit.(In this first greeting a Bishop, instead of "The Lord be with you", says: Peace be with you.)

d) The Priest, or a Deacon, or another minister, may very briefly introduce the faithful to the Mass of the day.

e) Penitential Act:

Then follows the Penitential Act, to which the Priest invites the faithful, saying: Brethren (brothers and sisters), let us acknowledge our sins, and so prepare ourselves to celebrate the sacred mysteries. A brief pause for silence follows. Then all recite together the formula of general confession: I confess to almighty God and to you, my brothers and sisters, that I have greatly sinned, in my thoughts and in my words, in what I have done and in what I have failed to do. And, striking their breast, they say: through my fault, through my fault, through my most grievous fault; Then they continue: therefore I ask blessed Mary ever-Virgin, all the Angels and Saints, and you, my brothers and sisters, to pray for me to the Lord our God.

The absolution by the Priest follows: May almighty God have mercy on us, forgive us our sins, and bring us to everlasting life.

The people reply: Amen.

Or Penitential Act:

The Priest invites the faithful to make the Penitential Act: Brethren (brothers and sisters), let us acknowledge our sins, and so prepare ourselves to celebrate the sacred mysteries. A brief pause for silence follows. The Priest then says: From time to time on Sundays, especially in Easter Time, instead of the customary Penitential Act: the blessing and sprinkling of water may take place as a reminder of Baptism. The Priest says, Have mercy on us, O Lord.

The people reply: For we have sinned against you.

The Priest: Show us, O Lord, your mercy.

The people: And grant us your salvation.

The absolution by the Priest follows: May almighty God have mercy on us, forgive us our sins, and bring us to everlasting life. The people reply: Amen.

Or The Priest invites the faithful to make the Penitential Act:
Brethren (brothers and sisters), let us acknowledge our sins, and so prepare ourselves to celebrate the sacred mysteries. A brief pause for silence follows. The Priest, or a Deacon or another minister, then says the following or other invocations with Kyrie, eleison (Lord, have mercy): You were sent to heal the contrite of heart: Lord, have mercy. Or: Kyrie, eleison. The people reply: Lord, have mercy. Or: Kyrie, eleison. The Priest: You came to call sinners: Christ, have mercy. Or: Christe, eleison. The people: Christ, have mercy. Or: Christe, eleison.

Or The Priest: You are seated at the right hand of the Father to intercede for us: Lord, have mercy. Or: Kyrie, eleison. The people: Lord, have mercy. Or: Kyrie, eleison. The absolution by the Priest follows: May almighty God have mercy on us, forgive us our sins, and bring us to everlasting life. The people reply: Amen.

The Kyrie eleison (Lord, have mercy) invocations follow, unless they have just occurred in a formula of the Penitential Act:

V. Lord, have mercy. R. Lord, have mercy.

V. Christ, have mercy. R. Christ, have mercy.

V. Lord, have mercy. R. Lord, have mercy. Or:

V. Kyrie, eleison. R. Kyrie, eleison.

V. Christe, eleison. R. Christe, eleison.

V. Kyrie, eleison. R. Kyrie, eleison.

The Kyrie and Gloria; We give honor to Christ and we turn our attention to praise and thanksgiving in beautiful and ancient prayers in honor of Christ.

f) Gloria:

Then, when it is prescribed, this hymn is either sung or said: Glory to God in the highest, and on earth peace to people of good will. We praise you, we bless you, we adore you, we glorify you, we give you thanks for your great glory, Lord God, heavenly King, O God, almighty Father. Lord Jesus Christ, Only Begotten Son, Lord God, Lamb of God, Son of the Father, you take away the sins of the world, have mercy on us; you take away the sins of the world, receive our prayer; you are seated at the right hand of the Father, have mercy on us. For you alone are the Holy One, you alone are the Lord, you alone are the Most High, Jesus Christ, with the Holy Spirit, in the glory of God the Father. Amen.

g) Collect(The opening prayer); We join in prayer together: When this hymn(Gloria) is concluded, the priest, with hands joined, says: Let us pray. And all pray in silence with the priest for a while. Then the priest, with hands extended, says the Collect prayer, at the end of which the people acclaim: Amen.

Through collect, the character of the celebration finds expression. This prayer literally "collects" the prayers of all who are gathered into one prayer led by the priest celebrant. The faithful bring to their prayer their cares, the concerns of their family, friends, and the whole world. The faithful then ratify the prayer with Amen.

2) The Liturgy of the Word

a) Then the reader goes to the ambo and reads the First Reading, while all sit and listen. To indicate the end of the reading, the reader acclaims: The word of the Lord. All reply: Thanks be to God. # The proclamation of God's Word is always centered on Jesus Christ. Jesus Christ is the Word of God Himself and the Author of Revelation. Hence, it is actually God Himself Who speaks to us when the Sacred Scriptures are liturgically proclaimed. Jesus Christ is present through His Word as the readings are proclaimed. The Old testament writings prepare for Him, and the New testament writings speak of Him directly.

b) The Responsorial Psalm: The psalmist or cantor sings or says the Psalm, with the people making the response. In the responsorial Psalm we reflect upon God's Words and respond to them.

After this, if there is to be a Second Reading, a reader reads it from the ambo, as above. To indicate the end of the reading, the reader acclaims: The word of the Lord. All reply: Thanks be to God. God speaks to us through the Apostles. We now listen to readings taken from the Letters of Paul and the other Apostles.

There follows the Alleluia or another chant laid down by the rubrics, as the liturgical time requires.(We praise Jesus Who comes to speak to us. Jesus will speak to us in the Gospel. We rise now out of respect and prepare for His message with the Alleluia verse) Meanwhile, if incense is used, the Priest puts some into the thurible.

c) The Gospel: After this, the Deacon who is to proclaim the Gospel, bowing profoundly before the Priest, asks for the blessing, saying in a low voice: Your blessing, Father. The Priest says in a low voice: May the Lord be in your heart and on your lips, that you may proclaim his Gospel worthily and well, in the name of the Father and of the Son and of the Holy Spirit. The Deacon signs himself with the Sign of the Cross and replies: Amen. If, however, a Deacon is not present, the Priest, bowing before the altar, says quietly: Cleanse my heart and my lips, Almighty God, that I may worthily proclaim your holy Gospel. The Deacon, or the Priest, then proceeds to the ambo, accompanied, if appropriate, by ministers with incense and candles. There he says: The Lord be with you. The people reply: And with your spirit. The Deacon, or the Priest: A reading from the holy Gospel according to N. and, at the same time, he makes the Sign of the Cross on the book and on his forehead, lips, and breast. The people acclaim: Glory to you, O Lord. Then the Deacon, or the Priest, incenses the book, if incense is used, and proclaims the Gospel. At the end of the Gospel, the Deacon, or the Priest, acclaims: The Gospel of the Lord. All reply: Praise to you, Lord Jesus Christ. Then he kisses the book, saying quietly: Through the words of the Gospel may our sins be wiped away. # God speaks to us through Jesus Christ. He comes to proclaim His Word (through the priest or deacon) to us here and now and to enable us to apply it to our lives today.

d) The Homily: Then follows the Homily, which is to be preached by a Priest or Deacon on all Sundays and Holydays of Obligation; on other days, it is recommended. # God speaks to us through the priest's Homily. God's Word is spoken again in the Homily. The Holy Spirit speaking through the lips of the preacher explains and applies the day's Biblical readings to the needs of a particular congregation. He calls us to respond to Jesus Christ through the life we lead.

e) The Profession of Faith(Creed; the Niceno-Constantinopolitan Creed): At the end of the Homily, the Symbol or Profession of Faith or Creed, when prescribed, is either sung or said: An alternate musical setting of the Creed may be found. I believe in one God, the Father almighty, maker of heaven and earth, of all things visible and invisible. I believe in one Lord Jesus Christ, the Only Begotten Son of God, born of the Father before all ages. God from God, Light from Light, true God from true God, begotten, not made, consubstantial with the Father; through him all things were made. For us men and for our salvation he came down from heaven, (At the words that follow up to and including and became man, all bow.) and by the Holy Spirit was incarnate of the Virgin Mary, and became man. For our sake he was crucified under Pontius Pilate, he suffered death and was buried, and rose again on the third day in accordance with the Scriptures. He ascended into heaven and is seated at the right hand of the Father. He will come again in glory to judge the living and the dead and his kingdom will have no end. I believe in the Holy Spirit, the Lord, the giver of life, who proceeds from the Father and the Son, who with the Father and the Son is adored and glorified, who has spoken through the prophets. I believe in one, holy, catholic and apostolic Church. I confess one Baptism for the forgiveness of sins and I look forward to the resurrection of the dead and the life of the world to come. Amen.

Apostle's Creed: Instead of the Niceno (or Nicene)-Constantinopolitan Creed, especially during Lent, Easter Time and in children's Masses, the baptismal Symbol of the Roman Church, known as the Apostles' Creed, may be used. I believe in God, the Father almighty, Creator of heaven and earth, and in Jesus Christ, his only Son, our Lord, (At the words that follow, up to and including the Virgin Mary, all bow.) who was conceived by the Holy Spirit, born of the Virgin Mary, suffered under Pontius Pilate, was crucified, died and was buried; he descended into hell; on the third day he rose again from the dead; he ascended into heaven, and is seated at the right hand of God, the Father almighty; from there he will come to judge the living and the dead. I believe in the Holy Spirit, the holy Catholic Church, the communion of saints, the forgiveness of sins, the resurrection of the body and life everlasting. Amen. # After listening to God's Word, reflecting on it, and responding in our hearts to it, we now make a corporate profession of faith. We publicly respond, assent, and adhere to that Word. This is a response not only to doctrinal propositions but also to the Person of Christ present in the Word. We now want to proclaim before everyone that we believe. We believe what God has told us; we believe that He has called us; we believe that He has loved us. To say all of this we profess our Faith with the Creed. The Niceno (or Nicene)-Constantinopolitan Creed is a summary of the Faith expressed by the Councils of Nicaea(AD 325) and of Constantinople(AD 381) as ratified by the Council of Chalcedon(AD 451).

f) The General Intercessions(Prayer of the Faithful): the Universal Prayer. Then the Universal Prayer follows, that is, the Prayer of the Faithful or Bidding Prayers. We pray for our brothers and sisters in Christ. We then close the first part of the Mass by saying the general Intercessions, also known as the prayer of the faithful. When we go to Mass, we pray not only for ourselves but also for all who need God's help. Instructed, moved and renewed by the Word of God, which brought Christ into our midst, we are now ready to exercise our priestly function by interceding for all mankind. We pray for the needs of the church and the world as well as the current needs of our local parish community. The substance of this prayer lies in the very simple invocations that all, both religious and lay members of the assembly, have to express. The celebrant sets the stage for the prayer and sums it up at the end, and the reader articulates its petitions, but it is the assembly that makes the prayer by its invocation.

3) The Liturgy of the Eucharist:

We enter now into the Eucharistic sacrifice itself, the Supper of the Lord. We are God's new people, the redeemed brothers and sisters of Christ, gathered around His table.

a) Preparation of the Gifts: The bread and wine for the Eucharist, with our gifts for the church and the poor, are brought to the altar. These are a symbol of our inner readiness to give God all of ourselves with our hopes and disappointments, our work and leisure, and our whole everyday lives. We prepare our hearts by song or in silence as the Lord's table is set. When all this has been done, the Offertory Chant begins. Meanwhile, the ministers place the corporal, the purificator, the chalice, the pall, and the Missal on the altar. It is desirable that the faithful express their participation by making an offering, bringing forward bread and wine for the celebration of the Eucharist and perhaps other gifts to relieve the needs of the Church and of the poor. The Priest, standing at the altar, takes the paten with the bread and holds it slightly raised above the altar with both hands, saying in a low voice:

Blessed are you, Lord God of all creation, for through your goodness we have received the bread we offer you: fruit of the earth and work of human hands, it will become for us the bread of life. Then he places the paten with the bread on the corporal. If, however, the Offertory Chant is not sung, the Priest may speak these words aloud; at the end, the people may acclaim: Blessed be God for ever. The Deacon, or the Priest, pours wine and a little water into the chalice, saying quietly: By the mystery of this water and wine may we come to share in the divinity of Christ who humbled himself to share in our humanity. The Priest then takes the chalice and holds it slightly raised above the altar with both hands, saying in a low voice: Blessed are you, Lord God of all creation, for through your goodness we have received the wine we offer you: fruit of the vine and work of human hands, it will become our spiritual drink. Then he places the chalice on the corporal. If, however, the Offertory Chant is not sung, the Priest may speak these words aloud; at the end, the people may acclaim: Blessed be God for ever. After this, the Priest, bowing profoundly, says quietly: With humble spirit and contrite heart may we be accepted by you, O Lord, and may our sacrifice in your sight this day be pleasing to you, Lord God. If appropriate, he also incenses the offerings, the cross, and the altar. A Deacon or other minister then incenses the Priest and the people. Then the Priest, standing at the side of the altar, washes his hands, saying quietly: Wash me, O Lord, from my iniquity and cleanse me from my sin.

The Prayer over the Gifts: Standing at the middle of the altar, facing the people, extending and then joining his hands, the priest says: Pray, brethren (brothers and sisters), that my sacrifice and yours may be acceptable to God, the almighty Father. The people rise and reply: May the Lord accept the sacrifice at your hands for the praise and glory of his name, for our good and the good of all his holy Church. Then the priest, with hands extended, says the prayer over the Offerings, at the end of which the people acclaim: Amen.

b) The Preface: Then the Priest begins the Eucharistic Prayer. Extending his hands, the priest says: The Lord be with you. The people reply: And with your spirit. The Priest, raising his hands, continues: Lift up your hearts. The people: We lift them up to the Lord. The Priest, with hands extended, adds: Let us give thanks to the Lord our God. The people: It is right and just. The Priest, with hands extended, continues the Preface.

c) Our prayer of thanksgiving. The priest then calls upon the Lord with a prayer of praise and thanksgiving. It gives the reason for praising God on the day in question.

d) The priest: It is truly right and just, our duty and salvation always and everywhere to give you thanks, Father most holy, through your beloved Son, Jesus Christ, your Word through whom you made all things, whom you sent as our Savior and Redeemer, incarnate by the Holy Spirit and born of the Virgin. Fulfilling your will and gaining for you a holy people, he stretched out his hands as he endured his Passion, so as to break the bonds of death and manifest the resurrection. And so, with the Angels and all the Saints we declare your glory, as with one voice we acclaim:

The Holy, Holy, Holy: we praise God in union with the angels. At the end we join our sentiments to those found in the Preface by voicing another praise of God with the magnificent Holy, Holy, Holy. We stress that the earth as well as heaven is filled with the glory of God and it will be more filled with glory as we continue our Eucharist. At the end of the Preface the priest joins his hands and concludes the Preface with the people, singing or saying aloud:

Holy, Holy, Holy, Lord God of hosts. Heaven and earth are full of your glory. Hosanna in the highest. Blessed is he who comes in the name of the Lord. Hosanna in the highest. Or: In all Masses, the Priest celebrant is permitted to sing parts of the Eucharistic Prayer provided with musical notation below, especially the principal parts.

e) The Priest, with hands extended, says: You are indeed Holy, O Lord, the fount of all holiness. He joins his hands and, holding them extended over the offerings, says: Make holy, therefore, these gifts, we pray, by sending down your Spirit upon them like the dewfall, He joins his hands and makes the Sign of the Cross once over the bread and the chalice together, saying: so that they may become for us the Body and † Blood of our Lord, Jesus Christ. He joins his hands.

In the formulas that follow, the words of the Lord should be pronounced clearly and distinctly, as the nature of these words requires. At the time he was betrayed and entered willingly into his Passion, He takes the bread and, holding it slightly raised above the altar, continues: he took bread and, giving thanks, broke it, and gave it to his disciples, saying: He bends slightly. TAKE THIS, ALL OF YOU, AND EAT OF IT, FOR THIS IS MY BODY, WHICH WILL BE GIVEN UP FOR YOU. He shows the consecrated host to the people, places it again on the paten, and genuflects in adoration.

After this, he continues: In a similar way, when supper was ended, He takes the chalice and, holding it slightly raised above the altar, continues: he took the chalice and, once more giving thanks, he gave it to his disciples, saying: He bends slightly. TAKE THIS, ALL OF YOU, AND DRINK FROM IT, FOR THIS IS THE CHALICE OF MY BLOOD, THE BLOOD OF THE NEW AND ETERNAL COVENANT, WHICH WILL BE POURED OUT FOR YOU AND FOR MANY FOR THE FORGIVENESS OF SINS. DO THIS IN MEMORY OF ME. He shows the chalice to the people, places it on the corporal, and genuflects in adoration.

f) The mystery of faith (The memorial acclamation): We proclaim the mystery of our faith. The people now praise Christ in the memorial acclamation. We celebrate the fact that Christ has redeemed us, is with us now to apply that redemption to each of us, and will return in glory to perfect that redemption for all. Then priest says the mystery of faith. And the people continue, acclaiming: We proclaim your Death, O Lord, and profess your Resurrection until you come again. Or: When we eat this Bread and drink this Cup, we proclaim your Death, O Lord, until you come again. Or: Save us, Savior of the world, for by your Cross and Resurrection you have set us free.

g) Then the Priest, with hands extended, says: Therefore, as we celebrate the memorial of his Death and Resurrection, we offer you, Lord, the Bread of life and the Chalice of salvation, giving thanks that you have held us worthy to be in your presence and minister to you. Humbly we pray that, partaking of the Body and Blood of Christ, we may be gathered into one by the Holy Spirit. Remember, Lord, your Church, spread throughout the world, and bring her to the fullness of charity, together with N. our Pope and N. our Bishop and all the clergy.(Mention may be made here of the Coadjutor Bishop, or Auxiliary Bishops, as noted in the General Instruction of the Roman Missal, n. 149).

In Masses for the Dead, the following may be added: Remember your servant N., whom you have called (today) from this world to yourself. Grant that he (she) who was united with your Son in a death like his, may also be one with him in his Resurrection.

Remember also our brothers and sisters who have fallen asleep in the hope of the resurrection, and all who have died in your mercy: welcome them into the light of your face. Have mercy on us all, we pray, that with the blessed Virgin Mary, Mother of God, with blessed Joseph, her Spouse, with the blessed Apostles, and all the Saints who have pleased you throughout the ages, we may merit to be co-heirs to eternal life, and may praise and glorify you (He joins his hands) through your Son, Jesus Christ.

h) The Great Amen: We give our assent to all that has taken place. The Eucharistic Prayer concludes with the final doxology, an explicit note of praise. The priest offers praise and honor to the Father through Christ Who is the High Priest, with Christ Who is really present in the sacrificial memorial, and in Christ Who gives Himself to the members of His body. We heartily endorse these sentiments by our Great Amen. This Amen says that we have joined in praising the Father for all His wonderful works and have offered ourselves with Jesus to Him; now we are ready to receive Jesus back from the Father in Communion. The priest takes the chalice and the paten with the host and, raising both, he says: Through him, and with him, and in him, O God, almighty Father, in the unity of the Holy Spirit, all glory and honor is yours, forever and ever. The people acclaim: Amen.

4) Communion Rite

The Communion Rite is the part when God gives a gift to us after we have presented our gift to Him. The key point is that the gift is in both cases the same, the Jesus Christ, the Son of God and Savior of the world. After the chalice and paten have been set down, the priest, with hands joined, says: At the Savior's command and formed by divine teaching, we dare to say: He extends his hands and, together with the people, continues:

a) Our Father, who art in heaven, hallowed be thy name; thy kingdom come, thy will be done on earth as it is in heaven. Give us this day our daily bread, and forgive us our trespasses, as we forgive those who trespass against us; and lead us not into temptation, but deliver us from evil. Or: Alternate musical settings of the Lord's Prayer may be sung. We speak to God, our Father in the Words Jesus taught us. The Lord's Prayer sums up all the petitions that have preceded and knocks at the door of the banquet of the Kingdom that communion anticipates. In the Our Father, we ask for our daily bread, the bread that gives access to eternity, the bread of Life. For this purpose, we beg forgiveness of our sins as we forgive others so that "holy things may be given to the holy."

With hands extended, the Priest alone continues, saying: Deliver us, Lord, we pray, from every evil, graciously grant peace in our days, that, by the help of your mercy, we may be always free from sin and safe from all distress, as we await the blessed hope and the coming of our Savior, Jesus Christ. He joins his hands. The people conclude the prayer, acclaiming: For the kingdom, the power and the glory are yours now and forever.

b) The Sign of Peace; Then the Priest, with hands extended, says aloud: Lord Jesus Christ, who said to your Apostles: Peace I leave you, my peace I give you; look not on our sins, but on the faith of your Church, and graciously grant her peace and unity in accordance with your will. He joins his hands. Who live and reign forever and ever. The people reply: Amen. The Priest, turned towards the people, extending and then joining his hands, adds: The peace of the Lord be with you always. The people reply: And with your spirit. Then, if appropriate, the Deacon, or the Priest, adds: Let us offer each other the sign of peace. And all offer one another a sign, in keeping with local customs, that expresses peace, communion, and charity. The Priest gives the sign of peace to a Deacon or minister.

c) The breaking of the Bread: Then he takes the host, breaks it over the paten, and places a small piece in the chalice, saying quietly: May this mingling of the Body and Blood of our Lord Jesus Christ bring eternal life to us who receive it. Meanwhile the following is sung or said: Lamb of God, you take away the sins of the world, have mercy on us. Lamb of God, you take away the sins of the world, have mercy on us. Lamb of God, you take away the sins of the world, grant us peace. Or: The invocation may even be repeated several times if the fraction is prolonged. Only the final time, however, is grant us peace said. Then the Priest, with hands joined, says quietly: Lord Jesus Christ, Son of the living God, who, by the will of the Father and the work of the Holy Spirit, through your Death gave life to the world, free me by this, your most holy Body and Blood, from all my sins and from every evil; keep me always faithful to your commandments, and never let me be parted from you. Or: May the receiving of your Body and Blood, Lord Jesus Christ, not bring me to judgment and condemnation, but through your loving mercy be for me protection in mind and body and a healing remedy.

d) Receiving Holy Communion: We receive the Body and Blood of Jesus. The Priest genuflects, takes the host and, holding it slightly raised above the paten or above the chalice, while facing the people, says aloud: Behold the Lamb of God, behold him who takes away the sins of the world. Blessed are those called to the supper of the Lamb. And together with the people he adds once: Lord, I am not worthy that you should enter under my roof, but only say the word and my soul shall be healed. The Priest, facing the altar, says quietly: May the Body of Christ keep me safe for eternal life. And he reverently consumes the Body of Christ. Then he takes the chalice and says quietly: May the Blood of Christ keep me safe for eternal life. And he reverently consumes the Blood of Christ. After this, he takes the paten or ciborium and approaches the communicants. The Priest raises a host slightly and shows it to each of the communicants, saying: The Body of Christ. The communicant replies: Amen. And receives Holy Communion. If a Deacon also distributes Holy Communion, he does so in the same manner. If any are present who are to receive Holy Communion under both kinds, the rite described in the proper place is to be followed. While the Priest is receiving the Body of Christ, the Communion Chant begins.

5) The Concluding Rites:

When the distribution of Communion is over, the Priest or a Deacon or an acolyte purifies the paten over the chalice and also the chalice itself. While he carries out the purification, the Priest says quietly: What has passed our lips as food, O Lord, may we possess in purity of heart, that what has been given to us in time may be our healing for eternity. Then the Priest may return to the chair. If appropriate, a sacred silence may be observed for a while, or a psalm or other canticle of praise or a hymn may be sung. Then, standing at the altar or at the chair and facing the people, with hands joined, the Priest says: Let us pray. All pray in silence with the Priest for a while, unless silence has just been observed. Then the Priest, with hands extended, says the Prayer after Communion, at the end of which the people acclaim: Amen..

a) The Blessing: We receive God's Blessing. If they are necessary, any brief announcements to the people follow here. Then the dismissal takes place. The Priest, facing the people and extending his hands, says: The Lord be with you. The people reply: And with your spirit. The Priest blesses the people, saying: May almighty God bless you, the Father, and the Son, and the Holy Spirit. The people reply: Amen. On certain days or occasions, this formula of blessing is preceded, in accordance with the rubrics, by another more solemn formula of blessing or by a prayer over the people. In a Pontifical Mass, the celebrant receives the miter and, extending his hands, says: The Lord be with you. All reply: And with your spirit. The celebrant says: Blessed be the name of the Lord. All reply: Now and forever. The celebrant says: Our help is in the name of the Lord. All reply: Who made heaven and earth. Then the celebrant receives the pastoral staff, if he uses it, and says: May almighty God bless you, making the Sign of the Cross over the people three times, he adds: the Father, and the Son, and the Holy Spirit. All: Amen. Then the Deacon, or the Priest himself, with hands joined and facing the people, says: Go forth, the Mass is ended. Or: Go and announce the Gospel of the Lord. Or: Go in peace, glorifying the Lord by your life. Or: Go in peace. The people reply: Thanks be to God. Then the Priest venerates the altar as usual with a kiss, as at the beginning. After making a profound bow with the ministers, he withdraws. If any liturgical action follows immediately, the rites of dismissal are omitted.

b) The Recessional: We conclude our celebration with song. The recessional usually takes place with a song that expresses praise or reflects the particular day or season. This song is our farewell to the ministers at the altar for being helpful in reenacting and re-presenting the wondrous mystery of the Mass. Then we depart to try to apply the Eucharist to our lives. # Now it is the time for us to leave to do good works, to praise and bless the Lord in our daily lives.

NORMS

1) In General

a) Arrangement of Liturgical Furnishings

The provision of furnishings for the celebration of Mass must be in complete accord with the requirements of the liturgical books. This is also true of the requirements for the altar, the ambo and the chair for the priest celebrant, use of which should neither be omitted nor duplicated. There is to be only one altar, one ambo and one chair for the priest celebrant.

b) Orientation

All televised Masses will be celebrated in such a way that when the priest is standing at the altar he is facing the faithful (versus populum). This practice, currently observed in all but a relatively few parishes throughout the dioceses of the United States, has proved its pastoral effectiveness. Any confusion caused by a television Mass at variance with the practice of the diocesan bishop will thus be avoided.

c) Live vs. Prerecorded Celebrations

Whenever possible, the liturgy should be telecast live. When, for serious reasons, this is not possible, consideration may be given to prerecording the liturgy. A liturgy that is prerecorded for delayed telecast should be taped as it is celebrated in a local worshiping community and then be telecast at a later time on the same day. If the transmission is not simultaneous with the actual celebration, that fact should be made plain to the viewers. Only when neither of these options is possible should the liturgy be taped in advance in a setting other than that of a regularly scheduled liturgy celebrated by a local worshiping community. In order to reflect the integrity of the liturgical year, a prerecorded liturgy should be taped on a date as close as possible to the date of the actual telecast. In order to preserve the sacred character of the liturgical celebration, only one celebration of the Mass should be recorded on a given day with the same group of people.

d) Time Constraints

The celebration of the liturgy should not be rushed nor should elements of the liturgy be omitted. Those responsible for planning, production and for presiding at the celebration need to be sensitive to the requirements of the liturgy as well as the time constraints of television. For the integrity of the liturgy, those who produce a delayed television broadcast of the celebration should be strongly discouraged from editing out parts of the Mass (e.g., the Gloria, one of the readings) or introducing musical or other elements not present at the original celebration. Planning and the careful choice of options can help to keep the celebration within a particular time frame.

e) Participation

In human terms, no other single factor affects the liturgy as much as the attitude, style and bearing of the celebrant. Therefore, the priest who is to preside at a televised liturgy should be carefully chosen and should take pains to ensure that he is prepared for this special work. Since the liturgy is the work of Christ and the work of the church, the televised Mass should always be celebrated within a living community of God's people whose presence reveals the full, conscious and active participation of the faithful. Even when the liturgy to be televised is taped apart from a regularly scheduled liturgy, there should always be a group of people present who participate in the liturgy as fully as possible by their prayer, song and presence. Their participation must be considered as being of prime importance, a goal which may be achieved by seating the assembly in such a way as to foster a sense of community and by the choice of liturgical music which is easily sung and known to the faithful present.

f) Liturgical Music

Music is very important in televising liturgical celebrations. The televised Mass should normally include the sung acclamations, i.e., Alleluia, Holy, Holy, Memorial Acclamation and Great Amen. If acclamations are to be sung in Latin, the text and/ or the music should be available to the faithful so they might have an opportunity for full and active participation in the liturgy. Ideally, the responsorial psalm should also be sung. Other appropriate songs may be sung in accordance with guidelines found in Music in Catholic Worship and Liturgical Music Today. Additional musical selections should correspond to their placement in the liturgy and not simply be used as occasions for performance. The use of prerecorded music, even to accompany the congregation's singing, is not appropriate for the liturgy.

g) Legitimate Diversity

In order that all may be nourished by the rich and beautiful treasures of the Roman Missal, full use of the various options provided in the order of Mass should be utilized. This is particularly true of the penitential rite and the choice of Eucharistic prayers, including the memorial acclamation. The traditional use of incense and of the blessing and sprinkling of holy water should be encouraged at least on occasion.

h) Visual Elements and the Privacy of Persons

As much as possible, the televised image should concentrate on the action of the rite. When the priest prays, the camera should show him praying. When the reader reads, the camera should show the reader reading. Extended shots of sacred images accompanied by the disembodied voice of the priest or the reader are to be avoided. The photographing of the faces of communicants as they ask for God's forgiveness in the penitential rite, receive holy communion or make their thanksgiving after holy communion is likewise inappropriate since it can infringe on their privacy at a highly personal moment of spiritual reflection.

i) Gestures

Only the gestures prescribed by the Roman Missal may be used at Mass. The introduction of extraneous gestures is to be strongly discouraged, especially given the importance assumed by televised Masses and public models for the celebration of the Eucharist. If the tabernacle is located in the sanctuary, the priest and ministers are to revere the reposed sacrament with a genuflection at the beginning and the end of Mass and when they approach it to remove or reserve the reserved sacrament at communion. No other reverence of the reserved blessed sacrament is called for in the course of the Mass.

j) Entrance Rites

The entrance procession, entrance song and introductory rites are to be followed precisely as they are described in the order of Mass. The Book of Gospels may be carried by the deacon or, in his absence, by the reader in the entrance procession. The Lectionary is never carried in procession.

k) Liturgy of the Word

Readings from sacred Scripture and the chants between the readings form the main part of the Liturgy of the Word. The homily, profession of faith and general intercessions or prayer of the faithful expand and complete this part of the Mass.

—Only the approved Lectionary for Mass for use in the dioceses of the United States may be used for the proclamation of the scriptural readings. Whenever there are several readings, a different reader should preferably proclaim each reading so as to bring out more clearly the differences in the text.

—Since the homily is an integral part of the liturgy and necessary for the nurturing of the Christian life, there should be a homily during a televised Mass. The homilist needs to be sensitive to the needs of the gathered assembly and of those who will be viewing the telecast. The homily should always be based on the scriptural or liturgical texts of the Mass and must not be preoccupied with non-liturgical and non-scriptural sectarian political subjects or other extraneous considerations. The character of the homily should be "a proclamation of God's wonderful works in the history of salvation, the mystery of Christ, ever made present and active within us, especially in the celebration of the liturgy." The requirements of the liturgical books regarding the Prayer of the Faithful are to be carefully followed. The priest should introduce the petitions and pray the closing prayer, while a deacon or a lay minister should offer the petitions themselves. The petitions should be short, universal in character and reflective of the broad needs of the church as laid down in the rubrics. The final prayer, after the petitions, is addressed to the Father. It should not be substituted with any prayer or petition otherwise directed.

l) Liturgy of the Eucharist

"At the Last Supper Christ instituted the sacrifice and paschal meal that make the sacrifice of the cross to be continuously present in the church, when the priest, representing Christ the Lord, carries out what the Lord did and handed over to his disciples to do in his memory."

—The use of Latin in a predominantly English-language Mass is appropriate when the meaning of the Latin text in question is understood by participants. The Eucharistic Prayer should be in English throughout in order to assist the faithful in their understanding and to emphasize the unity of the prayer from the introductory dialogue through the doxology. If on some special occasion the Eucharistic Prayer is used in Latin, that language should be used throughout, and in any case the bishop should be consulted previously.

The faithful are to receive holy communion which has been consecrated during the same Mass at which they are participants.
—In accord with liturgical law, the choice of the communicant to receive "on the tongue" or "in the hand" is to be respected absolutely. In the light of the faculties received by the conference of bishops, communicants are never to be obliged concerning the manner of reception of holy communion. The purification of vessels should take place in a timely manner at the side of the altar or at a side table. Sacred vessels are never purified at the center of the altar. # These norms are intended to apply to all Masses produced, televised or taped for later broadcast in the Diocese of Birmingham in Alabama. Given on the feast of the Chair of St. Peter the apostle, in the jubilee year of the birth of our Lord, Feb. 22, 2000.

Chapter 8 Prayers before Communion (영성체 전 드리는 기도)

A. Act of Faith

Lord Jesus Christ, I firmly believe that You are present in this Blessed Sacrament as true God and true Man, with Your Body, Blood, Soul and Divinity. My redeemer and my judge, I adore Your divine majesty together with the angels and saints. I believe, O Lord; increase my faith. Amen.

B. Act of Hope

Good Jesus, in You alone I place all my hope. You are my salvation and my strength, the source of all good. Through your mercy, through Your passion and death, I hope to obtain the pardon of my sins, the grace of final perseverance, and a happy eternity. Amen

C. Act of Contrition

O my Savior, I am truly sorry for having offended You because You are infinitely good and sin displeases You. I detest all the sins of my life and I desire to atone for them. Through the merits of Your precious Blood, wash me of all stain of sin, so that, cleansed in body and soul, I may worthily approach the Most Holy Sacrament of the altar. Amen.

D. Act of Desire

Jesus, my God and my all, my soul longs for You. My heart yearns to receive You in Holy Communion. Come, Bread of Heaven and Food of angels, to nourish my soul and to rejoice my heart. Come, most lovable Friend of my soul, to inflame me with such love that I may never again be separated from You. Amen.

E. Act of Love

Jesus, my God, I love You with my whole heart and above all things, because You are the one supreme Good and an infinitely perfect Being. You have given Your life for me, a poor sinner, and in Your mercy You have even offered Yourself as food for my soul. My God, I love You. Inflame my heart so that I may love You more. Amen. # Prayer source: Copyright of (A), (B), (C), (D) and (E) ©2003, 1997 by Catholic Book Publishing Corp., N.J. All rights reserved.

F. Act of Humility

O Divine Lord, how shall I dare approach Thee, who have so often offended Thee? Lord, Who art Thou, and who am I? Indeed, I know well who Thou art, that Thou give Thyself to me; but O Lord, I am not worthy that Thou should enter under my roof, yet speak only the word and my soul shall be healed. Amen. # Prayer source: From e-Catholic 2000. Catholics Online for the Third Millennium.

Chapter 9 Prayers after Communion (영성체 후 드리는 기도)

A. Act of Faith

Jesus, I firmly believe that You are present within me as God and Man, to enrich my soul with graces and to fill my heart with the happiness of the blessed. I believe that You are Christ, the Son of the living God! Amen.

B. Act of Adoration

With deepest humility, I adore You, my Lord and God; You have made my soul Your dwelling place. I adore You as my Creator from Whose hands I came and with Whom I long to be happy forever. Amen.

C. Act of Love

Dear Jesus, I love You with my whole heart, my whole soul, and all my strength. May the love of Your own Sacred Heart fill my soul and purify it so that I may die to the world for love of You, as You died on the Cross for love of me. My God, You are all mine; grant that I may be all Yours in time and in eternity. Amen.

D. Act of Thanksgiving

From the depths of my heart I thank You, dear Lord, for Your infinite kindness in coming to me. How good You are to me! With Your most holy Mother and all the angels, I praise Your mercy and generosity toward me, a poor sinner. I thank You for nourishing my soul with Your Sacred Body and precious Blood. I will try to show my gratitude to You in the Sacrament of Your love, by obedience to Your holy commandments, by fidelity to my duties, by kindness to my neighbor, and by an earnest endeavor to become like You in my daily conduct. Amen.

E. Prayer to Christ the King

O Christ Jesus, I acknowledge You as King of the universe. All that has been created has been made for You. Exercise upon me all Your rights. I renew my baptismal promises, renouncing Satan and all his works and promises. I promise to live a good Christian life and to be diligent in furthering the interests and teachings of Almighty God and Your Church. Amen.

F. The Holy Cross Prayer(성 십자가 기도)

Lord Jesus, from the height of Your throne of suffering You reveal the depth of Your love for us. Lifted up from the world on the Cross, You draw everyone to Yourself. The Cross is both the symbol and the act by which You raised up the world from all its sin and weakness. But You also ask for our cooperation. Help us to die to self so that we may live for You and our fellow human beings. Set us free from the slavery of our passions, our prejudices, and our selfishness. Enable us to endure the pains and trials of this life and really help to change the world in our own small way. Keep before our minds the conviction that in the Cross is salvation and life as well as defense against our enemies. Through the Cross heavenly grace is given us, our minds are strengthened, and we experience spiritual joy. In the Cross is the height of virtue and the perfection of all sanctity. Let us take up our cross, and follow You through earthly sorrow into eternal happiness in heaven. Amen. #Prayer source: Copyright of (from A to F) ©2003, 1997 by Catholic Book Publishing Corp., N.J. All rights reserved.

G. Prayer to Jesus Christ Crucified

Behold, O kind and most sweet Jesus, I cast myself upon my knees in Your sight, and with the most fervent desire of my soul I pray and beseech You that You would impress upon my heart lively sentiments of Faith, Hope and Charity, with true repentance for my sins, and a firm desire of amendment, while with deep affection and grief of soul I ponder within myself and mentally contemplate Your five most precious wounds; having before my eyes that which David spoke in prophecy of You, O good Jesus; They have pierced My hands and feet; they have numbered all My bones. Amen. # No Copyright©. Prayer Source: (1)Catholic Book Publishing

Corp., N.J. (2)Holy Lent by Eileen O'Callaghan, The Liturgical Press, Collegeville, Minnesota, 1975.

H. Prayer after Communion

May these mysteries, O Lord, in which we have participated, profit us, we pray, for even now, as we walk amid passing things, You teach us by them to love the things of heaven and hold fast to what endures. Through Christ our Lord. Amen. # Copyright ©2010 United States Conference of Catholic Bishops, Washington, D.C. Used with permission. All rights reserved.

I. Radiating Christ

Dear Jesus, help us to spread Your fragrance everywhere we go. Flood our souls with Your spirit and life. Penetrate and possess our whole being so utterly, that our lives may only be a radiance of Yours. Shine through us and be so in us, that every soul we come in contact with may feel Your presence in our soul. Let them look up and see no longer us but only Jesus! Stay with us and then we shall begin to shine, as You shine; so to shine as to be a light to others; the light O Jesus, will be all from You, none of it will be ours; it will be You shining on others through us. Let us thus praise You in the way You love best, by shining on those around us. Let us preach You by our words and by our example, by the catching force, the sympathetic influence of what we do, the evident fullness of the love our hearts bear to You. Amen. # This Prayer is adapted by St. Mother Teresa of Calcutta. Originally this prayer was written by John Henry Cardinal Newman, theologian and cardinal, Founder of the London Oratory from England(1801-1890) beautified in 2010 by Pope Benedict XVI.

J. Anima Christi; Prayer to our Redeemer; Refer to Chapter 10 Eucharistic Adoration # 2 (성체조배 2 양식). B. Meditation and Adoration (4).

The author of Anima Christi, according to the traditional prayer from the Roman Missal, is unknown. It has often been attributed to St. Ignatius of Loyola (1491-1556), for it was indeed a favorite of his and it appears at the beginning of his Spiritual Exercises. However, he could not have been its author for a copy of the prayer appears in a document from 1334, a good century and a half before St. Ignatius was born. Others have attributed it to Blessed Bernadine of Feltre (1439-1494), but again the prayer was around for at least a century before his time as well. The prayer is also known as the Prayer of St. Patrick and some scholars formerly placed the prayer's composition in seventh century Ireland. This too seems unlikely, since no copy that early is known to exist. The prayer carries a partial indulgence.

K. Thanksgiving

I give Thee thanks, Holy Lord, Father Almighty, everlasting God, Who has vouchsafed to feed me, a sinner, Thine unworthy servant, for no merits of my own, but only out of the goodness of Thy great mercy, with the precious Body and Blood of Thy Son, our Lord Jesus Christ; and I pray Thee, that this holy Communion may be to me, not guilt for punishment, but a saving intercession for pardon. Let it be to me an armor of faith and a shield of good will. Let it be to me a casting out of vices; a driving away of all evil desires and fleshly lusts; an increase in charity, patience, humility, obedience, and all virtues; a firm defense against the plots of all my enemies, both seen and unseen; a perfect quieting of all motions of sin, both in my flesh and in my spirit; a firm cleaving unto Thee, the only and true God, and a happy ending to my life. And I pray Thee to deign to bring me, a sinner, to that ineffable Feast, where Thou art with Thy Son and the Holy Spirit, art to Thy holy ones true light, full satisfaction, everlasting joy, consummate pleasure and perfect happiness. Amen. This prayer was written by St. Thomas Aquinas(1225-1274).

Chapter 10 Eucharistic Adoration # 1(성체조배 # 1 양식)

A. Opening Prayer(Eucharistic Adoration Opening Prayer):

O Lord, thank you for this hour of Eucharistic devotion. It comes as a time of peace, recollection, and healing. How privileged I am to spend an hour with you! It makes me feel like the apostles and the disciples who were able to speak quietly with you along the road, perhaps sitting under a tree in the evening.

What am I to say to you? You know everything about me. You know all my needs, all my failings and even my good intentions. In this hour I adore you as the infinite and Holy One of God. You and the Father are one and you have promised that we will be one in you. I give you thanks for all the blessings of my life which I so seldom think of. I thank you for life itself, material and spiritual.

I ask your forgiveness and healing for all my shortcomings and sins; all the times that unthinkingly I have failed you and fallen short of the grace that you gave me. And finally I place before you confidently everyone that I care about, every concern that I have, every need of my life. I promise to trust you no matter what happens to me. You will bring good out of even the worst of it. I do not ask you to change what is to be. Rather, in whatever there is to be, let me find your will, your holiness, and your opportunity for me to grow. I will try to say, "I know that you are with me." Finally, I direct my life, my desires, my hopes, to you, not only for myself but for all whom I care about and for the whole world. May your Kingdom come. May your Holy Spirit be with us. Send him constantly to us as you promised you would at the last Supper. As I look it this mysterious sign, the white host, my eyes tell me nothing of who is there, but faith affirms in my heart that you, my Lord and God, are there. I thank you for this precious gift of faith. Amen.

B. A visit at the start of the day

Jesus, the day begins, a new opportunity, a clean slate, new work to be done. The day is not yet marred by my weakness and distraction, by my impatience and self-love. It is fresh and new, your gift to me. I am so grateful this morning to be in your Eucharistic presence. It is like your apostles waking up to find themselves along the road in Galilee, perhaps having slept near you under a tree or in the shelter of an old building. I look at the tabernacle, toward its glowing candles. Your shining presence there invites me to a new day, to start afresh. Your love in giving me your Eucharistic presence, which is just as real as your presence at Nazareth, fills me with great confidence as the day begins. I ask you to come with me when I leave this church, when duty and responsibility call me forth to begin the day. I ask you to be the unseen presence in all that I do. I am well aware that I will not do it well, that there will be many shortcomings, perhaps even sins. But you put up with your apostles and disciples. Even when you called them to task you also forgave them. Come with me and call me back on the path by your providence. But especially be with me that I may show to others a small reflection of the wealth that you give us by being with us at the beginning of every day until the end of the world. Amen.

B-1. A visit during the day

O Lord Jesus Christ, this day is very busy. I am distracted and pulled in many directions. There are concerns, worries, even fears. I am troubled about duties, failures, things to do that are beyond me. I come to your presence from the din of life, the noise of the street, from the pleas and demands of others. And you are here. For a moment I am with you by the Sea of Galilee, on the Mount of Beatitudes, looking at the serene water and the green hills. You say, "Come to me, all you who are weary and find life burdensome, and I will refresh you." Your presence in the Eucharist reassures me that this is true. You will be with me when I leave the chapel, but then I will not know where to turn my eyes or how to lift my heart. But here I know. Your signature is on all of creation, on the world about us. But it is often impossible for me to read. But here in the silence I am with you. You invited your disciples, "Come apart and rest a while." I am here. Give me, in these few moments, the fullness of your Spirit that I may know that you are with me, that I may go back to the tasks of life assured that you are beside me. Then I shall be at peace to do your will.

Amen.

B-2. A visit at the end of the day

O Divine Master, I come before you as the evening shadows gather and the day ends. This day is like so many others; your presence, your gifts and the opportunities of your grace have been marred by my failings, by my self-centeredness. I have failed others today. I have responded in no way in proportion to the immense graces that you have given me. But here you are waiting for me in your silent presence! It is both a motive for contrition and a motive for hope. You wait for me in silence. You wait for each one. Even notorious sinners can come and kneel before your tabernacle. Jesus, you are the Father of the poor. You are the one who forgives the sinner. I come and place my day before you and again I know I shall be healed. I am absolutely sure of your forgiving love because you have chosen to be with us, every morning, every day, every evening until, finally, the last evening of this world comes and we pass from this place of change and time to the endless day of your divine presence. I place before you all who will die this day. Send your Holy Spirit upon them all. I place before you all of my family and my friends. Guide and enlighten each of us. I entrust to you all who have need of conversion. Take my tomorrow into your wounded hands and I will be able to rest securely. Amen.

C. Adoro Te Devote by St. Thomas Aquinas(성 토마스의 성체 찬미가)

Hidden God, devoutly I adore Thee, truly present underneath these veils; All my heart subdues itself before Thee; Since it all before Thee faints and fails. Not to sight, or taste or touch be credit, Hearing only do we trust secure; I believe, for God the Son has said it- Word of Truth that ever shall endure. On the Cross was veiled Thy Godhead's splendor, here Thy Manhood lies hidden too; Unto both alike my faith I render, and, as sued the contrite thief I sue. Though I look not on Thy wounds, with Thomas, Thee, my Lord, and Thee, my God I call; Make me more and more believe Thy promise, hope in Thee, and love Thee over all. O Memorial of my Savior dying, Living bread, that gives life to man; May my soul, its life from Thee supplying, taste Thy sweetness, as on earth it can. Deign, O Jesus, Pelican of heaven, me, a sinner, in Thy Blood to lave, to a single drop of which is given, all the world from all its sin to save.

Contemplating, Lord, Thy hidden presence, grant me what I thirst for and implore, in the revelation of Thine essence to behold Thy glory evermore. Amen.

D. Te Deum(성 암브로시오 사은 찬미가)

O God, we praise Thee, and acknowledge Thee to be the supreme Lord. Everlasting Father, all the earth worships Thee. All the Angels, the heavens and all angelic powers, all the Cherubim and Seraphim, continuously cry to Thee: Holy, Holy, Holy, Lord God of Hosts!

Heaven and earth are full of the Majesty of Thy glory. The glorious choir of the apostles, the wonderful company of prophets, the white-robed army of martyrs, praise Thee. Holy Church throughout the world acknowledges Thee: The Father of infinite Majesty; Thy adorable, true and only Son; Also the Holy Spirit, the Comforter. O Christ, Thou art the King of glory! Thou art the everlasting Son of the Father. When Thou took it upon Thyself to deliver man, Thou didst not disdain the Virgin's womb. Having overcome the sting of death, Thou opened the Kingdom of Heaven to all believers. Thou sit at the right hand of God in the glory of the Father. We believe that Thou will come to be our Judge. We, therefore, beg Thee to help Thy servants whom Thou hast redeemed with Thy Precious Blood. Let them be numbered with Thy Saints in everlasting glory.

V. Save Thy people, O Lord, and bless Thy inheritance!
R. Govern them, and raise them up forever.
V. Every day we thank Thee.
R. And we praise Thy Name forever, yes, forever and ever.
V. O Lord, deign to keep us from sin this day.
R. Have mercy on us, O Lord, have mercy on us.
V. Let Thy mercy, O Lord, be upon us, for we have hoped in Thee.
R. O Lord, in Thee I have put my trust; let me never be put to shame. Amen.

E. Thanksgiving # Please refer to Chapter 8 (K)

F. Act of Reparation to the Sacred Heart of Jesus

Adorable Heart of Jesus, glowing with love for us and inflamed with zeal for our salvation: O Sacred Heart! ever sensible of our misery and the wretchedness to which our sins have reduced us, infinitely rich in mercy to heal the wounds of our souls, behold us humbly prostrate before you to express the sorrow that fills our hearts for the coldness and indifference with which we have so long requited the numberless benefits that you have conferred upon us. With a deep sense of the outrages that have been heaped upon you by our sins and the sins of others, we come to make a solemn reparation of honor to your most sacred majesty. It was our sins that overwhelmed your Heart with bitterness; it was the weight of our iniquities that pressed down your face to the earth in the Garden of Olives, and caused you to expire in anguish and agony on the cross. But now, repenting and sorrowful, we cast ourselves at your feet, and implore forgiveness. Adorable Heart of Jesus, source of true contrition and ever merciful to the penitent sinner, impart to our hearts the spirit of penance, and give to our eyes a fountain of tears, that we may sincerely bewail our sins now and for the rest of our days. Oh, would that we could blot them out, even with our blood! Pardon them, O Lord, in your mercy, and pardon and convert to you all that have committed irreverence and sacrileges against you in the sacrament of your love, and thus give another proof that your mercy is above all your works. Divine Jesus, with you there are mercy and plentiful redemption, deliver us from our sins, accept the sincere desire we now entertain, and our holy resolution, relying on your assistance of your grace, henceforth to be faithful to you. And in order to repair the sins of ingratitude by which we have grieved your most tender and loving Heart, we are resolved in the future ever to love and honor you in the most adorable Sacrament of the Altar, where you art ever present to hear and grant our petitions, and to be the food and life of our souls. Be you, O compassionate Jesus, our Mediator with your heavenly Father, Whom we have so grievously offended, strengthen our weakness, confirm these our resolutions of amendment, and as your Sacred Heart is our refuge and our hope when we have sinned, so may it be the strength and support of our repentance, that nothing in life or death may ever again separate us from you. Amen. # This prayer was written by Saint Margaret Mary Alacoque.

F-1. Act of Consecration to the Sacred Heart of Jesus

I give myself and consecrate to the Sacred Heart of our Lord Jesus Christ, my person and my life, my actions, pains and sufferings, so that I may be unwilling to make use of any part of my being other than to honor, love and glorify the Sacred Heart. This is my unchanging purpose, namely, to be all His, and to do all things for the love of Him, at the same time renouncing with all my heart whatever is displeasing to Him. I therefore take You, O Sacred heart, to be the only object of my love, the guardian of my life, my assurance of salvation, the remedy of my weakness and inconstancy, the atonement for all the faults of my life and my sure refuge at the hour of death. Be, then, O Heart of goodness, my justification before God the Father, and turn away from me the strokes of his righteous anger. O Heart of love, I put all my confidence in You, for I fear everything from my own wickedness and frailty, but I hope for all things from Your goodness and bounty. Remove from me all that can displease You or resist Your holy will; let Your pure love imprint Your image so deeply upon my heart, that I shall never be able to forget You or to be separated from You. May I obtain from all Your loving kindness the grace of having my name written in Your Heart, for in You I desire to place all my happiness and glory, living and dying in bondage to You. Amen. # This prayer was written by St. Margaret Mary Alacoque.

F-2. Act of Reparation to the Sacred Heart of Jesus

Most sweet Jesus, whose overflowing charity for men is requited by so much forgetfulness, negligence and contempt, behold us prostrate before Thy altar eager to repair by a special act of homage the cruel indifference and injuries, to which Thy loving Heart is everywhere subject. Mindful alas! that we ourselves have had a share in such great indignities, which we now deplore from the depths of our hearts, we humbly ask Thy pardon and declare our readiness to atone by voluntary expiation not only for our own personal offenses, but also for the sins of those, who straying far from the path of salvation, refuse in their obstinate infidelity to follow Thee, their Shepherd and Leader, or, renouncing the vows of their baptism, have cast off the sweet yoke of Thy law. We are now resolved to expiate each and every deplorable outrage committed against Thee; we are determined to make amends for the manifold offenses against Christian modesty in unbecoming dress and behavior, for all the foul seduction laid to ensnare the feet of the innocent, for the frequent violation of Sundays and holidays, and the shocking blasphemies uttered against Thee and Thy Saints. We wish also to make amends for the insults to which Thy Vicar on earth and Thy priests are subjected, for the profanation, by conscious neglect or terrible acts of sacrilege, of the very Sacrament of Thy divine love; and lastly for the public crimes of nations who resist the rights and the teaching authority of the Church which Thou hast founded. Would, O divine Jesus, we were able to wash away such abominations with our blood! We now offer, in reparation for these violations of Thy divine honor, the satisfaction Thou didst once make to Thy eternal Father on the cross and which Thou dost continue to renew daily on our altars; we offer it in union with the acts of atonement of Thy Virgin Mother and all the Saints and of the pious faithful on earth; and we sincerely promise to make reparation, as far as we can with the help of Thy grace, for all neglect of Thy great love and for the sins we and others have committed in the past. Henceforth, we will live a life of unwavering faith, of purity of conduct, of perfect observance of the precepts of the gospel and especially that of charity. We promise to the best of our power to prevent others from offending Thee and to bring as many as possible to follow Thee. O loving Jesus, through the intercession of the Blessed Virgin Mary our model in reparation, deign to receive the voluntary offering we make of this act of expiation; and by the crowning gift of perseverance keep us faithful unto death in our duty and the allegiance we owe to Thee, so that we may all one day come to that happy home, where Thou with the Father and the Holy Spirit live and reign, one God, forever and ever. Amen. # This prayer was originally prescribed by Pope Pius XI to be recited on the feast of The Most Sacred Heart of Jesus.

G. An Act of Adoration and Reparation to Jesus in the Blessed Sacrament

(I) I adore Thee profoundly, O my Jesus, in Thy sacramental form; I acknowledge Thee to be true God and true Man, and by this act of adoration I intend to atone for the coldness of so many Christians who pass before Thy churches and sometimes before the very Tabernacle in which Thou art pleased to remain at all hours with loving impatience to give Thyself to Thy faithful people, and do not so much as bend the knee before Thee, and who, by their indifference proclaim that they grow weary of this heavenly manna, like the people of Israel in the wilderness. I offer Thee in reparation for this grievous negligence, the Most Precious Blood which Thou didst shed from Thy five wounds, and especially from Thy sacred Side, and entering therein, I repeat a thousand times with true recollection of spirit:

O Sacrament most holy! O Sacrament divine!
All praise and all thanksgiving be every moment Thine.
Our Father, Hail Mary, Glory Be.

(II) Profoundly I adore Thee, my Jesus; I acknowledge Thy presence in the Blessed Sacrament, and by this act of adoration I intend to atone for the carelessness of so many Christians who see Thee carried to poor sick people to strengthen them for the great journey to eternity, and leave Thee unescorted, nay, who scarcely give Thee any outward marks of reverence. I offer Thee in reparation for such coldness, the Most Precious Blood which Thou didst shed from Thy five wounds and especially from Thy sacred Side, and entering therein I say again and again with my heart full of devotion:

O Sacrament most holy! O Sacrament divine!
All praise and all thanksgiving be every moment Thine.
Our Father, Hail Mary, Glory Be.

(III) Profoundly I adore Thee, my Jesus, true Bread of life eternal, and by my adoration I intend to compensate Thee for the many wounds which Thy Heart suffers daily in the profaning of churches where Thou art pleased to dwell beneath the sacramental veils to be adored and loved by all Thy faithful people; and in reparation for so many acts of irreverence, I offer Thee the Most Precious Blood which Thou didst shed from Thy five wounds and especially from Thy sacred Side, and entering therein with recollected spirit I repeat every instant:

O Sacrament most holy! O Sacrament divine!
All praise and all thanksgiving be every moment Thine.
Our Father, Hail Mary, Glory Be.

(IV) Profoundly I adore Thee, my Jesus, the living Bread which cometh down from heaven, and by this act of adoration, I intend to atone for all the many acts of irreverence which are committed all day long by Thy faithful when they assist at Holy Mass, wherein through Thine exceeding love Thou dost renew in an unbloody manner the self-same sacrifice which Thou didst once offer on Calvary for our salvation. I offer Thee in atonement for such base ingratitude the Most Precious Blood which Thou didst shed from Thy five wounds and especially from Thy sacred Side, and entering therein with sincere devotion, I unite my voice to that of the angels who stand around Thee in adoration, saying with them:

O Sacrament most holy! O Sacrament divine!
All praise and all thanksgiving be every moment Thine.
Our Father, Hail Mary, Glory Be.

(V) Profoundly I adore Thee, my Jesus, true Victim of expiation for our sins, and I offer Thee this act of adoration to atone for the sacrilegious outrages Thou dost suffer from so many ungrateful Christians who dare to draw near to receive Thee with mortal sin upon their souls. In reparation for such hateful sacrileges I offer Thee the last drops of Thy Most Precious Blood, which Thou didst shed from Thy sacred wounds and especially from the wound in Thy sacred Side, and entering therein with a devout heart, I adore Thee, I bless and I love Thee, and I repeat with all the hearts who are devoted to the Blessed Sacrament:

O Sacrament most holy! O Sacrament divine!
All praise and all thanksgiving be every moment Thine.
Our Father, Hail Mary, Glory Be.

Chapter 11 Eucharistic Adoration # 2(성체조배 # 2 양식)

A. Beginning(Opening) Prayer

O Lord, Who is always with us, I believe firmly that You are here in person in the form of the Eucharist. Like meeting You face to face, grant me to see You and to bless You blissfully. Let me realize true love and forgiveness, and understand the mysteries of the cross.

Lord, I am not worthy for You but I kneel and implore You to forgive all my faults committed against You and against my neighbors. Warm my cold mind with the flaming love of Your Sacred Heart.

Lord, allow me peace and happiness that You give those who follow and serve You as Lord. Lord, my wish is to live with You always. Grant me my wish that I may give You glory and praise. Amen.

A-1 Beginning (Opening) Prayer

O Lord, I come before You here in the Eucharist. First of all, thank You for this hour of Eucharistic adoration. In this hour I adore You as the infinite and Holy One God. I believe in my heart and openly profess that the Blessed Sacrament placed upon the monstrance are by the mystery of the sacred prayer and the words of the Redeemer substantially changed into the true and life-giving Flesh and Blood of Jesus Christ Our Lord. On the cross was veiled Your Godhead's splendor, here Your manhood lies hidden too. But now I believe that You are looking at me and listening to my prayers. You are so great and so holy, I adore You. You have given us everything, I thank You always. But I have sinned against You and against my neighbors, and I ask Your pardon with heart full of sorrow, repentance and contrition. I also pledge to redirect my life, my desires and my hopes to You. You are rich in mercy; I ask You grant me all the graces that will help me draw closer to You. Amen.

B. Meditation and Adoration

(1) Meaning of the Eucharist

Since it was the will of God's only-begotten Son that human beings should share in His Divinity, He assumed our nature in order that by becoming human He might make humans gods. Moreover, when He took our flesh He dedicated the whole of its substance to our salvation. He offered His Body to God the Father on the altar of the cross as a sacrifice for our reconciliation. He shed His Blood for our ransom and purification, so that we might be redeemed from our wretched state of bondage and cleansed from all sin. But to ensure that the memory of so great a gift would abide with us forever, He left His Body as food and His Blood as drink for the faithful to consume in the form of bread and wine. O precious and wonderful banquet that brings us salvation and contains all sweetness! Could anything be of more intrinsic value? Under the old law it was the flesh of calves and goats that was offered, but here Christ Himself, the true God, is set before us as our food. What could be more wonderful than this? No other Sacrament has greater healing power; through it sins are purged away, virtues are increased, and the soul is enriched with an abundance of every spiritual gift. It is offered in the Church for the living and the dead, so that what was instituted for the salvation of all may benefit all. Yet, in the end, no one can fully express the sweetness of this Sacrament, in which spiritual delight is tasted at its source, and in which we renew the memory of that surpassing love for us, which Christ revealed in His passion. It was to impress the vastness of this love more firmly upon the hearts of the faithful that our Lord instituted this Sacrament at the Last Supper. As He was on the point of leaving the world to go to the Father, after celebrating the Passover with His disciples, He left it as a perpetual Memorial of His Passion. It was the fulfillment of ancient figures and the greatest of all His miracles, while for those who were to experience the sorrow of His departure, it was destined to be a unique and abiding consolation.
This was composed by St. Thomas Aquinas(AD 1225-1274).

(2) O sacred banquet

O sacred banquet, wherein Christ is received, the memory of His Passion is renewed, the mind is filled with grace, and the pledge of future glory is given us. # This prayer was composed by St. Thomas Aquinas(AD 1225-1274).

(3) The Divine Praises

Blessed be God.

Blessed be His Holy Name.

Blessed be Jesus Christ, true God and true Man.

Blessed be the Name of Jesus.

Blessed be His Most Sacred Heart.

Blessed be His Most Precious Blood.

Blessed be Jesus in the Most Holy Sacrament of the Altar.

Blessed be the Holy Spirit, the Paraclete.

Blessed be the great Mother of God, Mary most Holy.

Blessed be her Holy and Immaculate Conception.

Blessed be her Glorious Assumption.

Blessed be the name of Mary, Virgin and Mother.

Blessed be St. Joseph, her most chaste spouse.

Blessed be God in His Angels and in His Saints. Amen.

The Divine Praises traditionally follows the Benediction of the Blessed Sacrament at Church when it is prayed by the priest and the worshippers before our Lord (in the Host) is returned to the tabernacle following adoration. It was composed in a slightly shorter form by Luigi Felici, a Jesuit priest, in 1797, as a prayer to make reparation for blasphemy and profane language. You can recite it privately (or in group settings other than during the Benediction) for this purpose as a great way to show God, the Holy Family, and the Angels and Saints thanksgiving and praise. In an era when many people only refer to our Lord in an exclamatory fashion after some sort of accident, it is good for us to sing His Divine Praises here. As we say in the introduction to the Eucharistic prayer at Mass "it is right to give Him thanks and praise!" Saint Thomas Aquinas once noted that this can increase the fervor of our devotion to Him, and that thus "we praise God not for His benefit but for ours." This prayer reminds us of the glories of the Trinity, and of the key role our Blessed Mother, St. Joseph, and the angels and saints have played in our salvation as well.

(4) Anima Christi

Soul of Christ, sanctify me. Body of Christ, save me. Blood of Christ, inebriate me.

Water from the side of Christ, wash me. Passion of Christ, strengthen me. O good Jesus, hear me. Within Your wounds hide me. Separated from You, let me never be. From the evil one protect me. At the hour of my death, call me. And close to you bid me; that with Your saints, I may be praising You forever and ever. Amen.

(5) Litany of the Most Precious Blood

Lord, have mercy. Lord, have mercy.

Christ, have mercy. Christ, have mercy.

Lord, have mercy. Lord, have mercy.

Christ, hear us. Christ, graciously hear us.

God our Father in Heaven, Have mercy on us.

God the Son, Redeemer of the world, Have mercy on us.

God the Holy Spirit, Have mercy on us.

Holy Trinity, One God, Have mercy on us.

Blood of Christ, only Son of the Father, save us(be our salvation).

Blood of Christ, Incarnate Word of God, save us.

Blood of Christ, of the new and Eternal Covenant, save us.

Blood of Christ, falling upon the earth in the Agony, save us.

Blood of Christ, shed profusely in the Scourging, save us.

Blood of Christ, flowing forth in the Crowning with Thorns, save us.

Blood of Christ, poured out on the Cross, save us.

Blood of Christ, Price of our salvation, save us.

Blood of Christ, without which there is no forgiveness, save us.

Blood of Christ, Eucharistic drink and refreshment of souls, save us.

Blood of Christ, river of mercy, save us.

Blood of Christ, Victor over demons, save us.

Blood of Christ, Courage of martyrs, save us.

Blood of Christ, Strength of confessors, save us.

Blood of Christ, bringing forth virgins, save us.

Blood of Christ, Help of those in peril, save us.

Blood of Christ, Relief of the burdened, save us.

Blood of Christ, Solace in sorrow, save us.

Blood of Christ, Hope of the penitent, save us.

Blood of Christ, consolation of the dying, save us.

Blood of Christ, Peace and Tenderness of hearts, save us.

Blood of Christ, Pledge of Eternal Life, save us.

Blood of Christ, freeing souls from Purgatory, save us.

Blood of Christ, most worthy of all glory and honor, save us.

Lamb of God, Who takes away the sins of the world, Have mercy on us. Lamb of God, Who takes away the sins of the world, Have mercy on us. Lamb of God, Who takes away the sins of the world, Have mercy on us.

V. Lord, You redeemed us by Your Blood,

R. And You have made us a kingdom.

Let us pray.

Father, by the blood of your Son you have set us free and saved us from death. Continue your work of love within us, that by constantly celebrating the mystery of our salvation we may reach the eternal life it promises. We ask this through Christ our Lord. Amen. # This litany clearly traces the line of salvation history through a series of biblical references and passages. In its present form it was approved by St. Pope John XXIII on February 24, 1960.

(6) Litany of the Holy Name of Jesus

V. Lord, have mercy on us.

R. Christ, have mercy on us.

V. Lord, have mercy on us. Jesus, hear us.

R. Jesus, graciously hear us.

V. God the Father of Heaven

R. Have mercy on us.

V. God the Son, Redeemer of the world,

R. Have mercy on us.

V. God the Holy Spirit,

R. Have mercy on us.

V. Holy Trinity, one God,

R. Have mercy on us.

V. Jesus, Son of the living God, R. Have mercy on us.

Jesus, splendor of the Father, [etc.]

Jesus, brightness of eternal light.

Jesus, King of glory.

Jesus, sun of justice.

Jesus, Son of the Virgin Mary.

Jesus, most amiable.

Jesus, most admirable.

Jesus, the mighty God.

Jesus, Father of the world to come.

Jesus, angel of great counsel.

Jesus, most powerful.

Jesus, most patient.

Jesus, most obedient.

Jesus, meek and humble of heart.

Jesus, lover of chastity.

Jesus, lover of us.

Jesus, God of peace.

Jesus, author of life.

Jesus, example of virtues.

Jesus, zealous lover of souls.

Jesus, our God.

Jesus, our refuge.

Jesus, father of the poor.

Jesus, treasure of the faithful.

Jesus, good Shepherd.

Jesus, true light.

Jesus, eternal wisdom.

Jesus, infinite goodness.

Jesus, our way and our life.

Jesus, joy of Angels.

Jesus, King of the Patriarchs.

Jesus, Master of the Apostles.

Jesus, teacher of the Evangelists.

Jesus, strength of Martyrs.

Jesus, light of Confessors.

Jesus, purity of Virgins.

Jesus, crown of Saints.

V. Be merciful, R. spare us, O Jesus.

V. Be merciful, R. graciously hear us, O Jesus.

V. From all evil, R. deliver us, O Jesus.

From all sin, deliver us, O Jesus.

From Your wrath,

From the snares of the devil.

From the spirit of fornication.

From everlasting death.

From the neglect of Your inspirations.

By the mystery of Your holy Incarnation.

By Your Nativity.

By Your Infancy.

By Your most divine Life.

By Your labors.

By Your agony and passion.

By Your cross and dereliction.

By Your sufferings.

By Your death and burial.

By Your Resurrection.

By Your Ascension.

By Your institution of the most Holy Eucharist.

By Your joys.

By Your glory.

V. Lamb of God, who takes away the sins of the world,

R. spare us, O Jesus.

V. Lamb of God, who takes away the sins of the world,

R. graciously hear us, O Jesus.

V. Lamb of God, who takes away the sins of the world,

R. have mercy on us, O Jesus.

V. Jesus, hear us.

R. Jesus, graciously hear us.

Let us pray:

O Lord Jesus Christ, You have said, "Ask and you shall receive, seek, and you shall find, knock, and it shall be opened to you." Grant, we beg of You, to us who ask it, the gift of Your most divine love, that we may ever love You with our whole heart, in word and deed, and never cease praising You. Give us, O Lord, as much a lasting fear as a lasting love of Your Holy Name, for You, who live and are King forever and ever, never fail to govern those whom You have solidly established in Your love. Amen.

(7) Litany of the Sacred Heart of Jesus

Lord, have mercy	Lord, have mercy
Christ, have mercy	Christ, have mercy
Lord, have mercy	Lord, have mercy
God our Father in heaven	have mercy on us
God the Son, Redeemer of the world	have mercy on us
God the Holy Spirit	have mercy on us
Holy Trinity, one God	have mercy on us
Heart of Jesus, Son of the eternal Father	have mercy on us
Heart of Jesus, formed by the Holy Spirit in the womb of the Virgin Mother	have mercy on us
Heart of Jesus, one with the eternal Word	have mercy on us
Heart of Jesus, infinite in majesty	have mercy on us
Heart of Jesus, holy temple of God	have mercy on us
Heart of Jesus, tabernacle of the Most High	have mercy on us
Heart of Jesus, house of God and gate of heaven	have mercy on us
Heart of Jesus, aflame with love for us	have mercy on us
Heart of Jesus, source of justice and love	have mercy on us
Heart of Jesus, full of goodness and love	have mercy on us
Heart of Jesus, well-spring of all virtue	have mercy on us
Heart of Jesus, worthy of all praise	have mercy on us
Heart of Jesus, king and center of all hearts	have mercy on us

Heart of Jesus, treasure-house of wisdom and knowledge	have mercy on us
Heart of Jesus, in whom there dwells the fullness of God	have mercy on us
Heart of Jesus, in whom the Father is well pleased	have mercy on us
Heart of Jesus, from whose fullness we have all received	have mercy on us
Heart of Jesus, desire of the eternal hills	have mercy on us
Heart of Jesus, patient and full of mercy	have mercy on us
Heart of Jesus, generous to all who turn to you	have mercy on us
Heart of Jesus, fountain of life and holiness	have mercy on us
Heart of Jesus, atonement for our sins	have mercy on us
Heart of Jesus, overwhelmed with insults	have mercy on us
Heart of Jesus, broken for our sins	have mercy on us
Heart of Jesus, obedient even to death	have mercy on us
Heart of Jesus, pierced by a lance	have mercy on us
Heart of Jesus, source of all consolation	have mercy on us
Heart of Jesus, our life and resurrection	have mercy on us
Heart of Jesus, our peace and reconciliation have mercy on us	
Heart of Jesus, victim of our sins	have mercy on us
Heart of Jesus, salvation of all who trust in you	have mercy on us
Heart of Jesus, hope of all who die in you	have mercy on us
Heart of Jesus, delight of all the saints	have mercy on us
Lamb of God, you take away the sins of the world	have mercy on us
Lamb of God, you take away the sins of the world	have mercy on us
Lamb of God, you take away the sins of the world	have mercy on us
Jesus, gentle and humble of heart.	Touch our hearts and make them like your own.

Let us pray:

Father, we rejoice in the gifts of love we have received from the Heart of Jesus your Son. Open our hearts to share his life and continue to bless us with his love. We ask this in the name of Jesus the Lord. Amen. # In 1899 Pope Leo XIII approved this Litany of the Sacred Heart of Jesus for public use. This litany is actually a synthesis of several other litanies dating back to the 17th century. Father Croiset composed a litany in 1691 from which 17 invocations were used by Venerable Anne Madeleine Remuzat when she composed her litany in 1718 at Marseille. She joined an additional 10 invocations to those of Father Croiset, for a total of 27 invocations. Six more invocations written by Sister Madeleine Joly of Dijon in 1686 were added by the Sacred Congregation for Rites when it was approved for public use in 1899. This makes a total of 33 invocations, one for each year of life of our Lord Jesus Christ. A partial indulgence is attached to this litany.

(8) Litany of the Holy Eucharist

Lord, have mercy	Lord, have mercy
Christ, have mercy	Christ, have mercy
Lord, have mercy	Lord, have mercy
Jesus, the Most High	have mercy on us
Jesus, the holy One	have mercy on us
Jesus, Word of God	have mercy on us
Jesus, only Son of the Father	have mercy on us
Jesus, Son of Mary	have mercy on us
Jesus, crucified for us	have mercy on us
Jesus, risen from the dead	have mercy on us
Jesus, reigning in glory	have mercy on us
Jesus, coming in glory	have mercy on us
Jesus, our Lord	have mercy on us
Jesus, our hope	have mercy on us
Jesus, our peace	have mercy on us
Jesus, our Savior	have mercy on us
Jesus, our salvation	have mercy on us
Jesus, our resurrection	have mercy on us
Jesus, Judge of all	have mercy on us

Jesus, Lord of the Church	have mercy on us
Jesus, Lord of creation	have mercy on us
Jesus, Lover of all	have mercy on us
Jesus, life of the world	have mercy on us
Jesus, freedom for the imprisoned	have mercy on us
Jesus, joy of the sorrowing	have mercy on us
Jesus, giver of the Spirit	have mercy on us
Jesus, giver of good gifts	have mercy on us
Jesus, source of new life	have mercy on us
Jesus, Lord of life	have mercy on us
Jesus, eternal high priest	have mercy on us
Jesus, priest and victim	have mercy on us
Jesus, true Shepherd	have mercy on us
Jesus, true Light	have mercy on us
Jesus, bread of heaven	have mercy on us
Jesus, bread of life	have mercy on us
Jesus, bread of thanksgiving	have mercy on us
Jesus, life-giving bread	have mercy on us
Jesus, holy manna	have mercy on us
Jesus, new covenant	have mercy on us
Jesus, food for everlasting life	have mercy on us
Jesus, food for our journey	have mercy on us
Jesus, holy banquet	have mercy on us
Jesus, true sacrifice	have mercy on us
Jesus, perfect sacrifice	have mercy on us
Jesus, eternal sacrifice	have mercy on us
Jesus, divine Victim	have mercy on us
Jesus, Mediator of the new covenant	have mercy on us
Jesus, mystery of the altar	have mercy on us
Jesus, medicine of immortality	have mercy on us
Jesus, pledge of eternal glory	have mercy on us

Jesus, Lamb of God, you take away the sins of the world, have mercy on us

Jesus, Bearer of our sins, you take away the sins of the world, have mercy on us

Jesus, Redeemer of the world, you take away the sins of the world, have mercy on us

Christig hear us
Christ, graciously hear us
Lord Jesus, hear our prayer

Christ, hear us
Christ, graciously hear us
Lord Jesus, hear our prayer.

Let us pray:

Lord our God, in this great Sacrament we come into the presence of Jesus Christ, your Son, born of the Virgin Mary and crucified for our salvation. May we who declare our faith in this fountain of love and mercy drink from it the water of everlasting life. Amen.

(9) Act of Adoration

We adore You, Most Holy Lord, Jesus Christ, here and in all the churches of the world, and we bless You because by Your Cross You have redeemed the world. Have mercy on us. Amen. # This prayer was written by St. Francis of Assisi.

(10) Act of faith in the Divine Eucharist

I believe in my heart and openly profess that the bread and wine which are placed upon the altar are by the mystery of the sacred prayer and the words of the Redeemer substantially changed into the true and life-giving Flesh and Blood of Jesus Christ Our Lord and after the Consecration there is present the true Body of Christ which was born of the Virgin Mary and offered up for the salvation of the world, hung upon the Cross, and now sits at the right hand of the Father and there is present the true Blood of Christ which flowed from his side. They are present not only by means of a sign and of the efficacy of the Sacrament, but also in the very reality and truth of their nature and substance. Amen. # This prayer was written by St. Gregory VII.

(11) Desire for closer union

Lord Jesus Christ, pierce my soul with your love so that I may always long for you alone, who are the bread of angels and the fulfillment of the soul's deepest desires. May my heart always hunger and feed upon you so that my soul may be filled with the sweetness of your presence. May my soul thirst for you, who are the source of life, wisdom, knowledge, light and all the riches of God our Father. May I always seek and find you, think upon you, speak to you and do all things for honor and glory of your holy name. Be always my only hope, my peace, my refuge and my help in whom my heart is rooted so that I may never be separated from you. # This prayer was written by St. Bonaventure.

(12) Prayer before the reception of the Eucharist

O Lord Jesus Christ, Son of the Living God, who according to the will of the Father and with the cooperation of the Holy Spirit hast by Thy death given life unto the world, I adore and revere this Thy Holy Body and this Thy Holy Blood which was given over and poured forth for the many unto the remission of sins. O merciful Lord, I beg of Thy mercy that through the power of this Sacrament, Thou wilt make me one of that many. Through faith and love make me feel the power of these Sacraments so I may experience their saving power. Absolve and free from all sin and punishment of sin of Thy servants, Thy handmaids, myself, all who have confessed their sins to the priest, those whom I have promised or am obliged to pray for, and so too those who themselves hope or beg to be helped by my prayers with Thee. Make our Church rejoice in Thy constant protection and consolation. Amen. # This prayer was written by St. Anselm(AD 1033-1109).

(13) Support for Families

O Living Bread, that came down from heaven to give life to the world! O loving shepherd of our souls, from your throne of glory whence, a "hidden God", you pour out your grace upon families and peoples, we commend to you particularly the sick, the unhappy, the poor and all who beg for food and employment, imploring for all and every one the assistance of your providence; we commend to you the families, so that they may be fruitful centers of Christian life. May the abundance of your grace be poured over all. Amen.

(14) Food for service

O Jesus, present in the Sacrament of the altar, teach all the nations to serve you with willing hearts, knowing that to serve God is to reign. May Your Sacrament, O Jesus, be light to the mind, strength to the will, joy to the heart. May it be the support of the weak, the comfort of the suffering, the wayfaring bread of salvation for the dying and for all the pledge of future glory. Amen. # The prayers of (13) and (14) were written by St. Pope John XXIII(1881-1963).

(15) Prayer for a visit to the Blessed Sacrament

My Lord Jesus Christ, who for the love which You bear us, remain night and day in this Sacrament full of compassion and love, awaiting, calling, and welcoming all who come to visit You; I believe that You are present in the Sacrament of the altar; I adore You from the abyss of my own nothingness, and I thank You for all the graces You have bestowed upon me; and especially for having given me Yourself in this Sacrament, for having given me Your most holy Mother Mary as my Advocate; and for having called me to visit You in this church. I now salute Your most loving Heart; and this for three intentions: first, in thanksgiving for this great gift; secondly, to make amends to You for all the outrages which You receive in this Sacrament from all Your enemies; thirdly, I intend by this visit to adore You in all the places on earth in which You are present in this Sacrament and in which You are the least reserved and the most abandoned. My Jesus, I love You with all my heart. I grieve for having hitherto so many times offended Your infinite goodness. I purpose with the help of Your grace never more to offend You in the future; and at this moment, miserable and unworthy though I am, I consecrate myself wholly to You without reserve. I give You renounce my entire will, all my affections, all my desires, and all that I possess. Henceforward, dispose of me and of all that I have as You please. All that I ask of You and desire is Your holy love, final perseverance and the perfect accomplishment of Your will. I recommend to You the souls in purgatory, and especially those who had the greatest devotion to the most Blessed Sacrament and to the Most Blessed Virgin Mary. I also recommend to You all poor sinners. Finally, my dear Savior, I unite all my affections with the affections of Your most loving Heart, and I offer them, thus united, to Your eternal Father, and I pray Him in Your name to vouchsafe for your love, to accept and grant them. Amen. # This prayer was written by St. Alphonsus Liguori(1696-1787).

(16) Visit to the Blessed Sacrament before Meditation

I place myself in the presence of Him, in whose Incarnate Presence I am before I place myself there. I adore You, O my Savior, present here as God and as man, in soul and in body, in true flesh and blood. I acknowledge and confess that I kneel before that Sacred Humanity, which was conceived in Mary's womb, and lay in Mary's bosom; which grew up to twelve, wrought miracles, and spoke words of wisdom and peace; which in due season hung on the cross, lay in the tomb, rose from the dead, and now reigns in heaven. I praise, and bless, and give myself wholly to Him, who is the true Bread of my soul, and my everlasting joy. Amen. # This prayer was written by Blessed John Henry Cardinal Newman(1801-1890).

(17) How good it is to love You

My Jesus, from all eternity you were pleased to give yourself to us in love. And you planted within us a deep spiritual desire that can only be satisfied by yourself. I may go from here to the other end of the world, from one country to another, from riches to greater riches, from pleasure to pleasure, and still I shall not be content. All the world cannot satisfy the immortal soul. It would be like trying to feed a starving man with a single grain of wheat. We can only be satisfied by setting our hearts, imperfect as they are, on you. We are made to love you; you created us as your lovers. It sometimes happens that the more we know a neighbor, the less we love him. But with you it is quite the opposite. The more we know you, the more we love you. Knowledge of you kindles such a fire in our souls that we have no energy left for worldly desires. My Jesus, how good it is to love you. Let me be like your disciples on Mount Tabor, seeing nothing else but you. Let us be like two bosom friends, neither of whom can ever bear to offend the other. Amen. # This prayer was written by St. Jean-Baptiste Marie Vianney(1786-1859).

(18) Dedication to Jesus - St. Ignatius Loyola(1491-1556)

Lord Jesus Christ, take all my freedom, my memory, my understanding and my will. All that I have and cherish you have given me. I surrender it all to be guided by your will. Your love and your grace are wealth enough for me. Give me these, Lord Jesus, and I ask for nothing more. Amen.(Translation ©1973, ICEL. All rights reserved).

C. Closing Prayer; Prayer after the Eucharist Adoration

O Sacred Heart of Jesus, warm my cold mind with the heat of Your love and lighten my mind from darkness. Strengthen my will. Help me serve for the salvation of our neighbors by lightening my footsteps. Grant me to be a good neighbor of those who are shedding tears and trembling in loneliness in desperate situations. Lord of love, look down upon me with mercy, I beg You, prostrating myself before You, and send me Your eyes of love. You read my inner heart and know my problems and hopes. Strengthen my weak will and grant me to give You praise and glory by loving You more each day. Amen.

Glossary

Adoration

The adoration means that we acknowledge God as God, Creator and Savior, the Lord and Master of everything that exists. Also, we acknowledge God as infinite and merciful Love. Through worship and prayer, the Church and individual persons give to God the adoration which is the first act of the virtue of religion. The first commandment of the law obliges us to adore God. Adoration is the first attitude of man acknowledging that he is a creature before his creator. It exalts the greatness of the Lord who made us (Ps. 95, 1-6) and the almighty power of the savior who sets us free from evil. Adoration is homage of the spirit to the "King of Glory"(Ps. 24, 9-10), respectful silence in the presence of the "ever greater" God (cf. St. Augustine, En and Ps. 62, 1-6). Adoration of the thrice-holy and sovereign God of love blends with humility and gives assurance of our supplications. True adoration involves a docile heart, an assent to God's sovereignty over our lives, a constant posture of humility before Him, and gifts of love offered in homage.

Bless

Blessing expresses the basic movement of Christian prayer: it is an encounter between God and man. In blessing, God's gift and man's acceptance of it are united in dialogue with each other. The prayer of blessing is man's response to God's gifts: because God blesses, the human heart can in return bless the One who is the source of every blessing. Two fundamental forms express this movement: our prayer of blessing ascends in the Holy Spirit through Christ to the Father--we bless him for having blessed us (Eph 1, 3-14); it implores the grace of the Holy Spirit that descends through Christ from the Father--he blesses us (2 Cor 13, 14 and Rom 15, 5-6). Bless means praise, glorify, pronounce words in a religious rite to confer or invoke divine favor upon, held in reverence, honored in worship, highly favored or fortunate. This word has a variety of meanings in the sacred writings: It has taken in a sense that is synonymous with praise; thus the Psalmist, "I will bless the Lord at all times, His praise shall be always in my mouth"(Ps. 34, 2). Sun and moon, bless the Lord; praise and exalt him above all forever.(Daniel 3, 62). It is used to express a wish or desire that all good fortune, especially of a spiritual or supernatural kind, may go with the person or thing, as the Psalmist says: What your hands provide you will enjoy; you will be blessed and prosper.(Ps. 128, 2). It signifies the sanctification or dedication of a person or thing to some sacred purpose; While they were eating, Jesus took bread, said the blessing, broke it, and giving it to his disciples said, "Take and eat; this is my body." (Matthew 26:26). Finally it is employed to designate a gift so Naaman addresses Elisha: "Now I know that there is no God in all the earth, except in Israel. Please accept a gift(blessing) from your servant." (2 Kings 5:15).

Praise

Praise is the form of prayer which recognizes most immediately that God is God. It lauds God for his own sake and gives him glory, quite beyond what he does, but simply because HE IS. It shares in the blessed happiness of the pure of heart who love God in faith before seeing him in glory. By praise, the Spirit is joined to our spirits to bear witness that we are children of God, (Rom 8, 16) testifying to the only Son in whom we are adopted and by whom we glorify the Father. Praise embraces the other forms of prayer and carries them toward him who are all things and for whom we exist (1 Cor 8, 6).

Worship

Worship means that adoration and honor given to God, which is the first act of the virtue of religion. "You shall worship the Lord your God, and him only shall you serve," says Jesus, citing Deuteronomy (Lk 4, 8 and Deut 6, 13). Public worship is given to God in the Church by the celebration of the Paschal Mystery of Christ in the liturgy. One of the great errors in modern worship is making it worshiper centered. Worship is to be centered on praising God, not entertaining ourselves: Enter, let us bow down in worship; let us kneel before the LORD who made us (Ps 95, 6). The primary Hebrew word for worship: Shachah; to depress, i.e. prostrate (in homage to royalty or God); bow (self) down, crouch, fall down (flat), humbly beseech, do (make) obedience, do reverence, make to stoop, worship. Three Greek words: (a). Proskuneo; meaning to kiss, like a dog licking his master's hand, to fawn or crouch to, homage (do reverence to, adore): worship. It occurs 59 times in the New Testament. It originally carried with it the idea of subjects falling down to kiss the ground before a king or kiss their feet. (b). Sebomai; to reverence, hold in awe. It was used10 times in the New Testament. (c). Latreuo; to render religious service of homage. Also used 21 times in the New Testament.

Chapter 12 The Holy Hour (성시간)

A. The Holy Hour (성시간)

The following Holy Hour is a model and is based on the ritual book Holy Communion and Worship of the Eucharist Outside of Mass, which should be followed in all respects.

1) Entrance hymn or processional chant is sung.

2) Exposition and Incense Offering

After the entrance song or processional chant was sung, O Salutaris Hostia or another suitable song may be sung while the minister prepares the Holy Eucharist for adoration.

O Salutaris Hostia:
O saving Victim, open wide the gate of Heaven to man below; Our foes press on from every side; Your aid supply; Your strength bestow. To your great name be endless praise; Immortal Godhead, One in Three; O grant us endless length of days in our true native land with thee. Amen. # O Salutaris Hostia was translated from Latin to English by Edward Caswall(1814-1878). Caswall's father was Robert Clarke Caswall (Perpetual Curate of Yateley, and later Vicar of West Lavington, Wiltshire). His mother was a niece of Thomas Burgess, Bishop of St. David and later of Salisbury. Caswall attended Chigwell Grammar School in Essex, Marlborough School, and Brasenose College, Oxford, where he graduated with honors in 1836. Before leaving Oxford, he published, under the pseudonym of Scriblerus Redivivus, The Art of Pluck, in imitation of Aristotle, a satire on the ways of the careless college student. In 1838, Caswall was ordained a deacon, and 1839 an Anglican priest. In 1840 he became perpetual curate at Stratford-sub-Castle near Salisbury. By 1847, though, he had switched to Roman Catholicism and went to the Oratory of St. Philip Neri at Edgbaston, where he did most of his hymn work. Caswall is best remembered

as a translator of ancient hymns, though he also wrote original lyrics. His works include:
- Sketches of Young Ladies
- Morals from the Church Yard, 1838

3) After the Sign of the Cross, the minister tells the purpose of the Holy Hour.

4) Beginning(Opening) Prayer:

O Lord, thank you for this hour of Eucharistic devotion. It comes as a time of peace, recollection, and healing. How privileged I am to spend an hour with you! It makes me feel like the apostles and the disciples who were able to speak quietly with you along the road, perhaps sitting under a tree in the evening.

What am I to say to you? You know everything about me. You know all my needs, all my failings and even my good intentions. In this hour I adore you as the infinite and Holy One of God. You and the Father are one and you have promised that we will be one in you. I give you thanks for all the blessings of my life which I so seldom think of. I thank you for life itself, material and spiritual.

I ask Your forgiveness and healing for all my shortcomings and sins; all the times that unthinkingly I have failed you and fallen short of the grace that you gave me. And finally I place before you confidently everyone that I care about, every concern that I have, every need of my life. I promise to trust you no matter what happens to me. You will bring good out of even the worst of it. I do not ask you to change what is to be. Rather, in whatever there is to be, let me find your will, your holiness, and your opportunity for me to grow. I will try to say, "I know that you are with me." Finally, I direct my life, my desires, my hopes, to you, not only for myself but for all whom I care about and for the whole world. May your Kingdom come. May your Holy Spirit be with us. Send him constantly to us as you promised you would at the last Supper. As I look it this mysterious sign, the white host, my eyes tell me nothing of who is there, but faith affirms in my heart that you, my Lord and God, are there. I thank you for this precious gift of faith. Amen. Or other suitable prayer prepared by the minister.

5) Liturgy of the Word

- First Reading
- Responsorial Song or Psalm
- Gospel Acclamation
- Gospel
- Homily

6) Adoration: The faithful sit.

(a) Meditation; A prayer of silence, reflection and meditation.

(b) Adoro Te Devote by St. Thomas Aquinas(성 토마스의 성체 찬미가)

Hidden God, devoutly I adore Thee,

Truly present underneath these veils:

All my heart subdues itself before Thee,

Since it all before Thee faints and fails.

Not to sight, or taste, or touch be credit,

Hearing only do we trust secure;

I believe, for God the Son hath said it

Word of Truth that ever shall endure.

On the Cross was veiled Thy Godhead's splendor,

Here Thy manhood lies hidden too;

Unto both alike my faith I render,

And, as sued the contrite thief, I sue.

Though I look not on Thy wounds with Thomas,

Thee, my Lord, and Thee, my God, I call:

Make me more and more believe Thy promise,

Hope in Thee, and love Thee over all.

O Memorial of my Savior dying,

Living Bread that gives life to man;

May my soul, its life from Thee supplying,

Taste Thy sweetness, as on earth it can.

Deign, O Jesus, pelican* of heaven,

Me, a sinner, in Thy Blood to lave,

To a single drop of which is given
All the world from all its sin to save.
Contemplating Lord, Thy hidden presence,
Grant me what I thirst for and implore,
In the revelation of Thine essence
To behold Thy glory evermore. Amen.

(c) Act of Consecration of the Human Race to the Sacred Heart of Jesus(예수 성심께
천하만민을 바치는 기도)

Most sweet Jesus, Redeemer of the human race, look down upon us humbly prostrate before Thy altar. We are Thine, and Thine we wish to be; but, to be more surely united with Thee, behold each one of us freely consecrates himself today to Thy Most Sacred Heart. Many indeed have never known Thee; many too, despising Thy precepts, have rejected Thee. Have mercy on them all, most merciful Jesus, and draw them to Thy Sacred Heart. Be Thou King, O Lord, not only of the faithful who have never forsaken Thee, but also of the prodigal children who have abandoned Thee; grant that they may quickly return to their Father's house lest they die of wretchedness and hunger. Be Thou King of those who are deceived by erroneous opinions, or whom discord keeps aloof; call them back to the harbor of truth and unity of faith, so that soon there may be but one flock and one Shepherd. Be Thou King of all those who are still involved in the darkness of idolatry or of Islamism; refuse not to draw them all into the light and kingdom of God. Turn Thine eyes of mercy toward the children of that race, once Thy chosen people: of old they called down upon themselves the Blood of the Savior; may it now descend upon them a laver of redemption and of life. Grant, O Lord, to Thy Church assurance of freedom and immunity from harm; give peace and order to all nations, and make the earth resound from pole to pole with one cry: Praise to the Divine Heart that wrought our salvation; to It be glory and Honor forever. Amen.

(d) Tantum Ergo: The faithful kneel.
Down in adoration falling,
Lo! the sacred Host we hail(This great Sacrament we hail);
Lo! o'er ancient forms departing(Over ancient forms of worship),
Newer rites of grace prevail;

Faith for all defects supplying(Faith will tell us Christ is present),

Where the feeble senses fail(When our human senses fail).

To the everlasting Father,

And the Son who reigns on high(And the Son who made us free),

With the Holy Spirit proceeding(And the Holy Spirit, God proceeding)

Forth from each eternally(From them Each eternally),

Be salvation, honor, blessing, might and endless majesty. Amen.

7) Incense offering before benediction

8) Song and prayer before benediction

(a) Benediction song:

V. You have given them bread from heaven,

R. Having all delight within it. (Having within it all sweetness.)

(b) Prayer:

Let us pray,

O God, who in this wonderful Sacrament left us a memorial of your Passion: grant, we implore you, that we may so venerate the sacred mysteries of your Body and Blood, as always to be conscious of the fruit of your Redemption. Glory be to the Father, to the Son and to the Holy Spirit. As it was in the beginning, is now, and will be forever. Amen.

Or

Lord Jesus Christ, You gave us Eucharist as the memorial of Your suffering and death. May our worship of this Sacrament of Your Body and Blood help us to experience the salvation You won for us and the peace of the kingdom. Where You live with the Father and the Holy Spirit, one God, forever and ever. Amen.

(At the Eucharistic Blessing of the Holy Hour; If the minister is a priest or deacon, there may be a blessing. Before the Blessing, a prayer such as the above may be said.)

9) Eucharistic Blessing or Benediction of the Blessed Sacrament

10) The Divine Praises

Blessed be God.

Blessed be His Holy Name.

Blessed be Jesus Christ, true God and true Man.

Blessed be the Name of Jesus.

Blessed be His Most Sacred Heart.

Blessed be His Most Precious Blood.

Blessed be Jesus in the Most Holy Sacrament of the Altar.

Blessed be the Holy Spirit, the Paraclete.

Blessed be the great Mother of God, Mary most Holy.

Blessed be her Holy and Immaculate Conception.

Blessed be her Glorious Assumption.

Blessed be the name of Mary, Virgin and Mother.

Blessed be St. Joseph, her most chaste spouse.

Blessed be God in His Angels and in His Saints. Amen.

11) Reposition:

After the benediction and the Divine Draises are finished, the priest places the Blessed Sacrament in the tabernacle.

12) Dismissal hymn

The faithful shall sing "Holy God, we praise thy name" unless the priest designates other hymn.

B. Eucharistic Holy Hour for Divine Mercy Sunday

Cathedrals and parishes throughout the country are encouraged to join together in prayer and adoration seeking God's mercy for ourselves and for our nation for offenses against life, marriage, and religious liberty. The following Holy Hour is a basic model with suggested readings and prayers for this time. Other suitable prayers may be used by the presiding minister.

Procession/Exposition

1) Opening Hymn: "O Salutaris Hostia" or another suitable Eucharistic hymn

2) Opening Prayer

Presiding Minister: Lord our God, in this great sacrament we come into the presence of Jesus Christ, your Son, born of the Virgin Mary and crucified for our salvation. May we who declare our faith in this fountain of love and mercy drink from it the water of everlasting life. Through Christ our Lord. All: Amen.

3) Liturgy of the Word (select 1 or 2 readings and a passage from Luke's Gospel or a similar passage illustrating God's merciful love); #Jon 4:1-11 (Lectionary for Mass: LFM 463) And should I not pity Nineveh? # Psalm 103:1-14 (LFM 377) The Lord is kind and merciful #1 Pt 1:3-9 (LFM 347) The death and resurrection of Jesus has won us the hope of salvation # Eph 2:4-10 (LFM 32).God, who is rich in mercy, brought us to life in Christ # Rom 5:6-11 (LFM 91). Christ died for us while we were still sinners # Lk 15:3-7 (LFM 172) The Parable of the Lost Sheep # Lk 15:1-3, 11-32 (LFM 33) The Parable of the Prodigal Son.

4) Reflection/meditation on God's merciful love for mankind

The Presiding Minister may offer insights on the revelation of God's mercy throughout salvation history—in Scripture, through the writings of saints and, in a particular way, through the revelations recorded in the Diary of St. Faustina Kowalska. Attached is a brief description of Divine Mercy and the origin of devotions and the observance of Divine Mercy Sunday, along with selected quotations.

5) Period of Silent Reflection and Adoration

6) Recitation of the Chaplet of Divine Mercy (A pamphlet or the attached instruction sheet may be made available to congregants to enable full participation in the chaplet.)

7) Intercessions: Presiding Minister: God is the Father of all mercies. In him we place our faith as we pray the following petitions:

Deacon or Lector: For our Holy Father, Pope Francis, bishops, priests, and all the faithful: that each will bear witness to the love and mercy of God; We pray to the Lord: All: Lord, hear our prayer.

For all who have committed grave sin and who are afraid to go to confession: that their fears will dissolve in the face of Jesus's longing to forgive and be reconciled to them; We pray to the Lord: All: Lord, hear our prayer.

For those who serve in public office: that they govern with true compassion for the lives of the most vulnerable among us— especially unborn children, the elderly, and persons with disabilities; We pray to the Lord: All: Lord, hear our prayer.

For parents: that, by their guidance and the witness of their own lives, they will teach their children how to love and forgive when they have been wronged; We pray to the Lord: All: Lord, hear our prayer.

For the protection of conscience rights and religious liberty, and that all people of good will may work together against the increasing threats to these fundamental rights; We pray to the Lord: All: Lord, hear our prayer.

For peace throughout the world, and especially in areas of open conflict: that ancient prejudices and hatreds will be replaced by a spirit of mercy and brotherhood; We pray to the Lord: All: Lord, hear our prayer.

Presiding Minister: Almighty and merciful Father, we give you thanks for all of your many blessings, and we ask you to hear these petitions in the name of your Son, our Lord and Savior Jesus Christ, who lives and reigns with you in the unity of the Holy Spirit, one God, for ever and ever. All: Amen.

8) Benediction

"Tantum ergo" or another suitable Eucharistic hymn is sung as the Presiding Minister incenses the Blessed Sacrament.

(a) Song and prayer before benediction
(b) Benediction song:
V. You have given them bread from heaven,
R. Having all delight within it. (Having within it all sweetness.)

(c) Prayer:

Let us pray,

O God, who in this wonderful Sacrament left us a memorial of your Passion: grant, we implore you, that we may so venerate the sacred mysteries of your Body and Blood, as always to be conscious of the fruit of your Redemption. Glory be to the Father, to the Son and to the Holy Spirit. As it was in the beginning, is now, and will be forever. Amen.

Or

Lord Jesus Christ, You gave us Eucharist as the memorial of Your suffering and death. May our worship of this Sacrament of Your Body and Blood help us to experience the salvation You won for us and the peace of the kingdom. Where You live with the Father and the Holy Spirit, one God, forever and ever. Amen.

(At the Eucharistic Blessing of the Holy Hour; If the minister is a priest or deacon, there may be a blessing. Before the Blessing, a prayer such as the above may be said.)

9) Eucharistic Blessing or Benediction of the Blessed Sacrament

10) Reposition

Divine Praises: Blessed be God. Blessed be his Holy Name. Blessed be Jesus Christ, true God and true man. Blessed be the Name of Jesus. Blessed be his Most Sacred Heart. Blessed be his Most Precious Blood. Blessed be Jesus in the Most Holy Sacrament of the Altar. Blessed be the Holy Spirit, the Paraclete. Blessed be the great Mother of God, Mary most holy. Blessed be her holy and Immaculate Conception. Blessed be her glorious Assumption. Blessed be the name of Mary, Virgin and Mother. Blessed be St. Joseph, her most chaste spouse. Blessed be God in his angels and in his Saints.

11) Closing Hymn; "Holy God, We Praise Thy Name" or another suitable hymn

C. HOW TO PRAY THE CHAPLET OF DIVINE MERCY

Optional Opening Prayers: You expired, Jesus, but the source of life gushed forth for souls, and the ocean of mercy opened up for the whole world. O Fount of Life, unfathomable Divine Mercy, envelop the whole world and empty Yourself out upon us.

(Repeat 3 times) O Blood and Water, which gushed forth from the Heart of Jesus as a fountain of Mercy for us, I trust in You!

Our Father, Hail Mary and the Apostle's Creed

For each of the five decades (On each "Our Father" bead of the rosary, pray) Eternal Father, I offer you the Body and Blood, Soul and Divinity of Your Dearly Beloved Son, Our Lord, Jesus Christ, in atonement for our sins and those of the whole world.

(On each of the 10 "Hail Mary" beads, pray) For the sake of His sorrowful Passion, have mercy on us and on the whole world.

Concluding prayer (Repeat 3 times) Holy God, Holy Mighty One, Holy Immortal One, have mercy on us and on the whole world.

Optional Closing Prayer: Eternal God, in whom mercy is endless and the treasury of compassion inexhaustible, look kindly upon us and increase Your mercy in us, that in difficult moments we might not despair nor become despondent, but with great confidence submit ourselves to Your holy will, which is Love and Mercy itself. Copyright ©2013, United States Conference of Catholic Bishops. All rights reserved.

하느님 자비를 구하는 9일기도 (Divine Mercy Chaplet)

(1) (십자가를 쥐고) 성호경 기도를 바칩니다.

(2) 시작기도: (묵주기도 경우, 전능하신 천주 성부, 신앙고백 다음) 주님의 기도 묵주에서; First Opening Prayer(첫 번째 시작기도Optional선택사항): 예수님, 주님께서는 숨을 거두셨으나, 저희들의 영혼을 구원하시기 위하여 생명의 샘은 세차게 흘러나왔으며, 온 세상을 위하여 바다와 같이 넓고 크신 자비를 베풀어 주셨나이다. 하느님의 자비는 이루 헤아릴 수 없습니다. 오 생명의 샘, 하느님의 자비시여, 온 세상을 자비로 감싸주시고 저희를 위하여 당신 자신을 온전히 비워주소서.

(First Opening Prayer가 끝난 다음)

Second Opening Prayer(두 번째 시작 기도 Optional선택사항): 저희를 위한 자비의 샘, 예수성심에서 세차게 흘러나온, 오 피와 물이시여, 저는 주님의 자비에 의탁하옵니다.

(3) (작은 묵주 3개의 첫 번째 묵주에서) 주님의 기도를 바칩니다.

(4) (작은 묵주 3개의 두 번째 묵주에서) 성모송을 바칩니다.

(5) (작은 묵주 3개의 세 번째 묵주에서) 사도신경을 바칩니다.

(6) (묵주기도 1단) 주님의 기도 묵주 알에서 다음기도를 바칩니다.

영원하신 아버지, 저희가 지은 죄와 온 세상의 죄를 뉘우치는 마음으로, 하느님께서 지극히 사랑하시는 당신 아들 우리 주 예수 그리스도의 몸과 피, 영혼과 신성을 하느님께 바치나이다.

(7) 성모송을 바치는 매 단의 10개의 묵주 알에서 다음 기도문을 바칩니다.

예수님의 고통스러운 수난을 (생각해서라도, 고려해서라도, 위해서라도) 저희와 온 세상에 자비를 베풀어 주시옵소서

(8) 마침기도(This prayer, repeated three times in succession, concludes the Chaplet.)
5단을 모두 바친 후 다음 기도문을 마침 기도로 세 번 바칩니다.

거룩하신 하느님, 거룩하시고 전능하신 하느님, 거룩하시고 영원 불멸하신 하느님, 저희와 온 세상에 자비를 베풀어 주시옵소서.

(9) 추가 마침 기도(선택사항 Optional Additional Closing Prayer):

자비가 끝이 없으시고 무궁무진한 연민의 보고이신 영원하신 하느님, 저희를 어여삐 보시고, 저희에게 대자대비하신 자비를 베푸소서. 그로 인해 저희가 어려울 때에 절망하거나 낙담하지 않게 하시며 크나큰 확신을 가지고 사랑과 자비 그 자체이신 주님의 거룩한 뜻에 순명하게 하소서.

Chapter 13 Prayers to St. Joseph

A. Litany of St. Joseph

Lord, have mercy.	Lord, have mercy.
Christ, have mercy.	Christ, have mercy.
Lord, have mercy.	Lord, have mercy.
Jesus, hear us.	Jesus, graciously hear us.
God, the Father of Heaven,	have mercy on us.
God, the Son, Redeemer of the world,	have mercy on us.
God, the Holy Spirit,	have mercy on us.
Holy Trinity, One God,	have mercy on us.
Holy Mary,	pray for us.
St. Joseph,	pray for us.
Renowned offspring of David,	pray for us.
Light of Patriarchs,	pray for us.
Spouse of the Mother of God,	pray for us.
Chaste guardian of the Virgin,	pray for us.
Foster father of the Son of God,	pray for us.
Diligent protector of Christ,	pray for us.
Head of the Holy Family,	pray for us.
Joseph most just,	pray for us.
Joseph most chaste,	pray for us.
Joseph most prudent,	pray for us.
Joseph most strong,	pray for us.
Joseph most obedient,	pray for us.
Joseph most faithful,	pray for us.
Mirror of patience,	pray for us.
Lover of poverty,	pray for us.
Model of artisans,	pray for us.
Glory of home life,	pray for us.

Guardian of virgins,	pray for us.
Pillar of families,	pray for us.
Solace of the wretched,	pray for us.
Hope of the sick,	pray for us.
Patron of the dying,	pray for us.
Terror of demons,	pray for us.
Protector of Holy Church,	pray for us.

Lamb of God, who takes away the sins of the world,
spare us, O Lord.

Lamb of God, who takes away the sins of the world,
have mercy on us.

Lamb of God, who takes away the sins of the world,
graciously hear us, O Lord.

He made him the lord of his household. And prince over all
his possessions.

Let us pray,

O God, in Your ineffable providence you were pleased to choose Blessed Joseph to be the spouse of Your most Holy Mother; grant, we beg You, that we may be worthy to have him for our intercessor in heaven whom on earth we venerate as our Protector: You who live and reign forever and ever. St. Joseph, pray for us. Amen. # The Litany of Saint Joseph was approved for public use by Pope St. Pius X in 1909. It is modeled after the Litany of Loreto and contains 21 invocations to St. Joseph which describe his virtues and the part he played as the foster father of Jesus. The Litany is approved for public use and has a partial indulgence attached.

B. To Thee, O blessed Joseph or Devotion to St. Joseph or Prayer of Pope Leo XIII to St. Joseph

To you, O blessed Joseph, do we come in our tribulation, and having implored the help of your most holy spouse, we confidently invoke your patronage also. Through that charity which bound you to the Immaculate Virgin Mother of God and through the paternal love with which you embraced the Child Jesus, we humbly beg you graciously to regard the inheritance which Jesus Christ has purchased by his

Blood, and with your power and strength to aid us in our necessities. O most watchful Guardian of the Holy Family, defend the chosen children of Jesus Christ; O most loving father, ward off from us every contagion of error and corrupting influence; O our most mighty protector, be propitious to us and from heaven assist us in our struggle with the power of darkness; and, as once you rescued the Child Jesus from deadly peril, so now protect God's Holy Church from the snares of the enemy and from all adversity; shield, too, each one of us by your constant protection, so that, supported by your example and your aid, we may be able to live piously, to die holily, and to obtain eternal happiness in heaven. Amen. # This prayer was written by Pope Leo XIII, a partial indulgence is attached to this prayer. Prayer source: From the Raccolta #476 & Enchr. #6. The purpose of Pope Leo XIII's encyclical Quamquam Pluries: At a difficult time in the Church's history, Pope Pius IX, wishing to place Her under the powerful patronage of the holy patriarch Joseph, declared him "Patron of the Catholic Church." (Decree Quemadmodum Deus, December 8, 1870.)

C. Memorare to St. Joseph

Remember, O most chaste spouse of the Virgin Mary, that never was it known that anyone who implored your help and sought your intercession was left unassisted. Full of confidence in your power I fly unto you and beg your protection. Despise not, O guardian of the Redeemer, my humble supplication, but in your bounty, hear and answer me. Amen. # Based upon the Memorare to the Blessed Virgin Mary, this prayer was originally composed in Italy.

D. Act of Consecration to St. Joseph

O dearest St. Joseph, I consecrate myself to your honor and give myself to you, that you may always be my father, my protector and my guide in the way of salvation. Obtain for me a greater purity of heart and fervent love of the interior life. After your example may I do all my actions for the greater glory of God, in union with the Divine Heart of Jesus and the Immaculate Heart of Mary. O Blessed St. Joseph, pray for me, that I may share in the peace and joy of your holy death. Amen.

E. Prayer to St. Joseph

O blessed St. Joseph, faithful guardian of my Redeemer, Jesus Christ, protector of thy chaste spouse, the Virgin Mother of God, I choose thee this day to be my special patron and advocate and I firmly resolve to honor thee all the days of my life. Therefore I humbly beseech thee to receive me as thy client, to instruct me in every doubt, to comfort me in every affliction, to obtain for me and for all the knowledge and love of the Heart of Jesus, and finally to defend and protect me at the hour of my death. Amen. # Prayer source of (C) (D) & (E): From Eternal Word Television Network, Inc. Irondale, Alabama. No Copyright ©.

"I know by experience," says St. Teresa of Avila, "that the glorious St. Joseph assists us generally in all necessities. I never asked him for anything which he did not obtain for me."

F. Prayer to St. Joseph

Holy St. Joseph, you were always most just; make us relish what is right. You sustained Jesus and Mary in time of trial; sustain us by your help. You provided for all the needs of Jesus and Mary; help the needy of the whole world. You rescued Jesus from Herod when he sought to kill your child; save us from our many sins. You were the foster-father of Christ, the priest-victim; make priests faithful to their calling. You were the foster-father of Christ, the divine physician; sustain the sick and obtain relief for them. You died the holiest of deaths in the arms of Jesus and Mary; intercede for the dying. You were the intrepid guardian of the Holy Family; protect all Christian families. You cared for Jesus with true fatherly love; protect all children in the world. You were a dedicated an honest worker in your trade as a carpenter; teach us to labor for Jesus. You were the faithful and chaste spouse of the Blessed Virgin Mary; preserve in all hearts a love of fidelity and purity. You were a model single person and a model father later on; help all people to imitate your virtues. Amen. # Prayer source: Ffrom "My pocket prayer book, by Rev. Lawrence G. Lovasik, S.V.D." published by Catholic Book Publishing Corp. (New Jersey, U.S.A. in 2004).

F-1. Prayer For Those with Profound Disabilities

Lord Jesus Christ, You know the pain of brokenness, You took our weaknesses upon Your shoulders and bore it to the wood of the cross. Hear our prayers for our brothers and sisters whose bodies fail them and whose minds are crippled by the ravages of disease. Implant a love for them deep within our hearts, that we, disfigured and disabled by our sin, may treasure and nurture the gifts of their lives. May we find You in their weakness, and console You in our care for them. For You are Lord, forever and ever. Amen. # Prayer source: Eternal Word Television Network, Inc. Irondale, Alabama. & . No Copyright ©

G. Prayer to St. Joseph

St. Joseph, in the popular piety of the Church, has been considered the patron saint of those dying since he himself had the privilege of dying in the arms of Mary and Jesus. Since we all must die, we should cherish a special devotion to St. Joseph, that he may obtain for us a happy death. (St. Alphonsus Ligouri)

O Blessed St. Joseph, you gave your last breath in the loving embrace of Jesus and Mary. When the seal of death shall close my life, come with Jesus and Mary to aid me. Obtain for me this solace for that hour – to die with their holy arms around me. Jesus, Mary and Joseph, I commend my soul, living and dying, into your sacred arms. Amen. Copyright ©2010 United States Conference of Catholic Bishops, Washington, D.C. Used with permission. All rights reserved.

H. Prayer to God to attain the rewards You promised through St. Joseph

O God, Creator of all things, who laid down for the human race the law of work, graciously grant that by the example of St. Joseph and under his patronage we may complete the works you set us to do and attain the rewards You promise. Through our Lord Jesus Christ, Your Son, who lives and reigns with You in the unity of the Holy Spirit, one God, forever and ever. Amen. # Prayer source: From collect; Daily readings of USCCB on May 1, 2017.

I. Prayer to St Joseph in the Holy Month. Prayer to St. Joseph.

성 요셉 성월기도. 성 요셉께 바치는 기도

O blessed St. Joseph, father who reared Jesus Christ, chaste spouse of the Virgin Mary and patron Saint of the dying, we earnestly beg you to pray for us to God that we love our Lord Jesus and faithfully follow Him. Also, defend and protect us at the hour of our death. Amen. # Prayer source: The prayer book of Catholic Bishops Conference of Korea. (Page 30).

J. Prayer to St. Joseph for Protection

O St. Joseph whose protection is so great, so strong, so prompt before the Throne of God, I place in you all my interests and desires. O St. Joseph do assist me by your powerful intercession and obtain for me from your Divine Son all spiritual blessings through Jesus Christ, Our Lord; so that having engaged here below your Heavenly power I may offer my thanksgiving and homage to the most loving of Father. O St. Joseph, I never weary contemplating you and Jesus asleep in your arms. I dare not approach while He reposes near your heart. Press Him in my name and kiss His fine Head for me, and ask Him to return the kiss when I draw my dying breath. St. Joseph, patron of departing souls, pray for us. Amen.

O Blessed St. Joseph, faithful guardian and protector of virgins, to whom God entrusted Jesus and Mary, I implore you by the love which did bear them, to preserve me from every defilement of soul and body, that I may always serve them in holiness and purity of love. Amen. O St. Joseph, foster father of Jesus Christ and true spouse of the Virgin Mary pray for us and for those who will die this day (or night). This prayer was found in the fiftieth year of our Lord and Savior Jesus Christ. In 1500's it was sent by the Pope to Emperor Charles when he was going into battle. Whoever shall read this prayer or hear it or keep it about themselves shall never die a sudden death, or be drowned, nor shall poison take effect on them; neither shall they fall into the hands of the enemy, or shall be burned in any fire or shall be overpowered in battle. Say this prayer for nine mornings for anything you may desire. It has never been known to fail, so be sure you really want what you ask. # Prayer source: From Imprimatur Rev George W. Ahr, Bishop of Trenton.

Chapter 14   Prayers Before and After Reading the Bible

A. Prayers before reading the Bible

Grant me grace, O merciful God to desire ardently all that is pleasing to Thee, to examine it prudently, to acknowledge it truthfully and to accomplish it perfectly, for the praise and glory of Thy name. Amen. # St. Thomas Aquinas was accustomed to recite this prayer and the Bible before the image of Jesus Christ.

(A-1) Prayers before reading the Bible

Let your Scriptures be my chaste delight. O Lord, perfect me and reveal those pages to me! See, your voice is my joy. Give me what I love. May the inner secrets of your words be laid open to me when I knock. This I beg by our Lord Jesus Christ in whom are hidden all the treasures of wisdom and knowledge (Col 2:3). These are the treasures I seek in your books. Amen. # St. Augustine, Confessions, bk 11, ch 2, nos 2-4.

(A-2) Prayer before reading the Bible

Lord, inspire me to read your Scriptures and to meditate upon them day and night. I beg you to give me real understanding of what I need, that I in turn may put its precepts into practice. Yet, I know that understanding and good intentions are worthless, unless rooted in your graceful love. So I ask that the words of Scripture may also be not just signs on a page, but channels of grace into my heart. Amen. (Origin, 184-253 AD) # This prayer was used by Holy Name of Jesus Bible Study in Minnesota.

(A-3) Prayer before reading the Bible

Lord, Who gloriously ascended into heaven as the King of glory, do not leave us alone like an orphan, but send us the Holy Spirit as the Holy Father promised. Lord, we offer You our prayers, grant the Paraclete proceeding from the Holy Son, to enlighten our soul and to seal all truths deeply in it. O God, Father of our Lord

Jesus Christ, grant that Christ would dwell in our hearts through faith that is rooted and grounded in love. Also, let us know the love of Christ that surpasses human knowledge through the fullness of Your glory. Through Christ Our Lord. Amen. Copyright ©2003 by The Bible in 100 weeks in Korea. All rights reserved.

(A-4) Prayer before reading the Bible

God our Father, we praise and thank You for giving us this opportunity to study and grow through Your Holy Word. We ask that You send the Holy Spirit to open our minds and our hearts to receive what You have prepared for us this night. Help us to pass on "The Story" to our families, parishes and communities as we learn to imitate the faith and the obedience of our Mother Mary. May we come to trust You more, as we follow Your Son and Word. Jesus Christ. Amen! # This prayer was written by St. Matthew's Bible Study, Surrey, British Columbia.

(A-5) Prayer before reading the Bible

I am not trying, O Lord, to penetrate your loftiness, for I cannot begin to match my understanding with it, but I desire in some measure to understand your truth, which my heart believes and loves. For I do not seek to understand in order to believe, but I believe in order to understand. For this too I believe, that 'unless I believe, I shall not understand.' Teach me to seek you, and reveal yourself to me as I seek: For unless you instruct me I cannot seek you, and unless you reveal yourself I cannot find you. Let me seek you in desiring you: let me desire you in seeking you. Let me find you in loving you: let me love you in finding you. Amen. # A prayer of St. Anselm of Canterbury, which he prayed to God as he began one of his theological works. # This prayer was printed in the book by Loyola Press & William Barry, SJ.

(A-6) Prayer before reading the Bible

Lord, who can grasp all the wealth of just one of your words? What we understand is much less than we leave behind, like thirsty people who drink from a fountain. For your word, Lord, has many shades of meaning just as those who study it have many different points of view. The Lord has colored his word with many hues so that each person who studies it can see in it what he loves. He has hidden many treasures in his word so that each of us is enriched as we meditate on it. The word of God is a tree of life that from all its parts offers you fruit that is blessed. It is like that rock opened in the desert that from all its parts gave forth a spiritual drink. He who comes into contact with some share of its treasure should not think that the only thing contained in the word is what he himself has found. He should realize that he has only been able to find that one thing from among many others. Nor, because only that one part has become his, should he say that the word is void and empty and look down on it. But because he could not exhaust it, he should give thanks for its riches. Be glad that you are overcome and do not be sad that it overcame you. The thirsty man rejoices when he drinks and he is not downcast because he cannot empty the fountain. Rather let the fountain quench your thirst than have your thirst quench the fountain. Because if your thirst is quenched and the fountain is not exhausted, you can drink from it again whenever you are thirsty. But if when your thirst is quenched and the fountain is also dried up, your victory will bode evil for you. So be grateful for what you have received and don't grumble about the abundance left behind. What you have received and what you have reached is your share. What remains is your heritage. What at one time you were unable to receive because of your weakness, you will be able to receive at other times if you persevere. Do not have the presumption to try to take in one draft what cannot be taken in one draft and do not abandon out of laziness what can only be taken little by little. Amen. # This prayer was prepared by St. Ephraim.

(A-7) Prayer before reading the Bible

Lord, open our eyes to see Your ways with the Holy Spirit and open our ears to hear the Words of Life. Amen. Copyright © Bible Life in Korea. All rights reserved.

(A-8) Prayer before reading the Bible

Lord our God, we bless you. As we come together to ponder the Scriptures, we ask you in your kindness to fill us with the knowledge of your will so that, pleasing you in all things, we may grow in every good work. We ask this through Christ our Lord. Amen. # This prayer was prepared by Catholic Household Blessings and Prayers. Source: USCCB.

(A-9) Prayer before reading Sacred Scripture

Jesus Christ, our Master, you are the Way and the Truth and the Life. Grant that we may learn the sublime knowledge of your charity in the spirit of St. Paul the Apostle and of the Catholic Church. Send your Holy Spirit to teach us and remind us of what you have preached. # Prayer source: The Prayers of the Pauline Family.

B. Prayer after reading the Bible

Let me not, O Lord, be puffed up with worldly wisdom, which passes away, but grant me that love which never abates, that I may not choose to know anything among men but Jesus, and Him crucified. (1 Cor. 13:8; 2:2.) I pray Thee, loving Jesus that as Thou hast graciously given me to drink in with delight the words of Thy knowledge, so Thou would mercifully grant me to attain one day to Thee, the fountain of all wisdom and to appear forever before Thy face. Amen. # Prayer of St. Bede the Venerable. (AD 672-735). In 1899, Pope Leo XIII declared him a Doctor of the Church.

(B-1) Prayer after reading the Bible

Lord, grant us to believe, pray and proclaim the Holy Bible as the Words of Life. And grant us to enjoy peace and rejoice in the Holy Spirit. Amen. Copyright © BIble Life in Korea. All rights reserved.

(B-2) Prayer After Reading the Bible

God, our Savior, may the Words of the Holy Bible we have read (lectio) be rooted and grounded deeply in our soul and heart. Help us, through meditation (meditatio) on the Bible, give wisdom, knowledge, direction, guidance, prudence and instructions to our life. God our Creator, through our prayer (oratio) and our personal response to the Bible, grant us to offer praise, adoration, glory, thanksgiving and worship to You. Holy God, in contemplation (contemplatio), grant us to experience contact with You behind and beyond the Bible. Your Words impart great wisdom, knowledge and understanding to know the everlasting God in our hearts and spirit. Through Bible study, we count everything as loss because of the exceeding value of knowing God our Father, Creator of all things. Thank you for speaking to us through the Holy Bible. Through Christ Our Lord. Amen.

(B-3) Prayer after reading the Bible

All-powerful and ever-living God, thank You for Your presence as we read Your Words and meditated on them in our heart. Heavenly God, cast out from our hearts the darkness of ignorance, instead open our eyes to Your wisdom, knowledge, prudence, understanding and counsel. Grant us to prepare our hearts with the power of Your Spirit to receive Your Words with great grace and blessing and to have a deeper understanding of who You are. We have heard of You with our ears but now also You have opened our eyes to spiritual truths and understanding that we never had before through Bible study. Therefore, bring us to the light of the truth of Your Words and practice what You have revealed to us through the Bible study. Through Christ Our Lord. Amen.

(B-4) Prayer after reading Sacred Scripture

Jesus, Divine Master, you have Words of eternal life. I believe, O Lord and Truth, but increase my faith. I love you, O Lord and Way, with all my strength, because you have commanded us to observe your commandments perfectly. I pray to you, O Lord and Life. I adore you, I praise you, I beseech you, and I thank you for the gift of Sacred Scripture. With Mary, I shall remember and preserve your Words in my mind and I shall meditate on them in my heart. Jesus Master, Way and Truth and Life, have mercy on us., # Prayer source: The Prayers of the Pauline Family.

C. Indulgence that was granted by Pope Leo XIII in 1898 to all the faithful who "shall read for at least a quarter of an hour the books of the Sacred Scripture with the veneration due to the Divine Words and as spiritual reading, an indulgence of 300 days".(Preces et Pia opera, 645.)

An indulgence of three years is granted to the faithful who read the Books of the Bible for at least a quarter of an hour, with the reverence due to the Divine Words and as spiritual reading: To the faithful who piously read at least some verses of the Gospel and in addition, while kissing the Gospel Book, devoutly recite one of the following invocations: "May our sins be blotted out through the words of the Gospel,""May the reading of the Gospel be our salvation and our protection," and "May Christ, the Son of God, teach us the words of the Holy Gospel": an indulgence of 500 days is granted; a plenary indulgence under the usual conditions is granted to those who for a whole month daily act in the way indicated above; a plenary indulgence is granted at the hour of death to those who often during life have performed this pious exercise, provided they have confessed and received Communion, or at least having sorrow for their sins, they invoke the most holy name of Jesus with their lips, if possible, or at least in their hearts, and humbly accept death from the hand of God as the price of sin.(Enchiridion Indulgentiarum, 694).

Chapter 15 Prayers to Angels(천사들께 대한 기도)

A. Prayer to your guardian angel(수호천사께 대한 기도)

Angel of God, my guardian dear, to whom God's love commits me here, ever this day, be at my side, to light and guard, rule and guide. Amen. # "From infancy to death human life is surrounded by their (the angels) watchful care and intercession. Beside each believer stands an angel as protector and shepherd leading him to life. Already here on earth the Christian life shares by faith in the blessed company of angels and men united to God."; from the Catechism of the Catholic Church; 336. page 87.

B. Prayer to St. Michael, the Archangel(미카엘대천사께 대한 기도)

St. Michael the Archangel, defend us in battle. Be our defense against the wickedness and snares of the Devil. May God rebuke him, we humbly pray, and do thou, O Prince of the heavenly hosts, by the power of God, thrust into hell Satan, and all the evil spirits, who prowl about the world seeking the ruin of souls. Amen. One day, after celebrating Mass, the aged Pope Leo XIII (AD 1878-1903) was in conference with the Cardinals when suddenly he sank to the floor in a deep swoon. Physicians who hastened to his side could find no trace of his pulse and feared that he had expired. However, after a short interval the Holy Father regained consciousness and exclaimed with great emotion: "Oh, what a horrible picture I have been permitted to see!" He had been shown a vision of evil spirits who had been released from Hell and their efforts to destroy the Church. But in the midst of the horror the archangel St. Michael appeared and cast Satan and his legions into the abyss of hell. Soon afterwards Pope Leo XIII composed the following prayer to Saint Michael, which is the original version:

Original Prayer to St. Michael: "O Glorious Prince of the heavenly host, St. Michael the Archangel, defend us in the battle and in the terrible warfare that we are waging against the principalities and powers, against the rulers of this world of darkness, against the evil spirits. Come to the aid of man, whom Almighty God created immortal, made in His own image and likeness, and redeemed at a great price from the tyranny of Satan. "Fight this day the battle of the Lord, together with the holy angels, as already thou hast fought the leader of the proud angels, Lucifer, and his apostate host, who were powerless to resist thee, nor was there place for them any longer in Heaven. That cruel, ancient serpent, who is called the devil or Satan who seduces the whole world, was cast into the abyss with his angels. Behold, this primeval enemy and slayer of men has taken courage. Transformed into an angel of light, he wanders about with all the multitude of wicked spirits, invading the earth in order to blot out the name of God and of His Christ, to seize upon, slay and cast into eternal perdition souls destined for the crown of eternal glory. This wicked dragon pours out, as a most impure flood, the venom of his malice on men of depraved mind and corrupt heart, the spirit of lying, of impiety, of blasphemy, and the pestilent breath of impurity, and of every vice and iniquity. "These most crafty enemies have filled and inebriated with gall and bitterness the Church, the spouse of the immaculate Lamb, and have laid impious hands on her most sacred possessions. In the Holy Place itself, where the See of Holy Peter and the Chair of Truth has been set up as the light of the world, they have raised the throne of their abominable impiety, with the iniquitous design that when the Pastor has been struck, the sheep may be. "Arise then, O invincible Prince, bring help against the attacks of the lost spirits to the people of God, and give them the victory. They venerate thee as their protector and patron; in thee holy Church glories as her defense against the malicious power of hell; to thee has God entrusted the souls of men to be established in heavenly beatitude. Oh, pray to the God of peace that He may put Satan under our feet, so far conquered that he may no longer be able to hold men in captivity and harm the Church. Offer our prayers in the sight of the Most High, so that they may quickly find mercy in the sight of the Lord; and vanquishing the dragon, the ancient serpent, who is the devil and Satan, do thou again make him captive in the abyss, that he may no longer seduce the nations. Amen.

V. Behold the Cross of the Lord; be scattered you hostile powers.

R. The Lion of the tribe of Judah has conquered, the root of David.

V. Let Your mercies be upon us, O Lord.

R. As we have hoped in You.

V. O Lord, hear my prayer.

R. And let my cry come to You.

Let us pray.

O God, the Father of our Lord Jesus Christ, we call upon Your holy Name, and as supplicants, we implore Your clemency, that by the intercession of Mary, ever Virgin Immaculate and our Mother, and of the glorious St. Michael the Archangel, You wouldst deign to help us against Satan and all the other unclean spirits who wander about the world for the injury of the human race and the ruin of souls. Amen."

Prayer source: From Roman Raccolta, July 23, 1898, supplement approved July 31, 1902, London: Burnes, Oates & Washbourne Ltd., 1935, 12th edition.

C. The Feast of the Guardian Angels (Feast, October 2)

Not only do believers have faith on their side, but they have "witnesses" of God's Word. Holy Scripture contains numerous examples that witness to the existence of angels and their manifestations in relation to the fulfillment of particular missions. The well-known example of Mary's Annunciation involved an angel sent by God to announce that the moment had arrived for the fulfillment of the coming of God's Son: He would be conceived by the power of the Holy Spirit and born of Mary as man. Angels were also the witnesses and heralds of Jesus' Resurrection.

Sacred Scripture and angels

With Sacred Scripture as its foundation, the Church affirms the existence of angels and puts into light their mission in relation to collective salvation in history as well as individual salvation. In a Catechesis during the early years of his Pontificate, keeping in mind what is held by tradition, John Paul II affirmed that "the angels, as pure spirits, not only participate in the holiness of God himself, in the manner proper to them, but in the key moments they surround Christ and accompany him in the fulfillment of his salvific mission in regard to mankind" (General Audience, 30 July 1986; L'Osservatore Romano English Edition, 4 August, p. 1).

Holiness, therefore, as the fruit of grace and love, is shared by the angels. It is not shared by all, however, for in the beginning there was a rebellion, and those unfaithful to God and his project of salvation were excluded.

Without manipulating Scripture, we can say that participation in God's holiness can be understood in relation to the redemptive holiness which springs forth from Christ, by means of and in sight of which the angels were created. Such participation was held in a specific way by the angels.

Guardian angels

In the Catechesis mentioned above, John Paul also affirms that "in the key moments [the angels] surround Christ and accompany him in the fulfillment of his salvific mission in regard to mankind". This is a logical consequence of the aforementioned text. Angels, created by God according to the importance and necessity of each situation, therefore "accompany" and "surround" the Church, the Mystical Body of Christ. In this way the mission is complete, embracing the whole Christ, Head and Body.

This dynamic refers not only to the Ecclesial Community as such, but also individual Church members. But as part of the historical and ecclesiological profile it must also be mentioned that angels journey together with the Church in her mission of salvation and at the same time travel side-by-side with her members; all human beings have their own guardian angel to guard, protect and enlighten them.

The Catechism of the Catholic Church proclaims that "from infancy to death human life is surrounded by their [angels'] watchful care and intercession. Beside each believer stands an angel as protector and shepherd leading him to life. Already here on earth the Christian life shares by faith in the blessed company of angels and men united in God" (CCC, n. 336).

Such protection will benefit those who respond to the Holy Spirit's direction and for those who willingly collaborate. In her liturgy, the Church prays to the angels for herself and others, calling upon their protection and intercession: it is sufficient to follow the liturgy of the Mass to be convinced.

The same Church makes the special prayer to the guardian angel available to the faithful and to all who wish to recite it. As a result, praying it at least twice a day, morning and evening, should not be "an option".

D. The Angel Prayer by St. Pope John XXIII (AD 1881–1963)

"I myself say the prayer <Angel of God, My Guardian Dear> at least five times a day, and I often speak spiritually to him; it always gives me serenity and peace. "Looking at the great crowd of pilgrims, I used to think of the equally numerous crowds of invisible guardian angels present in the same square." Pope John attributed the idea of calling the ecumenical council (Vatican II) to an inspiration of his guardian angel.

Pope Paul VI testified: "Angels and the blessed in heaven are associated 'in different degrees' in God's government of the world; the saints intercede on men's behalf, while the guardian angels not only pray and intercede for men, but also act on them, and directly intervene." "May the angels inspire in the nations and in their leaders plans of peace." He approved (1970) the Feast of the Guardian Angels (October 2). Copyright of C & D © EWTN Inc. Irondale, Alabama. All rights reserved."

Chapter 16 Prayers before examinations, study, work and interviews

A. Prayer before Exams or Student's Prayer

Come, Holy Spirit, Divine Creator, true source of light and fountain of wisdom! Pour forth your brilliance upon my dense intellect, dissipate the darkness which covers me, that of sin and of ignorance. Grant me a penetrating mind to understand, a retentive memory method, ease in learning, the lucidity to comprehend, and abundant grace in expressing myself. Guide the beginning of my study, direct its progress, and bring it to successful completion. This I ask through Jesus Christ, true God and true man, living and reigning with You and the Father, forever and ever. Amen.

B. Prayer Before Study #1

Creator of all things, true Source of light and wisdom, lofty origin of all being, graciously let a ray of Your brilliance penetrate into the darkness of my understanding and take from me the double darkness in which I have been born, an obscurity of both sin and ignorance. Give me a sharp sense of understanding, a retentive memory, and the ability to grasp things correctly and fundamentally. Grant me the talent of being exact in my explanations, and the ability to express myself with thoroughness and charm. Point out the beginning, direct the progress, and help in completion. Through Christ our Lord. Amen.

C. Our Lady of Studies

O Mary, Seat of Wisdom, so many persons of common intellect have made through your intercession admirable progress in their studies. I hereby choose you as guardian and patron of my studies. I humbly ask You to obtain for me the grace of the Holy Spirit, so that from now on I could understand more quickly, retain more readily, and express myself more fluently. May the example of my life serve to honor you and your Son, Jesus. Amen.

D. Prayer before study # 2

O ineffable Creator, Who, out of the treasure of Thy wisdom, hast ordained three hierarchies of Angels, and placed them in wonderful order above the heavens, and has most wisely distributed the parts of the world; Thou, Who are called the true fountain of light and wisdom, and the highest beginning, vouchsafe to pour upon the darkness of my understanding, in which I was born, the double beam of Thy brightness, removing from me all darkness of sin and ignorance. Thou, Who makes eloquent the tongue of the dumb, instruct my tongue, and pour on my lips the grace of Thy blessing. Give me quickness of understanding, capacity of retaining, subtlety of interpreting, facility in learning, and copious grace of speaking. Guide my going in, direct my going forward, accomplish my going forth; through Christ our Lord. Amen.

E. Prayer to St. Thomas Aquinas for Catholic Schools

Saint Thomas Aquinas, you are called by Holy Mother Church, the Angel of the Schools. Your wisdom, gathered through long meditation from the source of all wisdom, the most holy Trinity, has long been a shining light in the Catholic Church. Ignorance of the things of God is a darkness now enveloping the minds of many of our countrymen. In this darkness, we need an angel like you who will protect, foster, and nourish the schools we have, and guide and strengthen us in establishing and building newer and more adequate schools for the instruction of our children in the ways of Christ. Help and bless the generous sisters, brothers, and priests who labor so unselfishly in the classroom to spread the knowledge of Christ. Inspire our Catholic men and women to be most generous in the support of the schools we have. Grant to parents the wise generosity they need to give their child back to God when that child wishes to follow a priestly or religious vocation. Help us, Saint Thomas, Angel of the Schools, to understand what you taught, and to follow your example. Amen.

F. Prayer to St. Thomas Aquinas for student #1

O great student of knowledge and wisdom, whose great efforts attempted to synthesize the greatest works of faith and reason; But knew with the greatest humility that compared to the Divine itself such works were 'like straw.' Pray that the Lord may grant us, the students of knowledge, a great love of Truth, limited only by a love of God. That we may have the faith to search for her in the storms of materialism and uncertainty, and that we may become the great protectors and preachers of Truth's beauty when we hold her in our midst. For this we pray. Amen.

G. Prayer to St. Thomas Aquinas for student #2

Angel of Schools, at the bidding of Peter, thousands today are saluting you thus. We too are claiming your care and your counsel, Angel of Schools, be an Angel to us. Come to our aid when you hear us calling, Light up the dark, Make the rough places plain, Bring to our thoughts the unknown or forgotten, Give us the words that we seek for in vain. Amen. # From (A) to (G) are the prayers of St. Thomas Aquinas. # Prayer source: From www.daily-prayers.org & Catholic Ireland. Net.

H. Prayer to St. Joseph of Cupertino for Success in Examinations

For success in examinations; This powerful prayer is very effective in examinations. It has to be said before appearing in the examination. There are two variants to this prayer. Both the prayers are equally effective. You can choose any one of these:
1) First Prayer for Success in Examinations: O Great St. Joseph of Cupertino who while on earth did obtain from God the grace to be asked at your examination only the questions you knew, obtain for me a like favor in the examinations for which I am now preparing. In return I promise to make you known and cause you to be invoked. Through Christ our Lord. St. Joseph of Cupertino, pray for us. Amen.

I. Second Prayer for Success in Examinations

O St. Joseph of Cupertino who by your prayer obtained from God to be asked at your examination, the only preposition you knew. Grant that I may like you succeed in the examination. (here mention the name of Examination, for example. Introductory Account) In return I promise to make you known and cause you to be invoked. O St. Joseph of Cupertino, pray for me. O Holy Spirit, Advocate of truth, enlighten me. Our Lady of Good Studies, pray for me. Sacred Head of Jesus, Seat of divine wisdom, enlighten me. Amen. #1: Remember, when you succeed in the exams then you should thank St. Joseph of Cupertino. # 2: St. Joseph of Cupertino(1603–1663); feast, 18 September. Joseph received his surname from Cupertino, a small village in the Diocese of Nardo, lying between Brindisi and Otranto in the Kingdom of Naples.

J. Prayer for Passing Examinations

O Savior of the world, thank you for your countless graces and blessings. I pray that you would help me pass this exam. Thank you for your guidance in leading me to this study and for sustaining me as I have studied for this examination. I earnestly beg now that Your Holy Spirit would lead me. Come sharpen my mind and memory skills. Lord of power and might, with full understanding, knowledge and learning help me to excel in this examination. May I be able to recall everything I need from my studies, wisdom, knowledge and understanding. Allow me to answer each question correctly in accordance with your guidance. Through Christ our Lord. Amen.

K. Prayer of Student Undertaking Examinations

Almighty God in heaven, you have given me a great day to rejoice. I praise you and believe in your loving kindness and help that will never fail. Lord God, I have prepared for my examinations, open to me the way to succeed in them. This is your own way where the just students who have prepared for the examinations may enter. I thank you for having answered me and for being my helper when I am faced with difficulties. Also, I always grateful for your many gifts of the Holy Spirit: wisdom, knowledge, talent, understanding and counsel. Grant the Holy Spirit to sit with me in my examinations not to forget to answer all the questions, to remember all that I have studied and to do my very best that I can succeed in the examinations. Through Christ our Lord Amen.

L. Prayer for Students Undertaking CSAT

God of wisdom and love, source of all good, I will take the college scholastic ability test(CSAT). I always thank You for the graces that You have bestowed upon me. Words cannot measure the boundaries of Your love. Also, I thank You for this test opportunity. I trust that You and the Holy Spirit will sit at my side during the test. I believe that You will have a perfect test fit for me. Lord God, grant me a calm attitude, a peaceful and clearheaded mind. Let Your wisdom, prudence and understanding flow out through my thoughts. Almighty God, my hope and my strength, without You I falter. But whatever the outcome of the test, grant all participants in the CSAT to feel happy to have had the test opportunity and this test be a blessing to those who join in taking the test. Lord God, grant also a blessing to me and my family who support my test. I trust You to work in me and through this CSAT process, to meet all my needs. Teach me to cherish Your blessings and gifts and bless those who will be participate in this CSAT. Also, grant them wisdom, knowledge, understanding, prudence, counsel, peaceful mind, lucidity and clarity. I trust in You and that You will not forsake my prayer. With that confidence, I will prepare thoroughly for the CSAT. Please encamp around me my guardian angel and the Holy Spirit to help me during the preparation process and while taking the test. Father in heaven, Creator of all, give success to the work of my hands. Make me love and obey You, so that the work of my hands during the CSAT may display what Your hands have done. Through Christ Our Lord. Amen.

M. Prayer for Students

Lord our God, in your wisdom and love you surround us with the mysteries of the universe. Send your Spirit upon these students and fill them with your wisdom and blessings. Grant that they may devote themselves to their studies and draw ever closer to you, the source of all knowledge. We ask this through Christ our Lord. Amen. # Prayer source: From Catholic Household Blessings and Prayers.

M-1. Parent's Prayer for Their Son, Daughter or Grandchildren

Almighty and ever-living God, you are source of unfailing light. I know you are with my (son, daughter or grandchildren) and love (him or her). Give him (her) true knowledge, wisdom, understanding, prudence and peace of mind as he (she) prepares for this time of study and exam. Help (mention his or her name), not only with this examination, but the many exams of life that are sure to come his (her) way. God our Father, watch over my (son, daughter, grandson or granddaughter) by day and by night. In the midst of (his or her) life's countless changes strengthen him (her) with your never-changing love. Help him (her) to focus on his (her) books and notes. Heavenly God, keep my (son, daughter or grandchildren) from all distractions so that (he or she) will make the best use of this time that is available to (him or her). Almighty God, you reward each one according to his (her) studies. Hear me as I pour out my hearts to you, seeking your grace and blessings. God our Father and protector, grant (him or her) insight that (he or she) might understand what (he or she) is studying, and help him (her) to remember it when the examination time comes. Almighty God, be gracious with what he (she) has overlooked. Help (him or her) to remain focused and clam, confident in the facts and in (his or her) ability. Almighty and Eternal God, I thank you for the ability to be able to study and for the many gifts of the Holy Spirit and talents you have given him (her). Almighty God, bless all students who will participate in this examination. Also, grant the Holy Spirit to sit with him (her) in (his or her) examinations not to forget to answer all the questions, to remember all that he (she) has studied and to do his (her) very best that he (she) can succeed in the examinations. Amen.

N. Prayer for Morning Resolve

O Lord God my Father, creator of all, You have taught us to overcome our sins by prayer, fasting and works of mercy. When we are discouraged by our weakness, give us confidence through Your love. I will try today to live a faithful and sincere life, repelling promptly every thought of ignorance, forgetfulness, obstinacy, prejudice, perversion, discontent, anxiety, hatred, discouragement, impurity, and self-seeking. I will cultivate cheerfulness, good taste, feelings and inclinations, magnanimity, charity, and the habit of holy silence and exercise economy in expenditure, generosity in giving, carefulness in conversation, diligence in appointed service, fidelity to every trust, and a childlike faith in God. In particular I will try to be faithful in those habits of prayer, work, study, physical exercise, eating, and sleep which I believe the Holy Spirit has shown me to be right. As I cannot with my own strength do this, nor even with a hope of success attempt it, O Lord God my Father, I am completely dependent on You. Lord, true light and source of all light, listen to our morning resolve. Turn our thoughts to what is holy and may we ever live in the light of Your love. We ask this through our Lord Jesus Christ, Your Son, Who lives and reigns with You and the Holy Spirit, one God, forever and ever. Amen.

O. On Waking Up

INVOCATION: V. To you I pray, O Lord, R. At dawn you hear my voice. (Ps 5:3).
REFLECTION: Each day is a new beginning, an opportunity to draw closer to Christ. Whatever the misery or glory of the past may have been, today offers another chance which will never come again to do God's work and will. Try to use it prudently.
PRAYER: Good Morning, Lord, and thank you for another day of life. Please help me to face whatever pains and problems it may bring and to enjoy whatever pleasures may come my way. In your kindness keep me close to you today and preserve me and all your other people from every evil. In the name of Christ, your Son, receive my morning prayer. Amen. SCRIPTURE READING: Matthew 20:1-16.

O-1. As You Wash and Dress

INVOCATION: V. Cleanse me of my sin that I may be purified, R. Wash me, and I shall be whiter than snow. (Ps 51:9)
REFLECTION: We make each day a special effort to make ourselves presentable in public by careful attention to our appearance, our persons and clothing. A similar effort is called for that we may make ourselves worthy in the eyes of God who sees all and knows everything.
PRAYER: Father in heaven, cleanse me of all my faults and sins of the past. By your favor wash away every blemish of mind, and stain of spirit. Merciful Lord, clothe me in righteousness so I may be without spot or wrinkle in your sight. Assist me now and all your other people to prepare for the day's happenings, and send your Holy Spirit to be with us today. We ask this in Christ's name. Amen.
SCRIPTURE READING: Ephesians 6:10-17.

O-2. At Breakfast

INVOCATION: V. The lowly shall eat their fill, R. They who seek the Lord shall praise Him. (Ps 22:27)
REFLECTION: Think how many men and women labored to bring your food to the table, and to make the dishes and utensils used. They are the hidden guests at every meal reminding us how we all depend on each other. How grateful we should be for abundant food and for the appetite to enjoy it! So many in the world go hungry

or cannot relish what they eat.

PRAYER: All-powerful Father, we thank you for your goodness in providing for our bodily needs. Bless all those whose work made this meal possible. May we always so eat and drink that we may be deemed worthy to sit down and share with you the food and fellowship of the heavenly banquet you are preparing for us. Through Christ, our Lord. Amen. SCRIPTURE READING: Luke 14:12-15. # Prayer source of (O, O-1 & O-2): From the Franciscan Mission Associates.

P. St. Pio's Prayer of Today for Tomorrow

Eternal Father, today, while I am fully conscious, totally lucid and completely free, I offer You my life with all its mystery and suffering. Indeed, Eternal Father, I offer You my life as an ultimate act of love, as an act of infinite gratitude, as an act of faith in Your mercy. My God and Father, accept this prayer I am making to You now for the day when You will call me back to You. If I am unconscious at the final moment of my life, if anguish and doubt assail me, if medication prevents me from thinking of You, I want my last heartbeat to be an act of perfect love, telling You with Jesus, "Into Your hands, I commend my spirit." Amen.

Q. Prayer after Work

O Most sweet Jesus, You are the fulfillment of all blessings. Fill my soul with joy and gladness and save me. Grant that your Name be glorified: for not to us, but to your Name are forever due honor, glory, and adoration. Amen.

Q-1. Prayer before Work

O Lord Jesus Christ, Only-begotten Son of your eternal Father: You have said with your holy lips: "Without Me, you can do nothing." My Lord, I embrace your words with my heart and soul, and bow before your goodness and say: Help me, your unworthy servant, to complete this, my present undertaking, in the name of the Father and of the Son, and the Holy Spirit. Amen. # The prayer source of (Q) and (Q-1) is from Eternal Word Television Network, Inc. Irondale, Alabama. No Copyright ©.

Q-2. Prayer before Work

My heavenly Father, as I enter this work place, I bring your presence with me. I speak your peace, your grace, your mercy and your perfect order into my work. I acknowledge your power over all that will be done, spoken, thought and decided within these walls. Lord, I thank you for the gifts you have blessed me with. I commit to use them responsibly in your honor. Give me a fresh supply of strength to do my job. Anoint my projects, ideas, and energy, so that even my smallest accomplishment may bring you glory. Lord, when I am confused, guide me. When I am weary, energize me. When I am burned out, infuse me with the light of the Holy Spirit. May the work that I do and the way I do it bring faith, joy and a smile to all that I come in contact with today. And oh Lord, when I leave this place, give me traveling mercy. Bless my family and home to be in order as I left it. Lord, I thank you for everything you've done, everything you are doing, and everything, you are going to do. In the name of Jesus I pray, with much love and thanksgiving. In the name of the Father, and of the Son, and of the Holy Spirit, Amen. # This prayer is from the Men of Emmaus a.k.a. The Church Guys are a group of men at St. Francis of Assisi Parish in Derwood, MD. # No Copyright ©.

Q-3. As You Go to Work

INVOCATION: V. May the gracious care of the Lord, our God, be ours,
R. Prosper the work of our hands for us. (Ps 90:17)
REFLECTION: Each of us has a job to do in life even when ill or retired. Blessed we are when we find our daily work something we look forward to each morning. There are many who lack any means of making a living. Even the humblest task is ennobled when done in God's sight and for His honor.
PRAYER: Lord and Creator of the universe, and all it contains, help me today in my daily tasks. May they be a worthy part of your eternal plan for the salvation of mankind. By my work I support myself and those dear to me with something left over to help the poor. My work benefits the community and my neighbors far and near. So in your goodness, Lord, assist me to do it better for your sake. May Christ, our Lord, in whose name I ask, be with us while we work. Amen.
SCRIPTURE READING: Luke 16:1-8.

Q-4. As the Day Progresses

INVOCATION: V. May the Lord bless and keep us,

R. May the Lord let His face shine upon us and be gracious to us. (Nm 6:24-25)

REFLECTION: The Lord, our God, watches over us with loving concern at every moment of the day. Even when our thoughts may be far from Him, He remains close to us. It is well at times during the day, when we pause in our work, to turn to our Creator and Redeemer, to acknowledge His presence, seek His help, and put ourselves under His protection.

PRAYER: Almighty Father, in our busyness let us not forget your abiding presence, your infinite majesty, and your unchanging love for us. Please teach us how to pray, when we are tired, and words will not come, to raise our hearts and minds to you. Christ, our Lord, knew weariness and loneliness during His life on earth. By His merits help us to love you despite our human weakness and frailty. Amen.

SCRIPTURE READING: John 4:4-42. # The prayer source: of (Q-3 & Q-4) is from the Franciscan Mission Associates.

R. Prayer to St. Jude for Employment

Lord Jesus, my desire to work is itself Your gift. You gave me talents so I could shine Your light to the world. Send Your Spirit to guide me to work that will provide security and joy, and most of all the ability to serve You in love. St. Jude, I do not know where I am going, and so I call upon You in my need. Bless my spirit with the determination to continue on with energy. Give my heart patience and fortitude. Help me, dear friend, to remember that God's plan for me is forged out of love. Amen. # The prayer source is from the National Shrine of St. Jude. © 2017 The Claretians.

S. Prayer for Job Seekers

Gracious and loving God, You know our need for meaningful work. Send Your Holy Spirit to guide those who are searching for employment. Help them to recognize the gifts and talents You have given them. Deepen their desire to follow Your will. Inspire them as they contact potential employers. Give them patience as they wait for responses. Shelter them from feelings of rejection. Protect them from discouragement. Give them courage to overcome fear. Shower on them the graces they need to persevere. Let this time of searching become an opportunity to grow in faith, to cultivate the virtue of hope, and to experience Your healing love. We ask this through Chirst our Lord. Amen. # Prayer source: From the folks at St. George Catholic Church.

T. Prayer for a Job Interview # 1

Almighty God, ever-loving Father, your love extends beyond the boundaries of time and space to the hearts of all who live. I thank you always for the love and joy you have prepared for me. Today, I will have a job interview for a position that would really change my career path in a good way. God our Father, grant me to do my best in the interview today. Hold me tight in your loving arms when I feel nervous. Take me in your loving embrace when I feel uneasy. Lord God, grant me wisdom, knowledge, prudence, counsel, courage and boldness to answer the questions I am asked wisely and in a honest and inspired way. During the job interview, increase Your Spirit within me, direct me in your path and bring me to the promising new job I desire. Through Christ our Lord. Amen.

U. Prayer for a Job Interview # 2

God of mercy and goodness, when Christ called out to You in torment, You heard Him and gave Him victory over death because of His love for You. I already know the affection and love You have for me. May You fill me with a greater love of Your name. Today, I will have a job interview for a position that would really change my career path in a good way. Before the interview, I am really nervous about interview issues and especially about the way of dealing with stress and anxiety during the interview. I am currently working at an IT product export company. My present career has seen me entrenched in roles where I deal with complaints and, frequently, aggressive and overbearing customers in the marketing division. This job is one that draws on my skills and experience, but I do not wish to deal with complaints anymore. If I would succeed in the job interview today, it will be a good opportunity that may not come again, and I am so hopeful to get the job. Lord God, gentle and humble of heart, never let anxiety reign in my heart during the interview, but may Your compassion and love reward and embrace me. Lord God, grant me wisdom, knowledge, prudence, counsel, courage and boldness that it all goes well. Also, grant me strong belief that You are always with me during my job interview. Through Christ our Lord. Amen.

V. Prayer for Charity in Truth

Father, your truth is made known in your Word. Guide us to seek the truth of the human person. Teach us the way to love because you are Love. Jesus, you embody Love and Truth. Help us to recognize your face in the poor. Enable us to live out our vocation to bring love and justice to your people. Holy Spirit, you inspire us to transform our world. Empower us to seek the common good for all persons. Give us a spirit of solidarity and make us one human family. We ask this through Christ our Lord. Amen. This prayer is based on Pope Benedict XVI's 2009 encyclical, Caritas in Veritate (Charity in Truth).

Chapter 17   Prayers for Family, Parents, Marriage, Pro-Life, Birthday, Rain, New Year, Journey, Safety and Souls Day

A. Prayer for the Whole Family
(Feast of the Holy Family First Sunday after Epiphany)

Dear Lord, bless our family. Be so kind as to give us the unity, peace, and mutual love that You found in Your own family in the little town of Nazareth. St. Joseph, bless the head of our family. Obtain for him the strength, the wisdom, and the prudence he needs to support and direct those under his care. Mother Mary, bless the mother of our family. Help her to be pure and kind, gentle and self-sacrificing. For the more she resembles you, the better will our family be. Lord Jesus, bless the children of our family. Help them to be obedient and devoted to their parents. Make them more and more like You. Let them grow, as You did, in wisdom and age and grace before God and man. Holy Family of Nazareth, make our family and home more and more like Yours, until we are all one family, happy and at peace in our true home with You. Amen. Copyright ©2017 Eternal Word Television Network, Inc. Irondale, Alabama. All rights reserved.

B. Prayer for family

A. Lord Jesus Christ, Who was obedient to Mary and St. Joseph and made Your family life holy, grant us our family life to be holy and to live in accordance with Your will by following the model of the holy family.

R. Holy Mary and St. Joseph, who are the proud model of family life, pray for our family life that the Lord grant our whole family to be healthy and happy and always live to serve Lord, to love our neighbors and to join the eternal heavenly family by the grace of the Lord. All. Amen. # Prayer source: The Prayer Book of the Catholic Bishops Conference of Korea (Page 105).

C. Mother Teresa's Nazareth Prayer for the Family

Heavenly Father, you have given us the model of life in the Holy Family of Nazareth. Help us, O Loving Father, to make our family another Nazareth where love, peace and joy reign. May it be deeply contemplative, intensely Eucharistic, revived with joy. Help us to stay together in joy and sorrow in family prayer. Teach us to see Jesus in the members of our families, especially in their distressing disguise. May the Eucharistic heart of Jesus make our hearts humble like his and help us to carry out our family duties in a holy way. May we love one another as God loves each one of us, more and more each day, and forgive faults each other as you forgive our sins. Help us, O Loving Father, to take whatever you give and give whatever you take with a big smile. Immaculate Heart of Mary, cause of our joy, pray for us. St. Joseph, pray for us. Holy Guardian Angels, be always with us, guide and protect us. Amen. # This prayer was composed by Mother Teresa of Calcutta.

D. Prayer for the Fervent Charity and Love among Families

Almighty God, our heavenly Father, grant continual care for the homes in which your families dwell. Keep far from them, we pray, every root of bitterness, hatred, obstinacy, prejudice, attachment, fickleness, sloth, enmity, bad habits, the desire for vainglory, and the pride of life. Fill them with faith, virtue, wisdom, understanding, knowledge, counsel, prudence, temperance, patience and godliness. Unite together in constant affection those who, in holy wedlock, have been made one flesh. Turn the hearts of parents to their children, and the hearts of children to their parents; and so enkindle fervent charity and love among families. God and Father of our Lord Jesus Christ, grant all family members to be more kindly and affectionate to one another. Through Christ our Lord. Amen.

E. Prayer for Families

We bless your name, O Lord, for sending your own incarnate Son, to become part of a family, so that, as he lived its life, he would experience its worries and its joys. We ask you, Lord, to protect and watch over this family, so that in the strength of your grace its members may enjoy prosperity, possess the priceless gift of your peace, and, as the Church alive in the home, bear witness in this world to your glory. We ask this through Christ our Lord. Amen. # Prayer Source: From Catholic Household Blessings and Prayers.

E-1. Prayer for Our Family

Our Father, we thank You for Your love and for the many things You have given to our family. Help us to show our gratitude by loving one another as You love us. Give us patience and understanding to bear with one another—generosity to share our joys and sorrows—honesty to admit our faults and correct them. We entrust our family to Your Fatherly care and protection. We ask that we may grow daily in wisdom and grace, that some of us be granted the privilege of following Your Divine Son in the priesthood or religious life, and that all of us may one day share with You the joys of heaven. Amen. # Prayer source: Franciscan Mission Associates.

F. Vocations prayer for parents

Loving God, you have given us the privilege as well as the responsibility of being loving parents. In the name of Jesus, we ask you to guide us as we invite our children to hear your call to service and leadership in our church. May our children respond with deep faith and generosity to the needs of God's people. Help us to be a source of encouragement to our children by our own desire to be committed people who serve with love and enthusiasm. Amen. # This prayer is from the Holy Trinity Catholic Church, Dalls, Texas.

G. Prayer for parents

Almighty God, you have commanded me to honor my father and my mother, that I may have a long life and that I may prosper in the land You are giving me. Lord God, from the depth of my soul I fervently beg you, hear my prayer and have mercy upon my parents, who have given birth to me and are bringing me up in your grace and love. I beg you to protect them from all evil, accidents, harm, hazards, disease and sickness; help them promote good health and mercifully pour forth your countless and bountiful graces and blessings upon them. Bless their lives and efforts; have mercy on them according to your great mercy. Also grant me to be worthy to bless, adore, worship, praise, glorify, serve and thank you through showing great respect to my parents. Amen.

H. Prayer for parents

Our Father, Who art in heaven, bless my father and mother, my guardians, and those who are in authority over me, for their love and tender care for me, and the benefits I receive at their hands. Help me, I pray you, to be respectful and obedient to them in all matters according to your will; and give me your grace to perform all my duties carefully and faithfully, to avoid undesirable company and influence, and resist all temptation that may come my way; that I may live a sober, righteous and godly life, ever praising you and glorifying your Holy Name. Amen. #Prayer source: From http:www. ocf.org.

I. Prayer for parents

O benevolent God, we will take care of our parents, fulfilling filial piety as You told us to love, respect and be thankful for hidden virtues. As our parents bear and rear us and overcome all difficulties gladly, now grant them lead a comfortable life to make their life worth living. Lord, bless our parents, keep them with grace and eventually enjoy eternal happiness with You. Through Christ our Lord. Amen. # Prayer source: The prayer book of Catholic Bishops Conference of Korea.(Page 107).

J. Parents' Thanksgiving Prayer

O God, we give you thanks for(N.), whom you have welcomed into our family. Bless this family. Confirm a lively sense of your presence with us, and grant us patience and wisdom, that our lives may show forth the love of Christ, as we bring N. up to love all that is good. We ask this through Christ our Lord. Amen. # Prayer source: From Catholic Household Blessings and Prayers.

K. Prayer for every family on earth

Lord, from You every family in heaven and on earth takes its name. Father, You are Love and Life. Through Your Son, Jesus Christ who was born of woman, and through the Holy Spirit, the fountain of divine charity, grant that every family on earth may become for each successive generation a true shrine of life and love. Grant that

Your grace may guide the thoughts and actions of husbands and wives for the good of their families and of all the families of the world. Grant that the young may find in the family solid support for their human dignity and for their growth in truth and love. Grant that love, strengthened by the grace of the sacrament of Marriage, may prove mightier than all the weaknesses and trials through which our families sometimes pass. Lord, through the intercession of the Holy Family of Nazareth, grant that the Church may fruitfully carry out her worldwide mission in the family and through the family. We ask this of You, who are Life, Truth, and Love with the Son and the Holy Spirit. Amen. (L'Osservatore Romano, 5-25-80, 19) Blessed is everyone who fears the Lord, who walks in His ways! Your wife will be like a fruitful vine within your house; Your children will be like olive shoots around your table. Lo, thus shall the man be blessed who fears the Lord. Psalm 128:1, 3-4.

L. Bless our home and family

Be pleased, Lord God, to bless our home and family this night. Let your holy angels stay here with us to keep us from evil and harm. In your mercy grant us a quiet night that we may sleep in the peace of Christ. May we by your mercy awake refreshed and invigorated in body, mind and spirit. We ask this in Christ's name. Amen.
Prayer source: Franciscan Mission Associates.

M. Parent's Prayer

Loving God, You are the giver of all we possess, the source of all of our blessings. We thank and praise you. Thank you for your countless graces and blessings and for the gift of our children. Help us to set boundaries for them, and yet encourage them to explore. Give us the strength and courage to treat each day as a fresh start. May our children come to know you, the one true God, and Jesus Christ, whom you have sent. May your Holy Spirit help them to grow in faith, hope, and love, so they may know peace, truth, and goodness. May their ears hear your voice. May their eyes see your presence in all things. May their lips proclaim your word. May their hearts be your dwelling place. May their hands do works of charity. May their feet walk in the way of Jesus Christ, your Son and our Lord. Amen. # Prayer source: From Loyola Press, A Jesuit Ministry.

N. Prayer of forgiveness for abusive parents

Dear Lord, My childhood was not the happy time that I would have liked it to be and my parents were certainly not the ideal example of parenthood – but Lord I know that in their way they tried to do their best for us, but it always seemed to go sour. Thank You Lord that in Your grace You lifted me out of this difficult and abusive family life to faith in Jesus – I praise You every day that You found me and brought me into Your family. Lord I bring my parents to You - Life seems to have passed them by and they need to know Jesus as their Savior. Lord I know that You died for them as well and forgave every sin they have committed, for You are a gracious and loving God and I praise You. Lord, I too want to forgive them for all that they did to me, I forgive both my parents and thank You that in Your grace You are taking me through a process of healing all the hurt and pain that I had to go through. Bless them both, dear Lord Jesus, and I pray that both of them will come to know You as their Savior. In Jesus name I pray. Amen. #From http://www. knowing-Jesus.com.

O. Prayer for my unbelieving parents

Father in heaven, I bring my dear mother and father to You - those who brought me into this world and gave me the gift of life. I do thank You for all the loving support and care they have given me throughout my life – but I am also aware that they do not know the Lord Jesus as their Savior. I do praise You that in Your grace You searched me out to become Your child and gave me the gift of eternal life – but Lord I long that my parents also come to that same saving faith in Jesus – and the older they get the more I realize that without You they have a sad future. Lord whatever it takes - I pray that in Your mercy, You will give both of them the sort of Damascus Road experience that Paul had, before it is too late. Draw them to Yourself I pray. Bring them Lord to an understanding of Who You are and what You have done for them - that You died on the cross to forgive their sins.. and all that they have to do is to believe in Jesus as their Savior. Use me Lord in whatever way You choose to point them to Christ. Let me not speak out of turn, but let me not miss an opportunity to share the gospel with them once more. Father I honor them as my parents and love them dearly – but Father- save them I pray – draw them with Your love – so that we may all be together in Your eternal home. Through Christ our Lord. Amen.

P. Prayer for my divorced parents.

Loving Lord, I bring both my parents to You and though it saddens my heart that they chose to go through a divorce. I love them both and pray that You would be gracious to them and draw them both closer into Your loving arms. As they each forge their own path through life , be with each of them to comfort and help, to lead and to guide. Be their strength in times of weakness, their hope in times of discouragement and their provision in times of need. Thank You Lord for my parents and the good times that we had together. Thank You for all that they taught me and the training that they gave me in my childhood and youth and Father – as they go their separate ways from each other – I pray that You would be their ever present companion and comforter in the days that lie ahead. In Jesus name I pray. Amen. #The prayer source of (O) & (P) is from http://www. knowing-Jesus.com.

Q. Prayer for Mothers

Good and gentle God, we pray in gratitude for our mothers and for all the women of theory who have joined with you in the wonder of bringing forth new life. You who became human through a woman, grant to all mothers the courage they need to face the uncertain future that life with children always brings. Give them the strength to live and to be loved in return, not perfectly, but humanly. Give them the faithful support of husband, family and friends as they care for the physical and spiritual growth of their children. Give them joy and delight in their children to sustain them through the trials of motherhood. God of mercy, give them the wisdom to turn to you for help when they need it most. Amen. # Prayer source; The Catholic Center at the University of Georgia. No Copyright ©

R. Prayer for the care of children

Almighty God, heavenly Father, You have blessed us with the joy and care of children. Grant us good taste, feelings and inclinations. Give us tolerant attitude, lenient mind, calm strength, patient wisdom, prudence, knowledge, counsel and wise understanding as we bring them up, that we may teach them to love whatever is just, true and good. Grant us to follow the example of our Savior Jesus Christ. Through Christ our Lord. Amen.

S. Prayer for our Children

Heavenly Father, please take our children, especially those who have turned from the ways of God and his Church, under your protection. Let them always remain faithful to their baptismal vows. Give them the strength to walk always in the ways of the Lord despite the temptations and false values they find in the world today. Grant that they may share with you the joys of eternal life. Amen. # Prayer source: Franciscan Mission Associates.

T. Prayer for Young People

I thank You for my life and for all the good qualities You have gifted me with. I thank You for friendships, family life and for so many opportunities to grow. I thank You for inviting me to walk closely with You and to continue to proclaim and deepen what You stand for; love, justice and peace. Thank You for living with me through your Holy Spirit and encouraging, loving, forgiving, healing and empowering me. Touch my heart and renew me with Your presence. Fill me with joy. Continue to mould and nurture me, so that I will never be afraid to respond to the needs of others and Your world, and turn to You in times of difficulty and distress. I trust You with my past life, my present situation and with my future. Today I decide again to accept You and You alone as my God. I truly desire to know You better. Amen. # This prayer was prepared by Bishop Joe Grech of Catholic Diocese of Sandhurst.

U. Prayer for the Aged

O God our Father, Your merciful care extends beyond the boundaries of race and nation to the hearts of all the aged. Almighty God, look with mercy on all the aged, whose increasing years bring them psychological distress, somatic health problems, socio-economic issues, spiritual and physical weakness, stress and isolation. Provide for them homes of love, reverence, dignity, joy and peace. All-powerful and ever-living God, grant them wisdom, understanding, the willingness to accept help, increasing their faith and assurance of Your love as their strength. We ask this through our Lord Jesus Christ, Your Son, who lives and reigns with You and the Holy Spirit, one God, forever and ever. Amen.

V. Prayer for the Elderly

Grant, O Lord of life, that we may be ever vividly aware of this and that we may savor every season of our lives as a gift filled with promise for the future. Grant that we may lovingly accept your will, and place ourselves each day in your merciful hands. And when the moment of our definitive "passage" comes, grant that we may face it with serenity, without regret for what we shall leave behind. For in meeting you, after having sought you for so long, we shall find once more every authentic good which we have known here on earth, in the company of all who have gone before us marked with the sign of faith and hope. Mary, Mother of pilgrim humanity, pray for us "now and at the hour of our death". Keep us ever close to Jesus, your beloved Son and our brother, the Lord of life and glory. Amen. # This prayer was prepared by St. Pope John Paul II. # From the Vatican on October 1, 1999.

W. Prayer for the Unborn Babies

Lord Jesus, You who faithfully visit and fulfill with your Presence the Church and the history of men; You who in the miraculous Sacrament of your Body and Blood render us participants in divine Life and allow us a foretaste of the joy of eternal Life; We adore and bless you. Prostrated before You, source and lover of Life, truly present and alive among us, we beg you. Reawaken in us respect for every unborn life, make us capable of seeing in the fruit of the maternal womb the miraculous work of the Creator, open our hearts to generously welcoming every child that comes into life. Bless all families, sanctify the union of spouses, render fruitful their love. Accompany the choices of legislative assemblies with the light of your Spirit, so that peoples and nations may recognize and respect the sacred nature of life, of every human life. Guide the work of scientists and doctors, so that all progress contributes to the integral well-being of the person, and no one endures suppression or injustice. Give creative charity to administrators and economists, so they may realize and promote sufficient conditions so that young families can serenely embrace the birth of new children. Console the married couples who suffer because they are unable to have children and in Your goodness provide for them. Teach us all to care for orphaned or abandoned children, so they may experience the warmth of your Charity, the consolation of your divine Heart. Together with Mary, Your Mother, the great believer, in whose womb you took on our human nature, we wait to receive from You, our Only True God and Savior, the strength to love and serve life, in anticipation of living forever in You, in communion with the Blessed Trinity. Amen. # This prayer was composed by Pope Benedict XVI.

X. Prayer to End Abortion

Lord God, I thank you today for the gift of my life, and for the lives of all my brothers and sisters. I know there is nothing that destroys more life than abortion, yet I rejoice that You have conquered death by the Resurrection of Your Son. I am ready to do my part in ending abortion. Today I commit myself NEVER to be silent, NEVER to be passive, NEVER to be forgetful of the unborn. I commit myself to be active in the pro-life movement, and never to stop defending life until all my brothers and sisters are protected, and our nation once again becomes a nation with liberty and justice not just for some, but for all, through Christ our Lord. Amen!

Y. Blessing of Parents before the Birth of Their Child

Gracious Father, Your Word, spoken in love, created the human family and, in the fullness of time, Your Son, conceived in love, restored it to Your friendship. Hear the prayers of Parents awaiting the birth of a child, calm their fears when they are anxious. Watch over and support these parents and bring their child into this world safely and in good health, so that as members of Your family they may praise You and glorify You through your Son, our Lord Jesus Christ, now and forever. Amen.

aa. Blessing of a Mother Before Childbirth

God has brought gladness and light to the world through the Virgin Mary's delivery of her child. May Christ fill your heart with His holy joy and keep you and your baby safe from harm. In the name of the Father, and of the Son, and of the Holy Spirit. Amen. # The over 56 million abortions since the 1973 decisions of Roe v. Wade and Doe v. Bolton reflect with heartbreaking magnitude what Pope Francis means by a "throwaway culture." However, we have great trust in God's providence. We are reminded time and again in Scripture to seek the Lord's help, and as people of faith, we believe that our prayers are heard. The General Instruction of the Roman Missal (GIRM), no. 373, designates January 22 as a particular day of prayer and penance, called the "Day of Prayer for the Legal Protection of Unborn Children": "In all the Dioceses of the United States of America, January 22 (or January 23, when January 22 falls on a Sunday) shall be observed as a particular day of prayer for the full restoration of the legal guarantee of the right to life and of penance for violations to the dignity of the human person committed through acts of abortion." As individuals, we are called to observe this day through the penitential practices of prayer, fasting and/or giving alms. Another way to take part is through participating in special events to observe the anniversary of Roe v. Wade. Call your local diocese or parish to find out what events might be taking place in your area. A great prayer for life is urgently needed, a prayer which will rise up throughout the world. Through special initiatives and in daily prayer, may an impassioned plea rise to God, the Creator and lover of life, from every Christian community, from every group and association, from every family and from the heart of every believer. Pope St. John Paul II, Evangelium Vitae, no. 100* # Copyright of (W)(X)(Y) and (aa) ©2017 Eternal Word Television Network, Inc. Irondale, Alabama. All rights reserved.

bb. Blessing of a Child in the Womb

God, author of all life, bless, we pray, this unborn child; give constant protection and grant a healthy birth that is the sign of our rebirth one day into the eternal rejoicing of heaven. Amen. The "Rite for the Blessing of a Child in the Womb" was crafted to support parents awaiting the birth of their child, to encourage parish prayers for -- and recognition of -- the precious gift of the child in the womb, and to foster respect for human life within society. It may be offered within the context of the Mass as well as outside of Mass. # Excerpt from the Prayer of Blessing. Copyright © 2010 United States Conference of Catholic Bishops, Washington, D.C. Used with permission. All rights reserved.

cc. Parents' Thanksgiving Prayer for a Newborn Child

O Saint Joseph, you witnessed the miracle of birth, seeing the infant Jesus born of your most holy spouse, the Virgin Mary. With wonder and awe, you took into your arms the Savior. With gratitude that only a parent can know, you glorified God for the birth of his Son, entrusted to your fatherly care. Like you, St. Joseph, I too give praise and glory to God for the birth of my child. This child's life is such a miraculous testimony of God's loving presence. My heart is filled with grateful joy. Join me dear St. Joseph, in offering thanks to God for the gift of my child. What great trust and confidence God placed in you, St. Joseph, by entrusting his only Son into your fatherly care. This inspires me to entrust the spiritual care and protection of my newborn child into your competent and loving hands. Teach, guide, and support me to fulfill well my awesome vocation to be a worthy parent to this child. Amen.

Prayer source: From The Oblates of St. Joseph. (2014). Prayers to St. Joseph. Retrieved from the Oblates of St. Joseph, a religious order of priests and brothers founded by St. Joseph Marello in 1878.

dd. Prayer in Defence of Marriage

God our Father, we give you thanks for the gift of marriage: the bond of life and love, and the font of the family. The love of husband and wife enriches your Church with children, fills the world with a multitude of spiritual fruitfulness and service, and is the sign of the love of your Son, Jesus Christ, for his Church. The grace of Jesus flowed forth at Cana at the request of the Blessed Mother. May your Son, through the intercession of Mary, pour out upon us a new measure of the Gifts of the Holy Spirit as we join with all people of good will to promote and protect the unique beauty of marriage. May your Holy Spirit enlighten our society to treasure the heroic love of husband and wife, and guide our leaders to sustain and protect the singular place of mothers and fathers in the lives of their children. Father, we ask that our prayers be joined to those of the Virgin Mary, that your Word may transform our service so as to safeguard the incomparable splendor of marriage.We ask all these things through Christ our Lord, Amen. Saints Joachim and Anne, pray for us. # Prayer source: From Catholic Household Blessings and Prayers of USCCB.

ee. Prayer for Husband and Wife

V. Benevolent God, our Father, thank You for bringing us together through the sacrament of matrimony and for looking after us.

R. Now, we beg You in keeping our mind upon the memory of our marriage vows, and according to them, to grant us to love, respect and keep faith each other, regardless of whether we are joyful and happy, are in pain, living well or not, enjoying good health or in illness. V. Also, we beg You that our lives of the husband and wife who are always praising You, Lord, become the sacrament to show the love of the Lord. Through Christ our Lord. All: Amen. # Prayer source: The Prayer Book of the Catholic Bishops Conference of Korea (Page 109).

ee-1. Prayer For A Married Couple

O God, who in creating the human race willed that man and wife should be one, keep, we pray, in a bond of inseparable love those who are united in the covenant of Marriage, so that, as you make their love fruitful, they may become, by your grace, witnesses to charity itself. Through Christ our Lord. Amen.

ee-2. Prayer Of A Couple On The Anniversary Of Marriage

We praise you, O God, we bless you, Creator of all things, who in the beginning made man and woman that they might form a communion of life and love. We also give you thanks for graciously blessing our family life so that it might present an image of Christ's union with the Church. Therefore look with kindness upon us today, and as you have sustained our communion amid joys and struggles, renew our Marriage covenant each day, increase our charity, and strengthen in us the bond of peace, so that we may for ever enjoy your blessing. Through Christ our Lord. Amen. # The prayer of the (ee-1) and (ee-2) was adapted from the English translation of The Order of Celebrating Matrimony ©2013, International Commission on English in the Liturgy Corporation. Also, Copyright © 2010 United States Conference of Catholic Bishops, Washington, D.C. Used with permission. All rights reserved.

ff. Birthday Prayer

Heavenly God, devoted to us as a Father, help us all to praise You and give You glory. Today we celebrate (for example) Ms Seo Young Mary Mun's birthday. I pray for Your blessings and joy for Seo Young Mary Mun. As You said to Jeremiah: Before I formed you in the womb, I knew you and before you were born I blessed you. Lord God, You know everything about Ms Seo Young Mary Mun. You created Ms Seo Young Mary Mun as a sign of Your power, and elected her Your handmaid to show Your goodness. Grant her rich blessings and peace. Save her from all accidents and harms. Let her feel confident and ready for the year ahead and continue to brighten her future. Sanctify her through Your life-giving Word. Consecrate her to find joy in every circumstance and continue to grow in Your grace, gifts, peace and love. Amen.

gg. Prayer for farmers

Almighty God, our creator, You gave us the earth to cultivate and the sun to serve our needs. We always thank you for your countless graces and blessings. Also, we always thank you that you made the earth fruitful, so that it might produce what is needed for life. Bless those who work in the farm fields; give us seasonable weather; and grant that the farmers may receive the reasonable compensation for their work, share the produce for the earth, and rejoicing in your goodness. Through Christ our Lord. Amen.

hh. Prayer for rain

Lord God, maker of heaven and earth and of all created things, we give You all the praise and glory. It is in Your power to send abundant rain on the earth and thus bless its inhabitants. God of the universe, look on our dry hills and fields. If our sins be the reason for this drought, Lord God, I plead for Your forgiveness. Graciously forgive us our sins and forget them according to the multitude of Your tender mercies. Lord God, have mercy on us and for a moment think about our plight. We are struggling for drinking water, crops failing and cattle dying. Our hearts have also grown weak, constantly anxious over the drought. But You have promised to all those who seek Your righteousness all things necessary to sustain their life. I strongly believe that You are in perfect control and You would definitely hear our prayers. God our Father, send rain to the parched land and more again across all the thirsty areas, we earnestly beseech You, in this time of need, such moderate rain and showers, that we may receive the fruits of the earth, to our comfort and to Your honor. And the land will rejoice, and the rivers will sing Your praises, and the hearts of men will be made glad. Through Christ our Lord. Amen.

ii. Prayer for rain

Almighty God, we are in need of rain. We realize now, looking up into the clear, blue sky, what a marvel even the least drop of rain really is. To think that so much water can fall out of the sky, which now is empty and clear! We place our trust in You. We are sure that You know our needs. But You want us to ask You anyway, to show You that we know we are dependent on You. Look on our dry hills and fields, dear God, and bless them with the living blessing of soft rain. Then the land will rejoice, and the rivers will sing Your praises, and the hearts of men will be made glad. Amen.

This prayer is from the lovely prayer book, the rural life prayer book, written and compiled by Alban J. Dachauer, S.J. and printed by the National Catholic Rural Life Conference in 1956 and recently reprinted by Tan books.

jj. Prayer for rain (Bishop Soto offers this simple prayer)

May God open the heavens and let His mercy rain down upon our fields and mountains. Let us especially pray for those most impacted by water shortages and for the wisdom and charity to be good stewards of this precious gift. May our political leaders seek the common good as we learn to care and share God's gift of water for the good of all. Amen.

Other prayers:

"O God, in Whom we live, move and have our being, grant us sufficient rain, so that, being supplied with what sustains us in this present life, we may seek more confidently what sustains us for eternity. Through our Lord Jesus Christ, your Son, who lives and reigns with you in the unity of the Holy Spirit, one God forever and ever." # Prayer Source: The Roman Missal of the Catholic Church, No. 35.

For those facing threats to their health, safety and well-being because of the lack of rainfall in Seoul area. May God bring us rain and snow to alleviate their struggles and to care for the water needs of the people in Seoul Korea. For this we pray to the Lord." Amen.

"For those who manage our water resources. May they be granted the wisdom and strength to balance the many needs of people and commerce as we share God's gift of water among all Koreans. For this we pray to the Lord." Amen.

kk. Prayer at the time of drought(excessive rain)

V. God, Who has created and is reigning over all creation, look on us in pity, suffering difficulties in this drought (excessive rain), bring rain (stop the rain) and grant us to reap the benefits of hard work by relieving our anxiety.

R. Grant us to obtain all things that people need to live, serving God peaceably and living diligently.

All. Amen. # Prayer source: The prayer book of the Catholic Bishops Conference of Korea. (Page 113).

ll. Prayer for embracing new year

V. Lord Jesus, the beginning and the end, thank You for the grace that You bestowed on us during the past year.

R. Lord Jesus, forgive us all the sins that we committed, bestow upon us even greater grace. And let us contribute to the development of our family and society in the new year by eliminating bad habits and doing our best in the responsibilities that we bear.

V. Also as we offer our thoughts, words and behavior to You, Lord, help us work diligently for the glory of God and the salvation of all.

All. Amen. # Prayer source: The prayer book of the Catholic Bishops Conference of Korea. (Page 113).

mm. Prayer for the New year

On New Year's Eve or New Year's Day, the household gathers at the table or at the Christmas tree or manger scene. Many people make New Year's Day a day of prayer for peace. All make the sign of the cross. The leader begins: Let us praise the Lord of days and seasons and years, saying: Glory to God in the highest!
R/. And peace to his people on earth!

The leader may use these or similar words to introduce the blessing: Our lives are made of days and nights, of seasons and years, for we are part of a universe of suns and moons and planets. We mark ends and we make beginnings and, in all, we praise God for the grace and mercy that fill our days. Then the Scripture is read,

Book of Genesis 1:14-19: A reading from the Book of Genesis: God said: "Let there be lights in the dome of the sky, to separate day from night. Let them mark the fixed times, the days and the years, and serve as luminaries in the dome of the sky, to shed light upon the earth." And so it happened: God made the two great lights, the greater one to govern the day, and the lesser one to govern the night; and he made the stars. God set them in the dome of the sky, to shed light upon the earth, to govern the day and the night, and to separate the light from the darkness. God saw how good it was. Evening came, and morning followed—the fourth day. (The family's Bible may be used for an alternate reading such as Psalm 90: 1-4)
Reader: The Word of the Lord.
R/. Thanks be to God.

After a time of silence, members of the household offer prayers of thanksgiving for the past year, and of intercession for the year to come. On January 1, it may be appropriate to conclude these prayers with the Litany of the Blessed Virgin Mary since this is the solemn feast of Mary, Mother of God. In conclusion, all join hands for the Lord's Prayer. Then the leader continues: Let us now pray for God's blessing in the new year. After a short silence, parents may place their hands on their children in blessing as the leader says: Remember us, O God; from age to age be our comforter. You have given us the wonder of time, blessings in days and nights, seasons and years. Bless your children at the turning of the year and fill the months ahead with the bright hope that is ours in the coming of Christ. You are our God, living and reigning, forever and ever. R/. Amen.

nn. Prayer for the New year

Another prayer for peace may be said(On New Year's Eve or New Year's Day,):
Lord, make me an instrument of your peace: where there is hatred, let me sow love; where there is injury, pardon; where there is doubt, faith; where there is despair, hope; where there is darkness, light; where there is sadness, joy. O divine Master, grant that I may not so much seek to be consoled as to console, to be understood as to understand, to be loved as to love. For it is in giving that we receive, it is in pardoning that we are pardoned, it is in dying that we are born to eternal life.
R/. Amen.

Attributed to St. Francis of Assisi. The leader says: Let us bless the Lord. All respond, making the sign of the cross: Thanks be to God. The prayer may conclude with the singing of a Christmas carol. # Prayer souece: (mm) & (nn) are from Catholic Household Blessings and Prayers of USCCB.

oo. Prayer for Travellers

O Almighty and merciful God, who hast commissioned Thy angels to guide and protect us, command them to be our assiduous companions from our setting out until our return; to clothe us with their invisible protection; to keep from us all danger of collision, of fire, of explosion, of fall and bruises, and finally, having preserved us from all evil, and especially from sin, to guide us to our heavenly home. Through Jesus Christ, our Lord. Amen. # "Whatever house you go into, let your first words be, 'Peace to this house!' And if a man of peace lives there, your peace will go and rest on him" (Lk 10,5-6). # Copyright © 2017 Eternal Word Television Network, Inc. Irondale, Alabama. All rights reserved.

pp. Litany of the Way, Prayer for the Journey

As Jesus sought the quiet of the desert, teach us to pray. As Jesus washed the feet of his disciples, teach us to love. As Jesus promised paradise to the thief on the cross, teach us to hope. As Jesus called Peter to walk to him across the water, teach us to believe. As the child Jesus sat among the elders in the temple, teach us to seek answers. As Jesus in the garden opened his mind and heart to God's will, teach us to listen. As Jesus reflected on the Law and the prophets, teach us to learn. As Jesus used parables to reveal the mysteries of the Kingdom, teach us to teach. Amen.

qq. Prayer for Safety

Strong and faithful God, keep our son/daughter safe from injury and harm and make him/her a blessing to all he/she meets today. R/. Amen. Prayer source: From Catholic Household Blessings and Prayers. Copyright of (pp& qq) © 2010 United States Conference of Catholic Bishops, Washington, D.C. Used with permission. All rights reserved.

rr. Prayer for Patience

Heavenly Father, you humbled the pride of our old enemy, the devil, by the patience of your only Son. We beg you to grant us a lively remembrance of all He suffered for us. By His example may we be enabled to bear patiently the trials we suffer. In His name we implore you. Amen.

ss. Prayer for Purity of Heart

O God, you know the secret thoughts of every heart, and nothing is hidden from your sight. Please purify our inmost desires so that we may love you perfectly, and praise you fittingly. We ask this in the name of Christ, your Son. Amen.

For Guidance of the Holy Spirit, O God, may the Holy Spirit who proceeds from you enlighten our minds, and lead us to perfect truth as Christ your Son promised. We ask in His name. Amen.

tt. Prayer for Special Friends

Father in Heaven, you fill the hearts of your faithful with love by the grace of the Holy Spirit. Grant in your goodness strength of mind and body to all for whom we beseech your mercy. May they love you with all their strength and with perfect charity, and always do what is pleasing to you. We ask this through our Lord, Jesus Christ, who lives and reigns with you and the same Spirit for all ages to come. Amen. # The prayer source of (rr, ss & tt) is from Franciscan Mission Associates.

uu. Prayer for Visiting a Country Cemetery on All Souls Day, Nov 2

Dear Lord, here lie in their last rest, the boys and girls, the men and women that worked on the land.

They knew the meaning of hard work.

They knew the joy and peace that is the product of labor. Now we trust they know the peace and happiness of everlasting life with You.

They watched the sun rise often, winter and summer, over these hills and fields. They worked hard by its light, and turned willingly to their rest at its setting. Now they walk in the light of a Sun that knows no setting. Lord, if they are still in the waiting room of heaven, in purgatory, bring them speedily to the light of Your peace and the happiness of Your presence. These men and women all their lives long labored to supply the food and drink necessary to sustain human life. Now, or soon, they enjoy in all its fullness the life that You, Lord, came down to earth to give men, and to give more abundantly. Dear Lord, bless us who labor now in the fields and hills where these dear dead have worked. Grant that we may remember them with charity and kindness, walking reverently in the ways that they have left behind them. Grant, too, that we may finally meet these men and women, these boys and girls, in the eternal mansions that You are even now preparing for us. Amen.

This prayer is from the lovely prayer book, The Rural Life Prayer Book, written and compiled by Alban J. Dachauer, S.J. and printed by the National Catholic Rural Life Conference in 1956 and recently reprinted by Tan books.

vv. Visiting a Cemetery on All Souls Day, Memorial Day, or on the Anniversary of Death or Burial

1734 This order is a solemn commemoration of the departed whose bodies lie in a cemetery. It may be used on All Souls Day, Memorial Day, on the anniversary of the death or burial of a particular deceased person, or when a gravestone or cemetery monument is erected. The service may also be adapted for use by individuals when they visit the grave of a relative or friend.

1735 The service may be used immediately following Mass or apart from Mass.

1736 If the service takes place immediately after Mass and there is to be a procession to the cemetery, the blessing and dismissal of the Mass are omitted. During the procession a psalm or other suitable song may be sung. The priest may wear the chasuble or a cope for the procession and for the service in the cemetery.

1737 This order may be used by a priest, deacon, or a lay minister.

1738 On those occasions when this service is used by a family, one of the family members takes the minister's parts.

ORDER FOR VISITING A CEMETERY

PROCESSION

1739 If the service is to take place immediately after Mass and the cemetery is close to the parish church, the blessing and dismissal of the Mass are omitted and the procession to the cemetery is formed. During the procession Psalm 25, Psalm 116, Psalm 118, or Psalm 42 may be sung. Other suitable songs may also be used. When all have reached the cemetery, the minister addresses the people, using the introduction in no. 1742, below.

If there is no procession, or the service takes place apart from Mass, a psalm or other suitable song may be sung after all have gathered at the cemetery.

GREETING

1740 A minister who is a priest or deacon greets the people in the following or other words preferably taken from Scripture: The grace and peace of God our Father, who raised Jesus from the dead, be with you always.

All reply: And also with your spirit.

1741 A lay minister greets those present in the following words: Praise be to God our Father, who raised Jesus Christ from the dead. Blessed be God for ever.

R. Blessed be God for ever.

1742 The minister using these or similar words, says: My dear friends, we gather today to pray for our brothers and sisters whose bodies lie here in rest. They have passed from death to life in company with the Lord Jesus, who died and rose to new life, and are purified now of their faults. We pray that God may welcome them among all the saints of heaven.

READING OF THE WORD OF GOD

1743 If Mass has not preceded, a reader, another person present, or the minister reads a text of sacred Scripture. Brothers and sisters, listen to the words of the first letter of Paul to the Thessalonians:

4:13-18 We shall stay with the Lord forever. We do not want you to be unaware, brothers and sisters, about those who have fallen asleep, so that you may not grieve like the rest, who have no hope. For if we believe that Jesus died and rose, so too will God, through Jesus, bring with him those who have fallen asleep. Indeed, we tell you this, on the word of the Lord, that we who are alive, who are left until the coming of the Lord, will surely not precede those who have fallen asleep. For the Lord himself, with a word of command, with the voice of an archangel and the trumpet of God, will come down from heaven, and the dead in Christ will rise first. Then we who are alive, who are left, will be caught up together with them in the clouds to meet the Lord in the air. Thus we shall always be with the Lord. Therefore, console one another with these words.

1744 Or one of the Scripture texts in Part III of the Order of Christian Funerals may be chosen.

1745 As circumstances suggest, one of the following responsorial psalms may be sung, or some other suitable song.

R. To you, 0 Lord, I lift up my soul.

Psalm 25 In you I trust; let me not be put to shame, let not my enemies exult over me. No one who waits for you shall be put to shame; those shall be put to shame who heedlessly break faith. R.

Your ways, O LORD, make known to me; teach me your paths, Guide me in your truth and teach me, for you are God my savior, and for you I wait all the day. R.

Remember that your compassion, O LORD, and your kindness are from of old. The sins of my youth and my frailties remember not; in your kindness remember me, because of your goodness, O LORD. R.

Good and upright is the LORD; thus he shows sinners the way. He guides the humble to justice, he teaches the humble his way. R.

All the paths of the LORD are kindness and constancy toward those who keep his covenant and his decrees. For your name's sake, O LORD, you will pardon my guilt, great as it is. R.

Psalm 27:1, 2, 3, 4, 13 R. (v. 1) The Lord is my light and my salvation.
Psalm 130:1-2, 3-4, 5-6, 7-8 R. (v. 5) My soul has hoped in the Lord.
Psalm 143:1-2, 3-4, 5-6, 7, 9-10, 11-12 R. (v. 1) 0 Lord, hear my prayer.

LITANY

1746 While the following litany is sung or recited, the minister sprinkles the graves with holy water and, if desired, may also incense them.

Lord, have mercy. Lord, have mercy.
Christ, have mercy. Christ, have mercy.
Lord, have mercy. Lord, have mercy.

Holy Mary, Mother of God, pray for them. Saint Michael, pray for them. Saint John the Baptist, pray for them. Saint Joseph, pray for them. Saint Peter, pray for them. Saint Paul, pray for them. Saint Andrew, pray for them. Saint Stephen, pray for them. Saint Ann, pray for them. Saint Teresa, pray for them. Saint Catherine, pray for them. Saint Frances Cabrini, pray for them. Saint Elizabeth Seton, pray for them. (The names of other saints may be added.) All holy men and women, pray for them.

Christ, pardon all their faults: Lord, hear our prayer: Christ, remember the good they have done: Lord, hear our prayer: Christ, receive them into eternal life: Lord, hear our prayer: Christ, comfort all those who mourn: Lord, hear our prayer.

Lord, have mercy. Lord, have mercy.
Christ, have mercy. Christ, have mercy.
Lord, have mercy. Lord, have mercy.

1747 The minister then invites those present to pray the Lord's Prayer, in these or similar words: With Christ there is mercy and fullness of redemption; let us pray as Jesus taught us:

All: Our Father ⋯

PRAYER

1748 The minister then says the following prayer or another taken from the Order of
     Christian Funerals, no. 398.

All-powerful God, whose mercy is never withheld from those who call upon you in
hope, look kindly on your servants (N. and N.), who departed this life confessing
your name, and number them among your saints for evermore. We ask this through
Christ our Lord. R. Amen.

1749 Or:
Almighty God and Father, by the mystery of the cross, you have made us strong; by
the sacrament of the resurrection you have sealed us as your own. Look kindly upon
your servants, now freed from the bonds of mortality, and count them among your
saints in heaven. We ask this through Christ our Lord. R. Amen.

1750 Or: For one person
Almighty God and Father, it is our certain faith that your Son, who died on the cross,
was raised from the dead, the first fruits of all who have fallen asleep. Grant that
through this mystery your servant N., who has gone to his/her rest in Christ, may
share in the joy of his resurrection. We ask this through Christ our Lord. R. Amen.

1751 Or: For the blessing of a gravestone or monument
O God, by whose mercy the faithful departed find rest, bless this gravestone with
which we mark the resting place of N. May he/she have everlasting life and rejoice
in you with your saints for ever. We ask this through Christ our Lord. R. Amen.

CONCLUDING RITE

1752 The minister says:
Eternal rest grant unto them, O Lord. R. And let perpetual light shine upon them.
May they rest in peace. R. Amen.
May their souls and the souls of the faithful departed, through the mercy of God, rest
in peace. R. Amen.

1753 A priest or deacon adds: May the peace of God, which is beyond all understanding, keep your hearts and minds in the knowledge and love of God and of his Son, our Lord Jesus Christ. R. Amen.

Then he blesses all present. And may almighty God bless you all, the Father, and the Son, + and the Holy Spirit. R. Amen.

1754 The service may be concluded by a suitable psalm or other song.

Prayer Source: Book of Blessings prepared by International Commission on English in the Liturgy; A Joint Commission of Catholic Bishops' Conferences, The Liturgical Press, Collegeville, Minnesota, 1989.

Chapter 18 Prayers of Saints, the Blessed and the Pope

A   Prayers related to St. Augustine of Hippo (AD 354-430)

A. Prayer to the Holy Spirit Or Breathe in me O Holy Spirit

Breathe in me O Holy Spirit, that my thoughts may all be holy.

Act in me O Holy Spirit, that my work, too, may be holy.

Draw my heart O Holy Spirit, that I love but what is holy.

Strengthen me O Holy Spirit, to defend all that is holy.

Guard me, then, O Holy Spirit, that I always may be holy. Amen.

B. Prayer for the Indwelling of the Spirit

Holy Spirit, powerful Consoler, sacred Bond of the Father and the Son, Hope of the afflicted, descend into my heart and establish in it your loving dominion. Enkindle in my tepid soul the fire of your Love so that I may be wholly subject to you. We believe that when you dwell in us, you also prepare a dwelling for the Father and the Son. Deign, therefore, to come to me, Consoler of abandoned souls, and Protector of the needy. Help the afflicted, strengthen the weak, and support the wavering. Come and purify me. Let no evil desire take possession of me. You love the humble and resist the proud. Come to me, glory of the living, and hope of the dying. Lead me by your grace that I may always be pleasing to you. Amen.

C. Too Late Have I Loved You Or Prayer on Finding God after a Long Search

Late have I loved you, beauty so old and so new: late have I loved you. And see, you were within and I was in the external world and sought you there, and in my unlovely state I plunged into those lovely created things which you made. You were with me, and I was not with you. The lovely things kept me far from you, though if they did not have their existence in you, they had no existence at all. You called and cried out loud and shattered my deafness. You were radiant and resplendent, you put to flight my blindness. You were fragrant, and I drew in my breath and now pant after you. I tasted you, and I feel but hunger and thirst for you. You touched me, and I am set on fire to attain the peace which is yours. Amen. ©1991 Henry Chadwick. St. Confessions X.27 of Augustine of Hippo. This prayer is translated by Henry Chadwick.

D. Prayer to Our Lady, Mother of Mercy

Blessed Virgin Mary, who can worthily repay you with praise and thanks for having rescued a fallen world by your generous consent! Receive our gratitude, and by your prayers obtain the pardon of our sins. Take our prayers into the sanctuary of heaven and enable them to make our peace with God. Holy Mary, help the miserable, strengthen the discouraged, comfort the sorrowful, pray for your people, plead for the clergy, intercede for all women consecrated to God. May all who venerate you feel now your help and protection. Be ready to help us when we pray, and bring back to us the answers to our prayers. Make it your continual concern to pray for the people of God, for you were blessed by God and were made worthy to bear the Redeemer of the world, who lives and reigns forever. Amen.

E. Prayer to St. Augustine

We humbly supplicate and beseech thee, O thrice-blessed Augustine, that thou wouldst be mindful of us poor sinners this day, daily, and at the hour of our death, that by thy merits and prayers we may be delivered from all evils, of soul as well as body, and daily increase in virtue and good works; obtain for us that we may know our God and know ourselves, that in His mercy He may cause us to love Him above all things in life and death; impart to us, we beseech thee, some share of that love with which thou so ardently glow, that our hearts being all inflamed with this divine love, happily departing out of this mortal pilgrimage, we may deserve to praise with thee the loving heart of Jesus for a never-ending eternity. Amen.

F. Act of Hope

For your mercies' sake, O Lord my God, tell me what you are to me. Say to my soul: "I am your salvation." So speak that I may hear, O Lord; my heart is listening; open it that it may hear you, and say to my soul: "I am your salvation." After hearing this word, may I come in haste to take hold of you. Hide not your face from me. Let me see your face even if I die, lest I die with longing to see it. The house of my soul is too small to receive you; let it be enlarged by you. It is all in ruins; do you repair it. There are thing in it, I confess and I know, that must offend your sight. But who shall cleanse it? Or to what others besides you shall I cry out? From my secret sins cleanse me, O Lord, and from those of others spare your servant. Amen.

G. Act of Petition

Give me yourself, O my God, give yourself to me. Behold I love you, and if my love is too weak a thing, grant me to love you more strongly. I cannot measure my love to know how much it falls short of being sufficient, but let my soul hasten to your embrace and never be turned away until it is hidden in the secret shelter of your presence. This only do I know, that it is not good for me when you are not with me, when you are only outside me. I want you in my very self. All the plenty in the world which is not my God is utter want. Amen.

H. Lord Jesus, Let Me Know Myself

Lord Jesus, let me know myself and know You, and desire nothing save only You.
Let me hate myself and love You.
Let me do everything for the sake of You.
Let me humble myself and exalt You.
Let me think of nothing except You.
Let me die to myself and live in You.
Let me accept whatever happens as from You.
Let me banish self and follow You, and ever desire to follow You.
Let me fly from myself and take refuge in You, that I may deserve to be defended by You.
Let me fear for myself, let me fear You, and let me be among those who are chosen by You.
Let me distrust myself and put my trust in You.
Let me be willing to obey for the sake of You.
Let me cling to nothing save only to You, and let me be poor because of You. Look upon me, that I may love You. Call me that I may see You, and forever enjoy You. Amen.

I. Prayer of Trust in God's Heavenly Promise

My God, let me know and love you, so that I may find my happiness in you. Since I cannot fully achieve this on earth, help me to improve daily until I may do so to the full enable me to know you ever more on earth, so that I may know you perfectly in heaven. Enable me to love you ever more on earth, so that I may love you perfectly in heaven. In that way my joy may be great on earth, and perfect with you in heaven. O God of truth, grant me the happiness of heaven so that my joy may be full in accord with your promise. In the meantime let my mind dwell on that happiness, my tongue speak of it, my heart pine for it, my mouth pronounce it, my soul hunger for it, my flesh thirst for it, and my entire being desire it until I enter through death in the joy of my Lord forever. Amen.

J. Prayer to seek God Continually

O Lord my God, I believe in You, Father, Son and Holy Spirit. Insofar as I can, insofar as you have given me the power, I have sought you. I became weary and I labored. O Lord my God, my sole hope, help me to believe and never to cease seeking you. Grant that I may always and ardently seek out your countenance. Give me the strength to seek you, for you help me to find you and you have more and more given me the hope of finding you. Here I am before you with my firmness and my infirmity. Preserve the first and heal the second. Here I am before you with my strength and my ignorance. Where you have opened the door to me, welcome me at the entrance; where you have closed the door to me, open to my cry; enable me to remember you, to understand you, and to love you. Amen.

K. St. Augustine of Hippo by St. Pope John Paul II

"Great Augustine, our father and teacher, knowledgeable in the luminous ways of God and also in the tortuous paths of men; we admire the wonders that divine grace wrought in you, making you a passionate witness of truth and goodness, at the service of brothers.

At the beginning of the new millennium marked by the cross of Christ, teach us to read history in the light of Divine Providence, which guides events toward the definitive encounter with the Father. Direct us toward peaceful ends, nourishing in our hearts your own longing for those values on which it is possible to build, with the strength that comes from God, the 'city' made to the measure of man. May the profound doctrine, that with loving and patient study you drew from the ever living sources of Scripture, enlighten all those tempted today by alienating illusions. Give them the courage to undertake the path toward that 'interior man' where the One awaits who alone can give peace to our restless hearts. Many of our contemporaries seem to have lost the hope of being able to reach -- amid the numerous opposing ideologies -- the truth, of which their innermost being still keeps a burning nostalgia. Teach them to never cease in their search, in the certainty that, in the end, their effort will be rewarded by the satisfying encounter with the supreme Truth who is source of all created truth. Finally, St. Augustine, transmit to us also a spark of that ardent love for the Church, the Catholic Mother of the Saints, which sustained and animated the toils of your long ministry." Have us, walking together under the guidance of legitimate pastors, reach the glory of the heavenly Homeland, where, with all the Saints, we will be able to join the new canticle of the everlasting alleluia. Amen. This prayer was prepared by St. Pope John Paul II In November 2004.

In November 2004 Pope John Paul II received the relics of St. Augustine in the Vatican. The initiative marked the celebration of the 1,650th anniversary of the birth of the bishop, philosopher and theologian, as well as one of the most influential Fathers of the Church of the West. The Holy Father was so moved when viewing the relics that he composed this prayer to St. Augustine.

B Prayers related to the St. Thomas Aquinas

A. Prayer for Steadfastness

Grant me, I beseech You, almighty and most merciful God, fervently to desire, wisely to search out, and perfectly to fulfill, all that is well-pleasing unto You. Order You my worldly condition to the glory of Your name; and, of all that You require me to do, grant me the knowledge, the desire, and the ability, that I may so fulfill it as I ought, and may my path to You, I pray, be safe, straightforward, and perfect to the end. Give me, O Lord, a steadfast heart, which no unworthy affection may drag downwards; give me an unconquered heart, which no tribulation can wear out; give me an upright heart, which no unworthy purpose may tempt aside. Bestow upon me also, O Lord my God, understanding to know You, diligence to seek You, wisdom to find You, and a faithfulness that may finally embrace Thee. Amen.

B. Adoro Te Devote; Refer to Chapter 11, (b) Adoro Te Devote (Page 195)

B-1. Pange Lingua Gloriosi

Sing, my tongue, the Savior's glory, Of His Flesh the mystery sing; Of His Blood, all price exceeding, Shed by our immortal King, Destined, for the world's redemption, From a noble womb to spring.

Of a pure and spotless Virgin Born for us on earth below, He, as Man, with man conversing, Stayed, the seeds of truth to sow; Then He closed in solemn order Wondrously His life of woe.

On the night of that Last Supper, Seated with His chosen band, He the Pascal victim eating, First fulfills the Law's command; Then as Food to His Apostles Gives Himself with His own hand.

Word made Flesh, the bread of nature By His word to Flesh He turns; Wine into His Blood He changes: What though sense no change discerns? Only be the heart in earnest, Faith her lesson quickly learns.

Down in adoration falling, Lo! the sacred Host we hail; Lo! o'er ancient forms departing, Newer rites of grace prevail; Faith for all defects supplying, Where the feeble sense fail.

To the everlasting Father, And the Son who reigns on high, With the Holy Spirit proceeding Forth from Each eternally, Be salvation, honor, blessing, Might and endless majesty. Amen.

C Prayer of St. Bonaventure

Pierce, O most sweet Lord Jesus, my inmost soul with the most joyous and healthful wound of Thy love, and with true, calm and most holy apostolic charity, that my soul may ever languish and melt with entire love and longing for Thee, may yearn for Thee and for thy courts, may long to be dissolved and to be with Thee. Grant that my soul may hunger after Thee, the Bread of Angels, the refreshment of holy souls, our daily and super substantial bread, having all sweetness and savor and every delightful taste. May my heart ever hunger after and feed upon Thee, Whom the angels desire to look upon, and may my inmost soul be filled with the sweetness of Thy savor; may it ever thirst for Thee, the fountain of life, the fountain of wisdom and knowledge, the fountain of eternal light, the torrent of pleasure, the fullness of the house of God; may it ever compass Thee, seek Thee, find Thee, run to Thee, come up to Thee, meditate on Thee, speak of Thee, and do all for the praise and glory of Thy name, with humility and discretion, with love and delight, with ease and affection, with perseverance to the end; and be Thou alone ever my hope, my entire confidence, my riches, my delight, my pleasure, my joy, my rest and tranquility, my peace, my sweetness, my food, my refreshment, my refuge, my help, my wisdom, my portion, my possession, my treasure; in Whom may my mind and my heart be ever fixed and firm and rooted immovably. Amen. No Copyright©.

D Prayers related to St. Cecilia

A. Prayer to St. Cecilia

Dear Saint Cecilia, one thing we know for certain about you is that you became a heroic martyr in fidelity to your divine Bridegroom. We do not know that you were a musician but we are told that you heard Angels sing. Inspire musicians to gladden the hearts of people by filling the air with God's gift of music and reminding them of the divine Musician who created all beauty. Amen. No Copyright©.

B. Prayer to St. Cecilia for help to be united with Christ

O glorious saint, who chose to die instead of denying your King, we pray you please to help us as His fair praise we sing. We lift our hearts in joyous song to honor Him this way. And while we sing, remembering, to sing is to doubly pray. At once in our hearts and in our tongues we offer double prayer sent heavenward on winged notes to praise God dwelling there. While in our hearts and tongues we try with song to praise God twice, we ask dear saint, to help us be united close to Christ! Amen. No Copyright©.

E Prayers related to St. Francis

A. Prayer of St. Francis for peace

Lord, make me a channel of thy peace,
that where there is hatred, I may bring love;
that where there is wrong, I may bring the spirit of forgiveness;
that where there is discord, I may bring harmony;
that where there is error, I may bring truth;
that where there is doubt, I may bring faith;
that where there is despair, I may bring hope;
that where there are shadows, I may bring light;
that where there is sadness, I may bring joy.
Lord, grant that I may seek rather to comfort than to be comforted;
to understand, than to be understood; to love, than to be loved.
For it is by self-forgetting that one finds.
It is by forgiving that one is forgiven.
It is by dying that one awakens to Eternal Life. Amen. #. The prayer is often attributed to St Francis Bernadone who was born in Assisi, Italy in 1181 or 1182. He lived and preached a life of poverty and love of God to all men. He founded the religious Order of the Franciscans; with St. Clare, he founded the Order of the Poor Clares; and the Third Order for lay people. After living a carefree childhood and young adulthood filled with wealthy entertainment and pleasure, Francis fell ill at the age of 20 and his thoughts began to focus on eternity and his relationship with God. Francis turned from his wealthy lifestyle and decided to give his life over to the church. He passed in 1226 after rekindling the love of God among many thousands of people.

B. Prayer through St. Francis

O God, who, through the merits of blessed Francis, didst give increase to Thy Church, by enriching her with new offspring: grant us, that following his example we may despise earthly goods and ever rejoice in partaking of Thy heavenly gifts. Through our Lord Jesus Christ, Thy Son, Who lives and reigns with You and Holy Spirit, one God, forever and ever. Amen.

C. Prayer of Saint Clare of Assisi

God of mercy, You inspired Saint Clare with the love of poverty. By the help of her prayers may we follow Christ in poverty of spirit and come to the joyful vision of Your glory in the Kingdom of heaven. We ask this through Our Lord Jesus Christ, Your Son, Who lives and reigns with you and the Holy Spirit, one God, forever and ever. Amen. "Saint Clare of Assisi expressed to Saint Francis the desire to consecrate herself to God. Together with him, she became the founder of the Franciscan Nuns of the Second Order: the "Poor Clares". Having governed her convent for forty-two years, she died in 1253." No Copyright©.

F   Prayers related to St. Ignatius of Loyola's

A. St. Ignatius of Loyola's Prayer against depression

O Christ Jesus, when all is darkness and we feel our weakness and helplessness, give us the sense of Your Presence, Your Love and Your Strength. Help us to have perfect trust in Your protecting love and strengthening power, so that nothing may frighten or worry us. For, living close to You, we shall see Your Hand, Your Purpose, Your Will through all things. Amen. No Copyright©.

B. Prayer of St. Ignatius of Loyola

Teach us, good Lord, to serve you as you deserve; to give, and not to count the cost, to fight, and not to heed the wounds, to toil, and not to seek for rest, to labor, and not to ask for reward, except that of knowing that we are doing your will. Amen. No Copyright©.

A. Thanksgiving Prayer

O Jesus, eternal God, I thank You for Your countless graces and blessings. Let every beat of my heart be a new hymn of thanksgiving to You, O God. Let every drop of my blood circulate for You, Lord. My soul is one hymn in adoration of Your mercy. I love You, God, for Yourself alone. (Diary 1794)

B. Prayer of St. Faustina Kowalska before the Eucharist

I adore You, Lord and Creator, hidden in the Most Blessed Sacrament. I adore You for all the works of Your hands, that reveal to me so much wisdom, goodness and mercy, O Lord. You have spread so much beauty over the earth and it tells me about Your beauty, even though these beautiful things are but a faint reflection of You, incomprehensible Beauty. And although You have hidden Yourself and concealed Your beauty, my eye, enlightened by faith, reaches You and my soul recognizes its Creator, its Highest Good, and my heart is completely immersed in prayer of adoration.

My Lord and Creator, Your goodness encourages me to converse with You. Your mercy abolishes the chasm which separates the Creator from the creature. To converse with You, O Lord, is the delight of my heart. In You I find everything that my heart could desire. Here Your light illumines my mind, enabling it to know You more and more deeply. Here streams of graces flow down upon my heart. Here my soul draws eternal life. O my Lord and Creator, You alone, beyond all these gifts, give Your own self to me and unite Yourself intimately with Your miserable creature.

O Christ, let my greatest delight be to see You loved and Your praise and glory proclaimed, especially the honor of Your mercy. O Christ, let me glorify Your goodness and mercy to the last moment of my life, with every drop of my blood and every beat of my heart. Would that I be transformed into a hymn of adoration of You. When I find myself on my deathbed, may the last beat of my heart be a loving hymn glorifying Your unfathomable mercy. Amen.

C. Prayer through Saint Faustina

O Jesus, Who filled Your handmaid Saint Faustina with profound veneration for Your boundless Mercy, deign, if it be Your holy will, to grant me, through her intercession, the grace for which I fervently pray (here make your request). My sins render me unworthy of Your Mercy, but be mindful of Saint Faustina's spirit of sacrifice and self-denial, and reward her virtue by granting the petition which, with childlike confidence, I present to You through her intercession. Amen.

D. The Hour of Great Mercy — 3 O'clock Prayer

At 3:00 PM, meditate on the Passion of Jesus no matter how brief, implore God's unconditional love and mercy especially for poor sinners, and say······You expired, Jesus, but the source of life gushed forth for souls, and the ocean of mercy opened up for the whole world. O Fount of Life, unfathomable Divine Mercy, envelop the whole world and empty Yourself out upon us. (Diary 1319) O Blood and Water, which gushed forth from the Heart of Jesus as a Fount of Mercy for us, I trust in You. (Diary 187) Holy God, Holy Mighty One, Holy Immortal One, have mercy on us and on the whole world. Amen. (Three times)

E. Prayer to the Holy Trinity

O Holy Trinity, Eternal God, I thank you for allowing me to know the greatness and the various degrees of glory to which souls attain···O Lord, immerse my soul in the ocean of Your divinity and grant me the grace of knowing You; for the better I know You, the more I desire You, and the more my love for You grows. Amen. (Diary 605)

F. Prayer To Be Merciful

O Most Holy Trinity! As many times as I breathe, as many times as my heart beats, as many times as my blood pulsates through my body, so many thousand times do I want to glorify Your mercy. I want to be completely transformed into Your mercy and to be Your living reflection, O Lord. May the greatest of all Divine attributes, that of Your unfathomable Mercy, pass through my heart and soul to my neighbor. Help me, O Lord, that my eyes may be merciful, so that I may never suspect or judge from appearances, but always look for what is beautiful in my neighbor's souls and come to their rescue. Help me, that my ears may be merciful, so that I may give heed to my neighbor's needs, and not be indifferent to their pains and moaning. Help me, O Lord, that my tongue may be merciful, so that I should never speak negatively of others, but have a word of comfort and forgiveness for all. Help me, O Lord, that my hands may be merciful and filled with good deeds, so that I may do only good to my neighbors and always try to take upon myself the more difficult and toilsome tasks. Help me, O Lord, that my feet may be merciful, so that I may hurry to assist my neighbor, overcoming my own fatigue and weariness. My true rest is in the service of my neighbor. Help me, O Lord, that my heart may be merciful, so that I myself may feel all the sufferings of my neighbor. I will refuse my heart to no one. I will be sincere even with those who, I know, will abuse my kindness. And I will lock myself up in the most merciful Heart of Jesus. I will bear my own suffering in silence. May your mercy, O Lord, rest upon me. Amen. (Diary 163)

G. Prayer for Divine Mercy for the World

O Greatly Merciful God, Infinite Goodness, today all mankind calls out from the abyss of its misery to Your mercy - to Your compassion, O God; and it is with its mighty voice of misery that it cries out. Gracious God, do not reject the prayer of this earth's exiles! O Lord, Goodness beyond our understanding, Who are acquainted with our misery through and through, and know that by our own power we cannot ascend to You. We implore You, anticipate us with Your grace and keep on increasing Your mercy in us, that we may faithfully do Your holy will all through our life and at death's hour. Let the omnipotence of Your mercy shield us from the darts of our salvation's enemies, that we may with confidence, as Your children, await Your final coming - that day known to You alone. And we expect to obtain everything promised us by Jesus in spite of all our wretchedness. For Jesus is our hope: Through His merciful Heart, as through an open gate, we pass through to heaven. Amen. (Diary 1570)

H Prayers to related to St. Jude

A. Prayer to St. Jude for hope in desperation.

Oh glorious apostle St. Jude, faithful servant and friend of Jesus, the name of the traitor who delivered thy beloved Master into the hands of His enemies has caused thee to be forgotten by many, but the Church honors and invokes thee universally as the patron of hopeless cases--of things despaired of. Pray for me who am so miserable; make use, I implore thee, of that particular privilege accorded thee of bringing visible and speedy help where help is almost despaired of. Come to my assistance in this great need, that I may receive the consolations and succor of heaven in all my necessities, tribulations and sufferings, particularly (mention your request), and that I may bless God with thee and all the elect throughout eternity. I promise thee, O blessed St. Jude, to be ever mindful of this great favor, and I will never cease to honor thee as my special and powerful patron, and to do all in my power to encourage devotion to thee. Amen. # No Copyright ©.

B. Prayer to St. Jude for help in difficult times

Most holy Apostle, Saint Jude Thaddeus, friend of Jesus, I place myself in your care at this difficult time. Help me know that I need not face my troubles alone. Please join me in my need, asking God to send me: consolation in my sorrow, courage in my fear, and healing in the midst of my suffering. Ask our loving Lord to fill me with the grace to accept whatever may lie ahead for me and my loved ones, and to strengthen my faith in God's healing powers. Thank you, Saint Jude Thaddeus, for the promise of hope you hold out to all who believe, and inspire me to give this gift of hope to others as it has been given to me.

V. Saint Jude, Apostle of Hope
R. Pray for us! Amen. # This prayer, courtesy of the Dominican Shrine of Saint Jude Dominican Friars, is wonderfully straightforward.

I Prayer to St. Maximillian Kolbe

A. Novena Prayer to St. Maximilian Kolbe

O Lord Jesus Christ, who said, "greater love than this no man has that a man lay down his life for his friends," through the intercession of St. Maximilian Kolbe whose life illustrated such love, we beseech you to grant us our petitions⋯(here mention the requests you have). Through the Militia Immaculata movement, which Maximilian founded, he spread a fervent devotion to Our Lady throughout the world. He gave up his life for a total stranger and loved his persecutors, giving us an example of unselfish love for all men - a love that was inspired by true devotion to Mary.

Grant, O Lord Jesus, that we too may give ourselves entirely without reserve to the love and service of our Heavenly Queen in order to better love and serve our fellowman in imitation of your humble servant, Maximilian. Amen. # St. Maximillian Kolbe is a modern-day saint who was killed in Auschwitz after he volunteered to take the place of a prisoner who was sentenced to be locked in a bunker and starved to death. St. Maximillian bravely led the men in the bunker in prayer and songs and was still alive days later. He was finally given a lethal injection. His feast day is celebrated on August 14th. # Copyright © 2017 Eternal Word Television Network, Inc. Irondale, Alabama. All rights reserved.

J Prayers related to St. Padre Pio

A. Stay with me; Prayer of St. Padre Pio after communion

Stay with me, Lord, for it is necessary to have You present so that I do not forget You. You know how easily I abandon You. Stay with me Lord, because I am weak, and I need Your strength, so that I may not fall so often. Stay with me Lord, for You are my life, and without You, I am without fervor. Stay with me Lord, for You are my light, and without you, I am in darkness. Stay with me Lord, to show me Your will. Stay with me Lord, so that I hear Your voice and follow You. Stay with me Lord, for I desire to love you very much, and always be in Your Company. Stay with me Lord, if You wish me to be faithful to You. Stay with me Lord, for as poor as my soul is, I want it to be a place of consolation for You, a nest of Love. Stay with me, Jesus, for it is getting late, and the day is coming to a close, and life passes, death, judgment, eternity approach. It is necessary to renew my strength, so that I will not stop along the way and for that, I need You. It is getting late and death approaches. I fear the darkness, the temptations, the dryness, the cross, the sorrows. O how I need You, my Jesus, in this night of exile. Stay with me tonight, Jesus, in life with all its dangers, I need You. Let me recognize You as Your disciples did at the breaking of bread, so that the Eucharistic Communion be the light which disperses the darkness, the force which sustains me, the unique joy of my heart. Stay with me Lord, because at the hour of my death, I want to remain united to you, if not by Communion, at least by grace and love. Stay with me Jesus, I do not ask for divine consolation because I do not merit it, but the gift of Your presence, oh yes, I ask this of You. Stay with me Lord, for it is You alone I look for, Your love, Your grace, Your will, Your heart, Your Spirit, because I love You and ask no other reward but to love You more and more. With a firm love, I will love You with all my heart while on earth and continue to love You perfectly during all eternity. Amen. # This prayer was written by St. Pio of Pietrelcina. # No Copyright ©

B. Prayer for the Intercession of St. Pio of Pietrelcina

Gracious God, You generously blessed Your servant, Padre Pio, with the gifts of the Spirit. You marked his body with the five wounds of Christ Crucified, as a powerful witness to the saving Passion and Death of Your Son, and as a stirring inspiration to many people of Your infinite mercy, forgiveness, and love. In the confessional, Padre Pio labored endlessly for the salvation of souls. Through his prayerful intercession, many who suffered were healed of sickness and disease. Endowed with the gift of discernment, he could read people's hearts. From the blood of his wounds came a perfumed fragrance, a special sign of Your Holy Presence. With dignity and intense devotion, he celebrated daily Mass, inviting countless men and women to a greater union with Jesus Christ, in the Sacrament of the Holy Eucharist. Through the intercession of Padre Pio, I confidently beseech You to grant me the grace of (here state your petition). Help me to imitate his example of prayerful holiness and compassion, so that I, too, may faithfully follow the Risen Lord, and one day rejoice in the Kingdom, where You live and reign forever and ever. Glory be to the Father (three times). Amen. # Prayer Source: Capuchin Franciscan Friars, 2003.

K Prayers of St. Mother Teresa of Calcutta

A. Radiating Christ; Refer to Chapter 8, I

B. Prayer to the Most Blessed Virgin Mary

Mary, give me your heart: so beautiful, so pure, so immaculate; your heart so full of love and humility that I may be able to receive Jesus in the Bread of Life and love

Him as you love Him and serve Him in the distressing guise of the poor. Amen.
This prayer was written by St. Mother Teresa of Calcutta.

C. St. Mother Teresa of Calcutta

Mother Teresa, known in the Catholic Church as Saint Teresa of Calcutta (born Anjezë Gonxhe Bojaxhiu; Albanian 1910 – 1997), was an Albanian Indian Roman Catholic nun and missionary. She was born in Skopie(now the capital of the Republic of Macedonia), then part of the Kosovo Vilayet of the Ottoman Empire. After living in Macedonia for eighteen years she moved to Ireland and then to India, where she lived for most of her life. In 1950 Teresa founded the Missionaries of Charity, a Roman Catholic religious congregation which had over 4,500 sisters and was active in 133 countries in 2012. The congregation manages for people dying of HIV/AIDS, leprosy and soup kitchens; dispensaries and mobile clinics; children's and family counseling programs; orphanages, and schools. Members, who take vows of chastity, poverty, and obedience, also profess a fourth vow: to give "wholehearted free service to the poorest of the poor". Teresa received a number of honors, including the 1962 Ramon Magsaysay Peace Prize and 1979 Nobel Peace Prize. She was canonized (Recognized by the church as a saint) on 4 September 2016, and the anniversary of her death (5 September) is her feast day. She was a controversial figure during her life and after her death. Teresa was admired by many for her charitable work. She was praised and criticized for her opposition to abortion, and criticized for poor conditions in her houses for the dying. Her authorized biography was written by Navin Chwala and published in 1992, and she has been the subject of films and other books.

L   Prayers related to St. Thérèse of Lisieux

A. Prayer to St. Thérèse of Lisieux for Guidance

Govern by all Thy Wisdom, O Lord, so that my soul may always be serving Thee as Thou dost Will, and not as I may choose. Do not punish me, I beseech Thee, by granting that which I wish or ask if it offended Thy Love, which would always live in me. Let me die to myself, so that I may love Thee. Let me live to Thee, Who art in Thyself, the True Life. Dear St. Thérèse of Lisieux, guide me in your little Way, so that

I may ascend to the heights and happiness of heaven. Amen. No Copyright ©

B. Prayer to St. Thérèse

O little St. Theresa of the Child Jesus, who during your short life on earth became a mirror of angelic purity, of love strong as death, and of wholehearted abandonment to God, now that you rejoice in the reward of your virtues, cast a glance of pity on me as I leave all things in your hands. Make my troubles your own - speak a word for me to our Lady Immaculate, whose flower of special love you were - to that Queen of heaven "who smiled on you at the dawn of life." Beg her as the Queen of the heart of Jesus to obtain for me by her powerful intercession, the grace I yearn for so ardently at this moment, and that she join with it a blessing that may strengthen me during life. Defend me at the hour of death, and lead me straight on to a happy eternity. Amen.

C. A Prayer of St. Thérèse

O Jesus, Who in Thy cruel Passion didst become the "Reproach of men and the Man of Sorrows," I worship Thy Divine Face. Once it shone with the beauty and sweetness of the Divinity: now for my sake it is become as the face of a leper. Yet in that disfigured Countenance I recognize Thy infinite Love, and I am consumed with the desire of loving Thee and of making Thee loved by all mankind. The tears that streamed in such abundance from Thy Eyes are to me as precious pearls which I delight to gather, that with their infinite worth I may ransom the souls of poor sinners. O Jesus, Whose Face is the sole beauty that ravishes my heart, I may not behold here upon earth the sweetness of Thy Glance, nor feel the ineffable tenderness of Thy Kiss. I bow to Thy Will - but I pray Thee to imprint in me Thy Divine Likeness, and I implore Thee so to inflame me with Thy Love, that it may quickly consume me and I may soon reach the Vision of Thy glorious Face in Heaven. Amen.

D. A Morning Prayer Written by St. Thérèse

O my God! I offer Thee all my actions of this day for the intentions and for the glory of the Sacred Heart of Jesus. I desire to sanctify every beat of my heart, my every thought, my simplest works, by uniting them to Its infinite merits; and I wish to make reparation for my sins by casting them into the furnace of Its Merciful Love. O my God! I ask of Thee for myself and for those whom I hold dear, the grace to fulfill perfectly Thy Holy Will, to accept for love of Thee the joys and sorrows of this passing life, so that we may one day be united together in heaven for all Eternity.

E. Little Flower Novena; St. Thérèse of the Child Jesus Novena

Prayers to be said each day:
Come Holy Spirit and fill the hearts of the faithful, and kindle in them the fire of divine love.
V. Send forth Your Spirit and they shall be created.
R. And You shall renew the face of the earth.

Let us pray: O God, who have instructed the hearts of the faithful by the light of the Holy Spirit; grant that by the gift of the same Spirit, we may be ever truly wise and rejoice in His consolation, through Christ our Lord. Amen.
Acts of Faith, Hope, and Love: O my God! I believe in Thee: strengthen my faith. All my hopes are in Thee: do Thou secure them. I love Thee: teach me to love Thee daily more and more.

The Act of Contrition: O my God! I am heartily sorry for having offended You, and I detest all my sins, because I dread the loss of heaven and the pains of hell, but most of all because they offend You, my God, who are all good and deserving of all my love. I firmly resolve, with the help of Your grace, to confess my sins, to do penance, and to amend my life. Amen.

Concluding Prayer Prayed Each Day:
O Lord, You have said: Unless you become as little children you shall not enter the kingdom of heaven; grant us, we beg You, so to follow, in humility and simplicity of heart, the footsteps of the Virgin blessed Thérèse, that we may attain to an everlasting reward. Amen.

First Day

St. Thérèse, privileged Little Flower of Jesus and Mary, I approach you with childlike confidence and deep humility. I lay before you my desires, and beg that through your intercession they may be realized. Did you not promise to spend your heaven doing good upon earth? Grant me according to this promise the favors I am asking from you. Intercede for us all the days of our life, but specially during this Novena and obtain for us from God the graces and favors we ask through your intercession. Amen.

Thought for the day: Confidence in God. We can never have too much confidence in the good God who is so powerful and so merciful. We obtain from Him as much as we hope for. If you are nothing, do you forget that Jesus is everything? You have only to lose your nothingness in His Infinity and think only of loving Him.

Concluding Prayer

Second Day

O dear little Saint, now that you see the crucified Jesus in heaven, still bearing the wounds caused by sin, you know still more clearly than you did upon earth the value of souls, and the priceless worth of that Precious Blood which He shed to save them. As I am one of those children for whom Christ died, obtain for me all the graces I need in order to profit by that Precious Blood. Use your great power with our divine Lord and pray for me. Intercede for us all the days of our life, but especially during this Novena and obtain for us from God the graces and favors we ask through your intercession. Amen.

Thought for the day: Sin. The only grace I ask, O Jesus, is never to offend Thee. By love and not by fear, does a soul avoid committing the least fault. Yes, even if I have on my conscience every possible crime, I should lose none of my confidence; my heart breaking with sorrow, I should go and throw myself into the arms of my Savior. The remembrance of my faults humbles me and makes me afraid to rely on my own strength, which is nothing but weakness.

Concluding Prayer

Third Day

Dear Little Flower, make all things lead me to heaven and God, whether I look at the sun, the moon, the stars and the vast expanse in which they float, or whether I look at the flowers of the field, the trees of the forest, the beauties of the earth so full of color and so glorious, may they speak to me of the love and power of God; may they all sing His praises in my ear. Like you may I daily love Him more and more in return for His gifts. Teach me often to deny myself in my dealings with others, that I may offer to Jesus many little sacrifices. Intercede for us all the days of our life, but especially during this Novena and obtain for us from God the graces and favors we ask through your intercession. Amen.

Thought for the day: The Use of God's Gifts. How much benefit have I received from the beauties of nature, bestowed in such abundance. How they raise me to Him who placed such wonders in this land of exile which is only to last a day. O sparkling nature, if I did not see God in you, you would be naught but a great tomb. With your little hand which caresses Mary, You sustain the universe and bestow life; and You think of me, O Jesus my little King. I do not wish creatures to have one atom of my love. I wish to give all to Jesus, since He has shown me that He alone is perfect happiness.
Concluding Prayer

Fourth Day

Dear Little Flower of Carmel, bearing so patiently the disappointments and delays allowed by God, and preserving in the depths of your soul an unchanging peace because you sought only God's will, ask for me complete conformity to that adorable Will in all the trials and disappointments of life. If the favors I am asking during this Novena are pleasing to God, obtain them for me. If not, it is true I shall feel the refusal keenly, but I too wish only God's Will, and pray in the words you used, that I "may ever be perfectly fulfilled in me." Intercede for us all the days of our life, but especially during this Novena and obtain for us from God the graces and favors we ask through your intercession. Amen.

Thought for the day: Abandonment to God. I fear only one thing---to keep my own will; take it, my God, for I choose all that You choose. The only happiness here below is to strive to be always content with what Jesus gives us. I can demand nothing with fervor, except the perfect accomplishment of God's will in my soul. O my Beloved, I offer myself to You, that You may perfectly accomplish in me Your holy designs, and I will not allow anything created to be an obstacle in their path.

Concluding Prayer

Fifth Day

Little Flower of Jesus, from the very first moment of your religious life you thought only of denying yourself in all things so as to follow Jesus more perfectly; help me to bear patiently the trials of my daily life. Teach me to make use of the trials, the sufferings, the humiliations, that come my way, to learn to know myself better and to love God more. Intercede for us all the days of our life, but especially during this Novena and obtain for us from God the graces and favors we ask through your intercession. Amen.

Thought for the day: Patience in Sufferings. I do not fear trials sent by Jesus, for even in the most bitter suffering we can see that it is His loving hand which causes it. When we are expecting nothing but suffering, we are quite surprised at the least joy; but then suffering itself becomes the greatest of joys when we seek it as a precious treasure. Far from resembling those beautiful saints who practiced all sorts of austerities from childhood, my penance consisted in breaking my self-will, in keeping back a sharp reply, in doing little kindnesses to those about me, but considering these deeds as nothing.

Concluding Prayer

Sixth Day

St. Thérèse, Patroness of the Missions, be a great missionary throughout the world to the end of time. Remind our Master of His own words, "The harvest is great, but the laborers are few." Your zeal for souls was so great, obtain a like zeal for those now working for souls, and beg God to multiply their numbers, that the millions to whom Jesus is yet unknown may be brought to know, love and follow Him. Intercede for us all the days of our life, but especially during this Novena and obtain for us from God the graces and favors we ask through your intercession. Amen.

Thought for the day: Zeal for souls. Let us work together for the salvation of souls. We have only the day of this life to save souls and to give them to the Lord as proofs of our love. I tell Jesus that I am glad not to be able to see, with the eyes of my soul, this beautiful heaven which awaits me, in order that He may vouchsafe to open it forever to poor unbelievers. I cannot perform brilliant works; I cannot preach the Gospel or shed my blood. But what matter? My brothers work in place of me, and I a little child, keep very close to the royal throne. I love for those who are carrying on the warfare. My deeds, my little sufferings, can make God loved all over the world.

Concluding Prayer

Seventh Day

O little martyr of Love, you know now even better than in the days of your pilgrimage that Love embraces all vocations; that it is Love alone which counts, which unites us perfectly to God and conforms our will with His. All you sought on earth was love; to love Jesus as He had never yet been loved. Use your power in heaven to make us love Him. If only we love Him we shall desire to make Him loved by others; we shall pray much for souls. We shall no longer fear death, for it will unite us to Him forever. Obtain for us the grace to do all for the love of God, to give Him pleasure, to love Him so well that He may be pleased with us as He was with you. Intercede for us all the days of our life, but especially during this Novena and obtain for us from God the graces and favors we ask through your intercession. Amen.

Thought for the day: Love of God. I will love God alone and will not have the misfortune of attaching myself to creatures, now that my heart perceive what He has in store for those who love Him. What attracts me to the kingdom of Heaven is the call of our Lord, the hope of loving Him as I have so desired and the thought that I shall be able to make Him loved by a great number of souls who will bless Him forever. When Christ said, "Give Me a Drink," it was the love of His poor creatures that He, the Creator of all things, desired. He thirsted for love. Remember that the dear Jesus is there in the tabernacle expressly for you, for you alone. Remember that He is consumed with a desire to come into your heart.

Concluding Prayer:

Eighth Day

Dear St. Thérèse, like you I have to die one day. I beseech you, obtain from God, by reminding Him of your own precious death, that I may have a holy death, strengthened by the Sacraments of the Church, entirely resigned to the most holy Will of God, and burning with love for Him. May my last words on earth be, "My God. I love You." Intercede for us all the days of our life, but especially during this Novena and obtain for us from God the graces and favors we ask through your intercession. Amen.

Thought for the day: Death. It says in the catechism that death is nothing but the separation of the soul and body. Well, I have no fear of a separation which will unite me forever with the good God. I am happy to die because I shall be able to help souls who are dear to me, far more than I can here below. Life is not sad; it is very joyous. If you say, "This exile is sad," I understand you. We are wrong to give the name "life" to something which will end; it is only to the things of Heaven that we should apply this beautiful name.

Concluding Prayer:

Ninth Day

Dear Little St. Thérèse, by love and suffering while you were on earth, you won the power with God which you now enjoy in heaven. Since your life there began, you have showered down countless blessings on this poor world; you have been an instrument made use of by your divine Spouse to work countless miracles. I beg of you to remember all my wants. Sufferings must come to me also, may I use them to love God more, and follow my Jesus better. You are especially the little missionary of love. Make me love Jesus more, and all others for His sake. With all my heart I thank the most Holy Trinity for the wonderful blessings conferred on you, and upon the world through you. Intercede for us all the days of our life, but especially during this Novena and obtain for us from God the graces and favors we ask through your intercession. Amen.

Thought for the day: The Mission of the Little Flower. I do not intend to remain inactive in Heaven. I want to work for the Church and for souls. I have asked this of God and I am certain that He will grant my request. I will spend my Heaven doing good upon earth. This is not impossible, since the angels though always enjoying the beatific vision, watch over us. No, I cannot be at rest until the end of the world. I beseech Thee, O Jesus, to cast Thy divine glance on a great number of little souls. I beg of Thee to choose in this world a legion of little victims, worthy of Thy Love.

Concluding Prayer

Lord, You have said: Unless you become as little children you shall not enter the kingdom of heaven; grant us, we beg You, so to follow, in humility and simplicity of heart, the footsteps of the Virgin blessed Thérèse, that we may attain to an everlasting reward. Amen. # Copyright © 2017 Eternal Word Television Network, Inc. Irondale, Alabama. All rights reserved.

F. Prayer to St. Thérèse of the Child Jesus

St Thérèse, the Little Flower of Jesus, please pick a rose from the heavenly garden, and send it to me with a message of love. I ask you to obtain for me the favors that I seek (here mention your request). Recommend my request to Mary, Queen of Heaven, so that she may intercede for me, with you, before her Son, our Lord Jesus Christ. If this favor is granted, I will love you more and more, and be better prepared to spend eternal happiness with you in heaven. Saint Thérèse of the Little Flower, pray for me. Amen. # No Copyright ©.

A-1　Prayers of the Blessed James Alberione

A. Conversation with Jesus Master after Receiving the Eucharist

I adore you present in me, Incarnate Word, only -begotten Son and splendor of the Father, born of Mary. I thank you, sole Master and truth, for coming to me. With Mary I offer you to the Father: through you, with you, in you, may there be eternal praise, thanksgiving, and petition for peace for all people. Enlighten my mind; make me a faithful disciple of the Church; make mine a life of faith. Give me an understanding of the Scriptures; make me your enthusiastic apostle. Let the light of your Gospel shine to the ends of the earth. Jesus, you are the Way I want to follow, the perfect model to imitate. I want my whole life to be configured to you. You were humble and obedient: make me similar to you. You loved unselfishly and with a pure heart: make me similar to you. You were poor in spirit and patient: make me similar to you. You loved everyone and sought to bring everyone to your father: make me similar to you. O Jesus, my life, my joy, and source of all good, I love you. May I more generously love you and the people you came to save. You are the vine and I am the branch; I want to remain united to you always so as to bear much fruit. You are the fount: pour out an ever greater abundance of grace to sanctify me. You are my head, I, your member: communicate to me your Holy Spirit with the Spirit's gifts; may your Kingdom come through Mary. Console and save all my dear ones. Bring those who have died into your presence. Assist all who share your mission of spreading the Good News. Bless the Church with many vocations to the priesthood and religious life.

B. Prayer for the gifts of the Holy Spirit

Divine Holy Spirit, eternal love of the Father and of the Son. I adore you, I thank you, I love you and I ask your forgiveness for all the times I have sinned against you and against my neighbor. Descend with many graces on those ordained as bishops and priests, on those consecrated as men and women religious, on those who receive the Sacrament of Confirmation. Be for them light, sanctity, and zeal. To you, Spirit of Truth, I dedicate my mind, imagination, and memory. Enlighten me. Bring me to fuller knowledge of Jesus Christ, and deeper understanding of the Gospel and the teaching of the Church. Increase in me the gifts of wisdom, knowledge, understanding, and counsel. To you, sanctifying Spirit, I dedicate my will. Guide me. Make me faithful in living fully the commandments and my vocation. Grant me the gifts of fortitude and holy fear of God. To you, life-giving Spirit, I dedicate my heart. Guard me from evil. Pour out on me an always greater abundance of your life. Bring to completion your work in me. Grant me the gift of piety. Amen.

C. Forgive Me Master

Jesus Master, here I am before your Tabernacle to give an account of my life, of my vocation, of my particular mission. Infinite Goodness, who with love is patient with my obstinacy, with my continual lack of correspondence, with my deafness, you have conquered me as you conquered Paul. I surrender; always with you, in you, for you. Forgive me Master! Don't be silent. I feel like you have brought me to this place of solitude to speak to me, to enlighten me. Forgive me, Master! Have the same mercy for me as you had with Peter, Magdalene, Matthew, and Thomas. Deign to receive your prodigal child, who has been unfaithful to your desires. I wasted all my gifts: my mind, my will, my heart, my time, my energies, my relationships, my health, my blessings and my merits. All needs to be reconstructed, since I lack the virtue and the faith that you desire. I lack sufficient piety and zeal for God and for souls. Rebuild in me yourself: I want to leave you free to do with me as you desire. Work in me "until Christ be formed in me," out of these ashes and ruins. I trust in you, Sacred Heart of the Master. I trust in you, Immaculate Heart of my Mother.

D. Live in Us, Jesus

Jesus, Divine Master, we adore you with the angels who sang the reasons for your Incarnation: glory to God and peace to all people. We thank you for having called us to share in your flame of love for God and for all humanity. Live in us so that we may radiate you through our prayer, suffering, and work, as well as by word, example, and deed. Send good laborers into your harvest. Enlighten preachers, teachers, and writers; infuse in them the Holy Spirit and the Spirit's seven gifts. Come, Master and Lord! Teach and reign, through Mary, Mother, Teacher, and Queen. Amen.
The prayers of (A), (B), (C) and (D) were written by Blessed James Alberione.
Copyright ©2003, Daughters of St. Paul. By Pauline Books & Media, 50 Saint Paul's Avenue, Boston, MA 02130-3491.

E. Help Me Trust in Darkness

Thank you, Lord, for everything, for my life and those you have given to me. Please keep everyone I love safe! Lord, help me to recognize you in all the "disguises" you wear, so that I never fail to feed the hungry, comfort the ill, visit the prisoners. I know

I was sent here to be a blazing spark of your love, to help you in your ever-continuing expression of creation. Keep my eyes and heart open so that I never fail to gasp at the wonder and beauty of your creation. I want to always trust you, even when I don't understand why you sometimes seem to have disappeared. Help me in dark times to remember that the other side of the cross is rebirth. I trust you in everything. Amen. # This prayer was written by Antoinette Bosco. Copyright ©2003, Daughters of St. Paul. By Pauline Books & Media, 50 Saint Paul's Avenue, Boston, MA 02130-3491.

F. We Adore You, Hidden God

We adore you, hidden God, in this Sacrament.

Christ our Savior and our King, truly present.

Humbly we come before you, hearts completely won,

lost in wonder at the great marvels you have done.

Sense alone will fail to grasp this great mystery.

Faith and love enable our human eyes to see.

We believe all the truth that God's own Son has shown.

Nothing can be truer than what he has made known.

On the cross was hidden your divinity,

Hidden here before us, too, is your humanity.

We in faith profess them both, one in our belief.

And we make our own the plea of the dying thief.

Thomas saw your wounds, O Lord; these we do not see.

Yet do we confess you, Lord and God to be.

May this faith of ours ever grow and our hope increase.

May our burning love for you, Jesus, never cease.

O most blest memorial of Christ's sacrifice, giver of eternal life--Bread of paradise!

You are food for our hungry souls; live in us, O Lord.

Be the only goal we seek; be our sole reward.

We are cleansed, Lord, by your blood; filled with grace and love.

One drop shed to save the world would have been enough.

Yet you suffered and died for us, mankind lost in sin.

O how great a price you paid to redemption win.

Jesus, whom we now behold veiled from human sight, grant us what we thirst for so: that one day we might face to face behold your vision, bliss you have in store, love surpassing space and time, joy forevermore. Amen. #This prayer was written by St. Thomas Aquinas and translated by Daughters of St. Paul.

G. SEQUENCE (Optional)

The sequence Laud, O Zion (Lauda Sion), or the shorter form beginning with the verse Lo! the angel's food is given, may be sung before the Gospel Acclamation. For a musical setting, see "Laud, O Zion" by Randall DeBruyn (edition 11500).

Laud, O Zion, your Salvation, Laud with hymns of exultation, Christ, your king and shepherd true: Bring him all the praise you know, He is more than you bestow. Never can you reach his due. Special theme for glad thanksgiving Is the quick'ning and the living Bread today before you set: From his hands of old partaken, As we know, by faith unshaken, Where the Twelve at supper met. Full and clear ring out your chanting, Joy nor sweetest grace be wanting, From your heart let praises burst: For today the feast is holden, When the institution olden Of that supper was rehearsed. Here the new law's new oblation, By the new king's revelation, Ends the form of ancient rite: Now the new the old effaces, Truth away the shadow chases, Light dispels the gloom of night. What he did at supper seated, Christ ordained to be repeated, His memorial ne'er to cease: And his rule for guidance taking, Bread and wine we hallow, making Thus our sacrifice of peace. This the truth each Christian learns, Bread into his flesh he turns, To his precious blood the wine: Sight has fail'd, nor thought conceives, But a dauntless faith believes, Resting on a pow'r divine.

Here beneath these signs are hidden Priceless things to sense forbidden; Signs, not things are all we see: Blood is poured and flesh is broken, Yet in either wondrous token Christ entire we know to be. Whoso of this food partakes, Does not rend the Lord nor breaks; Christ is whole to all that taste: Thousands are, as one, receivers, One, as thousands of believers, Eats of him who cannot waste. Bad and good the feast are sharing, Of what divers dooms preparing, Endless death, or endless life. Life to these, to those damnation, See how like participation Is with unlike issues rife. When the sacrament is broken, Doubt not, but believe 'tis spoken, That each sever'd outward token doth the very whole contain. Nought the precious gift divides, Breaking but the sign betides Jesus still the same abides, still unbroken does remain.

The shorter form of the sequence begins here. Lo! the angel's food is given To the pilgrim who has striven; See the children's bread from heaven, which on dogs may not be spent. Truth the ancient types fulfilling, Isaac bound, a victim willing, Paschal lamb, its lifeblood spilling, manna to the fathers sent. Very bread, good shepherd, tend us, Jesus, of your love befriend us, You refresh us, you defend us, Your eternal goodness send us in the land of life to see. You who all things can and know, who on earth such food bestow, grant us with your saints, though lowest, Where the heav'nly feast you show, fellow heirs and guests to be. Amen. Alleluia.

Chapter 19 The Gospel according to John

머리글

요한복음서 1장

1 한처음에 말씀이 계셨다. 말씀은 하느님과 함께 계셨는데 말씀은 하느님이셨다.

2 그분께서는 한처음에 하느님과 함께 계셨다.

3 모든 것이 그분을 통하여 생겨났고 그분 없이 생겨난 것은 하나도 없다.

4 그분 안에 생명이 있었으니 그 생명은 사람들의 빛이었다.

5 그 빛이 어둠 속에서 비치고 있지만 어둠은 그를 깨닫지 못하였다.

6 하느님께서 보내신 사람이 있었는데 그의 이름은 요한이었다.

7 그는 증언하러 왔다. 빛을 증언하여 자기를 통해 모든 사람이 믿게 하려는 것이었다.

8 그 사람은 빛이 아니었다. 빛을 증언하러 왔을 따름이다.

9 모든 사람을 비추는 참빛이 세상에 왔다.

10 그분께서 세상에 계셨고 세상이 그분을 통하여 생겨났지만 세상은 그분을 알아보지 못하였다.

11 그분께서 당신 땅에 오셨지만 그분의 백성은 그분을 맞아들이지 않았다.

12 그분께서는 당신을 받아들이는 이들, 당신의 이름을 믿는 모든 이에게 하느님의 자녀가 되는 권한을 주셨다.

13 이들은 혈통이나 육욕이나 남자의 욕망에서 난 것이 아니라 하느님에게서 난 사람들이다.

14 말씀이 사람이 되시어 우리 가운데 사셨다. 우리는 그분의 영광을 보았다. 은총과 진리가 충만하신 아버지의 외아드님으로서 지니신 영광을 보았다.

15 요한은 그분을 증언하여 외쳤다. "그분은 내가 이렇게 말한 분이시다. '내 뒤에 오시는 분은 내가 나기 전부터 계셨기에 나보다 앞서신 분이시다.'"

16 그분의 충만함에서 우리 모두 은총에 은총을 받았다.

17 율법은 모세를 통하여 주어졌지만 은총과 진리는 예수 그리스도를 통하여 왔다.

18 아무도 하느님을 본 적이 없다. 아버지와 가장 가까우신 외아드님 하느님이신 그분께서 알려 주셨다.

세례자 요한의 증언(마태 3, 1-12; 마르 1, 2-8; 루카 3, 1-9. 15-18)

19 요한의 증언은 이러하다. 유다인들이 예루살렘에서 사제들과 레위인들을 요한에게 보내어, "당신은 누구요?" 하고 물었을 때,

20 요한은 서슴지 않고 고백하였다. "나는 그리스도가 아니다." 하고 고백한 것이다.

21 그들이 "그러면 누구란 말이오? 엘리야요?" 하고 묻자, 요한은 "아니다." 하고 대답하였다. "그러면 그 예언자요?" 하고 물어도 다시 "아니다." 하고 대답하였다.

22 그래서 그들이 물었다. "당신은 누구요? 우리를 보낸 이들에게 우리가 대답을 해야 하오. 당신은 자신을 무엇이라고 말하는 것이오?"

23 요한이 말하였다. "나는 이사야 예언자가 말한 대로 '너희는 주님의 길을 곧게 내어라.' 하고 광야에서 외치는 이의 소리다."

24 그들은 바리사이들이 보낸 사람들이었다.

25 이들이 요한에게 물었다. "당신이 그리스도도 아니고 엘리야도 아니고 그 예언자도 아니라면, 세례는 왜 주는 것이오?"

26 그러자 요한이 그들에게 대답하였다. "나는 물로 세례를 준다. 그런데 너희 가운데에는 너희가 모르는 분이 서 계신다.

27 내 뒤에 오시는 분이신데, 나는 그분의 신발 끈을 풀어 드리기에도 합당하지 않다."

28 이는 요한이 세례를 주던 요르단 강 건너편 베타니아에서 일어난 일이다.

하느님의 어린양

29 이튿날 요한은 예수님께서 자기 쪽으로 오시는 것을 보고 말하였다. "보라, 세상의 죄를 없애시는 하느님의 어린양이시다.

30 저분은, '내 뒤에 한 분이 오시는데, 내가 나기 전부터 계셨기에 나보다 앞서신 분이시다.' 하고 내가 전에 말한 분이시다.

31 나도 저분을 알지 못하였다. 내가 와서 물로 세례를 준 것은, 저분께서 이스라엘에 알려지시게 하려는 것이었다."

32 요한은 또 증언하였다. "나는 성령께서 비둘기처럼 하늘에서 내려오시어 저분 위에 머무르시는 것을 보았다.

33 나도 저분을 알지 못하였다. 그러나 물로 세례를 주라고 나를 보내신 그분께서 나에게 일러 주셨다. '성령이 내려와 어떤 분 위에 머무르는 것을 네가 볼 터인데, 바로 그분이 성령으로 세례를 주시는 분이다.'

34 과연 나는 보았다. 그래서 저분이 하느님의 아드님이시라고 내가 증언하였다."

첫 제자들

35 이튿날 요한이 자기 제자 두 사람과 함께 그곳에 다시 서 있다가,

36 예수님께서 지나가시는 것을 눈여겨보며 말하였다. "보라, 하느님의 어린양이시다."

37 그 두 제자는 요한이 말하는 것을 듣고 예수님을 따라갔다.

38 예수님께서 돌아서시어 그들이 따라오는 것을 보시고, "무엇을 찾느냐?" 하고 물으시자, 그들이

"라삐, 어디에 묵고 계십니까?" 하고 말하였다. '라삐'는 번역하면 '스승님'이라는 말이다.

39 예수님께서 그들에게 "와서 보아라." 하시니, 그들이 함께 가 예수님께서 묵으시는 곳을 보고 그날 그분과 함께 묵었다. 때는 오후 네 시쯤이었다.

40 요한의 말을 듣고 예수님을 따라간 두 사람 가운데 하나는 시몬 베드로의 동생 안드레아였다.

41 그는 먼저 자기 형 시몬을 만나, "우리는 메시아를 만났소." 하고 말하였다. '메시아'는 번역하면 '그리스도'이다.

42 그가 시몬을 예수님께 데려가자, 예수님께서 시몬을 눈여겨보며 이르셨다. "너는 요한의 아들 시몬이구나. 앞으로 너는 케파라고 불릴 것이다." '케파'는 '베드로'라고 번역되는 말이다.

필립보와 나타나엘을 부르시다

43 이튿날 예수님께서는 갈릴래아에 가기로 작정하셨다. 그때에 필립보를 만나시자 그에게 "나를 따라라." 하고 이르셨다.

44 필립보는 안드레아와 베드로의 고향인 벳사이다 출신이었다.

45 이 필립보가 나타나엘을 만나 말하였다. "우리는 모세가 율법에 기록하고 예언자들도 기록한 분을 만났소. 나자렛 출신으로 요셉의 아들 예수라는 분이시오."

46 나타나엘은 필립보에게, "나자렛에서 무슨 좋은 것이 나올 수 있겠소?" 하였다. 그러자 필립보가 나타나엘에게 "와서 보시오." 하고 말하였다.

47 예수님께서는 나타나엘이 당신 쪽으로 오는 것을 보시고 그에 대하여 말씀하셨다. "보라, 저 사람이야말로 참으로 이스라엘 사람이다. 저 사람은 거짓이 없다."

48 나타나엘이 예수님께 "저를 어떻게 아십니까?" 하고 물으니, 예수님께서 그에게 "필립보가 너를 부르기 전에, 네가 무화과나무 아래에 있는 것을 내가 보았다." 하고 대답하셨다.

49 그러자 나타나엘이 예수님께 말하였다. "스승님, 스승님은 하느님의 아드님이십니다. 이스라엘의 임금님이십니다."

50 예수님께서 나타나엘에게 이르셨다. "네가 무화과나무 아래에 있는 것을 보았다고 해서 나를 믿느냐? 앞으로 그보다 더 큰 일을 보게 될 것이다."

51 이어서 그에게 또 말씀하셨다. "내가 진실로 진실로 너희에게 말한다. 너희는 하늘이 열리고 하느님의 천사들이 사람의 아들 위에서 오르내리는 것을 보게 될 것이다."

Prologue

John Chapter 1

1 In the beginning was the Word, and the Word was with God, and the Word was God. 2 He was in the beginning with God. 3 All things came to be through him, and without him nothing came to be. What came to be 4 through him was life, and this life was the light of the human race; 5 the light shines in the darkness, and the darkness has not overcome it. 6 A man named John was sent from God. 7 He came for testimony, to testify to the light, so that all might believe through him. 8 He was not the light, but came to testify to the light. 9 The true light, which enlightens everyone, was coming into the world. 10 He was in the world, and the world came to be through him, but the world did not know him. 11 He came to what was his own, but his own people did not accept him. 12 But to those who did accept him he gave power to become children of God, to those who believe in his name, 13 who were born not by natural generation nor by human choice nor by a man's decision but of God. 14 And the Word became flesh and made his dwelling among us, and we saw his glory, the glory as of the Father's only Son, full of grace and truth. 15 John testified to him and cried out, saying, "This was he of whom I said, 'The one who is coming after me ranks ahead of me because he existed before me.'" 16 From his fullness we have all received, grace in place of grace, 17 because while the law was given through Moses, grace and truth came through Jesus Christ. 18 No one has ever seen God. The only Son, God, who is at the Father's side, has revealed him.

The Book of Signs

John the Baptist's Testimony to Himself

19 And this is the testimony of John. When the Jews from Jerusalem sent priests and Levites (to him) to ask him, "Who are you?" 20 he admitted and did not deny it, but admitted, "I am not the Messiah." 21 So they asked him, "What are you then? Are you Elijah?" And he said, "I am not." "Are you the Prophet?" He answered, "No." 22 So they said to him, "Who are you, so we can give an answer to those who sent us? What do you have to say for yourself?" 23 He said: "I am 'the voice of one crying out in the desert, "Make straight the way of the Lord,"' as Isaiah the prophet said." 24 Some Pharisees were also sent. 25 They asked him, "Why then do you baptize if you are not the Messiah or Elijah or the Prophet?" 26 John answered them, "I baptize

with water; but there is one among you whom you do not recognize, 27 the one who is coming after me, whose sandal strap I am not worthy to untie." 28 This happened in Bethany across the Jordan, where John was baptizing.

John the Baptist's Testimony to Jesus

29 The next day he saw Jesus coming toward him and said, "Behold, the Lamb of God, who takes away the sin of the world. 30 He is the one of whom I said, 'A man is coming after me who ranks ahead of me because he existed before me.' 31 I did not know him, but the reason why I came baptizing with water was that he might be made known to Israel." 32 John testified further, saying, "I saw the Spirit come down like a dove from the sky and remain upon him.33 I did not know him, but the one who sent me to baptize with water told me, 'On whomever you see the Spirit come down and remain, he is the one who will baptize with the holy Spirit.' 34 Now I have seen and testified that he is the Son of God."

The First Disciples

35 The next day John was there again with two of his disciples, 36 and as he watched Jesus walk by, he said, "Behold, the Lamb of God." 37 The two disciples heard what he said and followed Jesus. 38 Jesus turned and saw them following him and said to them, "What are you looking for?" They said to him, "Rabbi" (which translated means Teacher), "where are you staying?" 39 He said to them,"Come, and you will see." So they went and saw where he was staying, and they stayed with him that day. It was about four in the afternoon. 40 Andrew, the brother of Simon Peter, was one of the two who heard John and followed Jesus.41 He first found his own brother Simon and told him, "We have found the Messiah" (which is translated Anointed). 42 Then he brought him to Jesus. Jesus looked at him and said, "You are Simon the son of John; you will be called Cephas" (which is translated Peter). 43 The next day he decided to go to Galilee, and he found Philip. And Jesus said to him, "Follow me." 44 Now Philip was from Bethsaida, the town of Andrew and Peter.45 Philip found Nathanael and told him, "We have found the one about whom Moses wrote in the law, and also the prophets, Jesus, son of Joseph, from Nazareth." 46 But Nathanael said to him, "Can anything good come from Nazareth?" Philip said to him, "Come and see." 47 Jesus saw Nathanael coming toward him and said of him, "Here is a true Israelite. There is no duplicity in him." 48 Nathanael said to him, "How do you

know me?" Jesus answered and said to him, "Before Philip called you, I saw you under the fig tree." 49 Nathanael answered him, "Rabbi, you are the Son of God; you are the King of Israel." 50 Jesus answered and said to him, "Do you believe because I told you that I saw you under the fig tree? You will see greater things than this." 51 And he said to him, "Amen, amen, I say to you, you will see the sky opened and the angels of God ascending and descending on the Son of Man."

(3절)How the universe was created is still a mistery.우주가 어떻게 생겨났는지는 여전히 미스테리다. stem from.생겨나다. grow up.서서히 생겨나다. spring up.우후죽순 처럼 생겨나다. In him was life, and that life was the light of men.그분 안에 생명이 있었으니 그 생명은 사람들의 빛이었다. What came to be through him was life, and this life was the light of the human race.그분을 통하여 생겨난 것은 생명이었는데 이 생명은 인류의 빛이었다. (5절)~ darkness, but the darkness has not comprehended(understood) it.그 빛이 어둠속에서 비치고 있지만 어둠은 그를 깨닫지 못하였다. ~ darkness, and the darkness has not overcome it.그 빛이 어둠속에서 비치고 있는데 어둠은 그분을 이기지 못하였다. overcome.이기다, 압도하다, 극복하다, 물리치다. (6절)There was a man who was sent from God; his name was John.하느님께서 보내신 사람이 있었는데 그의 이름은 요한이었다. A man named John was sent from God.하느님께서 요한이라고 불리는 사람을 보내셨다. or 요한이라고 불리는 사람이 하느님으로 부터 파견되었다. (7절)through himself.자기를 통해, 자기로 말미암아. through him.그를 통해. (8절)not~but.~이 아니고 ~이다. but은 연결어로써 의미가 없음. He was not the light; he came only to testify to the light.그 사람은 빛이 아니었다. 빛을 증언하러 왔을 따름이다. (9절)enlighten(inláitn)계몽(교화)하다 (instruct), 뜻 등을 밝히다, 설명하다, 가르치다, (고어·시어) 빛을 비추다(=give light to everyone, illuminate everyone, throws a light on everyone). ~came into the world. 세상에 왔다. ~was coming into the world.세상에 오고 있었다. (10절)recognize, identify, make out, appreciate, judge.알아보다. ~did not recognize him.그분을 알아보지 못하였다. ~did not know him.그분을 알지 못하였다. (11절)receive.단체의 구성원으로 (받아, 맞아)들이다. accept.사람을 며느리(사위, 이웃, 이민자)로 (받아, 맞아)들이다. He came to what(=that which) was his own, but his own people did not accept him.그분께서 그분 소유물(그분 피조물, 그분이 창조하신 곳)에 오셨지만 그분 자신의 백성은 그분을 (맞아, 받아) 들이지않았다. ~come to his land.당신 땅에 오다. (12절)But.그러나. (13절)descent(disént). 혈통, 가문, 가계, 내리막, 내려오기, 내려가기, 하강, 강하. natural descent.자연적인 혈통. natural generation.자연적인 (혈통, 가계, 출산, 생식, 발생). sensual (appetites, pleasure), lust, one's passion, carnal (desire, appetites), carnality.육욕. fleshly temptation.

육욕의 유혹. human choice.인간의 선택. but of God=but born of God.~난, 태어난. a desire; a craving; an appetite.욕망. want.욕구. will.소망, 욕구, 의지, 의욕, 의도. Ambition. 야망. power, authority, right, jurisdiction, competence.권한. one's (choice, decision). 멋대로, 좋을 대로, 자유롭게, 특히 좋아서.(14절)have, keep, carry, retain.지니다. made his dwelling=lived. ~the glory that has as of.~으로서 지니신 영광. ~the glory as of.~ 으로서의 영광. (15절)~cried out, saying.외쳤는데 다음과 같이 말했다. This is he of whom I said.이분이 내가 (말했던, 말한) 바로 그분이시다. ahead of.앞서 있다. ranks second in the world.2위를 차지하다. rank.(순위, 위치)를 차지하다. before me.나보다 먼저, 내 앞에. exist.존재하다, 살다, 살아가다. ~he existed before me= ~he was (before my birth, before I was born, before me).그분은 내가 나기 전부터 계셨기에. (16절)We have all. 우리는 모두. We have all grown up, knowing that people are different.우리는 모두 사람이 서로 다르다는 사실을 알면서 성장했다. one grace after another grace.은총에 은총을 연하여. in place of.대신에. Grace in place of grace.은총에 은총을 받았다, 은총 대신에 은총을 받았다, 은총을 받고 또 받았다. (17절)because.왜냐하면. came through.(말미암아, 통하여) 생겨났다. (18절)The only Son, God, who is at the Father's side, has revealed him.(성부, 아버지) 곁에 계시는 하느님이시며 외아드님이신 외아드님께서 (그분, 하느님)을 (우리에게) 드러내 보여주셨다. 의역: (성부, 아버지) 곁에 계시는 외아드님이요(동시에) 하느님이신 (예수님께서, 외아드님께서) (그분, 하느님)을 (우리에게) 드러내 보여주셨다. The only Son, God, who is the nearest to Father, has made him known.아버지와 가장 가까우신 외 아드님, 하느님이신 그분께서 알려주셨다. at one's side.곁에. reveal. 비밀 등을 (드러내다, 밝히다, 폭로하다, 나타내 보이다); 보이지 않던 것을 드러내 보이다. (19절)And. 그런데, 자, 그리고. (20절)admit. 자신의 행동 때문에 보통 좋지 못하거나 잘못된 것으로 여겨지는 일이 일어났음을 (인정, 고백, 자백, 시인, 허용)할 때 쓴다. confess.수치스럽거나 당혹스럽게 여기는 것을 (고백, 자백, 시인, 인정)하다. without (hesitation, flinching).서슴지 않다. He confessed it without hesitation, and confessed, "I am not the Christ." (22절) So they said to him, "Who are you, so we can give an answer to those who sent us? What do you have to say for yourself?"→ So they asked him, "Who are you?" We have to give an answer to those who sent us? What do you say about yourself? (24 절)Some Pharisees were also sent.몇몇 바리사이들이 또한 (세례자 요한에게) 보내졌다 (의역: 또한 유다인들이 몇 사람의 바리사이들을 세례자 요한에게 보냈다. They were sent by Pharisees.그들은 바리사이들이 보낸 사람들이었다. (26절)recognize.어떤 사람·사물을 보거나 듣고 누구·무엇인지 (알아보다, 알아내다, 알다), 존재·진실성을 (인정, 인식)하다, 공로를 (인정, 표창)하다. do not know.모르다. ~but there is one among you whom you do not recognize.→ ~but there is one whom you do not know stands among you. (27

절)strap.(가죽, 신발)끈, 혁대. (29절)Lamb.인류의 죄를 대신 짊어지신 예수님을 의미함. 어린 양, (유순한, 천진난만한, 잘 속는)사람. (32절)further. 추가로, 더. (34절)Now.지금, 이제, 자, 그런데, 곧, 당장. indeed, sure enough, really.과연. (35절) stood there.그곳에 서 있다가. were there.그곳에 있다가. (36절)watch.시간과 관심을 기울이며 보다, 지켜보다, 주시하다, 눈여겨보다. (39절)Come and see.와서 보아라. Come, and you will see.와라. 그러면 너희들이 보게 될 것이다. (41절)find.우연히 만나다, 찾다, 찾아내다, 찾아보다, 알아보다, 알아내다, 발견하다. Messiah(misáiə).예수 그리스도, 구세주, 메시아, 유다인이 대망하는 메시아. (42절)케파. 아람어, 바위. (43절)And Jesus.그러자 예수님께서는. (44절)Now. 그런데. (46절)But. 그러나. (47절)There is nothing false in him.저 사람은 거짓이 없다. There is no duplicity in him.저 사람은 이중성이 없다. duplicity(dju:plísiti).이중성, 표리부동, 속임수, 일구이언, 불성실.

Footnotes

(1-18절)The prologue states the main themes of the gospel: life, light, truth, the world, testimony, and the preexistence of Jesus Christ, the incarnate Logos, who reveals God the Father. In origin, 원래it was probably an early Christian hymn그리스도를 믿는 이들의 찬미가. Its closest parallel 가장 밀접한 병행문은 is in other christological hymns,다른 예수찬미가 Col 1:15-20 and Philippians 2:6-11. Its core (John 1:1-5, 10-11, 14) is poetic in structure, with short phrases짧은 구절 linked by "staircase parallelism,"계단식 대치법 in which the last word of one phrase becomes the first word of the next. Prose inserts (at least John 1:6-8, 15) deal with John the Baptist.(1절) In the beginning: also the first words of the Old Testament (Genesis 1:1). Was: this verb is used three times with different meanings in this verse: existence, relationship, and predication. The Word (Greek logos): this term combines God's dynamic, creative word (Genesis), personified preexistent Wisdom as the instrument of God's creative activity (Proverbs), and the ultimate intelligibility of reality (Hellenistic philosophy). With God: the Greek preposition here connotes communication친교를 의미한다 with another. Was God: lack of a definite article with "God" in Greek signifies predication rather than identification.그리스어에 있어서 하느님에 정관사가 없는 것은 동일시 보다는 단정을 의미함. (1-18절)Logos.하느님의 말씀(the Word), 삼위일체의 제2위인 그리스도(Christ), 이성, 로고스. the incarnate Logos.육화된 말씀. parallelism.유사성; 유사점, 대치법(對峙法), 균형법이라고도 함, predication.술어적 서술, 술어, 단정, 단언. intelligibility.이해할 수 있음, 알기 쉬움, 명료도, 명료한 것. (1절)What came to be: while the oldest manuscripts have no punctuation here, the corrector of Bodmer Papyrus P75, some manuscripts, and the Ante-Nicene Fathers take this phrase with what follows, as staircase parallelism. Connection with John 1:3 reflects fourth-century anti-Arianism. (5절)The ethical dualism of light and darkness is paralleled in intertestamental literature and in the Dead Sea Scrolls. 빛과 어둠의 윤리적 이원성은 구약과 신약

사이의 문학과 사해 두루마리에서와 같이 유사하다. Overcome: "comprehend" is another possible translation, but cf John 12:35; Wisdom 7:29-30.이기다;"이해하다"의 의미를 담고 있으며 또 다른 가능한 번역임. The intertestamental period is a term used to refer to a period of time between the writings of the Christian "Old" and "New Testament" texts (both terms being associated with Su persessionism(sjùːpərséʃənizm).대신 들어서기, 대체, 교체. Traditionally, it is considered to be a roughly four hundred year period, spanning the ministry of Malachi (c. 420 BC), the last of the Old Testament prophets, and the appearance of John the Baptist in the early 1st century. parallel:아주 유사한 병행하는, 평행한. dualism:이원론, 이원(이중)성. (6절)John was sent just as Jesus was "sent" (John 4:34) in divine mission. Other references to John the Baptist in this gospel emphasize the differences between them and John's subordinate role.예수님이 하느님의 사명가운데(사명을 받고)파견된 것처럼 세례자 요한도 보냄을 받았다. subordinate:종속된, 부차(부수)적인. John's subordinate role.세례자 요한의 상하관계 역할. (7절)Testimony: the testimony theme of John is introduced, which portrays Jesus as if on trial throughout his ministry.예수님의 활동(사목, 선교)내내 예수님께서 재판을 받는 것처럼 묘사하는 것이 세례자요한의 증언의 주제임. All testify to Jesus: John the Baptist, the Samaritan woman, scripture, his works, the crowds, the Spirit, and his disciples.(11절)What was his own⋯his own people: first a neuter, literally, "his own property; possession" (probably=Israel), then a masculine, "his own people" (the Israelites). neuter. 중성의, 중립의, 효과를 못 내게 하다, 무력화시키다. feminine(fémənin), female, womanly, male, mannish. (13절) Believers in Jesus become children of God not through any of the three natural causes(육욕, 혈통, 사람의 욕망) mentioned but through God who is the immediate cause of the new spiritual life. Were born: the Greek verb can mean "begotten" (by a male) or "born" (from a female or of parents). The variant "he who was begotten," asserting Jesus' virginal conception 동정잉태, is weakly attested in Old Latin and Syriac versions.옛 라틴어 번역본이나 시리아 번역본에서 그 의미가 약화되었다(약화된 것으로 입증되었다). (14절) Flesh: the whole person, used probably against docetic tendencies (cf 1 John 4:2; 1:7). Made his dwelling: literally, "pitched his tent/ tabernacle." Cf the tabernacle or tent of meeting that was the place of God's presence among his people (Exodus 25:8-9). The incarnate Word is the new mode of God's presence among his people. The Greek verb has the same consonants as the Aramaic word for God's presence (Shekinah). Glory: God's visible manifestation of majesty in power, which once filled the tabernacle (Exodus 40:34) and the temple (1 Kings 8:10-11, 27), is now centered in Jesus. Only Son: Greek, monogenes, but see the note on John 1:18. Grace and truth: these words may represent two Old Testament terms describing Yahweh in covenant relationship with Israel (cf Exodus 34:6), thus God's "love" and "fidelity." The Word shares Yahweh's covenant qualities. docetism; docetic.강생하신 예수님께서 지니신 육신의 실재를 부정하고 궁극적으로는 예수님께서 하늘의 실체임을 주장. monogenesis. 일원 발생설, 단성(單性), 무성(無性) 생식. (15절)This verse, interrupting John 1:14, 16 seems drawn from John 1:30.(16절)Grace in place of grace.은총에 은총을 받았다

(은총 대신에 은총을 받았다, 은총을 받고 또 받았다): replacement of the Old Covenant with the New (cf John 1:17).구약의 은총(율법) 다음에 신약의 복음의 은총을 받았다(구약을 대체하는 신약의 은총). Other possible translations are "grace upon grace" (accumulation은총위에 은총; 축적) and "grace for grace" (correspondence은총을 위한 은총; 대응)(18절) The only Son, God: while the vast majority of later textual witnesses.후기 원문 가운데 대부분의 방대한 증언에는 다른 표현(reading)으로 되어 있는 반면 위의 번역은 가장 뛰어난 최초의 사본들인 단성신지학(monogenes theos)을 따르고 있음. ~have another reading, "the Son, the only one" or "the only Son," the translation above follows the best and earliest manuscripts, monogenes theos, but takes the first term to mean not just "Only One" but to include a filial relationship with the Father, as at Luke 9:38 ("only child") or Hebrews 11:17 ("only son") and as translated at John 1:14. 그러나 독생자만을 의미하는 것이 아니라 아버지와의 친자관계를 포함하는 첫번째 표현을 취하고 있다. The Logos is thus "only Son" and God but not Father(God).로고스는 외아들이신 하느님이며 아버지이신 하느님이 아니다. textual.원문(본문)의, 원전. theo.하느님과 관련 있음을 나타냄. theosophic.신지학(神智學)상의. theosophy.신지학. (19-51절) The testimony of John the Baptist about the Messiah and Jesus' self-revelation to the first disciples. This section constitutes the introduction to the gospel proper복음서 고유부분(엄밀한 의미의 복음) and is connected with the prose inserts in the prologue. It develops the major theme of testimony in four scenes: John's negative testimony about himself; his positive testimony about Jesus; the revelation of Jesus to Andrew and Peter; the revelation of Jesus to Philip and Nathanael. proper엄밀한 의미의, 적절한, 제대로 된, 제대로 된, 참된, 고유의. (19절)The Jews: throughout most of the gospel, the "Jews" does not refer to the Jewish people as such but to the hostile authorities, both Pharisees and Sadducees, particularly in Jerusalem, who refuse to believe in Jesus. The usage reflects the atmosphere, at the end of the first century, of polemics between church and synagogue, or possibly it refers to Jews as representative of a hostile world (John 1:10-11). polemic. 격렬한 비판, 옹호, 논쟁, 격론; 논쟁술 (20절) Messiah: the anointed agent of Yahweh야훼의 기름 부음 받은 대리자, usually considered to be of Davidic descent. See further the note on John 1:41. (21절) Elijah: the Baptist did not claim to be Elijah returned to earth (cf Malachi 3:23; Matthew 11:14). The Prophet: probably the prophet like Moses (Deut 18:15; cf Acts 3:22). (23절)This is a repunctuation and reinterpretation (as in the synoptic gospels and Septuagint) of the Hebrew text of Isaiah 40:3 which reads, "A voice cries out: In the desert prepare the way of the Lord." Septuagint.70인역(譯) 성서; 그리스어역 구약 성서; 이집트왕 Ptolemy Philadelphus(기원전 3세기)의 명에 의하여 알렉산드리아에서 70(72)명의 유다인이 70(72)일간에 번역해 냈다고 전해짐. punctuate.간간이 끼어들다, 문장에 구두점을 찍다. repunctuation. 새로운 해석, 새로이 문장에 구두점을 찍다. (24절) Some Pharisees: other translations, such as "Now they had been sent from the Pharisees," misunderstand the grammatical construction. This is a different group from that in John 1:19; the priests and Levites would have been Sadducees, not Pharisees. (26절) I baptize with water: the synoptics add "but he will baptize you with the holy Spirit" (Mark 1:8) or "…holy Spirit and fire" (Matthew 3:11; Luke 3:16). John's emphasis is on purification and preparation for a better baptism. (28절) Bethany across the Jordan: site unknown. Another reading is "Bethabara." (29절) The Lamb of God: the background for this title may be the victorious apocalyptic lamb who would destroy evil in the world (Rev 5-7; 17:14); the paschal lamb, whose blood saved Israel (Exodus 12); and/or the suffering servant led like a lamb to the slaughter as a sin-offering (Isaiah 53:7, 10). apocalyptic. 종말론적, 세상에 종말이 온 듯한. (30절)He existed before me: possibly as Elijah (to come, John 1:27); for the evangelist and his audience, Jesus' preexistence would be implied (see the note on John 1:1).evangelist 전도사, 복음사가, 4대 복음서의 저자 중 한 명.(31절) I did not know him: this gospel shows no knowledge of the tradition (Luke 1) about the kinship of Jesus and John the Baptist. The reason why I came baptizing with water: in this gospel, John's baptism is not connected with forgiveness of sins; its purpose is revelatory, that Jesus may be made known to Israel. revelatory. 계시적인. (32절)Like a dove: a symbol of the new creation (Genesis 8:8) or the community of Israel (Hosea 11:11). Remain: the first use of a favorite verb in John, emphasizing the permanency of the relationship between Father and Son (as here) and between the Son and the Christian. Jesus is the permanent bearer of the Spirit. bearer. 소지자, 나르는 사람, 운반인. 메시지 등의 전달자, 전통 등의 전수자. (34절)The Son of God: this reading is supported by good Greek manuscripts 훌륭한 그리스어 사본들, including the Chester Beatty and Bodmer Papyri and the Vatican Codex, but is suspect because it harmonizes this passage with the synoptic version: "This is my beloved Son" (Matthew 3:17; Mark 1:11; Luke 3:22). The poorly attested alternate reading, "God's chosen One," is probably a reference to the Servant of Yahweh (Isaiah 42:1). Codex. 책의 형태로 된 고문서(필사본). poorly. 좋지 못하게, 저조하게, 형편없이. (36절)John the Baptist's testimony makes his disciples' following of Jesus plausible. plausible. 그럴싸하게 만든다, 타당한 것 같은, 이치에 맞는, 그럴듯한, 특히 남을 속일 때 그럴듯하게 구는. (37절)The two disciples: Andrew (John 1:40) and, traditionally, John, son of Zebedee (see the note on John 13:23).(39절)Four in the afternoon: literally, the tenth hour, from sunrise, in the Roman calculation of time. Some suggest that the next day, beginning at sunset, was the sabbath; they would have stayed with Jesus to avoid travel on it. 해가 지면 시작되는 다음날이 안식이었기에 안식일에 여행하는 것을 피하기 위하여 예수님과 함께 머물렀을 것이라고 몇몇 학자들은 제안하고 있다. suggest. 시사(암시)하다, 넌지시 · 간접적으로 말하다, (뜻을) 비치다, 아이디어 · 계획을 제안(제의, 추천)하다. (41절) Messiah: the Hebrew word masiah, "anointed one" (see the note on Luke 2:11), appears in Greek as the transliterated messias only here and in John 4:25. Elsewhere the Greek translation christos is used. transliterate. 다른 문자(글자)로 옮기다. (42절)Simon, the son of John: in Matthew 16:17, Simon is called Bariona, "son of Jonah," a different tradition for the name of Simon's father. Cephas:in Aramaic=the Rock; cf Matthew 16:18. Neither the Greek equivalent Petros nor, with one isolated exception, Cephas is attested as a personal name before Christian times.(43절)He:grammatically, could be Peter, but logically is probably Jesus.(47절)A true Israelite. There is no duplicity in him: Jacob was the first to bear the name "Israel" (Genesis 32:29), but Jacob was a man of duplicity (Genesis 27:35-36).(48절)Under the fig tree: a symbol of messianic peace (cf Micah 4:4; Zechariah 3:10).(49절)Son of God: this title is used in the Old Testament, among other ways, as a title of adoption for the Davidic king (2 Sam 7:14; Psalm 2:7; 89:27), and thus here, with King of Israel, in a messianic sense. For the evangelist, Son of God also points to Jesus' divinity (cf John 20:28).(50절)Possibly a statement: "You(singular) believe because I saw you under the fig tree." (51절)The double "Amen"(진실로, 진실로) is characteristic of John. You is plural in Greek. The allusion is to Jacob's ladder (Genesis 28:12).야곱의 사다리에 관한 암시는 예수님을 통하여 하느님이 지상에 현존하심을 저희들 모두에게 알려줍니다.

요한복음서 2장

카나의 혼인 잔치

1 사흘째 되는 날, 갈릴래아 카나에서 혼인 잔치가 있었는데, 예수님의 어머니도 거기에 계셨다.

2 예수님도 제자들과 함께 그 혼인 잔치에 초대를 받으셨다.

3 그런데 포도주가 떨어지자 예수님의 어머니가 예수님께 "포도주가 없구나." 하였다.

4 예수님께서 어머니에게 말씀하셨다. "여인이시여, 저에게 무엇을 바라십니까? 아직 저의 때가 오지 않았습니다."

5 그분의 어머니는 일꾼들에게 "무엇이든지 그가 시키는 대로 하여라." 하고 말하였다.

6 거기에는 유다인들의 정결례에 쓰는 돌로 된 물독 여섯 개가 놓여 있었는데, 모두 두세 동이들이였다.

7 예수님께서 일꾼들에게 "물독에 물을 채워라." 하고 말씀하셨다. 그들이 물독마다 가득 채우자,

8 예수님께서 그들에게 다시, "이제는 그것을 퍼서 과방장에게 날라다 주어라." 하셨다. 그들은 곧 그것을 날라 갔다.

9 과방장은 포도주가 된 물을 맛보고 그것이 어디에서 났는지 알지 못하였지만, 물을 퍼 간 일꾼들은 알고 있었다. 그래서 과방장이 신랑을 불러

10 그에게 말하였다. "누구든지 먼저 좋은 포도주를 내놓고, 손님들이 취하면 그보다 못한 것을 내놓는데, 지금까지 좋은 포도주를 남겨 두셨군요."

11 이렇게 예수님께서는 처음으로 갈릴래아 카나에서 표징을 일으키시어, 당신의 영광을 드러내셨다. 그리하여 제자들은 예수님을 믿게 되었다.

12 그 뒤에 예수님께서는 어머니와 형제들과 제자들과 함께 카파르나움으로 내려가셨다. 그러나 그곳에 여러 날 머무르지는 않으셨다.

성전을 정화하시다(마태 21, 12-13; 마르 11, 15-17; 루카 19, 45-48)

13 유다인들의 파스카 축제가 가까워지자 예수님께서는 예루살렘에 올라가셨다.

14 그리고 성전에 소와 양과 비둘기를 파는 자들과 환전꾼들이 앉아 있는 것을 보시고,

15 끈으로 채찍을 만드시어 양과 소와 함께 그들을 모두 성전에서 쫓아내셨다. 또 환전상들의 돈을 쏟아 버리시고 탁자들을 엎어 버리셨다.

16 비둘기를 파는 자들에게는, "이것들을 여기에서 치워라. 내 아버지의 집을 장사하는 집으로 만들지 마라." 하고 이르셨다.

17 그러자 제자들은 "당신 집에 대한 열정이 저를 집어삼킬 것입니다."라고 성경에 기록된 말씀이 생각났다.

18 그때에 유다인들이 예수님께, "당신이 이런 일을 해도 된다는 무슨 표징을 보여 줄 수 있소?" 하고 말하였다.

19 그러자 예수님께서 그들에게 대답하셨다. "이 성전을 허물어라. 그러면 내가 사흘 안에 다시 세우겠다."

20 유다인들이 말하였다. "이 성전을 마흔여섯 해나 걸려 지었는데, 당신이 사흘 안에 다시 세우겠다는 말이오?"

21 그러나 그분께서 성전이라고 하신 것은 당신 몸을 두고 하신 말씀이었다.

22 예수님께서 죽은 이들 가운데에서 되살아나신 뒤에야, 제자들은 예수님께서 이 말씀을 하신 것을 기억하고, 성경과 그분께서 이르신 말씀을 믿게 되었다.

모든 사람을 아시는 예수님

23 파스카 축제 때에 예수님께서 예루살렘에 계시는 동안, 많은 사람이 그분께서 일으키신 표징들을 보고 그분의 이름을 믿었다.

24 그러나 예수님께서는 그들을 신뢰하지 않으셨다. 그분께서 모든 사람을 다 알고 계셨기 때문이다.

25 그분께는 사람에 관하여 누가 증언해 드릴 필요가 없었다. 사실 예수님께서는 사람 속에 들어 있는 것까지 알고 계셨다.

The Wedding of Cana

John Chapter 2

1 On the third day there was a wedding in Cana in Galilee, and the mother of Jesus was there. 2 Jesus and his disciples were also invited to the wedding. 3 When the wine ran short, the mother of Jesus said to him, "They have no wine." 4 (And) Jesus said to her, "Woman, how does your concern affect me? My hour has not yet come." 5 His mother said to the servers, "Do whatever he tells you." 6 Now there were six stone water jars there for Jewish ceremonial washings, each holding twenty to thirty gallons. 7 Jesus told them, "Fill the jars with water." So they filled them to the brim.8 Then he told them, "Draw some out now and take it to the headwaiter." So they took it.9 And when the headwaiter tasted the water that had become wine, without knowing where it came from (although the servers who had drawn the water knew), the headwaiter called the bridegroom 10 and said to him, "Everyone serves good wine first, and then when people have drunk freely, an inferior one; but you have kept the good wine until now."11Jesus did this as the beginning of his signs in Cana in Galilee and so revealed his glory, and his disciples began to believe in him. 12 After this, he and his mother, (his) brothers, and his disciples went down to Capernaum and stayed there only a few days.

Cleansing of the Temple

13 Since the Passover of the Jews was near, Jesus went up to Jerusalem. 14 He found in the temple area those who sold oxen, sheep, and doves, as well as the money-changers seated there.15 He made a whip out of cords and drove them all out of the temple area, with the sheep and oxen, and spilled the coins of the money-changers and overturned their tables, 16 and to those who sold doves he said, "Take these out of here, and stop making my Father's house a marketplace." 17 His disciples recalled the words of scripture, "Zeal for your house will consume me." 18 At this the Jews answered and said to him, "What sign can you show us for doing this?" 19 Jesus answered and said to them, "Destroy this temple and in three days I will raise it up." 20 The Jews said, "This temple has been under construction for forty-six years, and you will raise it up in three days?" 21 But he was speaking about the temple of his body. 22 Therefore, when he was raised from the dead, his disciples remembered that he had said this, and they came to believe the scripture and the word Jesus had spoken. 23 While he was in Jerusalem for the feast of Passover, many began to believe in his name when they saw the signs he was doing. 24 But Jesus would not trust himself to them because he knew them all, 25 and did not need anyone to testify about human nature. He himself understood it well.

(2절)Jesus and his disciples.예수님과 그분의 제자들도(함께). (3절)run short.~이 (떨어, 없어)지다, ~이 (부족하다, 부족하게 되다). They have no wine.그들에게 포도주가 없구나. (4절)concern.관계, 관심, 상관, 걱정, 근심, 배려, 중요한 것. Woman, how does your concern affect me?여인이시여, 어머님께서 걱정하시는 것이 저에게 무슨 상관이 있습니까?→ Woman, what do you want from me?여인이시여, 저에게 무엇을 바라십니까? affect(əfékt), affectability, affectable, affective.영향을 미치다, 작용하다, 와 상관이 있다. (5절)tell.말 (이야기, 표현, 분부, 명, 주의, 충고, 비밀 등을 누설, 털어놓고 이야기)하다, 시키다. (make, have, let)(sb do), get (sb to do).남에게 어떤 일을 하게 시키다. (force, compel) (sb to do).원하지 않는 일을 강제로 시키다. (order, tell) (sb to do).시키다, (지시, 명령)하다. (6절) hold.(그릇, 용기)에 액체 등을 담다, (그릇, 용기)에 들어가다, 방 등이 사람을 (수용, 포함)하다. This jar held two liters of cooking oil.이 단지 (항아리)에는 2리터의 요리용 기름이 들어있다. This room can hold ten people.이 방에는 10명 들어갈 수 있다. ~each(stone water jar) holding twenty to thirty gallons.각각의 물독은 이십에서 삼십 갤론들이었다; 각각 20 내지 30갤론을 담을 수 있는 물동이들이었다. a jar, an earthenware jar.동이. a water jar.물동이. two or three.두세. a bottle capable of containing 4 hop.4홉들이 병. This bottle holds a pound.이 병은 1파운드들이입니다. (7절)brim.단지, 항아리, 컵 등의 가장자리, 언저리, 테두리, 모자의 챙. full to the brim.넘칠 만큼, 가득 찬. fill A to the brim.넘칠듯이 A를 가득 채우다. So 그래서. (8절)Then.그러자, 그런 다음에. draw out.(퍼, 꺼, 떠)내다. headwaiter(hédwèitər). (수석, 책임자) 웨이터. (9절) So. 그런데. So they took it.그래서 그들은 그것을(포도주를) 가져갔다(날라갔다). server(séːrvər).섬기는 사람, 봉사자, 근무자, 급사, 일(시중)꾼, 미사에서 사제를 돕는 복사. serve food; serve wine; offer tea; set cake before a person.(음식, 와인, 차, 케이크)을 내놓다. (10절)and then.그러고는, 그런 다음, 그리고 나서, 그 다음에, 게다가. drink freely. (많이, 취하도록) 마시다. but you.그런데 당신은. (11절)Jesus did this as the beginning of his signs in Cana in Galilee.예수님께서는 그분의 표징의 시작으로서 이렇게 갈릴래아 카나에서 표징을 일으기셨다. Jesus performed his first signs in Cana in Galilee like this.이렇게 예수님께서는 처음으로 갈릴래아 카나에서 표징을 일으기셨다. For the first time.처음으로. Like this, Jesus performed signs for the first time in Cana in Galilee.이렇게 예수님께서는 처음으로 갈릴래아 카나에서 표징을 일으기셨다. (13절)Since. (가까워지고) 있으므로. When(가까워지)자. (14절)in the temple area.성전 뜰. in the temple.성전. (15절)Drive out.내어쫓다. Money Changer.환전상(로마와 그리스 화폐를 Jewish 화폐로 교환해주고 환차익을 얻음). pour out; spill; drop; empty; be bent on. 쏟다. dash water over the ground.땅 위에 물을 쏟다. empty out the water from a pail.통의 물을 쏟다. Someone has upset the inkstand.누가 잉크를 쏟아 놓았다. spill. 엎지르다, 흘뜨리다. without spilling a drop.한 방울도 흘리지 않고. spill milk.우유를 엎지르다. dump out the gravel.자갈을 와르르 쏟아 버리다. (16절)marketplace(márket·plàce).시장, 장터. (17절)consume.불사를 것입니다. pick up and swallow; drink in.집어삼키다. gulp down; swallow at one gulp.한 입에 꿀꺽 집어삼키다. (18절)What sign can you show us to prove that you may do such things(this)?→ What sign can you show us for doing this? (19절)(pull, tear, break, take) down, destroy, demolish.허물다. (22절)Therefore. 그러므로. (23절)for the feast of passover.파스카 축제를 (지내, 축하하, 기념, 참여)시기 위하여. at the feast of passover.파스카 축제 때에. (25절)For he himself.사실 예수님 자신께서는.

Footnotes

(2:1-6:71절)Signs revealing Jesus as the Messiah to all Israel. "Sign" (semeion세메이온) is John's symbolic term for Jesus' wondrous deeds (see Introduction). 예수님의 경이로운 행업의 상징적 용어임. The Old Testament background lies in the Exodus story (cf Deut 11:3; 29:2). John is interested primarily in what the semeia signify: God's intervention in human history in a new way through Jesus. intervention. 개입. (1-11절)The first sign. This story of replacement of Jewish ceremonial washings (John 2:6) presents the initial revelation about Jesus at the outset of his ministry. He manifests his glory; the disciples believe. There is no synoptic parallel. outset.착수, 시초, 발단. initial.처음의, 초기의, 이름의 첫 글자, 머리글자. (1절)Cana: unknown from the Old Testament. The mother of Jesus: she is never named in John. (4절)This verse may seek to show that Jesus did not work miracles to help his family and friends, as in the apocryphal gospels. Woman: a normal, polite form of address, but unattested in reference to one's mother. Cf also John 19:26. How does your concern affect me?: literally, "What is this to me and to you?" 이것이 나와 당신에게 무슨 상관이 있습니까? A Hebrew expression! of either hostility (Judges 11:12; 2 Chron 35:21; 1 Kings 17:18) or denial of common interest (Hosea 14:9; 2 Kings 3:13). Cf Mark 1:24; 5:7 used by demons to Jesus. My hour has not yet come: the translation as a question ("Has not my hour now come?"), while preferable grammatically and supported by Greek Fathers, seems unlikely from a comparison with John 7:6, 30. The "hour" is that of Jesus' passion, death, resurrection, and ascension (John 13:1).아직 저의 때가 오지 않았습니다. 이 문장을 제때가 아직 오지 않았지 않습니까?의 의문문으로 만드는 것이 문법적으로 바람직하고 그리스 교부들에 의해 지지받고 있지만 7장 6절 30절과 비교해 보면 그렇지 않은 것으로 보인다. (6절)Twenty to thirty gallons: literally, "two or three measures"; the Attic liquid measure contained 39.39 liters.(아테네의 액체 측정단위로서). The vast quantity recalls prophecies of abundance in the last days; cf Amos 9:13-14; Hosea 14:7; Jeremiah 31:12.이렇게 많은(방대한) 양은 마지막 날(종말)에 있을 풍성함에 대한 예언을 상기시켜준다. (8절) Headwaiter: used of the official who managed a banquet, but there is no evidence of such a functionary in Palestine. Perhaps here a friend of the family acted as master of ceremonies; cf Sirach 32:1. (11절)The beginning of his signs: the first of seven (see Introduction).(2:12-3:21절)The next three episodes take place in Jerusalem. Only the first is paralleled in the synoptic gospels.(12절)This transitional verse(과도기적 구절) may be a harmonization with the synoptic tradition in Luke 4:31 and Matthew 4:13. There are many textual variants. John depicts no extended ministry in Capernaum as do the synoptics.요한은 공관 복음서에서 서술한 것과 같이 카파르나움에 까지 확대된 공생활의 활동을 묘사하지 않는다. (13-22절) This episode indicates the post-resurrectional replacement of the temple by the person of Jesus. (13절)Passover: this is the first Passover mentioned in John; a second is mentioned in John 6:4 a third in John 13:1. Taken literally, they point to a ministry of at least two years. (14-22

절)The other gospels place the cleansing of the temple in the last days of Jesus' life (Matthew, on the day Jesus entered Jerusalem; Mark, on the next day). The order of events in the gospel narratives is often determined by theological motives rather than by chronological data. (14절) Oxen, sheep, and doves: intended for sacrifice. The doves were the offerings of the poor (Lev 5:7). Money-changers: for a temple tax paid by every male Jew more than nineteen years of age, with a half-shekel coin (Exodus 30:11-16), in Syrian currency. See the note on Matthew 17:24. (17절)Psalm 69:10, changed to future tense to apply to Jesus. (19절)This saying about the destruction of the temple occurs in various forms (Matthew 24:2; 27:40; Mark 13:2; 15:29; Luke 21:6; cf Acts 6:14). Matthew 26:61 has: "I can destroy the temple of God."; see the note there. In Mark 14:58, there is a metaphorical contrast with a new temple: "I will destroy this temple made with hands and within three days I will build another not made with hands." Here it is symbolic of Jesus' resurrection and the resulting community (see John 2:21 and Rev 21:2). In three days: an Old Testament expression! for a short, indefinite period of time; cf Hosea 6:2. (짧고 한정적인 시간을 나타내는 구약성서적인 표현). (20절)Forty-six years: based on references in Josephus (Jewish Wars 1,21,1 #401; Antiquities 15,11,1 #380), possibly the spring of A.D. 28. Cf the note on Luke 3:1.

요한복음서 3장

니코데모와 이야기하시다

1 바리사이 가운데 니코데모라는 사람이 있었다. 그는 유다인들의 최고 의회 의원이었다.

2 그 사람이 밤에 예수님께 와서 말하였다. "스승님, 저희는 스승님이 하느님에게서 오신 스승이심을 알고 있습니다. 하느님께서 함께 계시지 않으면, 당신께서 일으키시는 그러한 표징들을 아무도 일으킬 수 없기 때문입니다."

3 그러자 예수님께서 그에게 이르셨다. "내가 진실로 진실로 너에게 말한다. 누구든지 위로부터 태어나지 않으면 하느님의 나라를 볼 수 없다."

4 니코데모가 예수님께 말하였다. "이미 늙은 사람이 어떻게 또 태어날 수 있겠습니까? 어머니 배 속에 다시 들어갔다가 태어날 수야 없지 않습니까?"

5 예수님께서 대답하셨다. "내가 진실로 진실로 너에게 말한다. 누구든지 물과 성령으로 태어나지 않으면, 하느님 나라에 들어갈 수 없다.

6 육에서 태어난 것은 육이고 영에서 태어난 것은 영이다.

7 '너희는 위로부터 태어나야 한다.'고 내가 말하였다고 놀라지 마라.

8 바람은 불고 싶은 데로 분다. 너는 그 소리를 들어도 어디에서 와 어디로 가는지 모른다. 영에서 태어난 이도 다 이와 같다."

9 니코데모가 예수님께 "그런 일이 어떻게 이루어질 수 있습니까?" 하자,

10 예수님께서 그에게 대답하셨다. "너는 이스라엘의 스승이면서 그런 것도 모르느냐?

11 내가 진실로 진실로 너에게 말한다. 우리는 우리가 아는 것을 말하고 본 것을 증언한다. 그러나 너희는 우리의 증언을 받아들이지 않는다.

12 내가 세상일을 말하여도 너희가 믿지 않는데, 하물며 하늘 일을 말하면 어찌 믿겠느냐?

13 하늘에서 내려온 이, 곧 사람의 아들 말고는 하늘로 올라간 이가 없다.

14 모세가 광야에서 뱀을 들어 올린 것처럼, 사람의 아들도 들어 올려져야 한다.

15 믿는 사람은 누구나 사람의 아들 안에서 영원한 생명을 얻게 하려는 것이다.

16 하느님께서는 세상을 너무나 사랑하신 나머지 외아들을 내주시어, 그를 믿는 사람은 누구나 멸망하지 않고 영원한 생명을 얻게 하셨다.

17 하느님께서 아들을 세상에 보내신 것은, 세상을 심판하시려는 것이 아니라 세상이 아들을 통하여 구원을 받게 하시려는 것이다.

18 아들을 믿는 사람은 심판을 받지 않는다. 그러나 믿지 않는 자는 이미 심판을 받았다. 하느님의 외아들의 이름을 믿지 않았기 때문이다.

19 그 심판은 이러하다. 빛이 이 세상에 왔지만, 사람들은 빛보다 어둠을 더 사랑하였다. 그들이 하는 일이 악하였기 때문이다.

20 악을 저지르는 자는 누구나 빛을 미워하고 빛으로 나아가지 않는다. 자기가 한 일이 드러나지 않게 하려는 것이다.

21 그러나 진리를 실천하는 이는 빛으로 나아간다. 자기가 한 일이 하느님 안에서 이루어졌음을 드러내려는 것이다."

예수님과 세례자 요한

22 그 뒤에 예수님께서는 제자들과 함께 유다 땅으로 가시어, 그곳에서 제자들과 함께 머무르시며 세례를 주셨다.

23 요한도 살림에 가까운 애논에 물이 많아, 거기에서 세례를 주고 있었다. 그리하여 사람들이 가서 세례를 받았다.

24 그때는 요한이 감옥에 갇히기 전이었다.

25 그런데 요한의 제자들과 어떤 유다인 사이에 정결례를 두고 말다툼이 벌어졌다.

26 그래서 그 제자들이 요한에게 가서 말하였다. "스승님, 요르단 강 건너편에서 스승님과 함께 계시던 분, 스승님께서 증언하신 분, 바로 그분이 세례를 주시는데 사람들이 모두 그분께 가고 있습니다."

27 그러자 요한이 대답하였다. "하늘로부터 주어지지 않으면 사람은 아무것도 받을 수 없다.

28 '나는 그리스도가 아니라 그분에 앞서 파견된 사람일 따름이다.' 하고 내가 말한 사실에 관하여, 너희 자신이 내 증인이다.

29 신부를 차지하는 이는 신랑이다. 신랑 친구는 신랑의 소리를 들으려고 서 있다가, 그의 목소리를 듣게 되면 크게 기뻐한다. 내 기쁨도 그렇게 충만하다.

30 그분은 커지셔야 하고 나는 작아져야 한다."

하늘에서 오시는 분

31 위에서 오시는 분은 모든 것 위에 계신다. 땅에서 난 사람은 땅에 속하고 땅에 속한 것을 말하는데, 하늘에서 오시는 분은 모든 것 위에 계신다.

32 그분께서는 친히 보고 들으신 것을 증언하신다. 그러나 아무도 그분의 증언을 받아들이지 않는다.

33 그분의 증언을 받아들이는 사람은 하느님께서 참되심을 확증한 것이다.

34 하느님께서 보내신 분께서는 하느님의 말씀을 하신다. 하느님께서 한량없이 성령을 주시기 때문이다.

35 아버지께서는 아드님을 사랑하시고 모든 것을 그분 손에 내주셨다.

36 아드님을 믿는 이는 영원한 생명을 얻는다. 그러나 아드님께 순종하지 않는 자는 생명을 보지 못할 뿐만 아니라, 하느님의 진노가 그 사람 위에 머무르게 된다.

Nicodemus

John Chapter 3

1 Now there was a Pharisee named Nicodemus, a ruler of the Jews. 2 He came to Jesus at night and said to him, "Rabbi, we know that you are a teacher who has come from God, for no one can do these signs that you are doing unless God is with him." 3 Jesus answered and said to him, "Amen, amen, I say to you, no one can see the kingdom of God without being born from above." 4 Nicodemus said to him, "How can a person once grown old be born again? Surely he cannot reenter his mother's womb and be born again, can he?" 5 Jesus answered, "Amen, amen, I say to you, no one can enter the kingdom of God without being born of water and Spirit. 6 What is born of flesh is flesh and what is born of spirit is spirit. 7 Do not be amazed that I told you, 'You must be born from above.' 8 The wind blows where it wills, and you can hear the sound it makes, but you do not know where it comes from or where it goes; so it is with everyone who is born of the Spirit." 9 Nicodemus answered and said to him, "How can this happen?" 10 Jesus answered and said to him, "You are the teacher of Israel and you do not understand this? 11 Amen, amen, I say to you, we speak of what we know and we testify to what we have seen, but you people do not accept our testimony. 12 If I tell you about earthly things and you do not believe, how will you believe if I tell you about heavenly things? 13 No one has gone up to heaven except the one who has come down from heaven, the Son of Man. 14 And just as Moses lifted up the serpent in the desert, so must the Son of Man be lifted up, 15 so that everyone who believes in him may have eternal life." 16 For God so loved the world that he gave his only Son, so that everyone who believes in him might not perish but might have eternal life. 17 For God did not send his Son into the world to condemn the world, but that the world might be saved through him. 18 Whoever believes in him will not be condemned, but whoever does not believe has already been condemned, because he has not believed in the name of the only Son of God. 19 And this is the verdict, that the light came into the world, but people preferred darkness to light, because their works were evil. 20 For everyone who does wicked things hates the light and does not come toward the light, so that his works might not be exposed. 21 But whoever lives the truth comes to the light, so that his works may be clearly seen as done in God.

Final Witness of the Baptist

22 After this, Jesus and his disciples went into the region of Judea, where he spent some time with them baptizing. 23 John was also baptizing in Aenon near Salim, because there was an abundance of water there, and people came to be baptized,24 for John had not yet been imprisoned. 25 Now a dispute arose between the disciples of John and a Jew about ceremonial washings. 26 So they came to John and said to him, "Rabbi, the one who was with you across the Jordan, to whom you testified, here he is baptizing and everyone is coming to him." 27 John answered and said, "No one can receive anything except what has been given him from heaven. 28 You yourselves can testify that I said (that) I am not the Messiah, but that I was sent before him. 29 The one who has the bride is the bridegroom; the best man, who stands and listens for him, rejoices greatly at the bridegroom's voice. So this joy of mine has been made complete. 30 He must increase; I must decrease."

The One from Heaven

31The one who comes from above is above all. The one who is of the earth is earthly and speaks of earthly things. But the one who comes from heaven (is above all). 32 He testifies to what he has seen and heard, but no one accepts his testimony. 33 Whoever does accept his testimony certifies that God is trustworthy. 34 For the one whom God sent speaks the words of God. He does not ration his gift of the Spirit. 35 The Father loves the Son and has given everything over to him. 36 Whoever believes in the Son has eternal life, but whoever disobeys the Son will not see life, but the wrath of God remains upon him.

(1절) Now:말머리를 바꾸던가 요구를 할 때 감탄사적으로: 한데, 그런데, 그렇다면, 자. a ruler of the Jews.유다인들의 통치자. Sanhedrin(sænhédrin).산헤드린; 유다의 최고 입법 및 사법 기관; 의회겸 법원. a(member) councillor of the Jewish Sanhedrin.유다인들의 최고의회 의원. Now there was a Pharisee named Nicodemus,그런데, 거기에 니코데모라는 바리사이 사람이 있었다.→ There was a man of the Pharisee named Nicodemus. 바리사이 가운데 니코데모라는 사람이 있었다. (4절)How can a person once grown old be born again?사람이 일단 늙으면 어떻게 또(다시) 태어날 수 있겠습니까? once.부정·조건문에서; 한 번도 ~안하다. 한 번이라도~하면, 일단~하면, 하기만 하면(ever, at all). womb. 자궁, 자궁(uterus);배, 태내. abdomen(ǽbdəmən).배, 복부(belly). (5절)without:단순한 조건; 이 없으면, 없이는. No one can enter the kingdom of God without being born of water and Spirit.물과 성령으로 태어나지 않으면 아무도 하느님 나라에 들어갈 수 없다.→He can not enter the kingdom of God unless anyone is born of water and Spirit.누구든지 물과 성령으로 태어나지 않으면 하느님 나라에 들어갈 수 없다. born of a rich family. 부유한 집안 태생이다. (9절)Nicodemus answered and said to him.→ Nicodemus asked him, "How can this happen?" (10절)understand→ know. (14절)and.추가적으로 보충하여; 더욱이, 그것도. And just as.더욱이 모세가~ 들어 올린 것처럼. (15절)~so that everyone who believes in him may have eternal life.(그래서, 그 결과) 그를 믿는 사람은 누구나 영원한 생명을 얻게 하려는 것이다. (16절)For God.하느님으로서는, 과연 하느님께서는. (18절)condemn.선고를 내리다, 단죄하다, 좋지 않은 상황에 처하게 만들다, 유죄 판결을 내리다. (19절)verdict(və:rdikt).평결, 판결, 숙고 뒤에 내린 결정. (20절)For. 사실. (21절)live by something= live something.신조 · 원칙에 따라 살다. live the truth=I ive by the truth. 진리에 따라 살다, 진리를 실천하며 살아가다, 진리를 따라 살아가다. his works.자기 행실이. ~(that) what he has done.자기가 한 일이. to be seen.보이다, 드러내다, 비춰지다, 여겨지다. (22절)spend some time.얼마동안 지내다, 시간 좀 내다, 시간을 보내다. region.지방, 지역, 지대, 범위, 인체의 (부위, 부분), 영역, 행정구. a district, an area, a place, a territory, a land.땅. (24절)~for John had not yet been imprisoned.→ That time was before John was put in prison. (26절)here.여기에(로), 여기서(까지), 이쪽으로, 이 점에서(는); 지금, 이 시점에, 이 기회(에), 이 순간에, 이때(에), (문두에 두어 남의 주의를 끌고자 할 때 써서) 저봐, 이봐, 자. (27절)soon, then, thereupon, and.그러자. except.을 제외하고, 이외는, 이 아니면 (unless), 이 없으면. (28절)You yourselves can testify that.너희들 자신이 that 이하를 증언할 수 있다. Messiah= Christ. before=ahead of.보다 앞서, 앞서. (29절)The friend of the bridegroom stands to listen for him, and rejoices greatly if he hears the bridegroom's voice.→ ~the best man, who stands and listens for him, rejoices greatly at the bridegroom's voice. The best man.신랑 들러리, 최적임자, 강자. the best man for; the very man for; just the man for.최적임자. Mr. Rick Carter was best man at the wedding of Mr. Robert Steffes.스테페스군의 결혼식에서 릭 카터군은 신랑 들러리 노릇을 했다. My joy is also complete like that.내 기쁨도 그렇게 충만하다. like that, so, in that manner, in that way.그렇게. (30절)He must become greater; I must become less= He must increase; I must decrease. (31절)above all.모든 것 위에 계신다, 만물보다 높으시다. Health is above all else.건강이 제일이다. Your remarkable conduct is above all praise.너의 훌륭한 행동은 칭찬할 말이 없다. The one who is of(from) the earth.땅에서 난 사람은. belongs to the earth.땅에 속하고 and speaks of things which belongs to the earth.땅에 속한 것을 말하는데. (33절)certify.(증명, 보증)하다. trustworthy.(신뢰할, 믿을)수 있는. true, real, sincere, truthful, genuine.참되다. (34절)For.사실, 때문에, 으로(인하여),

하였기 때문에. For God gives the Spirit without limit. 하느님께서 한량 없이 성령을 주시기 때문입니다. He does not ration his gift of the Spirit.하느님께서는(예수님께, 성자께) 성령의 은사를 아끼지 않으십니다. 의역: 아끼지 않고 주십니다. ration(ræ∫ən).식량 등이 부족할 때 공급량을 제한하다, 배급을 주다, (배급, 할당, 식)량, (군인) 하루분의 양식, 소비를 제한하다, 말 등을 조심해서 쓰다, 아끼다. (35절)~has given everything over to him.→ ~has given everything in his hands.~그분 손에 내주셨다. give, offer, yield, hand over.내주다.

Footnotes

(1-21절)Jesus instructs Nicodemus on the necessity of a new birth from above. This scene in Jerusalem at Passover exemplifies the faith engendered by signs (John 2:23). It continues the self-manifestation of Jesus in Jerusalem begun in John 2(2장). This is the first of the Johannine discourses, shifting from dialogue to monologue (John 3:11-15) to reflection of the evangelist (John 3:16-21). The shift from singular through John 3:10 to plural in John 3:11 may reflect the early church's controversy with the Jews. engender. 어떤 감정·상황을 낳다(불러일으키다).self-manifestation. 자기현시, 자기 자신을 드러냄. discourse. 담론, 요점, 강론, 이야기. reflection. 거울 등에 비친 상(모습, 빛·열·소리 등의) 반사, 반향, 상태·속성 등의 반영, 심사숙고, 특정 주제·화제에 대해 말·글에 반영된 생각. (1절) A ruler of the Jews: most likely a member of the Jewish council, the Sanhedrin; see the note on Mark 8:31. (3절)Born: see the note on John 1:13. From above: the Greek adverb anothen (그리스 부사, 아노덴은 위로부터) means both "from above" and "again." Jesus means "from above" (see John 3:31) but Nicodemus misunderstands it as "again." This misunderstanding serves as a springboard for further instruction. springboard. 다이빙대; 체조의 도약판, 어떤 활동의 발판, 출발점. (8절)Wind: the Greek word pneuma (as well as the Hebrew ruah) means both "wind" and "spirit." In the play on the double meaning, "wind" is primary. In the play.두 가지 뜻을 다룸에 있어, 상황을 처리하다. (14절)Lifted up: in Numbers 21:9 Moses simply "mounted" a serpent upon a pole. John here substitutes a verb implying glorification. Jesus, exalted to glory at his cross and resurrection, represents healing for all. (15절)Eternal life: used here for the first time in John, this term stresses quality of life rather than duration. (16절)Gave: as a gift in the incarnation, and also "over to death" in the crucifixion; cf Romans 8:32. 또한, 십자가상 죽음의 극복으로서. (17-19절)Condemn; the Greek root means both judgment and condemnation. Jesus' purpose is to save, but his coming provokes judgment.심판을 가져온다. ~some condemn themselves by turning from the light. provoke.특정한 반응을 (유발하다, 가져오다), (화나게, 짜증나게) 하다, 도발하다. (19절)Judgment is not only future but is partially realized here and now. (22-26절)Jesus' ministry in Judea is only loosely connected with John 2:13-3:21; cf John 1:19-36. Perhaps John the Baptist's further testimony was transposed here to give meaning to "water" in John 3:5. Jesus is depicted as baptizing (John 3:22); contrast John

4:2. loosely.느슨하게, 막연하게, 헐겁게. transpose.순서를 뒤바꾸다, 음악에서 조옮김하다, 다른 장소 · 환경으로 바꾸다, 이동시키다. ~was transposed here.이곳으로 옮겨졌다. (23절)Aenon near Salim: site uncertain, either in the upper Jordan valley or in Samaria. (24절)A remark probably intended to avoid objections based on a chronology like that of the synoptics (Matthew 4:12; Mark 1:14). (25절)A Jew: some think Jesus is meant. Many manuscripts read "Jews." (29절)The best man: literally, "the friend of the groom," the shoshben of Jewish tradition, who arranged the wedding. Competition between him and the groom would be unthinkable.쇼쉬벤은 결혼을 조정한 신랑 들러리, 신랑과 들러리의 경쟁은 생각할 수 없다. (31-36절)It is uncertain whether these are words by the Baptist, Jesus, or the evangelist. They are reflections on the two preceding scenes. reflection.거울 등에 비친 (상, 모습, 빛 · 열 · 소리) 등의 반사, 반향, 상태 · 속성 등의 반영, 특정 주제 · 화제에 대해 말 · 글에 반영된 생각. (34절)His gift: of God or to Jesus, perhaps both. This verse echoes John 5:8.예수님께서는 구약의 예언자들과는 달리 직접 하느님의 말씀을 하신다는 뜻임.

요한복음서 4장

사마리아 여인과 이야기하시다

1 예수님께서는 당신이 요한보다 더 많은 사람을 제자로 만들고 세례를 준다는 소문을 바리사이들이 들었다는 것을 알게 되셨다.

2 사실은 예수님께서 친히 세례를 주신 것이 아니라 제자들이 준 것이다.

3 그래서 예수님께서는 유다를 떠나 다시 갈릴래아로 가셨다.

4 그때에 사마리아를 가로질러 가셔야 했다.

5 그렇게 하여 예수님께서는 야곱이 자기 아들 요셉에게 준 땅에서 가까운 시카르라는 사마리아의 한 고을에 이르셨다.

6 그곳에는 야곱의 우물이 있었다. 길을 걷느라 지치신 예수님께서는 그 우물가에 앉으셨다. 때는 정오 무렵이었다.

7 마침 사마리아 여자 하나가 물을 길으러 왔다. 그러자 예수님께서 "나에게 마실 물을 좀 다오." 하고 그 여자에게 말씀하셨다.

8 제자들은 먹을 것을 사러 고을에 가 있었다.

9 사마리아 여자가 예수님께 말하였다. "선생님은 어떻게 유다 사람이시면서 사마리아 여자인 저에게 마실 물을 청하십니까?" 사실 유다인들은 사마리아인들과 상종하지 않았다.

10 예수님께서 그 여자에게 대답하셨다. "네가 하느님의 선물을 알고 또 '나에게 마실 물을 좀 다오.' 하고 너에게 말하는 이가 누구인지 알았더라면, 오히려 네가 그에게 청하고 그는 너에게 생수를 주었을 것이다."

11 그러자 그 여자가 예수님께 말하였다. "선생님, 두레박도 가지고 계시지 않고 우물도 깊은데, 어디에서 그 생수를 마련하시렵니까?

12 선생님이 저희 조상 야곱보다 더 훌륭한 분이시라는 말씀입니까? 그분께서 저희에게 이 우물을 주셨습니다. 그분은 물론 그분의 자녀들과 가축들도 이 우물물을 마셨습니다."

13 예수님께서 그 여자에게 이르셨다. "이 물을 마시는 자는 누구나 다시 목마를 것이다.

14 그러나 내가 주는 물을 마시는 사람은 영원히 목마르지 않을 것이다. 내가 주는 물은 그 사람 안에서 물이 솟는 샘이 되어 영원한 생명을 누리게 할 것이다."

15 그러자 그 여자가 예수님께 말하였다. "선생님, 그 물을 저에게 주십시오. 그러면 제가 목마르지도 않고, 또 물을 길으러 이리 나오지 않아도 되겠습니다."

16 예수님께서 그 여자에게, "가서 네 남편을 불러 이리 함께 오너라." 하고 말씀하셨다.

17 그 여자가 "저는 남편이 없습니다." 하고 대답하자, 예수님께서 말씀하셨다. "저는 남편이 없습니다.' 한 것은 맞는 말이다.

18 너는 남편이 다섯이나 있었지만 지금 함께 사는 남자도 남편이 아니니, 너는 바른대로 말하였다."

19 여자가 예수님께 말하였다. "선생님, 이제 보니 선생님은 예언자시군요.

20 저희 조상들은 이 산에서 예배를 드렸습니다. 그런데 선생님네는 예배를 드려야 하는 곳이 예루살렘에 있다고 말합니다."

21 예수님께서 그 여자에게 말씀하셨다. "여인아, 내 말을 믿어라. 너희가 이 산도 아니고 예루살렘도 아닌 곳에서 아버지께 예배를 드릴 때가 온다.

22 너희는 알지도 못하는 분께 예배를 드리지만, 우리는 우리가 아는 분께 예배를 드린다. 구원은 유다인들에게서 오기 때문이다.

23 그러나 진실한 예배자들이 영과 진리 안에서 아버지께 예배를 드릴 때가 온다. 지금이 바로 그때다. 사실 아버지께서는 이렇게 예배를 드리는 이들을 찾으신다.

24 하느님은 영이시다. 그러므로 그분께 예배를 드리는 이는 영과 진리 안에서 예배를 드려야 한다."

25 그 여자가 예수님께, "저는 그리스도라고도 하는 메시아께서 오신다는 것을 압니다. 그분께서 오시면 우리에게 모든 것을 알려 주시겠지요." 하였다.

26 그러자 예수님께서 그 여자에게 말씀하셨다. "너와 말하고 있는 내가 바로 그 사람이다."

27 바로 그때에 제자들이 돌아와 예수님께서 여자와 이야기하시는 것을 보고 놀랐다. 그러나 아무도 "무엇을 찾고 계십니까?", 또는 "저 여자와 무슨 이야기를 하십니까?" 하고 묻지 않았다.

28 그 여자는 물동이를 버려두고 고을로 가서 사람들에게 말하였다.

29 "제가 한 일을 모두 알아맞힌 사람이 있습니다. 와서 보십시오. 그분이 그리스도가 아니실까요?"

30 그리하여 그들이 고을에서 나와 예수님께 모여 왔다.

31 그러는 동안 제자들은 예수님께 "스승님, 잡수십시오." 하고 권하였다.

32 그러나 예수님께서 "나에게는 너희가 모르는 먹을 양식이 있다." 하시자,

33 제자들은 서로 "누가 스승님께 잡수실 것을 갖다 드리기라도 하였다는 말인가?" 하고 말하였다.

34 예수님께서 다시 그들에게 말씀하셨다. "내 양식은 나를 보내신 분의 뜻을 실천하고, 그분의 일을 완수하는 것이다.

35 너희는 '아직도 넉 달이 지나야 수확 때가 온다.' 하고 말하지 않느냐? 자, 내가 너희에게 말한다. 눈을 들어 저 밭들을 보아라. 곡식이 다 익어 수확 때가 되었다. 이미

36 수확하는 이가 삯을 받고, 영원한 생명에 들어갈 알곡을 거두어들이고 있다. 그리하여 씨 뿌리는 이도 수확하는 이와 함께 기뻐하게 되었다.

37 과연 '씨 뿌리는 이가 다르고 수확하는 이가 다르다.'는 말이 옳다.

38 나는 너희가 애쓰지 않은 것을 수확하라고 너희를 보냈다. 사실 수고는 다른 이들이 하였는데, 너희가 그 수고의 열매를 거두는 것이다."

39 그 고을에 사는 많은 사마리아인들이 예수님을 믿게 되었다. 그 여자가 "저분은 제가 한 일을 모두 알아맞혔습니다." 하고 증언하는 말을 하였기 때문이다.

40 이 사마리아인들이 예수님께 와서 자기들과 함께 머무르시기를 청하자, 그분께서는 거기에서 이틀을 머무르셨다.

41 그리하여 더 많은 사람이 그분의 말씀을 듣고 믿게 되었다.

42 그들이 그 여자에게 말하였다. "우리가 믿는 것은 이제 당신이 한 말 때문이 아니오. 우리가 직접 듣고 이분께서 참으로 세상의 구원자이심을 알게 되었소."

왕실 관리의 아들을 살리시다(마태 8, 5-13; 루카 7, 1-10)

43 이틀 뒤에 예수님께서는 그곳을 떠나 갈릴래아로 가셨다.

44 예수님께서는 친히, 예언자는 자기 고향에서 존경을 받지 못한다고 증언하신 적이 있다.

45 예수님께서 갈릴래아에 가시자 갈릴래아 사람들이 그분을 맞아들였다. 그들도 축제를 지내러 예루살렘에 갔다가, 예수님께서 축제 때에 그곳에서 하신 모든 일을 보았기 때문이다.

46 예수님께서는 물을 포도주로 만드신 적이 있는 갈릴래아 카나로 다시 가셨다. 거기에 왕실 관리가 한 사람 있었는데, 그의 아들이 카파르나움에서 앓아누워 있었다.

47 그는 예수님께서 유다를 떠나 갈릴래아에 오셨다는 말을 듣고 예수님을 찾아와, 자기 아들이 죽게 되었으니 카파르나움으로 내려가시어 아들을 고쳐 주십사고 청하였다.

48 예수님께서는 그에게 이르셨다. "너희는 표징과 이적을 보지 않으면 믿지 않을 것이다."

49 그래도 그 왕실 관리는 예수님께 "주님, 제 아이가 죽기 전에 같이 내려가 주십시오." 하고 말하였다.

50 그러자 예수님께서 그에게 말씀하셨다. "가거라. 네 아들은 살아날 것이다." 그 사람은 예수님께서 자기에게 이르신 말씀을 믿고 떠나갔다.

51 그가 내려가는 도중에 그의 종들이 마주 와서 아이가 살아났다고 말하였다.

52 그래서 그가 종들에게 아이가 나아지기 시작한 시간을 묻자, "어제 오후 한 시에 열이 떨어졌습니다." 하고 대답하는 것이었다.

53 그 아버지는 바로 그 시간에 예수님께서 자기에게, "네 아들은 살아날 것이다." 하고 말씀하신 것을 알았다. 그리하여 그와 그의 온 집안이 믿게 되었다.

54 이렇게 예수님께서는 유다를 떠나 갈릴래아로 가시어 두 번째 표징을 일으키셨다.

John Chapter 4

1 Now when Jesus learned that the Pharisees had heard that Jesus was making and baptizing more disciples than John 2 (although Jesus himself was not baptizing, just his disciples), 3 he left Judea and returned to Galilee.

The Samaritan Woman

4 He had to pass through Samaria. 5 So he came to a town of Samaria called Sychar, near the plot of land that Jacob had given to his son Joseph. 6 Jacob's well was there. Jesus, tired from his journey, sat down there at the well. It was about noon. 7 A woman of Samaria came to draw water. Jesus said to her, "Give me a drink." 8 His disciples had gone into the town to buy food. 9 The Samaritan woman said to him, "How can you, a Jew, ask me, a Samaritan woman, for a drink?" (For Jews use nothing in common with Samaritans.) 10 Jesus answered and said to her, "If you knew the gift of God and who is saying to you, 'Give me a drink,' you would have asked him and he would have given you living water." 11 (The woman) said to him, "Sir, you do not even have a bucket and the cistern is deep; where then can you get this living water? 12 Are you greater than our father Jacob, who gave us this cistern and drank from it himself with his children and his flocks?" 13 Jesus answered and said to her, "Everyone who drinks this water will be thirsty again; 14 but whoever drinks the water I shall give will never thirst; the water I shall give will become in him a spring of water welling up to eternal life." 15 The woman said to him, "Sir, give me this water, so that I may not be thirsty or have to keep coming here to draw water." 16 Jesus said to her, "Go call your husband and come back." 17 The woman answered and said to him, "I do not have a husband." Jesus answered her, "You are right in saying, 'I do not have a husband.' 18 For you have had five husbands, and the one you have now is not your husband. What you have said is true." 19 The woman said to him, "Sir, I can see that you are a prophet. 20 Our ancestors worshiped on this mountain; but you people say that the place to worship is in Jerusalem." 21 Jesus said to her, "Believe me, woman, the hour is coming when you will worship the Father neither on this mountain nor in Jerusalem. 22 You people worship what you do not understand; we worship what we understand, because salvation is from the Jews. 23 But the hour is coming, and is now here, when true worshipers will worship the Father in Spirit and truth; and indeed the Father seeks such people to worship him. 24 God is Spirit, and those who worship him must worship in Spirit and truth."

25 The woman said to him, "I know that the Messiah is coming, the one called the Anointed; when he comes, he will tell us everything." 26 Jesus said to her, "I am he, the one who is speaking with you." 27 At that moment his disciples returned, and were amazed that he was talking with a woman, but still no one said, "What are you looking for?" or "Why are you talking with her?" 28 The woman left her water jar and went into the town and said to the people, 29 "Come see a man who told me everything I have done. Could he possibly be the Messiah?" 30 They went out of the town and came to him. 31 Meanwhile, the disciples urged him, "Rabbi, eat." 32 But he said to them, "I have food to eat of which you do not know." 33 So the disciples said to one another, "Could someone have brought him something to eat?" 34 Jesus said to them, "My food is to do the will of the one who sent me and to finish his work. 35 Do you not say, 'In four months the harvest will be here'? I tell you, look up and see the fields ripe for the harvest. 36 The reaper is already receiving his payment and gathering crops for eternal life, so that the sower and reaper can rejoice together. 37 For here the saying is verified that 'One sows and another reaps.' 38 I sent you to reap what you have not worked for; others have done the work, and you are sharing the fruits of their work." 39 Many of the Samaritans of that town began to believe in him because of the word of the woman who testified, "He told me everything I have done." 40 When the Samaritans came to him, they invited him to stay with them; and he stayed there two days. 41 Many more began to believe in him because of his word, 42 and they said to the woman, "We no longer believe because of your word; for we have heard for ourselves, and we know that this is truly the savior of the world."

Return to Galilee

43 After the two days, he left there for Galilee. 44 For Jesus himself testified that a prophet has no honor in his native place. 45 When he came into Galilee, the Galileans welcomed him, since they had seen all he had done in Jerusalem at the feast; for they themselves had gone to the feast.

Second Sign at Cana

46 Then he returned to Cana in Galilee, where he had made the water wine. Now there was a royal official whose son was ill in Capernaum. 47 When he heard that Jesus had arrived in Galilee from Judea, he went to him and asked him to come

down and heal his son, who was near death. 48 Jesus said to him, "Unless you people see signs and wonders, you will not believe." 49 The royal official said to him, "Sir, come down before my child dies." 50 Jesus said to him, "You may go; your son will live." The man believed what Jesus said to him and left. 51 While he was on his way back, his slaves met him and told him that his boy would live. 52 He asked them when he began to recover. They told him, "The fever left him yesterday, about one in the afternoon." 53 The father realized that just at that time Jesus had said to him, "Your son will live," and he and his whole household came to believe. 54 (Now) this was the second sign Jesus did when he came to Galilee from Judea.

(1절)Now.한데, 그런데, 그렇다면. when. 하고자, 하면. (3절)returned to Galilee→ went back again to Galilee. (5절)사마리아 여인은 구원의 보편성을 설명해준다. (5절)At that time he had to pass~그때에~. cross, through, traverse, go(cut) across, intersect. 가로지르다. 가로질러가다. pass through.통과하다, 거쳐지나가다. go through.겪다, 통과하다, 거치다, 보내다. There is a lot of red tape when you go through U.S. custom.미세관 통관시 많은 행정 절차가 있다. plot. 음모, 소설 등의 (구성, 줄거리), 작은 땅, 터, 대지. plot of land.작은 대지. (6절)Jesus, tired from his walking on the road.길을 걷느라 지치신 예수님께서는. ~there at the well= by the well. 여기에서 there는 어떤 것이 존재하거나 발생함을 의미. (7절)Just then.마침. And Jesus.그러자 예수님께서. (9절)(associate, keep company) with.상종하다. in common.공동으로. For Jews did not associate with Samaritans. (10절)~you would rather. (11절)bucket(bʌkit).두레박, 양동이, 두레박, 들통. (12절)flock. 염소·거위·오리·새 등의 떼. herd. 소, 말 등 발굽이 있으며 함께 생활하는 가축·동물의 무리. flocks and herds.가축들. ~himself, of course, with his children and his flocks? (14절)well up.분출하다, 솟아나다. up to. 까지, 어떤 지경, 정도에 이르기 까지. ~will become in him a spring of water welling up to eternal life.그 사람 안에서 영원한 (생명에 이르기, 생명을 누리기) 까지 솟아나는 샘이 될 것이다; 영원한 생명을 누릴 것이라는 번역은 너무 비약적인 번역임. 의역; 영원한 생명에 이르게 하는 샘이 될 것이다. (15절)그러자. redundant번역임. ~may not have to keep coming here.이리 계속 나오지 않아도 되겠습니다. (16절)이리 함께 오너라.→ 돌아오너라. (18절)For.사실. (21절)believe me.내 말을 믿어라, 정말이야, 정말로, (저를, 저의 말을) 믿어주십시오, 정말이라고요. (22절)understand.→ know. (23절)~and is now here.(때가 오고 있으니) 지금 이 자리가 그 때이다. (27절)just then, just at that time(moment), at that (very) minute, at the (very) moment.바로 그때. but still. 그러나, 하지만, 아직은. Why are you talking with her?(왜 그 여자와, 저 여자와 무슨, 어찌하여 그 여자와) 이야기를 하십니까? (29절)guess right; make a good guess.알아맞히다. possibly.아마, 혹시, 어쩌면, 어떻게든지, 과연. ~who told me everything.➝ ~who made a good guess about me. (34절)다시 redundant번역. (35절)아직도 redundant번역. (36절)payment.➝ wages. grain.알곡. gather.거두어들이다. harvest crops.곡식을 거두어들이다. 영원한 생명에 들어갈. ➝영원한 생명을 위한, 영원한 생명에 이르는. (37절)indeed, sure enough.과연. right, proper, correct.옳다. Indeed, the saying "one sows and another reaps" is right.과연 "씨 뿌리는 이가 다르고 수확하는 이가 다르다"는 말이 옳다. For(사실) here the saying is verified that 'One sows and another reaps.' verify(vérəfài).증거를 대다, (증명, 입증, 확증, 조회, 확인)하다, 사실·행위, 예언·약속 등을 (실, 입)증하다. Saying is one thing and doing (is) another.말하는 것과 행동하는 것은 다른 것이다. 언행이란 흔히 상반하기 마련이다. 언행이 일치하지 않는다. (38절)~the work, and you are sharing the fruits of their work.➝ ~the hard work, and you are reaping the fruits of the hard work. (41절)and, then, so, now.그리하여. (46절)then.그 다음에, 그리고 나서, 그 후에, 그래서. Now.그런데. again, once again, once more.다시. all over again.처음부터 다시. Again he went to Cana. (47절)~was close to death=was near death. (49절)그래도 redundant번역. nevertheless, (but) still, for all that, and(but) yet, even so, none the less.그래도.

Footnotes

(1-42절)당시, 사마리아인들은 요르단 서부, 유다인들은 남부, 갈릴래아인들은 북부에 살았음. 기원전 722년 아시리아에 의해 북이스라엘이 멸망하였을 때 사마리아인들은 이방인들의 신과 관습을 받아들여 혈통과 신앙의 순수성을 잃었음. 사마리아인들은 유일신 하느님을 믿는다고 하면서 이스라엘 성지 순례를 하지 않았고 게리짐 산에다 신당을 차렸음. 유다인들은 사마리아인들을 증오하였으며 공공장소에서 여인과의 대화는 당시 유다 문화에서 용납되지 않았음. 그러나 예수님은 사회적 편견을 무시하시고 사마리아 여인과 말씀을 나누셨음. (1-42절)Jesus in Samaria. The self-revelation of Jesus continues with his second discourse, on his mission to "half-Jews." 이복 유다인, 배 다른 유다인. It continues the theme of replacement, here with regard to cult (John 4:21). Water (John 4:7-15) serves as a symbol (as at Cana and in the Nicodemus episode).하느님께서 자녀들에게 주시는 선물인 생명수. (2절)An editorial refinement of John 3:22, perhaps directed against followers of John the Baptist who claimed that Jesus imitated him.아마, 사도 요한의 편집자적인 세련된 정리로서 예수님이 세례를 주시는데 있어 세례자요한을 흉내 냈다고 주장한 세례자요한을 따르는 사람들을 겨냥한 것임. refinement. 작은 변화를 통한 개선, 개량, 정제, 제련, 교양, 품위, 세련, 고상함. (4절)He had to: a theological necessity; geographically, Jews often bypassed Samaria by taking a route across the Jordan. 거쳐야만했다, 신학적인 필연성을 강조함. 유다인들은 사마리아인들을 증오하여 사마리아를 우회하여 요르단을 건너다님. (5절)Sychar: Jerome identifies this with Shechem, a reading found in Syriac manuscripts.시카르. 예로니모는 이곳을 세켐이라고 확인하였다. 시리아 사본에서 발견된 해석임. reading. 성경, 책·상황 등에 대한 이해, 해석. 1.5키로 거리에 야곱의 우물이 있음. (9절)Samaritan women were regarded by Jews as ritually impure.(의식적으로 부정하다고 여겼다), and therefore Jews were forbidden to drink from any vessel they had handled. (10절)Living water:샘솟는 물: the water of life, i.e., the revelation that Jesus brings.예수님이 가져다주시는 계시, 즉, 생명수; the woman thinks of "flowing water," so much more desirable than stagnant cistern water. On John's device of such misunderstanding, cf the note on John 3:3. (11절)Sir: the Greek kyrios means "master" or "lord," as a respectful mode of address for a human being or a deity; cf John 4:19.그리스어 키리오스는 스승 또는 주님이라는 의미로 사람이나 신에게 붙이는 정중한 (방법, 표현). It is also the word used in the Septuagint for the Hebrew 'adonai, substituted for the tetragrammaton YHWH. (20절) This mountain: Gerizim, on which a temple was erected in the fourth century B.C. by Samaritans to rival Matthew. Zion in Jerusalem; cf Deut 27:4 (Mount Ebal = the Jews' term for Gerizim). (23절) In Spirit and truth: not a reference to an interior worship within one's own spirit. 마음속에서 우러나오는 내적인 예배를 가리키는 것이 아니다. The Spirit is the spirit given by God that reveals truth and enables one to worship God appropriately (John 14:16-17). Cf "born of water and Spirit (John 3:5) (23절)appropriately. 합당하게. (25절)The expectations of the Samaritans are expressed here in Jewish terminology.유다인들의 용어로. They did not expect a messianic king of the house of David but a prophet like Moses(Deut 18:15). (26절)I am he: it could also be translated "I am," an Old Testament self-designation of Yahweh (Isaiah 43:1 - 3, 10, 13 탈출기 3:14, 이사야서 41:4, 10, 14); cf John 6:20; 8:24, 28, 58; 13:19; 18:5-6, 8. See the note on Mark 6:50. (27절)Talking with a woman: a religious and social restriction that Jesus is pictured treating as unimportant.예수님이 종교적, 사회적 제한 규정을 중요하지 않게 여기셨음을 보여준다. 당시 남자는 집밖에서 다른 여자와 이야기 하는 것은 물론 자기 아내와 이야기하는 것도 옳지 않은 것으로 여김. (35절) In four months: probably a proverb; cf Matthew 9:37-38.아마도 격언임. 곡식을 파종하고 수확하는 데는 오랜 시간이 소요되지만 영혼을 구원하는 영적 추수는 즉각적임을 표현하는 것임. (36절) Already: this word may go with the preceding verse rather than with John 4:36. (39절) The woman is presented as a missionary, described in virtually the same words as the disciples are in Jesus' prayer (John 17:20). (39절)missionary.외국에 파견되는 선교사. (43-54절)Jesus' arrival in Cana in Galilee; the second sign. This section introduces another theme, that of the life-giving word of Jesus. It is explicitly linked to the first sign (John 2:11). The royal official believes (John 4:50). The natural life given his son is a sign of eternal life.그의 아들에게 주어진 자연적인 생명은 영원한 생명의 표징이다. (44절)Probably a reminiscence of a tradition as in Mark 6:4. Cf Gospel of Thomas John 4:31: "No prophet is acceptable in his village, no physician heals those who know him." (46-54절)The story of the cure of the royal official's son may be a third version of the cure of the centurion's son (Matthew 8:5-13) or servant (Luke 7:1-10). Cf also Matthew 15:21-28; Mark 7:24-30.

요한복음서 5장

벳자타 못 가에서 병자를 고치시다

1 그 뒤에 유다인들의 축제 때가 되어 예수님께서 예루살렘에 올라가셨다.

2 예루살렘의 '양 문' 곁에는 히브리 말로 벳자타라고 불리는 못이 있었다. 그 못에는 주랑이 다섯 채 딸렸는데,

3 그 안에는 눈먼 이, 다리저는 이, 팔다리가 말라비틀어진 이 같은 병자들이 많이 누워 있었다.

4 Footnotes 4절 참조 (Page 450).

5 거기에는 서른여덟 해나 앓는 사람도 있었다.

6 예수님께서 그가 누워 있는 것을 보시고 또 이미 오래 그렇게 지낸다는 것을 아시고는, "건강해지고 싶으냐?" 하고 그에게 물으셨다.

7 그 병자가 예수님께 대답하였다. "선생님, 물이 출렁거릴 때에 저를 못 속에 넣어 줄 사람이 없습니다. 그래서 제가 가는 동안에 다른 이가 저보다 먼저 내려갑니다."

8 예수님께서 그에게 말씀하셨다. "일어나 네 들것을 들고 걸어가거라."

9 그러자 그 사람은 곧 건강하게 되어 자기 들것을 들고 걸어갔다. 그날은 안식일이었다.

10 그래서 유다인들이 병이 나은 그 사람에게, "오늘은 안식일이오. 들것을 들고 다니는 것은 합당하지 않소." 하고 말하였다.

11 그가 "나를 건강하게 해 주신 그분께서 나에게, '네 들것을 들고 걸어가라.' 하셨습니다." 하고 대답하자,

12 그들이 물었다. "당신에게 '그것을 들고 걸어가라.' 한 사람이 누구요?"

13 그러나 병이 나은 이는 그분이 누구이신지 알지 못하였다. 그곳에 군중이 몰려 있어 예수님께서 몰래 자리를 뜨셨기 때문이다.

14 그 뒤에 예수님께서 그 사람을 성전에서 만나시자 그에게 이르셨다. "자, 너는 건강하게 되었다. 더 나쁜 일이 너에게 일어나지 않도록 다시는 죄를 짓지 마라."

15 그 사람은 물러가서 자기를 건강하게 만들어 주신 분은 예수님이시라고 유다인들에게 알렸다.

16 그리하여 유다인들은 예수님께서 안식일에 그러한 일을 하셨다고 하여, 그분을 박해하기 시작하였다.

17 그러나 예수님께서는 그들에게, "내 아버지께서 여태 일하고 계시니 나도 일하는 것이다." 하고 말씀하셨다.

18 이 때문에 유다인들은 더욱 예수님을 죽이려고 하였다. 그분께서 안식일을 어기실 뿐만 아니라, 하느님을 당신 아버지라고 하시면서 당신 자신을 하느님과 대등하게 만드셨기 때문이다.

아드님의 권한

19 예수님께서 그들에게 말씀하셨다. "내가 진실로 진실로 너희에게 말한다. 아버지께서 하시는 것을

보지 않고서 아들이 스스로 할 수 있는 것은 하나도 없다. 그분께서 하시는 것을 아들도 그대로 할 따름이다.

20 아버지께서는 아들을 사랑하시어 당신께서 하시는 모든 것을 아들에게 보여 주신다. 그리고 앞으로 그보다 더 큰 일들을 아들에게 보여 주시어, 너희를 놀라게 하실 것이다.

21 아버지께서 죽은 이들을 일으켜 다시 살리시는 것처럼, 아들도 자기가 원하는 이들을 다시 살린다.

22 아버지께서는 아무도 심판하지 않으시고, 심판하는 일을 모두 아들에게 넘기셨다.

23 모든 사람이 아버지를 공경하듯이 아들도 공경하게 하시려는 것이다. 아들을 공경하지 않는 자는 아들을 보내신 아버지도 공경하지 않는다.

24 내가 진실로 진실로 너희에게 말한다. 내 말을 듣고 나를 보내신 분을 믿는 이는 영생을 얻고 심판을 받지 않는다. 그는 이미 죽음에서 생명으로 건너갔다.

25 내가 진실로 진실로 너희에게 말한다. 죽은 이들이 하느님 아들의 목소리를 듣고 또 그렇게 들은 이들이 살아날 때가 온다. 지금이 바로 그때다.

26 아버지께서 당신 안에 생명을 가지고 계신 것처럼, 아들도 그 안에 생명을 가지게 해 주셨기 때문이다.

27 아버지께서는 또 그가 사람의 아들이므로 심판을 하는 권한도 주셨다.

28 이 말에 놀라지 마라. 무덤 속에 있는 모든 사람이 그의 목소리를 듣는 때가 온다.

29 그들이 무덤에서 나와, 선을 행한 이들은 부활하여 생명을 얻고 악을 저지른 자들은 부활하여 심판을 받을 것이다.

30 나는 아무것도 스스로 할 수 없다. 나는 듣는 대로 심판할 따름이다. 그래서 내 심판은 올바르다. 내가 내 뜻이 아니라 나를 보내신 분의 뜻을 추구하기 때문이다.”

예수님을 믿게 하는 증언

31 “내가 나 자신을 위하여 증언하면 내 증언은 유효하지 못하다.

32 그러나 나를 위하여 증언하시는 분이 따로 계시다. 나는 나를 위하여 증언하시는 그분의 증언이 유효하다는 것을 알고 있다.

33 너희가 요한에게 사람들을 보냈을 때에 그는 진리를 증언하였다.

34 나는 사람의 증언을 필요로 하지 않는다. 그런데도 이러한 말을 하는 것은 너희가 구원을 받게 하려는 것이다.

35 요한은 타오르며 빛을 내는 등불이었다. 너희는 한때 그 빛 속에서 즐거움을 누리려고 하였다.

36 그러나 나에게는 요한의 증언보다 더 큰 증언이 있다. 아버지께서 나에게 완수하도록 맡기신 일들이다. 그래서 내가 하고 있는 일들이 나를 위하여 증언한다. 아버지께서 나를 보내셨다는 것이다.

37 그리고 나를 보내신 아버지께서도 나를 위하여 증언해 주셨다. 너희는 그분의 목소리를 들은 적이 한 번도 없고 그분의 모습을 본 적도 없다.

38 너희는 또 그분의 말씀이 너희 안에 머무르게 하지 않는다. 그분께서 보내신 이를 너희가 믿지 않기 때문이다.

39 너희는 성경에서 영원한 생명을 찾아 얻겠다는 생각으로 성경을 연구한다. 바로 그 성경이 나를 위하여 증언한다.

40 그런데도 너희는 나에게 와서 생명을 얻으려고 하지 않는다.

41 나는 사람들에게서 영광을 받지 않는다.

42 그리고 나는 너희에게 하느님을 사랑하는 마음이 없다는 것을 안다.

43 나는 내 아버지의 이름으로 왔다. 그런데도 너희는 나를 받아들이지 않는다. 다른 이가 자기 이름으로 오면, 너희는 그를 받아들일 것이다.

44 자기들끼리 영광을 주고받으면서 한 분이신 하느님에게서 받는 영광은 추구하지 않으니, 너희가 어떻게 믿을 수 있겠느냐?

45 그러나 내가 너희를 아버지께 고소하리라고 생각하지는 마라. 너희를 고소하는 이는 너희가 희망을 걸어 온 모세이다.

46 너희가 모세를 믿었더라면 나를 믿었을 것이다. 그가 나에 관하여 성경에 기록하였기 때문이다.

47 그런데 너희가 그의 글을 믿지 않는다면 나의 말을 어떻게 믿겠느냐?"

Cure on a Sabbath

John Chapter 5

1 After this, there was a feast of the Jews, and Jesus went up to Jerusalem. 2 Now there is in Jerusalem at the Sheep (Gate) a pool called in Hebrew Bethesda, with five porticoes. 3 In these lay a large number of ill, blind, lame, and crippled.5 One man was there who had been ill for thirty-eight years. 6 When Jesus saw him lying there and knew that he had been ill for a long time, he said to him, "Do you want to be well?" 7 The sick man answered him, "Sir, I have no one to put me into the pool when the water is stirred up; while I am on my way, someone else gets down there before me." 8 Jesus said to him, "Rise, take up your mat, and walk." 9 Immediately the man became well, took up his mat, and walked. Now that day was a sabbath. 10 So the Jews said to the man who was cured, "It is the sabbath, and it is not lawful for you to carry your mat." 11 He answered them, "The man who made me well told me, 'Take up your mat and walk.'" 12 They asked him, "Who is the man who told you, 'Take it up and walk'?" 13 The man who was healed did not know who it was, for Jesus had

slipped away, since there was a crowd there. 14 After this Jesus found him in the temple area and said to him, "Look, you are well; do not sin any more, so that nothing worse may happen to you." 15 The man went and told the Jews that Jesus was the one who had made him well. 16 Therefore, the Jews began to persecute Jesus because he did this on a sabbath. 17 But Jesus answered them, "My Father is at work until now, so I am at work." 18 For this reason the Jews tried all the more to kill him, because he not only broke the sabbath but he also called God his own father, making himself equal to God.

The Work of the Son

19 Jesus answered and said to them, "Amen, amen, I say to you, a son cannot do anything on his own, but only what he sees his father doing; for what he does, his son will do also. 20 For the Father loves his Son and shows him everything that he himself does, and he will show him greater works than these, so that you may be amazed. 21 For just as the Father raises the dead and gives life,so also does the Son give life to whomever he wishes. 22 Nor does the Father judge anyone, but he has given all judgment to his Son, 23 so that all may honor the Son just as they honor the Father. Whoever does not honor the Son does not honor the Father who sent him. 24 Amen, amen, I say to you, whoever hears my word and believes in the one who sent me has eternal life and will not come to condemnation, but has passed from death to life. 25 Amen, amen, I say to you, the hour is coming and is now here when the dead will hear the voice of the Son of God, and those who hear will live. 26 For just as the Father has life in himself, so also he gave to his Son the possession of life in himself. 27 And he gave him power to exercise judgment, because he is the Son of Man. 28 Do not be amazed at this, because the hour is coming in which all who are in the tombs will hear his voice 29 and will come out, those who have done good deeds to the resurrection of life, but those who have done wicked deeds to the resurrection of condemnation. 30 "I cannot do anything on my own; I judge as I hear, and my judgment is just, because I do not seek my own will but the will of the one who sent me.

Witnesses to Jesus

31 "If I testify on my own behalf, my testimony cannot be verified. 32 But there is another who testifies on my behalf, and I know that the testimony he gives on my behalf is true. 33 You sent emissaries to John, and he testified to the truth. 34 I do not accept testimony from a human being, but I say this so that you may be saved. 35 He was a burning and shining lamp, and for a while you were content to rejoice in his light. 36 But I have testimony greater than John's. The works that the Father gave me to accomplish, these works that I perform testify on my behalf that the Father has sent me. 37 Moreover, the Father who sent me has testified on my behalf. But you have never heard his voice nor seen his form, 38 and you do not have his word remaining in you, because you do not believe in the one whom he has sent. 39 You search the scriptures, because you think you have eternal life through them; even they testify on my behalf. 40 But you do not want to come to me to have life.

Unbelief of Jesus' Hearers

41 "I do not accept human praise; 42 moreover, I know that you do not have the love of God in you. 43 I came in the name of my Father, but you do not accept me; yet if another comes in his own name, you will accept him. 44 How can you believe, when you accept praise from one another and do not seek the praise that comes from the only God? 45 Do not think that I will accuse you before the Father: the one who will accuse you is Moses, in whom you have placed your hope. 46 For if you had believed Moses, you would have believed me, because he wrote about me. 47 But if you do not believe his writings, how will you believe my words?"

(1절)Afterwards, subsequently, with that, thence.그 뒤에. after this.이후는, 금후, (이 번, 지금) 부터(는), 이런 일이 있은 후. since (then), since that time, ever since, from that time on.그 뒤. (2절)Now there is in Jerusalem at(near) the Sheep.그런데 예루살렘의 양문 곁에는 ~이 있다. with, be attached to, belong to.딸리다. portico(pɔ́ːrtəkòu). 포르티코; 특히 대형 건물 입구에 기둥을 받쳐 만든 현관 지붕. (4절)a sick person, a patient, the sick, the sick man.병자. lame.다리 저는 사람, 절름발이의, 절뚝거리는. crippled. 다리를 저는, 불구의, 지체가 부자유한, 절름발이의. In these lay a large number of ill, blind, lame, and crippled.(거기에는, 그 주랑 안에는) 병자들, 눈먼 이들, 다리 저는 이들, 팔다리가 비틀어진 이들이 많이 누워 있었다. (7절)그래서 redundant한 번역임. lap(against), slop, slash, roll, swell, jiggle, tumbled in a cascade, bounce.출렁거리다. jiggle:아래위 양

옆으로 빠르게 움직이다, 출렁거리다, 흔들다, 까불다. stir:휘젓다, 젓다, 저어가며 섞다, 소용돌이치다, 움직이다, 불러일으키다, 동요시키다, 자극하다. (7절)go(first, before) me, go ahead of me.나보다 먼저 가다. (9절)그러자 redundant한 번역. (10절)Now.그런데. lawful(lɔ́:fəl), lawfully, lawfulness.(합법, 적법)의, 법률이 인정하는, (정당, 타당, 합당)한, 법률에(의해 허가·인가되어 있는, 위반되지 않는). (13절)slipped away.사라지다, 빠져나가다, 가로새다, 도망쳤다, 딴 데로 샜다, 살짝 가버렸다. left, excuse oneself, Ask to be excused from the seat, rose from the seat.자리를 뜨다. (14절)Look.이봐, 자, 자기 말에 주의를 기울이라는 뜻. You got(were) well. You were healthier. You (became, got) healthy. 건강해졌다. (15절)withdraw from; leave; move backward; (fall, draw, step) back. 물러가다. (18절)For this reason.이 때문에, 이런 까닭에. (20절)For.문두에서 사실, 실상, 과연, 왜냐하면 ~이니까, 그 까닭은 ~이므로, 이기 때문이다. 문어적이며 회화에서는 쓰지 않음. (21절)For.실상, 사실. (24절)condemn.(판정을, 선고를) 내리다; (단죄, 유죄를 시사)하다; (규탄, 비난)하다. passed= crossed over.(건너, 옮겨)갔다. ~will not be condemned= ~will not come to condemnation. (26절)possess(pəzés).(소유, 점유)하다, 가지다, 손에 넣다. ~so also he gave to his Son the possession of life in himself.= ~he has also granted his Son to have life in himself.(왜냐하면) ~(그렇게 아들에게도 생명을 주셔서) 아들도 그 안에 생명을 가지게 해 주셨기 때문이다. For.~기 때문이다. (27절)exercise.권력 등을 행사하다, 위력 등을 휘두르다, 맡은 일을 다 하다(discharge), 좋은 일 등을 행하다(practice). power.권능, 권한. authority.권한, 당국. (29절)done good deeds.(선행, 미덕)을 행하다. done good.선을 행하다. (31절)behalf(bihǽf). 이익, 원조, 자기 편들기. on one's own behalf.자신의 이익을 위하여, 자신을 위하여, 을 대신하여, 대표하여, 을 위하여. for myself.나 자신을 위하여. verify.(확인, 검증. 입증, 증명)하다, (진실이라고 · 정확하다고) (확인해, 말해) 주다. ~is not valid.유효하지 못하다. on one's behalf.을 대신하여, 대표하여, 을 위하여. on behalf of.~(을, 남을) (대신, 대표)하여, 을 위하여, 때문에, 을 도우려고. somebody else. 누군가 다른 사람. (33절)emissary(émɔsèri).사절, 특사, 밀사, 사자(messenger). 사람들.➜ 특사들. (34절)I do not accept testimony.➜ I do not need testimony. (35절)~and you did for a while to enjoy the pleasure in the light.너희는 한때 그 빛 속에서 즐거움을 누리려고 하였다. be content to rejoice.기꺼이 기뻐하다, 기뻐하며 (만족, 흡족해)하였다. (36절)~these works that I perform testify on my behalf that the Father has sent me.내가 수행하는 일들이 아버지께서 나를 보내셨다는 것을 내 대신 증언한다. (37절) Moreover.더욱이, 게다가. And.그리고. (39절)너희는 성경을 통하여 영원한 생명을 얻겠다는 생각을 하기 때문에 성경을 연구한다. ~even they testify on my behalf.성경마저도 내대신 증언한다. ~precisely the scripture testify for my behalf.바로 그 성경이 나를 위하여 증언한다. (40절)But you do not want to come to me to have life. 그러나 너희는 생명을

얻기 위하여 나에게 오려고 하지 않는다. (41절)I do not accept human praise.나는 사람의 찬양을 받지 않는다. I do not accept glory from men.나는 사람들에게서 영광을 받지 않는다. (42절)Moreover I know that you do not have the love of God in you.더욱이, 나는 너희 안에 하느님의 사랑이 없다는 것을 안다. 더욱이 나는 너희들이 너희 안에 하느님의 사랑을 지니고 있지 않다는 것을 안다. (43절)~yet if그러나 ~하면. (44절)How can you believe, when you accept praise from one another and do not seek the praise that comes from the only God? 너희가 자기들 끼리 찬양을 받아들이고 유일한 하느님에게서 오는 찬양은 추구하지 않을 때에 어떻게 믿을 수 있겠느냐?; 어떻게 나의 말을 믿을 수 있겠느냐? (45절) before the Father.아버지 (앞에서, 면전에서).

Footnotes

(1-47절)The self-revelation of Jesus continues in Jerusalem at a feast. The third sign (cf John 2:11; 4:54) is performed, the cure of a paralytic by Jesus' life-giving word. The water of the pool fails to bring life; Jesus' word does. (1절)The reference in John 5:45-46 to Moses suggests that the feast was Pentecost. The connection of that feast with the giving of the law to Moses on Sinai, attested in later Judaism, may already have been made in the first century. The feast could also be Passover (cf John 6:4). John stresses that the day was a sabbath (John 5:9). (2절)There is no noun with Sheep. "Gate" is supplied on the grounds that there must have been a gate in the NE wall of the temple area where animals for sacrifice were brought in; cf Nehemiah 3:1, 32; 12:39. Hebrew: more precisely, Aramaic. Bethesda(House of Grace은총의 집): preferred to variants "Be(th)zatha" and "Bethsaida"; bet-esdatayin is given as the name of a double pool northeast of the temple area in the Qumran Copper Roll. Five porticoes: a pool excavated in Jerusalem actually has five porticoes.벳자타 연못은 기원전 2세기경 예루살렘 성전에 깨끗한 물을 대기 위해 만들어졌음. excavated.(발굴, 출토)하다. (3절)The Caesarean and Western recensions, followed by the Vulgate, add "waiting for the movement of the water." Apparently an intermittent spring in the pool bubbled up occasionally (see John 5:7). This turbulence was believed to cure.불가타 사본에 이은 시저와 서구 사본에서는 물의 움직임을 기다렸다는 구절이 추가된다. recension. 교정, 교정(본, 판). intermittent.간헐적인, 간간이 일어나는. (4절)Toward the end of the second century in the West and among the fourth-century Greek Fathers, an additional verse was known: "For (from time to time) an angel of the Lord used to come down into the pool; and the water was stirred up, so the first one to get in (after the stirring of the water) was healed of whatever disease afflicted him." The angel was a popular explanation of the turbulence and the healing powers attributed to it. This verse is missing from all early Greek manuscripts and the earliest versions, including the original Vulgate. Its vocabulary is markedly non-Johannine. (14 절)While the cure of the paralytic in Mark 2:1-12 is associated with the forgiveness of sins, Jesus never drew a one-to-one connection between sin and suffering (cf John 9:3; Luke 12:1-5), as did Ezekiel 18:20.예수님께서는 죄와 고통의 연관성을 1대1로 결부시키지 않으십니다. (17절)Sabbath observance (10절)~was based on God's resting on the seventh day (cf Genesis 2:2-3; Exodus 20:11). Philo and some rabbis insisted that God's providence remains active on the sabbath, keeping all things in existence, giving life in birth and taking it away in death. Other rabbis taught that God rested from creating, but not from judging (=ruling, governing). 하느님께서 심판하시고 다스리시고 통치하시는 일에서는 쉬지 않으셨다고 가르쳤다. Jesus here claims the same authority to work as the Father, and, in the discourse that follows, the same divine prerogatives: power over life and death (John 5:21, 24-26) and judgment (John 5:22, 27).예수님께서는 여기서 하느님처럼 일할 수 있는 똑같은 권위를 주장하시고 이어지는 다음 설교에서는 생명과 죽음을 다스리시는 권능과 심판 등 하느님과 똑같은 특권을 주장하십니다. (19절)This proverb or parable is taken from apprenticeship in a trade.상거래에서의 도제제도. ~the activity of a son is modeled on that of his father. Jesus' dependence on the Father is justification for doing what the Father does. (21절) Gives life: in the Old Testament, a divine prerogative (Deut 32:39; 1 Sam 2:6; 2 Kings 5:7; Tobit 13:2; Isaiah 26:19; Daniel 12:2). (22절)Judgment: another divine prerogative, often expressed as acquittal or condemnation (Deut 32:36; Psalm 43:1). (28-29절)While John 5:19-27 present realized eschatology, John 5:28-29 are future eschatology; cf Daniel 12:2. (32절)Another: likely the Father, who in four different ways gives testimony to Jesus, as indicated in the verse groupings John 5:33-34, 36, 37-38, 39-40. (35절)Lamp: cf. Psalm 132:17. "I will place a lamp for my anointed (= David)," and possibly the description of Elijah in Sirach 48:1. But only for a while, indicating the temporary and subordinate nature of John's mission.내가 (세운, 기름 부운) 왕(다윗)의 등잔에 불을 켜 주리라, 그리고 아마(최대한 가능한 대로) 집회서의 엘리야에 대한 서술을 참조하라. 그러나 단지 (한때, 잠시 동안, 일시)는 요한의 사명이 가지는 순간적이고 종속적인 (본질, 성격) 을 가리킨다. 등불도 태양이 뜨면 필요 없듯이 세례자 요한도 세상의 빛이신 예수님이 나타나실 때 까지 어두운 세상을 잠시 비추었던 빛이었다. (39절)You search: this may be an imperative: "Search the scriptures, because you think that you have eternal life through them." (41절)Praise: the same Greek word means "praise.찬양, 칭찬" or "honor.예우, 명예, 영예, 영광, 광영, 특권." (from others) and "glory" (from God). There is a play (역할, 기량, 내용) on this in John 5:44.이에 대해서는 요한복음서 5장 44절에 역할이 있다.

요한복음서 6장

오천 명을 먹이시다(마태 14, 13-21; 마르 6, 30-44; 루카 9, 10-17)

1 그 뒤에 예수님께서 갈릴래아 호수 곧 티베리아스 호수 건너편으로 가셨는데,

2 많은 군중이 그분을 따라갔다. 그분께서 병자들에게 일으키신 표징들을 보았기 때문이다.

3 예수님께서는 산에 오르시어 제자들과 함께 그곳에 앉으셨다.

4 마침 유다인들의 축제인 파스카가 가까운 때였다.

5 예수님께서는 눈을 드시어 많은 군중이 당신께 오는 것을 보시고 필립보에게, "저 사람들이 먹을 빵을 우리가 어디에서 살 수 있겠느냐?" 하고 물으셨다.

6 이는 필립보를 시험해 보려고 하신 말씀이다. 그분께서는 당신이 하시려는 일을 이미 잘 알고 계셨다.

7 필립보가 예수님께 대답하였다. "저마다 조금씩이라도 받아 먹게 하자면 이백 데나리온어치 빵으로도 충분하지 않겠습니다."

8 그때에 제자들 가운데 하나인 시몬 베드로의 동생 안드레아가 예수님께 말하였다.

9 "여기 보리 빵 다섯 개와 물고기 두 마리를 가진 아이가 있습니다만, 저렇게 많은 사람에게 이것이 무슨 소용이 있겠습니까?"

10 그러자 예수님께서 "사람들을 자리 잡게 하여라." 하고 이르셨다. 그곳에는 풀이 많았다. 그리하여 사람들이 자리를 잡았는데, 장정만도 그 수가 오천 명쯤 되었다.

11 예수님께서는 빵을 손에 들고 감사를 드리신 다음, 자리를 잡은 이들에게 나누어 주셨다. 물고기도 그렇게 하시어 사람들이 원하는 대로 주셨다.

12 그들이 배불리 먹은 다음에 예수님께서는 제자들에게, "버려지는 것이 없도록 남은 조각을 모아라." 하고 말씀하셨다.

13 그래서 그들이 모았더니, 사람들이 보리 빵 다섯 개를 먹고 남긴 조각으로 열두 광주리가 가득 찼다.

14 사람들은 예수님께서 일으키신 표징을 보고, "이분은 정말 세상에 오시기로 되어 있는 그 예언자시다." 하고 말하였다.

15 예수님께서는 그들이 와서 당신을 억지로 모셔다가 임금으로 삼으려 한다는 것을 아시고, 혼자서 다시 산으로 물러가셨다.

물 위를 걸으시다(마태 14, 22-33; 마르 6, 45-52)

16 저녁때가 되자 제자들은 호수로 내려가서,

17 배를 타고 호수 건너편 카파르나움으로 떠났다. 이미 어두워졌는데도 예수님께서는 아직 그들에게 가지 않으셨다.

18 그때에 큰 바람이 불어 호수에 물결이 높게 일었다.

19 그들이 배를 스물다섯이나 서른 스타디온쯤 저어 갔을 때, 예수님께서 호수 위를 걸어 배에 가까이 오시는 것을 보고 두려워하였다.

20 예수님께서는 그들에게 말씀하셨다. "나다. 두려워하지 마라."

21 그래서 그들이 예수님을 배 안으로 모셔 들이려고 하는데, 배는 어느새 그들이 가려던 곳에 가 닿았다.

생명의 빵

22 이튿날, 호수 건너편에 남아 있던 군중은, 그곳에 배가 한 척밖에 없었는데 예수님께서 제자들과 함께 그 배를 타고 가지 않으시고 제자들만 떠났다는 것을 알게 되었다.

23 그런데 티베리아스에서 배 몇 척이, 주님께서 감사를 드리신 다음 빵을 나누어 먹이신 곳에 가까이 와 닿았다.

24 군중은 거기에 예수님도 계시지 않고 제자들도 없는 것을 알고서, 그 배들에 나누어 타고 예수님을 찾아 카파르나움으로 갔다.

25 그들은 호수 건너편에서 예수님을 찾아내고, "라삐, 언제 이곳에 오셨습니까?" 하고 물었다.

26 예수님께서 그들에게 대답하셨다. "내가 진실로 진실로 너희에게 말한다. 너희가 나를 찾는 것은 표징을 보았기 때문이 아니라 빵을 배불리 먹었기 때문이다.

27 너희는 썩어 없어질 양식을 얻으려고 힘쓰지 말고, 길이 남아 영원한 생명을 누리게 하는 양식을 얻으려고 힘써라. 그 양식은 사람의 아들이 너희에게 줄 것이다. 하느님 아버지께서 사람의 아들을 인정하셨기 때문이다."

28 그들이 "하느님의 일을 하려면 저희가 무엇을 해야 합니까?" 하고 묻자,

29 예수님께서 그들에게 대답하셨다. "하느님의 일은 그분께서 보내신 이를 너희가 믿는 것이다."

30 그들이 다시 물었다. "그러면 무슨 표징을 일으키시어 저희가 보고 선생님을 믿게 하시겠습니까? 무슨 일을 하시렵니까?

31 '그분께서는 하늘에서 그들에게 빵을 내리시어 먹게 하셨다.'는 성경 말씀대로, 우리 조상들은 광야에서 만나를 먹었습니다."

32 예수님께서 그들에게 이르셨다. "내가 진실로 진실로 너희에게 말한다. 하늘에서 너희에게 빵을 내려 준 이는 모세가 아니다. 하늘에서 너희에게 참된 빵을 내려 주시는 분은 내 아버지시다.

33 하느님의 빵은 하늘에서 내려와 세상에 생명을 주는 빵이다."

34 그들이 예수님께, "선생님, 그 빵을 늘 저희에게 주십시오." 하자,

35 예수님께서 그들에게 이르셨다. "내가 생명의 빵이다. 나에게 오는 사람은 결코 배고프지 않을 것이며, 나를 믿는 사람은 결코 목마르지 않을 것이다.

36 그러나 내가 이미 말한 대로, 너희는 나를 보고도 나를 믿지 않는다.

37 아버지께서 나에게 주시는 사람은 모두 나에게 올 것이고, 나에게 오는 사람을 나는 물리치지 않을 것이다.

38 나는 내 뜻이 아니라 나를 보내신 분의 뜻을 실천하려고 하늘에서 내려왔기 때문이다.

39 나를 보내신 분의 뜻은, 그분께서 나에게 주신 사람을 하나도 잃지 않고 마지막 날에 다시 살리는 것이다.

40 내 아버지의 뜻은 또, 아들을 보고 믿는 사람은 누구나 영원한 생명을 얻는 것이다. 나는 마지막 날에 그들을 다시 살릴 것이다."

41 예수님께서 "나는 하늘에서 내려온 빵이다." 하고 말씀하셨기 때문에, 유다인들이 그분을 두고 수군거리기 시작하였다.

42 그들이 말하였다. "저 사람은 요셉의 아들 예수가 아닌가? 그의 아버지와 어머니도 우리가 알고 있지 않는가? 그런데 저 사람이 어떻게 '나는 하늘에서 내려왔다.'고 말할 수 있는가?"

43 그러자 예수님께서 그들에게 대답하셨다. "너희끼리 수군거리지 마라.

44 나를 보내신 아버지께서 이끌어 주지 않으시면 아무도 나에게 올 수 없다. 그리고 나에게 오는 사람은 내가 마지막 날에 다시 살릴 것이다.

45 '그들은 모두 하느님께 가르침을 받을 것이다.'라고 예언서들에 기록되어 있다. 아버지의 말씀을 듣고 배운 사람은 누구나 나에게 온다.

46 그렇다고 하느님에게서 온 이 말고 누가 아버지를 보았다는 말은 아니다. 하느님에게서 온 이만 아버지를 보았다.

47 내가 진실로 진실로 너희에게 말한다. 믿는 사람은 영원한 생명을 얻는다.

48 나는 생명의 빵이다.

49 너희 조상들은 광야에서 만나를 먹고도 죽었다.

50 그러나 이 빵은 하늘에서 내려오는 것으로, 이 빵을 먹는 사람은 죽지 않는다.

51 나는 하늘에서 내려온 살아 있는 빵이다. 누구든지 이 빵을 먹으면 영원히 살 것이다. 내가 줄 빵은 세상에 생명을 주는 나의 살이다."

52 그러자 "저 사람이 어떻게 자기 살을 우리에게 먹으라고 줄 수 있단 말인가?" 하며, 유다인들 사이에 말다툼이 벌어졌다.

53 예수님께서 그들에게 이르셨다. "내가 진실로 진실로 너희에게 말한다. 너희가 사람의 아들의 살을 먹지 않고 그의 피를 마시지 않으면, 너희는 생명을 얻지 못한다.

54 그러나 내 살을 먹고 내 피를 마시는 사람은 영원한 생명을 얻고, 나도 마지막 날에 그를 다시 살릴 것이다.

55 내 살은 참된 양식이고 내 피는 참된 음료다.

56 내 살을 먹고 내 피를 마시는 사람은 내 안에 머무르고, 나도 그 사람 안에 머무른다.

57 살아 계신 아버지께서 나를 보내셨고 내가 아버지로 말미암아 사는 것과 같이, 나를 먹는 사람도 나로 말미암아 살 것이다.

58 이것이 하늘에서 내려온 빵이다. 너희 조상들이 먹고도 죽은 것과는 달리, 이 빵을 먹는 사람은 영원히 살 것이다."

59 이는 예수님께서 카파르나움 회당에서 가르치실 때에 하신 말씀이다.

영원한 생명의 말씀

60 제자들 가운데 많은 사람이 예수님께서 말씀하시는 것을 듣고 말하였다. "이 말씀은 듣기가 너무 거북하다. 누가 듣고 있을 수 있겠는가?"

61 예수님께서는 제자들이 당신의 말씀을 두고 투덜거리는 것을 속으로 아시고 그들에게 이르셨다. "이 말이 너희 귀에 거슬리느냐?

62 사람의 아들이 전에 있던 곳으로 올라가는 것을 보게 되면 어떻게 하겠느냐?

63 영은 생명을 준다. 그러나 육은 아무 쓸모가 없다. 내가 너희에게 한 말은 영이며 생명이다.

64 그러나 너희 가운데에는 믿지 않는 자들이 있다." 사실 예수님께서는 믿지 않는 자들이 누구이며 또 당신을 팔아넘길 자가 누구인지 처음부터 알고 계셨던 것이다.

65 이어서 또 말씀하셨다. "그렇기 때문에, 아버지께서 허락하지 않으시면 아무도 나에게 올 수 없다고 너희에게 말한 것이다."

66 이 일이 일어난 뒤로, 제자들 가운데에서 많은 사람이 되돌아가고 더 이상 예수님과 함께 다니지 않았다.

67 그래서 예수님께서는 열두 제자에게, "너희도 떠나고 싶으냐?" 하고 물으셨다.

68 그러자 시몬 베드로가 예수님께 대답하였다. "주님, 저희가 누구에게 가겠습니까? 주님께는 영원한 생명의 말씀이 있습니다.

69 스승님께서 하느님의 거룩하신 분이라고 저희는 믿어 왔고 또 그렇게 알고 있습니다."

70 예수님께서 그들에게 말씀하셨다. "내가 너희 열둘을 뽑지 않았느냐? 그러나 너희 가운데 하나는 악마다."

71 이는 시몬 이스카리옷의 아들 유다를 가리켜 하신 말씀이었다. 사실 그는 열두 제자 가운데 하나이면서도 머지않아 예수님을 팔아넘길 자였다.

Multiplication of the Loaves

John Chapter 6

1 After this, Jesus went across the Sea of Galilee (of Tiberias). 2 A large crowd followed him, because they saw the signs he was performing on the sick. 3 Jesus went up on the mountain, and there he sat down with his disciples. 4 The Jewish feast of Passover was near. 5 When Jesus raised his eyes and saw that a large crowd was coming to him, he said to Philip, "Where can we buy enough food for them to eat?" 6 He said this to test him, because he himself knew what he was going

to do. 7 Philip answered him, "Two hundred days' wages worth of food would not be enough for each of them to have a little (bit)." 8 One of his disciples, Andrew, the brother of Simon Peter, said to him, 9 "There is a boy here who has five barley loaves and two fish; but what good are these for so many?" 10 Jesus said, "Have the people recline." Now there was a great deal of grass in that place. So the men reclined, about five thousand in number. 11 Then Jesus took the loaves, gave thanks, and distributed them to those who were reclining, and also as much of the fish as they wanted. 12 When they had had their fill, he said to his disciples, "Gather the fragments left over, so that nothing will be wasted." 13 So they collected them, and filled twelve wicker baskets with fragments from the five barley loaves that had been more than they could eat. 14 When the people saw the sign he had done, they said, "This is truly the Prophet, the one who is to come into the world." 15 Since Jesus knew that they were going to come and carry him off to make him king, he withdrew again to the mountain alone.

Walking on the Water

16 When it was evening, his disciples went down to the sea, 17 embarked in a boat, and went across the sea to Capernaum. It had already grown dark, and Jesus had not yet come to them. 18 The sea was stirred up because a strong wind was blowing. 19 When they had rowed about three or four miles, they saw Jesus walking on the sea and coming near the boat, and they began to be afraid. 20 But he said to them, "It is I. Do not be afraid." 21 They wanted to take him into the boat, but the boat immediately arrived at the shore to which they were heading.

The Bread of Life Discourse

22 The next day, the crowd that remained across the sea saw that there had been only one boat there, and that Jesus had not gone along with his disciples in the boat, but only his disciples had left. 23 Other boats came from Tiberias near the place where they had eaten the bread when the Lord gave thanks.24 When the crowd saw that neither Jesus nor his disciples were there, they themselves got into boats and came to Capernaum looking for Jesus. 25 And when they found him across the sea they said to him, "Rabbi, when did you get here?" 26 Jesus answered them and said, "Amen, amen, I say to you, you are looking for me not because you saw signs but because you ate the loaves and were filled. 27 Do not work for food that perishes

but for the food that endures for eternal life, which the Son of Man will give you. For on him the Father, God, has set his seal." 28 So they said to him, "What can we do to accomplish the works of God?" 29 Jesus answered and said to them, "This is the work of God, that you believe in the one he sent." 30 So they said to him, "What sign can you do, that we may see and believe in you? What can you do? 31 Our ancestors ate manna in the desert, as it is written: 'He gave them bread from heaven to eat.'" 32 So Jesus said to them, "Amen, amen, I say to you, it was not Moses who gave the bread from heaven; my Father gives you the true bread from heaven. 33 For the bread of God is that which comes down from heaven and gives life to the world." 34 So they said to him, "Sir, give us this bread always." 35 Jesus said to them, "I am the bread of life; whoever comes to me will never hunger, and whoever believes in me will never thirst. 36 But I told you that although you have seen (me), you do not believe. 37 Everything that the Father gives me will come to me, and I will not reject anyone who comes to me, 38 because I came down from heaven not to do my own will but the will of the one who sent me. 39 And this is the will of the one who sent me, that I should not lose anything of what he gave me, but that I should raise it (on) the last day.40 For this is the will of my Father, that everyone who sees the Son and believes in him may have eternal life, and I shall raise him (on) the last day." 41 The Jews murmured about him because he said, "I am the bread that came down from heaven," 42 and they said, "Is this not Jesus, the son of Joseph? Do we not know his father and mother? Then how can he say, 'I have come down from heaven'?" 43 Jesus answered and said to them, "Stop murmuring among yourselves.44 No one can come to me unless the Father who sent me draw him, and I will raise him on the last day. 45 It is written in the prophets: 'They shall all be taught by God.' Everyone who listens to my Father and learns from him comes to me.46 Not that anyone has seen the Father except the one who is from God; he has seen the Father. 47 Amen, amen, I say to you, whoever believes has eternal life. 48 I am the bread of life. 49 Your ancestors ate the manna in the desert, but they died; 50 this is the bread that comes down from heaven so that one may eat it and not die.51 I am the living bread that came down from heaven; whoever eats this bread will live forever; and the bread that I will give is my flesh for the life of the world." 52 The Jews quarreled among themselves, saying, "How can this man give us (his) flesh to eat?" 53 Jesus said to them, "Amen, amen, I say to you, unless you eat the flesh of the Son of Man and drink his blood, you do not have life within you. 54 Whoever eats my flesh and drinks my blood has eternal life, and I will raise him on the last day.55 For my flesh is true food, and my blood is true drink. 56 Whoever eats my flesh and drinks my blood remains in me and I in him.57 Just as the living Father sent me and I have life because of the Father, so also the one who feeds on me will have life because of me.58 This is the bread that came down from heaven. Unlike your ancestors who ate and still died, whoever eats this bread will live forever." 59 These things he said while teaching in the synagogue in Capernaum.

The Words of Eternal Life

60 Then many of his disciples who were listening said, "This saying is hard; who can accept it?" 61Since Jesus knew that his disciples were murmuring about this, he said to them, "Does this shock you? 62 What if you were to see the Son of Man ascending to where he was before? 63 It is the spirit that gives life, while the flesh is of no avail. The words I have spoken to you are spirit and life.64 But there are some of you who do not believe." Jesus knew from the beginning the ones who would not believe and the one who would betray him. 65 And he said, "For this reason I have told you that no one can come to me unless it is granted him by my Father." 66 As a result of this, many (of) his disciples returned to their former way of life and no longer accompanied him.67 Jesus then said to the Twelve, "Do you also want to leave?" 68 Simon Peter answered him, "Master, to whom shall we go? You have the words of eternal life. 69 We have come to believe and are convinced that you are the Holy One of God." 70 Jesus answered them, "Did I not choose you twelve? Yet is not one of you a devil?" 71 He was referring to Judas, son of Simon the Iscariot; it was he who would betray him, one of the Twelve.

(1절)thence, afterwards, subsequently.그 뒤에. after this.이 후는, 이런 일이 있은 뒤에. (2절)work signs.표징을 일으키다. perform signs.표징을 (행, 이행, 실행)하다. (5절)enough food.(먹을)충분한 음식. (7절)Two hundred denarii worth of bread. (10절)recline(rikláin). 편안하게 비스듬히 (앉다, 기대다, 눕다). recline at table.식탁에 앉다. Miss June Thompson was reclining elegantly in a chair.쥰 탐슨양은 의자에 우아하게 앉아 있었다. Have the people(recline= sit down). So the men (reclined= sat down). (11절)~were reclining.→ ~were seated. (12절)have one's fill.실컷 먹다. fragment.조각, 파편. ~had had their fill.= ~had all had enough to eat. (13절)more than.보다 많은, 이상으로(의), 뿐만 아니라, 하고도 남음이 있다. ~fragments from the five barley loaves that had been left over by those who had eaten.사람들이 보리 빵 다섯 개를 먹고 남긴 조각으로 열두 광주리가 가득 찼다. wicker(wíkər).나긋나긋한 작은 가지, 버들가지, 고리버들 세공(제품). 작은 가지로 만든. wicker basket.광주리. (15절)force.억지로. carry one off.(데리고, 모시고) 가다. ~carry him off by force to make him king. (18절)stirred up.소용돌이치다, 휘젓다. The waves were high rising.물결이 높게 일었다. stir.젓다, (유발, 자극)하다, (움직, 뒤척)이다. The sea(lake) was stirred up because a strong wind was blowing.강한 바람이 불고 있었기 때문에 바다(호수)가 소용돌이 치고 있었다. At that time strong wind was blowing and (the waters grew rough, and the waves became high, the waves are high) on the lake.그때에 큰 바람이 불어 호수에 물결이 높게 일었다. (19절)스타디온(stadion).191.27m에 해당하고, 전설에는 제우스신의 600행보에 해당됨. 스타디움의 어원임. began to be afraid.두려워하기 시작하였다. (20절)But.그런데, 하지만. (25절)And.그런데. (27절)endure. 지속시키다, 오래 (가게하다, 누리다), (지속, 지탱)하다, 참다, 인내하다. enjoy.누리다. for.앞 문장의 부가적 설명 · 이유로서 왜냐하면 ~이니까(이기 때문이다), 그 까닭은 ~이므로. For on him the Father, God, has set his seal.왜냐하면 하느님 아버지께서 사람의 아들에게 (영원한 생명을 오래누리는 양식을 주도록) 인정해 주셨기 때문이다. set seal on.(승인, 인정)하다. (set, fix, stamp)a seal.도장을 찍다. (28절)So they said to him, "What can we do to accomplish the works of God?" 그래서 그들이 예수님께 말하였다, 하느님의 일을 완수하기 위하여 저희가 무엇을 할 수 있습니까?→ They asked him, "What must we do to do the works of God?" 그들이 하느님의 일을 하려면 저희가 무엇을 해야 합니까? 하고 물었다. (30절)(work, do, perform, make) (signs, miracles, marvels).기적을 일으키다. What can you do?→ What will you do? (32절)So.그러자. (33절)For.사실. (34절) So.그리하여. (36절)But as I told you, even though you have seen me and you do not believe. (37절)Everything, All.모든 것, 모두. reject.(거절, 거부)하다. refuse, reject, turn down, decline, defeat, beat, repel.물리치다. (39절)raise.일으키다, 인상하다, 부활시키다, 되살리다. anything.아무것도, 뭔가, 무엇이든, 뭐든. anyone.누구, 아무, 누구나, 누구든지, 누구한테도. ~that I should lose none of all that he gave me.그분께서 나에게 주신 사람을 하나도 잃지 않고. raise it(on). or raise them(on). (40절)For.과연, 사실. ~(may, shall) have eternal life.영원한 생명을 (얻게 하려는 것이다, 얻는 것이다). raise him.그들을 다시 살리다. 문맥상 "그들"로 번역. 200주년 성서에는 "그를"로 번역. (41절)whisper.수근 거리다. murmur.(중얼, 투덜)거리다, 속삭이다. grumble.투덜거리다, 불평하다. (47절)whoever believes.→ he who believes. (51절)~my flesh for the life of the world.세상의 생명을 위한 나의 살이다. 의역: 세상에 생명을 주는 나의 살이다. (52절)Then the Jews. (53절) 너희는 너희 안에 생명을 얻지 못한다. (54절)그러나 redundant번역임. whoever.누구든지, 누구나. (55절)For.사실. (57절)have life= live. because of, due to, owing to.말미암아.

(60절)Then.그런 다음에. feel ill at ease, feel quite embarrassed, uncomfortable, awkward, offensive.거북하다. (61절)shock you?너희들에게 충격적이냐? be offensive, be unpleasant.거슬리다. be (harsh, offensive) to the ear, jar upon the ear.귀에 거슬리다. be an eyesore.눈에 거슬리다. (63절)while.주절 뒤에서 반대 · 비교 · 대조를 뜻함; 그런데, 한편(으로는), 하지만, 동시에. of no avail.(쓸모가, 소용이) 없다. It is the Spirit that gives life.→ The Spirit gives life. (64절)For Jesus knew.사실 예수님께서는 ~알고 계셨던 것이다. (65절)go on to say.(이어서, 계속해서) 말하다. And he said.예수님께서 또 말씀하셨다. 그러자 예수님께서 말씀하셨다. (그리하여, 이렇게) 말씀하셨다. And He went on to say.또 이어서 말씀하셨다. for this reason.(이렇기, 그렇기) 때문에, 이러한 이유로 해서, 이러한 이유 때문에. (66절)go about together; accompany.함께 다니다, 동반하다. (Since, After) this happened.이 일이 일어난 뒤로. As a result of this.이에 대한 결과로, 이 일 때문에, 이 일의 결과로. way of life.생활 (양식, 방식), 삶의 (방식, 방법). As a result of this, many (of) his disciples returned to their former way of life and no~→ After this happened, many of his disciples turned back and no longer accompanied him. (67절)so, therefore, thereupon, and, then, accordingly.그래서. said to.→asked. (68절) And. 그러자. (69절)~are convinced. →know. (71절)before long, soon, shortly.머지않아. Yet is not one of you a devil?→ Yet one of you is a devil. ~for it was he who, though one of the Twelve, (was to betray him before long. was soon to betray him).

Footnotes

(1절)(Of Tiberias): the awkward apposition represents a later name of the Sea of Galilee. It was probably originally a marginal gloss. (1절)marginal gloss.여백에 쓴 주석. apposition.동격(同格). marginal.여백에 쓴, 난외의, 미미한, 한계, 주변부의, 주변적인. gloss.주석, 해설, 매끄러운 표면의 (윤, 광), 광택제. (1-15절)This story of the multiplication of the loaves is the fourth sign (cf the note on John 5:1-47). It is the only miracle story found in all four gospels (occurring twice in Mark and Matthew). See the notes on Matthew 14:13-21; 15:32-39. John differs on the roles of Philip and Andrew, the proximity of Passover (John 6:4) 과월절의 가까움, and the allusion to Elisha (see John 6:9).엘리사에 대한 암시. The story here symbolizes the food that is really available through Jesus. It connotes a new exodus and has eucharistic overtones. 여기에는 새로운 출애굽(탈출)과 성찬의 의미가 포함되어 있음. connote.어떤 의미를 함축하다. overtone.함축, 색채. (5절)Jesus takes the initiative (in the synoptics, the disciples do), possibly pictured as (cf John 6:14) the new Moses (cf Numbers 11:13). (6절)Probably the evangelist's comment; in this gospel Jesus is never portrayed as ignorant of anything. (7절)Days' wages: literally, "denarii"; a Roman denarius is a day's wage in Matthew 20:2. (9절)Barley loaves: the food of the poor. There seems an allusion to the story of Elisha multiplying the barley bread in 2 Kings 4:42-44. (10)Grass: implies springtime, and therefore Passover. Five thousand: so Mark 6:39, 44 and parallels. (13절) Baskets: the word describes the typically Palestinian wicker basket, as in Mark 6:43 and parallels. (14)The Prophet: probably the prophet like Moses (see the note on John 1:21). The one who is to come into the world: probably Elijah; cf Malachi 3:1, 23. (16-21절)The fifth sign is a nature miracle, portraying Jesus sharing Yahweh's power. Cf the parallel stories following the multiplication of the loaves in Mark 6:45-52 and Matthew 14:22-33. (19절)Walking on the sea: although the Greek (cf John 6:16) could mean "on the seashore" or "by the sea" (cf John 21:1), the parallels, especially Matthew 14:25, make clear that Jesus walked upon the water. John may allude to Job 9:8: God "treads upon the crests of the sea." (20절)It is I: literally, "I am." See also the notes on John 4:26 and Mark 6:50. (22-71절)Discourse on the bread of life; replacement of the manna. John 6:22-34 serve as an introduction, John 6:35-59 constitute the discourse proper, John 6:60-71 portray the reaction of the disciples and Peter's confession. (23절)Possibly a later interpolation, to explain how the crowd got to Capernaum. (27절)The food that endures for eternal life: cf John 4:14, on water "springing up to eternal life."(31절)Bread from heaven: cf Exodus 16:4, 15, 32-34 and the notes there; Psalm 78:24. The manna, thought to have been hidden by Jeremiah (2 Macc 2:5-8), was expected to reappear miraculously at Passover, in the last days. (35-59절)Up to John 6:50 "bread of life" is a figure for God's revelation in Jesus; in John 6:51-58, the eucharistic theme comes to the fore. There may thus be a break between John 6:50-51. (43절)Murmuring: the word may reflect the Greek of Exodus 16:2, 7-8. (54-58절) Eats: the verb used in these verses is not the classical Greek verb used of human eating, but that of animal eating: "munch," "gnaw." This may be part of John's emphasis on the reality of the flesh and blood of Jesus (cf John 6:55), but the same verb eventually became the ordinary verb in Greek meaning "eat." (60-71절)These verses refer more to themes of John 6:35-50 than to those of John 6:51-58 and seem to be addressed to members of the Johannine community who found it difficult to accept the high christology reflected in the bread of life discourse. (62 절)This unfinished conditional sentence is obscure. Probably there is a reference to John 6:49-51. Jesus claims to be the bread that comes down from heaven (John 6:50); this claim provokes incredulity (John 6:60); and so Jesus is pictured as asking what his disciples will say when he goes up to heaven. (63절)Spirit···flesh: probably not a reference to the eucharistic body of Jesus but to the supernatural and the natural, as in John 3:6. Spirit and life: all Jesus said about the bread of life is the revelation of the Spirit.

요한복음서 7장

예수님의 형제들이 믿지 않다

1 그 뒤에 예수님께서는 갈릴래아를 돌아다니셨다. 유다인들이 당신을 죽이려고 하였으므로, 유다에서는 돌아다니기를 원하지 않으셨던 것이다.

2 마침 유다인들의 초막절이 가까웠다.

3 그래서 예수님의 형제들이 그분께 말하였다. "이곳을 떠나 유다로 가서, 하시는 일들을 제자들도 보게 하십시오.

4 널리 알려지기를 바라면서 남몰래 일하는 사람은 없습니다. 이런 일들을 할 바에는 자신을 세상에 드러내십시오."

5 사실 예수님의 형제들은 그분을 믿지 않았다.

6 그래서 예수님께서는 그들에게 말씀하셨다. "너희에게는 아무 때라도 상관없지만 나의 때는 아직 오지 않았다.

7 세상이 너희를 미워할 수는 없다. 그러나 세상은 나를 미워한다. 내가 세상을 두고 그 일이 악하다고 증언하기 때문이다.

8 너희나 축제를 지내러 올라가라. 나는 이번 축제에는 올라가지 않겠다. 나의 때가 아직 차지 않았기 때문이다."

9 예수님께서는 이렇게 말씀하시고 나서 갈릴래아에 머무르셨다.

초막절에 가르치시다

10 형제들이 축제를 지내러 올라가고 난 뒤에 예수님께서도 올라가셨다. 그러나 드러나지 않게 남몰래 올라가셨다.

11 그래서 유다인들은 축제 동안에, "그 사람은 어디 있나?" 하면서 예수님을 찾았다.

12 군중 사이에서는 예수님을 두고 수군거리는 말들이 많았다. "그는 선한 사람이오." 하는 이들이 있는가 하면, "아니오. 그는 군중을 속이고 있소." 하는 이들도 있었다.

13 그러나 유다인들이 두려워 그분에 관하여 드러내 놓고 말하는 사람은 없었다.

14 축제가 이미 중반을 지날 때, 예수님께서는 성전에 올라가 가르치셨다.

15 그러자 유다인들이 놀라워하며, "저 사람은 배우지도 않았는데 어떻게 성경을 잘 알까?" 하였다.

16 예수님께서 그들에게 이르셨다. "나의 가르침은 내 것이 아니라 나를 보내신 분의 것이다.

17 누구나 하느님의 뜻을 실천하려고만 하면, 이 가르침이 하느님에게서 오는 것인지 내가 스스로 말하는 것인지 알게 될 것이다.

18 스스로 나서서 말하는 자는 자기의 영광을 찾는다. 그러나 자기를 보내신 분의 영광을 찾는 이는 참되고, 또 그 사람 안에는 불의가 없다.

19 모세가 너희에게 율법을 주지 않았느냐? 그런데도 너희 가운데 율법을 지키는 자가 하나도 없다.

도대체 너희는 왜 나를 죽이려고 하느냐?"

20 군중이 "당신은 마귀가 들렸군. 누가 당신을 죽이려 한단 말이오?" 하고 대답하자,

21 예수님께서 그들에게 이르셨다. "내가 한 가지 일을 하였을 뿐인데 너희는 모두 놀라워한다.

22 모세가 너희에게 할례를 하라고 명령하였다. — 사실 할례는 모세가 아니라 선조들에게서 비롯되었다. — 아무튼 너희는 안식일에도 사람들에게 할례를 베푼다.

23 모세의 율법을 어기지 않으려고 안식일에도 할례를 받는데, 어째서 내가 안식일에 한 사람의 온몸을 건강하게 만들어 준 것을 가지고 나에게 화를 내느냐?

24 겉모습을 보고 판단하지 말고 올바로 판단하여라."

저분이 그리스도이신가

25 예루살렘 주민들 가운데 몇 사람이 말하였다. "그들이 죽이려고 하는 이가 저 사람 아닙니까?

26 그런데 보십시오. 저 사람이 드러내 놓고 이야기하는데 그들은 아무 말도 하지 못합니다. 최고 의회 의원들이 정말 저 사람을 메시아로 알고 있는 것은 아닐까요?

27 그러나 메시아께서 오실 때에는 그분이 어디에서 오시는지 아무도 알지 못할 터인데, 우리는 저 사람이 어디에서 왔는지 알고 있지 않습니까?"

28 그래서 예수님께서는 성전에서 가르치시며 큰 소리로 말씀하셨다. "너희는 나를 알고 또 내가 어디에서 왔는지도 알고 있다. 그러나 나는 나 스스로 온 것이 아니다. 나를 보내신 분은 참되신데 너희는 그분을 알지 못한다.

29 나는 그분을 안다. 내가 그분에게서 왔고 그분께서 나를 보내셨기 때문이다."

30 그러자 그들은 예수님을 잡으려고 하였지만, 그분께 손을 대는 자는 아무도 없었다. 그분의 때가 아직 오지 않았기 때문이다.

31 그러나 군중 가운데에는, "메시아가 오시더라도 저분께서 일으키신 것보다 더 많은 표징을 일으키시겠는가?" 하며 예수님을 믿는 사람이 많았다.

예수님을 잡으려고 하다

32 군중이 예수님을 두고 이렇게 수군거리는 소리를 바리사이들이 들었다. 그리하여 수석 사제들과 바리사이들이 예수님을 잡아 오라고 성전 경비병들을 보냈다.

33 그러자 예수님께서 이르셨다. "나는 잠시 동안만 너희와 함께 있다가, 나를 보내신 분께 간다.

34 그러면 너희가 나를 찾아도 찾아내지 못할 것이다. 또 내가 있는 곳에 너희는 올 수 없다."

35 그러자 유다인들이 서로 말하였다. "저 사람이 어디에 가려고 하기에 우리가 자기를 찾아내지 못한다는 말인가? 그리스인들 사이에 흩어져 사는 동포들에게 가서 그리스인들을 가르치겠다는 말인가?

36 그리고 '너희가 나를 찾아도 찾아내지 못할 것이다. 또 내가 있는 곳에 너희는 올 수 없다.'는 말은 무슨 뜻인가?"

목마른 사람은 나에게 오라

37 축제의 가장 중요한 날인 마지막 날에 예수님께서는 일어서시어 큰 소리로 말씀하셨다. "목마른 사람은 다 나에게 와서 마셔라.

38 나를 믿는 사람은 성경 말씀대로 '그 속에서부터 생수의 강들이 흘러나올 것이다.'"

39 이는 당신을 믿는 이들이 받게 될 성령을 가리켜 하신 말씀이었다. 예수님께서 영광스럽게 되지 않으셨기 때문에, 성령께서 아직 와 계시지 않았던 것이다.

예수님에 관한 여러 가지 생각

40 이 말씀을 들은 군중 가운데 어떤 이들은, "저분은 참으로 그 예언자시다." 하고,

41 어떤 이들은 "저분은 메시아시다." 하였다. 그러나 이렇게 말하는 이들도 있었다. "메시아가 갈릴래아에서 나올 리가 없지 않은가?

42 성경에 메시아는 다윗의 후손 가운데에서, 그리고 다윗이 살았던 베들레헴에서 나온다고 하지 않았는가?"

43 이렇게 군중 가운데에서 예수님 때문에 논란이 일어났다.

44 그들 가운데 몇몇은 예수님을 잡으려고 하였지만, 그분께 손을 대는 자는 아무도 없었다.

예수님을 믿지 않는 지도자들

45 성전 경비병들이 돌아오자 수석 사제들과 바리사이들이, "왜 그 사람을 끌고 오지 않았느냐?" 하고 그들에게 물었다.

46 "그분처럼 말하는 사람은 지금까지 하나도 없었습니다." 하고 성전 경비병들이 대답하자,

47 바리사이들이 그들에게 말하였다. "너희도 속은 것이 아니냐?

48 최고 의회 의원들이나 바리사이들 가운데에서 누가 그를 믿더냐?

49 율법을 모르는 저 군중은 저주받은 자들이다."

50 그들 가운데 한 사람으로 전에 예수님을 찾아왔던 니코데모가 그들에게 말하였다.

51 "우리 율법에는 먼저 본인의 말을 들어 보고 또 그가 하는 일을 알아보고 난 뒤에야, 그 사람을 심판하게 되어 있지 않습니까?"

52 그러자 그들이 니코데모에게 대답하였다. "당신도 갈릴래아 출신이라는 말이오? 성경을 연구해 보시오. 갈릴래아에서는 예언자가 나지 않소."

간음하다 잡힌 여자

53 그들은 저마다 집으로 돌아가고

The Feast of Tabernacles

John Chapter 7

1After this, Jesus moved about within Galilee; but he did not wish to travel in Judea, because the Jews were trying to kill him. 2 But the Jewish feast of Tabernacles was near. 3 So his brothers said to him, "Leave here and go to Judea, so that your disciples also may see the works you are doing. 4 No one works in secret if he wants to be known publicly. If you do these things, manifest yourself to the world." 5. For his brothers did not believe in him. 6 So Jesus said to them, "My time is not yet here, but the time is always right for you. 7 The world cannot hate you, but it hates me, because I testify to it that its works are evil. 8 You go up to the feast. I am not going up to this feast, because my time has not yet been fulfilled." 9 After he had said this, he stayed on in Galilee. 10 But when his brothers had gone up to the feast, he himself also went up, not openly but (as it were) in secret. 11 The Jews were looking for him at the feast and saying, "Where is he?" 12 And there was considerable murmuring about him in the crowds. Some said, "He is a good man," (while) others said, "No; on the contrary, he misleads the crowd." 13 Still, no one spoke openly about him because they were afraid of the Jews.

The First Dialogue

14 When the feast was already half over, Jesus went up into the temple area and began to teach. 15 The Jews were amazed and said, "How does he know scripture without having studied?"16 Jesus answered them and said, "My teaching is not my own but is from the one who sent me. 17 Whoever chooses to do his will shall know whether my teaching is from God or whether I speak on my own. 18 Whoever speaks on his own seeks his own glory, but whoever seeks the glory of the one who sent him is truthful, and there is no wrong in him. 19 Did not Moses give you the law? Yet none of you keeps the law. Why are you trying to kill me?" 20 The crowd answered, "You are possessed! Who is trying to kill you?" 21 Jesus answered and said to them, "I performed one work and all of you are amazed 22 because of it. Moses gave you circumcision--not that it came from Moses but rather from the patriarchs--and you circumcise a man on the sabbath. 23 If a man can receive circumcision on a sabbath so that the law of Moses may not be broken, are you angry with me because I made a whole person well on a sabbath? 24 Stop judging by appearances, but judge

justly." 25 So some of the inhabitants of Jerusalem said, "Is he not the one they are trying to kill? 26 And look, he is speaking openly and they say nothing to him. Could the authorities have realized that he is the Messiah? 27 But we know where he is from. When the Messiah comes, no one will know where he is from." 28 So Jesus cried out in the temple area as he was teaching and said, "You know me and also know where I am from. Yet I did not come on my own, but the one who sent me, whom you do not know, is true. 29 I know him, because I am from him, and he sent me." 30 So they tried to arrest him, but no one laid a hand upon him, because his hour had not yet come. 31 But many of the crowd began to believe in him, and said, "When the Messiah comes, will he perform more signs than this man has done?"

Officers Sent to Arrest Jesus

32 The Pharisees heard the crowd murmuring about him to this effect, and the chief priests and the Pharisees sent guards to arrest him. 33 So Jesus said, "I will be with you only a little while longer, and then I will go to the one who sent me. 34 You will look for me but not find (me), and where I am you cannot come." 35 So the Jews said to one another, "Where is he going that we will not find him? Surely he is not going to the dispersion among the Greeks to teach the Greeks, is he? 36 What is the meaning of his saying, 'You will look for me and not find (me), and where I am you cannot come'?"

Rivers of Living Water

37 On the last and greatest day of the feast, Jesus stood up and exclaimed, "Let anyone who thirsts come to me and drink. 38 Whoever believes in me, as scripture says: 'Rivers of living water will flow from within him.'" 39 He said this in reference to the Spirit that those who came to believe in him were to receive. There was, of course, no Spirit yet, because Jesus had not yet been glorified.

Discussion about the Origins of the Messiah

40 Some in the crowd who heard these words said, "This is truly the Prophet." 41 Others said, "This is the Messiah." But others said, "The Messiah will not come from Galilee, will he? 42 Does not scripture say that the Messiah will be of David's family and come from Bethlehem, the village where David lived?" 43 So a division occurred in the crowd because of him. 44 Some of them even wanted to arrest him, but no one laid hands on him.45 So the guards went to the chief priests and Pharisees, who

asked them, "Why did you not bring him?" 46 The guards answered, "Never before has anyone spoken like this one." 47 So the Pharisees answered them, "Have you also been deceived? 48 Have any of the authorities or the Pharisees believed in him? 49 But this crowd, which does not know the law, is accursed." 50 Nicodemus, one of their members who had come to him earlier, said to them, 51 "Does our law condemn a person before it first hears him and finds out what he is doing?" 52 They answered and said to him, "You are not from Galilee also, are you? Look and see that no prophet arises from Galilee."

(1절)subsequently, afterwards, thence.그 뒤에. wander(roam) about, go around, move about(around).돌아다니다. travel.(여행, 통과, 이동, 기계 등이 왕복 운동을) 하다. go to and from(a place), go to (a place) and back, make a trip to and from(a place), walk about(around) (the street).다니다. ~wish to go around in Judea. (2절)just, Just then, exactly, favorably, fortunately, opportunely, in the (very) nick of time.마침. however, but, (and) yet.그런데. (4절)widely, broadly, extensively, far and wide.널리. publicly.공개적으로, 공식적으로. If you do, than to do, whatever you do.할 바에는. If you do it at all.이왕 할 바에야. Whatever you do.무엇이든 할 바에는. I would sooner die than do it.그것을 할 바엔 차라리 죽는 것이 낫다. (manifest, show) yourself.(드러, 나타)내 보이다, 드러내다. (6절)here.목적지에 도착했을 때, 시간을 나타낼 때 "오다"의 뜻을 의미. Here we are.자 (우리가) 왔다. Here I am.다녀왔습니다. My time is not yet here= My time has not yet come. Any time do not matter for you.너희에게는 아무 때라도 상관없다. ~but the time is always right for you. ~but any time is right for you.너희에게는 언제나 (알맞 은, 적절한) 때이지만; 너희들의 때는 언제나 좋게 마련이지만; 너희들은 아무 때나 축제에 가도 좋다는 뜻. I will tell you when the time is right.알맞은 때에 너한테 말해줄게. (8절) fulfill.(달성, 이행, 완료)하다, 시간이 차다, 채우다. (10절)(celebrate, keep, observe) a feast.축제를 지내다. (10절)But when.그러나 형제들이 축제에 갔을 때에. (11절)at the feast. 축제에서. during the feast.축제 동안에. (12절)No; on the contrary.아니오; 반대로. misleads.오도하고 있소, 그르치고 있소. deceives.속이고 있소. (13절)But=Still.아직은, 그러나. Still.아직도(계속해서), 그런데도, 그럼에도 불구하고, 훨씬, 고요한. but, however, still, yet.그러나 (14절)~went up into the temple area.올라가셔서 성전 뜰 안으로 들어가셨다.→ ~went up to the temple.성전에 올라가. courts, area.뜰. began to teach. 가르치기 시작하셨다. (15절)그러자 redundant번역임. without having studied.(제대로) 배우지도 않았는데. (16절)~is from= comes from.~에서(부터) 오다, 의 것이다. ~에서 (나오, [비롯되다, ;생산되다), 출신이다, 에서 생겨나다. (17절)chooses to do.(행, 실천)하다, 하려고

결단하다. Whoever chooses to do his will.누구든지 하느님의 뜻을 (행, 실천)하는 사람은. → If anyone only chooses to do his will.누구나 하느님의 뜻을 (행, 실천)하려고만 하면. on one's own.스스로, 혼자서, 단독으로(alone). (18)unrighteousness, wrong, injustice. 불의. (19절)but, however, yet, now, by the way.그런데. (20절)demon-possessed, possessed.마귀가 들리다. (21절)performed only one work.한 가지 일을 하였을 뿐인데. (22절)Moses gave you circumcision.모세가 너희에게 (할례를, 할례 법을, 할례의 계명을) 주었다.→ Moses commanded you to perform circumcision.모세가 너희에게 할례를 하라고 명령하였다. originate, arise, come from.비롯되다. (came, began) from.에서 나오다, 비롯되다, 출신이다. anyway, in any case, anyhow.아무튼. (24절)justly.바르게, (정당, 타당, 공정, 정확)하게. make a right judgment.올바로 판단하여라. (25절)So.그래서. (26절) The councillors of the Sanhedrin.최고의회 의원들. authorities.복수로 사용하여, 당국. realized.→ known. (32절)to this effect.(이런, 저런, 같은)취지로. like this, in this way.이렇게. so, therefore, accordingly, consequently, thus, for (that, this) reason, on that (account, score).그리하여. and.그래서, 그러면. (33절)thereupon, and, so, then, soon.그러자. only a little while longer.(단지, 다만) 조금 더, 얼마 더. for only a short time. 잠시 동안만. (35절)dispersion(dispə:rʒən).흩어짐, 흩뜨림, 살포, (분, 이, 확)산. 여기서 the dispersion= the diaspora(daiǽspərə) 임. Where is he going that we will not find him?→ Where does this man intend to go that we can not find him? Surely he is not going to the dispersion among the Greeks to teach the Greeks, is he?= Will he go to our people who live scattered among the Greeks, and teach the Greeks? (37절)the greatest= the most important. exclaimed→ said in a loud voice. (38절)flow from within him.(그분 안에서, 그분 안에서부터, 그분에게서, 그의 속에서) 흘러나올 것이다. (39절) in reference to.과 관련하여, 에 관하여. ~this in allusion to the Spirit.→ ~this in pointing out the Spirit.이는 ~성령을 가리키며. 물론 성령께서 아직(믿는 이들에게) 계시지 않았던 것이다. (40절)This is truly= This man is truly.이분은 참으로. (43절)controversy, dispute, argument. 논란. division.분열, 분란, 의견 등의 차이, 불일치. (45절)So.그래서. (47절) So.그러자. (48절)The councillors of the Sanhedrin.최고의회 의원들. authorities.복수로 사용하여, 당국. (49절)But.그러나. accursed.저주받은. (51절)condemn.(규탄, 비난, 단죄) 하다, (선고, 판정, 판결)을 내리다, 유죄판결을 내리다. (52절)You are not from Galilee also, are you?→ Are you from Galilee too? Look into the scripture, and you will see that no prophet comes out of Galilee or Study into the scripture, and you will see that no prophet comes out of Galilee. (53절)Then each went to his own house.그런 다음에 (그들은) 저마다 그들 자신의 집으로 돌아갔다.

Footnotes

(John 7-8절)These chapters contain events about the feast of Tabernacles (Sukkoth, Ingathering: Exodus 23:16; Tents, Booths: Deut 16:13-16), with its symbols of booths (originally built to shelter harvesters), rain (water from Siloam poured on the temple altar), and lights (illumination of the four torches in the Court of the Women). They continue the theme of the replacement of feasts (Passover, John 2:13; 6:4; Hanukkah, John 10:22; Pentecost, John 5:1), here accomplished by Jesus as the Living Water. These chapters comprise seven miscellaneous controversies and dialogues. There is a literary inclusion with Jesus in hiding in John 7:4, 10; 8:59. There are frequent references to attempts on his life: John 7:1, 13, 19, 25, 30, 32, 44; 8:37, 40, 59.(3절) Brothers: these relatives (cf John 2:12 and see the note on Mark 6:3) are never portrayed as disciples until after the resurrection (Acts 1:14). Matthew 13:55 and Mark 6:3 give the names of four of them. Jesus has already performed works/signs in Judea; cf John 2:23; 3:2; 4:45; 5:8. (6절)Time: the Greek word means "opportune time," here a synonym for Jesus' "hour" (see the note on John 2:4), his death and resurrection. In the wordplay, any time is suitable for Jesus' brothers, because they are not dependent on God's will. (8절)I am not going up: an early attested reading "not yet" seems a correction, since Jesus in the story does go up to the feast. "Go up," in a play on words, refers not only to going up to Jerusalem but also to exaltation at the cross, resurrection, and ascension; cf John 3:14; 6:62; 20:17.(14-31)Jesus teaches in the temple; debate with the Jews. (15절)Without having studied: literally, "How does he know letters without having learned?" Children were taught to read and write by means of the scriptures. But here more than Jesus' literacy is being discussed; the people are wondering how he can teach like a rabbi. Rabbis were trained by other rabbis and traditionally quoted their teachers.(17절) To do his will: presumably a reference back to the "work" of John 6:29: belief in the one whom God has sent. (20절)You are possessed: literally, "You have a demon." The insane were thought to be possessed by a demoniacal spirit. (21절)One work: the cure of the paralytic (John 5:1-9) because of the reference to the sabbath (John 7:22; 5:9-10). (26절)The authorities: the members of the Sanhedrin (same term as John 3:1). (32-36절)Jesus announces his approaching departure (cf also John 8:21; 12:36; 13:33) and complete control over his destiny. (35절) Dispersion: or "diaspora": Jews living outside Palestine. Greeks: probably refers to the Gentiles in the Mediterranean area; cf John 12:20. (37,39절)Promise of living water through the Spirit. (38절)Living water: not an exact quotation from any Old Testament passage; in the gospel context the gift of the Spirit is meant; cf John 3:5. From within him: either Jesus or the believer; if Jesus, it continues the Jesus-Moses motif (water from the rock, Exodus 17:6; Numbers 20:11) as well as Jesus as the new temple (cf Ezekiel 47:1). Grammatically, it goes better with the believer. (39절)No Spirit yet: Codex Vaticanus and early Latin, Syriac, and Coptic versions add "given." In this gospel, the sending of the Spirit cannot take place until Jesus' glorification through his death, resurrection, and ascension; cf John 20:22. (40-53절)Discussion of the Davidic lineage of the Messiah.(7:53-8:11). The story of the woman caught in adultery is a later insertion here, missing from all early Greek manuscripts. A Western text-type insertion, attested mainly in Old Latin translations, it is found in different places in different manuscripts: here, or after John 7:36 or at the end of this gospel, or after Luke 21:38, or at the end of that gospel. There are many non-Johannine features in the language, and there are also many doubtful readings within the passage. The style and motifs are similar to those of Luke, and it fits better with the general situation at the end of Luke 21:but it was probably inserted here because of the allusion to Jeremiah 17:13 (cf the note on John John 8:6) and the statement, "I do not judge anyone," in John 8:15. The Catholic Church accepts this passage as canonical scripture.

요한복음서 8장

1 예수님께서는 올리브 산으로 가셨다.

2 이른 아침에 예수님께서 다시 성전에 가시니 온 백성이 그분께 모여들었다. 그래서 그분께서는 앉으셔서 그들을 가르치셨다.

3 그때에 율법 학자들과 바리사이들이 간음하다 붙잡힌 여자를 끌고 와서 가운데에 세워 놓고,

4 예수님께 말하였다. "스승님, 이 여자가 간음하다 현장에서 붙잡혔습니다.

5 모세는 율법에서 이런 여자에게 돌을 던져 죽이라고 우리에게 명령하였습니다. 스승님 생각은 어떠하십니까?"

6 그들은 예수님을 시험하여 고소할 구실을 만들려고 그렇게 말한 것이다. 그러나 예수님께서는 몸을 굽히시어 손가락으로 땅에 무엇인가 쓰기 시작하셨다.

7 그들이 줄곧 물어 대자 예수님께서 몸을 일으키시어 그들에게 이르셨다. "너희 가운데 죄 없는 자가 먼저 저 여자에게 돌을 던져라."

8 그리고 다시 몸을 굽히시어 땅에 무엇인가 쓰셨다.

9 그들은 이 말씀을 듣고 나이 많은 자들부터 시작하여 하나씩 하나씩 떠나갔다. 마침내 예수님만 남으시고 여자는 가운데에 그대로 서 있었다.

10 예수님께서 몸을 일으키시고 그 여자에게, "여인아, 그자들이 어디 있느냐? 너를 단죄한 자가 아무도 없느냐?" 하고 물으셨다.

11 그 여자가 "선생님, 아무도 없습니다." 하고 대답하자, 예수님께서 이르셨다. "나도 너를 단죄하지 않는다. 가거라. 그리고 이제부터 다시는 죄짓지 마라."

나는 세상의 빛이다

12 예수님께서 다시 그들에게 말씀하셨다. "나는 세상의 빛이다. 나를 따르는 이는 어둠 속을 걷지 않고 생명의 빛을 얻을 것이다."

13 바리사이들이 "당신이 자신에 관하여 증언하고 있으니, 당신의 증언은 유효하지 않소." 하고 말하자,

14 예수님께서 그들에게 이르셨다. "내가 나 자신에 관하여 증언하여도 나의 증언은 유효하다. 내가 어디에서 왔고 어디로 가는지 알기 때문이다. 그러나 너희는 내가 어디에서 왔는지, 또 내가 어디로 가는지 알지 못한다.

15 너희는 사람의 기준으로 심판하지만 나는 아무도 심판하지 않는다.

16 그리고 내가 심판을 하여도 내 심판은 유효하다. 나 혼자가 아니라, 나와 나를 보내신 아버지께서 함께 심판하시기 때문이다.

17 너희의 율법에도 두 사람의 증언은 유효하다고 기록되어 있다.

18 바로 내가 나 자신에 관하여 증언하고 또 나를 보내신 아버지께서도 나에 관하여 증언하신다."

19 그들이 예수님께 "당신의 아버지가 어디 있소?" 하고 묻자, 예수님께서 대답하셨다. "너희는 나를

알지 못할 뿐만 아니라 나의 아버지도 알지 못한다. 너희가 나를 알았더라면 나의 아버지도 알았을 것이다."

20 이는 예수님께서 성전에서 가르치실 때에 헌금함 곁에서 하신 말씀이다. 그러나 아무도 그분을 잡지 않았다. 그분의 때가 아직 오지 않았기 때문이다.

예수님의 신원

21 예수님께서 다시 그들에게 이르셨다. "나는 간다. 너희가 나를 찾겠지만 너희는 자기 죄 속에서 죽을 것이다. 내가 가는 곳에 너희는 올 수 없다."

22 그러자 유다인들이 "'내가 가는 곳에 너희는 올 수 없다.' 하니, 자살하겠다는 말인가?" 하였다.

23 예수님께서 그들에게 말씀하셨다. "너희는 아래에서 왔고 나는 위에서 왔다. 너희는 이 세상에 속하지만 나는 이 세상에 속하지 않는다.

24 그래서 너희는 자기 죄 속에서 죽을 것이라고 내가 말하였다. 정녕 내가 나임을 믿지 않으면, 너희는 자기 죄 속에서 죽을 것이다."

25 그러자 그들이 예수님께 "당신이 누구요?" 하고 물었다. 예수님께서 그들에게 이르셨다. 처음부터 내가 너희에게 말해 오지 않았느냐?

26 나는 너희에 관하여 이야기할 것도, 심판할 것도 많다. 그러나 나를 보내신 분께서는 참되시기에, 나는 그분에게서 들은 것을 이 세상에 이야기할 따름이다."

27 그들은 예수님께서 아버지를 가리켜 말씀하신 줄을 깨닫지 못하였다.

28 그래서 예수님께서 다시 그들에게 이르셨다. "너희는 사람의 아들을 들어 올린 뒤에야 내가 나임을 깨달을 뿐만 아니라, 내가 스스로는 아무것도 하지 않고 아버지께서 가르쳐 주신 대로만 말한다는 것을 깨달을 것이다.

29 나를 보내신 분께서는 나와 함께 계시고 나를 혼자 버려두지 않으신다. 내가 언제나 그분 마음에 드는 일을 하기 때문이다."

30 예수님께서 이렇게 말씀하시자 많은 사람이 그분을 믿었다.

아브라함의 참된 자손

31 예수님께서 당신을 믿는 유다인들에게 말씀하셨다. "너희가 내 말 안에 머무르면 참으로 나의 제자가 된다.

32 그러면 너희가 진리를 깨닫게 될 것이다. 그리고 진리가 너희를 자유롭게 할 것이다."

33 그들이 예수님께 말하였다. "우리는 아브라함의 후손으로서 아무에게도 종노릇 한 적이 없습니다. 그런데 어찌 '너희가 자유롭게 될 것이다.' 하고 말씀하십니까?"

34 예수님께서 그들에게 대답하셨다. "내가 진실로 진실로 너희에게 말한다. 죄를 짓는 자는 누구나 죄의 종이다.

35 종은 언제까지나 집에 머무르지 못하지만, 아들은 언제까지나 집에 머무른다.

36 그러므로 아들이 너희를 자유롭게 하면 너희는 정녕 자유롭게 될 것이다.

37 나는 너희가 아브라함의 후손임을 알고 있다. 그런데 너희는 나를 죽이려고 한다. 내 말이 너희 안에 있을 자리가 없기 때문이다.

38 나는 내 아버지에게서 본 것을 이야기하고, 너희는 너희 아비에게서 들은 것을 실천한다."

39 그들이 "우리 조상은 아브라함이오." 하자, 예수님께서 그들에게 말씀하셨다. "너희가 아브라함의 자손이라면 아브라함이 한 일을 따라 해야 할 것이다.

40 그런데 너희는 지금, 하느님에게서 들은 진리를 너희에게 이야기해 준 사람인 나를 죽이려고 한다. 아브라함은 그런 짓을 하지 않았다.

41 그러니 너희는 너희 아비가 한 일을 따라 하는 것이다." 그래서 그들이 예수님께 말하였다. "우리는 사생아가 아니오. 우리 아버지는 오직 한 분, 하느님이시오."

42 예수님께서 그들에게 이르셨다. "하느님께서 너희 아버지시라면 너희가 나를 사랑할 것이다. 내가 하느님에게서 나와 여기에 와 있기 때문이다. 나는 나 스스로 온 것이 아니라 그분께서 나를 보내신 것이다.

43 어찌하여 너희는 내 이야기를 깨닫지 못하느냐? 너희가 내 말을 들을 줄 모르기 때문이다.

44 너희는 너희 아비인 악마에게서 났고, 너희 아비의 욕망대로 하기를 원한다. 그는 처음부터 살인자로서, 진리 편에 서 본 적이 없다. 그 안에 진리가 없기 때문이다. 그가 거짓을 말할 때에는 본성에서 그렇게 말하는 것이다. 그가 거짓말쟁이며 거짓의 아비기 때문이다.

45 내가 진리를 말하기 때문에 너희는 나를 믿지 않는다.

46 너희 가운데 누가 나에게 죄가 있다고 입증할 수 있느냐? 내가 진리를 말하고 있다면, 너희는 어찌하여 나를 믿지 않느냐?

47 하느님에게서 난 이는 하느님의 말씀을 듣는다. 그러므로 너희가 그 말씀을 듣지 않는 것은, 너희가 하느님에게서 나지 않았기 때문이다."

아브라함 전부터 계신 분

48 유다인들이 예수님께, "우리가 당신을 사마리아인이고 마귀 들린 자라고 하는 것이 당연하지 않소?" 하였다.

49 그러자 예수님께서 대답하셨다. "나는 마귀 들린 것이 아니라 내 아버지를 공경하는 것이다. 그런데도 너희는 나를 모욕한다.

50 나는 내 영광을 찾지 않는다. 그것을 찾아 주시고 또 심판해 주시는 분이 계시다.

51 내가 진실로 진실로 너희에게 말한다. 내 말을 지키는 이는 영원히 죽음을 보지 않을 것이다."

52 유다인들이 예수님께 말하였다. "이제 우리는 당신이 마귀 들렸다는 것을 알았소. 아브라함도 죽고 예언자들도 그러하였는데, 당신은 '내 말을 지키는 이는 영원히 죽음을 맛보지 않을 것이다.' 하고 말하고 있소.

53 우리 조상 아브라함도 죽었는데 당신이 그분보다 훌륭하다는 말이오? 예언자들도 죽었소. 그런데

당신은 누구로 자처하는 것이오?"

54 예수님께서 대답하셨다. "내가 나 자신을 영광스럽게 한다면 나의 영광은 아무것도 아니다. 나를 영광스럽게 하시는 분은 내 아버지시다. 너희가 '그분은 우리의 하느님이시다.' 하고 말하는 바로 그분이시다.

55 너희는 그분을 알지 못하지만 나는 그분을 안다. 내가 그분을 알지 못한다고 말하면 나도 너희와 같은 거짓말쟁이가 될 것이다. 그러나 나는 그분을 알고 또 그분의 말씀을 지킨다.

56 너희 조상 아브라함은 나의 날을 보리라고 즐거워하였다. 그리고 그것을 보고 기뻐하였다."

57 유다인들이 예수님께 말하였다. "당신은 아직 쉰 살도 되지 않았는데 아브라함을 보았다는 말이오?"

58 예수님께서 그들에게 이르셨다. "내가 진실로 진실로 너희에게 말한다. 나는 아브라함이 태어나기 전부터 있었다."

59 그러자 그들은 돌을 들어 예수님께 던지려고 하였다. 그러나 예수님께서는 몸을 숨겨 성전 밖으로 나가셨다.

A Woman Caught in Adultery

John Chapter 8

53 Then each went to his own house, 1 while Jesus went to the Mount of Olives. 2 But early in the morning he arrived again in the temple area, and all the people started coming to him, and he sat down and taught them. 3 Then the scribes and the Pharisees brought a woman who had been caught in adultery and made her stand in the middle. 4 They said to him, "Teacher, this woman was caught in the very act of committing adultery. 5 Now in the law, Moses commanded us to stone such women. So what do you say?" 6 They said this to test him, so that they could have some charge to bring against him. Jesus bent down and began to write on the ground with his finger. 7 But when they continued asking him, he straightened up and said to them, "Let the one among you who is without sin be the first to throw a stone at her." 8 Again he bent down and wrote on the ground. 9 And in response, they went away one by one, beginning with the elders. So he was left alone with the woman before him.10 Then Jesus straightened up and said to her, "Woman, where are they? Has no one condemned you?" 11 She replied, "No one, sir." Then Jesus said, "Neither do I condemn you. Go, (and) from now on do not sin any more."

The Light of the World

12 Jesus spoke to them again, saying, "I am the light of the world. Whoever follows me will not walk in darkness, but will have the light of life." 13 So the Pharisees said to him, "You testify on your own behalf, so your testimony cannot be verified." 14 Jesus answered and said to them, "Even if I do testify on my own behalf, my testimony can be verified, because I know where I came from and where I am going. But you do not know where I come from or where I am going. 15 You judge by appearances, but I do not judge anyone. 16 And even if I should judge, my judgment is valid, because I am not alone, but it is I and the Father who sent me. 17 Even in your law it is written that the testimony of two men can be verified. 18 I testify on my behalf and so does the Father who sent me." 19 So they said to him, "Where is your father?" Jesus answered, "You know neither me nor my Father. If you knew me, you would know my Father also." 20 He spoke these words while teaching in the treasury in the temple area. But no one arrested him, because his hour had not yet come.

Jesus, the Father's Ambassador

21 He said to them again, "I am going away and you will look for me, but you will die in your sin. Where I am going you cannot come." 22 So the Jews said, "He is not going to kill himself, is he, because he said, 'Where I am going you cannot come?'" 23 He said to them, "You belong to what is below, I belong to what is above. You belong to this world, but I do not belong to this world. 24 That is why I told you that you will die in your sins. For if you do not believe that I AM, you will die in your sins." 25 So they said to him, "Who are you?" Jesus said to them, "What I told you from the beginning. 26 I have much to say about you in condemnation. But the one who sent me is true, and what I heard from him I tell the world." 27 They did not realize that he was speaking to them of the Father. 28 So Jesus said (to them), "When you lift up the Son of Man, then you will realize that I AM, and that I do nothing on my own, but I say only what the Father taught me. 29 The one who sent me is with me. He has not left me alone, because I always do what is pleasing to him." 30 Because he spoke this way, many came to believe in him.

Jesus and Abraham

31 Jesus then said to those Jews who believed in him, "If you remain in my word, you will truly be my disciples, 32 and you will know the truth, and the truth will set you

free." 33 They answered him, "We are descendants of Abraham and have never been enslaved to anyone. How can you say, 'You will become free'?" 34 Jesus answered them, "Amen, amen, I say to you, everyone who commits sin is a slave of sin. 35 A slave does not remain in a household forever, but a son always remains. 36 So if a son frees you, then you will truly be free. 37 I know that you are descendants of Abraham. But you are trying to kill me, because my word has no room among you. 38 I tell you what I have seen in the Father's presence; then do what you have heard from the Father." 39 They answered and said to him, "Our father is Abraham." Jesus said to them, "If you were Abraham's children, you would be doing the works of Abraham. 40 But now you are trying to kill me, a man who has told you the truth that I heard from God; Abraham did not do this. 41 You are doing the works of your father!" (So) they said to him, "We are not illegitimate. We have one Father, God." 42 Jesus said to them, "If God were your Father, you would love me, for I came from God and am here; I did not come on my own, but he sent me. 43 Why do you not understand what I am saying? Because you cannot bear to hear my word.44 You belong to your father the devil and you willingly carry out your father's desires. He was a murderer from the beginning and does not stand in truth, because there is no truth in him. When he tells a lie, he speaks in character, because he is a liar and the father of lies. 45 But because I speak the truth, you do not believe me. 46 Can any of you charge me with sin? If I am telling the truth, why do you not believe me? 47 Whoever belongs to God hears the words of God; for this reason you do not listen, because you do not belong to God." 48 The Jews answered and said to him, "Are we not right in saying that you are a Samaritan and are possessed?" 49 Jesus answered, "I am not possessed; I honor my Father, but you dishonor me. 50 I do not seek my own glory; there is one who seeks it and he is the one who judges. 51 Amen, amen, I say to you, whoever keeps my word will never see death." 52 (So) the Jews said to him, "Now we are sure that you are possessed. Abraham died, as did the prophets, yet you say, 'Whoever keeps my word will never taste death.' 53 Are you greater than our father Abraham, who died? Or the prophets, who died? Who do you make yourself out to be?" 54 Jesus answered, "If I glorify myself, my glory is worth nothing; but it is my Father who glorifies me, of whom you say, 'He is our God.' 55 You do not know him, but I know him. And if I should say that I do not know him, I would be like you a liar. But I do know him and I keep his word. 56 Abraham your father rejoiced to see my day; he saw it and was glad. 57 So the Jews said to him,

"You are not yet fifty years old and you have seen Abraham?" 58 Jesus said to them, "Amen, amen, I say to you, before Abraham came to be, I AM." 59 So they picked up stones to throw at him; but Jesus hid and went out of the temple area.

(1절)한편 예수님께서는. 그러나 이른 아침. (2절)temple area= temple courts.성전 뜰. ~people gathered around him.그분께 모여들었다.→ ~people started coming to him. 사람들이 그분께 오기 시작하였다. (4절)in the (very) act (of).현행범으로, ~하는 현장에서, 범죄 행위 따위를 하는 도중에, 막 ~하려고 하여. (5절)Now.그런데. So what do you say? 그러므로 선생님(생각은 어떻습니까?, 은 어떻게 생각하십니까?, 어때요?) What do you think?스승님 생각은(어때요, 어떠하십니까?), 스승님은(무엇이라고 생각하십니까?, 어떻게 생각하십니까?) (6절)bring(level) a charge against= accuse somebody of a crime.죄를 묻다. (make, find, invent, trump up) (an excuse, a pretext (of)), (concoct, cook up) an excuse(for delay).구실을 (만들다, 만들어 대다). They said this to test him, so that they could make an excuse for accusing him. But Jesus~그들은 예수님을 시험하여 (그 결과 그분을) 고소할 구실을 만들려고 그렇게 말한 것이다. 그러나 예수님께서는~. accuse (sb of doing, sb of sth), charge (sb with sth).고소하다. (bring, press, prefer) charges against sb.~를 (고소, 기소)하다. (7절)But when they.그러나 그들이 (줄곧 물어대자). straighten. 자세를 똑바르게 하다, 바로하다. straighten up.자세를 똑바로 하다. (push, raise, pick) himself up; (erect, heave, lift, push) oneself.몸을 일으키다. (8절)Again.→ And again. (9절)response.대답, 응답, 회신, 답장, 반응. And in response.그래서 (이 말씀을 들은) (응답, 답, 반응)으로; (호응, 답)하여. one by one= one at a time.하나씩 하나씩. After hearing this, they went away one by one; They heard this word and went away one by one; When they heard this word, they went away one by one.그들은 이 말씀을 듣고 하나씩 하나씩 떠나갔다. And in response, they went away one by one.그러자 그들은 이에 대한 응답으로 하나씩 하나씩 떠나갔다. So he was left alone with the woman before him. 그래서 예수님은 그 여자와 함께 홀로 남으셨는데 그 여자는 예수님 앞에 있었다.→ At last Jesus was left alone with the woman standing in the middle as it is.마침내 예수님만 남으시고 여자는 가운데에 그대로 서 있었다. (10절)Then Jesus.그때에 예수님께서. ~said to her.→ asked her. (11절)anymore(ènimɔːr)= any more.(더, 그, 이) 이상. 부정문: 다시는, 이제는, 이미, (이, 그) 이상 많이, 이젠 달라, 이젠 안 그래. sin again= sin any more. (12절) Whoever follows.→ Those who follow. (13절)on one's own behalf.자신의 이익을 위하여, 자신에 관해. on one's behalf= on a person's behalf= on behalf of.을 대신하여, 대표하여, 을 위하여, 자신에 관해. ~can not be verified.→ ~is not valid. ~can be verified.(확인, 입증, 검증)해줄 수 있다, 진실이라고, 정확하다고 입증될 수 있다. valid, available, good, effective, remain in effect, remain, stand.유효하다. My offer is still (valid or stands).내 제안은 아직도 유효합니다. So.그러자, so.(뒤의)그러므로. (14절)Jesus answered and said to them.예수님께서 대답하시며 이르셨다. = ~대답하시며 (이렇게) 말씀하셨다. (15절)judge by appearances.(겉모양만, 겉모습, 외관)으로 (심판, 판단)하다. You judge by human standards.너희는 사람의 기준으로 심판한다. (16절)(because)~ but it(여기서 it는 심판하는 사람을 지칭하는 대명사임) is I and the Father who sent me.심판하는 사람은 나와 나를 보내신 아버지시기 때문이다.→ (because)~ but I and the Father who sent me judge together.나와 나를 보내신 아버지께서 함께 심판하시기 때문이다. (17절)~can be verified.→ ~is valid. (18절)on my behalf.내 대신. He did it on my behalf.내 대신 그가 했다. for myself.나 자신에 관하여. speaking for myself.나 자신에 관하여 말하자면. I testify for(about) myself.내가 나 자신에 관하여 증언하다. precisely, even now.바로. Precisely I testify on my behalf and so does~ (19절)So(그래서) they said to him.→They asked him. (20절)(collection, offertory) box.헌금함. He spoke these words while teaching (by, near, beside) the offertory box in the temple.이는 예수님께서 성전에서 가르치실 때에 헌금함 곁에서 하신 말씀이다.→ He spoke these words while teaching in the treasury in the temple area.이는 예수님께서 성전 뜰 안의 금고가 있는 곳에서 가르치실 때에 하신 말씀이다. treasury(trézəri). 국고, 공공 단체의 금고. (22절)So가 문두에 놓여 사실을 믿지 않을 때: 그러면, 그렇다면(then). He is not going to kill himself, is he?→ Will he kill himself? thereupon, and, soon, then, so, in turn, upon that.그러자. (23절)You belong to what is below, I belong to what is above.→ You are from below, I am from above. (24절)That is why.그것이~ 이유이다, 그런 까닭으로~ 한다(이다), 그것이 이유야, 왜냐하면~ 때문입니다, 그것이 바로 이유야, 그래서 하는거야. That is why I told you that you will die in your sins.→ So I told you that you will die in your sins. (25절)So they said to him.→ So they asked him. Jesus said to them, "What I told you from the beginning."→ Jesus said to them, "That who I Am I told you from the beginning."="I told you from the beginning that who I Am.". tell you용법: I told you! 그것 봐, 내가 말한 그대로지!; (구어): (단언, 장담)하다. It is there, I tell you.거기에 있다니까. What(that who I Am) I told you from the beginning.(내가 나임을; 내가 누구인지를; 나의 정체성을) 처음부터 내가 말한 그대로다. 처음부터 내가 누구인지를 내가 너희에게 말해주었다. (26절)condemnation(kàndemnéiʃən).유죄 선고(판결), 비난, 견책, 책망. I have much to say about you in condemnation (of you).나는 너희를 단죄하는데 있어 너희에게(너희에 대하여) 이야기 할 것이 많다. 여기서는 "에게"로 번역하는 것이 타당함.→ I have much to say about you and to judge you.나는 너희에게(너희에 관하여) 이야기할 것도 심판할 것도 많다. (30절)Because.때문에.→ When.(말씀)하시자. come to believe.믿게 되었다. come to.결국~

이 되다. (31절)Then.그런 다음에, 그 때에. You will truly be my disciples.➝ You become truly my disciples. (32절)know.➝ realize. (33절)They answered him.➝ They said to him. But how.그런데 어찌. (38절)in the Father's presence.하느님의 면전(앞)에서. (39절) They answered and said to him.그들이 예수님께 대답하며 말하였다. doing the works of Abraham.➝ doing the works Abraham did. (41절)an illegitimate child.사생아, 적출이 아닌. (43절)Because you can not bear to hear my word.➝ Because you do not know to hear my word. bear. 검사 · 시험 등에(~하기에) 적합하다, 할 수 있다(be capable of), 할 만하다, 할 필요가 있다. bear the test.검사에 합격하다. This cloth will bear washing.이 천은 빨 수 있다. ~can not bear to hear.들을 수가 없다. I can not bear to see it.나는 그것을 눈뜨고 볼 수가 없다. (44절)belong to.소유, ~의 것, 차지, 세상 소속, ~에 속하다. in character.성격, 인격. (선천, 천성)적으로. by nature, 본래, 본성에서. (46절) prove, verify, give proof, establish(a fact), substantiate, bear out.입증하다. Can any of you prove me guilty of sin?너희 가운데 누가 나에게 죄가 있다고 입증할 수 있느냐? 너희 가운데 누가 나에게 죄의 유죄를 입증할 수 있느냐? Can any of you charge me with sin? 너희 가운데 누가 나에게 죄가 있다고 고소할 수 있느냐? or 너희 가운데 누가 나에게 죄를 씌울 수 있느냐? (47절)He who was begotten by God hears the words of God; therefore, the reason why you do not listen to the words(of God) is because you were not begotten by God. for that(this) reason.이런(그런) 이유 때문에, 그런 만큼, (그, 이)러한 까닭에. 그(이) 때문에. (48절)The Jews answered and said to him.유다인들이 예수님께 대답하며 말하였다. (49절)Then Jesus.그러자 예수님께서. dishonor(disánə).불명예, 망신, 모욕(insult), 치욕, 망신시키는 것, 굴욕, 어음의 부도. (52절)~will never taste death.결코 죽음을 맛보지 않을 것이다. (53절)think of oneself (as), consider(fancy) oneself (as), make one out(to be).자처하다. make one out.~라고 주장하다. Who do you think of yourself?= Who do you think you are?= Who do you make yourself out to be? 당신은 누구라고 자처하오? (54절)mean nothing; nothing.아무것도 아니다. ~is worth nothing.무가치하다, 아무 가치도 없다. ~lose one's temper for nothing.아무것도 아닌 일에 화내다. My work is nothing to what you've done.내가 한 일은 당신이 한 일에 비하면 아무것도 아닙니다. Don't make a big deal out of nothing.아무것도 아닌 걸로 너무 과장하지 마라. a small(trifling) matter, nothing serious, a trifle.아무것도 아닌 일. (57절)So the Jews.그러자(그래서) 유다인들이. (58절)~before Abraham came to be, I AM.나는 아브라함이 (있기, 생겨나기) 전부터 있었다. ~before Abraham was born, I AM.나는 아브라함이 태어나기 전부터 있었다. came to be.생겨나다(요한복음 1:3). ~was born. 태어나다.

Footnotes

(1절)Mount of Olives: not mentioned elsewhere in the gospel tradition outside of passion week. 수난 주간이 아닌 경우 복음서 전승에서는 아무데서도 언급되지 않았다. (5절)Lev 20:10 and Deut 22:22 mention only death, but Deut 22:23-24 prescribes stoning for a betrothed virgin.(6절)Cf Jeremiah 17:13 (RSV): "Those who turn away from thee shall be written in the earth, for they have forsaken thee, the fountain of living water"; cf John 7:38.생명수의 샘인 하느님을 저버린 자, 주님을 저버린 자는 땅에 이름이 적혀질 것이다. (7절)The first stones were to be thrown by the witnesses (Deut 17:7). (12-20절)Jesus the light of the world. Jesus replaces the four torches of the illumination of the temple as the light of joy.예수님은 세상의 빛이시다. 예수님은 기쁨을 주는 빛으로서 성전을 조명하는 네개의 횃불을 대신하신다. (14절)My testimony can be verified: this seems to contradict John 5:31 but the emphasis here is on Jesus' origin from the Father and his divine destiny. 여기에서 강조하는 것은 예수님의 기원이 하느님에게서 온다는 것과 예수님의 신성을 지니신 운명을 타고 나셨다는 것이다. Where I am going: indicates Jesus' passion and glorification. (15절) By appearances: literally, "according to the flesh." I do not judge anyone: superficial contradiction of John 5:22, 27, 30; here the emphasis is that the judgment is not by material standards.겉모양만(겉모습)으로라는 뜻은 문자(말)그대로 육적인 기준(사람의 기준)에 따라 예수님께서는 누구도 심판하지 않으십니다. John 5:22, 27, 30과 피상(표면)적인 모순이나 여기서는 심판이 물질적인 기준에 의해 이뤄지지 않는다는 것을 강조함. (15절)literally.문자(말) 그대로.   superficial.깊이 없는, 얄팍한, 피상(표면)적인. (17절)Your law: a reflection of later controversy between church and synagogue.훗날에 있을 교회와 회당의 논쟁을 반영. (21-30절)He whose ambassador I am is with me. Jesus' origin is from God; he can reveal God.예수님은 하느님의 사절이시기에 하느님은 예수님과 함께 계십니다. 예수님의 기원은 하느님으로 부터 오셨으므로 예수님은 하느님을 보여주실 수가 있으십니다. (21-30절)ambassador.사절, 대사. (21절)You will die in your sin: i.e., of disbelief; cf John 8:24. Where I am going you cannot come: except through faith in Jesus' passion- resurrection. (22절)The Jews suspect that he is referring to his death. Johannine irony is apparent here; Jesus' death will not be self-inflicted but destined by God.여기에서 요한적인 아이러니가 분명한데 예수님의 죽음은 자초되지 않고 하느님에 의해 운명되어진 것이다. (22절)self-inflicted.자초한. (24,28절)I AM: an expression that late Jewish tradition understood as Yahweh's own self-designation (Isaiah 43:10); see the note on John 4:26. Jesus is here placed on a par with Yahweh. (25절)What I told you from the beginning: this verse seems textually corrupt, with several other possible translations: "(I am) what I say to you"; "Why do I speak to you at all?" The earliest attested reading (Bodmer Papyrus P66) has (in a second hand), "I told you at the beginning what I am also telling you (now)." The answer here (cf Proverb 8:22) seems to hinge on a misunderstanding of John 8:24 "that I AM" as "what I am." (31-59절)Jesus' origin ("before Abraham") and destiny are developed; the truth will free them from sin (John 8:34) and death (John 8:51). (31절)Those

Jews who believed in him: a rough editorial suture, since in John 8:37 they are described as trying to kill Jesus. (33절)Have never been enslaved to anyone: since, historically, the Jews were enslaved almost continuously, this verse is probably Johannine irony, about slavery to sin. (35절)A slave···a son: an allusion to Ishmael and Isaac (Genesis 16; 21), or to the release of a slave after six years (Exodus 21:2; Deut 15:12).(38절)The Father: i.e., God. It is also possible, however, to understand the second part of the verse as a sarcastic reference to descent of the Jews from the devil (John 8:44), "You do what you have heard from(your)father."아버지는 곧 하느님이시다. 그러나 이 절의 두번째 부분은 악마의 자식인 유다인의 자손들에 대한 야유적인 언급으로 또한 이해할 수 있다. (39절)The works of Abraham: Abraham believed; cf Romans 4:11-17; James 2:21-23. (48절)Samaritan: therefore interested in magical powers; cf Acts 7:14-24. (53절)Are you greater than our father Abraham?: cf John 4:12. (56절)He saw it: this seems a reference to the birth of Isaac (Genesis 17:7; 21:6), the beginning of the fulfillment of promises about Abraham's seed. (57절)The evidence of the third-century Bodmer Papyrus P75 and the first hand of Codex Sinaiticus indicates that the text originally read: "How can Abraham have seen you?" (58절)Came to be, I AM: the Greek word used for "came to be" is the one used of all creation in the prologue, while the word used for "am" is the one reserved for the Logos.생겨나기 전, 나는 나이다(나는 야훼 하느님이시다): "생 겨나기 전"이라는 말로 사용된 그리스말은 서두(요한복음 1:3)에서 "모든 창조물이 생겨났다"에서 사용된 것이다, 한편 "이다"라는 말로 사용된 말은 예수님의 신성을 (나타내기)위해 사용되는 전용적인 언어이다.

요한복음서 9장

태어나면서부터 눈먼 사람을 고쳐 주시다

1 예수님께서 길을 가시다가 태어나면서부터 눈먼 사람을 보셨다.

2 제자들이 예수님께 물었다. "스승님, 누가 죄를 지었기에 저이가 눈먼 사람으로 태어났습니까? 저 사람입니까, 그의 부모입니까?"

3 예수님께서 대답하셨다. "저 사람이 죄를 지은 것도 아니고 그 부모가 죄를 지은 것도 아니다. 하느님의 일이 저 사람에게서 드러나려고 그리된 것이다.

4 나를 보내신 분의 일을 우리는 낮 동안에 해야 한다. 이제 밤이 올 터인데 그때에는 아무도 일하지 못한다.

5 내가 이 세상에 있는 동안 나는 세상의 빛이다."

6 예수님께서는 이렇게 말씀하시고 나서, 땅에 침을 뱉고 그것으로 진흙을 개어 그 사람의 눈에 바르신 다음,

7 "실로암 못으로 가서 씻어라." 하고 그에게 이르셨다. '실로암'은 '파견된 이'라고 번역되는 말이다. 그가 가서 씻고 앞을 보게 되어 돌아왔다.

8 이웃 사람들이, 그리고 그가 전에 거지였던 것을 보아 온 이들이 말하였다. "저 사람은 앉아서 구걸하던 이가 아닌가?"

9 어떤 이들은 "그 사람이오." 하고, 또 어떤 이들은 "아니오. 그와 닮은 사람이오." 하였다. 그 사람은 "내가 바로 그 사람입니다." 하고 말하였다.

10 그들이 "그러면 어떻게 눈을 뜨게 되었소?" 하고 묻자,

11 그 사람이 대답하였다. "예수님이라는 분이 진흙을 개어 내 눈에 바르신 다음, '실로암 못으로 가서 씻어라.' 하고 나에게 이르셨습니다. 그래서 내가 가서 씻었더니 보게 되었습니다."

12 그들이 "그 사람이 어디 있소?" 하고 물으니, 그가 "모르겠습니다." 하고 대답하였다.

바리사이들이 개입하다

13 그들은 전에 눈이 멀었던 그 사람을 바리사이들에게 데리고 갔다.

14 그런데 예수님께서 진흙을 개어 그 사람의 눈을 뜨게 해 주신 날은 안식일이었다.

15 그래서 바리사이들도 그에게 어떻게 보게 되었는지 다시 물었다. 그는 "그분이 제 눈에 진흙을 붙여 주신 다음, 제가 씻었더니 보게 되었습니다." 하고 대답하였다.

16 바리사이들 가운데에서 몇몇은 "그는 안식일을 지키지 않으므로 하느님에게서 온 사람이 아니오." 하고, 어떤 이들은 "죄인이 어떻게 그런 표징을 일으킬 수 있겠소?" 하여, 그들 사이에 논란이 일어났다.

17 그리하여 그들이 눈이 멀었던 이에게 다시 물었다. "그가 당신 눈을 뜨게 해 주었는데, 당신은 그를 어떻게 생각하오?" 그러자 그가 대답하였다. "그분은 예언자이십니다."

18 유다인들은 그가 눈이 멀었었는데 이제는 보게 되었다는 사실을 믿으려고 하지 않았다. 그리하여 앞을 볼 수 있게 된 그 사람의 부모를 불러,

19 그들에게 물었다. "이 사람이 태어날 때부터 눈이 멀었다는 당신네 아들이오? 그런데 지금은 어떻게 보게 되었소?"

20 그의 부모가 대답하였다. "이 아이가 우리 아들이라는 것과 태어날 때부터 눈이 멀었다는 것은 우리가 압니다.

21 그러나 지금 어떻게 해서 보게 되었는지는 모릅니다. 누가 그의 눈을 뜨게 해 주었는지도 우리는 모릅니다. 그에게 물어보십시오. 나이를 먹었으니 제 일은 스스로 이야기할 것입니다."

22 그의 부모는 유다인들이 두려워 이렇게 말하였다. 누구든지 예수님을 메시아라고 고백하면 회당에서 내쫓기로 유다인들이 이미 합의하였기 때문이다.

23 그래서 그의 부모가 "나이를 먹었으니 그에게 물어보십시오." 하고 말한 것이다.

24 그리하여 바리사이들은 눈이 멀었던 그 사람을 다시 불러, "하느님께 영광을 드리시오. 우리는 그자가 죄인임을 알고 있소." 하고 말하였다.

25 그 사람이 대답하였다. "그분이 죄인인지 아닌지 저는 모릅니다. 그러나 이 한 가지, 제가 눈이 멀었는데 이제는 보게 되었다는 것은 압니다."

26 "그가 당신에게 무엇을 하였소? 그가 어떻게 해서 당신의 눈을 뜨게 하였소?" 하고 그들이 물으니,

27 그가 대답하였다. "제가 이미 여러분에게 말씀드렸는데 여러분은 들으려고 하지 않으셨습니다. 어째서 다시 들으려고 하십니까? 여러분도 그분의 제자가 되고 싶다는 말씀입니까?"

28 그러자 그들은 그에게 욕설을 퍼부으며 말하였다. "당신은 그자의 제자지만 우리는 모세의 제자요.

29 우리는 하느님께서 모세에게 말씀하셨다는 것을 아오. 그러나 그자가 어디에서 왔는지는 우리가 알지 못하오."

30 그 사람이 그들에게 대답하였다. "그분이 제 눈을 뜨게 해 주셨는데 여러분은 그분이 어디에서 오셨는지 모르신다니, 그것 정말 놀라운 일입니다.

31 하느님께서는 죄인들의 말을 들어 주지 않으신다는 것을 우리는 압니다. 그러나 누가 하느님을 경외하고 그분의 뜻을 실천하면, 그 사람의 말은 들어 주십니다.

32 태어날 때부터 눈이 먼 사람의 눈을 누가 뜨게 해 주었다는 말을 일찍이 들어 본 적이 없습니다.

33 그분이 하느님에게서 오지 않으셨으면 아무것도 하실 수 없었을 것입니다."

34 그러자 그들은 "당신은 완전히 죄 중에 태어났으면서 우리를 가르치려고 드는 것이오?" 하며, 그를 밖으로 내쫓아 버렸다.

참으로 눈이 먼 사람

35 그가 밖으로 내쫓겼다는 말을 들으신 예수님께서는 그를 만나시자, "너는 사람의 아들을 믿느냐?" 하고 물으셨다.

36 그 사람이 "선생님, 그분이 누구이십니까? 제가 그분을 믿을 수 있도록 말씀해 주십시오." 하고

대답하자,

37 예수님께서 그에게 이르셨다. "너는 이미 그를 보았다. 너와 말하는 사람이 바로 그다."

38 그는 "주님, 저는 믿습니다." 하며 예수님께 경배하였다.

39 그때에 예수님께서 이르셨다. "나는 이 세상을 심판하러 왔다. 보지 못하는 이들은 보고, 보는 이들은 눈먼 자가 되게 하려는 것이다."

40 예수님과 함께 있던 몇몇 바리사이가 이 말씀을 듣고 예수님께, "우리도 눈먼 자라는 말은 아니겠지요?" 하고 말하였다.

41 예수님께서 그들에게 이르셨다. "너희가 눈먼 사람이었으면 오히려 죄가 없었을 것이다. 그러나 지금 너희가 '우리는 잘 본다.' 하고 있으니, 너희 죄는 그대로 남아 있다."

The Man Born Blind

John Chapter 9

1 As he passed by he saw a man blind from birth. 2 His disciples asked him, "Rabbi, who sinned, this man or his parents, that he was born blind?" 3 Jesus answered, "Neither he nor his parents sinned; it is so that the works of God might be made visible through him. 4 We have to do the works of the one who sent me while it is day. Night is coming when no one can work.5 While I am in the world, I am the light of the world." 6 When he had said this, he spat on the ground and made clay with the saliva, and smeared the clay on his eyes,7 and said to him, "Go wash in the Pool of Siloam" (which means Sent). So he went and washed, and came back able to see. 8 His neighbors and those who had seen him earlier as a beggar said, "Isn't this the one who used to sit and beg?" 9 Some said, "It is," but others said, "No, he just looks like him." He said, "I am." 10 So they said to him, "(So) how were your eyes opened?" 11 He replied, "The man called Jesus made clay and anointed my eyes and told me, 'Go to Siloam and wash.' So I went there and washed and was able to see." 12 And they said to him, "Where is he?" He said, "I don't know." 13 They brought the one who was once blind to the Pharisees. 14 Now Jesus had made clay and opened his eyes on a sabbath. 15 So then the Pharisees also asked him how he was able to see. He said to them, "He put clay on my eyes, and I washed, and now I can see." 16 So some of the Pharisees said, "This man is not from God, because he does not keep the sabbath." (But) others said, "How can a sinful man do such signs?" And there was a division among them. 17 So they said to the blind man again, "What do

you have to say about him, since he opened your eyes?" He said, "He is a prophet." 18 Now the Jews did not believe that he had been blind and gained his sight until they summoned the parents of the one who had gained his sight. 19 They asked them, "Is this your son, who you say was born blind? How does he now see?" 20 His parents answered and said, "We know that this is our son and that he was born blind. 21 We do not know how he sees now, nor do we know who opened his eyes. Ask him, he is of age; he can speak for himself." 22 His parents said this because they were afraid of the Jews, for the Jews had already agreed that if anyone acknowledged him as the Messiah, he would be expelled from the synagogue. 23 For this reason his parents said, "He is of age; question him." 24 So a second time they called the man who had been blind and said to him, "Give God the praise! We know that this man is a sinner." 25 He replied, "If he is a sinner, I do not know. One thing I do know is that I was blind and now I see." 26 So they said to him, "What did he do to you? How did he open your eyes?" 27 He answered them, "I told you already and you did not listen. Why do you want to hear it again? Do you want to become his disciples, too?" 28 They ridiculed him and said, "You are that man's disciple; we are disciples of Moses! 29 We know that God spoke to Moses, but we do not know where this one is from." 30 The man answered and said to them, "This is what is so amazing, that you do not know where he is from, yet he opened my eyes. 31 We know that God does not listen to sinners, but if one is devout and does his will, he listens to him. 32 It is unheard of that anyone ever opened the eyes of a person born blind. 33 If this man were not from God, he would not be able to do anything." 34 They answered and said to him, "You were born totally in sin, and are you trying to teach us?" Then they threw him out.35 When Jesus heard that they had thrown him out, he found him and said, "Do you believe in the Son of Man?" 36 He answered and said, "Who is he, sir, that I may believe in him?" 37 Jesus said to him, "You have seen him and the one speaking with you is he." 38 He said, "I do believe, Lord," and he worshiped him. 39 Then Jesus said, "I came into this world for judgment, so that those who do not see might see, and those who do see might become blind." 40 Some of the Pharisees who were with him heard this and said to him, "Surely we are not also blind, are we?" 41 Jesus said to them, "If you were blind, you would have no sin; but now you are saying, 'We see,' so your sin remains.

(1절)as.하고 있을 때, 하자마자, 하다가, 하면서, 하는 동안, 하는 사이, 하면. as는 when보다 동시성의 뜻이 강하며, while과 거의 같은 뜻으로 씀. 길을 가시다가= 길을 가시고 있었을 때에.

(3절)~be made visible.알아볼 수 있게 하다, 보이게 하다. ~be displayed= be revealed. 드러내다, 드러내 보이다. ~be displayed in(from)him.그에게서 드러나려고. (4절)Night is coming when no one can work= Night when no one can work is coming.아무도 일할 수 없는 밤이 오고 있다. (6절)make clay(mud).(찰흙, 점토)를 만들다. clay. 점토, 찰흙. mud. 진흙. (temper, pug) (mud, clay).(진흙, 찰흙)을 개다. saliva(səláivə).침, 타액. smear.(바, 문지)르다, 비방하다. (7절)그래서 그가 가서. (9절)"I am.".→ "I am very the man." (10절) So they said to him.그래서 그들이 그(눈뜬 사람)에게 말하였다. They asked him.그들이 그 (눈뜬 사람)에게 묻자. How then were~. (12절)And they said to him.그러자 그들이 그에게 말하였다.→ They asked him그들이 그에게 물었다. (14절)Now the day on which Jesus had tempered the mud and opened his eyes was a sabbath. (15절)so then.그래서, 그러면, 그러므로, 그렇다면, 그럼, 그렇게 지금, 그러니까, 그렇다 치고. (16절)So.그래서 And. 그러자. a sinful man= sinner. (17절)What do you have to say about him?당신은 그에 대해 무엇이라 하겠소? 당신은 그에 대해 어떤 말을 하겠는가? 의역: 당신은 그를 어떻게 생각하오. 그러자 그가 대답하였다. 여기서 "그러자"는 redundant한 번역임. (18절)Now. 그런데. received= gained sight.시력을(얻다, 찾다). 부정어와 함께 쓰여: ~까지는 ~하지 않다, ~이 되어서야 (겨우, 간신히, 비로소) ~부모를 부를 때까지 믿지 않았다. ~부모를 부르고 나서야 비로소 믿게 되었다. (19절)How does he now see?그가 지금 어떻게 보는가? But how is it that now he can see?그런데 (그가) 지금은 어떻게 보게 되었소? (21절)~he is af age.성년에 달했으니, 나이를 먹었으니, 장성했으니. for himself.스스로, 혼자 힘으로. ~how he sees now.→ ~how he can see now. (23절)for this reason.(이, 그)렇기 때문에, (이, 그)러한 (이유로 해서, 이유 때문에). (24절)and, thus, then, so, now, now and then. 그리하여. Then again.그리하여 다시. So a second time.그리하여 (재차, 두번째로). Give glory to God= Give God the glory.하느님께 영광을 드리시오. Give God the praise. 하느님께 찬미를 드리시오. (25절)보게 되었다는.→ 본다는. If he is a sinner= Whether he is a sinner or not. (28절)rain abuses, launch into abuses against, hurled insults at him.욕설을 퍼부으며. ridiculed.조롱하며, 비웃으며. (30절)This is what.이것이 (바로) ~ 이다. yet.그런데도, 부정문과 함께 강조적으로 ~는데도 않다, (뿐만 아니라) ~까지도(않다). (31 절)godly.신앙심 깊은, 독실한. devout(diváut).독실한, 경건한. in awe(ɔ:)of, fear.경외하다. ~but if one fear God. (32절) early, ever.일찍이. earlier, once, at one time, formerly. 이전에. It is unheard of.선례가 없는, 들어보지 못한. (Anybody has never heard, Nobody has ever heard) of that anyone opened the eyes of a person born blind. (34절)They answered and said to him.→ So(그러자) they said to him. Then.그런 다음에. throw one out.쫓아내다. 내쫓다, (내)던져버리다. (35절)When.하자, 하고, 한 후에 (문 두에서). found= meet. (36절)He answered and said, "Who is he, sir, that I may believe in him?"→ He answered, "Who is he, sir? Tell me so that I may believe in him. 그 사람이 "선생님 그분이 누구이십니까? 제가 그분을 믿을 수 있도록 말씀해 주십시오." 하고 대답하였다. (37절)~have already seen. (41절)but now that.이므로, 이기 때문에, 하고 있으므로. ~but now you are saying, "We see", so your sin remains.→ but now that you are saying, "We see well", your sin remains.

Footnotes

(9:1-10:21절)Sabbath healing of the man born blind. This sixth sign is introduced to illustrate the saying, "I am the light of the world" (John 8:12; 9:5). The narrative of conflict about Jesus contrasts Jesus (light) with the Jews (blindness, John 9:39-41). The theme of water is reintroduced in the reference to the pool of Siloam. Ironically, Jesus is being judged by the Jews, yet the Jews are judged by the Light of the world; cf John 3:19-21. (2절)See the note on John 5:14, and Exodus 20:5, that parents' sins were visited upon their children. Jesus denies such a cause and emphasizes the purpose: the infirmity was providential. (7절)Go wash: perhaps a test of faith; cf 2 Kings 5:10-14. The water tunnel Siloam (= Sent) is used as a symbol of Jesus, sent by his Father. (14절)In using spittle, kneading clay, and healing, Jesus had broken the sabbath rules laid down by Jewish tradition. (22절)This comment of the evangelist (in terms used again in John 12:42; John 16:2) envisages a situation after Jesus' ministry. Rejection/excommunication from the synagogue of Jews who confessed Jesus as Messiah seems to have begun ca. A.D. 85, when the curse against the minim or heretics was introduced into the "Eighteen Benedictions." (24절)Give God the praise!: an Old Testament formula of adjuration to tell the truth; cf Joshua 7:19; 1 Sam 6:5 LXX. Cf John 5:41. (32절)A person born blind: the only Old Testament cure from blindness is found in Tobit (cf Tobit 7:7; 11:7-13; 14:1-2), but Tobit was not born blind. (39-41절)These verses spell out the symbolic meaning of the cure; the Pharisees are not the innocent blind, willing to accept the testimony of others.

요한복음서 10장

목자의 비유

1 "내가 진실로 진실로 너희에게 말한다. 양 우리에 들어갈 때에 문으로 들어가지 않고 다른 데로 넘어 들어가는 자는 도둑이며 강도다.

2 그러나 문으로 들어가는 이는 양들의 목자다.

3 문지기는 목자에게 문을 열어 주고, 양들은 그의 목소리를 알아듣는다. 그리고 목자는 자기 양들의 이름을 하나하나 불러 밖으로 데리고 나간다.

4 이렇게 자기 양들을 모두 밖으로 이끌어 낸 다음, 그는 앞장서 가고 양들은 그를 따른다. 양들이 그의 목소리를 알기 때문이다.

5 그러나 낯선 사람은 따르지 않고 오히려 피해 달아난다. 낯선 사람들의 목소리를 알지 못하기 때문이다.

6 예수님께서 그들에게 이 비유를 말씀하셨다. 그러나 그들은 예수님께서 자기들에게 이야기하시는 것이 무슨 뜻인지 깨닫지 못하였다.

나는 착한 목자다

7 예수님께서 다시 이르셨다. "내가 진실로 진실로 너희에게 말한다. 나는 양들의 문이다.

8 나보다 먼저 온 자들은 모두 도둑이며 강도이다. 그래서 양들은 그들의 말을 듣지 않았다.

9 나는 문이다. 누구든지 나를 통하여 들어오면 구원을 받고, 또 드나들며 풀밭을 찾아 얻을 것이다.

10 도둑은 다만 훔치고 죽이고 멸망시키려고 올 뿐이다. 그러나 나는 양들이 생명을 얻고 또 얻어 넘치게 하려고 왔다.

11 나는 착한 목자다. 착한 목자는 양들을 위하여 자기 목숨을 내놓는다.

12 삯꾼은 목자가 아니고 양도 자기 것이 아니기 때문에, 이리가 오는 것을 보면 양들을 버리고 달아난다. 그러면 이리는 양들을 물어가고 양 떼를 흩어 버린다.

13 그는 삯꾼이어서 양들에게 관심이 없기 때문이다.

14 나는 착한 목자다. 나는 내 양들을 알고 내 양들은 나를 안다.

15 이는 아버지께서 나를 아시고 내가 아버지를 아는 것과 같다. 나는 양들을 위하여 목숨을 내놓는다.

16 그러나 나에게는 이 우리 안에 들지 않는 양들도 있다. 나는 그들도 데려와야 한다. 그들도 내 목소리를 알아듣고 마침내 한 목자 아래 한 양 떼가 될 것이다.

17 아버지께서는 내가 목숨을 내놓기 때문에 나를 사랑하신다. 그렇게 하여 나는 목숨을 다시 얻는다.

18 아무도 나에게서 목숨을 빼앗지 못한다. 내가 스스로 그것을 내놓는 것이다. 나는 목숨을 내놓을 권한도 있고 그것을 다시 얻을 권한도 있다. 이것이 내가 내 아버지에게서 받은 명령이다."

19 이 말씀 때문에 유다인들 사이에 다시 논란이 일어났다.

20 그들 가운데 많은 사람이, "그는 마귀가 들려 미쳤소. 무엇 때문에 그 사람의 말을 듣고들 있소?"

하였다.

21 그러나 또 다른 이들은, "그가 한 말은 마귀 들린 자의 말이 아니오. 마귀는 눈먼 이들의 눈을 뜨게 할 수가 없지 않소?" 하고 말하였다.

유다인들이 예수님을 배척하다

22 그 때에 예루살렘에서는 성전 봉헌 축제가 벌어지고 있었다. 때는 겨울이었다.

23 예수님께서는 성전 안에 있는 솔로몬 주랑을 거닐고 계셨는데,

24 유다인들이 그분을 둘러싸고 말하였다. "당신은 언제까지 우리 속을 태울 작정이오? 당신이 메시아라면 분명히 말해 주시오."

25 그러자 예수님께서 그들에게 대답하셨다. "내가 이미 말하였는데도 너희는 믿지 않는다. 내가 내 아버지의 이름으로 하는 일들이 나를 증언한다.

26 그러나 너희는 믿지 않는다. 너희가 내 양이 아니기 때문이다.

27 내 양들은 내 목소리를 알아 듣는다. 나는 그들을 알고 그들은 나를 따른다.

28 나는 그들에게 영원한 생명을 준다. 그리하여 그들은 영원토록 멸망하지 않을 것이고, 또 아무도 그들을 내 손에서 빼앗아 가지 못할 것이다.

29 그들을 나에게 주신 내 아버지께서는 누구보다도 위대하시어, 아무도 그들을 내 아버지의 손에서 빼앗아 갈 수 없다.

30 아버지와 나는 하나다."

31 그러자 유다인들이 돌을 집어 예수님께 던지려고 하였다.

32 예수님께서 그들에게 말씀하셨다. "나는 아버지의 분부에 따라 너희에게 좋은 일을 많이 보여 주었다. 그 가운데에서 어떤 일로 나에게 돌을 던지려고 하느냐?"

33 유다인들이 예수님께, "좋은 일을 하였기 때문이 아니라 하느님을 모독하였기 때문에 당신에게 돌을 던지려는 것이오. 당신은 사람이면서 하느님으로 자처하고 있소." 하고 대답하자,

34 예수님께서 그들에게 말씀하셨다. "너희 율법에 '내가 이르건대 너희는 신이다.' 라고 기록되어 있지 않느냐?

35 폐기될 수 없는 성경에서, 하느님의 말씀을 받은 이들을 신이라고 하였는데,

36 아버지께서 거룩하게 하시어 이 세상에 보내신 내가 '나는 하느님의 아들이다.' 하였다 해서, '당신은 하느님을 모독하고 있소.' 하고 말할 수 있느냐?

37 내가 내 아버지의 일들을 하고 있지 않다면 나를 믿지 않아도 좋다.

38 그러나 내가 그 일들을 하고 있다면, 나를 믿지 않더라도 그 일들은 믿어라. 그러면 아버지께서 내 안에 계시고 내가 아버지 안에 있다는 것을 너희가 깨달아 알게 될 것이다."

39 그러자 유다인들이 다시 예수님을 잡으려고 하였지만, 예수님께서는 그들의 손을 벗어나셨다.

요르단 강 건너편으로 가시다

40 예수님께서는 다시 요르단 강 건너편, 요한이 전에 세례를 주던 곳으로 물러가시어 그 곳에 머무르셨다.

41 그러자 많은 사람이 그분께 몰려와 서로 말하였다. "요한은 표징을 하나도 일으키지 않았지만, 그가 저분에 관하여 한 말은 모두 사실이었다."

42 그 곳에서 많은 사람이 예수님을 믿었다.

The Good Shepherd

John Chapter 10

1 "Amen, amen, I say to you, whoever does not enter a sheepfold through the gate but climbs over elsewhere is a thief and a robber. 2 But whoever enters through the gate is the shepherd of the sheep. 3 The gatekeeper opens it for him, and the sheep hear his voice, as he calls his own sheep by name and leads them out. 4 When he has driven out all his own, he walks ahead of them, and the sheep follow him, because they recognize his voice. 5 But they will not follow a stranger; they will run away from him, because they do not recognize the voice of strangers." 6Although Jesus used this figure of speech, they did not realize what he was trying to tell them. 7 So Jesus said again, "Amen, amen, I say to you, I am the gate for the sheep. 8 All who came [before me] are thieves and robbers, but the sheep did not listen to them. 9 I am the gate. Whoever enters through me will be saved, and will come in and go out and find pasture. 10 A thief comes only to steal and slaughter and destroy; I came so that they might have life and have it more abundantly. 11 I am the good shepherd. A good shepherd lays down his life for the sheep. 12 A hired man, who is not a shepherd and whose sheep are not his own, sees a wolf coming and leaves the sheep and runs away, and the wolf catches and scatters them. 13 This is because he works for pay and has no concern for the sheep.14 I am the good shepherd, and I know mine and mine know me, 15 just as the Father knows me and I know the Father; and I will lay down my life for the sheep. 16 I have other sheep that do not belong to this fold. These also I must lead, and they will hear my voice, and there will be one flock, one shepherd. 17 This is why the Father loves me, because I lay down my life in order to take it up again. 18 No one takes it from me, but I lay it down on my own. I have power to lay it down, and power to take it up again. This

command I have received from my Father." 19 Again there was a division among the Jews because of these words. 20 Many of them said, "He is possessed and out of his mind; why listen to him?" 21 Others said, "These are not the words of one possessed; surely a demon cannot open the eyes of the blind, can he?"

Feast of the Dedication

22 The feast of the Dedication was then taking place in Jerusalem. It was winter. 23 And Jesus walked about in the temple area on the Portico of Solomon. 24 So the Jews gathered around him and said to him, "How long are you going to keep us in suspense? If you are the Messiah, tell us plainly." 25 Jesus answered them, "I told you and you do not believe. The works I do in my Father's name testify to me. 26 But you do not believe, because you are not among my sheep. 27 My sheep hear my voice; I know them, and they follow me. 28 I give them eternal life, and they shall never perish. No one can take them out of my hand. 29 My Father, who has given them to me, is greater than all, and no one can take them out of the Father's hand. 30 The Father and I are one." 31 The Jews again picked up rocks to stone him.32 Jesus answered them, "I have shown you many good works from my Father. For which of these are you trying to stone me?" 33 The Jews answered him, "We are not stoning you for a good work but for blasphemy. You, a man, are making yourself God." 34 Jesus answered them, "Is it not written in your law, 'I said, "You are gods"'? 35 If it calls them gods to whom the word of God came, and scripture cannot be set aside, 36 can you say that the one whom the Father has consecrated and sent into the world blasphemes because I said, 'I am the Son of God'? 37 If I do not perform my Father's works, do not believe me; 38 but if I perform them, even if you do not believe me, believe the works, so that you may realize (and understand) that the Father is in me and I am in the Father."39 (Then) they tried again to arrest him; but he escaped from their power. 40 He went back across the Jordan to the place where John first baptized, and there he remained. 41 Many came to him and said, "John performed no sign, but everything John said about this man was true." 42 And many there began to believe in him.

(1절)(go, pass) through a (door, gate).문으로 들어가다. (3절)call by name.이름을 부르다. one by one, one at a time.하나하나, 하나씩. ~calls each and every one of his own sheep by name. or ~calls his own sheep by name one by one.자기 양들의 이름을

하나하나 불러. (4절)when.때를 나타내는 부사절을 만들어 특정한 때를 나타냄. ~한 후, 하(니, 고, 자, 면), 할(때에, 때는). drive out.(가축을, 차를) 몰고 나가다, (추방, 배격)하다, 차로 외출하다, 드라이브하러 나가다, 쫓아내다. ahead of.보다 먼저. go (ahead, first), go before, be ahead of.앞서가다. recognize.외면 · 특징으로 ~을 알다, 알아보다, 분간하다(진행형 불가). know.~을 알다. (5절)~rather, they will run away. run away.사람 · 동물이 ~에서 달아나다. flee, outrun.피해 달아난다. (6절)figure.숫자, 인물, 도표. figure of speech.비유, (비유, 수사)적 표현, 말의 수식. Although Jesus used this figure of speech.예수님께서 이 비유를 (사용, 활용)하셨지만.→ Jesus said to them this figure of speech, but~.예수님께서 그들에게 이 비유를 말씀하셨다. 그러나~. (7절)So.그래서. (8절)before me.나보다 (앞서, 먼저), 내 앞에서. but.강조 구문 또는 감동 표현 등 뒤에 별 뜻이 없는 연결어로서 사용되었음. Why didn't you go?" "Oh(Ah), but I did." 왜 가지 않았지? 아니야, 난 갔었어. Excuse me, but will you show me the way to the museum? 죄송합니다. 박물관으로 가는 길을 가리켜 주시겠습니까? "그래서"는 redundant 번역임.(10절)kill, slaughter(slɔ´:tər).가축의 도살, 대학살, 살육. destroy.(파괴, 멸망)시키다. have it more abundantly.더욱 풍성하게 얻게 하려고. have it to the full.(마음껏, 최대한으로 가득)얻게 하려고. have it full to overflowing. 얻어 넘치게 하려고. (11절)lay down.목숨을 내놓다, 생명을 던지다, (쉬, 휴식하)려고 눕다, (아래, 땅)에 내려놓다. (12절)leaves.뒤에 남기다, 방치하다.→ abandons.버리다. ~runs away, and the wolf catches and scatters them.(달아나고, 달아난 다음에) 이리는 양들을 잡아가고 양떼를 흩어버린다.→ ~runs away. Then the wolf bites and scatters them. (달아나고, 달아난 다음에) 그러면 이리는 양들을 물어 가고 양떼를 흩어버린다. 여기서 and는 (동시성, ~와 동시에의 의미임) "또, 하고 (나서), 그 다음에, 하면서"의 뜻임. (13절)~he works for pay.그가 (삯일을 하기에, 임금을 받고 일을 하기에)→ ~he is a hired man(= hired hand). 그가 (삯꾼이기에, 삯꾼이어서). have no concern.에 아무 관심(관계)도 없다. (14절)mine= my sheep. (15절)just as.꼭 ~처럼, 바로 할 때에. (16절)But.그러나. fold= pen. These also I must lead.→ I must bring them also. lead.선두에 서서 남을 인도하다, 이끌다, 길 안내를 하다; 동물을 손 · 고삐 등을 잡고 데리고 가다. (bring, go and fetch).데려오다. one flock and one shepherd= one flock, one shepherd.한 목자 아래 하나의 양떼. recognize, understand, see, be intelligible, get.알아듣다. (17절)This is why 이것이 ~이유이다, 그런 까닭으로 ~한다(이다). This is why the Father loves me, because I lay down my life in order to take it up again.아버지께서 나를 사랑하시는 이유는 이러하다. 내가 목숨을 다시 얻으려고 목숨을 내 놓기 때문이다. (18절)on my own= of my own record.스스로, (독단적, 혼자함, 자발적)으로, 자진하여. This command I have received from my Father.(이, 이러한) 명령을 나는 내 아버지에게서 받았습니다. (19절)division분열, 분할. adverse criticism, charge, denunciation, censure, disproof, debating, attack (by arguments).

논란. (21절)Others.➞ But others. (23절)And.그리고. ~walking in the Portico of Solomon in the temple area.= ~walking about on the Portico of Solomon in the temple area. (23절)portico(pɔ́ːrtikou).포르티코; 특히 대형 건물 입구에 기둥을 받쳐 만든 현관 지붕. (24절)So.그래서. besiege, (gather, sit) around, lay siege to, surround, be encircled, enclose, environ.둘러싸다, 에워싸다. keep us in suspense.애태우다, 마음졸이게하다. plainly.분명히, 솔직하게, 숨김없이. worry (oneself), cause (worry, anxiety) to, make nervous, agitate oneself, be (worried, anxious, agonized, anguished, distressed, nervous), burn with anguish.속을 태우다. (25절)(Then, And).그러자. (26절)~you are not among my sheep.➞ ~you are not my sheep. 알아듣는다.➞ 듣는다. (28절)(take them= snatch them) out of my hand.빼앗아가다, 를 낚아채다. (29절)greater than all. 우주에 존재하는 (모든 것, 만유) 보다 위대하시어. (31절)그러자 redundant번역. (32절) answered.➞ said to them. in obedience to (your, his, her) (wishes, instructions). 분부에 따라, 분부대로. be (ordered, told).분부를 받다. obey order, toe the (line, mark, scratch).분부에 따르다. from my Father.아버지로(부터, 에게서) (맡은, 명령받은) (많은~) (33절)You, a mere man, are thinking of yourself as God.당신은 (단지)사람이면서 하느님으로 자처하고 있다= You, a man, are making yourself God.일개(하나의) 사람인 당신이 스스로 당신을 하느님으로 내 세우고 있다; 하느님이라고(주 장하고 있다, 하였다). think of oneself as, consider oneself as, flatter oneself, fancy oneself as.자처하다. (34절)answered.➞ said to. (35절)come to.에게 내려오다, (총계, 합계)가 ~이 되다, 받다, 받게 되는 상황이 되다, (알게, 하게) 되다, 들다, 닻을 내리다. disuse, discard, abolish, abandon, renounce, abrogate, repeal, dissolve, denounce.(습관, 법, 조약) 등을 폐기하다. set aside.을 한쪽으로 치우다, 그만두다, 제쳐놓다, (포기, 파기, 제외, 폐기, 제거)하다. (36절) consecrated. 종교 의식을 통해 (축성, 봉헌)하다, 종교적 목적으로 바치다, 성직자로 임명되다, 빵과 포도주를 성별(聖別)하다, 거룩하게 하시다, 성별: 신성한 일에 쓰기 위하여 보통의 것과 구별하는 일. 제사장이나 물건, 지역 따위를 구별한다. (37절)Do not believe me.나를 믿지 마라.➞ You may not believe me. or You had better not believe me.(너희들은) 나를 믿지 않아도 좋다. (38절)realize and understand.(알아차리고, 인식하고) 깨닫다.➞ understand and know.깨달아 알다. (39절)seize.잡다. arrest.(체포, 구속, 검거, 억류)하다, power.(물리적 힘, 영향력, 지배력, 재능, 능력, 권력, 권능, 정권, 힘)➞ hands. (40절)~where John first baptized.요한이 처음에 세례를 주던 곳.➞ ~where John baptized before.요한이 전에 세례를 주던 곳. (41절)그러자 redundant번역. (42절)And.그래서.

Footnotes

(1-21절)The good shepherd discourse continues the theme of attack on the Pharisees that ends John 9. The figure is allegorical: the hired hands are the Pharisees who excommunicated the cured blind man. It serves as a commentary on John 9. 이 부분은 9장에 대한 주해 역할을 제공한다. For the shepherd motif, used of Yahweh in the Old Testament, cf Exodus 34; Genesis 48:15; 49:24; Micah 7:14; Psalm 23:1-4; 80:1. allegorical.우화의, 우화적인, 우의(寓意)의. motif. 문학·음악 작품 속에서 반복, 전개되는 주제(모티프), 장식용 디자인(무늬). commentary.라디오·텔레비전의 실황 방송, 책·연극·글에 대해 글로 쓴 주석(해설), 비판, 논의, 흔적. (1절)Sheepfold: a low stone wall open to the sky.양우리: 나지막한 돌담 울타리로 하늘로 열려져 있음. (4절)Recognize his voice: the Pharisees do not recognize Jesus, but the people of God, symbolized by the blind man, do. (6절)Figure of speech: John uses a different word for illustrative speech than the "parable" of the synoptics, but the idea is similar. (7-10절)In John 10:7-8, the figure is of a gate for the shepherd to come to the sheep; in John 10:9-10, the figure is of a gate for the sheep to come in and go out. (8절)Before me: these words are omitted in many good early manuscripts and versions.나보다 먼저: 이 말씀은 초기의 많은 훌륭한 사본과 번역본에서 생략되어 있다. version. 번역본: 다른 언어로 된 것을 번역하거나 다른 예술 작품 형태로 된 것을 영화·연극·음악 작품 등으로 만든 것. 어떤 사건에 대해 특정한 입장에서 밝힌 설명, 견해. (16절)Other sheep: the Gentiles, possibly a reference to "God's dispersed children" of John 11:52 destined to be gathered into one, or "apostolic Christians" at odds with the community of the beloved disciple at odds with.다툰다, 갈등을 겪다, 티격태격하다, 대립하다, 뜻이 안 맞는다. (18절)Power to take it up again: contrast the role of the Father as the efficient cause of the resurrection in Acts 2:24; 4:10; etc.; Romans 1:4; 4:24. Yet even here is added: This command I have received from my Father. efficient cause. 동력인(動力因), 작용인; Aristotle이 말한 운동의 4대 원인의 하나. (22절)Feast of the Dedication: an eight-day festival of lights (Hebrew, Hanukkah) held in December, three months after the feast of Tabernacles (John 7:2), to celebrate the Maccabees' rededication of the altar and reconsecration of the temple in 164 B.C., after their desecration by Antiochus IV Epiphanes (Daniel 8:13; 9:27; cf 1 Macc 4:36-59; 2 Macc 1:18-2:19; 10:1-8). (23절)Portico of Solomon: on the east side of the temple area, offering protection against the cold winds from the desert. (24절)Keep us in suspense.우리의 속을 태울 작정이오. (우리의 마음을 조이게 하실 것입니까?): literally, "How long will you take away our life?" Cf John 11:48-50. If you are the Messiah, tell us plainly: cf Luke 22:67. This is the climax of Jesus' encounters with the Jewish authorities. There has never yet been an open confession before them.얼마동안 우리의 생명을 빼앗아 가렵니까? encounter.특히 반갑지 않은 일에 맞닥뜨리다, 부딪히다, 접하다, 마주치다. (25절)I told you: probably at John 8:25 which was an evasive answer. (29절)The textual evidence for the first clause is very divided; it may also be translated: "As for the Father, what he has given me is greater than all," or "My Father is greater than all, in what he has given me." 첫번째 절의 성경 본문 증거가 분분해서. (30절)This is justification for John 10:29; it asserts unity of power and reveals that the words and deeds of Jesus are the words and deeds of God.이 부분은 10장 29절의 정당한 이유가 된다. 예수님의 말씀과 행위는 하느님의 말씀과 행위임을 드러내 주며 아버지와 나는 하나라는 말씀은 힘의 일치를 주장한다. (34절)This is a reference to the judges of Israel who, since they exercised the divine prerogative to judge (Deut 1:17), were called "gods"; cf Exodus 21:6, besides Psalm 82:6 from which the quotation comes.이 절은 판관들이 남을 심판할 수 있는 하느님의 특권을 행사하였으므로 "신들"이라고 불려졌던 이스라엘의 판관들에 대한 언급이다. 인용문 나온 (출 처인) Exodus 21:6와 Psalm 82:6을 참조할 것. (36절)Consecrated. 거룩하게 하시다: This may be a reference to the rededicated altar at the Hanukkah feast; see the note on John 10:22. (41절) Performed no sign: this is to stress the inferior role of John the Baptist. The Transjordan topography recalls the great witness of John the Baptist to Jesus, as opposed to the hostility of the authorities in Jerusalem.

요한복음서 11장

라자로가 죽다

1 어떤 이가 병을 앓고 있었는데, 그는 마리아와 그 언니 마르타가 사는 베타니아 마을의 라자로였다.

2 마리아는 주님께 향유를 붓고 자기 머리카락으로 그분의 발을 닦아 드린 여자인데, 그의 오빠 라자로가 병을 앓고 있었던 것이다.

3 그리하여 그 자매가 예수님께 사람을 보내어, "주님, 주님께서 사랑하시는 이가 병을 앓고 있습니다." 하고 말하였다.

4 예수님께서 그 말을 듣고 이르셨다. "그 병은 죽을 병이 아니라 오히려 하느님의 영광을 위한 것이다. 그 병으로 말미암아 하느님의 아들이 영광스럽게 될 것이다."

5 예수님께서는 마르타와 그 여동생과 라자로를 사랑하셨다.

6 그러나 라자로가 병을 앓고 있다는 말을 들으시고도, 계시던 곳에 이틀을 더 머무르셨다.

7 예수님께서는 그런 뒤에야 제자들에게, "다시 유다로 가자." 하고 말씀하셨다.

8 제자들이 예수님께, "스승님, 바로 얼마 전에 유다인들이 스승님께 돌을 던지려고 하였는데, 다시 그리로 가시렵니까?" 하자,

9 예수님께서 대답하셨다. "낮은 열두 시간이나 되지 않느냐? 사람이 낮에 걸어 다니면 이 세상의 빛을 보므로 어디에 걸려 넘어지지 않는다.

10 그러나 밤에 걸어 다니면 그 사람 안에 빛이 없으므로 걸려 넘어진다."

11 이렇게 말씀하신 다음에 이어서, "우리의 친구 라자로가 잠들었다. 내가 가서 그를 깨우겠다." 하고 그들에게 말씀하셨다.

12 그러자 제자들이 예수님께, "주님, 그가 잠들었다면 곧 일어나겠지요." 하였다.

13 예수님께서는 라자로가 죽었다고 하셨는데, 제자들은 그냥 잠을 잔다고 말씀하시는 것으로 생각하였다.

14 그제야 예수님께서 그들에게 분명히 이르셨다. 라자로는 죽었다.

15 내가 거기에 없었으므로 너희가 믿게 될 터이니, "나는 너희 때문에 기쁘다. 이제 라자로에게 가자."

16 그러자 '쌍둥이'라고 불리는 토마스가 동료 제자들에게, "우리도 스승님과 함께 죽으러 갑시다." 하고 말하였다.

부활이며 생명이신 예수님

17 예수님께서 가서 보시니, 라자로가 무덤에 묻힌 지 벌써 나흘이나 지나 있었다.

18 베타니아는 예루살렘에서 열다섯 스타디온쯤 되는 가까운 곳이어서,

19 많은 유다인이 마르타와 마리아를 그 오빠 일 때문에 위로하러 와 있었다.

20 마르타는 예수님께서 오신다는 말을 듣고 그분을 맞으러 나가고, 마리아는 그냥 집에 앉아 있었다.

21 마르타가 예수님께 말하였다. "주님, 주님께서 여기에 계셨더라면 제 오빠가 죽지 않았을 것입니다.

22 그러나 하느님께서는 주님께서 청하시는 것은 무엇이나 들어주신다는 것을 저는 지금도 알고 있습니다."

23 예수님께서 마르타에게, "네 오빠는 다시 살아날 것이다." 하시니,

24 마르타가 "마지막 날 부활 때에 오빠도 다시 살아나리라는 것을 알고 있습니다." 하였다.

25 그러자 예수님께서 그에게 이르셨다. "나는 부활이요 생명이다. 나를 믿는 사람은 죽더라도 살고,

26 또 살아서 나를 믿는 모든 사람은 영원히 죽지 않을 것이다. 너는 이것을 믿느냐?"

27 마르타가 대답하였다. "예, 주님! 저는 주님께서 이 세상에 오시기로 되어 있는 메시아시며 하느님의 아드님이심을 믿습니다."

눈물을 흘리시다

28 이렇게 말하고 나서 마르타는 돌아가 자기 동생 마리아를 불러, "스승님께서 오셨는데 너를 부르신다." 하고 가만히 말하였다.

29 마리아는 이 말을 듣고 얼른 일어나 예수님께 갔다.

30 예수님께서는 마을로 들어가지 않으시고, 마르타가 당신을 맞으러 나왔던 곳에 그냥 계셨다.

31 마리아와 함께 집에 있으면서 그를 위로하던 유다인들은, 마리아가 급히 일어나 나가는 것을 보고 그를 따라갔다. 무덤에 가서 울려는 줄 알았던 것이다.

32 마리아는 예수님께서 계신 곳으로 가서 그분을 뵙고 그 발 앞에 엎드려, "주님, 주님께서 여기에 계셨더라면 제 오빠가 죽지 않았을 것입니다." 하고 말하였다.

33 마리아도 울고 또 그와 함께 온 유다인들도 우는 것을 보신 예수님께서는 마음이 북받치고 산란해지셨다.

34 예수님께서 "그를 어디에 묻었느냐?" 하고 물으시니, 그들이 "주님, 와서 보십시오." 하고 대답하였다.

35 예수님께서는 눈물을 흘리셨다.

36 그러자 유다인들이 "보시오, 저분이 라자로를 얼마나 사랑하셨는지!" 하고 말하였다.

37 그러나 그들 가운데 몇몇은, "눈먼 사람의 눈을 뜨게 해 주신 저분이 이 사람을 죽지 않게 해 주실 수는 없었는가?" 하였다.

라자로를 다시 살리시다

38 예수님께서는 다시 속이 북받치시어 무덤으로 가셨다. 무덤은 동굴인데 그 입구에 돌이 놓여 있었다.

39 예수님께서 "돌을 치워라." 하시니, 죽은 사람의 누이 마르타가 "주님, 죽은 지 나흘이나 되어 벌써 냄새가 납니다." 하였다.

40 예수님께서 마르타에게 말씀하셨다. "네가 믿으면 하느님의 영광을 보리라고 내가 말하지

않았느냐?"

41 그러자 사람들이 돌을 치웠다. 예수님께서는 하늘을 우러러보시며 말씀하셨다. "아버지, 제 말씀을 들어 주셨으니 아버지께 감사드립니다.

42 아버지께서 언제나 제 말씀을 들어 주신다는 것을 저는 알고 있습니다. 그러나 이렇게 말씀드린 것은, 여기 둘러선 군중이 아버지께서 저를 보내셨다는 것을 믿게 하려는 것입니다."

43 예수님께서는 이렇게 말씀하시고 나서 큰 소리로 외치셨다. "라자로야, 이리 나와라."

44 그러자 죽었던 이가 손과 발은 천으로 감기고 얼굴은 수건으로 감싸인 채 나왔다. 예수님께서 사람들에게, "그를 풀어 주어 걸어가게 하여라." 하고 말씀하셨다.

최고 의회가 예수님을 죽이기로 결의하다(마태 26,1-5; 마르 14,1-2; 루카 22,1-2)

45 마리아에게 갔다가 예수님께서 하신 일을 본 유다인들 가운데에서 많은 사람이 예수님을 믿게 되었다.

46 그러나 그들 가운데 몇 사람은 바리사이들에게 가서, 예수님께서 하신 일을 알렸다.

47 그리하여 수석 사제들과 바리사이들이 의회를 소집하고 이렇게 말하였다. "저 사람이 저렇게 많은 표징을 일으키고 있으니, 우리가 어떻게 하면 좋겠소?

48 저자를 그대로 내버려 두면 모두 그를 믿을 것이고, 또 로마인들이 와서 우리의 이 거룩한 곳과 우리 민족을 짓밟고 말 것이오."

49 그들 가운데 한 사람으로서 그해의 대사제인 카야파가 말하였다. "여러분은 아무것도 모르는군요.

50 온 민족이 멸망하는 것보다 한 사람이 백성을 위하여 죽는 것이 여러분에게 더 낫다는 사실을 여러분은 헤아리지 못하고 있소."

51 이 말은 카야파가 자기 생각으로 한 것이 아니라, 그해의 대사제로서 예언한 셈이다. 곧 예수님께서 민족을 위하여 돌아가시리라는 것과,

52 이 민족만이 아니라 흩어져 있는 하느님의 자녀들을 하나로 모으시려고 돌아가시리라는 것이다.

53 이렇게 하여 그날 그들은 예수님을 죽이기로 결의하였다.

54 그래서 예수님께서는 더 이상 유다인들 가운데로 드러나게 다니지 않으시고, 그곳을 떠나 광야에 가까운 고장의 에프라임이라는 고을에 가시어, 제자들과 함께 그곳에 머무르셨다.

55 유다인들의 파스카 축제가 가까워지자, 많은 사람이 자신을 정결하게 하려고 파스카 축제 전에 시골에서 예루살렘으로 올라갔다.

56 그들은 예수님을 찾다가 성전 안에 모여 서서 서로 말하였다. "여러분은 어떻게 생각하시오? 그가 축제를 지내러 오지 않겠소?"

57 수석 사제들과 바리사이들은 예수님을 잡으려고, 누구든지 예수님께서 계신 곳을 알면 신고하라는 명령을 내려 두었다.

The Raising of Lazarus

John Chapter 11

1 Now a man was ill, Lazarus from Bethany, the village of Mary and her sister Martha.2 Mary was the one who had anointed the Lord with perfumed oil and dried his feet with her hair; it was her brother Lazarus who was ill. 3 So the sisters sent word to him, saying, "Master, the one you love is ill." 4 When Jesus heard this he said, "This illness is not to end in death, but is for the glory of God, that the Son of God may be glorified through it." 5 Now Jesus loved Martha and her sister and Lazarus. 6 So when he heard that he was ill, he remained for two days in the place where he was. 7 Then after this he said to his disciples, "Let us go back to Judea." 8 The disciples said to him, "Rabbi, the Jews were just trying to stone you, and you want to go back there?" 9 Jesus answered, "Are there not twelve hours in a day? If one walks during the day, he does not stumble, because he sees the light of this world. 10 But if one walks at night, he stumbles, because the light is not in him." 11 He said this, and then told them, "Our friend Lazarus is asleep, but I am going to awaken him." 12 So the disciples said to him, "Master, if he is asleep, he will be saved." 13 But Jesus was talking about his death, while they thought that he meant ordinary sleep. 14 So then Jesus said to them clearly, "Lazarus has died. 15 And I am glad for you that I was not there, that you may believe. Let us go to him." 16 So Thomas, called Didymus, said to his fellow disciples, "Let us also go to die with him." 17 When Jesus arrived, he found that Lazarus had already been in the tomb for four days. 18 Now Bethany was near Jerusalem, only about two miles away. 19 And many of the Jews had come to Martha and Mary to comfort them about their brother. 20 When Martha heard that Jesus was coming, she went to meet him; but Mary sat at home. 21 Martha said to Jesus, "Lord, if you had been here, my brother would not have died. 22 (But) even now I know that whatever you ask of God, God will give you." 23 Jesus said to her, "Your brother will rise." 24 Martha said to him, "I know he will rise, in the resurrection on the last day." 25 Jesus told her, "I am the resurrection and the life; whoever believes in me, even if he dies, will live, 26 and everyone who lives and believes in me will never die. Do you believe this?" 27 She said to him, "Yes, Lord. I have come to believe that you are the Messiah, the Son of God, the one who is coming into the world." 28. When she had said this, she went and called her sister Mary secretly, saying, "The teacher is here and is asking for you." 29 As soon

as she heard this, she rose quickly and went to him. 30 For Jesus had not yet come into the village, but was still where Martha had met him. 31 So when the Jews who were with her in the house comforting her saw Mary get up quickly and go out, they followed her, presuming that she was going to the tomb to weep there. 32 When Mary came to where Jesus was and saw him, she fell at his feet and said to him, "Lord, if you had been here, my brother would not have died." 33 When Jesus saw her weeping and the Jews who had come with her weeping, he became perturbed and deeply troubled, 34 and said, "Where have you laid him?" They said to him, "Sir, come and see." 35 And Jesus wept. 36 So the Jews said, "See how he loved him." 37 But some of them said, "Could not the one who opened the eyes of the blind man have done something so that this man would not have died?" 38 So Jesus, perturbed again, came to the tomb. It was a cave, and a stone lay across it. 39 Jesus said, "Take away the stone." Martha, the dead man's sister, said to him, "Lord, by now there will be a stench; he has been dead for four days." 40 Jesus said to her, "Did I not tell you that if you believe you will see the glory of God?" 41 So they took away the stone. And Jesus raised his eyes and said, "Father, I thank you for hearing me. 42 I know that you always hear me; but because of the crowd here I have said this, that they may believe that you sent me." 43 And when he had said this, he cried out in a loud voice, "Lazarus, come out!" 44 The dead man came out, tied hand and foot with burial bands, and his face was wrapped in a cloth. So Jesus said to them, "Untie him and let him go."

Session of the Sanhedrin

45 Now many of the Jews who had come to Mary and seen what he had done began to believe in him.46 But some of them went to the Pharisees and told them what Jesus had done.47 So the chief priests and the Pharisees convened the Sanhedrin and said, "What are we going to do? This man is performing many signs. 48 If we leave him alone, all will believe in him, and the Romans will come and take away both our land and our nation." 49 But one of them, Caiaphas, who was high priest that year, said to them, "You know nothing, 50 nor do you consider that it is better for you that one man should die instead of the people, so that the whole nation may not perish." 51 He did not say this on his own, but since he was high priest for that year, he prophesied that Jesus was going to die for the nation,52 and not only for the nation, but also to gather into one the dispersed children of God. 53 So from

that day on they planned to kill him. 54 So Jesus no longer walked about in public among the Jews, but he left for the region near the desert, to a town called Ephraim, and there he remained with his disciples.

The Last Passover

55 Now the Passover of the Jews was near, and many went up from the country to Jerusalem before Passover to purify themselves. 56 They looked for Jesus and said to one another as they were in the temple area, "What do you think? That he will not come to the feast?" 57 For the chief priests and the Pharisees had given orders that if anyone knew where he was, he should inform them, so that they might arrest him.

(1절)Now.자, 그런데, 그럼, 그래서; 부탁을 하거나 화제를 바꿀 때; 어떤 이가 병을 앓고 있었는데. from Bethany.~그는 마리아와 그 언니 마르타가 사는 마을, 베타니아 출신 라자로였다. from.기원·유래에서 (온, 따온 등); 출신의, 산(産)의; 으로 부터의. These oranges (come, are) from Florida.이 오렌지는 플로리다산이다. (3절)sent word.기별하다, 에게 말을 전하다. Master= Lord. (4절)not to end in death.결국에는 (죽, 죽음으로 끝나)게 되어 있지 않다. (5절)Now.자, 그런데. (6절)So when he heard.실제 (라자로가 병을 앓고 있다는 소식을) 들으시고.→ (But, Yet) even when he heard.그러나 ~들으시고도. so+ 주어 +(조)동사의 어순으로, 선행의 진술에 대하여 동의·확인을 나타내어: 정말로, 참으로, 실제. (7절)Then after this.그 다음에, 그리고 나서, 그 후, 그 때에, 그런 뒤에야, 이런 일이 있은 후. (8절)just.이제 방금, 막. just(not long ago; some time ago; not too long ago; a short while ago).바로 얼마 전에. (11절)and then.그러고는, 그런 다음, 그 다음에, 그리고 나서, 하고 나서, 게다가, 그때에. He said this, and then told them.~이렇게 말씀하신 다음에 그들에게 말씀하셨다.→ After he said this, he went on to tell them.~이렇게 말씀하신 다음에 이어서 ~그들에게 말씀하셨다. ~but ~to (awaken him =wake him up).~(하지만, 그렇지만) ~(내가 가서 그를 깨우겠다). (12절)thereupon, and, so, soon, then, in turn, upon that.그러자. ~he will be saved.→ ~he will get up soon. (13절)Jesus said of his death, while his disciples thought that he meant just ordinary sleep.예수님께서는 라자로가 죽었다고 하셨는데, 제자들은 그냥 잠을 잔다고 말씀하시는 것으로 생각하였다. ordinary:일상의, 통상의. as it (is, stands); just.그냥, 그저. (14절)for the first time, only when(after, then), not ~until, at last, at length.그제야. so then.그러면, 그러므로, 그래서, 그렇다면, 그럼, 그렇게 지금, 그러니까, 그렇다 치고. (15절)And.그런데. ~glad(for you= for your sake).너희 때문에 기쁘다. Let us.→ Now let us. (16절)Then.그러자. So.그러자, 그래서. (17절)When Jesus arrived, he found.→ (When Jesus went and saw it= When Jesus came by and had a look at it), (~four days had already passed since Lazarus was buried in the tomb). found.자체가 "가서 보니"의 뜻이 있음. (18절)Now.그런데. about two miles away.약 2마일 정도되는. About two miles: literally, "about fifteen stades"; a (stade, stadion) was 607 feet.약 185.4미터; 경기장을 일컫는 스타디움은 stadion에서 유래되었음. (19절)And그러자. about.(그들의 오빠)일로. ~because of their brother.그들의 오빠 일 때문에. (20절)나가고, 마리아는.→ 나갔으나, 마리아는. (23절)rise, rose, risen.높은 위치·수준 등으로 오르다, 올라가다, 죽은 사람이 되살아나다, (부활, 소생)하다. (26절)~will never die.결코 죽지 않을 것이다. 의역; 영원히 살 것이다. (27절)She said to him.→ Martha answered him. I have come to believe that~.나는 ~라고 믿게 되었다.→ I believe that.나는 ~라고 믿습니다. ~who is coming.오시기로 되어 있는. (28절)(And) After she had said this, she went back and called her sister Mary. "The teacher is here," she said secretly, "and is asking for you." ask for.찾다, (부탁, 요청, 요구, 초대)하다, 부르다(invite), 을 달라고 (부탁, 청)하다, 에게 면회를 청하다. stealthily, on the sly, secretly, in secret, privately.가만히, 살짝·몰래. (29절)As soon as she heard this.→ When Mary heard this. rose= got up= arose. (30절)For Jesus.사실 예수님께서는. 마을로.→ 아직 마을로. 그냥.→ 여전히. (31절) 마리아와 함께.→ 그래서 마리아와 함께. presume.실질적인 증거는 없지만 사실일 것이라고 (추정하다, 여기다, 생각하다), 무엇을 사실로 간주하다. So when.그래서 ~보고. presuming that.→ knowing that.알았던 것이다. (33절)become deeply moved.깊이 감동을 받다, 몹시 동요되다. perturbed(pərtə́:rbd).(심란, 산란)하게 하다, 교란하다, 혼란된, 동요한, 불안한. surge up; gush forth; well up; have a fit of(anger); be filled with emotion. 북받치다. (be) discomposed; perturbed; distracted; restless.산란하다, 산란한. be troubled.(괴로워, 걱정, 불안해)하다, 근심스러운, 괴로운, (곤란, 불안, 지역 등이 소란)한, 고통을 받다, 금전 문제로 골치를 앓다, 시달리다, 부대끼다, 골머리를 앓다, 머릿살이 아프다. 마음이 북받치고 산란해지셨다.→ 마음이 산란하여 괴로워하셨다. (34절)said.→ asked. ~answered him.→ said to him. Sir.→ Lord. lay= bury.묻다, 매장하다. (35절)And그러자. (36절)So. 그러니까. (38절)So Jesus, perturbed again.그래서 예수님께서는 다시 마음이 산란해지셔서. 의역; 연민으로 마음깊이 감명을 받아; 연민으로 마음깊이 동요되어. across it.→ across the entrance. (39절)Lord, by now there will be a stench.주님, 지금쯤은 악취가 (풍길, 날) 것입니다.→ Lord, there is already a odor.주님, 벌써 냄새가 납니다. odor(óudər)냄새(특히 악취), 기미, 낌새, 평판. (42절)~but what I have said to you like this for the crowd standing here, that they may~.그러나 이렇게 말씀드린 것은, 여기 둘러선 군중이 아버지께서 저를 보내셨다는 것을 믿게 하려는 것입니다. (43절)And when. 그러자 예수님께서는. (44절)그러자 죽었던; "그러자"는 redundant번역임. be (twined; wound; wrapped; coiled; bound).감기다. ~tied hand and foot with burial bands.손과

발은 장례용 끈으로 묶이고. ~wrapped hand and foot with a cloth.손과 발은 천으로 감기고. towel; washcloth; facecloth.수건. ~and his face was wrapped in a cloth.그리고 그의 얼굴은 천으로 감기인 채 나왔다. So Jesus.그러자 예수님께서. go.→ walk. (45절)Now. 한데, 그런데, 그렇다면, 자. ~began to believe.→came to believe. (47절)What are we going to do?우리가 어떻게 하면 좋겠습니까? 우리가 (어떻게 할까요?, 어떻게 해야만 합니까?) convened the Sanhedrin= called a meeting of the Sanhedrin. (48절)take away. 빼앗다; 강탈하다; 없애주다. trample(on, over), (stamp, step)on.짓밟다. both our land and our nation.→ both this holy place of ours and our nation. (49절)But. 그런데. (50 절)~nor do you consider that it is better for you that one man should die instead of the people, so that the whole nation may not perish.또한, 한 사람이 백성을 대신하여 죽는 것이 여러분에게 더 낫다는 것을 여러분은 헤아리지 못하고 있소. (그 러면, 그 결과) 온 민족이 멸망하지 않을지 모릅니다. (You know nothing). You do not consider that it is better for you that one man should die for the people than that the whole nation perish.온 민족이 멸망하는 것보다 한 사람이 백성을 위하여 죽는 것이 여러분에게 더 낫다는 사실을 여러분은 헤아리지 못하고 있소. consider; weigh; ponder; deliberate.헤아리다, 고려하다. (51절)~but since he was high priest for that year, he prophesied that.~ 아니라 그가 그해의 대사제였으므로 ~돌아가시리라는 것을 예언한 셈이다. ~but as high priest for that year he prophesied that(not..but의 용법; ~이 아니라 ~이다). (53절)So from that day.그래서 그날로 부터. resolved, adopted a resolution.결의하였다. (54절)region.→ village(town). (55절)Now.그런데. (56절)~as they were.→ as they gathered and stood. 그들이 모여 서서. Isn't he coming to the feast?그가 축제에 오지 않겠지요? 의역: 그가 축제에 오지 않겠소? Do you think that he will not come to the feast?그가 축제에 안 올까요? 그가 축제에 오지 않겠다고 생각하오? 의역: 그가 축제에 오지 않겠소? Don't you think.생각하지 않니? Very fine! Don't you think so? 정말 멋지다! 그렇게 생각하지 않니? (celebrate, keep, observe) a festival.축제를 지내다.

Footnotes

(1-44절)The raising of Lazarus, the longest continuous narrative in John outside of the passion account, is the climax of the signs. It leads directly to the decision of the Sanhedrin to kill Jesus. The theme of life predominates. Lazarus is a token of the real life that Jesus dead and raised will give to all who believe in him. Johannine irony is found in the fact that Jesus' gift of life leads to his own death. The story is not found in the synoptics, but cf Mark 5:21 and parallels; Luke 7:11-17. There are also parallels between this story and Luke's parable of the rich man and poor Lazarus (Luke 16:19-31). In both a man named Lazarus dies; in Luke, there is a request that he return to convince his contemporaries of the need for faith and repentance, while in John, Lazarus does return and some believe but others do not. (4절)Not to end in death: this is misunderstood by the disciples as referring to physical death, but it is meant as spiritual death. (10절)The light is not in him: the ancients apparently did not grasp clearly the entry of light through the eye; they seem to have thought of it as being in the eye; cf Luke 11:34; Matthew 6:23. (16절)Called Didymus: Didymus is the Greek word for twin. Thomas is derived from the Aramaic word for twin; in an ancient Syriac version and in the Gospel of Thomas (#80: 11-12) his given name, Judas, is supplied. (18절)About two miles: literally, "about fifteen stades"; a stade was 607 feet. (27절)The titles here are a summary of titles given to Jesus earlier in the gospel. (33절)Became perturbed: a startling phrase in Greek, literally, "He snorted in spirit," perhaps in anger at the presence of evil (death). (41절)Father: in Aramaic, abba. See the note on Mark 14:36. (43절)Cried out in a loud voice: a dramatization of John 5:28; "the hour is coming when all who are in the tombs will hear his voice." (48절)The Romans will come: Johannine irony; this is precisely what happened after Jesus' death. (49절)That year: emphasizes the conjunction of the office and the year. Actually, Caiaphas was high priest A.D. 18-36. The Jews attributed a gift of prophecy, sometimes unconscious, to the high priest. (52절)Dispersed children of God: perhaps the "other sheep" of John 10:16. (54절)Ephraim is usually located about twelve miles northeast of Jerusalem, where the mountains descend into the Jordan valley. (55절)Purify: prescriptions for purity were based on Exodus 19:10-11, 15; Numbers 9:6-14; 2 Chron 30:1-3, 15-18.

요한복음서 12장

마리아가 예수님의 발에 향유를 붓다(마태 26,6-13; 마르 14,3-9)

1 예수님께서는 파스카 축제 엿새 전에 베타니아로 가셨다. 그곳에는 예수님께서 죽은 이들 가운데에서 다시 일으키신 라자로가 살고 있었다.

2 거기에서 예수님을 위한 잔치가 베풀어졌는데, 마르타는 시중을 들고 라자로는 예수님과 더불어 식탁에 앉은 이들 가운데 끼여 있었다.

3 그런데 마리아가 비싼 순 나르드 향유 한 리트라를 가져와서, 예수님의 발에 붓고 자기 머리카락으로 그 발을 닦아 드렸다. 그러자 온 집 안에 향유 냄새가 가득하였다.

4 제자들 가운데 하나로서 나중에 예수님을 팔아넘길 유다 이스카리옷이 말하였다.

5 "어찌하여 저 향유를 삼백 데나리온에 팔아 가난한 이들에게 나누어 주지 않는가?"

6 그가 이렇게 말한 것은, 가난한 이들에게 관심이 있어서가 아니라 도둑이었기 때문이다. 그는 돈주머니를 맡고 있으면서 거기에 든 돈을 가로채곤 하였다.

7 예수님께서 이르셨다. "이 여자를 그냥 놔두어라. 그리하여 내 장례 날을 위하여 이 기름을 간직하게 하여라.

8 사실 가난한 이들은 늘 너희 곁에 있지만, 나는 늘 너희 곁에 있지는 않을 것이다."

유다인들이 라자로까지 죽이기로 결의하다

9 예수님께서 그곳에 계시다는 것을 알고 많은 유다인들의 무리가 몰려왔다. 예수님 때문만이 아니라, 그분께서 죽은 이들 가운데에서 다시 일으키신 라자로도 보려는 것이었다.

10 그리하여 수석 사제들은 라자로도 죽이기로 결의하였다.

11 라자로 때문에 많은 유다인이 떨어져 나가 예수님을 믿었기 때문이다.

예루살렘에 입성하시다(마태 21, 1-11; 마르 11, 1-11; 루카 19, 28-38)

12 이튿날, 축제를 지내러 온 많은 군중이 예수님께서 예루살렘에 오신다는 말을 듣고서,

13 종려나무 가지를 들고 그분을 맞으러 나가 이렇게 외쳤다. "'호산나! 주님의 이름으로 오시는 분은 복되시어라.' 이스라엘의 임금님은 복되시어라."

14 예수님께서는 나귀를 보시고 그 위에 올라앉으셨다. 이는 성경에 기록된 그대로였다.

15 "딸 시온아, 두려워하지 마라. 보라, 너의 임금님이 오신다. 어린 나귀를 타고 오신다."

16 제자들은 처음에 이 일을 깨닫지 못하였다. 그러나 예수님께서 영광스럽게 되신 뒤에, 이 일이 예수님을 두고 성경에 기록되고 또 사람들이 그분께 그대로 해 드렸다는 것을 기억하게 되었다.

17 그리고 예수님께서 라자로를 무덤에서 불러내시어 죽은 이들 가운데에서 다시 일으키실 때에 그분과 함께 있던 군중이 그 일을 줄곧 증언하였다.

18 군중이 이렇게 예수님을 맞으러 나온 것은, 그분께서 그 표징을 일으키셨다는 말을 들었기

때문이다.

19 그러자 바리사이들이 서로 말하였다. "이제 다 글렀소. 보시오, 온 세상이 그의 뒤를 따라가고 있소."

그리스인들이 예수님을 찾다

20 축제 때에 예배를 드리러 올라온 이들 가운데 그리스 사람도 몇 명 있었다.

21 그들은 갈릴래아의 벳사이다 출신 필립보에게 다가가, "선생님, 예수님을 뵙고 싶습니다." 하고 청하였다.

22 필립보가 안드레아에게 가서 말하고 안드레아와 필립보가 예수님께 가서 말씀드리자,

23 예수님께서 그들에게 대답하셨다. "사람의 아들이 영광스럽게 될 때가 왔다.

24 내가 진실로 진실로 너희에게 말한다. 밀알 하나가 땅에 떨어져 죽지 않으면 한 알 그대로 남고, 죽으면 많은 열매를 맺는다.

25 자기 목숨을 사랑하는 사람은 목숨을 잃을 것이고, 이 세상에서 자기 목숨을 미워하는 사람은 영원한 생명에 이르도록 목숨을 간직할 것이다.

26 누구든지 나를 섬기려면 나를 따라야 한다. 내가 있는 곳에 나를 섬기는 사람도 함께 있을 것이다. 누구든지 나를 섬기면 아버지께서 그를 존중해 주실 것이다."

사람의 아들은 들어 올려져야 한다

27 "이제 제 마음이 산란합니다. 무슨 말씀을 드려야 합니까? '아버지, 이때를 벗어나게 해 주십시오.' 하고 말할까요? 그러나 저는 바로 이때를 위하여 온 것입니다.

28 아버지, 아버지의 이름을 영광스럽게 하십시오." 그러자 하늘에서 "나는 이미 그것을 영광스럽게 하였고 또다시 영광스럽게 하겠다."는 소리가 들려왔다.

29 그곳에 서 있다가 이 소리를 들은 군중은 천둥이 울렸다고 하였다. 그러나 "천사가 저분에게 말하였다." 하는 이들도 있었다.

30 예수님께서 이르셨다. "그 소리는 내가 아니라 너희를 위하여 내린 것이다.

31 이제 이 세상은 심판을 받는다. 이제 이 세상의 우두머리가 밖으로 쫓겨날 것이다.

32 나는 땅에서 들어 올려지면 모든 사람을 나에게 이끌어 들일 것이다."

33 예수님께서는 이 말씀으로, 당신께서 어떻게 죽임을 당하실 것인지 가리키신 것이다.

34 그때에 군중이 예수님께 말하였다. "우리는 율법에서 메시아는 영원히 사실 것이라고 들었는데, 어떻게 선생님은 사람의 아들이 들어 올려져야 한다고 말씀하십니까? 그 사람의 아들이 누구입니까?"

35 그러자 예수님께서 그들에게 이르셨다. "빛이 너희 가운데에 있는 것도 잠시뿐이다. 빛이 너희 곁에 있는 동안에 걸어가거라. 그래서 어둠이 너희를 덮치지 못하게 하여라. 어둠 속을 걸어가는 사람은 자기가 어디로 가는지 모른다.

36 빛이 너희 곁에 있는 동안에 그 빛을 믿어, 빛의 자녀가 되어라." 예수님께서는 이렇게 말씀하시고 나서 그들을 떠나 몸을 숨기셨다.

유다인들의 불신

37 예수님께서는 그들 앞에서 그토록 많은 표징을 일으키셨지만, 그들은 그분을 믿지 않았다.

38 이는 이사야 예언자가 한 말이 이루어지려고 그리된 것이다. "주님, 저희가 전한 말을 누가 믿었습니까? 주님의 권능이 누구에게 드러났습니까?"

39 그들이 믿을 수 없었던 까닭을 이사야는 또 이렇게 말하였다.

40 "주님이 그들의 눈을 멀게 하고 그들의 마음을 무디게 하였다. 이는 그들이 눈으로 보고 마음으로 깨닫고서는 돌아와 내가 그들을 고쳐 주는 일이 없게 하려는 것이다."

41 이사야가 이렇게 말한 것은, 그가 예수님의 영광을 보았기 때문이다. 그는 그분에 관하여 이야기한 것이다.

42 사실 지도자들 가운데에서도 많은 사람이 예수님을 믿었지만, 바리사이들 때문에 회당에서 내쫓길까 두려워 그것을 고백하지 못하였다.

43 그들이 하느님에게서 받는 영광보다 사람에게서 받는 영광을 더 사랑하였기 때문이다.

예수님의 말씀과 심판

44 예수님께서 큰 소리로 말씀하셨다. "나를 믿는 사람은 나를 믿는 것이 아니라 나를 보내신 분을 믿는 것이다.

45 그리고 나를 보는 사람은 나를 보내신 분을 보는 것이다.

46 나는 빛으로서 이 세상에 왔다. 나를 믿는 사람은 누구나 어둠 속에 머무르지 않게 하려는 것이다.

47 누가 내 말을 듣고 그것을 지키지 않는다 하여도, 나는 그를 심판하지 않는다. 나는 세상을 심판하러 온 것이 아니라 세상을 구원하러 왔기 때문이다.

48 나를 물리치고 내 말을 받아들이지 않는 자를 심판하는 것이 따로 있다. 내가 한 바로 그 말이 마지막 날에 그를 심판할 것이다.

49 내가 스스로 말하지 않고, 나를 보내신 아버지께서 무엇을 말하고 무엇을 이야기할 것인지 친히 나에게 명령하셨기 때문이다.

50 나는 그분의 명령이 영원한 생명임을 안다. 그래서 내가 하는 말은 아버지께서 나에게 말씀하신 그대로 하는 말이다."

The Anointing at Bethany

John Chapter 12

1 Six days before Passover Jesus came to Bethany, where Lazarus was, whom Jesus had raised from the dead. 2 They gave a dinner for him there, and Martha served, while Lazarus was one of those reclining at table with him. 3 Mary took a liter of costly perfumed oil made from genuine aromatic nard and anointed the feet of Jesus and dried them with her hair; the house was filled with the fragrance of the oil. 4 Then Judas the Iscariot, one (of) his disciples, and the one who would betray him, said, 5 "Why was this oil not sold for three hundred days' wages and given to the poor?" 6 He said this not because he cared about the poor but because he was a thief and held the money bag and used to steal the contributions. 7 So Jesus said, "Leave her alone. Let her keep this for the day of my burial. 8 You always have the poor with you, but you do not always have me." 9 (The) large crowd of the Jews found out that he was there and came, not only because of Jesus, but also to see Lazarus, whom he had raised from the dead. 10 And the chief priests plotted to kill Lazarus too, 11 because many of the Jews were turning away and believing in Jesus because of him.

The Entry into Jerusalem

12 On the next day, when the great crowd that had come to the feast heard that Jesus was coming to Jerusalem, 13 they took palm branches and went out to meet him, and cried out: "Hosanna! Blessed is he who comes in the name of the Lord, (even) the king of Israel." 14 Jesus found an ass and sat upon it, as is written: 15 "Fear no more, O daughter Zion; see, your king comes, seated upon an ass's colt." 16 His disciples did not understand this at first, but when Jesus had been glorified they remembered that these things were written about him and that they had done this for him. 17 So the crowd that was with him when he called Lazarus from the tomb and raised him from death continued to testify. 18 This was (also) why the crowd went to meet him, because they heard that he had done this sign. 19 So the Pharisees said to one another, "You see that you are gaining nothing. Look, the whole world has gone after him."

The Coming of Jesus' Hour

20 Now there were some Greeks among those who had come up to worship at the feast. 21 They came to Philip, who was from Bethsaida in Galilee, and asked him, "Sir, we would like to see Jesus." 22 Philip went and told Andrew; then Andrew and Philip went and told Jesus. 23 Jesus answered them, "The hour has come for the Son of Man to be glorified. 24 Amen, amen, I say to you, unless a grain of wheat falls to the ground and dies, it remains just a grain of wheat; but if it dies, it produces much fruit. 25 Whoever loves his life loses it, and whoever hates his life in this world will preserve it for eternal life. 26 Whoever serves me must follow me, and where I am, there also will my servant be. The Father will honor whoever serves me. 27 "I am troubled now. Yet what should I say? 'Father, save me from this hour'? But it was for this purpose that I came to this hour. 28 Father, glorify your name." Then a voice came from heaven, "I have glorified it and will glorify it again." 29 The crowd there heard it and said it was thunder; but others said, "An angel has spoken to him." 30 Jesus answered and said, "This voice did not come for my sake but for yours. 31 Now is the time of judgment on this world; now the ruler of this world will be driven out. 32 And when I am lifted up from the earth, I will draw everyone to myself." 33 He said this indicating the kind of death he would die. 34 So the crowd answered him, "We have heard from the law that the Messiah remains forever. Then how can you say that the Son of Man must be lifted up? Who is this Son of Man?" 35 Jesus said to them, "The light will be among you only a little while. Walk while you have the light, so that darkness may not overcome you. Whoever walks in the dark does not know where he is going. 36 While you have the light, believe in the light, so that you may become children of the light."

Unbelief and Belief among the Jews

After he had said this, Jesus left and hid from them. 37 Although he had performed so many signs in their presence they did not believe in him, 38 in order that the word which Isaiah the prophet spoke might be fulfilled: "Lord, who has believed our preaching, to whom has the might of the Lord been revealed?" 39 For this reason they could not believe, because again Isaiah said: 40 "He blinded their eyes and hardened their heart, so that they might not see with their eyes and understand with their heart and be converted, and I would heal them." 41 Isaiah said this because he saw his glory and spoke about him. 42 Nevertheless, many, even among the authorities, believed in him, but because of the Pharisees they did not acknowledge it openly in order not to be expelled from the synagogue. 43 For they preferred human praise to the glory of God.

Recapitulation

44 Jesus cried out and said, "Whoever believes in me believes not only in me but also in the one who sent me, 45 and whoever sees me sees the one who sent me. 46 I came into the world as light, so that everyone who believes in me might not remain in darkness. 47 And if anyone hears my words and does not observe them, I do not condemn him, for I did not come to condemn the world but to save the world. 48 Whoever rejects me and does not accept my words has something to judge him: the word that I spoke, it will condemn him on the last day, 49 because I did not speak on my own, but the Father who sent me commanded me what to say and speak. 50 And I know that his commandment is eternal life. So what I say, I say as the Father told me."

(1절)Lazarus was.→ Lazarus lived. raise.들어 올리다, 일으키다, 부활시키다, 살리다. 되살리다, 소생시키다. the+dead(형용사)= 복수명사(죽은 이들). raise question.(의문, 질문) 을 (제기하다, 끄집어내다). fund raising.기금모금, 자금조달. (2절)give a dinner.(잔치, 만찬회, 축하연)을 (열다, 베풀다), 저녁을 (한턱내다, 제공하다). ~was among those= ~was joining those.이들 가운데 끼여 있었다. ~was one of those.이들 가운데 하나였었다. be put(held) between; be caught in; get jammed(hemmed) in; be sandwiched between. 물건사이에 끼이다. (be, lie) between.양자사이에 끼이다. take one's place among; rank with.끼이다, 참여하다. (3절)Litra.그리스의 용량단위; same as one pint(paint).0.47리터. Then Mary took a litra of costly genuine(pure) perfumed nard oil and poured it on the feet of Jesus and wiped them with her hair.그런데 마리아가 비싼 순 나르드 향유 한 리트라를 가져와서, 예수님의 발에 붓고 자기 머리카락으로 그 발을 닦아드렸다. fragrance (fréigrəns).향기로움, 향기, 방향(芳香), 꽃다운 향기. (aromatic, perfumed) oil.향유. And (그러자) the whole house was filled with the (fragrance, smell) of the perfumed oil. 그러자 온 집안에 향유 (향기, 냄새)가 가득하였다. (4절)Then.그때에. ~would betray.→ ~would later betray. (5절)~this oil.→ ~this perfumed oil. ~distribute sth among sb.나누어 주다. Days' wages: literally, "denarii." A denarius is a day's wage in Matthew 20:2; See the note on John 6:7. (6절)care about.~에 (마음, 신경을) 쓰다, 에 관심을 가지다. used to steal.훔치곤 하였다. 가로채곤하였다. steal, embezzle, misappropriate, help oneself to, snatch, interrupt, cut in.가로채다. ~used to (steal the money or help himself to) the money that was put into it(money bag).거기에 든 돈을 가로채곤 하였다. help oneself to.(횡령, 착복)하다, 가로채다, 을 마음대로 쓰다. contribution.기부금, 성금, 기여금. (7절)So Jesus said.그래서 예수님께서 이르셨다. Let her keep this for~.그 여자가 (내 장례 날을 위하여) 이 것(기름)을 간직하(도록, 게) 하여라. (그냥 나둬라). (So, Therefore 그리하여) let her (save, keep, store) this(perfumed) oil for.그리하여 그 여자가 내 장례 날을 위하여 이 기름을 간직하게 하여라. (8절)by, beside, with.곁에. near, (close, hard, near) by.곁에, 가까이. ~but you do not always have me.너희는 (늘, 언제나) 나와 함께 있는 것이 아니다. ~but you will not always have me. or ~but I will not always with you. 나는 늘 너희 곁에 있지는 않을 것이다. (9절)come in (crowds, flocks, swarms, packs, shoals); flock; throng; come crowding; storm (a place).(몰려, 떼지어)오다. People come crowding. or People pour in(into)(a place).사람이 몰려온다. find out.임을 (알아, 찾아)내다, 발견하다. (10절)resolved, adopted a resolution.결의하였다. plotted.음모를 꾸미다. (11절)detached from; fall away; peeled off; dropped out; separated from. 떨어져나가다. turn away.(외면, 거절, 퇴)하다, 등을 돌리다, 돌아서다. I have a sister who has long been fallen away from the practice of our faith.나는 우리의 믿음을 실천하지 못하고 떨어져 나간 누이가 하나 있다. (12절)the (next, following)day; the day after; the second day (of the month).이튿날, 다음날. the next morning.(초이틀, 이튿날) 아침. ~was coming to; drawing near(=approaching).오다, 다가오다. Mount of Olive.(올리브, 감람)나무가 많은 예루살렘 동편 산. palm branch.종려나무 가지. Olive branch.평화 · 화해의 상징; Noah의 방주에서 날려 보낸 비둘기가 올리브의 가지를 물고 왔다는 내용에서 인용. Hosanna(houzǽnə)= Oh, Grant us salvation.오, 저희에게 구원을 허락하여 주소서. ~even the king of Israel.이스라엘의 임금님(도, 조차도, 마저) (복되시어라). (17절)So.그래서 from death.→ from the dead. (19절)It's all domino with one(us).이제 (우리는) 다 글렀다. (be) hopeless; be(done for, all over, all fouled up); have had it.글렀다. gain nothing.득 될 것 없다, 헛수고였다, 얻는 것은 하나도 없다, 아무 소용없어요. See + that절, See + wh-절, See + wh- to do(발언 등에서) ~임을 알다, 알고 있다(진행형은 쓰지 않음). (20절)Now. 그런데. (22절)then.그런 다음에. (24절)(bear, produce) fruits, fructify, make fruitful, produce a result, come to fruition, be brought to fruition.열매를 맺다. a grain of wheat, a kernel(kəˊːrnl) of wheat.한 알. (25절)~ will preserve it(life) for eternal life.영원한 생명에 이르도록 목숨을 (간직, 보존)할 것이다. hold; keep; harbor; cherish; preserve. 간직하다. (26절)If anyone wants to serve me.누구든지 나를 섬기려면. Whoever serves me.나를 섬기는 사람은. The Father will honor whoever serves me.아버지께서는 나를 섬기는 사람은 누구든지 존중해 주실 것이다. The Father will honor him if he serves me.누구든지 나를 섬기면 아버지께서 그를 존중해 주실 것이다. (27절)I am troubled now. or Now my heart is troubled.이제 제 마음이 시달리고 있습니다, 지금(이제) 내 마음이 괴롭습니다. be distracted with the thought (of), heart is torn by, be (deranged, unhinged) in mind, be upset by.산란해지다. Now my heart is distracted.이제 제 마음이 산란합니다. Yet what.이제 무슨. from.에서. ~save me from this hour'?(이 시간, 이때)에서 저를 구원해 주십시오. ~let me bail out of this hour.이 때를 벗어나게 해 주십시오. (get, keep, bail) out of, escape from.벗어나다. But it was for this purpose that I came to this hour.그러나 이 시간에 도달한 (다다른) 것은 이런 목적(아버지의 이름을 영광스럽게 하는 것)을 위한 것이었습니다. 의역; 내가(바로) 이 목적을 위하여 이 시간에 왔습니다.(이 시간에 귀착하였습니다) very, exactly, just.바로. (29절)The crowd there heard it and said it was thunder.→ The crowd standing there heard it and said it had thundered. (30절)answered and said.대답하시며 이르셨다. give, be handed down, issue, proclaim, have.(은총, 명령, 허가 등을) 내리다. ring, go, sound.소리가 나다. voice come.소리가 (들려오다, 나다). ~not come for my sake.(그 소리는) 나를 위하여 (들려오지, 나지) 않았다. (31절)Now is the time of judgment on this world.지금이 이 세상에 대한 심판의 때이다. be judged.심판을 받다. ruler.통치자, 지배자, 사탄. (32절)And when.그래서 ~하면. (33절)~indicating the kind of death he would die.예수님께서 죽게 되실 죽임의 종류를 (가리키신, 암시하신) 것이다; 예수님께서 죽게 되실 죽임이 어느 편인가를 (가리키, 암시하)시면서 (이 말씀을 하셨다): 의역, 예수님께서 어떤 죽임을 당하실 것인지 (가리키, 암시하)시면서 (이 말씀을 하셨다). (34절)So the crowd answered him.(그런 까닭으로, 그래서, 그러자) 군중이 예수님께 대답하였다. remain.(처리, 이행 등을 해야 할 일이) 남아 있다, 아직 ~해야 한다, (계속, 여전히) ~이다, 지내다, 체류하다, 유지하다. live, dwell, be alive, (lead, live, have) a life.살다. (35절)Then Jesus.그러자 예수님께서. The light will be among you only a little while.빛이 단지 얼마 동안은 너희 가운데 있을 것이다. raid, attack, overtake, swoop(on).덮치다, 습격하다. ~while you have the light near you~곁에 있는 동안에. overtake.앞지르다, (능가, 추월)하다, 불쾌한 일이 사람에게 불시에 (덮치다, 닥치다, 엄습하다). this, like this.이렇게. (39절)For this reason they could not believe, because again Isaiah said.(이러한 이유로 해서, 이유 때문에) 그들은 믿을 수 없었다. 왜냐하면 이사야는 또 (이렇게) 말하였기 때문입니다; 문장 앞에 콤마가 있는 경우, 보통 앞에서 부터 내리 번역해서 (왜냐하면 ~때문으로 번역합니다). (40절)~so that they might not see with their eyes and(might not) understand with their heart and (might not) be converted, and I would heal them.그래서 (그들이, 그들의) 눈으로 보지 못하게 하고 그들의 마음으로 (이 해하, 깨닫)지 못하게 하며 그들이 (회심하, 돌이키, 돌아오)지 못하게 하려는 것이다. 그리하여 내가 그들을 고쳐주지 못하게 하려는 것이다. ~and (if they were converted) I would heal them.그래서

그들이 회심하였다면 내가 그들을 고쳐주었을 것이다. 그런데 그들이 (회심하지 못하게 하여, 돌아오지 못하게 하여) 내가 그들을 고쳐주는 일이 없게 하려는 것이다. (41절)speak about. 대해 이야기 하다, 에 관해서 말하다, 소문 이야기를 하다. (42절)Nevertheless, many, even among the authorities, believed in him, ~they did not acknowledge it openly in order not to be expelled from the synagogue.→ In fact, many, even among the leaders, believed in him, ~they did not confess their faith(it) for fear they would be expelled from the synagogue. (43절)~preferred human praise to the glory of God.→ ~loved the glory received from men more than the glory received from God. (44절)Jesus cried out and said.예수님께서 외치시며 말씀하셨다. cry out.외치다, 소리치다, 부르짖다. (47절) observe→ keep. condemn→ judge. (49절)personally, in person 친히. (50절)And. 그래서. So.그러므로.

Footnotes

(1-8절)This is probably the same scene of anointing found in Mark 14:3-9 (see the note there) and Matthew 26:6-13. The anointing by a penitent woman in Luke 7:36-38 is different. Details from these various episodes have become interchanged.(3절)The feet of Jesus: so Mark 14:3; but in Matthew 26:6, Mary anoints Jesus' head as a sign of regal, messianic anointing. (5)Days' wages: literally, "denarii." A denarius is a day's wage in Matthew 20:2; see the note on John 6:7. (7절)Jesus' response reflects the rabbinical discussion of what was the greatest act of mercy, almsgiving or burying the dead. Those who favored proper burial of the dead thought it an essential condition for sharing in the resurrection.(12-19절)In John, the entry into Jerusalem follows the anointing whereas in the synoptics it precedes. In John, the crowd, not the disciples, are responsible for the triumphal procession.(13절)Palm branches: used to welcome great conquerors; cf 1 Macc 13:51; 2 Macc 10:7. They may be related to the lulab, the twig bundles used at the feast of Tabernacles. Hosanna: see Psalm 118:25-26. The Hebrew word means: "(O Lord), grant salvation." He who comes in the name of the Lord: referred in Psalm 118:26 to a pilgrim entering the temple gates, but here a title for Jesus (see the notes on Matthew 11:3 and John 6:14; 11:27). The king of Israel: perhaps from Zephaniah 3:14-15 in connection with the next quotation from Zechariah 9:9. (15) Daughter Zion: Jerusalem. Ass's colt: symbol of peace, as opposed to the war horse.(16절)They had done this: the antecedent of they is ambiguous.(17-18절)There seem to be two different crowds in these verses. There are some good witnesses to the text that have another reading for John 12:17: "Then the crowd that was with him began to testify that he had called Lazarus out of the tomb and raised him from the dead." (19절)The whole world: the sense is that everyone is following Jesus, but John has an ironic play on world; he alludes to the universality of salvation (John 3:17; 4:42). (20-36) This announcement of glorification by death is an illustration of "the whole world" (19) going after him.(20절)Greeks: not used here in a nationalistic sense. These are probably Gentile proselytes to Judaism; cf John 7:35.(21-22절)Philip···Andrew: the approach is made through disciples who have distinctly Greek names, suggesting that access to Jesus was mediated to the Greek world through his disciples. Philip and Andrew were from Bethsaida (John 1:44); Galileans were mostly bilingual. See: here seems to mean "have an interview with." (23)Jesus' response suggests that only after the crucifixion could the gospel encompass both Jew and Gentile.(24절)This verse implies that through his death Jesus will be accessible to all. It remains just a grain of wheat: this saying is found in the synoptic triple and double traditions (Mark 8:35; Matthew 16:25; Luke 9:24; Matthew 10:39; Luke 17:33). John adds the phrases (John 12:25) in this world and for eternal life.(25절)His life: the Greek word psyche refers to a person's natural life. It does not mean "soul," for Hebrew anthropology did not postulate body/soul dualism in the way that is familiar to us.(27절)I am troubled: perhaps an allusion to the Gethsemane agony scene of the synoptics.(31절)Ruler of this world: Satan.(34절)There is no passage in the Old Testament that states precisely that the Messiah remains forever. Perhaps the closest is Psalm 89:37.(37-50절)These verses, on unbelief of the Jews, provide an epilogue to the Book of Signs.(38-41절)John gives a historical explanation of the disbelief of the Jewish people, not a psychological one. The Old Testament had to be fulfilled; the disbelief that met Isaiah's message was a foreshadowing of the disbelief that Jesus encountered. In John 12:42 and also in John 3:20 we see that there is no negation of freedom.(41절)His glory: Isaiah saw the glory of Yahweh enthroned in the heavenly temple, but in John the antecedent of his is Jesus.

요한복음서 13장

제자들의 발을 씻어 주시다

1 파스카 축제가 시작되기 전, 예수님께서는 이 세상에서 아버지께로 건너가실 때가 온 것을 아셨다. 그분께서는 이 세상에서 사랑하신 당신의 사람들을 끝까지 사랑하셨다.

2 만찬 때의 일이다. 악마가 이미 시몬 이스카리옷의 아들 유다의 마음속에 예수님을 팔아넘길 생각을 불어넣었다.

3 예수님께서는 아버지께서 모든 것을 당신 손에 내주셨다는 것을, 또 당신이 하느님에게서 나왔다가 하느님께 돌아간다는 것을 아시고,

4 식탁에서 일어나시어 겉옷을 벗으시고 수건을 들어 허리에 두르셨다.

5 그리고 대야에 물을 부어 제자들의 발을 씻어 주시고, 허리에 두르신 수건으로 닦기 시작하셨다.

6 그렇게 하여 예수님께서 시몬 베드로에게 이르시자 베드로가, "주님, 주님께서 제 발을 씻으시렵니까?" 하고 말하였다.

7 예수님께서는 "내가 하는 일을 네가 지금은 알지 못하지만 나중에는 깨닫게 될 것이다." 하고 대답하셨다.

8 그래도 베드로가 예수님께 "제 발은 절대로 씻지 못하십니다." 하니, 예수님께서 그에게 대답하셨다. "내가 너를 씻어 주지 않으면 너는 나와 함께 아무런 몫도 나누어 받지 못한다."

9 그러자 시몬 베드로가 예수님께 말하였다. "주님, 제 발만 아니라 손과 머리도 씻어 주십시오."

10 예수님께서 그에게 말씀하셨다. "목욕을 한 이는 온몸이 깨끗하니 발만 씻으면 된다. 너희는 깨끗하다. 그러나 다 그렇지는 않다."

11 예수님께서는 이미 당신을 팔아넘길 자를 알고 계셨다. 그래서 "너희가 다 깨끗한 것은 아니다." 하고 말씀하신 것이다.

12 예수님께서는 제자들의 발을 씻어 주신 다음, 겉옷을 입으시고 다시 식탁에 앉으셔서 그들에게 이르셨다. "내가 너희에게 한 일을 깨닫겠느냐?

13 너희가 나를 '스승님', 또 '주님' 하고 부르는데, 그렇게 하는 것이 옳다. 나는 사실 그러하다.

14 주님이며 스승인 내가 너희의 발을 씻었으면, 너희도 서로 발을 씻어 주어야 한다.

15 내가 너희에게 한 것처럼 너희도 하라고, 내가 본을 보여 준 것이다.

16 내가 진실로 진실로 너희에게 말한다. 종은 주인보다 높지 않고, 파견된 이는 파견한 이보다 높지 않다.

17 이것을 알고 그대로 실천하면 너희는 행복하다.

18 내가 너희를 모두 가리켜 말하는 것은 아니다. 내가 뽑은 이들을 나는 안다. 그러나 '제 빵을 먹던 그가 발꿈치를 치켜들며 저에게 대들었습니다.'라는 성경 말씀이 이루어져야 한다.

19 일이 일어나기 전에 내가 미리 너희에게 말해 둔다. 일이 일어날 때에 내가 나임을 너희가 믿게 하려는 것이다.

20 내가 진실로 진실로 너희에게 말한다. 내가 보내는 이를 맞아들이는 사람은 나를 맞아들이는 것이고, 나를 맞아들이는 사람은 나를 보내신 분을 맞아들이는 것이다."

유다가 배신할 것을 예고하시다(마태 26, 20-25; 마르 14, 17-21; 루카 22, 21-23)

21 예수님께서는 이렇게 이르시고 나서 마음이 산란하시어 드러내 놓고 말씀하셨다. "내가 진실로 진실로 너희에게 말한다. 너희 가운데 한 사람이 나를 팔아넘길 것이다."

22 제자들은 누구를 두고 하시는 말씀인지 몰라 어리둥절하여 서로 바라보기만 하였다.

23 제자 가운데 한 사람이 예수님 품에 기대어 앉아 있었는데, 그는 예수님께서 사랑하시는 제자였다.

24 그래서 시몬 베드로가 그에게 고갯짓을 하여, 예수님께서 말씀하시는 사람이 누구인지 여쭈어 보게 하였다.

25 그 제자가 예수님께 더 다가가, "주님, 그가 누구입니까?" 하고 물었다.

26 예수님께서는 "내가 빵을 적셔서 주는 자가 바로 그 사람이다." 하고 대답하셨다. 그리고 빵을 적신 다음 그것을 들어 시몬 이스카리옷의 아들 유다에게 주셨다.

27 유다가 그 빵을 받자 사탄이 그에게 들어갔다. 그때에 예수님께서 유다에게 말씀하셨다. "네가 하려는 일을 어서 하여라."

28 식탁에 함께 앉은 이들은 예수님께서 그에게 왜 그런 말씀을 하셨는지 아무도 몰랐다.

29 어떤 이들은 유다가 돈주머니를 가지고 있었으므로, 예수님께서 그에게 축제에 필요한 것을 사라고 하셨거나, 또는 가난한 이들에게 무엇을 주라고 말씀하신 것이려니 생각하였다.

30 유다는 빵을 받고 바로 밖으로 나갔다. 때는 밤이었다.

새 계명

31 유다가 나간 뒤에 예수님께서 말씀하셨다. "이제 사람의 아들이 영광스럽게 되었고, 또 사람의 아들을 통하여 하느님께서도 영광스럽게 되셨다.

32 하느님께서 사람의 아들을 통하여 영광스럽게 되셨으면, 하느님께서도 몸소 사람의 아들을 영광스럽게 하실 것이다. 이제 곧 그를 영광스럽게 하실 것이다.

33 얘들아, 내가 너희와 함께 있는 것도 잠시뿐이다. 너희는 나를 찾을 터인데, 내가 유다인들에게 말한 것처럼 이제 너희에게도 말한다. '내가 가는 곳에 너희는 올 수 없다.'

34 내가 너희에게 새 계명을 준다. 서로 사랑하여라. 내가 너희를 사랑한 것처럼 너희도 서로 사랑하여라.

35 너희가 서로 사랑하면, 모든 사람이 그것을 보고 너희가 내 제자라는 것을 알게 될 것이다."

베드로가 당신을 모른다고 할 것을 예고하시다(마태 26,31-35; 마르 14,27-31; 루카 22,31-34)

36 시몬 베드로가 예수님께 "주님, 어디로 가십니까?" 하고 물었다. 예수님께서는 그에게, "내가 가는 곳에 네가 지금은 따라올 수 없다. 그러나 나중에는 따라오게 될 것이다." 하고 대답하셨다.

37 베드로가 다시 "주님, 어찌하여 지금은 주님을 따라갈 수 없습니까? 주님을 위해서라면 저는

목숨까지 내놓겠습니다." 하자,

38 예수님께서 대답하셨다. "나를 위하여 목숨을 내놓겠다는 말이냐? 내가 진실로 진실로 너에게 말한다. 닭이 울기 전에 너는 세 번이나 나를 모른다고 할 것이다."

The Book of Glory

The Washing of the Disciples' Feet

John Chapter 13

1 Before the feast of Passover, Jesus knew that his hour had come to pass from this world to the Father. He loved his own in the world and he loved them to the end. 2 The devil had already induced Judas, son of Simon the Iscariot, to hand him over. So, during supper, 3 fully aware that the Father had put everything into his power and that he had come from God and was returning to God, 4 he rose from supper and took off his outer garments. He took a towel and tied it around his waist. 5 Then he poured water into a basin and began to wash the disciples' feet and dry them with the towel around his waist. 6 He came to Simon Peter, who said to him, "Master, are you going to wash my feet?" 7 Jesus answered and said to him, "What I am doing, you do not understand now, but you will understand later." 8 Peter said to him, "You will never wash my feet." Jesus answered him, "Unless I wash you, you will have no inheritance with me." 9 Simon Peter said to him, "Master, then not only my feet, but my hands and head as well." 10 Jesus said to him, "Whoever has bathed has no need except to have his feet washed, for he is clean all over; so you are clean, but not all." 11 For he knew who would betray him; for this reason, he said, "Not all of you are clean." 12 So when he had washed their feet (and) put his garments back on and reclined at table again, he said to them, "Do you realize what I have done for you? 13 You call me 'teacher' and 'master,' and rightly so, for indeed I am. 14 If I, therefore, the master and teacher, have washed your feet, you ought to wash one another's feet. 15 I have given you a model to follow, so that as I have done for you, you should also do. 16 Amen, amen, I say to you, no slave is greater than his master nor any messenger greater than the one who sent him. 17 If you understand this, blessed are you if you do it. 18 I am not speaking of all of you. I know those whom I have chosen. But so that the scripture might be fulfilled, 'The one who ate

my food has raised his heel against me.' 19 From now on I am telling you before it happens, so that when it happens you may believe that I AM. 20 Amen, amen, I say to you, whoever receives the one I send receives me, and whoever receives me receives the one who sent me."

Announcement of Judas' Betrayal

21 When he had said this, Jesus was deeply troubled and testified, "Amen, amen, I say to you, one of you will betray me." 22 The disciples looked at one another, at a loss as to whom he meant. 23 One of his disciples, the one whom Jesus loved, was reclining at Jesus' side. 24 So Simon Peter nodded to him to find out whom he meant. 25 He leaned back against Jesus' chest and said to him, "Master, who is it?" 26 Jesus answered, "It is the one to whom I hand the morsel after I have dipped it." So he dipped the morsel and (took it and) handed it to Judas, son of Simon the Iscariot. 27 After he took the morsel, Satan entered him. So Jesus said to him, "What you are going to do, do quickly." 28 (Now) none of those reclining at table realized why he said this to him. 29 Some thought that since Judas kept the money bag, Jesus had told him, "Buy what we need for the feast," or to give something to the poor. 30 So he took the morsel and left at once. And it was night.

The New Commandment

31 When he had left, Jesus said, "Now is the Son of Man glorified, and God is glorified in him. 32 (If God is glorified in him,) God will also glorify him in himself, and he will glorify him at once.33 My children, I will be with you only a little while longer. You will look for me, and as I told the Jews, 'Where I go you cannot come,' so now I say it to you. 34 I give you a new commandment: love one another. As I have loved you, so you also should love one another. 35 This is how all will know that you are my disciples, if you have love for one another."

Peter's Denial Predicted

36 Simon Peter said to him, "Master, where are you going?" Jesus answered (him), "Where I am going, you cannot follow me now, though you will follow later." 37 Peter said to him, "Master, why can't I follow you now? I will lay down my life for you." 38 Jesus answered, "Will you lay down your life for me? Amen, amen, I say to you, the cock will not crow before you deny me three times."

(1절)Before the feast of Passover.파스카 축제 전에. Before the beginning of the Passover Feast.파스카 축제가 시작되기 전. pass, (go, pass, cross, put) over, (get, go) across.건너가다. his own(people).그분 자신의 사람들. (2절)The devil had already induced Judas, son of Simon the Iscariot, to hand him over.악마가 이미 시몬 이스카리옷의 아들 유다가 예수님을 넘겨주도록 꾀었다(설득하였다). induce(indjú:s). 에게 ~을 하게(권유)하다, 꾀다, (설득, 권)하여 ~시키다(persuade). It is (a matter, a thing, an affair) during the supper.만찬 때의 일이다. to hand him over.예수님을 넘겨줄. to betray.을 팔아넘기다, (배신, 배반, 밀고)하다, 드러내다. inspire, imbue, instill, infuse, put. 불어넣다. It is a matter during the supper. The devil had already infused thoughts into Judas' heart, son of Simon the Iscariot, to sell off him.만찬때의 일이다 악마가 이미 시몬 이스카리옷의 아들 유다의 마음속에 예수님을 팔아넘길 생각을 불어넣었다. in one's power.(권능, 수중, 지배 하, 손안)에. The devil had already induced Judas, son of Simon the Iscariot, to hand him over. So, during supper, fully aware that the Father had put everything into his power and that he had come from God and was returning to God.악마가 예수님을 (최고의회에) 넘겨주도록 시몬 이스카리옷의 아들 유다를 이미 유인하였다. 그래서 만찬 중(때)에 예수님께서는 아버지께서 모든 것을 당신 수중(손)에 내주셨다는 것과 당신이 하느님에게서 나왔다가 하느님께 돌아간다는 것을 (충분, 완전)히 아시고. (4절)~he rose from supper.예수님께서는 만찬(자리)에서 일어나시어. wrap, put around, enclose, encircle, surround.싸서 두르다, 두르다. wear about(one), wrap, put. 옷을 두르다, 감싸다, 걸치다. tie.묶다, 매다. ~he got up from the table.예수님께서는 식탁에서 일어나시어. (5절)And.그리고. then.그런 다음에, 그리고 나서, 그 후에, 그래서. ~with the towel that was wrapped around his waist.허리에 두르신 수건. (6절)그렇게 하여.Redundant번역임. Master→ Lord. (7절)understand→ (know, realize) (8절)그래도. Redundant번역임. ~you will have no inheritance with me.나와 함께 상속을 받지 못할 것이다. ~you will not receive any share with me that are divided up.나와 함께 아무런 몫도 나누어 받지 못한다. (9절)Then.문장 서두에 나오면 대개, 그러자. 여기서는 Master뒤에 나왔으므로 "주님 그렇다면"으로 번역되어야 함. (10절)need only to, have only to, all one has to do is (to), only have to.단지 ~하기만 하면 된다. Whoever has bathed has no need except to have his feet washed, for he is clean all over.→ A person who has bathed, as his whole body is clean, needs only to wash his feet. (11절)For he already knew.(사실, 실상, 과연) 예수님께서는 이미 ~알고 계셨다. for this reason.이러한 이유로 해서, 이러한 이유 때문에, 이 때문에, 그래서. (12절)when이 부사절을 만들 때: 하고, 할 때, 하고 나서, 하니, 하자, 하면. So when he had washed.그래서 예수님께서는(제자들의 발을) 씻어 주시고 (의역, 씻어 주신 다음). After he had washed.예수님께서는(제자들의 발을)씻어

주신 다음. (13절)Master; Lord. ~for indeed I am.사실 나는 정말로 그러하다. (14절) therefore.그러므로. (15절)give you a model= set you an example.좋은 모범을 보이다, 본을 보여주다. I have given you a model to follow, so that as I have done for you, you should also do.내가 너희가 따라야할 본을 보여주었으므로 너희도 내가 너희에게 한 것처럼 하여야 한다. I have given you a model that you should do as I have done for you.내가 너희에게 한 것처럼 너희도 하라고, 내가 본을 보여 준 것이다. (16절)messenger(mésindʒər). 직업적으로 메시지를 전하는 전달자, 전령, 심부름꾼, 배달원, 파견된 (사람, 사자). (17절)do it.(실천, 실행)하다. understand→ know. (18절)I am not referring to all of you.내가 너희를 모두 가리켜 말하는 것은 아니다. (raised, lifted) his heel against me.나를 발로 차다; 의역 (배신하다). (raise, lift) the heel against, lift up one's heel against.을 발로 차다, 을 뒷발로 걷어차려 하다, 괴롭히다. raised his heel against me.나를 거슬러 발꿈치를 들었다; 의역, 나를 배반하였다. food→ bread. But so that the scripture might be fulfilled, "The one who ate my food has raised his heel against me"→ But the scripture should be fulfilled, "He who used to eat my bread has raised his heel against me" (19절) from now on.앞으로는(쪽), (지금, 이제, 다음)부터(는). Be more careful from now on.다음부터 더욱 조심해라. From now on I am telling you before it happens.이제부터 (그것, 그런 일)이 일어나기 전에 미리 너희에게 말해 주고 있는 것이다. I am distracted now. 이제 제 마음이 산란합니다. (21절)When= After.하고 나서, 한 다음에. ~was deeply troubled.몹시 (괴로워, 번민)하시며. 번민하다(마음이 번거롭고 답답하여 괴로워하다). (23절) side→ chest. 여기서 his side는 "예수님의 옆에"라는 뜻임. (=was reclining next to Him). (24절)to find out→ to ask. (25절)leaned back.기대다, 뒤로 젖혀 ~에게 기대다. He leaned back against Jesus' chest and said to him.그가 예수님의 가슴에 기대며 말하였다. The disciple got closer to Jesus and asked him.그 제자가 예수님께 더 다가가 ~ 하고 물었다. (26절)hand= give. morsel(mɔ:sl)작은 (양, 조각). morsel→ bread. So→ And after. handed→ gave. (27절)After. 받은 후에. When or As soon as.받자. So Jesus.그래서 예수님께서. Then(At that time) Jesus.그때에 예수님께서. (28절)Now. 그런데. (30절)So he.그러자 유다는. After he.유다는 빵을 받고. ~left at once→ ~went out at once. And it was night.그런데 때는 밤이었다. (31절)When he had left.유다가 떠나(자, 고, 니). After he had gone out.유다가 나간 뒤에. ~is glorified in him.사람의 아들로 말미암아 영광스럽게 되셨다. in.~로(인해, 말미암아). ~is glorified through him.사람의 아들을 통하여 영광스럽게 되셨다. (32절)in oneself, personally, in person, in body, in the flesh.몸소, 친히. Miss June Thompson has heard that the king is coming here in the flesh.쥰 탐슨양은 왕이 몸소 이곳으로 오신다고 들었다. in himself.몸소, 자기 자신의, 자기 자신을 통하여. (33절)a little while longer.조금 더, 좀 더, 아주 (잠깐, 잠시) 동안, 잠시. My children ~.내 애들아, ~

그래서 이제 너희에게도. (34절)~것처럼 너희도 또한 그렇게 서로 사랑하여야 한다. (35절) If you love one another, all men will see it and will know that you are my disciples. 너희가 서로 사랑하면, 모든 사람이 그것을 보고 너희가 내 제자라는 것을 알게 될 것이다. This is how all will know that you are my disciples, if you have love for one another.너희가 서로 사랑하면 그것 때문에 모든 사람이 너희가 내 제자라는 것을 알게 될 것이다. This is how. 이렇습니다, 이렇게 하였습니다. 이것 때문에 ~하였다. 이렇게 해서 ~하였다, 이것이 ~한 방법입니다. (사연, 사단)은 이러하다, 이런 식으로 ~했다, 과정은 이렇습니다, 이리하여 된 것이다. (37절)~said to → asked. (38절)~before the cock crows, you will deny me three times.닭이 울기 전에 너는 세번이나 나를 모른다고 할 것이다. deny(dinái).사실이 아니라고 말하다, (부인, 부정, 거부, 거절)하다, (인정하지, 받아들이지, 허락하지) 않다. I read the Bible three times in all.저는 성경을 다해서 세 번이나 읽었어요.

Footnotes

(13:1-19:42절)The Book of Glory. There is a major break here; the word "sign" is used again only in John 20:30. In this phase of Jesus' return to the Father, the discourses (John 13-17) precede the traditional narrative of the passion (John 18-20) to interpret them for the Christian reader. This is the only extended example of esoteric(esətérik 비밀의, 은밀한, 심원한, 난해한) teaching of disciples in John. (1-20절)Washing of the disciples' feet. This episode occurs in John at the place of the narration of the institution of the Eucharist in the synoptics. It may be a dramatization of Luke 22:27--"I am your servant." It is presented as a "model" ("pattern") of the crucifixion. It symbolizes cleansing from sin by sacrificial death. (1절)Before the feast of Passover: this would be Thursday evening, before the day of preparation; in the synoptics, the Last Supper is a Passover meal taking place, in John's chronology, on Friday evening. To the end: or, "completely." (2절)Induced: literally, "The devil put into the heart that Judas should hand him over." (5절)The act of washing another's feet was one that could not be required of the lowliest Jewish slave. It is an allusion to the humiliating death of the crucifixion.(10절)Bathed: many have suggested that this passage is a symbolic reference to baptism. The Greek root involved is used in baptismal contexts in 1 Cor 6:11; Eph 5:26; Titus 3:5; Hebrews 10:22. (16절) Messenger: the Greek has apostolos, the only occurrence of the term in John. It is not used in the technical sense here. (23절)The one whom Jesus loved: also mentioned in John 19:26; 20:2; 21:7. A disciple, called "another disciple" or "the other disciple," is mentioned in John 18:15 and John 20:2; in the latter reference he is identified with the disciple whom Jesus loved. There is also an unnamed disciple in John 1:35-40; see the note on John 1:37. (26절)Morsel: probably the bitter herb dipped in salt water. (13:31-17:26절)Two farewell discourses and a prayer. These seem to be Johannine compositions, including sayings of Jesus at the Last

Supper and on other occasions, modeled on similar farewell discourses in Greek literature and the Old Testament (of Moses, Joshua, David). (31-38절)Introduction: departure and return. Terms of coming and going redominate. These verses form an introduction to the last discourse of Jesus, which extends through John 14-17. In it John has collected Jesus' words to his own (John 13:1). There are indications that several speeches have been fused together, e.g., in John 14:31 and John 17:1. (34절)I give you a new commandment: this puts Jesus on a par with Yahweh. The commandment itself is not new; cf Lev 19:18 and the note there.

요한복음서 14장

아버지께 가는 길

1 "너희 마음이 산란해지는 일이 없도록 하여라. 하느님을 믿고 또 나를 믿어라.

2 내 아버지의 집에는 거처할 곳이 많다. 그렇지 않으면 내가 너희를 위하여 자리를 마련하러 간다고 말하였겠느냐?

3 내가 가서 너희를 위하여 자리를 마련하면, 다시 와서 너희를 데려다가 내가 있는 곳에 너희도 같이 있게 하겠다.

4 너희는 내가 어디로 가는지 그 길을 알고 있다."

5 그러자 토마스가 예수님께 말하였다. "주님, 저희는 주님께서 어디로 가시는지 알지도 못하는데, 어떻게 그 길을 알 수 있겠습니까?"

6 예수님께서 그에게 말씀하셨다. "나는 길이요 진리요 생명이다. 나를 통하지 않고서는 아무도 아버지께 갈 수 없다.

7 너희가 나를 알게 되었으니 내 아버지도 알게 될 것이다. 이제부터 너희는 그분을 아는 것이고, 또 그분을 이미 뵌 것이다."

8 필립보가 예수님께, "주님, 저희가 아버지를 뵙게 해 주십시오. 저희에게는 그것으로 충분하겠습니다." 하자,

9 예수님께서 그에게 말씀하셨다. "필립보야, 내가 이토록 오랫동안 너희와 함께 지냈는데도, 너는 나를 모른다는 말이냐? 나를 본 사람은 곧 아버지를 뵌 것이다. 그런데 너는 어찌하여 '저희가 아버지를 뵙게 해 주십시오.' 하느냐?

10 내가 아버지 안에 있고 아버지께서 내 안에 계시다는 것을 너는 믿지 않느냐? 내가 너희에게 하는 말은 나 스스로 하는 말이 아니다. 내 안에 머무르시는 아버지께서 당신의 일을 하시는 것이다.

11 내가 아버지 안에 있고 아버지께서 내 안에 계시다고 한 말을 믿어라. 믿지 못하겠거든 이 일들을 보아서라도 믿어라.

12 내가 진실로 진실로 너희에게 말한다. 나를 믿는 사람은 내가 하는 일을 할 뿐만 아니라, 그보다 더 큰 일도 하게 될 것이다. 내가 아버지께 가기 때문이다.

13 너희가 내 이름으로 청하는 것은 무엇이든지 내가 다 이루어 주겠다. 그리하여 아버지께서 아들을 통하여 영광스럽게 되시도록 하겠다.

14 너희가 내 이름으로 청하면 내가 다 이루어 주겠다."

성령을 약속하시다

15 "너희가 나를 사랑하면 내 계명을 지킬 것이다.

16 그리고 내가 아버지께 청하면, 아버지께서는 다른 보호자를 너희에게 보내시어, 영원히 너희와 함께 있도록 하실 것이다.

17 그분은 진리의 영이시다. 세상은 그분을 보지도 못하고 알지도 못하기 때문에 그분을 받아들이지 못하지만, 너희는 그분을 알고 있다. 그분께서 너희와 함께 머무르시고 너희 안에 계시기 때문이다.

18 나는 너희를 고아로 버려두지 않고 너희에게 다시 오겠다.

19 이제 조금만 있으면, 세상은 나를 보지 못하겠지만 너희는 나를 보게 될 것이다. 내가 살아 있고 너희도 살아 있을 것이기 때문이다.

20 그날, 너희는 내가 아버지 안에 있고 또 너희가 내 안에 있으며 내가 너희 안에 있음을 깨닫게 될 것이다.

21 내 계명을 받아 지키는 이야말로 나를 사랑하는 사람이다. 나를 사랑하는 사람은 내 아버지께 사랑을 받을 것이다. 그리고 나도 그를 사랑하고 그에게 나 자신을 드러내 보일 것이다."

22 이스카리옷이 아닌 다른 유다가 예수님께, "주님, 저희에게는 주님 자신을 드러내시고 세상에는 드러내지 않으시겠다니 무슨 까닭입니까?" 하자,

23 예수님께서 그에게 대답하셨다. "누구든지 나를 사랑하면 내 말을 지킬 것이다. 그러면 내 아버지께서 그를 사랑하시고, 우리가 그에게 가서 그와 함께 살 것이다.

24 그러나 나를 사랑하지 않는 사람은 내 말을 지키지 않는다. 너희가 듣는 말은 내 말이 아니라 나를 보내신 아버지의 말씀이다.

25 나는 너희와 함께 있는 동안에 이것들을 이야기하였다.

26 보호자, 곧 아버지께서 내 이름으로 보내실 성령께서 너희에게 모든 것을 가르치시고 내가 너희에게 말한 모든 것을 기억하게 해 주실 것이다.

27 나는 너희에게 평화를 남기고 간다. 내 평화를 너희에게 준다. 내가 주는 평화는 세상이 주는 평화와 같지 않다. 너희 마음이 산란해지는 일도, 겁을 내는 일도 없도록 하여라.

28 '나는 갔다가 너희에게 돌아온다.'고 한 내 말을 너희는 들었다. 너희가 나를 사랑한다면 내가 아버지께 가는 것을 기뻐할 것이다. 아버지께서 나보다 위대하신 분이시기 때문이다.

29 나는 일이 일어나기 전에 너희에게 미리 말하였다. 일이 일어날 때에 너희가 믿게 하려는 것이다.

30 나는 너희와 더 이상 많은 이야기를 나누지 않겠다. 이 세상의 우두머리가 오고 있기 때문이다. 그는 나에게 아무 권한도 없다.

31 그러나 내가 아버지를 사랑한다는 것과 아버지께서 명령하신 대로 내가 한다는 것을 세상이 알아야 한다. 일어나 가자."

Last Supper Discourse

John Chapter 14

1 "Do not let your hearts be troubled. You have faith in God; have faith also in me. 2 In my Father's house there are many dwelling places. If there were not, would I have told you that I am going to prepare a place for you? 3 And if I go and prepare a place for you, I will come back again and take you to myself, so that where I am you also may be. 4 Where (I) am going you know the way." 5 Thomas said to him, "Master, we do not know where you are going; how can we know the way?" 6 Jesus said to him, "I am the way and the truth and the life. No one comes to the Father except through me. 7 If you know me, then you will also know my Father. From now on you do know him and have seen him." 8 Philip said to him, "Master, show us the Father, and that will be enough for us." 9 Jesus said to him, "Have I been with you for so long a time and you still do not know me, Philip? Whoever has seen me has seen the Father. How can you say, 'Show us the Father'? 10 Do you not believe that I am in the Father and the Father is in me? The words that I speak to you I do not speak on my own. The Father who dwells in me is doing his works. 11 Believe me that I am in the Father and the Father is in me, or else, believe because of the works themselves. 12 Amen, amen, I say to you, whoever believes in me will do the works that I do, and will do greater ones than these, because I am going to the Father. 13 And whatever you ask in my name, I will do, so that the Father may be glorified in the Son. 14 If you ask anything of me in my name, I will do it.

The Advocate

15 "If you love me, you will keep my commandments. 16 And I will ask the Father, and he will give you another Advocate to be with you always, 17 the Spirit of truth, which the world cannot accept, because it neither sees nor knows it. But you know it, because it remains with you, and will be in you. 18 I will not leave you orphans; I will come to you. 19 In a little while the world will no longer see me, but you will see me, because I live and you will live. 20 On that day you will realize that I am in my Father and you are in me and I in you. 21 Whoever has my commandments and observes them is the one who loves me. And whoever loves me will be loved by my Father, and I will love him and reveal myself to him." 22 Judas, not the Iscariot, said to him, "Master, (then) what happened that you will reveal yourself to us and not to

the world?" 23 Jesus answered and said to him, "Whoever loves me will keep my word, and my Father will love him, and we will come to him and make our dwelling with him. 24 Whoever does not love me does not keep my words; yet the word you hear is not mine but that of the Father who sent me. 25 "I have told you this while I am with you. 26 The Advocate, the holy Spirit that the Father will send in my name-- he will teach you everything and remind you of all that (I) told you. 27 Peace I leave with you; my peace I give to you. Not as the world gives do I give it to you. Do not let your hearts be troubled or afraid. 28 You heard me tell you, 'I am going away and I will come back to you.' If you loved me, you would rejoice that I am going to the Father; for the Father is greater than I. 29 And now I have told you this before it happens, so that when it happens you may believe. 30 I will no longer speak much with you, for the ruler of the world is coming. He has no power over me, 31 but the world must know that I love the Father and that I do just as the Father has commanded me. Get up, let us go.

(1절)be troubled.(걱정, 괴로워, 불안해, 근심)하다, 고통을 받다, 힘든, 문제가 많은, 뒤숭숭한. become deeply moved.깊이 감동을 받다, 몹시 동요되다. perturbed.(동요, 심란하게) 되다. (surge, spring, well, gush)up.북받치다. distracted, deranged.산란하다. have faith in.을 (믿고 있다, 믿다), (신앙, 확신)하다. believe in God.= have faith in God.하느님을 믿다. 여기서 You have= Have.명령문임. 보통 You가 생략됨. (2절)If there were not, would I have told you that I am going to prepare a place for you?가정법 과거로 현재의 사실과 반대 개념을 나타냄. (3절)And.그런데. ~take you to myself.너희를 나에게로 데려다가 (너희 도 같이 있게 하겠다). 여기서 "같이"는 redundant번역임. (5절)Then.그러자. (7절)If.~할 때는 (언제든지, 언제나), ~한다면. if.현재형을 써서 현재나 미래에 관한 추측을 나타냄. If you know me, then you will also know my Father.(너희가 나를 알 때에는 언제든지, 너희가 나를 안다면) 동시에 너희가 내 아버지도 알게 될 것이다. then은 여기서 "동시에"로 번역됨. ~이미 뵌 것이다. 여기서 "이미"는 redundant번역임. (8절)~저희에게 아버지를 보여주십시오. (9절) Even after.그렇게 까지 했는데. Jesus said to him, "Philip, don't you know me, even after I have been with you for so long a time? Whoever.~하는 사람은 누구나(anyone who), 누가 ~이라도(no matter who). He who.~사람은 (본 것이다). (10절)on one's(his) own.스스로, 혼자서, 자기 나름대로, 자기 (생각, 혼자 힘, 독단, 단독)으로. (11절)명령문 뒤에서 종종 or else는 부정 조건의 결과를 나타냄. 그렇지 (않으면, 않다면), ~이 아니면. (13 절)And. 그리고. in the Son.아들로 (말미암아, 인해). through the Son.아들을 통하여. through.통하여, (원인, 동기, 이유) ~ 때문에, 말미암아, 인해, ~의 이유로(by reason of). (14

절) I will do it.내가 해 주겠다. 의역: 내가 다 이루어 주겠다. (16절)And I will ask the Father, and he will give you another Advocate to be with you always그리고 내가 아버지께 청할 것이다, 그러면(만약 그리하면) 아버지께서는 다른 보호자를 너희와 항상 함께 있도록 보내 주실 것이다. 두번째 and는 명령법 또는 그에 상당하는 어구 다음에 써서 "만약 그리하면, 그러면, 할 터인데"의 뜻으로 쓰임. always→ forever. (18절)~to you again. (21절)have.~을 (얻, 받, 사)다. have a part in a play.연극에서 배역을 받다. (22절)What happened? 무슨 일이니? 무슨 일인가요? 어떻게 된 (겁, 일 입)니까? 어떻게 된 영문인가! Why is it?, why, Why is it that, How's that, How is it, for what reason, on what ground, for some reason.무슨 까닭이냐?, 무슨 까닭으로. Why is it that: that이하가 무슨 까닭이냐? 여기서 "무슨 까닭 입니까?로 번역된 것은 Why is it that을 번역한 것임. (23절)make a dwelling.거처를 만들다. make a home.가정을 (이루다, 가지다). ~and live with him.그와 함께 살 것이다. (24절)Whoever→ But he who. yet.그러나. (25절)this→ these. (26절)remind.상기시키다, 생각나게 하다, 기억하도록 다시 한 번 알려주다. remind A of B. A에게 B를 생각나게 하다. (27절)Peace I leave with you.나는 너희에게 평화를 남겨준다. 의역: 평화를 남기고 간다. 마음이 산란해지는 일도→ 마음에 (근심, 괴로워)하는 일도. (28절) I am going away.나는 떠나 갈 것이다. (29절)and now.그리고 (지금, 이제, 당장). (30절)the head, the chief, the chieftain, the top, a leader, the boss, the commander.우두머리, 사령관, 장(長). ruler: 통치자.

Footnotes

(1-31절)Jesus' departure and return. This section is a dialogue marked off by a literary inclusion in John 14:1, 27: "Do not let your hearts be troubled." (1절)You have faith: could also be imperative: "Have faith." (3절)Come back again: a rare Johannine reference to the parousia; cf 1 John 2:28. (4절)The way: here, of Jesus himself; also a designation of Christianity in Acts 9:2; 19:9, 23; 22:4; 24:14, 22. (6절)The truth: in John, the divinely revealed reality of the Father manifested in the person and works of Jesus. The possession of truth confers knowledge and liberation from sin (John 8:32). (7절)An alternative reading, "If you knew me, then you would have known my Father also," would be a rebuke, as in John 8:19. (8절)Show us the Father: Philip is pictured asking for a theophany like Exodus 24:9-10; 33:18. (16절)Another Advocate: Jesus is the first advocate (paraclete); see 1 John 2:1, where Jesus is an advocate in the sense of intercessor in heaven. The Greek term derives from legal terminology for an advocate or defense attorney, and can mean spokesman, mediator, intercessor, comforter, consoler, although no one of these terms encompasses the meaning in John. The Paraclete in John is a teacher, a witness to Jesus, and a prosecutor of the world, who represents the continued presence on earth of the Jesus who has returned to the Father. (17절)The Spirit of truth: this term is also used at Qumran, where it is a moral force put into a person by God, as opposed to the spirit of perversity. It is more personal in John; it will teach the realities of the new order (John 14:26), and testify to the truth (John 14:6). While it has been customary to use masculine personal pronouns in English for the Advocate, the Greek word for "spirit" is neuter, and the Greek text and manuscript variants fluctuate between masculine and neuter pronouns.(18절)I will come to you: indwelling, not parousia. (22절)Judas, not the Iscariot: probably not the brother of Jesus in Mark 6:3 // Matthew 13:55 or the apostle named Jude in Luke 6:16 but Thomas (see the note on John 11:16), although other readings have "Judas the Cananean." (27절)Peace: the traditional Hebrew salutation salom; but Jesus' "Shalom" is a gift of salvation, connoting the bounty of messianic blessing. (28절)The Father is greater than I: because he sent, gave, etc., and Jesus is "a man who has told you the truth that I heard from God" (John 8:40). (30절)The ruler of the world: Satan; cf John 12:31; 16:11.

요한복음서 15장

나는 참포도나무다

1 "나는 참포도나무요 나의 아버지는 농부이시다.

2 나에게 붙어 있으면서 열매를 맺지 않는 가지는 아버지께서 다 쳐 내시고, 열매를 맺는 가지는 모두 깨끗이 손질하시어 더 많은 열매를 맺게 하신다.

3 너희는 내가 너희에게 한 말로 이미 깨끗하게 되었다.

4 내 안에 머물러라. 나도 너희 안에 머무르겠다. 가지가 포도나무에 붙어 있지 않으면 스스로 열매를 맺을 수 없는 것처럼, 너희도 내 안에 머무르지 않으면 열매를 맺지 못한다.

5 나는 포도나무요 너희는 가지다. 내 안에 머무르고 나도 그 안에 머무르는 사람은 많은 열매를 맺는다. 너희는 나 없이 아무것도 하지 못한다.

6 내 안에 머무르지 않으면 잘린 가지처럼 밖에 던져져 말라 버린다. 그러면 사람들이 그런 가지들을 모아 불에 던져 태워 버린다.

7 너희가 내 안에 머무르고 내 말이 너희 안에 머무르면, 너희가 원하는 것은 무엇이든지 청하여라. 너희에게 그대로 이루어질 것이다.

8 너희가 많은 열매를 맺고 내 제자가 되면, 그것으로 내 아버지께서 영광스럽게 되실 것이다.

9 아버지께서 나를 사랑하신 것처럼 나도 너희를 사랑하였다. 너희는 내 사랑 안에 머물러라.

10 내가 내 아버지의 계명을 지켜 그분의 사랑 안에 머무르는 것처럼, 너희도 내 계명을 지키면 내 사랑 안에 머무를 것이다.

11 내가 너희에게 이 말을 한 이유는, 내 기쁨이 너희 안에 있고 또 너희 기쁨이 충만하게 하려는 것이다.

12 이것이 나의 계명이다. 내가 너희를 사랑한 것처럼 너희도 서로 사랑하여라.

13 친구들을 위하여 목숨을 내놓는 것보다 더 큰 사랑은 없다.

14 내가 너희에게 명령하는 것을 실천하면 너희는 나의 친구가 된다.

15 나는 너희를 더 이상 종이라고 부르지 않는다. 종은 주인이 하는 일을 모르기 때문이다. 나는 너희를 친구라고 불렀다. 내가 내 아버지에게서 들은 것을 너희에게 모두 알려 주었기 때문이다.

16 너희가 나를 뽑은 것이 아니라 내가 너희를 뽑아 세웠다. 너희가 가서 열매를 맺어 너희의 그 열매가 언제나 남아 있게 하려는 것이다. 그리하여 너희가 내 이름으로 아버지께 청하는 것을 그분께서 너희에게 주시게 하려는 것이다.

17 내가 너희에게 명령하는 것은 이것이다. 서로 사랑하여라."

세상이 너희를 미워할 것이다

18 "세상이 너희를 미워하거든 너희보다 먼저 나를 미워하였다는 것을 알아라.

19 너희가 세상에 속한다면 세상은 너희를 자기 사람으로 사랑할 것이다. 그러나 너희가 세상에

속하지 않을 뿐만 아니라 내가 너희를 세상에서 뽑았기 때문에, 세상이 너희를 미워하는 것이다.

20 '종은 주인보다 높지 않다.'고 내가 너희에게 한 말을 기억하여라. 사람들이 나를 박해하였으면 너희도 박해할 것이고, 내 말을 지켰으면 너희 말도 지킬 것이다.

21 그러나 그들은 내 이름 때문에 너희에게 그 모든 일을 저지를 것이다. 그들이 나를 보내신 분을 알지 못하기 때문이다.

22 내가 와서 그들에게 말하지 않았으면 그들은 죄가 없었을 것이다. 그러나 이제는 자기들의 죄를 변명할 구실이 없다.

23 나를 미워하는 자는 내 아버지까지 미워한다.

24 일찍이 다른 그 누구도 하지 못한 일들을 내가 그들 가운데에서 하지 않았으면, 그들은 죄가 없었을 것이다. 그러나 그들은 내가 한 일을 보고 나와 내 아버지까지 미워하였다.

25 이는 그들의 율법에 '그들은 까닭 없이 저를 미워하였습니다.'라고 기록된 말이 이루어지려고 그리된 것이다.

26 내가 아버지에게서 너희에게로 보낼 보호자, 곧 아버지에게서 나오시는 진리의 영이 오시면, 그분께서 나를 증언하실 것이다.

27 그리고 너희도 처음부터 나와 함께 있었으므로 나를 증언할 것이다."

The Vine and the Branches

John Chapter 15

1 "I am the true vine, and my Father is the vine grower. 2 He takes away every branch in me that does not bear fruit, and everyone that does he prunes so that it bears more fruit. 3 You are already pruned because of the word that I spoke to you. 4 Remain in me, as I remain in you. Just as a branch cannot bear fruit on its own unless it remains on the vine, so neither can you unless you remain in me. 5 I am the vine, you are the branches. Whoever remains in me and I in him will bear much fruit, because without me you can do nothing. 6 Anyone who does not remain in me will be thrown out like a branch and wither; people will gather them and throw them into a fire and they will be burned. 7 If you remain in me and my words remain in you, ask for whatever you want and it will be done for you. 8 By this is my Father glorified, that you bear much fruit and become my disciples. 9 As the Father loves me, so I also love you. Remain in my love. 10 If you keep my commandments, you will remain in my love, just as I have kept my Father's commandments and remain in his love. 11 "I have told you this so that my joy may be in you and your joy may be complete. 12

This is my commandment: love one another as I love you. 13 No one has greater love than this, to lay down one's life for one's friends. 14 You are my friends if you do what I command you. 15 I no longer call you slaves, because a slave does not know what his master is doing. I have called you friends, because I have told you everything I have heard from my Father.16 It was not you who chose me, but I who chose you and appointed you to go and bear fruit that will remain, so that whatever you ask the Father in my name he may give you.17 This I command you: love one another.

The World's Hatred

18 "If the world hates you, realize that it hated me first. 19 If you belonged to the world, the world would love its own; but because you do not belong to the world, and I have chosen you out of the world, the world hates you. 20 Remember the word I spoke to you, 'No slave is greater than his master.' If they persecuted me, they will also persecute you. If they kept my word, they will also keep yours. 21 And they will do all these things to you on account of my name, because they do not know the one who sent me. 22 If I had not come and spoken to them, they would have no sin; but as it is they have no excuse for their sin. 23 Whoever hates me also hates my Father. 24 If I had not done works among them that no one else ever did, they would not have sin; but as it is, they have seen and hated both me and my Father. 25 But in order that the word written in their law might be fulfilled, 'They hated me without cause.' 26 "When the Advocate comes whom I will send you from the Father, the Spirit of truth that proceeds from the Father, he will testify to me. 27 And you also testify, because you have been with me from the beginning.

(1절)vine= grapevine.포도나무, 포도덩굴. grower.재배자, 경작자, 자라는 식물. fast or quick(slow) grower.(조생, 만생)식물. (2절)cuts off.자르다, 잘라내다, 쳐내다. take away. 없애다, 없애주다. prune.가지치기 하다, 전지하다, 가지를 (쳐내, 잘라내, 치)다. handle with care, care for, trim, repair, mend, do up, fix up, patch up, give it a clean.손질하다. (3절)~already pruned.→ ~already clean. (4절)~as I remain in you.→ ~and I will remain in you.나도 너희 안에 머무르겠다. 여기서 and는 명령문 또는 그에 상당하는 어구 다음의 용법으로써, "그러면, 만약 그리하면"으로 번역되어야 함; 그러면 내가 너희 안에 머무르겠다. stick to, adhere to, cling to.붙다, 붙어있다. Remain in me= Abide in me.내 안에 머무르라. (5절)Whoever→ ~He who. ~because without me you can do nothing.왜냐하면 너희는 나 없이 아무것도 할 수 없기 때문이다(하지 못한다). 5절에서 because없이 without(apart from) me.로 시작되는 문장을 번역하였음. (6절)Anyone who does not remain in me will be thrown out like a branch and wither.→ If anyone does not remain in me, like a branch that is cut off, is thrown out and withers. (7절)be done.이루어지다. (8절)By this is my Father glorified, that you bear much fruit and become my disciples.→ If you bear much fruit and become my disciples, my Father will be glorified by this. (11절)complete.완벽한, 완전한. be full of, be filled with, replete.충만하다. I have told you this so that~ → The reason why I have told you this(words) is that~. (13절)one.총칭 인칭임; 누구나, 사람, 세상사람. No one has greater love than this, to lay down one's life for one's friends.누구나 자신의 친구들을 위하여 목숨을 내 놓는 것, 그보다 더 큰 사랑을 지니지 못합니다. (14절)친구가 된다.→ 친구들이다. (16절)It was not you who chose me, but I who chose you and appointed you to go and bear fruit that will remain always.나를 뽑은 것이 너희가 아니고 너희를 뽑아 너희가 가서 언제나 남아있게 될 열매를 맺도록 임명한 것은 나였다(not ~but의 용법).→ You did not choose me, but I chose you and appointed, so that you may go and bear fruit that will remain always.너희가 나를 뽑은 것이 아니라 내가 너희를 뽑아 세웠다. (그리하여) 너희가 가서 열매를 맺어 너희의 그 열매가 언제나 남아있게 하려는 것이다. (18절)realize→ know. (19절)~love its own. → ~love you as its own. (21절)And. 그래서. (22절)have excuse for.을(를) 위해 변명하다, 핑게를 대다. as it is. 사실은, 있는 그대로, 정말로 말하면, (그러나)(실제로는, 사실), 실상은, 지금 대로도, 이대로. (24절)~but as it is, they have seen and hated both me and my Father.그러나 그들은 있는 그대로 보았으며 나와 나의 아버지를 미워하였다. ~but they have seen what I have done and have hated me and even my Father.그러나 그들은 내가 한일을 보고 나와 내 아버지까지 미워하였다. (25절)without (reason, good cause, sake), without provocation, causelessly.까닭 없이. But in order that the word written in their law might be fulfilled, "They hated me without cause." 하지만, "그들은 까닭 없이 저를 미워하였습니다."라고 그들의 율법에 기록된 말이 이루어지게 하려는 것이다(나와 나의 아버지를 미워하게 하려는 것이다).→ This has become so(become that way) in order that the word written in their law might be fulfilled, "They hated me without cause."이는 그들의 율법에 "그들은 까닭 없이 저를 미워하였습니다."라고 기록된 말이 이루어지려고 그리된 것이다. (26절)when이 부사절을 만들 때; 하니, 하자, 하면, 하고, 할 때에, 할 때는, 한 후에. proceed.생기다, (발생, 유래, 발)하다. ~that goes out from.아버지에게서 나오는. testify to(about) me.나(에 관하여, 에 대해, 를 위하여)증언하다. (27절)And you also testify, because you have been with me from the beginning.그리고 너희가 처음부터 나와 함께 있었으므로(있었기 때문에) 너희도 또한 나를 증언하여라. "you also testify"는 명령문임(=And also testify). 문맥상으로는 And you also must testify.의 뜻임. "나를 증언할 것이다"는 오역임. ~"(있었으므로, 있었기 때문에) 너희도 또한 나를 증언하여야만 한다."로 번역되어야 함.

Footnotes

(15:1-16:4절)Discourse on the union of Jesus with his disciples. His words become a monologue and go beyond the immediate crisis of the departure of Jesus.(1-17절)Like John 10:1-5, this passage resembles a parable. Israel is spoken of as a vineyard at Isaiah 5:1-7; Matthew 21:33-46 and as a vine at Psalm 80:9-17; Jeremiah 2:21; Ezekiel 15:2; 17:5-10; 19:10; Hosea 10:1. The identification of the vine as the Son of Man in Psalm 80:15 and Wisdom's description of herself as a vine in Sirach 24:17 are further background for portrayal of Jesus by this figure. There may be secondary eucharistic symbolism here; cf Mark 14:25 "the fruit of the vine." (2절) Takes away···prunes: in Greek there is a play on two related verbs. (6절)Branches were cut off and dried on the wall of the vineyard for later use as fuel.(13절)For one's friends: or: "those whom one loves." In John 15:9-13a, the words for love are related to the Greek agapao. In John 15:13b-15, the words for love are related to the Greek phileo. For John, the two roots seem synonymous and mean "to love"; cf also John 21:15-17. The word philos is used here. (15절) Slaves···friends: in the Old Testament, Moses (Deut 34:5), Joshua (Joshua 24:29), and David (Psalm 89:21) were called "servants" or "slaves of Yahweh"; only Abraham (Isaiah 41:8; 2 Chron 20:7; cf James 2:23) was called a "friend of God." (15:18-16:4절)The hostile reaction of the world. There are synoptic parallels, predicting persecution, especially at Matthew 10:17-25; 24:9-10. (20절)The word I spoke to you: a reference to John 13:16. (21절)On account of my name: the idea of persecution for Jesus' name is frequent in the New Testament (Matthew 10:22; 24:9; Acts 9:14). For John, association with Jesus' name implies union with Jesus. (22&24절)Jesus' words (spoken) and deeds)works) are the great motives of credibility. They have seen and hated: probably means that they have seen his works and still have hated; but the Greek can be read: "have seen both me and my Father and still have hated both me and my Father." Works···that no one else ever did: so Yahweh in Deut 4:32-33. (25절)In their law: law is here used as a larger concept than the Pentateuch, for the reference is to Psalm 35:19 or Psalm 69:5. See the notes on John 10:34; 12:34. Their law reflects the argument of the church with the synagogue. (26절)Whom I will send: in John 14:16, 26 the Paraclete is to be sent by the Father, at the request of Jesus. Here the Spirit comes from both Jesus and the Father in mission; there is no reference here to the eternal procession of the Spirit.

요한복음서 16장

1 "내가 너희에게 이 말을 한 이유는 너희가 떨어져 나가지 않게 하려는 것이다.

2 사람들이 너희를 회당에서 내쫓을 것이다. 게다가 너희를 죽이는 자마다 하느님께 봉사한다고 생각할 때가 온다.

3 그들은 아버지도 나도 알지 못하기 때문에 그러한 짓을 할 것이다.

4 내가 너희에게 이 말을 한 이유는, 그들의 때가 오면 내가 너희에게 한 말을 기억하게 하려는 것이다."

성령께서 하시는 일

4 "내가 처음부터 이 말을 너희에게 하지 않은 것은 내가 너희와 함께 있었기 때문이다.

5 이제 나는 나를 보내신 분께 간다. 그런데도 '어디로 가십니까?' 하고 묻는 사람이 너희 가운데 아무도 없다.

6 오히려 내가 이 말을 하였기 때문에 너희 마음에 근심이 가득 찼다.

7 그러나 너희에게 진실을 말하는데, 내가 떠나는 것이 너희에게 이롭다. 내가 떠나지 않으면 보호자께서 너희에게 오지 않으신다. 그러나 내가 가면 그분을 너희에게 보내겠다.

8 보호자께서 오시면 죄와 의로움과 심판에 관한 세상의 그릇된 생각을 밝히실 것이다.

9 그들이 죄에 관하여 잘못 생각하는 것은 나를 믿지 않기 때문이고,

10 그들이 의로움에 관하여 잘못 생각하는 것은 내가 아버지께 가고 너희가 더 이상 나를 보지 못할 것이기 때문이며,

11 그들이 심판에 관하여 잘못 생각하는 것은 이 세상의 우두머리가 이미 심판을 받았기 때문이다.

12 내가 너희에게 할 말이 아직도 많지만 너희가 지금은 그것을 감당하지 못한다.

13 그러나 그분 곧 진리의 영께서 오시면 너희를 모든 진리 안으로 이끌어 주실 것이다. 그분께서는 스스로 이야기하지 않으시고 들으시는 것만 이야기하시며, 또 앞으로 올 일들을 너희에게 알려 주실 것이다.

14 그분께서 나를 영광스럽게 하실 것이다. 나에게서 받아 너희에게 알려 주실 것이기 때문이다.

15 아버지께서 가지고 계신 것은 모두 나의 것이다. 그렇기 때문에 성령께서 나에게서 받아 너희에게 알려 주실 것이라고 내가 말하였다."

이별의 슬픔과 재회의 기쁨

16 "조금 있으면 너희는 나를 더 이상 보지 못할 것이다. 그러나 다시 조금 더 있으면 나를 보게 될 것이다."

17 그러자 제자들 가운데 몇 사람이 서로 말하였다. "'조금 있으면 너희는 나를 보지 못할 것이다. 그러나 다시 조금 더 있으면 나를 보게 될 것이다.', 또 '내가 아버지께 가기 때문이다.' 하고 우리에게 말씀하시는데, 그것이 무슨 뜻일까?"

18 그들은 또 "'조금 있으면'이라고 말씀하시는데, 그것이 무슨 뜻일까? 무슨 이야기를 하시는지 알 수가 없군." 하고 말하였다.

19 예수님께서는 제자들이 묻고 싶어 하는 것을 아시고 그들에게 이르셨다. "'조금 있으면 너희는 나를 보지 못할 것이다. 그러나 다시 조금 더 있으면 나를 보게 될 것이다.' 하고 내가 말한 것을 가지고 서로 묻고 있느냐?

20 내가 진실로 진실로 너희에게 말한다. 너희는 울며 애통해하겠지만 세상은 기뻐할 것이다. 너희가 근심하겠지만, 그러나 너희의 근심은 기쁨으로 바뀔 것이다.

21 해산할 때에 여자는 근심에 싸인다. 진통의 시간이 왔기 때문이다. 그러나 아이를 낳으면, 사람 하나가 이 세상에 태어났다는 기쁨으로 그 고통을 잊어버린다.

22 이처럼 너희도 지금은 근심에 싸여 있다. 그러나 내가 너희를 다시 보게 되면 너희 마음이 기뻐할 것이고, 그 기쁨을 아무도 너희에게서 빼앗지 못할 것이다.

23 그날에는 너희가 나에게 아무것도 묻지 않을 것이다. 내가 진실로 진실로 너희에게 말한다. 너희가 내 이름으로 아버지께 청하는 것은 무엇이든지 그분께서 너희에게 주실 것이다.

24 지금까지 너희는 내 이름으로 아무것도 청하지 않았다. 청하여라. 받을 것이다. 그리하여 너희 기쁨이 충만해질 것이다."

내가 세상을 이겼다

25 "나는 지금까지 너희에게 이런 것들을 비유로 이야기하였다. 그러나 더 이상 너희에게 비유로 이야기하지 않고 아버지에 관하여 드러내 놓고 너희에게 알려 줄 때가 온다.

26 그날에 너희는 내 이름으로 청할 것이다. 내가 너희를 위하여 아버지께 청하겠다는 말이 아니다.

27 바로 아버지께서 너희를 사랑하신다. 너희가 나를 사랑하고 또 내가 하느님에게서 나왔다는 것을 믿었기 때문이다.

28 나는 아버지에게서 나와 세상에 왔다가, 다시 세상을 떠나 아버지께 간다."

29 그러자 제자들이 말하였다. "이제는 드러내 놓고 이야기하시고 비유는 말씀하지 않으시는군요.

30 저희는 스승님께서 모든 것을 아시고, 또 누가 스승님께 물을 필요도 없다는 것을 이제 알았습니다. 이로써 저희는 스승님께서 하느님에게서 나오셨다는 것을 믿습니다."

31 예수님께서 그들에게 대답하셨다. "이제는 너희가 믿느냐?

32 그러나 너희가 나를 혼자 버려두고 저마다 제 갈 곳으로 흩어질 때가 온다. 아니, 이미 왔다. 그러나 나는 혼자가 아니다. 아버지께서 나와 함께 계시다.

33 내가 너희에게 이 말을 한 이유는, 너희가 내 안에서 평화를 얻게 하려는 것이다. 너희는 세상에서 고난을 겪을 것이다. 그러나 용기를 내어라. 내가 세상을 이겼다."

John Chapter 16

1 "I have told you this so that you may not fall away. 2 They will expel you from the synagogues; in fact, the hour is coming when everyone who kills you will think he is offering worship to God. 3 They will do this because they have not known either the Father or me. 4 I have told you this so that when their hour comes you may remember that I told you.

Jesus' Departure; Coming of the Advocate

"I did not tell you this from the beginning, because I was with you. 5 But now I am going to the one who sent me, and not one of you asks me, 'Where are you going?' 6 But because I told you this, grief has filled your hearts. 7 But I tell you the truth, it is better for you that I go. For if I do not go, the Advocate will not come to you. But if I go, I will send him to you. 8 And when he comes he will convict the world in regard to sin and righteousness and condemnation: 9 sin, because they do not believe in me; 10 righteousness, because I am going to the Father and you will no longer see me; 11 condemnation, because the ruler of this world has been condemned. 12 "I have much more to tell you, but you cannot bear it now. 13 But when he comes, the Spirit of truth, he will guide you to all truth. He will not speak on his own, but he will speak what he hears, and will declare to you the things that are coming. 14 He will glorify me, because he will take from what is mine and declare it to you. 15 Everything that the Father has is mine; for this reason I told you that he will take from what is mine and declare it to you. 16 "A little while and you will no longer see me, and again a little while later and you will see me." 17 So some of his disciples said to one another, "What does this mean that he is saying to us, 'A little while and you will not see me, and again a little while and you will see me,' and 'Because I am going to the Father'?" 18 So they said, "What is this 'little while' (of which he speaks)? We do not know what he means." 19 Jesus knew that they wanted to ask him, so he said to them, "Are you discussing with one another what I said, 'A little while and you will not see me, and again a little while and you will see me'? 20 Amen, amen, I say to you, you will weep and mourn, while the world rejoices; you will grieve, but your grief will become joy. 21 When a woman is in labor, she is in anguish because her hour has arrived; but when she has given birth to a child, she no longer remembers the pain because of her joy that a child has been born into the world. 22 So you also are now in anguish. But I will see you again, and your hearts will rejoice, and no one will take your joy away from you. 23 On that day you will not question me about anything. Amen, amen, I say to you, whatever you ask the Father in my name he will give you. 24 Until now you have not asked anything in my name; ask and you will receive, so that your joy may be complete. 25 "I have told you this in figures of speech. The hour is coming when I will no longer speak to you in figures but I will tell you clearly about the Father. 26 On that day you will ask in my name, and I do not tell you that I will ask the Father for you. 27 For the Father himself loves you, because you have loved me and have come to believe that I came from God. 28 I came from the Father and have come into the world. Now I am leaving the world and going back to the Father." 29 His disciples said, "Now you are talking plainly, and not in any figure of speech. 30 Now we realize that you know everything and that you do not need to have anyone question you. Because of this we believe that you came from God." 31 Jesus answered them, "Do you believe now? 32 Behold, the hour is coming and has arrived when each of you will be scattered to his own home and you will leave me alone. But I am not alone, because the Father is with me. 33 I have told you this so that you might have peace in me. In the world you will have trouble, but take courage, I have conquered the world."

(1절)I have told you this so that you may not fall away.나는 너희가 떨어져 나가지 않게 하려고 이런 일을 너희에게 말한 것이다. The reason why I have told you this is that you may not fall away. (2절)furthermore, besides, In addition, and then, moreover.게다가. each, every, everyone, all, at an interval of, whenever.마다. ~in fact, the hour is coming when ~ think he is offering worship to God.사실 너희를 죽이는 자마다 하느님께 예배를 봉헌하는 것이라고 생각할 때가 온다.→ ~furthermore, the hour is coming when ~ think he is serving God.게다가 너희를 죽이는 자마다 하느님께 봉사한다고 생각할 때가 온다. (3절)either.부정어와 함께: ~도 아니고, ~도 아니다(않다). (4절)I have told you this so that when their~ →The reason that I have told you this is that when their~. ~when their hour.그들의 때가 오면. (6절)But→ Rather. (7절)For if I do not go.사실 내가 가지 않으면. If I do not go away.내가 떠나지 않으면. (8절)And when he comes he will convict the world in regard to sin and righteousness and condemnation.그래서 보호자께서 오시면 죄와 의로움과 단죄(심판)에 관하여 세상에 유죄 판결을 내리실 것이다. When he comes he will make an erroneous conceptions of the world clear in regard to sin and righteousness and judgment.보호자께서 오시면 죄와 의로움과 심판에 관한 세상의 그릇된 생각을 밝히실 것이다. (10절)의로움: 죄가 없으신 예수님께서 비록 죄인 취급을 받아 치욕스럽게

십자가에서 돌아가셨다 하더라도 아버지께 되 돌아 가셨기 때문에 실제로 의로움이 승리하였다는 것임. (11절)chief, leader, boss, head.우두머리. ruler.통치자, 지배자. (12절)bear.견디다, (감당, 지탱)하다, 참다, 떠맡다. (13절)이끌어→ 인도해. declare.(선언, 말, 선고, 주장, 신고, 공표, 포고, 단언, 언명,) 하다. ~을 (밝히다, 분명하게 하다), ~을 (드러내다, 나타내다).→ tell. (14절)declare it to you.→ make it known to you. 나에게서→ (나의, 내) 것을. (18절)~what he means.→ ~what he is saying. (19절)discussing with one→ asking one. (20절)~become joy.기쁨이 될 것이다.→ ~(turn, be changed) to joy.기쁨으로 (바뀔, 변할) 것이다. anguish(ǽŋgwiʃ).괴로움, 비통, 고뇌, 번민, 심신의 격통. grief.비탄, 비통, 큰 슬픔. anxiety, concern, solicitude, uneasiness, fear, care, worry, apprehension, trouble. 근심. (24절)~will be abundant.충만해질 것이다. be full(of), be (filled, crowded, saturated) (with), (be) abundant, be replete.충만하다. complete(kəmplíːt)완전한, 완벽한, 완성된. (25절)openly, before one's very eyes.드러내 놓고. figure of speech.(비유, 수사)적 표현, 말의 수식. But the hour is ~ longer will (speak to→ tell) ~(tell you clearly → make it known to you clearly)~. talk, speak, converse, chat(over), have a (talk, chat) (with).이야기하다. (29절)plainly.분명히, 숨김없이, 소박하게, 솔직히 있는 그대로. (32절)~will be scattered to his own place to go.제 갈 곳으로 흩어지다. (33절) win, (win, gain) a victory (over), triumph (over), overcome, beat, defeat.이기다. conquered→ overcome.

Footnotes

(2절)Hour: of persecution, not Jesus' "hour" (see the note on John 2:4). (4b-33절)A duplicate of John 14:1-31 on departure and return. (5절)Not one of you asks me: the difficulty of reconciling this with Simon Peter's question in John 13:36 and Thomas' words in John 14:5 strengthens the supposition that the last discourse has been made up of several collections of Johannine material. (8-11절)These verses illustrate the forensic character of the Paraclete's role.이절들은 성령의 역할에 관한 변론적인 특징을 (설명, 예증, 예시)한다. in the forum of the disciples' conscience he prosecutes the world.성령님께서는 제자들의 양심의 재판에서 세상을 고발한다. He leads believers to see (a) that the basic sin was and is refusal to believe in Jesus; (b) that, although Jesus was found guilty and apparently died in disgrace, in reality righteousness has triumphed, for Jesus has returned to his Father; (c) finally, that it is the ruler of this world, Satan, who has been condemned through Jesus' death (John 12:32). (13절)Declare to you the things that are coming: not a reference to new predictions about the future, but interpretation of what has already occurred or been said. (25절)See the note on John 10:6. Here, possibly a reference to John 15:1-16 or John 16:21. (30절)The reference is seemingly to the fact that Jesus could anticipate their question in John 16:19. The disciples naively think they have the full understanding that is the climax of "the hour" of Jesus' death, resurrection, and ascension (John 16:25), but the only part of the hour that is at hand for them is their share in the passion (John 16:32). (32절)You will be scattered: cf Mark 14:27 and Matthew 26:31, where both cite Zechariah 13:7 about the sheep being dispersed.

요한복음서 17장

당신 자신을 위하여 기도하시다

1 예수님께서는 이렇게 이르시고 나서 하늘을 향하여 눈을 들어 말씀하셨다. "아버지, 때가 왔습니다. 아들이 아버지를 영광스럽게 하도록 아버지의 아들을 영광스럽게 해 주십시오.

2 아버지께서는 아들이 아버지께서 주신 모든 이에게 영원한 생명을 주도록 아들에게 모든 사람에 대한 권한을 주셨습니다.

3 영원한 생명이란 홀로 참하느님이신 아버지를 알고 아버지께서 보내신 예수 그리스도를 아는 것입니다.

4 아버지께서 저에게 하라고 맡기신 일을 완수하여, 저는 땅에서 아버지를 영광스럽게 하였습니다.

5 아버지, 세상이 생기기 전에 제가 아버지 앞에서 누리던 그 영광으로, 이제 다시 아버지 앞에서 저를 영광스럽게 해 주십시오."

제자들을 위하여 기도하시다

6 "아버지께서 세상에서 뽑으시어 저에게 주신 이 사람들에게 저는 아버지의 이름을 드러냈습니다. 이들은 아버지의 사람들이었는데 아버지께서 저에게 주셨습니다. 그래서 이들은 아버지의 말씀을 지켰습니다.

7 이제 이들은 아버지께서 저에게 주신 모든 것이 아버지에게서 왔다는 것을 알고 있습니다.

8 아버지께서 저에게 주신 말씀을 제가 이들에게 주고, 이들은 또 그것을 받아들였기 때문입니다. 그리하여 이들은 제가 아버지에게서 나왔다는 것을 참으로 알고, 아버지께서 저를 보내셨다는 것을 믿게 되었습니다.

9 저는 이들을 위하여 빕니다. 세상을 위해서가 아니라 아버지께서 저에게 주신 이들을 위하여 빕니다. 이들은 아버지의 사람들이기 때문입니다.

10 저의 것은 다 아버지의 것이고 아버지의 것은 제 것입니다. 이 사람들을 통하여 제가 영광스럽게 되었습니다.

11 저는 더 이상 세상에 있지 않지만 이들은 세상에 있습니다. 저는 아버지께 갑니다. 거룩하신 아버지, 아버지께서 저에게 주신 이름으로 이들을 지키시어, 이들도 우리처럼 하나가 되게 해 주십시오.

12 저는 이들과 함께 있는 동안, 아버지께서 저에게 주신 이름으로 이들을 지켰습니다. 제가 그렇게 이들을 보호하여, 성경 말씀이 이루어지려고 멸망하도록 정해진 자 말고는 아무도 멸망하지 않았습니다.

13 이제 저는 아버지께 갑니다. 제가 세상에 있으면서 이런 말씀을 드리는 이유는, 이들이 속으로 저의 기쁨을 충만히 누리게 하려는 것입니다.

14 저는 이들에게 아버지의 말씀을 주었는데, 세상은 이들을 미워하였습니다. 제가 세상에 속하지 않은 것처럼 이들도 세상에 속하지 않기 때문입니다.

15 이들을 세상에서 데려가시라고 비는 것이 아니라, 이들을 악에서 지켜 주십사고 빕니다.

16 제가 세상에 속하지 않은 것처럼 이들도 세상에 속하지 않습니다.

17 이들을 진리로 거룩하게 해 주십시오. 아버지의 말씀이 진리입니다.

18 아버지께서 저를 세상에 보내신 것처럼 저도 이들을 세상에 보냈습니다.

19 그리고 저는 이들을 위하여 저 자신을 거룩하게 합니다. 이들도 진리로 거룩해지게 하려는 것입니다.”

믿는 이들을 위하여 기도하시다

20 “저는 이들만이 아니라 이들의 말을 듣고 저를 믿는 이들을 위해서도 빕니다.

21 그들이 모두 하나가 되게 해 주십시오. 아버지, 아버지께서 제 안에 계시고 제가 아버지 안에 있듯이, 그들도 우리 안에 있게 해 주십시오. 그리하여 아버지께서 저를 보내셨다는 것을 세상이 믿게 하십시오.

22 아버지께서 저에게 주신 영광을 저도 그들에게 주었습니다. 우리가 하나인 것처럼 그들도 하나가 되게 하려는 것입니다.

23 저는 그들 안에 있고 아버지께서는 제 안에 계십니다. 이는 그들이 완전히 하나가 되게 하려는 것입니다. 그리고 아버지께서 저를 보내시고, 또 저를 사랑하셨듯이 그들도 사랑하셨다는 것을 세상이 알게 하려는 것입니다.

24 아버지, 아버지께서 저에게 주신 이들도 제가 있는 곳에 저와 함께 있게 되기를 바랍니다. 세상 창조 이전부터 아버지께서 저를 사랑하시어 저에게 주신 영광을 그들도 보게 되기를 바랍니다.

25 의로우신 아버지, 세상은 아버지를 알지 못하였지만 저는 아버지를 알고 있었습니다. 그들도 아버지께서 저를 보내셨다는 것을 알게 되었습니다.

26 저는 그들에게 아버지의 이름을 알려 주었고 앞으로도 알려 주겠습니다. 아버지께서 저를 사랑하신 그 사랑이 그들 안에 있고 저도 그들 안에 있게 하려는 것입니다.”

The Prayer of Jesus

John Chapter 17

1 When Jesus had said this, he raised his eyes to heaven and said, "Father, the hour has come. Give glory to your son, so that your son may glorify you, 2 just as you gave him authority over all people, so that he may give eternal life to all you gave him. 3 Now this is eternal life, that they should know you, the only true God, and the

one whom you sent, Jesus Christ. 4 I glorified you on earth by accomplishing the work that you gave me to do. 5 Now glorify me, Father, with you, with the glory that I had with you before the world began. 6 "I revealed your name to those whom you gave me out of the world. They belonged to you, and you gave them to me, and they have kept your word. 7 Now they know that everything you gave me is from you, 8 because the words you gave to me I have given to them, and they accepted them and truly understood that I came from you, and they have believed that you sent me. 9 I pray for them. I do not pray for the world but for the ones you have given me, because they are yours, 10 and everything of mine is yours and everything of yours is mine, and I have been glorified in them. 11 And now I will no longer be in the world, but they are in the world, while I am coming to you. Holy Father, keep them in your name that you have given me, so that they may be one just as we are. 12 When I was with them I protected them in your name that you gave me, and I guarded them, and none of them was lost except the son of destruction, in order that the scripture might be fulfilled. 13 But now I am coming to you. I speak this in the world so that they may share my joy completely. 14 I gave them your word, and the world hated them, because they do not belong to the world any more than I belong to the world. 15 I do not ask that you take them out of the world but that you keep them from the evil one. 16 They do not belong to the world any more than I belong to the world. 17 Consecrate them in the truth. Your word is truth. 18 As you sent me into the world, so I sent them into the world. 19 And I consecrate myself for them, so that they also may be consecrated in truth. 20 "I pray not only for them, but also for those who will believe in me through their word, 21 so that they may all be one, as you, Father, are in me and I in you, that they also may be in us, that the world may believe that you sent me. 22 And I have given them the glory you gave me, so that they may be one, as we are one, 23 I in them and you in me, that they may be brought to perfection as one, that the world may know that you sent me, and that you loved them even as you loved me. 24 Father, they are your gift to me. I wish that where I am they also may be with me, that they may see my glory that you gave me, because you loved me before the foundation of the world. 25 Righteous Father, the world also does not know you, but I know you, and they know that you sent me. 26 I made known to them your name and I will make it known, that the love with which you loved me may be in them and I in them."

(1절)to heaven→ toward heaven. Give glory to your son.→ Glorify your son. (3절) Now. 그런데. (4절)entrusted(intrʌstid).맡기신. gave주신. (5절)~before the world began. 세상이 시작되기 전에. ~before the world came to be.세상이 생기기 전에. Now glorify me, Father, with you, with the glory that I had with you before the world began.→Now again, Father, glorify me in your presence with the glory that I had before you before the world came to be. (6절)out of the world.세상으로부터, 세상에서 이끌어 내어. out of.출처를 의미(~에서 부터). 의역; 세상에서 이끌어 내어 제게 주신. (8절)understood→ knew. (10절)in.~로 말미암아. through.(원인, 동기, 이유) ~때문에, ~의 이유로(by reason of),~로 말미암아. (수단, 매개) ~에 의하여(by means of), 덕택에. (11절)And now.자, 이제. while.그런데, 한편(으로는), 동시에. in.도구, 재료, 표현 양식 등을 나타내어; 으로(로), 을 사용하여, 을 가지고, 으로 만든. in your name.아버지의 이름으로. (12절)When I→ While I. ~except the son of destruction.→ ~except the one doomed to destruction. lost→ destroyed. be(destroyed, ruined), become extinct, fall.멸망하다. (13절)But now.그러나 이제. ~may share my joy completely.→ ~may enjoy my joy fully within them. enjoy, have, be blessed with.누리다. I speak this.→ The reason that I speak(to you) this~ (14절)A does not belong to B any more than C belongs to D.A가 B가 아닌 (것처럼, 것과 같이, 것과 마찬가지로) C도 D가 아니다. (15절)I do not ask that.→ My prayer is not that~ (17절)in(=by)로. (21절)~so that they may all be one.그래서 그들 모두가 하나가 되게 하려는 것입니다. (23절)(bring, come) to perfection as one.완전히 하나가 되다. even as.~과 꼭 마찬가지로. (24절)Father, they are your gift to me. I wish that where I am they also may be with me, that they may see my glory that you gave me.→ Father, I wish those you have given me to be with me where I am, and to see my glory, the glory that you have given me.여기서 "they are your gift to me.그들은 저에게는 아버지의 선물입니다." 가 번역이 안 되어 있음.

Footnotes

(1-26절)Climax of the last discourse(s). Since the sixteenth century, this chapter has been called the "high priestly prayer" of Jesus. He speaks as intercessor, with words addressed directly to the Father and not to the disciples, who supposedly only overhear. Yet the prayer is one of petition, for immediate (John 17:6-19) and future (John 17:20-21) disciples. Many phrases reminiscent of the Lord's Prayer occur. Although still in the world (John 17:13), Jesus looks on his earthly ministry as a thing of the past (John 17:4, 12). Whereas Jesus has up to this time stated that the disciples could follow him (John 13:33, 36), now he wishes them to be with him in union with the Father (John 17:12-14).immediate family.직계 가족. immediate disciples.

아주 가까운(친밀한)제자. whereas=while on the other hand, 이므로, 라는 사실에서 보면, 인 까닭에 (since), 반면에, 에 반하여, 그런데, 그러나, 사실은. (1절)The action of looking up to heaven and the address Father are typical of Jesus at prayer; cf John 11:41 and Luke 11:2. (2절)Another possible interpretation is to treat the first line of the verse as parenthetical(삽입어구로 제시된) and the second as an appositive (동격의) to the clause that ends v 1: so that your son may glorify you (just as…all people), so that he may give eternal life…(3절)This verse was clearly added in the editing of the gospel as a reflection on the preceding verse; Jesus nowhere else refers to himself as Jesus Christ. (6절)I revealed your name: perhaps the name I AM; cf John 8:24, 28, 58; 13:19. (15절)Note the resemblance to the petition of the Lord's Prayer, "deliver us from the evil one." Both probably refer to the devil rather than to abstract evil. (24절)Where I am: Jesus prays for the believers ultimately to join him in heaven. Then they will not see his glory as in a mirror but clearly (2 Cor 3:18; 1 John 3:2). (26절)I will make it known: through the Advocate.

요한복음서 18장

잡히시다(마태 26, 47-56; 마르 14, 43-50; 루카 22, 47-53)

1 예수님께서는 이렇게 말씀하신 뒤에 제자들과 함께 키드론 골짜기 건너편으로 가셨다. 거기에 정원이 하나 있었는데 제자들과 함께 그곳에 들어가셨다.

2 예수님께서 제자들과 함께 여러 번 거기에 모이셨기 때문에, 그분을 팔아넘길 유다도 그곳을 알고 있었다.

3 그래서 유다는 군대와 함께, 수석 사제들과 바리사이들이 보낸 성전 경비병들을 데리고 그리로 갔다. 그들은 등불과 횃불과 무기를 들고 있었다.

4 예수님께서는 당신께 닥쳐오는 모든 일을 아시고 앞으로 나서시며 그들에게, "누구를 찾느냐?" 하고 물으셨다.

5 그들이 "나자렛 사람 예수요." 하고 대답하자, 예수님께서 그들에게 "나다." 하고 말씀하셨다. 예수님을 팔아넘길 유다도 그들과 함께 서 있었다.

6 예수님께서 "나다." 하실 때, 그들은 뒷걸음치다가 땅에 넘어졌다.

7 예수님께서 다시 그들에게 "누구를 찾느냐?" 하고 물으시니, 그들이 "나자렛 사람 예수요." 하고 대답하였다.

8 예수님께서 말씀하셨다. "'나다.' 하지 않았느냐? 너희가 나를 찾는다면 이 사람들은 가게 내버려 두어라."

9 이는 "아버지께서 저에게 주신 사람들 가운데 하나도 잃지 않았습니다." 하고 당신께서 전에 하신 말씀이 이루어지게 하려는 것이었다.

10 그때에 시몬 베드로가 가지고 있던 칼을 뽑아, 대사제의 종을 내리쳐 오른쪽 귀를 잘라 버렸다. 그 종의 이름은 말코스였다.

11 그러자 예수님께서 베드로에게 이르셨다. "그 칼을 칼집에 꽂아라. 아버지께서 나에게 주신 이 잔을 내가 마셔야 하지 않겠느냐?"

한나스의 신문과 베드로의 부인(마태 26, 57-75; 마르 14, 53-72; 루카 22, 54-71)

12 군대와 그 대장과 유다인들의 성전 경비병들은 예수님을 붙잡아 결박하고,

13 먼저 한나스에게 데려갔다. 한나스는 그해의 대사제 카야파의 장인이었다.

14 카야파는 백성을 위하여 한 사람이 죽는 것이 낫다고 유다인들에게 충고한 자다.

15 시몬 베드로와 또 다른 제자 하나가 예수님을 따라갔다. 그 제자는 대사제와 아는 사이여서, 예수님과 함께 대사제의 저택 안뜰에 들어갔다.

16 베드로는 대문 밖에 서 있었는데, 대사제와 아는 사이인 그 다른 제자가 나와서 문지기 하녀에게 말하여 베드로를 데리고 들어갔다.

17 그때에 그 문지기 하녀가 "당신도 저 사람의 제자 가운데 하나가 아닌가요?" 하자, 베드로가 "나는

아니오." 하고 말하였다.

18 날이 추워 종들과 성전 경비병들이 숯불을 피워 놓고 서서 불을 쬐고 있었는데, 베드로도 그들과 함께 서서 불을 쬐었다.

19 대사제는 예수님께 그분의 제자들과 가르침에 관하여 물었다.

20 예수님께서 그에게 대답하셨다. "나는 세상 사람들에게 드러내 놓고 이야기하였다. 나는 언제나 모든 유다인이 모이는 회당과 성전에서 가르쳤다. 은밀히 이야기한 것은 하나도 없다.

21 그런데 왜 나에게 묻느냐? 내가 무슨 말을 하였는지 들은 이들에게 물어보아라. 내가 말한 것을 그들이 알고 있다."

22 예수님께서 이렇게 말씀하시자, 곁에 서 있던 성전 경비병 하나가 예수님의 뺨을 치며, "대사제께 그따위로 대답하느냐?" 하였다.

23 예수님께서 그에게 대답하셨다. "내가 잘못 이야기하였다면 그 잘못의 증거를 대 보아라. 그러나 내가 옳게 이야기하였다면 왜 나를 치느냐?"

24 한나스는 예수님을 결박한 채로 카야파 대사제에게 보냈다.

25 시몬 베드로는 서서 불을 쬐고 있었다. 사람들이 그에게 "당신도 저 사람의 제자 가운데 하나가 아니오?" 하고 물었다. 베드로는 "나는 아니오." 하며 부인하였다.

26 대사제의 종 가운데 하나로서, 베드로가 귀를 잘라 버린 자의 친척이 말하였다. "당신이 정원에서 저 사람과 함께 있는 것을 내가 보지 않았소?"

27 베드로가 다시 아니라고 부인하자 곧 닭이 울었다.

빌라도에게 신문을 받으시다(마태 27, 1-2. 11-14; 마르 15, 1-5; 루카 23, 1-5)

28 사람들이 예수님을 카야파의 저택에서 총독 관저로 끌고 갔다. 때는 이른 아침이었다. 그들은 몸이 더러워져서 파스카 음식을 먹지 못할까 두려워, 총독 관저 안으로 들어가지 않았다.

29 그래서 빌라도가 그들이 있는 곳으로 나와, "무슨 일로 저 사람을 고소하는 것이오?" 하고 물었다.

30 그들이 빌라도에게, "저자가 범죄자가 아니라면 우리가 총독께 넘기지 않았을 것이오." 하고 대답하였다.

31 빌라도가 그들에게 "여러분이 데리고 가서 여러분의 법대로 재판하시오." 하자, 유다인들이 "우리는 누구를 죽일 권한이 없소." 하고 말하였다.

32 이는 예수님께서 당신이 어떻게 죽임을 당할 것인지 가리키며 하신 말씀이 이루어지려고 그리된 것이다.

33 그리하여 빌라도가 다시 총독 관저 안으로 들어가 예수님을 불러, "당신이 유다인들의 임금이오?" 하고 물었다.

34 예수님께서는 "그것은 네 생각으로 하는 말이냐? 아니면 다른 사람들이 나에 관하여 너에게 말해 준 것이냐?" 하고 되물으셨다.

35 "나야 유다인이 아니잖소? 당신의 동족과 수석 사제들이 당신을 나에게 넘긴 것이오. 당신은 무슨

일을 저질렀소?" 하고 빌라도가 다시 물었다.

36 예수님께서 대답하셨다. "내 나라는 이 세상에 속하지 않는다. 내 나라가 이 세상에 속한다면, 내 신하들이 싸워 내가 유다인들에게 넘어가지 않게 하였을 것이다. 그러나 내 나라는 여기에 속하지 않는다."

37 빌라도가 "아무튼 당신이 임금이라는 말 아니오?" 하고 묻자, 예수님께서 그에게 대답하셨다. "내가 임금이라고 네가 말하고 있다. 나는 진리를 증언하려고 태어났으며, 진리를 증언하려고 세상에 왔다. 진리에 속한 사람은 누구나 내 목소리를 듣는다."

38 빌라도가 예수님께 말하였다. "진리가 무엇이오?"

사형 선고를 받으시다(마태 27, 15-31; 마르 15, 6-20; 루카 23, 13-25)

38 빌라도는 이 말을 하고 다시 유다인들이 있는 곳으로 나가 그들에게 말하였다. "나는 저 사람에게서 아무런 죄목도 찾지 못하겠소.

39 그런데 여러분에게는 내가 파스카 축제 때에 죄수 하나를 풀어 주는 관습이 있소. 내가 유다인들의 임금을 풀어 주기를 원하오?"

40 그러자 그들이 다시 "그 사람이 아니라 바라빠를 풀어 주시오." 하고 외쳤다. 바라빠는 강도였다.

Jesus Arrested

John Chapter 18

1 When he had said this, Jesus went out with his disciples across the Kidron valley to where there was a garden, into which he and his disciples entered. 2 Judas his betrayer also knew the place, because Jesus had often met there with his disciples. 3 So Judas got a band of soldiers and guards from the chief priests and the Pharisees and went there with lanterns, torches, and weapons. 4 Jesus, knowing everything that was going to happen to him, went out and said to them, "Whom are you looking for?" 5 They answered him, "Jesus the Nazorean." He said to them, "I AM." Judas his betrayer was also with them. 6 When he said to them, "I AM," they turned away and fell to the ground. 7 So he again asked them, "Whom are you looking for?" They said, "Jesus the Nazorean." 8 Jesus answered, "I told you that I AM. So if you are looking for me, let these men go." 9 This was to fulfill what he had said, "I have not lost any of those you gave me." 10 Then Simon Peter, who had a sword, drew it, struck the high priest's slave, and cut off his right ear. The slave's name was Malchus. 11 Jesus said to Peter, "Put your sword into its scabbard. Shall I not drink the cup that the Father gave me?" 12 So the band of soldiers, the tribune, and the

Jewish guards seized Jesus, bound him, 13 and brought him to Annas first. He was the father-in-law of Caiaphas, who was high priest that year. 14 It was Caiaphas who had counseled the Jews that it was better that one man should die rather than the people.

Peter's First Denial

15 Simon Peter and another disciple followed Jesus. Now the other disciple was known to the high priest, and he entered the courtyard of the high priest with Jesus. 16 But Peter stood at the gate outside. So the other disciple, the acquaintance of the high priest, went out and spoke to the gatekeeper and brought Peter in. 17 Then the maid who was the gatekeeper said to Peter, "You are not one of this man's disciples, are you?" He said, "I am not." 18 Now the slaves and the guards were standing around a charcoal fire that they had made, because it was cold, and were warming themselves. Peter was also standing there keeping warm.

The Inquiry before Annas

19 The high priest questioned Jesus about his disciples and about his doctrine. 20 Jesus answered him, "I have spoken publicly to the world. I have always taught in a synagogue or in the temple area where all the Jews gather, and in secret I have said nothing. 21 Why ask me? Ask those who heard me what I said to them. They know what I said." 22 When he had said this, one of the temple guards standing there struck Jesus and said, "Is this the way you answer the high priest?" 23 Jesus answered him, "If I have spoken wrongly, testify to the wrong; but if I have spoken rightly, why do you strike me?" 24 Then Annas sent him bound to Caiaphas the high priest.

Peter Denies Jesus Again

25 Now Simon Peter was standing there keeping warm. And they said to him, "You are not one of his disciples, are you?" He denied it and said, "I am not." 26 One of the slaves of the high priest, a relative of the one whose ear Peter had cut off, said, "Didn't I see you in the garden with him?" 27 Again Peter denied it. And immediately the cock crowed.

The Trial before Pilate

28 Then they brought Jesus from Caiaphas to the praetorium. It was morning. And

they themselves did not enter the praetorium, in order not to be defiled so that they could eat the Passover. 29 So Pilate came out to them and said, "What charge do you bring (against) this man?" 30 They answered and said to him, "If he were not a criminal, we would not have handed him over to you." 31 At this, Pilate said to them, "Take him yourselves, and judge him according to your law." The Jews answered him, "We do not have the right to execute anyone," 32 in order that the word of Jesus might be fulfilled that he said indicating the kind of death he would die. 33 So Pilate went back into the praetorium and summoned Jesus and said to him, "Are you the King of the Jews?" 34 Jesus answered, "Do you say this on your own or have others told you about me?" 35 Pilate answered, "I am not a Jew, am I? Your own nation and the chief priests handed you over to me. What have you done?" 36 Jesus answered, "My kingdom does not belong to this world. If my kingdom did belong to this world, my attendants (would) be fighting to keep me from being handed over to the Jews. But as it is, my kingdom is not here." 37 So Pilate said to him, "Then you are a king?" Jesus answered, "You say I am a king. For this I was born and for this I came into the world, to testify to the truth. Everyone who belongs to the truth listens to my voice." 38 Pilate said to him, "What is truth?" When he had said this, he again went out to the Jews and said to them, "I find no guilt in him. 39 But you have a custom that I release one prisoner to you at Passover. Do you want me to release to you the King of the Jews?" 40 They cried out again, "Not this one but Barabbas!" Now Barabbas was a revolutionary.

(1절)across= on the other side.건너편, 맞은편에, 반대쪽에. When he had said this, Jesus went out with his disciples across the Kidron valley to where there was a garden, into which he and his disciples entered.예수님께서 이렇게 (말씀하시고, 말씀하신 뒤에) 제자들과 함께 키드론 골짜기 건너편에 있는 한 정원으로 나가셔서 그곳으로 들어가셨다. (3절)a band of.무리, (일, 악)당. get soldiers.(데려, 가져, 불러)오다. So Judas got a band of soldiers and guards from the chief priests and the Pharisees and went there with lanterns, torches, and weapons.그래서 유다는 수석사제들과 바리사이들에게서 등불과 횃불과 무기를 (가지고 있는, 든) 한 무리의 군대와 경비병들을 데리고 그리로 갔다. So Judas brought temple guards sent from the chief priests and the Pharisees with soldiers went there. They were carrying lanterns, torches, and weapons; So Judas went there, bringing temple guards sent from the chief priests and the Pharisees with soldiers. They were carrying lanterns, torches, and weapons. 그래서

유다는 군대와 함께 수석사제들과 바리사이들이 보낸 성전 경비병들을 데리고 그리로 갔다. 그들은 등불과 횃불과 무기를 들고 있었다. take, bring, get.데리고 가다. get.입수하다, 얻다, "데리고 가다"의 가장 일반적인 말로서 손에 넣기 위한 노력과 의지의 유무와는 관계가 없다. get a job.일자리를 얻다. gain.자신에게 도움이 되는 것, 필요한 것을 노력하여 얻다, 또는 조금씩 손에 넣다. gain fame.명성을 얻다. obtain.몹시 원하는 것을 노력하여 손에 넣다. He has obtained aid.그는 도움을 얻었다. acquire.시간을 들여 손에 넣다. He acquired a fine education.그는 훌륭한 교육을 받았다. (5절)I AM.나다, 나는 나다. I am he.내가 그 사람이다. (5절)~was also with them.→ ~was also standing with them. (6절)turn away.(시선, 고개)를 돌리다, 외면하다. fell to the ground.땅에 쓰러지다, 넘어지다, 땅에 엎드리다. They stepped backward(stepped back) from him and= They were back away from him and= They drew back and.그들은 뒷걸음치다가. (8절)So. 그러므로.(9절)~had said before. (12절)So the band of soldiers, the tribune, and the Jewish guards seized Jesus, bound him, and brought him to Annas first.그래서 한 무리의 군대와 호민관과 유다인들의 경비병들은 예수님을 붙잡아 결박하고 먼저 한나스에게 데려갔다. Soldiers, its commander and the Jewish temple guards seized Jesus, bound him, and brought him to Annas first.군대와 그 대장과 유다인들의 성전 경비병들은 예수님을 붙잡아 결박하고 먼저 한나스에게 데려갔다. tribune(tríbju:n).호민관, 부대장, 민중지도자, 군단 사령관, 인민의 (보호, 옹호)자. (14절)It was Caiaphas who had counseled the Jews that it was better that one man should die rather than the people.백성이 죽는 것 보다 오히려 한사람이 죽어야만 하는(죽는) 것이 낫다고 유다인들에게 충고한 사람은 카야파였었다.→ Caiaphas was the one who had advised the Jews that it would be better that one man should die for the people.카야파는 백성을 위하여 한사람이 죽는 것이 낫다고 유다인들에게 충고한 자다. counsel(káunsəl).원로나 전문가에 의한 (조언, 충고, 의논, 상의), 변호인 또는 변호인단, 전문적인 상담을(충고, 조언)하다. (15절)(be, get, become) acquainted with, (make, seek) the acquaintance of a person= (make, seek) a person's acquaintance, be known to, know.아는 사이가 되다. (16절)gatekeeper→ maid servant gatekeeper. (18절)warm oneself by the fire, enjoy the fire, warm over a fire, toast oneself.불을 쬐다. slaves→ servants. (19절)doctrine. 원칙, 독트린, 교리, 신조, 정책. teachings, lesson.가르침. (20절)publicly(pʌ́blikli).공공연하게, 공개적으로, 공적으로, 여론에 의해. openly, before one's very eyes.드러내 놓고. (21절)But= By the way.그런데. (22절) standing beside him→ standing there. struck Jesus→ struck Jesus in the face. like that.그 따위로. a thing, a thing like that, that sort of thing.그 따위 것. Is this the way~. 이런 식으로, 이렇게, (고작)이런 식으로, 의역(paraphrase): 이따위로. (24절)him bound. 목적격 보어가 과거분사인 경우 "채로, 상태로"로 번역됨. (25절)stand keeping warm=stand warming himself. (25절)Now Simon Peter.자(그런데) 시몬 베드로는. (28절)Then they. 그때에 사람들이. And they.그런데 그들은. be hauled, frogmarched.끌고가다. bring. 데리고 가다, 데려오다. morning→ early morning. They were afraid that if their body would be defiled, they could not eat the Passover. And they themselves did not enter the praetorium. (29절)Pilate.빌라도; 도덕적 책임을 회피한 사람이라는 뜻. (32절) execute(éksikju:t).(실행, 수행, 달성)하다(carry out), 사형에 (처, 처형)하다, 사람을 죽이다. (34절)said to him→ asked him. Jesus answered→ Jesus asked again. own→ own idea. (35절)the same (race, tribe).동족. (36절)subject, attendant, retainer, courtier, vassal(væsl), follower, attendant.신하. attendant.(안내, 수행)원, 신하, 간병인, 시중드는 사람. But as it is, my kingdom is not here.그러나 (사실은, 정말로 말하면) 내 나라는 여기에 있지 않다. But my kingdom does not belong to here.그러나 내나라는 여기에 속하지 않는다. (37절)So Pilate said to him→ Pilate asked him. (38절)I find no guilt in him.나는 그에게서 그가 유죄임을 찾지 못하겠소. I find no basis for a charge against him.나는 그를 고소할 만한 아무런 근거도 찾지 못하겠소. I find no charges from that man.나는 저 사람에게서 아무런 죄목도 찾지 못하겠소. guilt.유죄(임), 죄책감. the name of a (crime, an offense), a charge.죄목. on (the, a) charge of fraud, charged with fraud.사기의 죄목으로. (40절)revolutionary.혁명가, 혁명의, 혁명적인. robber(rábr:rɔ́b).강도.

Footnotes

(1-14절)John does not mention the agony in the garden and the kiss of Judas, nor does he identify the place as Gethsemane or the Mount of Olives. (1절)Jesus went out: see John 14:31 where it seems he is leaving the supper room. Kidron valley: literally, "the winter-flowing Kidron" 문자 그대로 "겨울에 물이 흐르는 키드론"; this wadi has water only during the winter rains. wadi, wady(wɑ́:di, wɔ́di) 아라비아의 골짜기, 와디:사막 지방의 개울; 우기(雨期) 이외에는 말라 있음. (3절) Band of soldiers: seems to refer to Roman troops, either the full cohort of 600 men (1/10 of a legion), or more likely the maniple(보병부대) of 200 under their tribune (John 18:12). In this case, John is hinting at Roman collusion in the action against Jesus before he was brought to Pilate. The lanterns and torches may be symbolic of the hour of darkness. cohort(kɔuho:rt).고대 로마 보병대: legion을 10등분한 한 부대로 300명 내지 600명. (5절)Nazorean: the form found in Matthew 26:71 (see the note on Matthew 2:23) is here used, not Nazarene of Mark. I AM: or "I am he," but probably intended by the evangelist as an expression of divinity (cf their appropriate response in John 18:6); see the note on John 8:24. John sets the confusion of the arresting party against the background of Jesus' divine majesty. (9절)The citation may refer to John 6:39; 10:28; or John 17:12. (10절)Only John gives the names of the two antagonists; both John and

Luke mention the right ear. (11절)The theme of the cup is found in the synoptic account of the agony (Mark 14:36 and parallels). (13절)Annas: only John mentions an inquiry before Annas; cf John 18:16, 19-24; see the note on Luke 3:2. It is unlikely that this nighttime interrogation before Annas is the same as the trial before Caiaphas placed by Matthew and Mark at night and by Luke in the morning. (15-16절)Another disciple···the other disciple: see the note on John 13:23. (20절)I have always taught···in the temple area: cf Mark 14:49 for a similar statement. (24절)Caiaphas: see Matthew 26:3, 57; Luke 3:2; and the notes there. John may leave room here for the trial before Caiaphas described in the synoptic gospels. (27절)Cockcrow was the third Roman division of the night, lasting from midnight to 3 A.M. (28절)Praetorium: see the note on Matthew 27:27. Morning: literally, "the early hour," or fourth Roman division of the night, 3 to 6 A.M. The Passover: the synoptic gospels give the impression that the Thursday night supper was the Passover meal (Mark 14:12); for John that meal is still to be eaten Friday night. (31절) We do not have the right to execute anyone: only John gives this reason for their bringing Jesus to Pilate. Jewish sources are not clear on the competence of the Sanhedrin at this period to sentence and to execute for political crimes. (32절)The Jewish punishment for blasphemy was stoning (Lev 24:16). In coming to the Romans to ensure that Jesus would be crucified, the Jewish authorities fulfilled his prophecy that he would be exalted (John 3:14; 12:32-33). There is some historical evidence, however, for Jews crucifying Jews. (37절)You say I am a king: see Matthew 26:64 for a similar response to the high priest. It is at best a reluctant affirmative. (39 절)See the note on Matthew 27:15. (40절)Barabbas: see the note on Matthew 27:16-17. Revolutionary: a guerrilla warrior fighting for nationalistic aims, though the term can also denote a robber. See the note on Matthew 27:38.

요한복음서 19장

1 그리하여 빌라도는 예수님을 데려다가 군사들에게 채찍질을 하게 하였다.

2 군사들은 또 가시나무로 관을 엮어 예수님 머리에 씌우고 자주색 옷을 입히고 나서,

3 그분께 다가가 "유다인들의 임금님, 만세!" 하며 그분의 뺨을 쳐 댔다.

4 빌라도가 다시 나와 그들에게 말하였다. "보시오, 내가 저 사람을 여러분 앞으로 데리고 나오겠소. 내가 저 사람에게서 아무런 죄목도 찾지 못하였다는 것을 여러분도 알라는 것이오."

5 이윽고 예수님께서 가시나무 관을 쓰시고 자주색 옷을 입으신 채 밖으로 나오셨다. 그러자 빌라도가 그들에게 "자, 이 사람이오." 하고 말하였다.

6 그때에 수석 사제들과 성전 경비병들은 예수님을 보고, "십자가에 못 박으시오! 십자가에 못 박으시오!" 하고 외쳤다. 빌라도가 그들에게 "여러분이 데려다가 십자가에 못 박으시오. 나는 이 사람에게서 죄목을 찾지 못하겠소." 하자,

7 유다인들이 그에게 대답하였다. "우리에게는 율법이 있소. 이 율법에 따르면 그자는 죽어 마땅하오. 자기가 하느님의 아들이라고 자처하였기 때문이오."

8 빌라도는 이 말을 듣고 더욱 두려운 생각이 들었다.

9 그리하여 다시 총독 관저로 들어가 예수님께, "당신은 어디서 왔소?" 하고 물었다. 그러나 예수님께서는 그에게 아무 대답도 하지 않으셨다.

10 그러자 빌라도가 예수님께 말하였다. "나에게 말을 하지 않을 작정이오? 나는 당신을 풀어 줄 권한도 있고 당신을 십자가에 못 박을 권한도 있다는 것을 모르시오?"

11 예수님께서 그에게 대답하셨다. "네가 위로부터 받지 않았으면 나에 대해 아무런 권한도 없었을 것이다. 그러므로 나를 너에게 넘긴 자의 죄가 더 크다."

12 그때부터 빌라도는 예수님을 풀어 줄 방도를 찾았다. 그러나 유다인들은 "그 사람을 풀어 주면 총독께서는 황제의 친구가 아니오. 누구든지 자기가 임금이라고 자처하는 자는 황제에게 대항하는 것이오." 하고 외쳤다.

13 빌라도는 이 말을 듣고 예수님을 밖으로 데리고 나가 리토스트로토스라고 하는 곳에 있는 재판석에 앉았다. 리토스트로토스는 히브리 말로 가빠타라고 한다.

14 그날은 파스카 축제 준비일이었고 때는 낮 열두 시쯤이었다. 빌라도가 유다인들에게 말하였다. "보시오, 여러분의 임금이오."

15 그러자 그들이 외쳤다. "없애 버리시오. 없애 버리시오. 그를 십자가에 못 박으시오." 빌라도가 그들에게 "여러분의 임금을 십자가에 못 박으라는 말이오?" 하고 물으니, 수석 사제들이 "우리 임금은 황제뿐이오." 하고 대답하였다.

16 그리하여 빌라도는 예수님을 십자가에 못 박으라고 그들에게 넘겨주었다.

십자가에 못 박히시다(마태 27, 32-44; 마르 15, 21-32; 루카 23, 26-43)

16 그들은 예수님을 넘겨받았다.

17 예수님께서는 몸소 십자가를 지시고 '해골 터'라는 곳으로 나가셨다. 그곳은 히브리 말로 골고타라고 한다.

18 거기에서 그들은 예수님을 십자가에 못 박았다. 그리고 다른 두 사람도 예수님을 가운데로 하여 이쪽저쪽에 하나씩 못 박았다.

19 빌라도는 명패를 써서 십자가 위에 달게 하였는데, 거기에는 '유다인들의 임금 나자렛 사람 예수'라고 쓰여 있었다.

20 예수님께서 십자가에 못 박히신 곳이 도성에서 가까웠기 때문에, 많은 유다인이 그 명패를 읽게 되었다. 그것은 히브리 말, 라틴 말, 그리스 말로 쓰여 있었다.

21 그래서 유다인들의 수석 사제들이 빌라도에게 말하였다. "'유다인들의 임금'이라고 쓸 것이 아니라, '나는 유다인들의 임금이다.' 하고 저자가 말하였다고 쓰시오."

22 그러나 빌라도는 "내가 한번 썼으면 그만이오." 하고 대답하였다.

23 군사들은 예수님을 십자가에 못 박고 나서, 그분의 옷을 가져다가 네 몫으로 나누어 저마다 한몫씩 차지하였다. 속옷도 가져갔는데 그것은 솔기가 없이 위에서부터 통으로 짠 것이었다.

24 그래서 그들은 서로, "이것은 찢지 말고 누구 차지가 될지 제비를 뽑자." 하고 말하였다. "그들이 제 옷을 저희끼리 나누어 가지고 제 속옷을 놓고서는 제비를 뽑았습니다." 하신 성경 말씀이 이루어지려고 그리된 것이다. 그래서 군사들이 그렇게 하였다.

25 예수님의 십자가 곁에는 그분의 어머니와 이모, 클로파스의 아내 마리아와 마리아 막달레나가 서 있었다.

26 예수님께서는 당신의 어머니와 그 곁에 선 사랑하시는 제자를 보시고, 어머니에게 말씀하셨다. "여인이시여, 이 사람이 어머니의 아들입니다."

27 이어서 그 제자에게 "이분이 네 어머니시다." 하고 말씀하셨다. 그때부터 그 제자가 그분을 자기 집에 모셨다.

숨을 거두시다(마태 27, 45-56; 마르 15, 33-41; 루카 23, 44-49)

28 그 뒤에 이미 모든 일이 다 이루어졌음을 아신 예수님께서는 성경 말씀이 이루어지게 하시려고 "목마르다." 하고 말씀하셨다.

29 거기에는 신 포도주가 가득 담긴 그릇이 놓여 있었다. 그래서 사람들이 신 포도주를 듬뿍 적신 해면을 우슬초 가지에 꽂아 예수님의 입에 갖다 대었다.

30 예수님께서는 신 포도주를 드신 다음에 말씀하셨다. "다 이루어졌다." 이어서 고개를 숙이시며 숨을 거두셨다.

군사들이 예수님의 옆구리를 창으로 찌르다

31 그날은 준비일이었고 이튿날 안식일은 큰 축일이었으므로, 유다인들은 안식일에 시신이 십자가에 매달려 있지 않게 하려고, 십자가에 못 박힌 이들의 다리를 부러뜨리고 시신을 치우게 하라고 빌라도에게 요청하였다.

32 그리하여 군사들이 가서 예수님과 함께 십자가에 못 박힌 첫째 사람과 또 다른 사람의 다리를 부러뜨렸다.

33 예수님께 가서는 이미 숨지신 것을 보고 다리를 부러뜨리는 대신,

34 군사 하나가 창으로 그분의 옆구리를 찔렀다. 그러자 곧 피와 물이 흘러나왔다.

35 이는 직접 본 사람이 증언하는 것이므로 그의 증언은 참되다. 그리고 그는 여러분이 믿도록 자기가 진실을 말한다는 것을 알고 있다.

36 "그의 뼈가 하나도 부러지지 않을 것이다." 하신 성경 말씀이 이루어지려고 이런 일들이 일어난 것이다.

37 또 다른 성경 구절은 "그들은 자기들이 찌른 이를 바라볼 것이다." 하고 말한다.

묻히시다(마태 27, 57-61; 마르 15, 42-47; 루카 23, 50-56)

38 그 뒤에 아리마태아 출신 요셉이 예수님의 시신을 거두게 해 달라고 빌라도에게 청하였다. 그는 예수님의 제자였지만 유다인들이 두려워 그 사실을 숨기고 있었다. 빌라도가 허락하자 그가 가서 그분의 시신을 거두었다.

39 언젠가 밤에 예수님을 찾아왔던 니코데모도 몰약과 침향을 섞은 것을 백 리트라쯤 가지고 왔다.

40 그들은 예수님의 시신을 모셔다가 유다인들의 장례 관습에 따라, 향료와 함께 아마포로 감쌌다.

41 예수님께서 십자가에 못 박히신 곳에 정원이 있었는데, 그 정원에는 아직 아무도 묻힌 적이 없는 새 무덤이 있었다.

42 그날은 유다인들의 준비일이었고 또 무덤이 가까이 있었으므로, 그들은 예수님을 그곳에 모셨다.

John Chapter 19

1 Then Pilate took Jesus and had him scourged. 2 And the soldiers wove a crown out of thorns and placed it on his head, and clothed him in a purple cloak, 3 and they came to him and said, "Hail, King of the Jews!" And they struck him repeatedly. 4 Once more Pilate went out and said to them, "Look, I am bringing him out to you, so that you may know that I find no guilt in him." 5 So Jesus came out, wearing the crown of thorns and the purple cloak. And he said to them, "Behold, the man!" 6 When the chief priests and the guards saw him they cried out, "Crucify him, crucify

him!" Pilate said to them, "Take him yourselves and crucify him. I find no guilt in him." 7 The Jews answered, "We have a law, and according to that law he ought to die, because he made himself the Son of God." 8 Now when Pilate heard this statement, he became even more afraid, 9 and went back into the praetorium and said to Jesus, "Where are you from?" Jesus did not answer him. 10 So Pilate said to him, "Do you not speak to me? Do you not know that I have power to release you and I have power to crucify you?" 11 Jesus answered (him), "You would have no power over me if it had not been given to you from above. For this reason the one who handed me over to you has the greater sin." 12 Consequently, Pilate tried to release him; but the Jews cried out, "If you release him, you are not a Friend of Caesar. Everyone who makes himself a king opposes Caesar." 13 When Pilate heard these words he brought Jesus out and seated him on the judge's bench in the place called Stone Pavement, in Hebrew, Gabbatha. 14 It was preparation day for Passover, and it was about noon. And he said to the Jews, "Behold, your king!" 15 They cried out, "Take him away, take him away! Crucify him!" Pilate said to them, "Shall I crucify your king?" The chief priests answered, "We have no king but Caesar." 16 Then he handed him over to them to be crucified.

The Crucifixion of Jesus

So they took Jesus, 17 and carrying the cross himself he went out to what is called the Place of the Skull, in Hebrew, Golgotha. 18 There they crucified him, and with him two others, one on either side, with Jesus in the middle. 19 Pilate also had an inscription written and put on the cross. It read, "Jesus the Nazorean, the King of the Jews." 20 Now many of the Jews read this inscription, because the place where Jesus was crucified was near the city; and it was written in Hebrew, Latin, and Greek. 21 So the chief priests of the Jews said to Pilate, "Do not write 'The King of the Jews,' but that he said, 'I am the King of the Jews.'" 22 Pilate answered, "What I have written, I have written." 23 When the soldiers had crucified Jesus, they took his clothes and divided them into four shares, a share for each soldier. They also took his tunic, but the tunic was seamless, woven in one piece from the top down. 24 So they said to one another, "Let's not tear it, but cast lots for it to see whose it will be," in order that the passage of scripture might be fulfilled (that says): "They divided my garments among them, and for my vesture they cast lots." This is what the soldiers did. 25 Standing by the cross of Jesus were his mother and his mother's sister, Mary the wife of Clopas, and Mary of Magdala. 26 When Jesus saw his mother and the disciple there whom he loved, he said to his mother, "Woman, behold, your son." 27 Then he said to the disciple, "Behold, your mother." And from that hour the disciple took her into his home. 28 After this, aware that everything was now finished, in order that the scripture might be fulfilled, Jesus said, "I thirst." 29 There was a vessel filled with common wine. So they put a sponge soaked in wine on a sprig of hyssop and put it up to his mouth. 30 When Jesus had taken the wine, he said, "It is finished." And bowing his head, he handed over the spirit.

The Blood and Water

31 Now since it was preparation day, in order that the bodies might not remain on the cross on the sabbath, for the sabbath day of that week was a solemn one, the Jews asked Pilate that their legs be broken and they be taken down. 32 So the soldiers came and broke the legs of the first and then of the other one who was crucified with Jesus. 33 But when they came to Jesus and saw that he was already dead, they did not break his legs, 34 but one soldier thrust his lance into his side, and immediately blood and water flowed out. 35 An eyewitness has testified, and his testimony is true; he knows that he is speaking the truth, so that you also may (come to) believe. 36 For this happened so that the scripture passage might be fulfilled: "Not a bone of it will be broken." 37 And again another passage says: "They will look upon him whom they have pierced."

The Burial of Jesus

38 After this, Joseph of Arimathea, secretly a disciple of Jesus for fear of the Jews, asked Pilate if he could remove the body of Jesus. And Pilate permitted it. So he came and took his body. 39 Nicodemus, the one who had first come to him at night, also came bringing a mixture of myrrh and aloes weighing about one hundred pounds. 40 They took the body of Jesus and bound it with burial cloths along with the spices, according to the Jewish burial custom. 41 Now in the place where he had been crucified there was a garden, and in the garden a new tomb, in which no one had yet been buried. 42 So they laid Jesus there because of the Jewish preparation day; for the tomb was close by.

(1절)Then.그리하여, 그러더니, 그때에. ~had him scourged.→ ~let the soldiers scourge him. put, cover, lay.씌우다. place.사람, 물건을 어떤 상태 또는 위치에 (두다, 놓다, 배열하다), 왕관을 씌우다, 수갑을 채우다. (3절)hail(héil).만세, 행복하기를(환영·축복의 인사). Hail to the king!국왕만세! All hail=Hail to you! 만세, 환영! 동음어 hale(완전한, 건강한). ~struck him repeatedly.→ ~struck him in the face repeatedly. Once more한번 더; 다시 한번. I find no guilt in him.나는 그에게서 그가 유죄임을 찾지 못하겠소.→ I find no charges from that man.나는 저 사람에게서 아무런 죄목도 찾지 못하겠소. guilt유죄(임), 죄책감. (5절)after a while, before long, soon after, in a short time(course), by and by, then, presently, shortly.이윽고. Behold the man.이 사람을 보시오.→ Here is the man.자 이 사람이오. (6절)When.할 때에, 하고.→ At that time, Then.그때에. (7절)~because he made himself the Son of God.하느님의 아들이라 하였기 때문이오.→ because he claimed to be the Son of God.하느님의 아들이라 자처하였기 때문이오. (think of, consider, fancy) oneself (as), claim to be, refers to oneself, set up as. 자처하다. (8절)Now when Pilate. 그런데 빌라도는 듣고. statement(stéitmənt).말, 말씀, (표현, 진술)법, 말하는 방식, 성명서. (9절)~went back into.안으로 되돌아가다. (10절)Do you not speak to me?당신은 나에게 말하지 않겠소?→ Do you intend not to speak to me?당신은 나에게 말을 하지 않을 작정이오? (11절)Therefore.그러므로. for this reason.이러한 이유로 해서, 이러한 이유 때문에, 이 때문에. (12절)Consequently.그 결과, 따라서. Since then, And then, From then on, From then, from that time.그때부터. (13절)Stone Pavement.돌을 깔아 만든 포장지역, 돌로 만든 보도. (14절)It(=The day or That day). And he.그래서 빌라도가. (15절)take him away= away with him.그를 제거하라, 그를 없애라. (17절)그래서 그들은. took, took over, be given.넘겨받다. (19절)a nameplate, name tag, tablet.명패. inscription.책, 금석에 (적힌, 새겨진) 글, 비명. read.문장이 ~이라고 씌어 있다, ~로 해석되다. A rule that reads several ways.여러 가지 뜻으로 해석되는 규칙. It read as follows.(거 기에는, 그것은) 다음과 같이 쓰여 있었다. (20절)Now. 그런데. (22절)But Pilate answered, "What I have written, I have written".내가 쓴 것은 (이미) 내가 다 썼다; 내가 (쓸 것, 써야만 하는 것)을 내가 다 썼다. 의역: 내가 쓴 것은 (이미) 내가 다 썼으니 그만이오. (23절)tunic.엉덩이 위까지 내려오는 여성용 상의. 소매가 없고 무릎까지 내려오는 헐렁한 웃옷. seamless.솔기가 없는, 아주 매끄러운. seam.솔기; 옷이나 이부자리를 지을 때 두 폭을 맞대고 꿰맨 줄. underwear, underclothes, undergarments, lingerie.속옷. (24절)vesture.집합적 의복, 의류, 옷. This is what~군사들이 그렇게 하였다.→ So (that, this) is what~그래서 군사들이 그렇게 하였다. (cast, draw) lots, draw cuts, cut lots.제비를 뽑다. (25절)by, beside, with, neighborhood, vicinity, side.곁에. (26절)Woman, behold, your son.→ Dear woman, here is your son. And from that (hour =time).그래서 그때부터. This is.이분이 ~누구이시다. (27절)then.그때에, 곧이어, 그 무렵, 방금, (그, 바로) 뒤에, 이윽고, 그때부터 곧, 그 경우에는,

사정이 그렇다면. subsequently, continuously, successively, continuing, going on, following, next, (soon) after.이어서. Behold→ Here is~ (28절)now.과거시제 문장에서 이미, 그때 이미, 이제야, 그때, 그리고 나서, 다음에, 조금아까. finish.일 등을 끝내다, 끝마치다, (완료, 완수, 완성, 종료)하다, 과정·시기 등을 마치다. be (completed, achieved, attained, effected, realized, fulfilled, accomplished, done)이루어지다. (29절)vessel.배(보통 boat보다 큼), 용기, 그릇. sour wine.신포도주. common.흔한, 보통의, 평범한. sprig. 잔가지. sour wine= wine vinegar. hyssop.박하과의 작은 풀, 히쏩 풀, 유다인들이 귀신이나 재앙을 쫓으려고 제물의 피를 묻혀 뿌리는데 쓴 식물. (30절)bow.머리를 숙이다. handed over the spirit=gave up his spirit. (31절)Now since it was preparation day, in order that the bodies might not remain on the cross on the sabbath, for the sabbath day of that week was a solemn one, the Jews asked Pilate that their legs be broken and they be taken down.그런데 그날은 준비일이었고 그 주간의 안식일은 (장엄한, 엄숙한, 근엄한) 안식일이었으므로 유다인들은 안식일에 시신이 십자가에 남아있지 않게 하려고 십자가에 못 박힌 이들의 다리를 부러뜨리고 시신을 내리게 해달라고 빌라도에게 요청하였다. Since it was preparation day and the sabbath on the next day was a great feast, the Jews asked Pilate that their legs be broken and the bodies be taken down in order that the bodies might not remain on the cross on the sabbath day. (31절)~not remain on the cross= not be hung on the cross.십자가에 매달려있다. hung; hung. 매달려있다. hanged; hanged.교수형에 처하다. (33절)But. 그러나. (34절)thrust(θrʌst). 찌르다, 꿰찌르다(into, with, through), 세게 밀치다, 쑤셔 넣다, (떠, 와락)밀다. but one= instead one. (35절)An eyewitness has testified.(이는) (본 사람이, 증인이, 목격자가) 증언하는 것이므로. As the man who saw it in person has given this testimony. or As this is the testimony by the man who saw it in person.이는 직접 본 사람이 증언하는 것이므로. (37절)And again.그리고 또. (38절)After this.이 일이 있은 후에. Afterwards, after this, thence, subsequently.그 뒤에. (38절)After this(Afterwards), Joseph of Arimathea asked Pilate for removing the body of Jesus. He was a disciple of Jesus, but he hid the fact for fear of the Jews. When Pilate permitted it, he came and took his body.→ After this, Joseph of Arimathea, a disciple of Jesus for fear of the Jews, secretly asked Pilate if he could remove the body of Jesus. And Pilate permitted it. So he came and took his body.이 후에(그 뒤에, 이 일이 있은 후에) 예수님의 제자인 아리마태아 출신 요셉은 유다인들을 두려워한 나머지 은밀하게(비 밀리에) 예수님의 시신을 거둘(치울) 수 있는지를 빌라도에게 (청하였다, 물었다). 그러자 빌라도가 그것을 허락하였다. 그래서 요셉은 가서 예수님의 시신을 거두었다. (39절)Nicodemus, the one who had first come to him at night.→ Nicodemus who had at (one time, one day, before) visited

Jesus. or who had (made his visit Jesus= one day come to Jesus) at night. Pound; Litra.약 75 파운드, 32키로. weighing.무게가 나가는, 무게가 ~되는. (40절)~bound it with burial cloths.예수님의 시신을 수의로 묶었다. ~wrapped him in the linen cloths.예수님의 시신을 아마포로 감쌌다. (41절)Now. 그런데. (42절)So they laid Jesus there because of the Jewish preparation day; for the tomb was close by. → It(That day) was the Jewish preparation day and since the tomb was (close, near) by, they laid Jesus there.

Footnotes

(1절)Luke places the mockery of Jesus at the midpoint in the trial when Jesus was sent to Herod. Mark and Matthew place the scourging and mockery at the end of the trial after the sentence of death. Scourging was an integral part of the crucifixion penalty. (7절)Made himself the Son of God: this question was not raised in John's account of the Jewish interrogations of Jesus as it was in the synoptic account. Nevertheless, see John 5:18; 8:53; 10:36. (12절)Friend of Caesar: a Roman honorific title bestowed upon high-ranking officials for merit. (13절)Seated him: others translate "(Pilate) sat down." In John's thought, Jesus is the real judge of the world, and John may here be portraying him seated on the judgment bench. Stone Pavement: in Greek lithostrotos; under the fortress Antonia, one of the conjectured locations of the praetorium, a massive stone pavement has been excavated. Gabbatha (Aramaic rather than Hebrew) probably means "ridge, elevation." (14절)Noon: Mark 15:25 has Jesus crucified "at the third hour," which means either 9 A.M. or the period from 9 to 12. Noon, the time when, according to John, Jesus was sentenced to death, was the hour at which the priests began to slaughter Passover lambs in the temple; see John 1:29. (16절)He handed him over to them to be crucified: in context this would seem to mean "handed him over to the chief priests." Luke 23:25 has a similar ambiguity. There is a polemic tendency in the gospels to place the guilt of the crucifixion on the Jewish authorities and to exonerate the Romans from blame. But John later mentions the Roman soldiers (John 19:23), and it was to these soldiers that Pilate handed Jesus over. (17절) Carrying the cross himself: a different picture from that of the synoptics, especially Luke 23:26 where Simon of Cyrene is made to carry the cross, walking behind Jesus. In John's theology, Jesus remained in complete control and master of his destiny (cf John 10:18). Place of the Skull: the Latin word for skull is Calvaria; hence "Calvary." Golgotha is actually an Aramaic rather than a Hebrew word. (19절)The inscription differs with slightly different words in each of the four gospels. John's form is fullest and gives the equivalent of the Latin INRI = Iesus Nazarenus Rex Iudaeorum. Only John mentions its polyglot character (John 19:20) and Pilate's role in keeping the title unchanged (John 19:21-22). (23-25a절)While all four gospels describe the soldiers casting lots to divide Jesus' garments (see the note on Matthew 27:35), only John quotes the underlying passage from Psalm 22:19, and only John sees each line of the poetic parallelism literally carried out in two separate actions (John 19:23-24). (25절)It is not clear whether four women are meant, or three (i.e., Mary the wife of Cl[e]opas [cf Luke 24:18] is in apposition with his mother's sister) or two (his mother and his mother's sister, i.e., Mary of Cl[e]opas and Mary of Magdala). Only John mentions the mother of Jesus here. The synoptics have a group of women looking on from a distance at the cross (Mark 15:40). (26-27절)This scene has been interpreted literally, of Jesus' concern for his mother; and symbolically, e.g., in the light of the Cana story in John 2 (the presence of the mother of Jesus, the address woman, and the mention of the hour) and of the upper room in John 13 (the presence of the beloved disciple; the hour). Now that the hour has come (John 19:28), Mary (a symbol of the church?) is given a role as the mother of Christians (personified by the beloved disciple); or, as a representative of those seeking salvation, she is supported by the disciple who interprets Jesus' revelation; or Jewish and Gentile Christianity (or Israel and the Christian community) are reconciled. (28절)The scripture ~fulfilled: either in the scene of John 19:25-27, or in the I thirst of John 19:28. If the latter, Psalm 22:16; 69:22 deserve consideration. (29절)Wine: John does not mention the drugged wine, a narcotic that Jesus refused as the crucifixion began (Mark 15:23), but only this final gesture of kindness at the end (Mark 15:36). Hyssop, a small plant, is scarcely suitable for carrying a sponge (Mark mentions a reed) and may be a symbolic reference to the hyssop used to daub the blood of the paschal lamb on the doorpost of the Hebrews (Exodus 12:22). (30절)Handed over the spirit: there is a double nuance of dying (giving up the last breath or spirit) and that of passing on the holy Spirit; see John 7:39 which connects the giving of the Spirit with Jesus' glorious return to the Father, and John 20:22 where the author portrays the conferral of the Spirit. (34-35절)John probably emphasizes these verses to show the reality of Jesus' death, against the Docetist heretics. In the blood and water there may also be a symbolic reference to the Eucharist and baptism. (35절)He knows: it is not certain from the Greek that this he is the eyewitness of the first part of the sentence. May(come to)believe: see the note on John 20:31. (38-42절)In the first three gospels there is no anointing on Friday. In Matthew and Luke the women come to the tomb on Sunday morning precisely to anoint Jesus.

요한복음서 20장

부활하시다(마태 28, 1-8; 마르 16, 1-8; 루카 24, 1-12)

1 주간 첫날 이른 아침, 아직도 어두울 때에 마리아 막달레나가 무덤에 가서 보니, 무덤을 막았던 돌이 치워져 있었다.

2 그래서 그 여자는 시몬 베드로와 예수님께서 사랑하신 다른 제자에게 달려가서 말하였다. "누가 주님을 무덤에서 꺼내 갔습니다. 어디에 모셨는지 모르겠습니다."

3 베드로와 다른 제자는 밖으로 나와 무덤으로 갔다.

4 두 사람이 함께 달렸는데, 다른 제자가 베드로보다 빨리 달려 무덤에 먼저 다다랐다.

5 그는 몸을 굽혀 아마포가 놓여 있는 것을 보기는 하였지만, 안으로 들어가지는 않았다.

6 시몬 베드로가 뒤따라와서 무덤으로 들어가 아마포가 놓여 있는 것을 보았다.

7 예수님의 얼굴을 쌌던 수건은 아마포와 함께 놓여 있지 않고, 따로 한곳에 개켜져 있었다.

8 그제야 무덤에 먼저 다다른 다른 제자도 들어갔다. 그리고 보고 믿었다.

9 사실 그들은 예수님께서 죽은 이들 가운데에서 다시 살아나셔야 한다는 성경 말씀을 아직 깨닫지 못하고 있었던 것이다.

10 그 제자들은 다시 집으로 돌아갔다.

마리아 막달레나에게 나타나시다(마태 28, 9-10; 마르 16, 9-11)

11 마리아는 무덤 밖에 서서 울고 있었다. 그렇게 울면서 무덤 쪽으로 몸을 굽혀

12 들여다보니 하얀 옷을 입은 두 천사가 앉아 있었다. 한 천사는 예수님의 시신이 놓였던 자리 머리맡에, 다른 천사는 발치에 있었다.

13 그들이 마리아에게 "여인아, 왜 우느냐?" 하고 묻자, 마리아가 그들에게 대답하였다. "누가 저의 주님을 꺼내 갔습니다. 어디에 모셨는지 모르겠습니다."

14 이렇게 말하고 나서 뒤로 돌아선 마리아는 예수님께서 서 계신 것을 보았다. 그러나 예수님이신 줄은 몰랐다.

15 예수님께서 마리아에게 "여인아, 왜 우느냐? 누구를 찾느냐?" 하고 물으셨다. 마리아는 그분을 정원지기로 생각하고, "선생님, 선생님께서 그분을 옮겨 가셨으면 어디에 모셨는지 저에게 말씀해 주십시오. 제가 모셔 가겠습니다." 하고 말하였다.

16 예수님께서 "마리아야!" 하고 부르셨다. 마리아는 돌아서서 히브리 말로 "라뿌니!" 하고 불렀다. 이는 '스승님!'이라는 뜻이다.

17 예수님께서 마리아에게 말씀하셨다. "내가 아직 아버지께 올라가지 않았으니 나를 더 이상 붙들지 마라. 내 형제들에게 가서, '나는 내 아버지시며 너희의 아버지신 분, 내 하느님이시며 너희의 하느님이신 분께 올라간다.' 하고 전하여라."

18 마리아 막달레나는 제자들에게 가서 "제가 주님을 뵈었습니다." 하면서, 예수님께서 자기에게

하신 이 말씀을 전하였다.

제자들에게 나타나시어 사명을 부여하시다(마태 28, 16-20; 마르 16, 14-18; 루카 24, 36-49)

19 그날 곧 주간 첫날 저녁이 되자, 제자들은 유다인들이 두려워 문을 모두 잠가 놓고 있었다. 그런데 예수님께서 오시어 가운데에 서시며, "평화가 너희와 함께!" 하고 그들에게 말씀하셨다.

20 이렇게 말씀하시고 나서 당신의 두 손과 옆구리를 그들에게 보여 주셨다. 제자들은 주님을 뵙고 기뻐하였다.

21 예수님께서 다시 그들에게 이르셨다. "평화가 너희와 함께! 아버지께서 나를 보내신 것처럼 나도 너희를 보낸다."

22 이렇게 이르시고 나서 그들에게 숨을 불어넣으며 말씀하셨다. "성령을 받아라.

23 너희가 누구의 죄든지 용서해 주면 그가 용서를 받을 것이고, 그대로 두면 그대로 남아 있을 것이다."

예수님과 토마스

24 열두 제자 가운데 하나로서 '쌍둥이'라고 불리는 토마스는 예수님께서 오셨을 때에 그들과 함께 있지 않았다.

25 그래서 다른 제자들이 그에게 "우리는 주님을 뵈었소." 하고 말하였다. 그러나 토마스는 그들에게, "나는 그분의 손에 있는 못 자국을 직접 보고 그 못 자국에 내 손가락을 넣어 보고 또 그분 옆구리에 내 손을 넣어 보지 않고는 결코 믿지 못하겠소." 하고 말하였다.

26 여드레 뒤에 제자들이 다시 집 안에 모여 있었는데 토마스도 그들과 함께 있었다. 문이 다 잠겨 있었는데도 예수님께서 오시어 가운데에 서시며, "평화가 너희와 함께!" 하고 말씀하셨다.

27 그리고 나서 토마스에게 이르셨다. "네 손가락을 여기 대 보고 내 손을 보아라. 네 손을 뻗어 내 옆구리에 넣어 보아라. 그리고 의심을 버리고 믿어라."

28 토마스가 예수님께 대답하였다. "저의 주님, 저의 하느님!"

29 그러자 예수님께서 토마스에게 말씀하셨다. "너는 나를 보고서야 믿느냐? 보지 않고도 믿는 사람은 행복하다."

복음서를 쓴 목적

30 예수님께서는 이 책에 기록되지 않은 다른 많은 표징도 제자들 앞에서 일으키셨다.

31 이것들을 기록한 목적은 예수님께서 메시아시며 하느님의 아드님이심을 여러분이 믿고, 또 그렇게 믿어서 그분의 이름으로 생명을 얻게 하려는 것이다.

The Empty Tomb

John Chapter 20

1 On the first day of the week, Mary of Magdala came to the tomb early in the morning, while it was still dark, and saw the stone removed from the tomb. 2 So she ran and went to Simon Peter and to the other disciple whom Jesus loved, and told them, "They have taken the Lord from the tomb, and we don't know where they put him." 3 So Peter and the other disciple went out and came to the tomb. 4 They both ran, but the other disciple ran faster than Peter and arrived at the tomb first; 5 he bent down and saw the burial cloths there, but did not go in. 6 When Simon Peter arrived after him, he went into the tomb and saw the burial cloths there, 7 and the cloth that had covered his head, not with the burial cloths but rolled up in a separate place. 8 Then the other disciple also went in, the one who had arrived at the tomb first, and he saw and believed. 9 For they did not yet understand the scripture that he had to rise from the dead. 10 Then the disciples returned home.

The Appearance to Mary Magdala

11 But Mary stayed outside the tomb weeping. And as she wept, she bent over into the tomb 12 and saw two angels in white sitting there, one at the head and one at the feet where the body of Jesus had been. 13 And they said to her, "Woman, why are you weeping?" She said to them, "They have taken my Lord, and I don't know where they laid him." 14 When she had said this, she turned around and saw Jesus there, but did not know it was Jesus. 15 Jesus said to her, "Woman, why are you weeping? Whom are you looking for?" She thought it was the gardener and said to him, "Sir, if you carried him away, tell me where you laid him, and I will take him." 16 Jesus said to her, "Mary!" She turned and said to him in Hebrew, "Rabbouni," which means Teacher. 17 Jesus said to her, "Stop holding on to me, for I have not yet ascended to the Father. But go to my brothers and tell them, 'I am going to my Father and your Father, to my God and your God.'" 18 Mary of Magdala went and announced to the disciples, "I have seen the Lord," and what he told her.

Appearance to the Disciples

19 On the evening of that first day of the week, when the doors were locked, where the disciples were, for fear of the Jews, Jesus came and stood in their midst and

said to them, "Peace be with you." 20 When he had said this, he showed them his hands and his side. The disciples rejoiced when they saw the Lord. 21 (Jesus) said to them again, "Peace be with you. As the Father has sent me, so I send you." 22 And when he had said this, he breathed on them and said to them, "Receive the holy Spirit. 23 Whose sins you forgive are forgiven them, and whose sins you retain are retained."

Thomas

24 Thomas, called Didymus, one of the Twelve, was not with them when Jesus came. 25 So the other disciples said to him, "We have seen the Lord." But he said to them, "Unless I see the mark of the nails in his hands and put my finger into the nailmarks and put my hand into his side, I will not believe." 26 Now a week later his disciples were again inside and Thomas was with them. Jesus came, although the doors were locked, and stood in their midst and said, "Peace be with you." 27 Then he said to Thomas, "Put your finger here and see my hands, and bring your hand and put it into my side, and do not be unbelieving, but believe." 28 Thomas answered and said to him, "My Lord and my God!" 29 Jesus said to him, "Have you come to believe because you have seen me? Blessed are those who have not seen and have believed."

Conclusion

30 Now Jesus did many other signs in the presence of (his) disciples that are not written in this book. 31 But these are written that you may (come to) believe that Jesus is the Messiah, the Son of God, and that through this belief you may have life in his name.

(1절)~stone stopped up(the entrance to) the tomb had been removed from the tomb. (2절)They→ Someone. (3절)So.그래서. (5절)(bent =stooping) down. ~saw the burial cloths there.→ ~saw the linen cloths lying there. (7절)cloth(klɔ:θ).옷감, 직물, 특정 용도의 천. towel.수건. rolled up.접거나 개다, 감아올리다, 걷어붙이다, (둘둘, 돌돌) 말다, 긁어모으다, 모습을 드러내다, 모여들다. fold up.개키다, (말아, 걷어)올리다, 둥글게 감다, 접다, 말다, 둘러싸다. (10절)Then.그리고 나서 realize, notice, grasp, become (aware, conscious) of, find, perceive.깨닫다. understand.이해하다, 알다, 알아듣다. 무엇의 의미나 중요성을 처음으로 이해하게 되는 것을 나타낼 때는 understand나 grasp을 쓸

수 있다. 언어, 단어들, 글의 의미를 이해하는 것에 대해서는 understand만 쓸 수 있다. again, once more, once again.다시. return."다시 돌아가다"라는 뜻이므로 접두사 "re"가 있는 단어를 사용하는 경우에 again을 추가로 문장에 쓸 필요가 없다. (11절)But Mary.그러나 마리아는. stayed→ stood. And as she wept.그리고 그녀가 (울면서, 우는 채로). and. (시간적 전후 관계를 나타내어) 그리고, 그리고는(and then). as.(상태) ~대로, ~인 채로 ~면서. bend over.구부리다, 굽히다. (13절)And.그러자, 그랬더니. take, bring, (pull, draw, take, bring, pick) out.꺼내가다, 꺼내다. ~said to her.→ ~asked her.(그런데 그들이) 마리아에게 묻자. ~said to them.→ ~answered them. They.누가→ (말하는 사람이 속하지 않는 한 무리의) 사람들 또는 당국자. (14절)turn around.뒤돌아서다, 뒤로 돌아보다, 방향을 바꾸다. (15절)~said to her.→ ~asked her. (16절)~said to her, "Mary".~그녀에게 '마리아야'하고 말씀하셨다. 의역; ~그녀에게 '마리아야'하고 부르셨다. (17절)hold on.(붙들, 잡)다. But. 하지만. (18절)~하신 이 말씀을.→ ~하신 말씀을. (19절)~제자들은 유다인들이 두려워 그들이 있던 곳에서 문을 모두 잠가 놓고 (있었는데, 있었을 때에, 있자니) 예수님께서 오시어 가운데에 서시며, "평화가 너희와 함께!" 하고 그들에게 말씀하셨다. (23절)keep(leave) as it is.그대로 (두다, 유지하다, 간직하다). retain(ritéin).계속 (유지, 계속 함유, 간직, 보유)하다, 그대로 두다, 남아있다, 변호사 등과 지속적인 계약관계를 유지하다. "Whose sins you forgive are forgiven them, and whose sins you retain are retained. or Whosever sins you forgive, they are forgiven unto them; and whosever sins you retain, they are retained."→ If you forgive anyone his sins, they will be forgiven; if you retain them, they will be retained. remain.남아있다. (26절)Now a week later.그런데 한 주일 후에. After eight days.여드레 뒤에. again inside=again in the house. (27절)(brush, sweep) away doubts= Put off your doubts= rid the mind of doubt= stop doubting.의심을 버리다. ~bring your hand.네 손을 가져와→ ~reach out your hand.네 손을 뻗어. (reach, stretch, put) out one's hand, reach for.손을 뻗다. (28절)~answered and said to.대답하여 말하기를. (29절)Then.그러자. ~because you have seen me?너는 나를 보았으므로→ ~after you have seen me?너는 나를 보고서야~ (30절)Now Jesus.그런데 예수님께서는. in the presence of.~의 면전에서, ~의 앞에서, ~가 있는데서. (31절)But these are written that.그러나 ~을 위하여 이것들이 (집필되었다, 기록되었다, 작성되었다, 쓰여졌다). The purpose of recording these.이것들을 기록한 목적은. ~and that through this belief~또 이 믿음을 통하여. ~and that by believing like that~또 그렇게 믿어. in his name.그분의 이름으로.

Footnotes

(1-31절)The risen Jesus reveals his glory and confers the Spirit. This story fulfills the basic need for testimony to the resurrection. What we have here is not a record but a series of single stories. (1-10절)The story of the empty tomb is found in both the Matthean and the Lucan traditions; John's version seems to be a fusion of the two. (1절)Still dark: according to Mark the sun had risen, Matthew describes it as "dawning," and Luke refers to early dawn. Mary sees the stone removed, not the empty tomb. (2절)Mary runs away, not directed by an angel/young man as in the synoptic accounts. The plural "we" in the second part of her statement might reflect a tradition of more women going to the tomb. (3-10절)The basic narrative is told of Peter alone in Luke 24:12, a verse missing in important manuscripts and which may be borrowed from tradition similar to John. Cf also Luke 24:24. (6-8절)Some special feature about the state of the burial cloths caused the beloved disciple to believe. Perhaps the details emphasized that the grave had not been robbed. (9절)Probably a general reference to the scriptures is intended, as in Luke 24:26 and 1 Cor 15:4. Some individual Old Testament passages suggested are Psalm 16:10; Hosea 6:2; Jonah 2:1, 2, 10. (11-18절)This appearance to Mary is found only in John, but cf Matthew 28:8-10 and Mark 16:9-11. (16절)Rabbouni: Hebrew or Aramaic for "my master." (17절)Stop holding on to me: see Matthew 28:9, where the women take hold of his feet. I have not yet ascended: for John and many of the New Testament writers, the ascension in the theological sense of going to the Father to be glorified took place with the resurrection as one action. This scene in John dramatizes such an understanding, for by Easter night Jesus is glorified and can give the Spirit. Therefore his ascension takes place immediately after he has talked to Mary. In such a view, the ascension after forty days described in Acts 1:1-11 would be simply a termination of earthly appearances or, perhaps better, an introduction to the conferral of the Spirit upon the early church, modeled on Elisha's being able to have a (double) share in the spirit of Elijah if he saw him being taken up (same verb as ascending) into heaven (2 Kings 2:9-12). To my Father and your Father, to my God and your God: this echoes Ruth 1:16: "Your people shall be my people, and your God my God." The Father of Jesus will now become the Father of the disciples because, once ascended, Jesus can give them the Spirit that comes from the Father and they can be reborn as God's children (John 3:5). That is why he calls them my brothers. (19-29절)The appearances to the disciples, without or with Thomas (cf John 11:16; 14:5), have rough parallels in the other gospels only for John 20:19-23; cf Luke 24:36-39; Mark 16:14-18. (19절)The disciples: by implication from John 20:24 this means ten of the Twelve, presumably in Jerusalem. Peace be with you: although this could be an ordinary greeting, John intends here to echo John 14:27. The theme of rejoicing in John 20:20 echoes John 16:22. (20절)Hands and⋯side: Luke 24:39-40 mentions "hands and feet," based on

Psalm 22:17. (21절)By means of this sending, the Eleven were made apostles, that is, "those sent" (cf John 17:18), though John does not use the noun in reference to them (see the note on John 13:16). A solemn mission or "sending" is also the subject of the post-resurrection appearances to the Eleven in Matthew 28:19; Luke 24:47; Mark 16:15. (22절)This action recalls Genesis 2:7, where God breathed on the first man and gave him life; just as Adam's life came from God, so now the disciples' new spiritual life comes from Jesus. Cf also the revivification of the dry bones in Ezekial 37. This is the author's version of Pentecost. Cf also the note on John 19:30. (23절)The Council of Trent defined that this power to forgive sins is exercised in the sacrament of penance. See Matthew 16:19; Matthew 18:18. (28절)My Lord and my God: this forms a literary inclusion with the first verse of the gospel: "and the Word was God." (29절)This verse is a beatitude on future generations; faith, not sight, matters. (30-31절)These verses are clearly a conclusion to the gospel and express its purpose. While many manuscripts read come to believe, possibly implying a missionary purpose for John's gospel, a small number of quite early ones read "continue to believe," suggesting that the audience consists of Christians whose faith is to be deepened by the book; cf John 19:35

요한복음서 21장

일곱 제자에게 나타나시다

1 그 뒤에 예수님께서는 티베리아스 호숫가에서 다시 제자들에게 당신 자신을 드러내셨는데, 이렇게 드러내셨다.

2 시몬 베드로와 '쌍둥이'라고 불리는 토마스, 갈릴래아 카나 출신 나타나엘과 제베대오의 아들들, 그리고 그분의 다른 두 제자가 함께 있었다.

3 시몬 베드로가 그들에게 "나는 고기 잡으러 가네." 하고 말하자, 그들이 "우리도 함께 가겠소." 하였다. 그들이 밖으로 나가 배를 탔지만 그날 밤에는 아무것도 잡지 못하였다.

4 어느덧 아침이 될 무렵, 예수님께서 물가에 서 계셨다. 그러나 제자들은 그분이 예수님이신 줄을 알지 못하였다.

5 예수님께서 그들에게, "얘들아, 무얼 좀 잡았느냐?" 하시자, 그들이 대답하였다. "못 잡았습니다."

6 예수님께서 그들에게 이르셨다. "그물을 배 오른쪽에 던져라. 그러면 고기가 잡힐 것이다." 그래서 제자들이 그물을 던졌더니, 고기가 너무 많이 걸려 그물을 끌어 올릴 수가 없었다.

7 예수님께서 사랑하신 그 제자가 베드로에게 "주님이십니다." 하고 말하였다. 주님이시라는 말을 듣자, 옷을 벗고 있던 베드로는 겉옷을 두르고 호수로 뛰어들었다.

8 다른 제자들은 그 작은 배로 고기가 든 그물을 끌고 왔다. 그들은 뭍에서 백 미터쯤밖에 떨어져 있지 않았던 것이다.

9 그들이 뭍에 내려서 보니, 숯불이 있고 그 위에 물고기가 놓여 있고 빵도 있었다.

10 예수님께서 그들에게 말씀하셨다. "방금 잡은 고기를 몇 마리 가져오너라."

11 그러자 시몬 베드로가 배에 올라 그물을 뭍으로 끌어 올렸다. 그 안에는 큰 고기가 백쉰세 마리나 가득 들어 있었다. 고기가 그토록 많은데도 그물이 찢어지지 않았다.

12 예수님께서 그들에게 "와서 아침을 먹어라." 하고 말씀하셨다. 제자들 가운데에는 "누구 십니까?" 하고 감히 묻는 사람이 없었다. 그분이 주님이시라는 것을 알고 있었기 때문이다.

13 예수님께서는 다가가셔서 빵을 들어 그들에게 주시고 고기도 그렇게 주셨다.

14 이렇게 예수님께서는 죽은 이들 가운데에서 되살아나신 뒤에 세 번째로 제자들에게 나타나셨다.

예수님과 베드로

15 그들이 아침을 먹은 다음에 예수님께서 시몬 베드로에게 물으셨다. "요한의 아들 시몬아, 너는 이들이 나를 사랑하는 것보다 더 나를 사랑하느냐?" 베드로가 "예, 주님! 제가 주님을 사랑하는 줄을 주님께서 아십니다." 하고 대답하자, 예수님께서 그에게 말씀하셨다. "내 어린양들을 돌보아라."

16 예수님께서 다시 두 번째로 베드로에게 물으셨다. "요한의 아들 시몬아, 너는 나를 사랑하느냐?" 베드로가 "예, 주님! 제가 주님을 사랑하는 줄을 주님께서 아십니다." 하고 대답하자, 예수님께서

그에게 말씀하셨다. "내 양들을 돌보아라."

17 예수님께서 세 번째로 베드로에게 물으셨다. "요한의 아들 시몬아, 너는 나를 사랑하느냐?" 베드로는 예수님께서 세 번이나 "나를 사랑하느냐?" 하고 물으시므로 슬퍼하며 대답하였다. "주님, 주님께서는 모든 것을 아십니다. 제가 주님을 사랑하는 줄을 주님께서는 알고 계십니다." 그러자 예수님께서 베드로에게 말씀하셨다. "내 양들을 돌보아라.

18 내가 진실로 진실로 너에게 말한다. 네가 젊었을 때에는 스스로 허리띠를 매고 원하는 곳으로 다녔다. 그러나 늙어서는 네가 두 팔을 벌리면 다른 이들이 너에게 허리띠를 매어 주고서, 네가 원하지 않는 곳으로 데려갈 것이다."

19 예수님께서는 이렇게 말씀하시어, 베드로가 어떠한 죽음으로 하느님을 영광스럽게 할 것인지 가리키신 것이다. 이렇게 이르신 다음에 예수님께서는 베드로에게 "나를 따라라." 하고 말씀하셨다.

예수님께서 사랑하신 제자와 베드로

20 베드로가 돌아서서 보니 예수님께서 사랑하시는 제자가 따라오고 있었다. 그 제자는 만찬 때에 예수님 가슴에 기대어 앉아 있다가, "주님, 주님을 팔아넘길 자가 누구입니까?" 하고 물었던 사람이다.

21 그 제자를 본 베드로가 예수님께, "주님, 이 사람은 어떻게 되겠습니까?" 하고 물었다.

22 예수님께서는 "내가 올 때까지 그가 살아 있기를 내가 바란다 할지라도, 그것이 너와 무슨 상관이 있느냐? 너는 나를 따라라." 하고 말씀하셨다.

23 그래서 형제들 사이에 이 제자가 죽지 않으리라는 말이 퍼져 나갔다. 그러나 예수님께서는 그가 죽지 않으리라고 말씀하신 것이 아니라, "내가 올 때까지 그가 살아 있기를 내가 바란다 할지라도, 그것이 너와 무슨 상관이 있느냐?" 하고 말씀하신 것이다.

엮은이의 맺음말

24 이 제자가 이 일들을 증언하고 또 기록한 사람이다. 우리는 그의 증언이 참되다는 것을 알고 있다.

25 예수님께서 하신 일은 이 밖에도 많이 있다. 그래서 그것들을 낱낱이 기록하면, 온 세상이라도 그렇게 기록된 책들을 다 담아 내지 못하리라고 나는 생각한다.

Epilogue

The Resurrection Appearance in Galilee

The Appearance to the Seven Disciples

John Chapter 21

1 After this, Jesus revealed himself again to his disciples at the Sea of Tiberias. He revealed himself in this way. 2 Together were Simon Peter, Thomas called Didymus, Nathanael from Cana in Galilee, Zebedee's sons, and two others of his disciples. 3 Simon Peter said to them, "I am going fishing." They said to him, "We also will come with you." So they went out and got into the boat, but that night they caught nothing. 4 When it was already dawn, Jesus was standing on the shore; but the disciples did not realize that it was Jesus. 5 Jesus said to them, "Children, have you caught anything to eat?" They answered him, "No." 6 So he said to them, "Cast the net over the right side of the boat and you will find something." So they cast it, and were not able to pull it in because of the number of fish. 7 So the disciple whom Jesus loved said to Peter, "It is the Lord." When Simon Peter heard that it was the Lord, he tucked in his garment, for he was lightly clad, and jumped into the sea. 8 The other disciples came in the boat, for they were not far from shore, only about a hundred yards, dragging the net with the fish. 9 When they climbed out on shore, they saw a charcoal fire with fish on it and bread. 10 Jesus said to them, "Bring some of the fish you just caught." 11 So Simon Peter went over and dragged the net ashore full of one hundred fifty-three large fish. Even though there were so many, the net was not torn. 12 Jesus said to them, "Come, have breakfast." And none of the disciples dared to ask him, "Who are you?" because they realized it was the Lord. 13 Jesus came over and took the bread and gave it to them, and in like manner the fish. 14 This was now the third time Jesus was revealed to his disciples after being raised from the dead.

Jesus and Peter

15 When they had finished breakfast, Jesus said to Simon Peter, "Simon, son of John, do you love me more than these?" He said to him, "Yes, Lord, you know that I love you." He said to him, "Feed my lambs." 16 He then said to him a second time, "Simon, son of John, do you love me?" He said to him, "Yes, Lord, you know that I

love you." He said to him, "Tend my sheep." 17 He said to him the third time, "Simon, son of John, do you love me?" Peter was distressed that he had said to him a third time, "Do you love me?" and he said to him, "Lord, you know everything; you know that I love you." (Jesus) said to him, "Feed my sheep. 18 Amen, amen, I say to you, when you were younger, you used to dress yourself and go where you wanted; but when you grow old, you will stretch out your hands, and someone else will dress you and lead you where you do not want to go." 19 He said this signifying by what kind of death he would glorify God. And when he had said this, he said to him, "Follow me."

The Beloved Disciple

20 Peter turned and saw the disciple following whom Jesus loved, the one who had also reclined upon his chest during the supper and had said, "Master, who is the one who will betray you?" 21 When Peter saw him, he said to Jesus, "Lord, what about him?" 22 Jesus said to him, "What if I want him to remain until I come? What concern is it of yours? You follow me." 23 So the word spread among the brothers that that disciple would not die. But Jesus had not told him that he would not die, just "What if I want him to remain until I come? (What concern is it of yours?)"

Conclusion

24 It is this disciple who testifies to these things and has written them, and we know that his testimony is true. 25 There are also many other things that Jesus did, but if these were to be described individually, I do not think the whole world would contain the books that would be written.

(1절)sea→ lake. (3절)So.그래서. (4절)~was already dawn.이미 동틀 무렵에.→ ~was already early in the morning.어느덧 아침이 될 무렵. realize. 깨닫다, 알아차리다, 알다, (인식, 자각, 달성, 실현)하다. (5절)먹을 것을 무얼. (6절)So. 그러자. ~because of many fishes= because of the large number of fish= because of the number of fish.잡힌 고기가 많기 때문에; 의역: 고기가 너무 많이 걸려. caught in the net.그물에 걸리다. (7절)So.그러자. tuck.포근히 감싸주다, 덮어주다. ~he tucked in his garment= ~he wrapped his outer garment around him.(그는) 겉옷을 두르고. ~for he was lightly clad.옷을 가볍게 입었던= 가벼운 옷차림의. ~for he had taken garment off.옷을 벗고 있던. (8절)The other disciples came in the boat, for they were not far from shore, only about a hundred yards, dragging the net with the fish.배안에 있던 다른 제자들은 고기가 든 그물을 끌고 왔다. 왜냐하면 그들은 뭍에서 부터 단지 91.44(약 100 야드) 미터쯤 밖에 있어, 멀리 떨어져 있지 않았기 때문이다. (9절)When they climbed out on shore= When they landed on shore. 그들이 (물가= 뭍)에 내려서 보니. shore, land.뭍. climb out of.배, 자동차 등에서 내리다. (11 절)So Simon Peter went over and dragged.그러자 베드로가 (배위로 넘어가) 배로 가서 ~ 끌어 올렸다. So Simon Peter climbed aboard the boat and dragged.그러자 베드로가 배에 올라 ~끌어 올렸다. aboard.배, 비행기 등에 탑승하다. (12절)And none.그러자 아무도. realized= knew. (13절)in like manner.마찬가지로, 똑같이, 다름없이, 그렇게, 그런 모양으로. (14절)now.때를 나타내는 말과 함께 (지금부터 세어서) 벌써. 이렇게 예수님께서는 죽은 이들 가운데에서 되살아나신 뒤에 세 번째로 제자들에게 나타나셨다.→ 예수님께서는 죽은 이들 가운데에서 되살아나신 뒤에 제자들에게 나타나셨는데 이번이 벌써 세 번째였다. (15절) When,~한 후에, 하니, 하자, 하고. ~said to Simon→ asked Simon. He said to him→ He answered him. feed.먹여 살리다, 부양하다, 먹이를 주다. tend my sheep.내양들을 돌보아라. (16절)He then said to him→ He asked him. He said to him, "Yes"→ He answered him, "Yes". (17절)distress.(걱정, 괴로워, 고통스러워)하다, 곤경에 빠지다. (grieved, mourned) over.슬퍼하다. Peter was distressed that he had said to him a third time→ Peter was grieved because Jesus asked him the third time. feed→ tend. (Jesus)→ Then Jesus. (18절)dress oneself.옷을(차려) 입다, (단장, 정장, 몸차림)하다, (19 절)signify.의미하다, 뜻하다, 나타내다. →indicating.가리키다. And when ~said this. 그리고 이렇게 이르신 다음에. (20절)Master→ Lord. (21절)~he said to Jesus→ ~he asked Jesus. "Lord, what about him?""주님, 이 사람은 어떻게 되겠습니까?" (22절) remain→ alive. What concern is it of yours?너와 무슨 관계가 있느냐? What if I want~ (바란다 할지라도, 바란다 한들, 바란다면) (무슨 상관이 있느냐?, 무슨 일이라도 되느냐?, 무슨 일이 되느냐?) (24절)그리고 우리는~ (25절)in addition, other, additionally.이밖에도. ~were to be described.→ ~were written down. or ~were recorded.기록하면. individually.개인적으로, 개별적으로, 각자에게, 하나하나, 낱낱이. even the whole world.온 세상이라도. contain, serve, include, put sth in(into) bag, have room for, capture. 담아내다. contain.(무엇의 안에 또는 그 일부로) ~이 (들어, 함유되어) 있다, 포함하다, 담다, 함유하다, 담고 있다, 억누르다, 억제하다, 참다. one by one, piece by piece, singly, individually, in everything, entirely, in every case, every one of, in detail, fully, in full, each and everyone.낱낱이.

Footnotes

(1-23절)There are many non-Johannine peculiarities in this chapter, some suggesting Lucan Greek style; yet this passage is closer to John than John 7:53-8:11. There are many Johannine features as well. Its closest parallels in the synoptic gospels are found in Luke 5:1-11 and Matthew 14:28-31.Perhaps the tradition was ultimately derived from John but preserved by some disciple other than the writer of the rest of the gospel. The appearances narrated seem to be independent of those in John 20. Even if a later addition, the chapter was added before publication of the gospel, for it appears in all manuscripts. (2절)Zebedee's sons: the only reference to James and John in this gospel (but see the note on John 1:37). Perhaps the phrase was originally a gloss to identify, among the five, the two others of his disciples. The anonymity of the latter phrase is more Johannine (John 1:35). The total of seven may suggest the community of the disciples in its fullness. (3-6절)This may be a variant of Luke's account of the catch of fish; see the note on Luke 5:1-11. (9,12-13절)It is strange that Jesus already has fish since none have yet been brought ashore. This meal may have had eucharistic significance for early Christians since John 21:13 recalls John 6:11 which uses the vocabulary of Jesus' action at the Last Supper; but see also the note on Matthew 14:19. (11절)The exact number 153 is probably meant to have a symbolic meaning in relation to the apostles' universal mission; Jerome claims that Greek zoologists catalogued 153 species of fish. Or 153 is the sum of the numbers from 1 to 17. Others invoke Ezekiel 47:10. 153마리라는 숫자는 사도들의 보편적인 사명과 관련하여 상징적인 의미를 갖는 것을 뜻함. 예로니모 성인은 그리스 동물학자들이 153가지의 물고기 목록을 만들은 것에 기초한다고 주장함. 1에서 17까지의 숫자의 합계가 153임. 17은 많다는 의미의 10과 완전 숫자이자 하느님과 인간의 만남을 의미하는 7의 조합입니다. 153마리라는 숫자는 제자들이 많은 비신자들을 하느님과 만나게 하는 사명을 받았으며 실천해야 함을 상징함. 나머지 부분은 에제키엘서 47장 10절을 언급함. (12절) None ~dared to ask him: is Jesus' appearance strange to them? Cf Luke 24:16; Mark 16:12; John 20:14. The disciples do, however, recognize Jesus before the breaking of the bread (opposed to Luke 24:35). (14절)This verse connects John 20 and 21; cf John 20:19, 26. (15-23절)This section constitutes Peter's rehabilitation and emphasizes his role in the church.이 부분은 베드로 사도의 명예회복으로 여겨지며(성립, 구성하며)교회에서의 그의 역할을 강조한다. (15-17절)In these three verses there is a remarkable variety of synonyms: two different Greek verbs for love (see the note on John 15:13); two verbs for feed/tend; two nouns for sheep; two verbs for know. But apparently there is no difference of meaning. The threefold confession of Peter is meant to counteract his earlier threefold denial (John 18:17, 25, 27). The First Vatican Council cited these verses in defining that Jesus after his resurrection gave Peter the jurisdiction of supreme shepherd and ruler over the whole flock. (15절)More than these: probably "more than these disciples do" rather than "more than you love them" or "more than you love these things (fishing, etc.)." 베드로의 세 번의 고백은 그의 초기 세 번에 걸친 부인을 상쇄(대응)시킨다는 의미가 있음. 제1차 바티칸 공의회는 예수님께서 부활하신 후에 베드로에게 최고 목자로서의, 그리고 모든 양떼를 다스리는 통치자로서의 권한을 주셨다고 정의할 때 이 세 절을 인용하였음. (15-17절) (18절)Originally probably a proverb about old age, now used as a figurative reference to the crucifixion of Peter. (21절)"Lord, what about him?" "주님, 이 사람은 어떻게 되겠습니까?" KJV:"Lord, what shall this man do?" (22절)Until I come: a reference to the parousia. (23절)This whole scene takes on more significance if the disciple is already dead. The death of the apostolic generation caused problems in the church because of a belief that Jesus was to have returned first. Loss of faith sometimes resulted; cf 2 Peter 3:4. (24절) Who → ~has written them: this does not necessarily mean he wrote them with his own hand. The same expression is used in John 19:22 of Pilate, who certainly would not have written the inscription himself. We know: i.e., the Christian community; cf John 1:14, 16.

기도 맛들이기

초판인쇄 | 2025년 5월 8일
초판발행 | 2025년 5월 15일

저   자 | 문석호
펴낸이 | 서영애
펴낸곳 | 대양미디어

04559 서울시 중구 퇴계로45길 22-6(일호빌딩) 602호
전화 | (02)2276-0078
팩스 | (02)2267-7888

ISBN 979-11-6072-145-4 93230
값 35,000원

＊ 잘못된 책은 교환해 드립니다.